Inset map (upper right):

Bethel
Ai
Aiath
Michmash
Beeroth (Berea)
Ramah
Geba
Azmaveth
Anathoth
Ananiah
Mizpah
Adasa
Hazor
Meronoth
Gibeon
Chephirah
Kiriath-jearim
Elasa
Capharsalama
Jerusalem

10 Miles
10 Kilometres

Main map labels:

LEBANON S
AMMON
NABATAEANS
Gadara
Jazer
Philadelphia (Rabbah)
('Araq el-Emir)
Samaga
Heshbon
Medeba
Dabaloth
Libba
Machaerus
R. Arnon
Lake Asphalt-itis (Dead Sea)

Shiloh
Rathamin (Ramathaim)
Berzeth (Berzetho)
Mahalcema
Seilah
Beth-gilgal (Gilgal)
Doko
Jericho
Khirbet Qumran)
'Ain Feshkha
Bethel
Gophna
Geba
Anathoth
Beeroth
Mizpah
Gibeon
Jerusalem
Bethlehem
Beth-haccherem
Beth-basi
Netophah
Tekoa
En-gedi
Masada

JUDAH (JUDEA)
JOPPA
Ono
Nebalat
Hadid
Lod (Lydda) Modein
Gath Beth-horon
Gazara (Gezer)
Emmaus
Kiriath-jearim
Kedron
Ekron
Zorah
Zanoah
Jarmuth
Azekah Beth-zechariah
Harim
Keilah
Adullam
Beth-zaith
Nebo
Beth-zur
Elam
Hebron (Kiriath-arba)
Adoraim
Marisa
Lachish
Eglon
Jamnia (Jabneel)
Ashdod (Azotus)
Ashkelon (Ascalon)
Anthedon
Gaza
Gerar
Ziklag
Jekabzeel
Moladah
Beer-sheba
Jeshua
En-rimmon
Hazar-shual
Hormah
Raphia
IDUMEA
LAND OF THE PHILISTINES

River (Jordan River)

V W X Y
5 6 7

© Oxford University Press

# THE NEW OXFORD
# ANNOTATED APOCRYPHA
# THIRD EDITION

*New Revised Standard Version*

# THE NEW OXFORD
# ANNOTATED
# APOCRYPHA

## THIRD EDITION

❧❧

## MICHAEL D. COOGAN

### EDITOR

Marc Z. Brettler, Carol A. Newsom, Pheme Perkins

#### ASSOCIATE EDITORS

*New Revised Standard Version*

OXFORD
UNIVERSITY PRESS

# OXFORD
UNIVERSITY PRESS

Oxford   New York

Athens   Auckland   Bangkok   Bogota   Buenos Aires   Calcutta
Cape Town   Chennai   Dar es Salaam   Delhi   Florence   Hong Kong   Istanbul
Karachi   Kuala Lumpur   Madrid   Melbourne   Mexico City   Mumbai
Nairobi   Paris   Sao Paulo   Shanghai   Singapore   Taipei   Tokyo   Toronto   Warsaw
and associated companies in
Berlin   Ibadan

Published by Oxford University Press, Inc.
198 Madison Avenue, New York, New York 10016
http://www.oup-usa.org

Oxford is a registered trademark of Oxford University Press

The Apocryphal/Deuterocanonical Books of the Old Testament are taken from the
New Revised Standard Version Bible, copyright © 1989,
Division of Christian Education of the National Council of the Churches
of Christ in the United States of America

7   9   10   8   6

Printed in the United States of America

# Contributors

Theodore A. Bergren: *2 Esdras*

Mark E. Biddle: *Letter of Jeremiah, Baruch*

Mary Chilton Callaway: *1 and 2 Maccabees*

John J. Collins: *3 Maccabees*

Linda Day: *Judith*

Tamara Cohn Eskenazi: *1 Esdras*

John S. Kselman: *Psalm 151, Prayer of Manasseh*

Mary Joan Winn Leith: *Greek Esther*

Amy-Jill Levine: *Tobit, Additions to Daniel*

Harold C. Washington: *Sirach*

Walter T. Wilson: *Wisdom of Solomon, 4 Maccabees*

Michael D. Coogan: *The Geography of the Bible*

Carol A. Newsom: *Introduction to
the Apocryphal/Deuterocanonical Books;
The Persian and Hellenistic Periods*

# Contents

## The Apocryphal/Deuterocanonical Books

The Apocryphal/Deuterocanonical Books are listed here in four groupings, as follows:

(c) In the Slavonic Bible and in the Latin Vulgate Appendix

   2 Esdras (3 Esdras in Slavonic, 4 Esdras in Vulgate Appendix), 320 AP

   (*Note:* In the Latin Vulgate, Ezra–Nehemiah are 1 and 2 Esdras.)

(d) In an Appendix to the Greek Bible

   4 Maccabees, 362 AP

## List of Maps

# Alphabetical Listing
## of the Apocryphal/Deuterocanonical Books

# Alphabetical Listing
## of the Apocryphal/Deuterocanonical Books

# List of Abbreviations

The following abbreviations are used for the Apocryphal/Deuterocanonical Books:

| | | | |
|---|---|---|---|
| Tob | Tobit | Song of Thr | Prayer of Azariah |
| Jdt | Judith | | and the Song of the Three Jews |
| Add Esth | Additions to Esther | Sus | Susanna |
| Wis | Wisdom | Bel | Bel and the Dragon |
| Sir | Sirach (Ecclesiasticus) | 1 Macc | 1 Maccabees |
| Bar | Baruch | 2 Macc | 2 Maccabees |
| 1 Esd | 1 Esdras | 3 Macc | 3 Maccabees |
| 2 Esd | 2 Esdras | 4 Macc | 4 Maccabees |
| Let Jer | Letter of Jeremiah | Pr Man | Prayer of Manasseh |

In the notes to the Apocryphal/Deuterocanonical Books
the following abbreviations are used:

| | |
|---|---|
| *Ant.* | Josephus, *Antiquities of the Jews* |
| Aram | Aramaic |
| Ch, chs | Chapter, chapters |
| Cn | Correction; made where the text has suffered in transmission and the versions provide no satisfactory restoration but where the Standard Bible Committee agrees with the judgment of competent scholars as to the most probable reconstruction of the original text. |
| Gk | Septuagint, Greek version of the Old Testament |
| Heb | Hebrew of the consonantal Masoretic Text of the Old Testament |
| Josephus | Flavius Josephus (Jewish historian, ca. 37–95 CE) |
| Macc | The book(s) of the Maccabees |
| Ms(s) | Manuscript(s) |
| MT | The Hebrew of the pointed Masoretic Text of the Old Testament |
| OL | Old Latin |
| Q Ms(s) | Manuscript(s) found at Qumran by the Dead Sea |
| Sam | Samaritan Hebrew text of the Old Testament |
| Syr | Syriac Version of the Old Testament |
| Syr H | Syriac Version of Origen's Hexapla |
| Tg | Targum |
| Vg | Vulgate, Latin Version of the Old Testament |

| | |
|---|---|
| *Sifre Num.* | *Sifre Numbers* |
| *Sib. Or.* | *Sibylline Oracles* |
| *T. Jud. (Test. Jud.)* | *Testament of Judah* |
| *T. Moses* | *Testament of Moses* |
| *T. Reuben* | *Testament of Reuben* |
| *Tr. Eruv.* | Babylonian Talmud, *Tractate Eruvim* (see *b. Eruv.*) |
| *y.* | Jerusalem Talmud |
| *y. Sot.* | Jerusalem Talmud, *Sotah* |

*Note:* The abbreviation "Q," unless specified as "Quelle" ("Source") for the posited New Testament document of non-Markan common material in Matthew and Luke, refers to Qumran, and manuscripts from Qumran are identified by the cave number, which precedes the Q, and the official manuscript number, which follows it; thus, 1Q34 = Manuscript 34 from Cave 1 at Qumran; 4Q174 = Manuscript 174 from Cave 4; etc.

# The Editors' Preface

For nearly four decades *The Oxford Annotated Bible* has served generations of readers and students as a study Bible. That extraordinary longevity alone is eloquent testimony to its success. This new edition retains the format and features that have proven so attractive. At the same time, the field of biblical studies has not been static, and this edition is a thoroughgoing revision of the previous ones. In particular, the editors have recruited contributors from a wide diversity of backgrounds and of scholarly approaches to the biblical traditions. In order to present this diversity more fully, the space devoted to introductions to the biblical books, to the annotations, and to the study materials at the end of the book has been increased by over 30 percent.

We recognize that no single interpretation or approach is sufficient for informed reading of these ancient texts, and have aimed at inclusivity of interpretive strategies. On a great number of issues there is a consensus among scholars, and the contributors have been encouraged to present such consensus when it exists. Where it has broken down, and has not yet re-formed, alternatives are mentioned. Moreover, in order to respect the canonical status of various parts of the Bible for different communities, and to avoid privileging any book or part of the Bible, we have kept both introductions and annotations roughly proportionate to the length of the books, while recognizing that some parts require more elaboration than others.

The editorial process was collaborative. Each contribution was read in its entirety by at least three of the editors, and revised with a view toward consistency of tone, coherence of approach, and completeness of coverage. We have also wanted to allow the contributors' own voices to be heard, and we have avoided imposing a superficial uniformity of style and approach. Throughout, we have kept the needs of the general audience firmly in mind during the editorial stages, and our aim has been a congruity of experience as a reader turns from book to book and from section to section of the finished volume.

## CONTENTS OF THE ANNOTATED BIBLE

The biblical text stands apart from any editorial contributions, in both placement and format. This will enable anyone who wishes to do so to read the text unprejudiced by editorial judgments.

The footnotes that are part of the New Revised Standard Version (indicated by an italic superscript letter after the word or phrase in question) are printed at the bottom of the right-hand column of the biblical text on each page where they occur. In these notes, divergent textual readings and alternate translations are printed in italics. The phrase "Other ancient authorities read" means that the reading (i.e., the wording) of the passage is different in various manuscripts and early versions, and the word "Or" signifies that the Hebrew, Aramaic, Greek, or Latin text permits an alternate rendering besides the one given in the text.

Each book is preceded by its own introduction, which sketches the book's structure, main themes, literary history, and historical context, as well as broad lines of interpretation. As mentioned above, these introductions are in most cases considerably longer than in previous editions; they therefore present a clear overview and guide to reading.

At the bottom of each page of the biblical text, in a different font from it and in a single column, are the annotations. The annotations are just that, notes rather than paraphrase or commentary, although these genres admittedly overlap. They are intended to enhance the reader's understanding of the text, providing essential information, background, and interpretation, rather than only summarizing what it says. The boldface headings delineate the larger units of the book, and provide a detailed consecutive outline of its contents. The word or phrase being glossed is given in italics. Quotation marks are used for words quoted from elsewhere in the Bible as well as for transliterations of ancient languages. Since we desire each book to stand on its own, as much as possible the annotations are self-contained. We have thus tried to avoid both cross-references to fuller discussions elsewhere, and the misconception that a book or larger part of the Bible is merely a perfunctory reworking of other material, or that a particular passage can only be understood fully in the light of later biblical traditions. At the same time, we recognize that the Bible is often a progressive text, and that later parts of the Bible often contain the oldest interpretations of earlier traditions. The best starting point for interpreting a particular passage is often another passage, and we have encouraged contributors to point out interconnections in the biblical material by means of cross-references. (The cross-references that end with "n." refer to the annotation as well as to the biblical text.)

A listing of abbreviations for the books of the Bible used in this edition is found on p. xxv below. The chapter and verse divisions in a reference are separated by a period; thus, Gen 3.8 refers to the book of Genesis, chapter 3, verse 8. Inclusive references are used for both chapters and verses; thus, Ex 1–15 refers to the first fifteen chapters of the book of Exodus; Rom 11.33–36 to verses 33 through 36 of chapter 11 of the letter to the Romans; and so forth. When a book of the Bible is referred to within an annotation on that book, the name of the book is not repeated unless there is ambiguity.

In keeping with our general desire to take account of the diversity of the users of this study Bible, we have adopted two widely accepted conventions: We have referred to the first portion of the text as "the Hebrew Bible," since it is a collection preserved by the Jewish community and that is how Jews regard it; and we have cited all dates in the notes as BCE or CE ("Before the Common Era" and "Common Era") instead of BC or AD ("Before Christ" and "Anno Domini" ["in the year of the Lord"]), which imply a Christian view of the status of Jesus of Nazareth. Use of the title "Old Testament" for those books here designated as "the Hebrew Bible" is confined to instances expressing the historical view of various Christian interpreters. These conventions are followed in the study materials that we have produced; the translation has its own conventions which we are not at liberty to alter.

## ACKNOWLEDGMENTS

It remains to express our gratitude, first and above all to the contributors, whose learning has made this a work of which we are immensely proud, and whose uncommon patience with the editorial process made our task light. Allen D. Callahan was of assistance early in the development of the edition. Donald Kraus, Executive Editor in the Bible department at Oxford University Press, U.S.A., has guided this edition from its inception with wisdom and tact. Deborah Darcy, Michele McEnroe, Penelope Anderson, and Jennifer Grady, the editorial staff at the Press, have been meticulous in dealing with the complexities of an editorial process that went through many stages. Katrina Gettman carefully and conscientiously prepared the edited materials for the compositor. Leslie Phillips created the page design and oversaw every detail of the entire typesetting process, as well as providing the maps within the text. Peachtree Editorial and Proofreading Service proofread the entire text with extraordinary care and speed. The Scriptorium prepared the very useful index. We thank them all.

MICHAEL D. COOGAN

MARC Z. BRETTLER

CAROL A. NEWSOM

PHEME PERKINS

# To the Reader

When the King James or Authorized Version of the Bible was published in 1611, it contained, between the Old and the New Testaments, the books of the Apocrypha. These are books and portions of books that appear in the Latin Vulgate, either as part of the Old Testament or as an appendix, but are not in the Hebrew Bible. With the exception of 2 Esdras, these books appear also in the Greek version of the Old Testament that is known as the Septuagint.

In the course of time printers began to issue editions of the King James Bible without the books of the Apocrypha, and when the American Standard Version of the Bible was published in 1901, it did not include the Apocrypha. After the Revised Standard Version of the Bible was published in 1952, a request came from the General Convention of the Protestant Episcopal Church that the Standard Bible Committee undertake also the revision of the English translation of the Apocrypha. This work was accomplished in 1957. It was on the basis of this version that the text of a "Common Bible" (approved by both Roman Catholics and Protestants, was issued in 1973. Subsequently, in order to include all the texts accepted as Deuterocanonical by Eastern Orthodox Churches, the Standard Bible Committee prepared a version of 3 and 4 Maccabees and Psalm 151. These were issued in 1977, and the expanded edition of the Apocryphal/Deuterocanonical Books was endorsed by representatives of Orthodox communions. Since the contents of the collection known as Deuterocanonical Books vary among the churches that recognize them as authoritative, in the interest of clear identification they have been arranged in the New Revised Standard Version in four sections (see the Table of Contents).

For the translation of the Apocryphal/Deuterocanonical Books the Committee made use of a number of texts. In the case of most of the books the basic text was the standard edition of the Greek Septuagint prepared by Alfred Rahlfs and published by the Wurttemberg Bible Society (Stuttgart, 1935). For several of the books the more recently published individual volumes of Göttingen Septuagint project were utilized. For the book of Tobit it was decided to follow the form of the Greek text found in codex Sinaiticus (supported as it is by evidence from Qumran); where this text is defective, it was supplemented and corrected by other Greek manuscripts. For the three Additions to Daniel (namely, Susanna, the Prayer of Azariah and the Song of the Three Jews, and Bel and the Dragon) the Committee continued to use the Greek version attributed to Theodotion (the so-called "Theodotion-Daniel"). In translating Ecclesiasticus (Sirach), while constant reference was made to the Hebrew fragments of a large portion of this book (those discovered at Qumran and Masada as well as those recovered from the Cairo Geniza), the Committee generally followed the Greek text (including verse numbers) published by Joseph Ziegler in the Göttingen Septuagint (1965). But in many places the Committee has translated the Hebrew text when this provides a reading that is clearly superior to the Greek; the Syriac and Latin versions were also consulted throughout and occasionally adopted. The basic text adopted in rendering 2 Esdras is the Latin version given in the Biblia Sacra, edited by Robert Weber (Stuttgart, 1971). This was supplemented by consulting the Latin text as edited by R.L. Bensly (1895) and by Bruno Violet (1910), as well as the several Oriental versions of 2 Esdras, namely, the Syriac, Ethiopic, Arabic (two forms, referred to as

Arabic 1 and Arabic 2), Armenian, and Georgian versions. Finally, since the Additions to the Book of Esther are disjointed and unintelligible as they stand in most editions of the Apocrypha, we have provided them with their original context by translating the whole of the Greek version of Esther from Robert Hanhart's Göttingen edition (1983).

*For the Committee,*
BRUCE M. METZGER

# The Geography of the Bible

The geographical territory encompassed by the Bible (if one includes all identifiable places that are at least mentioned) includes most countries that border the Mediterranean Sea as well as those to its east. The majority of the narratives of the Hebrew Bible and the Apocrypha, as well as the Gospels in the New Testament, are set in that subregion of the Middle East known as the Levant and now governed by Lebanon, Syria, Jordan, Israel, and the Palestinian Authority. Egypt to the southwest and Mesopotamia (largely modern Iraq) and Persia (Iran) to the northeast are also part of the biblical landscape.

In Mesopotamia—the Greek term for the region between the Euphrates and Tigris Rivers (see color Maps 6 and 14 at the end of this volume)—as in Egypt, urban civilization developed by the fourth millennium BCE in the river valleys that provided the essential water for a region where rainfall was at best seasonal and at worst, especially in the case of Egypt, insufficient for agriculture. The regular summer flooding of the Nile Valley enabled the early and continuous existence of a remarkably long-lasting culture in Egypt, which because of its proximity to the Middle East was an important player in that region's history, and the locale for a number of key episodes in biblical narrative, most notably the Exodus. In Mesopotamia the inhabitants had harnessed the two rivers to provide, by means of an elaborate irrigation system, sufficient water for agriculture as well as for consumption. The several successive imperial powers that originated in Mesopotamia were able to use this productive region as a base for expansion, especially to the west, over which they exercised control throughout most of the first millennium BCE, until the Hellenistic period.

Although surrounded by vast deserts, there is a narrow stretch of land where agriculture can flourish that extends from the Nile Valley around to the Persian Gulf. The western part of this "fertile crescent," the Levant, has the same environment as much of the rest of the region adjacent to the Mediterranean, which today as for the last several millennia is characterized by almost ideal growing conditions for grapes and olives and for raising sheep and goats; grains and legumes and other fruits can also be grown in much of the region. Its climate is moderate, without excessively high or low temperatures for the most part, and with abundant rainfall that occurs mainly during the winter months. Jerusalem, for example, receives on average about 550 mm (22 in) of rain annually, most of it falling between November and February, with January being the rainiest month. Higher elevations to the north receive still more rainfall, and the southern and easternmost regions considerably less.

Within the Levant itself, the primary focus of biblical narratives, there is a wide variety of environments, the result of the geological substructure of the region, which presents dramatic changes in a relatively small area. Moving from west to east, the Mediterranean coast is occupied by a coastal plain that is about 25 km (15 mi) wide in the south but narrows as one moves north. It is interrupted by Mount Carmel, which juts into it, and virtually disappears in northen Israel and Lebanon. The coast itself has several excellent harbors in the north, from which the Canaanites and their successors the Phoenicians conducted a flourishing maritime trade. Farther south, the coast is relatively even, and there are few natural harbors. Phoenician influence eventually extended to such port cities as Acco, Dor, Joppa, and Ashkelon, and in the late first century Herod the Great constructed an impressive artificial harbor at Caesarea. Along the coastal plain was a major route, known as "the way of the sea" (Isa 9.1), used by traders and by armies of conquest between Egypt and Damascus. This route ran to the point where the coast narrows below Mount Carmel, from which passes led from the coastal plain to the Jezreel (Esdraelon) Valley; from there, several routes could be taken to the northeast.

Adjacent to the coastal plain in the south is an uplift of smaller, gentler hills called "the Shephelah" ("lowland"). As the natural western boundary of the kingdom of Judah in the Iron Age, and of other entities in the same region before and after, it was protected by a number of important cities, including Lachish and Gezer. The Shephelah forms the foothills of the mountainous region immediately to its east. This is the "hill country" of the biblical writers, with higher elevations to the north. For example, Jerusalem, about 55 km (35 mi) east of the Mediterranean, is 760 m (2,500 ft) above sea level, and many mountains in northern Galilee have elevations of over 1,000 m (3,300 ft). The highest peak in the region is Mount Hermon, which is 2,800 m (9,200 ft) high and for that reason is snow-covered year-round. The hill country is the setting for many of the key locales in biblical narrative, including the relatively inaccessible sites of Jerusalem, the capital of the kingdom of Judah (later Judea), and Samaria, the capital of the Northern Kingdom of Israel and later of the province with the same name. This central mountainous ridge is bisected by the broad, fertile Jezreel Valley, the major route to the interior and hence the location of a number of important ancient cities, including Jokneam, Megiddo, Taanach, Ibleam, and Jezreel. Mount Tabor rises from the floor of the Jezreel Valley in splendid isolation to an elevation of 588 m (1,929 ft) above sea level. The village of Nazareth, home of Jesus, is in the hills immediately north of the valley.

To the north of the Jezreel Valley lies Galilee. Because of its abundant springs, Galilee was dotted by settlements from prehistoric times, but it plays little role in biblical narratives until the end of the first millennium BCE, when it is the setting both for some of the campaigns of the Maccabees and, in the early first century CE, of the ministry of Jesus in the Gospels.

Just east of this central mountainous region is the Rift Valley. This major depression in the earth's crust extends from southern Turkey into East Africa; in Israel and Jordan it is almost entirely below sea level. Included in it are the Huleh Basin in northern Galilee, 70 m (230 ft) above sea level, where the site of Hazor was a major fortified city from early in the second millennium BCE until its destruction by the Assyrians in 732 BCE. Some 20 km (12 mi) south of Lake Huleh is the Sea of Chinnereth, or the Sea of Galilee (also called the Sea of Tiberias), a large lake about 20 km (12 mi) long that fills the valley. It lies 210 m (700 ft) below sea level, and is fed by the Jordan River, which flows into it from the north. It is habitat to nearly two dozen species of fish, and the fishing industry has been an important part of the local economy since prehistoric times. Many of the events narrated in the Gospels are set in the many towns and cities near the lake, and the region was a center of resistance against the Romans during the First Jewish Revolt of 66–73 CE.

The Jordan River continues its flow south from the Sea of Galilee 105 km (65 mi) to the Dead Sea. The valley itself is about 20 km (12 mi) wide and is entirely below sea level, with a semi-tropical climate that produces lush vegetation, even though because of its low elevation it receives relatively little rain. Important cities in the valley include Beth-shan (later Scythopolis) in the north and Jericho in the south. The valley was an important subsidiary route, especially during the Roman period, when Jews often avoided the district controlled by the Samaritans between Galilee and Judea.

The Dead Sea, lying 400 m (1,300 ft) below sea level, is the lowest point on the land mass of the earth. Because of evaporation due to high temperatures (a record 51° C [124° F] was measured here), the composition of the water is about 25 percent salt and other minerals, making organic life impossible and giving this lake its ancient name, "the salt sea" (Num 34.3,12; NRSV "Dead Sea"). The desolate region that surrounds it is the narrative setting for the legendary cities of Sodom and Gomorrah. On its western shore are Qumran, where the Dead Sea Scrolls were found, and Masada, a palace constructed by Herod that was the last Jewish outpost to be captured in the First Jewish Revolt.

East of the Rift Valley there is a rapid rise to the relatively level Transjordanian plateau to the east, with the elevation of modern Amman (ancient Rabbah, later Philadelphia) at ca. 820 m (2,700 ft) about average. This region too receives sufficient rainfall to sustain agriculture, and moreover is watered by two tributaries of the Jordan, the Yarmuk and the Jabbok, and by the Arnon, which flows into the Dead Sea. The northern part of the plateau, biblical Bashan, was famous for its cattle and for its oak forests, and in the Hellenistic and Roman periods was the location of several of the cities of the Decapolis. Traversing the Transjordanian plateau from south to north is a major route, called in the Bible the "King's Highway" (Num 20.17), used throughout antiquity as a conduit for the incense and spice trade from Arabia to Damascus. East of the plateau is a vast desert region, a continuation of the Arabian desert that extends northward to the Euphrates Valley, and thus limits the Fertile Crescent on both east and west. Apart from a few oases, especially Tadmor (later Palmyra) northeast of Damascus, this desert was essentially uninhabited in historic times.

South of the hill country of Judah lies the Negeb, a region of limited rainfall and hence marginal agriculture. The city of Beer-sheba is located in the extreme northern Negeb, just south of the Judean hill country. The Negeb merges into the Sinai peninsula, which is formed by the two northern arms of the Red Sea, separating the Sinai from the North African desert to its west and the Arabian desert to its east.

The small size of this region is out of proportion to its importance in ancient times and to the importance of the biblical texts which are set in it. West of the Jordan, the traditional boundaries of ancient Israel were Dan in the north and Beer-sheba in the south, separated by a distance of about 240 km (150 mi). Between these two cities, and between the Mediterranean and the Rift Valley, is a region with an area approximately the same as that of the state of Vermont. From another perspective, Jerusalem is about 55 km (35 mi) east of the Mediterranean and 25 km (16 mi) west of the Dead Sea. In the right conditions, both bodies of water are visible from Jerusalem's hills.

# The Persian and Hellenistic Periods

The Babylonian exile and the period of Persian domination that followed was a time of great transformation for Judean institutions, religious practices, and culture, but it was equally a time in which the fundamental continuity with preexilic traditions was reaffirmed and secured. When Nebuchadnezzar put down the rebellion of Judah in 586 BCE, he exiled to Babylonia a portion of the population, including the ruling class and the skilled artisans. Most, however, remained in Judah, where a subsistence economy was soon reestablished. Although the system of regular sacrifices at the Temple was disrupted, the ruined Temple remained a focus for religious observances. The book of Lamentations may preserve liturgical poems used on days commemorating the destruction of Jerusalem and its Temple. Little is known about the circumstances of those who went into exile, although it appears that the exiles were settled in a number of local communities in Babylonia, where they were able to oversee their own internal and cultural affairs under the leadership of Jewish elders and prophets (see Ezekiel; Isa 40–55).

The conquest of Babylon by the Persian king Cyrus the Great in 539 BCE brought significant changes. In keeping with his policy of respecting the various deities worshiped throughout the empire, a decree by Cyrus in 538 (see Ezra 1.1–4; 6.1–5) authorized the rebuilding of the Temple in Jerusalem and the return of the Temple vessels captured by Nebuchadnezzar. In addition, Cyrus allowed any of the exiles who wished to return to Judah to do so. Within the exilic community in Babylon the anonymous prophet known as "Second Isaiah" (Isa 40–55) strongly supported Cyrus and urged the exiles to return to Judah. Although historical sources are few and not always easy to interpret, it appears that only a small minority of the exiles and their descendants returned to Judah, most choosing to remain in Babylonia. This latter group became the nucleus of a large and highly significant Jewish Diaspora community (Jews of "the dispersion," that is, living outside Palestine), which strongly influenced the development of Judaism and Jewish culture during the following centuries.

Despite the decree of Cyrus, the Temple in Jerusalem was not rebuilt until 520–515 BCE. The reasons for the delay were various. Persian control over the western territories may actually have been tentative until after the Persians conquered Egypt in 525. The economy of Yehud (the name by which the Persian province of Judah was known) was weak, and there appears to have been friction between the population that had remained in the land and the small but powerful group who returned from exile with the authorization and financial backing of the Persian king. Conflicts with the neighboring territories of Samaria and Geshur and Ammon in Transjordan also complicated the situation. Within the Bible the prophetic books of Haggai and Zechariah and portions of Ezra 1–6 refer to this period, but these sources have to be read and interpreted critically, for they are neither consistent with one another nor easy to understand on their own terms. At least during the early part of Persian rule the governors of Judah appear to have been prominent Jews from the Diaspora community, one of whom, Zerubbabel, was actually a member of the Davidic royal family. The province of Yehud itself was very small, consisting of Jerusalem and the territory surrounding it within a radius of about 24–32 km (15–20 mi).

Once the Temple was rebuilt, it became the nucleus of the restored community, and consequently a focus of conflict (Isa 56–66; Malachi). The high priestly family, which had also returned from the Diaspora, became very powerful, and at least on occasion was in conflict with the governor appointed by the Persian king. Although the details are often not clear, there appears to have been continuing conflict during the fifth century between those Jews whose ancestors had been in exile and those whose ancestors had remained in the land. Those who returned from the Diaspora styled themselves the "children of the exile" and referred rather contemptuously to the rest as "people of the land," as though their very status as Jews was in question. In fact, the question of the limits of the community was one of the most contentious issues of the period, reflected both in the controversy over mixed marriages between Jewish men and ethnically foreign women (Ezra 10; Neh 13) and also in conflicts within the Jewish community over who had the right to claim the traditional identity as descendants of "Abraham" and "Israel" (see Isa 63.16 and more generally "Third Isaiah," Isa 56–66). Although the conflicts between various contending groups in early Persian period Yehud are largely cast in religious terms, there is no question that they were also in part socioeconomic (see Neh 5). All of these conflicts and efforts toward redefinition of the community, however, took place within the reality of Persian imperial control. Thus it is not by accident that the two most prominent figures involved in various reforms of mid-fifth century Yehud, Ezra and Nehemiah, were Diaspora Jews of high standing, carrying out tasks that had been specifically authorized by the Persian kings.

Because this was a period of self-conscious reconstruction, it was also a time of immense literary activity, as traditional materials were collected, revised, and edited, and new works composed. Although much of the Pentateuch may have existed in various forms during the time of the monarchy, it was probably reworked during the Persian period into something close to its final form. Indeed, some have suggested that this revision may have been undertaken under the sponsorship of the Persian government, reflecting Persia's interest in achieving stability throughout its empire by means of religious and legal reforms in the provinces. Although a history of Israel and Judah known as the Deuteronomistic History (Deuteronomy through 2 Kings) had been composed during the latter years of the monarchy and updated during the exile, a new version of that history, 1–2 Chronicles, was prepared during the Persian period (ca. 350 BCE). It clearly reflects the concerns of the postexilic community, focusing almost exclusively on the history of Judah and giving particular emphasis to the institution of the Temple. The books of Ezra and Nehemiah interpret events from the decree of Cyrus in 538 until the late fifth century.

In addition to the prophetic books composed at this time (Isa 56–66, Haggai, Zechariah, Malachi, and perhaps Joel), there is evidence that the texts of older prophets were also edited and reinterpreted. Psalmody had been an important element of worship at the First Temple, but appears to have taken on an even more significant role in the Second Temple. Although the expansion and revision of the book of Psalms may have continued until well into the Hellenistic or even Roman period, an important shaping of the psalter, perhaps including its division into five "books," was part of Persian period activity. Wisdom writing, too, flourished during this time. The book of Job, parts of the book of Proverbs, and perhaps Ecclesiastes were likely composed then.

THE HELLENISTIC PERIOD (333–363 BCE)

The westward expansion of the Persian Empire into the area of Asia Minor had brought it into conflict with Greece, since many of the cities of Asia Minor which came under Persian control had been founded and populated by Greeks. Twice the Persians had even invaded the Greek mainland, but were defeated on both occasions. Eventually, Philip of Macedon developed a plan to free the Greek cities of Asia Minor from Persian domination. Although he died before he could undertake the campaign, it was taken up by his son Alexander the Great in 334 BCE. Alexander, however, did not stop with the accomplishment of that initial goal. In 333 he continued down the Phoenician coast, subduing any city that resisted, conquered Egypt, then turned to the Persian heartland, defeating Darius III, the last Persian emperor, in 331. Alexander continued his conquest into the eastern reaches of the Persian Empire before returning in 324 to Babylon, which he apparently intended to establish as the capital of the empire he now controlled. He died in 323, however, before he could successfully organize his enormous territory. After Alexander's death, his generals fought for control of portions of the empire. By 301 an agreement gave Egypt to Ptolemy and Mesopotamia and Syria-Palestine to Seleucus. Ptolemy, however, occupied Palestine and southern Syria. Through a series of five wars extending over more than a hundred years, the Ptolemaic kings managed to hold onto their Palestinian territory, finally losing it to the Seleucids in 198 BCE.

Jerusalem had surrendered to Alexander in 333 and was relatively undisturbed by the events of his conquest. Samaria, too, surrendered, but rebelled in 332 and was severely punished, its inhabitants killed or sold into slavery, and the city refounded as a Macedonian military colony. Documents belonging to a group of Samaritans who fled and were later tracked down and killed by Alexander's troops have been excavated from the Wadi Daliyeh in the Jordan Valley. In contrast to the relatively settled conditions following Alexander's conquest, however, the dispute between the Ptolemies and the Seleucids over control of Palestine had serious consequences for Jerusalem and Judea. Not only did the wars sometimes affect Judean territory, but the nation's leaders had to make difficult choices concerning which power to support. The conflict between pro-Ptolemaic and pro-Seleucid factions within the Judean community was a significant factor in internal politics during the third century BCE.

Although the high priest was the primary representative of the Judeans, the Ptolemaic system of government and taxation had significant effects on the power structure of the country. The Ptolemies considered their territories primarily as a source of revenue. Rather than collecting funds directly, they employed "tax farmers," often local persons who bought the right to collect taxes for a specified area. Their profit was the difference between the amount they raised and the amount they had pledged to the government. Some of these positions were quite lucrative. Moreover, the Ptolemies also engaged prominent landowners to keep the peace as the heads of locally organized military villages. The Jewish historian Josephus preserves a long account of the Tobiad family, which served the Ptolemaic government in both capacities. From his lively narrative one has a sense not only of the power and wealth such positions could afford but also of the dangers and conflict they often entailed.

Culturally, the most significant effect of Ptolemaic rule was the establishment of a large Jewish Diaspora community in Egypt, centered in the new city of Alexandria, founded by Alexander the Great. Jews had often migrated to Egypt during times of economic or political trouble (see Jer 42–44). In the fifth century a Jewish military colony in the service of the Persian army was established at Elephantine (near modern Aswan). They had their own temple, though they remained in correspondence with Jerusalem concerning various religious matters, including the proper celebration of Passover and assistance in securing Persian permission for the rebuilding of the Elephantine temple after it was destroyed by local Egyptians. The various Aramaic documents found there (letters, contracts, marriage documents, records of legal disputes, etc.) provide an important glimpse into the daily life of this Jewish community in Egypt. Among the papyri was a copy of the book of Ahikar, a legendary story about an official in the Assyrian court at the time of Sennacherib and Esarhaddon (late eighth to early seventh century). Although the story was not Jewish in origin, it became popular among the Jews. The book of Tobit in the Apocrypha makes reference to Ahikar, even calling him Tobit's nephew (Tob 1.21–22).

The Hellenistic era Egyptian Diaspora, however, was much larger and more influential than the previous small communities of Jews living in Egypt. Its origins are not clear, but during the initial Ptolemaic conquest of Palestine, Ptolemy I apparently captured Jerusalem and took many prisoners back to Egypt, where they settled. Later many other Jews migrated there, presumably for economic reasons. The community continued to grow, both in numbers and in prosperity, until in the Roman period the Jewish population numbered in the hundreds of thousands, including many wealthy and prominent families.

By the middle of the third century BCE the Jewish community in Egypt had translated the books of the Torah (Genesis–Deuteronomy) into Greek, and over the next century or so, the other books of the Hebrew Bible were also translated. A legendary account of this project is contained in the *Letter of Aristeas*. According to that narrative, the impetus for the project came from the king himself, Ptolemy II Philadelphus (285–246 BCE), who wished to have a copy for the library of Alexandria. Seventy-two Jewish translators were brought to Egypt from Jerusalem for the task; hence the translation came to be known as the Septuagint, from the Greek word for "seventy." Scholars largely reject this account as unhistorical and maintain that the translation was undertaken for the religious needs of a Jewish community that no longer understood Hebrew.

In addition to the translation of the scriptures, the Jewish Diaspora in Egypt produced a rich and varied literature in Greek. One should not assume, however, that every Jewish writing in Greek originated in Alexandria, for during the Hellenistic period Greek became the most important international language. Educated Jews in Palestine and in the eastern Diaspora were nearly as likely to speak Greek as their counterparts in Egypt. Nevertheless, Alexandria remained unparalleled in the richness of its intellectual culture.

Throughout the Hellenistic world the increasing contact between different ethnic groups led to a new self-consciousness within communities about their own historical traditions and how these traditions related to those of other peoples. Thus historiographical writing, from the scholarly to the popular, became an important type of literary activity. In the late third century BCE an Alexandrian Jew named Demetrius investigated the chronologies of the biblical tradition, attempting to explain apparent contradictions and logical inconsistencies. A more entertaining work is Eupolemus's *Concerning the Kings in Judea*. A friend of Judas Maccabeus (see below), Eupolemus retold the biblical narrative with many embellishments and legendary details in an attempt to glorify Israel's traditions and accomplishments. In Eupolemus's history Moses appears as a culture-bringer, the inventor of the alphabet, which the Phoenicians and the Greeks later borrowed. Eupolemus particularly emphasizes the power and influence of the Israelite kingdom under David and Solomon, as well as the splendor of the Solomonic Temple. Not only was the Temple decorated with gifts from the kings of Tyre and Egypt, but Solomon reciprocated, sending a golden pillar to the temple of Zeus in Tyre.

The tendency to make connections between one's own traditions and those of other ethnic groups and to claim priority in the arts of civilization is reflected in the highly legendary history written in the second century BCE by an anonymous Samaritan. He identifies Enoch with Greek Atlas and claims that Abraham was the inventor of astrology, which he taught to the Egyptians when he sojourned there. A similar tendency is evident in the work of Artapanus. In his history Moses becomes the inventor of the technologies basic to civilization. Moreover, this Moses serves as a general in the Egyptian army, organizes Egyptian religion, and comes to be treated virtually as a god by the Egyptians, who identify him with Hermes (the Greek equivalent of the Egyptian god Thoth). The interest of Egyptian Jews in the biblical figure of Joseph is reflected in the romance, *Joseph and Asenath*, which tells the story of Joseph's marriage to the Egyptian noblewoman Asenath. She is depicted as a model convert to Judaism, and the story depicts some of the complications that attended Jewish-Gentile relations in Hellenistic Egypt.

Jewish poetic works composed in Greek also reflect a blending of cultural traditions. The Hellenistic genre of poetry praising cities and countries is represented in the work of Theodotus and

Philo the Epic Poet, who wrote poems about Shechem and Jerusalem, respectively. Even more ambitious was the work of Ezekiel the Tragedian, whose play *The Exodus* retold the account of Ex 1–15 in a style influenced by the Greek dramatists Aeschylus and Euripedes.

Greek philosophy, too, left its imprint on Hellenistic Jewish culture. Already in the second century BCE an Alexandrian Jew named Aristobulus produced a philosophical commentary on the Torah in which he claimed that the law of Moses anticipated many of the fundamental tenets of Greek philosophy and that the Greek philosophers Pythagoras, Socrates, and Plato derived their ideas from the Jewish law. Written toward the end of the Hellenistic period, the Wisdom of Solomon continues the biblical tradition of wisdom books like Proverbs but incorporates many elements of Greek rhetoric, philosophy, and literary style.

Less is known about the Jews of the eastern Diaspora who remained under Seleucid control than about the Jews of Egypt and Palestine, but it appears that peoples of various ethnic groups had access to economic and political advancement within the Seleucid Empire. Several writings from this time—Tobit, Dan 1–6, and Esther—suggest something of the outlook of Jews in the eastern Diaspora. Written originally in Hebrew or Aramaic, and later enlarged when they were translated into Greek, these books are works of fiction, edifying entertainments that tell the stories of Jews who achieved high status in foreign courts, were threatened by jealous rivals, and yet succeeded in securing personal power and the good will of the king. Though the stories are all set in the pre-Hellenistic period (Tobit in the Assyrian Empire, Daniel in the Babylonian exile, and Esther in the Persian court) they were probably written during the Seleucid period. While they acknowledge that faithful Jews may be vulnerable because of their religion, on the whole these are optimistic stories with a positive view of the Gentile kings.

The eastern Diaspora was also the conduit for important religious developments that arose from the contact between Judaism and the religions of Babylon and Persia. This influence is most clearly seen in the development of apocalyptic literature. Parts of the book of *1 Enoch* composed in the third century BCE reflect astronomical lore and traditions about antediluvian sages that derive from Babylonian sources. Although it is more difficult to trace the path of influence in its earliest stages, the dualistic religious beliefs of Persian Zoroastrianism almost certainly contributed to the development of Jewish apocalyptic thought and to some of the ideas of the sectarians at Qumran.

The eventual triumph of the Seleucid kingdom over the Ptolemies in the fifth Syrian war (198 BCE) obviously had a greater significance for the Jews of Judea than for those of Egypt. The Seleucid ruler Antiochus III treated the Judeans generously in appreciation for the support he received from the pro-Seleucid faction, granting an allowance for the Temple and various tax concessions, as well as confirming the Judeans' right to live "according to the laws of their country." Although relations began well, the difference in the way the Seleucid Empire governed its territories set the stage for a terrible conflict. Unlike the Ptolemaic system of centralized government administered with the cooperation of local leaders, the Seleucid regime was more decentralized. It derived some unity, however, from a network of Greek cities established throughout the empire. These were not necessarily ethnically Greek but were cities that had received a charter to organize as a *polis*, the Greek form of city government. Cultural prestige and economic advantages often led the leadership of Near Eastern cities to request such a charter.

The events leading up to the conflict between Judea and the Seleucid king Antiochus IV Epiphanes (175–164 BCE) are complex and not fully understood. In part they involved a struggle for succession to the high priesthood and the attempts of various contenders to secure the support of the king by paying him large sums of money. The first of the contenders, Jason, also paid to have Jerusalem established as a Greek *polis*, Antioch at Jerusalem. Neither of these acts in itself seems to have aroused much opposition in Jerusalem. The conflict was not a cultural conflict between Judaism and Hellenism, for Palestinian Jews had already incorporated significant elements of Hellenistic culture, which they considered quite compatible with their religious identity.

The crisis was sparked by the attempt by another contender, Menelaus, to buy the office of high priest. When he promised the king more than he could pay, he attempted to raise the money by taking golden vessels from the Temple. At this, a riot broke out in Jerusalem. Subsequent fighting between the forces of Jason and Menelaus convinced Antiochus that Judea was in revolt, and he retook the city and plundered the Temple, either in 169 or 168. Sometime later there were further disturbances, and Antiochus sent Syrian troops, which remained garrisoned in Jerusalem. Whether the status of Jerusalem at this point was a *polis* or a military colony is uncertain, but in either case in 167 the Temple was reorganized to accommodate the religious needs of the Syrian troops. A dedication was made to Zeus Olympius, the Greek name for the Syrian god Baal Shamem, and an altar established for sacrifice. Though Menelaus continued to preside as high priest, most Jews considered these actions to have profaned the Temple. In addition, the traditional practice of Judaism was suppressed by Antiochus, perhaps with the cooperation of Menelaus. Since religious persecution was virtually unknown in antiquity, it is difficult to know how Antiochus understood this repression and what he hoped to accomplish by it. Its actual result was to ignite the resistance known as the Maccabean revolt.

The Hasmoneans, Mattathias and his sons Judas Maccabeus, Jonathan, Simon, John, and Eleazar, were the leaders of the revolt. Although Judas managed to retake control of the Temple in 164 (its rededication being the occasion for the institution of the festival of Hannukah), it was not until 142 that the last of the Seleucid army was expelled and actual independence was secured by Simon. From then until the Roman conquest of Judea in 63 BCE the small kingdom was ruled by the Hasmonean family, which in addition to ruling as kings also assumed the office of high priest.

Religious and cultural life in Judea during the Seleucid and Hasmonean periods was rich and varied, with a remarkable quantity of literature produced in Hebrew, Aramaic, and to some extent in Greek. Sirach (Ecclesiasticus), Jesus Ben Sira's book of wisdom teachings, was probably composed in Hebrew about 180 BCE. Though largely traditional, it embodies several innovations: Ben Sira's identification of wisdom with the law of Moses, his praise of the contemporary high priest Simon II, and his own explicit claim to authorship. Ben Sira disapproved of apocalyptic speculation, but the crisis under Antiochus IV produced an upsurge in apocalyptic writings, not only Dan 7–12, but also *1 Enoch* 83–90 and *The Testament of Moses*. After the establishment of the Hasmonean monarchy, a supporter of the dynasty composed an account of the war in Hebrew (1 Maccabees), modeling it after the earlier books of Kings and Chronicles. An Egyptian Jewish writer, Jason of Cyrene, also wrote a history of the war in Greek (2 Maccabees), which was strongly influenced by forms of Hellenistic history writing.

Our knowledge of the literature of this time has been greatly increased by the discovery of the Dead Sea Scrolls at Qumran. Although this library was the property of a sectarian religious group related to the Essenes, it contained many Hebrew and Aramaic texts that were not sectarian compositions. Several of these scrolls contain noncanonical psalms, blessings, and other liturgical material. There are also many examples of what is called "the rewritten Bible," fairly free retellings of parts of the biblical story, embellished with new narrative episodes, prayers, and other elements (e.g., *Jubilees, The Genesis Apocryphon, The Apocryphon of Joshua*). Some texts elaborate on the apocalyptic elements of the books of Ezekiel and Daniel or place apocalyptic pronouncements in the mouths of other biblical figures, such as Levi, Qahat, and Amram. A number of texts, often having to do with matters of religious law, purport to be discourses of Moses. Perhaps the most remarkable document is the Temple Scroll, which apparently takes the form of an address by God to Moses. Although it incorporates material from the books of Exodus through Deuteronomy, it also contains much new material, including detailed instructions for building the Temple.

These documents and others pertaining to the Qumran sect itself help to clarify a number of issues of religious controversy that shaped the period of Hasmonean rule. The Temple and the Torah were central institutions for Judaism, which made them focal points for conflict. The Qumran scrolls show that conflict over the proper calendar (i.e., a solar or lunar calendar) for the conduct of Temple sacrifices was a major issue dividing the Qumran Essenes from their rivals, the Pharisees. Though the Hasmoneans were not always on good terms with the Pharisees, they adopted the lunar calendar favored by them. Many other writings from Qumran also elaborate their understanding of disputed issues such as purity, marriage, and sabbath observance, concerning which they were at odds with the Pharisees. Although the Qumran community did not compose apocalypses (i.e., reports of revelatory visions), they were strongly influenced by apocalyptic ideas and considered themselves to be living in the last times, just before God would intervene to restore proper order to the world. They supported their ideas in part by writing commentaries (*pesharim*) on biblical texts, which they read as referring to themselves and their opponents.

In general, the Hellenistic period presents a picture of Judaism that is much more diverse than is often imagined. Not only did Jews live in a vast range of lands from Egypt to Parthia, they also creatively adapted many elements from the varied Hellenistic cultures of these lands. Nevertheless, important symbols and institutions, including the Temple in Jerusalem, the scriptures, and common religious practices based in the Torah, provided a sense of unity and common identity.

# Calendar

The year was composed of twelve lunar months (beginning on the day of the new moon), with an intercalary month added periodically (see perhaps 1 Kings 12.33). In some traditions, and perhaps originally, the year began in the fall, at the autumnal equinox (see Ex 23.16; 34.22). In others, following Babylonian practice, the new year was celebrated in the spring. The fall new year became standard in postbiblical Judaism.

Months in the Bible are usually identified by ordinal numbers, beginning with the spring new year. Some months (in boldface in the following list) are also designated with names derived either from a Canaanite calendar or, in postexilic texts, from a Babylonian one; the names of months not found in the Bible are known from other ancient sources.

| | CANAANITE NAME | BABYLONIAN NAME | MODERN EQUIVALENT |
|---|---|---|---|
| First | **Abib** | **Nisan** | March–April |
| Second | **Ziv** | Iyyar | April–May |
| Third | | **Sivan** | May–June |
| Fourth | | Tammuz | June–July |
| Fifth | | Ab | July–August |
| Sixth | | **Elul** | August–September |
| Seventh | **Ethanim** | Tishri | September–October |
| Eighth | **Bul** | Marheshvan | October–November |
| Ninth | | Chislev | November–December |
| Tenth | | **Tebeth** | December–January |
| Eleventh | | **Shebat** | January–February |
| Twelfth | | **Adar** | February–March |

# Chronological Table of Rulers

| DATE | EGYPT | SYRIA |
|---|---|---|
| | HELLENISTIC PERIOD | Alexander (the Great) (336–323) |
| 300 BCE | Ptolemy I Soter (305–282) | Seleucus I Nicator (305–281) |
| | Ptolemy II Philadelphus (285–246) | Antiochus I Soter (281–261) |
| | | Antiochus II Theos (261–246) |
| | Ptolemy III Euergetes (246–221) | Seleucus II Callinicus (246–225) |
| | **Ptolemy IV Philopator (221–204)** | Seleucus III Soter Ceraunos (225–223) |
| | Ptolemy V Epiphanes (204–180); | Antiochus III (the Great) (223–187) |
| | Cleopatra I (180–176) | **Seleucus IV Philopator (187–175)** |
| | | **Antiochus IV Epiphanes (175–164)** |
| | **Ptolemy VI Philometor (180–145)**; | **Antiochus V Eupator (164–162)** |
| | **Cleopatra II (175–116)** | Demetrius I Soter (162–150) |
| | | **Alexander Epiphanes (Balas) (150–145)** |
| | **Ptolemy VII Neos Philopator (145)** | **Demetrius II Nicator (145–141 and 129–125)** |
| | **Ptolemy VIII Euergetes II Physcon (170–116)** | **Antiochus VI Epiphanes (145–142)** |
| | | **Trypho (142–138)** |
| | | **Antiochus VII Sidetes (138–129)** |
| | | Cleopatra Thea (126–121) |
| | | Antiochus VIII Grypus (125–121 and 121–96) |
| | Cleopatra III (116–101) | Seleucus V (125) |
| | Ptolemy IX Soter II (116–107 and 88–80) | Antiochus IX Cyzicenus (115–95) |
| 100 BCE | Ptolemy X Alexander I (107–88) | Seleucus VI (95) |
| | | Antiochus X Eusebes (95–83) |
| | | Antiochus XI Philadelphus (95) |
| | Cleopatra Berenice (101–88) | Demetrius III Eukairos (95–88) |
| | | Philip I Epiphanes Philadelphus (95–84) |
| | Ptolemy XI Alexander II (80) | Antiochus XII Dionysus Epiphanes (87–84) |
| | | Philip II (67–66) |
| | Ptolemy XII Auletes (80–59 and 55–51) | Antiochus XIII |
| 50 BCE | Cleopatra VII (51–30) | |
| | Ptolemy XIII (51–47) | |
| | Ptolemy XIV (47–44) | |

*Note:* Names in boldface occur in the Bible. Overlapping dates indicate coregencies. Date ranges are reigns, not life spans.

| DATE | PALESTINE |
|------|-----------|
| 300 BCE | |
| | **HASMONEAN RULERS** |
| | [Mattathias d. 166] |
| | **Judas Maccabeus,** son of Mattathias (165–160) |
| | **Jonathan,** son of Mattathias (160–142) |
| | **Simon,** son of Mattathias (142–135) |
| | **John** Hyrcanus I, son of Simon (135–104) |
| | Judah Aristobulus I , son of John Hyrcanus (104–103) |
| 100 BCE | Alexander Janneus, son of John Hyrcanus (103–76) |
| | Salome Alexandra, wife of Alexander Jannaeus (76–67) |
| | Aristobulus II, son of Alexander Jannaeus and Salome Alexandra (67–63) |
| | Hyrcanus II, son of Alexander Jannaeus and Salome Alexandra (63–40) |
| 50 BCE | Mattathias Antigonus, son of Aristobulus II (40–37) |

# THE APOCRYPHA

THE APOCRYPHAL/DEUTEROCANONICAL
BOOKS OF THE OLD TESTAMENT

*New Revised Standard Version*

# INTRODUCTION
## to the Apocryphal/Deuterocanonical Books

### DEFINITIONS

AS THE TERMS are used in the New Revised Standard Version translation, the Apocryphal/Deuterocanonical books are those works that were included in the Septuagint, the ancient Greek translation of the Hebrew Bible with additions, or in the Old Latin and Vulgate translations, but are not included in the Hebrew text that forms both the canon for Judaism and the Protestant Old Testament. All of these works, whether they are individual books or additions to the Hebrew texts of Esther and Daniel, have been regarded as canonical by one or more Christian communities, but not by all. (The exception to this is 4 Maccabees, which appears in an appendix to the Greek Bible.)

"Apocrypha" means "hidden things," but it is not clear why the term was chosen to describe these books. It could mean that they were "hidden" or withdrawn from common use because they were viewed as containing mysterious or esoteric teaching, too profound to be communicated to any except the initiated (see 2 Esd 14.45–46). Or it could mean that such books deserved to be "hidden" because they were spurious or heretical. This ambivalence has continued into the present, although increasingly even scholars from traditions that do not regard these books as canonical consider them of great value for understanding Judaism in the Hellenistic and Roman periods, and thus in the wider contexts, both literary and historical, of the later books in the Hebrew Bible and of the New Testament as well.

"Deuterocanonical," along with its coordinate term "protocanonical," is used in Roman Catholic tradition to describe the status of the two groups of books of the Old Testament. The "protocanon" consists of the books of the Hebrew Bible and the "deuterocanon" of the books whose inspiration came to be recognized later, after the matter had been discussed among some theologians and local churches. This distinction, introduced by Sixtus of Sienna in 1566, acknowledges the differences between the two categories while making clear that Roman Catholics accept as fully canonical those books and parts of books that Protestants call the Apocrypha (except the Prayer of Manasseh, Psalm 151, 3 and 4 Maccabees, and 1 and 2 Esdras, which both groups regard as apocryphal). Thus, although the terms "Deuterocanonical" and "Apocryphal" can describe the same collection of writings, they clearly indicate the difference in the status of the writings among different groups. In the NRSV translation, subheadings in the table of contents for these books, and in the text itself, explain the differing canonical status of various writings.

### THE ROMAN CATHOLIC, ORTHODOX, AND PROTESTANT CANONS
### OF THE OLD TESTAMENT

Toward the end of the fourth century CE, Pope Damasus commissioned Jerome, the most learned Christian biblical scholar of his day, to prepare a standard Latin version of the scriptures (the translation that was to become known as the Latin Vulgate). In the Old Testament Jerome followed the Hebrew canon; though he also translated the apocryphal books, he called attention to their distinct status in prefaces. Subsequent copyists of the Latin Bible, however, did not always include Jerome's prefaces, and during the medieval period the Western Church generally regarded these books as part of the holy scriptures without differentiation. In 1546 the Council of Trent decreed that the canon of the Old Testament includes them (with the exceptions as listed above). Subsequent editions of the Latin Vulgate text, officially approved by the Roman Catholic Church, place these books within the Christian sequence of the Old Testament books. Thus Tobit and Judith come after Nehemiah; the

Wisdom of Solomon and Ecclesiasticus come after the Song of Solomon; Baruch (with the Letter of Jeremiah as chapter 6) comes after Lamentations; and 1 and 2 Maccabees conclude the books of the Old Testament. Esther is given in its longer (Greek) form rather than in the version based solely on the Hebrew text; the Prayer of Azariah and Song of the Three Jews appear as vv. 24–90 of ch 3 of Daniel, and the stories of Susanna and Bel and the Dragon as chs 13 and 14 of Daniel. An appendix after the New Testament contains the Prayer of Manasseh and 1 and 2 Esdras, without implying canonical status.

The Eastern Orthodox Churches recognize several other books as authoritative. Editions of the Old Testament approved by the Holy Synod of the Greek Orthodox Church contain, besides the Roman Catholic Deuterocanonical books, 1 Esdras, Psalm 151, the Prayer of Manasseh, and 3 Maccabees, while 4 Maccabees appears in an appendix. Slavonic Bibles approved by the Russian Orthodox Church contain, besides the Deuterocanonical books, 1 and 2 Esdras (called 2 and 3 Esdras), Psalm 151, and 3 Maccabees.

Protestant Bibles have followed the Hebrew canon, though in a different order (see the essay, "The Canons of the Bible" on p. 453). The disputed books, if they are included at all, have generally been placed in a separate section, usually bound between the Old and New Testaments, but occasionally placed after the close of the New Testament.

## THE STATUS OF THE APOCRYPHAL/DEUTEROCANONICAL BOOKS IN CHRISTIANITY

During the first centuries of the Common Era, early Christian theologians (most of whom knew no Hebrew) quoted, in Greek, passages both from books in the Hebrew canon and from these additional works without making any distinction between them. Such citations were usually preceded by a word or phrase making it clear that the writer regarded the text being cited as canonical. During this time, only a few thinkers investigated the Jewish canon or distinguished between, for instance, the Hebrew text of Daniel and the addition of the story of Susanna in the Greek version.

By the fourth century, theologians in the eastern (Greek) churches had begun to recognize a distinction between the books in the Hebrew canon and the rest, though they continued to cite all of them as scripture. During the following centuries the matter was debated and, consequently, practice varied in the East, but at the Synod of Jerusalem in 1672 (which expressed the Orthodox churches' reaction to the Protestant Reformation), Tobit, Judith, Ecclesiasticus, Wisdom, Additions to Daniel, and 1 and 2 Maccabees were expressly designated as canonical.

In the western (Latin) church, on the other hand, though there has been some variety of opinion, in general theologians have regarded these books as canonical. More than one local synodical council (e.g., Hippo, 393, and Carthage, 397 and 419) justified and authorized their use as scripture. The so-called *Decretum Gelasianum*, a Latin document probably dating to the sixth century, contains lists of the books to be read as scripture and of books to be avoided as apocryphal. The former list, which is not present in all the manuscripts, includes among the biblical books Tobit, Judith, Wisdom, Ecclesiasticus, and 1 and 2 Maccabees.

Occasionally, however, theologians questioned the status of these books. Jerome, near the end of the fourth century, thought that books not in the Hebrew canon should be classed as apocryphal, and other thinkers, though always a minority, followed his view, at least theoretically. Toward the close of the fourteenth century John Wycliffe and his disciples produced the first English version of the Bible. This translation of the Latin Vulgate included all of the disputed books, with the exception of 2 Esdras. In the Prologue to the Old Testament, however, it makes a distinction between the books of the Hebrew canon, listed there, and the others which, the writer says, "shall be set among apocrypha, that is, without authority of belief." In the books of Esther and Daniel, the translators included a rendering of Jerome's notes calling the reader's attention to the additions.

At the time of the Reformation, Protestant thinkers came to the conclusion fairly early that they would need to determine which books were authoritative for the establishment of doctrine and which were not. For instance, disputes over the doctrine of Purgatory and of the usefulness of prayers and Masses for the dead involved the authority of 2 Maccabees, which contains what was held to be scriptural warrant for them (12.43–45). The first extensive Protestant discussion of the canon was Andreas Bodenstein's treatise *De Canonicis Scripturis Libellus* (1520). Bodenstein (or Carlstadt, after his place of birth) distinguished the books of the Hebrew Old Testament from the books of the Apocrypha, classifying the Apocrypha into two divisions. Concerning Wisdom, Sirach (Ecclesiasticus), Judith, Tobit, and 1 and 2 Maccabees, he says, "These are Apocrypha, that is, are outside the Hebrew canon; yet they are holy writings" (sect. 114). He continues:

> What they contain is not to be despised at once; still it is not right that Christians should relieve, much less slake, their thirst with them. . . . Before all things the best books must be read, that is, those that are canonical beyond all controversy; afterwards, if one has the time, it is allowed to peruse the controverted books, provided that you have the set purpose of comparing and collating the non-canonical books with those which are truly canonical (sect. 118).

The second group, 1 and 2 Esdras, Baruch, Prayer of Manasseh, and the Additions to Daniel, he declared without worth.

The first Bible in a modern vernacular language to segregate the apocryphal books from the others was the Dutch Bible published by Jacob van Liesveldt in 1526 at Antwerp. After Malachi there follows a section embodying the Apocrypha, which is titled, "The books which are not in the canon, that is to say, which one does not find among the Jews in the Hebrew."

The first edition of the Swiss-German Bible was published in six volumes (Zurich, 1527–29), the fifth of which contains the Apocrypha. The title page of this volume states, "These are the books which are not reckoned as biblical by the ancients, nor are found among the Hebrews." A one-volume edition of the Zurich Bible, which appeared in 1530, contains the apocryphal books grouped together after the New Testament. One Swiss reformer, Oecolampadius, declared in 1530: "We do not despise Judith, Tobit, Ecclesiasticus, Baruch, the last two books of Esdras, the three books of Maccabees, the Additions to Daniel; but we do not allow them divine authority with the others."

In reaction to Protestant criticism of the disputed books, on April 8, 1546, the Council of Trent gave what is regarded by Roman Catholics as the definitive declaration on the canon of the holy scriptures. After enumerating the books, which in the Old Testament include Tobit, Judith, Wisdom, Ecclesiasticus, Baruch, and the two books of Maccabees, the decree pronounces an anathema upon anyone who "does not accept as sacred and canonical the aforesaid books in their entirety and with all their parts, as they have been accustomed to be read in the Catholic Church and as they are contained in the old Latin Vulgate Edition" (trans. by Father H. J. Schroeder). The reference to "books in their entirety and with all their parts" is intended to cover the Letter of Jeremiah as chapter 6 of Baruch, the Additions to Esther, and the chapters in Daniel including the Prayer of Azariah, the Song of the Three Jews, Susanna, and Bel and the Dragon. It is noteworthy, however, that the Prayer of Manasseh and 1 and 2 Esdras, though included in some manuscripts of the Latin Vulgate, were denied canonical status by the Council. In the official edition of the Vulgate, published in 1592, these three are printed as an appendix after the New Testament, "lest they should perish altogether."

In England, though Protestants were unanimous in declaring that the apocryphal books were not to be used to establish any doctrine, differences arose as to the proper use and place of noncanonical books. A milder view prevailed in the Church of England, and the lectionary attached to the Book of Common Prayer, from 1549 onward, has always contained prescribed lessons from the Apocrypha. In addition, portions of the Song of the Three Jews are used as a canticle, or song of praise, alongside selected Psalms in the service of Morning Prayer. In reply to those who urged the discontinuance of reading lessons from apocryphal books, as being inconsistent with the sufficiency of scripture, the bishops at the Savoy Conference, held in 1661, replied that the same objection could be raised against the preaching of sermons, and that it was much to be desired that all sermons should give as useful instruction as did the chapters selected from the Apocrypha.

The Puritans took a stricter view and eventually published certain Geneva Bibles, printed in 1599 mainly in the Low Countries, that excluded the Apocrypha. The omission of the Apocrypha was presumably due to those responsible for binding the copies, since the titles of the apocryphal books occur in the table of contents at the beginning. During subsequent centuries Bibles that lacked the books of the Apocrypha came to outnumber those that included them, and soon it became difficult to obtain ordinary editions of the King James Version containing the Apocrypha.

For a more complete account of the formation of the various canons of scripture, see the essay on "The Canons of the Bible" on p. 453 ES.

THE HISTORICAL BACKGROUND TO THE APOCRYPHAL/
DEUTEROCANONICAL BOOKS

With the destruction of Jerusalem and the Temple by the Babylonians in 586 BCE, and the subsequent exile of the leading citizens of Judah in Babylon, the history of Israel underwent a decisive break. Henceforth there would always be Jewish communities outside the land of Israel, and even after the Persian king Cyrus allowed the exiles to return in 538 BCE, large communities flourished in Babylon and elsewhere.

For two centuries the Persians controlled the Near East, but little is known about Jewish history during this time. The Persian period came to an end when Alexander the Great completed a series of conquests that put him in control of Greece, the former Persian Empire, and Egypt. When Alexander died in 323, his empire was divided among his warring generals, and two of them—Seleucus, king of Syria, and Ptolemy, king of Egypt—and their successors fought over the territory of Judah, which fell first under Ptolemaic and then Seleucid dynastic control. Despite the political changes, however, the overall cultural influence remained: This was the era of the triumph of Hellenistic culture, including the use of the Greek language as the standard for the whole empire.

There had already been, in the Hebrew Bible, contention about such issues as intermarriage (Ezra 9.1–10.44; Neh 13.23–31). Now, with large numbers of Jews living outside the land as minorities within much larger and more dominant cultures, this issue and those of other religious observances came to be much more important. Stories of faithfully observant Jews among non-Jewish populations (Tobit, 3 Maccabees) were joined by expanded versions of books that strengthened this point (Greek Esther, the Prayer of Azariah and Song of the Three Jews in ch 3 of Daniel).

The Seleucid kings increasingly pressured the Jews to adopt Hellenistic ways in their religious observance, and in fact had some success. This effort came to a head under Antiochus IV Epiphanes (175–164). He installed Hellenizing high priests (Jason and Menelaus), against whom observant Jews rebelled. In response, Antiochus invaded Jerusalem in 169; in 167 he effectively outlawed the Jewish religion, making the teaching of the Torah a crime and establishing polytheistic worship in the Temple. This final provocation led to the ultimately successful Jewish revolt under the Hasmonean family, led by Mattathias and his five sons, one of whom, Judas, was known as Maccabeus, "the hammer." The revolt and the subsequent establishment of a Jewish government (which took more than twenty years to accomplish) are therefore referred to as Maccabean. This rule lasted for eighty years, until (because of constant power struggles among the various factions of Jews) the Romans were able to intervene and take direct control of the territory in 63 BCE.

## KINDS OF LITERATURE IN THE APOCRYPHAL/DEUTEROCANONICAL BOOKS

The Apocryphal/Deuterocanonical books contain several different literary genres, including histories, historical fiction, wisdom, devotional writings, letters, and an apocalypse. Though several of the books combine more than one of these genres, most of the books can be classified as predominantly one type or another. Thus 1 Esdras, 1 Maccabees, and, in a certain sense, 2 Maccabees are histories. First Esdras summarizes 2 Chr 35.1–36.23 and reproduces all of Ezra and Neh 7.38–8.12. Only 1 Esd 3.1–5.6 is a significant addition. First Maccabees recounts the history of the Seleucid persecutions and the rebellion and rise of the Maccabees. Second Maccabees, with its bombastic rhetoric and abundant use of invectives against the Seleucid tyrants and Hellenizing Jews, is an example of a popular Hellenistic genre, the "pathetic history," which uses highly charged language, exhortation, exaggeration, and other methods to stimulate the imaginations and emotions ("pathos") of readers. Third Maccabees is misleadingly named: It actually has nothing to do with the Maccabean period or the Seleucid dynasty, but deals with a period a half-century earlier and concerns the sufferings of the Jewish community in Egypt under the Ptolemaic rulers. It is a religious novel, written in Greek by an Alexandrian Jew sometime between 100 BCE and 70 CE. Using legendary elements, it tells three stories of conflict between Ptolemy IV (221–205) and the Jewish community in Egypt. The most dramatic section (5.1–6.21) describes Ptolemy's scheme to martyr the Jews: They were to be herded into an arena near Alexandria to be trampled under the feet of five hundred intoxicated elephants. The king's plan was finally foiled when angelic intervention terrorized those supervising the persecutions and also frightened the elephants into turning upon the Egyptian soldiers.

Fourth Maccabees is not a historical narrative but rather a Greek philosophical treatise addressed to Jews on the supremacy of reason over the passions of body and soul. In the form of a Stoic diatribe, or popular address, it uses narratives of exemplary behavior, and the conversations and arguments of character in the narratives, to explore philosophical issues. The author begins with a philosophical exposition of his theme, which he then illustrates at length with examples of the martyrs drawn from 2 Maccabees, who preferred death to committing apostasy. The book was probably written by a Hellenistic Jew before 70 CE. In early Christianity the Maccabean martyrs were venerated as saints and eventually accorded a yearly festival in the ecclesiastical calendar (August 1).

Judith, Tobit, Susanna, and Bel and the Dragon are short historical fictions written to convey a moral point, as well as to entertain. Except for Judith, which is set in Judah, the rest are sometimes referred to as "Diaspora novels" since they are all set in the Jewish Diaspora of Mesopotamia. Yet they differ from one another in other respects. Like the canonical stories of Daniel 1–6, Bel and the Dragon are court tales, in which the hero's relationship with the king and other members of the court provides the conflict of the plot. The motif of the lion's den, which occurs in Daniel 6, also occurs in the story of the dragon. In contrast to the earlier Daniel tales, however, Bel and the Dragon is preoccupied with the theme of the exposure of idols as false gods and their priests as fraudulent (see also the Letter of Jeremiah). Bel and the Dragon and Susanna are sometimes referred to as ancient examples of the detective story. Whereas Daniel functioned as an interpreter of dreams and visions in Daniel 1–6, in these stories Daniel uses cleverness and logical deduction to disclose deception.

Although Tobit, like Daniel, is represented as a court official of a Mesopotamian king, the story is concerned with personal and family affairs, not a rivalry at court. Thematically, Tobit may be compared with the prose story of Job, since it concerns the suffering of the righteous (both Tobit and his daughter-in-law Sarah). The book of Tobit is distinguished by the use of various folktale motifs (e.g., the motifs of the grateful dead, the angel in disguise, the dangerous bride and the demon lover), and by its reference to Ahikar, the hero of a non-Jewish folktale from Mesopotamia.

Judith might seem to bear comparison with 1 and 2 Maccabees, since it concerns a threat to the people from a foreign army. But whereas 1 and 2 Maccabees are histories, the fictional nature of Judith is evident from the story's flagrant historical inaccuracies (describing Nebuchadnezzar as king of Assyria and the invasion as taking place after the people's return from exile!). A better comparison might be between Judith and Esther. Though set in Judah rather than the Diaspora, Judith, like Esther, tells how a courageous Jewish woman saves her people from enemies bent on destroying them.

Didactic literature is represented in the Apocrypha by the two treatises on wisdom: the Wisdom of Solomon, and the Wisdom of Jesus son of Sirach (also known as Ecclesiasticus). Sirach, which was originally composed in Hebrew ca. 180 BCE, shows particularly close connections with the style and content of the book of Proverbs in the Hebrew Bible, from which it is a natural development. The Wisdom of Solomon, by contrast, contains no proverbial material, such as characterizes the Hebrew wisdom tradition. It does, however, share with Proverbs and Sirach an interest in the figure of wisdom personified as a woman. What makes the Wisdom of Solomon distinctive is the strong influence of Greek literary styles and philosophical ideas. Thus, it comes from the Greek-speaking Diaspora, most probably from Alexandria.

The Prayer of Manasseh is a hymnic lament of great feeling and literary skill. The Prayer of Azariah and the Song of the Three Jews are both modeled on psalms that are liturgical in form. In addition to the 150 psalms comprising the Book of Psalms in the Hebrew Bible, during the Hellenistic and Roman periods such hymns were composed in Hebrew and in other languages; there are a number of such compositions in the Dead Sea Scrolls. Another, which celebrates the prowess of young David in slaying Goliath, is appended (as Ps 151) to the Psalter in Greek manuscripts.

The Hebrew Bible contains no books that are in the form of a letter, although letters (or excerpts) occur at various places. There are decrees (Ezra 1.1–6), diplomatic correspondence (1 Kings 5.2–6), royal commands (2 Sam 11.14–15), even forgeries (1 Kings 21.8–10), but all are used to advance the narratives in which they occur, or explain incidents that follow, so it is unclear how representative they are. Twenty-one of the twenty-seven books of the New Testament are in the form of letters, though some (for instance, Hebrews) are more like sermons than letters. The Letter of Jeremiah, which dates from the Hellenistic period, may have provided later, Christian writers with an example of how this literary form could be used for religious purposes, combining theological content with a direct personal approach.

Finally, 2 Esdras, a book that purports to reveal the future, is a specimen of apocalypse. An apocalypse is literally "an unveiling." Like the last six chapters of Daniel in the Hebrew Bible and the book of Revelation in the New Testament, which also are apocalypses, 2 Esdras uses metaphoric language, symbolic numbers and animals (including composites, like the eagle with three heads and numerous wings in ch 11), and angelic messengers who reveal hidden information.

Despite this diversity of genres, most of which parallel or are developed from similar ones in the Hebrew Bible, there is no correlative to classical prophecy. Even within the prophetic books of the Hebrew Bible, apocalyptic elements had already begun to supplant strict prophecy (for instance, Isaiah chs 24–27; Ezekiel chs 38–39; Joel ch 2; Zechariah chs 9–14). This absence perhaps supports the view that Josephus, the Jewish historian, expressed (Ag. Ap. 1.8), that "the exact succession of the prophets" had been broken after the Persian period; a similar idea is found in later rabbinic literature. Sometimes there is a direct statement that "prophets ceased to appear" (1 Macc 9.27); at other times the writers express the hope that prophecy might one day return (1 Macc 4.46; 14.41). When a writer imitates prophetic style, as in the book of Baruch, he repeats with slight modifications the language of the older prophets. But the introductory phrase, "Thus says the LORD," which occurs so frequently in the prophetic literature of the Hebrew Bible, is absent from the Apocryphal/Deuterocanonical Books.

## THE APOCRYPHAL/DEUTEROCANONICAL BOOKS WITHIN JUDAISM

All of the writings in the Apocryphal/Deuterocanonical books are Jewish in origin, but it is not clear that they were collected by any particular community of Jews. Some of them (for instance, Sirach) were quoted by rabbis, but for others no evidence exists that they were regarded as central to the Jewish community at any point. Some (Tobit, parts of Sirach, the Letter of Jeremiah, and Psalm 151) are among the Dead Sea Scrolls, and were therefore presumably of importance to the Essene community there, but whether or not they were considered "canonical" is not clear.

Nevertheless, influences from some of these works are apparent within Judaism. As mentioned above, rabbinic literature quotes and appropriates sayings from Sirach. The martyrdom of the woman and her seven sons (2 Macc 7.1–42; 4 Macc 8.3–18.24) is recounted in several places (Lam. Rab 1.50; Git. 57b; Seder Eliyahu R 29).

First and Second Maccabees (1 Macc 4.36–59; 2 Macc 10.1–8) provide the original accounts of the purification of the Temple in 164 BCE, which is commemorated in the festival of Hanukkah. The Talmudic legend (*Shab.* 21b) that oil in the Temple, though only enough for one day, nevertheless burned for eight—the supposed reason for the eight-day length of the observance—is not found in the books of Maccabees. Judith was, during the Middle Ages, associated with Hanukkah as well, on the grounds that both had to do with rallying an oppressed Jewish population to overthrow a threatening or occupying power.

Both Tobit and 2 Esdras influenced later Jewish literature and were popular during the Middle Ages. Baruch may have been read in synagogues at one time (see Bar 1.14), and Baruch himself, and therefore his writing, were regarded in some rabbinic writings as sharing Jeremiah's prophetic status (*Sifre Num 78*; *Seder Olam R 20*; *Bab Meg.* 14b; *Jer Sot.* 9.12). Susanna's story is recounted in the Babylonian Talmud (b. San. 93a).

## NEW TESTAMENT USES OF THE APOCRYPHAL/DEUTEROCANONICAL BOOKS

None of the books of the New Testament quote directly from any Apocryphal book, in distinction from the frequent quotation of the thirty-nine books in the Hebrew Bible. On the other hand, several New Testament writers make allusions to one or more apocryphal books. For example, what seem to be literary echoes from the Wisdom of Solomon are present in Paul's Letter to the Romans (compare Rom 1.20–29 with Wis 13.5, 8; 14.24, 27; and Rom 9.20–23 with Wis 12.12, 20; 15.7) and in his correspondence with the Corinthians (compare 2 Cor 5.1,4 with Wis 9.15). The short Letter of James, a typical bit of "wisdom literature" in the New Testament, contains allusions not only to the book of Proverbs in the Hebrew Bible but to gnomic sayings in Sirach as well (compare Jas 1.19 with Sir 5.11; and Jas 1.13 with Sir 15.11–12).

## THE FURTHER INFLUENCE OF THE APOCRYPHAL/DEUTEROCANONICAL BOOKS

The influence of the Apocrypha has been widespread, inspiring homilies, meditations, and liturgical forms, and providing subjects for poets, dramatists, composers, and artists. Some common expressions and proverbs have come from the Apocrypha. The sayings, "A good name endures forever" and "You can't touch pitch without being defiled," are derived from Sir 41.13 and 13.1. The affirmation in 1 Esd 4.41, "Great is Truth, and mighty above all things" (King James Version), or its Latin form, *Magna est veritas et praevalet*, has been used as a motto or maxim in a wide variety of contexts.

The importance of these books extends to the information they supply concerning the development of Jewish life and thought just prior to the beginning of the Common Era. The stirring political fortunes of the Jews in the time of the Maccabees; the rise of what has been called normative Judaism, and the emergence of the sects of the Pharisees and the Sadducees; the lush growth of popular belief in the activities of angels and demons, and the use of magic to drive away malevolent influences; the first reflections on "original sin" and its relation to the "evil inclination" present in every person; the blossoming of apocalyptic hopes relating to the messiah, the resurrection of the body, and the vindication of the righteous—all these and many other topics receive welcome light from the Apocryphal/Deuterocanonical books.

(a) The following books from Tobit through 2 Maccabees are recognized as Deuterocanonical Scripture by the Roman Catholic, Greek, and Russian Orthodox Churches.

# TOBIT

🙡 🙣

Combining ethical exhortation, prayers, and doxologies with broad humor, a rollicking plot, and vivid characters, the book of Tobit is a splendid example of the Jewish novella. In addition to its entertainment value, it offers to historians information about the postexilic period and to theologians a view of a God who tests the faithful, responds to prayers, and redeems the covenant community.

The title character, Tobit, was exiled with his wife Anna from the region in Galilee held by the tribe of Naphtali. Removed to Assyria, he eventually, like Joseph, Mordecai, and Daniel, found himself in the service of a foreign ruler—in Tobit's case, as an officer of the court of Shalmaneser. This pious Israelite too is tested: First he is removed from his official position and then he is persecuted by Shalmaneser's successor for his insistence on burying the corpses of his fellow Jews. Most ignominious of all: One evening, following yet another burial, Tobit is blinded by a bird with unfortunate aim. Forced to depend on others, including his wife, for support, and following an argument with her in which she questions the value of his piety, Tobit prays for death.

At the same time his relative Sarah is also praying for death. The demon Asmodeus, who has fallen in love with her, has killed each of her seven successive grooms on the wedding night. To resolve these somewhat improbable situations, the angel Raphael will escort Tobit's son, Tobias, first to Media to exorcise the demon and marry Sarah and then back to Nineveh to cure Tobit.

The relatively complex plot is tied together by the parallel situations of older father and bride-to-be, frequent doxologies, almost incessant references to almsgiving, and the shifting of scenes between Nineveh and Ecbatana. The humorous aspects of the tale—from the angel in disguise to the attack of a magical fish—make the stories of Tobit and Sarah border on the farcical and so prevent the book from becoming tragic or maudlin. Readers familiar with biblical motifs will recognize various genres and themes incorporated in the volume: wisdom sayings, the antipathy between Sarah of Genesis and her maidservant Hagar, the search for a bride for Isaac, the success of the Jew in the royal court, the problems of life in the Diaspora, Job's trials, the role of angels, the centrality of Jerusalem, the fulfillment of prophecy and, especially, the importance of charity. The numerous personal prayers, found also in the stories of Judith, Daniel and the Additions (Prayer of Azariah and Song of the Three Jews, Susanna, and Bel and the Dragon), the Greek Additions to Esther, and elsewhere in Jewish postexilic literature, emphasize the universal authority and righteousness of God.

The book of Tobit is also replete with information concerning family life, travel, burial and eating customs, gender roles, and medicine. More than mere data, these various matters testify to the author's interest in providing guidance for life in exile: Where Temple sacrifice is unavailable and the people are scattered, the story insists that Jews maintain their identity not only through piety and practice, but also through strong bonds between parents and children, between husbands and wives, and with family members and fellow Jews. To preserve the community, Tobit also insists that his son imitate Abraham, Isaac, and Jacob, who "took wives from among their kindred" (4.12–13).

In addition to its references to biblical prophecy, characters, and theology, the volume offers connections to well-known folktale motifs, including the dangerous bride, the monster in the nuptial chamber, the supernatural being in disguise, the miraculous animal, and the grateful dead. Specifically mentioned are the characters of Ahikar and his nephew, whose story was well known in antiquity; there may also be some hints of Homer's *Odyssey*.

Although the original language of the document was likely Aramaic, that text has not survived. The translation below is based on the Greek text of Codex Sinaiticus; other versions include the Old Latin, Jerome's Vulgate, a medieval Aramaic rendering, Coptic, Syriac, Ethiopic, Armenian, and even fragments in both Hebrew and Aramaic from Qumran (the Dead Sea Scrolls). The book dates to the early postexilic period, likely sometime in the third century BCE; its place of composition remains unknown, with plausible suggestions including the eastern Diaspora, Egypt, and Israel.

1 This book tells the story of Tobit son of Tobiel son of Hananiel son of Aduel son of Gabael son of Raphael son of Raguel of the descendants[a] of Asiel, of the tribe of Naphtali, 2 who in the days of King Shalmaneser[b] of the Assyrians was taken into captivity from Thisbe, which is to the south of Kedesh Naphtali in Upper Galilee, above Asher toward the west, and north of Phogor.

3 I, Tobit, walked in the ways of truth and righteousness all the days of my life. I performed many acts of charity for my kindred and my people who had gone with me in exile to Nineveh in the land of the Assyrians. 4 When I was in my own country, in the land of Israel, while I was still a young man, the whole tribe of my ancestor Naphtali deserted the house of David and Jerusalem. This city had been chosen from among all the tribes of Israel, where all the tribes of Israel should offer sacrifice and where the temple, the dwelling of God, had been consecrated and established for all generations forever.

5 All my kindred and our ancestral house of Naphtali sacrificed to the calf[c] that King Jeroboam of Israel had erected in Dan and on all the mountains of Galilee. 6 But I alone went often to Jerusalem for the festivals, as it is prescribed for all Israel by an everlasting decree. I would hurry off to Jerusalem with the first fruits of the crops and the firstlings of the flock, the tithes of the cattle, and the first shearings of the sheep. 7 I would give these to the priests, the sons of Aaron, at the altar; likewise the tenth of the grain, wine, olive oil, pome-

a Other ancient authorities lack *of Raphael son of Raguel of the descendants*  b Gk *Enemessaros*
c Other ancient authorities read *heifer*

**1.1–2: Exilic context.** The superscription establishes Tobit's location and genealogy. **1:** *Tobiel,* "God is my good"; the names of his family members have the suffix *el,* meaning "God." Genealogy becomes increasingly important in Second Temple Judaism (Jdt 8; Mt 1; Lk 3). **2:** *Shalmaneser,* 2 Kings 15.29 states that Tiglath-pileser III exiled the Naphtalites to Assyria; in 722 BCE, *Sargon of Assyria,* Shalmaneser's brother, conquered Samaria, Israel's capital, and resettled substantial portions of the population (2 Kings 17.1–6). *Kedesh,* in northern Galilee, defeated by Joshua (Josh 12.22; 19.37), was the home of Deborah's general Barak (Judg 4.6) and the site of a Maccabean victory (1 Macc 11.63,73). *Asher* may be a Greek spelling of Hazor, ca. 10 km (6 mi) south-southeast of Kedesh.
**1.3–9: Tobit's background. 3–4:** Tobit consistently emphasizes his own righteousness despite Israel's apostasy. **3:** *Nineveh,* the capital of Assyria. **4:** Tobit's lifespan, ranging from before 928 to after 722 BCE, indicates the tale's fictional nature (the book of Judith similarly displays chronological fiction). *Naphtali* was one of the ten northern tribes that rebelled against the Davidic house in 928 (1 Kings 12.19–20); Tobit nevertheless consistently expresses concern for Jerusalem, the capital of the southern kingdom. **5:** *Calf,* 1 Kings 12.28–29; *Dan* is not far northeast of Kedesh (1.2n.). **6:** Participation in the pilgrimage *festivals* (Deut 12.11) of Booths (Sukkot), Passover (Pesach), and Weeks (Shavuot/Pentecost) entailed the giving of *first fruits* (Deut 26.1–11), *firstlings* (Ex 13.12), *tithes of the cattle* (Lev 27.32), *first shearings of the sheep* (Deut 18.4). **7:** For tithing of produce, see Lev 27.30; Deut 14.22–29. **8:** *Deborah* indicates

granates, figs, and the rest of the fruits to the sons of Levi who ministered at Jerusalem. Also for six years I would save up a second tenth in money and go and distribute it in Jerusalem. 8 A third tenth[a] I would give to the orphans and widows and to the converts who had attached themselves to Israel. I would bring it and give it to them in the third year, and we would eat it according to the ordinance decreed concerning it in the law of Moses and according to the instructions of Deborah, the mother of my father Tobiel,[b] for my father had died and left me an orphan. 9 When I became a man I married a woman,[c] a member of our own family, and by her I became the father of a son whom I named Tobias.

10 After I was carried away captive to Assyria and came as a captive to Nineveh, everyone of my kindred and my people ate the food of the Gentiles, 11 but I kept myself from eating the food of the Gentiles. 12 Because I was mindful of God with all my heart, 13 the Most High gave me favor and good standing with Shalmaneser,[d] and I used to buy everything he needed. 14 Until his death I used to go into Media, and buy for him there. While in the country of Media I left bags of silver worth ten talents in trust with Gabael, the brother of Gabri. 15 But when Shalmaneser[d] died, and his son Sennacherib reigned in his place, the highways into Media became unsafe and I could no longer go there.

16 In the days of Shalmaneser[d] I performed many acts of charity to my kindred, those of my tribe. 17 I would give my food to the hungry and my clothing to the naked; and if I saw the dead body of any of my people thrown out behind the wall of Nineveh, I would bury it. 18 I also buried any whom King Sennacherib put to death when he came fleeing from Judea in those days of judgment that the king of heaven executed upon him because of his blasphemies. For in his anger he put to death many Israelites; but I would secretly remove the bodies and bury them. So when Sennacherib looked for them he could not find them. 19 Then one of the Ninevites went and informed the king about me, that I was burying them; so I hid myself. But when I realized that the king knew about me and that I was being searched for to be put to death, I was afraid and ran away. 20 Then all my property was confiscated; nothing was left to me that was not taken into the royal treasury except my wife Anna and my son Tobias.

21 But not forty[e] days passed before

a A third tenth added from other ancient authorities  b Lat: Gk Hananiel  c Other ancient authorities add Anna  d Gk Enemessaros  e Other ancient authorities read either forty-five or fifty

women's roles in religious education; the name may have some connection to Kedesh and Naphtali (Judg 4–5; Tob 1.2n.). 9: Endogamy, i.e., marriage within the kinship group, is a major theme (3.17; 4.12–13; 6.11–12; 7.10–11; Gen 11.29; 24.3–4; 27.46–28.2; Deut 7.3–4; Ezra 9–10; Neh 10.28–30; but contrast the marriages of Ruth and Esther); intermarriage became a particularly acute issue in the Diaspora.

1.10–22: Early captivity. The setting and Tobit's initial political success resemble that of Dan 1–6. Like Daniel and his companions (Dan 1.8–20), Esther (Add Esth 14.17), and Judith (Jdt 12.1–3), Tobit follows Jewish dietary laws (Lev 11). 13: Tobit regards his stewardship as a reward for righteousness; later events temporarily question such justice. 14: Media (northern Iran) is east of Assyria; on Israelites exiled there, see 2 Kings 17.6. Ten talents is approximately 350 kg (750 lb). 15: His son Shennacherib: Sargon II, not Shalmaneser, was Sennacherib's father (see 1.2n., 18–20n.). Similar historical inaccuracies mark the opening of the book of Judith. 16–17: Tobit continues his earlier charitable works (1.3). Burying corpses is his principal sign of righteousness (1.18–20; 2.3–8; 4.3–4; 6.15; 14.10–13; Deut 28.26; 1 Kings 14.11; 21.24; Jer 7.33; Ezek 29.5); their unburied presence indicates Assyria's brutality. Appropriately, among Christians in the Middle Ages Tobit was hailed as the patron saint of gravediggers. 18: Sennacherib succeeded his father Sargon II in 705 BCE. Fleeing . . . in those days of judgment, a reference to the defeat of Sennacherib by divine intervention; see 2 Kings 19.35–36. 19: Like Sophocles's Antigone, Tobit is threatened with death for burying the executed. 20: As in Daniel (Dan 3, 6), Tobit is victimized for practicing Jewish piety. 21: Killed him, see 2 Kings 19.37. Esar-haddon reigned 681–669 BCE.

two of Sennacherib's[a] sons killed him, and they fled to the mountains of Ararat, and his son Esar-haddon[b] reigned after him. He appointed Ahikar, the son of my brother Hanael[c] over all the accounts of his kingdom, and he had authority over the entire administration. 22 Ahikar interceded for me, and I returned to Nineveh. Now Ahikar was chief cupbearer, keeper of the signet, and in charge of administration of the accounts under King Sennacherib of Assyria; so Esar-haddon[b] reappointed him. He was my nephew and so a close relative.

2 Then during the reign of Esar-haddon[b] I returned home, and my wife Anna and my son Tobias were restored to me. At our festival of Pentecost, which is the sacred festival of weeks, a good dinner was prepared for me and I reclined to eat. 2 When the table was set for me and an abundance of food placed before me, I said to my son Tobias, "Go, my child, and bring whatever poor person you may find of our people among the exiles in Nineveh, who is wholeheartedly mindful of God,[d] and he shall eat together with me. I will wait for you, until you come back." 3 So Tobias went to look for some poor person of our people. When he had returned he said, "Father!" And I replied, "Here I am, my child." Then he went on to say, "Look, father, one of our own people has been murdered and thrown into the market place, and now he lies there strangled." 4 Then I sprang up, left the dinner before even tasting it, and removed the body[e] from the square[f] and laid it[e] in one of the rooms until sunset when I might bury it.[e] 5 When I returned, I washed myself and ate my food in sorrow. 6 Then I remembered the prophecy of Amos, how he said against Bethel,[g]

"Your festivals shall be turned into
    mourning,
    and all your songs into
    lamentation."
And I wept.

7 When the sun had set, I went and dug a grave and buried him. 8 And my neighbors laughed and said, "Is he still not afraid? He has already been hunted down to be put to death for doing this, and he ran away; yet here he is again burying the dead!" 9 That same night I washed myself and went into my courtyard and slept by the wall of the courtyard; and my face was uncovered because of the heat. 10 I did not know that there were sparrows on the wall; their fresh droppings fell into my eyes and produced white films. I went to physicians to be healed, but the more they treated me with ointments the more my vision was obscured by the white films, until I became completely blind. For four years I remained unable to see. All my kindred were sorry for me, and Ahikar took care of me for two years before he went to Elymais.

11 At that time, also, my wife Anna earned money at women's work. 12 She used to send what she made to the owners and they would pay wages to her. One day,

a Gk his    b Gk Sacherdonos    c Other authorities read Hananael    d Lat: Gk wholeheartedly mindful    e Gk him    f Other ancient authorities lack from the square    g Other ancient authorities read against Bethlehem

**21–22:** *Ahikar* is a well-known figure in Semitic stories; his relationship to Tobit, noted only in this book, enhances Tobit's status. Ahikar's own story is summarized in 14.10.

**2.1–10: Tobit's blindness.** Tobit's charity toward others results in his being blinded. **1:** *Pentecost,* the spring harvest (Lev 23.15–21; Deut 16.9–12; 2 Chr 8.13). **2:** Tobit consistently demonstrates charity toward his people in exile (see 4.7–11,16). **5:** *Washed,* Num 19.11–13 commands washing as purification after contact with a corpse. **6:** *Amos* 8.10, one of the few scriptural citations in the book and another sign of composition in the Second Temple period. **9:** It is unclear why Tobit sleeps outside, especially since after moving the corpse he did return home to eat dinner. A similar connection of dinner and gravedigging, but with humorous overtones, appears in 8.9–11. **10:** *Droppings,* Tobit is blinded in an ignominious and potentially farcical scene. *Elymais,* earlier Elam, was a region in northwestern Persia.

**2.11–14: The argument.** Now dependent on others, Tobit becomes increasingly despondent. **11:** *Women's work* is weaving; Tobit's earlier source of income, aside from investments, is unmentioned. **13:**

the seventh of Dystrus, when she cut off a piece she had woven and sent it to the owners, they paid her full wages and also gave her a young goat for a meal. 13 When she returned to me, the goat began to bleat. So I called her and said, "Where did you get this goat? It is surely not stolen, is it? Return it to the owners; for we have no right to eat anything stolen." 14 But she said to me, "It was given to me as a gift in addition to my wages." But I did not believe her, and told her to return it to the owners. I became flushed with anger against her over this. Then she replied to me, "Where are your acts of charity? Where are your righteous deeds? These things are known about you!"[a]

3 Then with much grief and anguish of heart I wept, and with groaning began to pray:
2 "You are righteous, O Lord,
    and all your deeds are just;
  all your ways are mercy and truth;
    you judge the world.[b]
3 And now, O Lord, remember me
    and look favorably upon me.
  Do not punish me for my sins
    and for my unwitting offenses
    and those that my ancestors
      committed before you.
  They sinned against you,
4   and disobeyed your
      commandments.
  So you gave us over to plunder, exile,
      and death,
    to become the talk, the byword,
      and an object of reproach
      among all the nations among whom
        you have dispersed us.
5 And now your many judgments are
      true
    in exacting penalty from me for my
      sins.
  For we have not kept your
      commandments
    and have not walked in accordance
      with truth before you.
6 So now deal with me as you will;
    command my spirit to be taken
      from me,
  so that I may be released from the
      face of the earth and become
      dust.
  For it is better for me to die than to
      live,
  because I have had to listen to
      undeserved insults,
    and great is the sorrow within me.
  Command, O Lord, that I be released
      from this distress;
  release me to go to the eternal
      home,
    and do not, O Lord, turn your face
      away from me.
  For it is better for me to die
    than to see so much distress in my
      life
    and to listen to insults."

7 On the same day, at Ecbatana in Me-

a Or to you; Gk with you    b Other ancient authorities read you render true and righteous judgment forever

The outburst nuances Tobit's claims of righteousness and may also reflect his disgrace in being supported by a woman (Sir 25.22). **14:** Like Job's wife (Job 2.9), Anna questions the relationship between good deeds and a good life.

**3.1–6: Tobit's prayer.** The fight coupled with Anna's observations about justice, not Tobit's blindness, causes him to seek death. Personal prayer is a major motif of this book (3.11–15; 8.4–8,15–17; 13.1–17) as well as Jewish-Hellenistic literature in general (see Jdt 9; Esth 14.1–9; Song of Thr; Sus; Bel; 1 Macc 7.37–38). **3–4:** Tobit admits sinning. The theology, which posits that plunder, exile, and death are occasioned by sin, is complicated by the plot, wherein the righteous Tobit and Sarah suffer. Attribution of the exile to the people's sin is a common biblical idea. **6:** *Undeserved insults* were directed at Tobit by his neighbors (2.8); Tobit does not reflect upon his undeserved insult to Anna. To *become dust* evokes Gen 3.19. The request for death is reminiscent of Job 3; cf. Jer 20.14–18.

**3.7–15: Sarah's plight and prayer.** The scene shifts to Ecbatana in Media, ca. 525 km (325 mi) east-southeast of Nineveh, and the narration shifts from first to third person as, *on the same day,* Sarah's plight dia, it also happened that Sarah, the daughter of Raguel, was reproached by one of her father's maids. [8] For she had been married to seven husbands, and the wicked demon Asmodeus had killed each of them before they had been with her as is customary for wives. So the maid said to her, "You are the one who kills[a] your husbands! See, you have already been married to seven husbands and have not borne the name of[b] a single one of them. [9] Why do you beat us? Because your husbands are dead? Go with them! May we never see a son or daughter of yours!"

10 On that day she was grieved in spirit and wept. When she had gone up to her father's upper room, she intended to hang herself. But she thought it over and said, "Never shall they reproach my father, saying to him, 'You had only one beloved daughter but she hanged herself because of her distress.' And I shall bring my father in his old age down in sorrow to Hades. It is better for me not to hang myself, but to pray the Lord that I may die and not listen to these reproaches anymore." [11] At that same time, with hands outstretched toward the window, she prayed and said,

"Blessed are you, merciful God!
    Blessed is your name forever;
    let all your works praise you
        forever.
12 And now, Lord,[c] I turn my face to
        you,
    and raise my eyes toward you.
13 Command that I be released from the
        earth

and not listen to such reproaches
        any more.
14 You know, O Master, that I am
        innocent
    of any defilement with a man,
15 and that I have not disgraced my
        name
    or the name of my father in the
        land of my exile.
I am my father's only child;
    he has no other child to be his heir;
and he has no close relative or other
        kindred
    for whom I should keep myself as
        wife.
Already seven husbands of mine have
        died.
    Why should I still live?
But if it is not pleasing to you,
        O Lord, to take my life,
    hear me in my disgrace."

16 At that very moment, the prayers of both of them were heard in the glorious presence of God. [17] So Raphael was sent to heal both of them: Tobit, by removing the white films from his eyes, so that he might see God's light with his eyes; and Sarah, daughter of Raguel, by giving her in marriage to Tobias son of Tobit, and by setting her free from the wicked demon Asmodeus. For Tobias was entitled to have her before all others who had desired to marry her. At the same time that Tobit returned from the courtyard into his house, Sarah daughter of

a Other ancient authorities read *strangles*    b Other ancient authorities read *have had no benefit from*    c Other ancient authorities lack *Lord*

parallels that of Tobit. **7:** *Reproached*, like Sarah of Gen 16.4–6, this Sarah also has no children and beats her tormentor. **8:** The earliest literary mention of *Asmodeus*, who will become a stock villain in later Jewish legend. **10:** Sarah *intended to hang herself*, but concern for her father prevents suicide. *Hades*, i.e., Sheol, the abode of the dead; cf. Gen 42.38; 44.29,31. Like Tobit, Sarah seeks to escape a woman's reproaches, but unlike Tobit, she does not issue a retort to her tormentors. **11:** *Hands outstretched* is a common posture for prayer (Ezra 9.5; Dan 6.10). *Blessed are you* is the traditional opening of Jewish prayers (8.5,15; Jdt 13.17). **13:** Sarah more quickly than Tobit pleads for death; in contrast to Tobit, she does not confess sins. **14–15:** Women's sexual purity and honor are also prominent themes of the stories of Judith and Susanna. A *close relative* suggests levirite law (Deut 25.5–10); Sarah is not aware that another relative and thus a potential husband, Tobias, exists.

**3.16–17: Divine response.** The fates of the supplicants are intertwined by Raphael's dual mission. **17:** *Raphael's* name means "God has healed." *Entitled*, by being a near relation (6.12; 3.14–15n.).

Raguel came down from her upper room.
That same day Tobit remembered the money that he had left in trust with Gabael at Rages in Media, ²and he said to himself, "Now I have asked for death. Why do I not call my son Tobias and explain to him about the money before I die?" ³Then he called his son Tobias, and when he came to him he said, "My son, when I die,ᵃ give me a proper burial. Honor your mother and do not abandon her all the days of her life. Do whatever pleases her, and do not grieve her in anything. ⁴Remember her, my son, because she faced many dangers for you while you were in her womb. And when she dies, bury her beside me in the same grave.

5 "Revere the Lord all your days, my son, and refuse to sin or to transgress his commandments. Live uprightly all the days of your life, and do not walk in the ways of wrongdoing; ⁶for those who act in accordance with truth will prosper in all their activities. To all those who practice righteousnessᵇ ⁷give alms from your possessions, and do not let your eye begrudge the gift when you make it. Do not turn your face away from anyone who is poor, and the face of God will not be turned away from you. ⁸If you have many possessions, make your gift from them in proportion; if few, do not be afraid to give according to the little you have. ⁹So you will be laying up a good treasure for yourself against the day of necessity. ¹⁰For almsgiving delivers from death and keeps you from going into the Darkness. ¹¹Indeed, almsgiving, for all who practice it, is an excellent offering in the presence of the Most High.

12 "Beware, my son, of every kind of fornication. First of all, marry a woman from among the descendants of your ancestors; do not marry a foreign woman, who is not of your father's tribe; for we are the descendants of the prophets. Remember, my son, that Noah, Abraham, Isaac, and Jacob, our ancestors of old, all took wives from among their kindred. They were blessed in their children, and their posterity will inherit the land. ¹³So now, my son, love your kindred, and in your heart do not disdain your kindred, the sons and daughters of your people, by refusing to take a wife for yourself from among them. For in pride there is ruin and great confusion. And in idleness there is loss and dire poverty, because idleness is the mother of famine.

14 "Do not keep over until the next day the wages of those who work for you, but pay them at once. If you serve God you will receive payment. Watch yourself, my son,

*a* Lat    *b* The text of codex Sinaiticus goes directly from verse 6 to verse 19, reading *To those who practice righteousness* ¹⁹*the Lord will give good counsel.* In order to fill the lacuna verses 7 to 18 are derived from other ancient authorities

**4.1–13: Tobit's advice on the family.** Tobit offers a testament, a common literary genre in early (Gen 49) as well as Hellenistic times (*1 Enoch* 81; *Testaments of the Twelve Patriarchs*), in which a father offers his children ethical advice and prophetic insight. Chapter 14 provides a second example. **1**: *Money,* see 1.14. *Rages* is just east of modern Teheran. **3**: *Burial,* Tobit asks for what he provided others (on this familial responsibility, see also Lk 9.59). *Honoring one's mother* is commanded in the Decalogue (Ex 20.12; Deut 5.16; Prov 23.22; Sir 3.12–16; 7.27). **6–7**: Tobit's circumstances (temporarily) conflict with the comments typical of wisdom literature (e.g., Prov 10.27–30). **8**: Giving what one can is a prominent motif in Jewish-Hellenistic (*Testament of Issachar*), early Christian (Lk 21.1–4; 2 Cor 8.12), and rabbinic (*b. Git.* 7a) writing. **10**: *Delivers from death* probably suggests a long life, not an eternal one. **11**: *Almsgiving* is consistently emphasized (12.8–9; 14.10–11; Lev 23.22; Ps 112.9; Prov 14.21,31; Isa 58.6–8; Sir 3.30–31; 35.4). **12–13**: Consistent with the instructions of wisdom literature (Prov 5.20; 6.24), Tobit warns about the evils of sexual sin and foreign women. *Fornication* refers to any intercourse outside of marriage. On endogamy, see 1.9n. Genesis does not record the ancestry of Noah's wife, although the *Book of Jubilees* (4.33), an early Second Temple text, does. The reference to *pride* echoes Prov 16.18.

**4.14–19: Popular wisdom.** Following instructions on marriage, Tobit returns to the conventional advice begun in 4.5–10. **14**: *Do not keep over,* see Lev 19.13; Deut 24.15. **15**: The "golden rule" appears in everything you do, and discipline yourself in all your conduct. 15 And what you hate, do not do to anyone. Do not drink wine to excess or let drunkenness go with you on your way. 16 Give some of your food to the hungry, and some of your clothing to the naked. Give all your surplus as alms, and do not let your eye begrudge your giving of alms. 17 Place your bread on the grave of the righteous, but give none to sinners. 18 Seek advice from every wise person and do not despise any useful counsel. 19 At all times bless the Lord God, and ask him that your ways may be made straight and that all your paths and plans may prosper. For none of the nations has understanding, but the Lord himself will give them good counsel; but if he chooses otherwise, he casts down to deepest Hades. So now, my child, remember these commandments, and do not let them be erased from your heart.

20 "And now, my son, let me explain to you that I left ten talents of silver in trust with Gabael son of Gabrias, at Rages in Media. 21 Do not be afraid, my son, because we have become poor. You have great wealth if you fear God and flee from every sin and do what is good in the sight of the Lord your God."

5 Then Tobias answered his father Tobit, "I will do everything that you have commanded me, father; 2 but how can I obtain the money[a] from him, since he does not know me and I do not know him?

What evidence[b] am I to give him so that he will recognize and trust me, and give me the money? Also, I do not know the roads to Media, or how to get there." 3 Then Tobit answered his son Tobias, "He gave me his bond and I gave him my bond. I[c] divided his in two; we each took one part, and I put one with the money. And now twenty years have passed since I left this money in trust. So now, my son, find yourself a trustworthy man to go with you, and we will pay him wages until you return. But get back the money from Gabael."[d]

4 So Tobias went out to look for a man to go with him to Media, someone who was acquainted with the way. He went out and found the angel Raphael standing in front of him; but he did not perceive that he was an angel of God. 5 Tobias[e] said to him, "Where do you come from, young man?" "From your kindred, the Israelites," he replied, "and I have come here to work." Then Tobias[f] said to him, "Do you know the way to go to Media?" 6 "Yes," he replied, "I have been there many times; I am acquainted with it and know all the roads. I have often traveled to Media, and would stay with our kinsman Gabael who lives in Rages of Media. It is a journey of two days from Ecbatana to Rages; for it lies in a mountainous area, while Ecbatana is in the middle of the

a Gk it    b Gk sign    c Other authorities read He
d Gk from him    e Gk He    f Gk he

throughout ancient writing (Ahikar; Mt 7.12; Lk 6.31; B. Shabb 31a). On drunkenness, see Prov 23.29–35; Sir 31.25–30; Tobit's point is not abstinence but avoiding excess. 17: The Tale of Ahikar (see 1.21–22n.) also mentions this forbidden (Deut 26.14) and decried (Sir 30.18) practice. 19: Ways . . . made straight, see Prov 3.6; 11.5; Ps 5.8; Isa 45.13. The view that none of the nations has understanding (see Deut 32.38) comports with the condition of exile. Hades, see 3.10n.

4.20–5.3: Obtaining funds left in trust. Tobias is to obtain wealth from righteousness and, more directly, from his father's banked funds. 20: Ten talents, see 1.14n. 5.1–2: Tobit's positive response echoes Ex 19.8; Ruth 3.5. However, like Moses (Ex 3), he also questions his commission.

5.4–17: Raphael's disguise. Disguised heavenly beings are a stock folkloric motif (cf. The Odyssey, in which Athena accompanies Telemachus), and angelic appearances are frequent in biblical stories (Gen 18.1–15; Judg 13). That readers know more than Tobit and his family adds to the entertainment of the tale. 5: Young man, Tobias better fits this description; the humor of mistaken identities continues. 6: Two days, Rages is 300 km (185 mi) from Ecbatana; this may be a journey of only two days, for an angel. Ecbatana is not in the middle of the plain, but in the mountains; the story is as loose with geographical as with chronological and historical details (see 1.4n.; 1.15n.). 10: Having prayed for death (3.6), Tobit plain." [7] Then Tobias said to him, "Wait for me, young man, until I go in and tell my father; for I do need you to travel with me, and I will pay you your wages." [8] He replied, "All right, I will wait; but do not take too long."

9 So Tobias[a] went in to tell his father Tobit and said to him, "I have just found a man who is one of our own Israelite kindred!" He replied, "Call the man in, my son, so that I may learn about his family and to what tribe he belongs, and whether he is trustworthy enough to go with you."

10 Then Tobias went out and called him, and said, "Young man, my father is calling for you." So he went in to him, and Tobit greeted him first. He replied, "Joyous greetings to you!" But Tobit retorted, "What joy is left for me any more? I am a man without eyesight; I cannot see the light of heaven, but I lie in darkness like the dead who no longer see the light. Although still alive, I am among the dead. I hear people but I cannot see them." But the young man[a] said, "Take courage; the time is near for God to heal you; take courage." Then Tobit said to him, "My son Tobias wishes to go to Media. Can you accompany him and guide him? I will pay your wages, brother." He answered, "I can go with him and I know all the roads, for I have often gone to Media and have crossed all its plains, and I am familiar with its mountains and all of its roads."

11 Then Tobit[a] said to him, "Brother, of what family are you and from what tribe? Tell me, brother." [12] He replied, "Why do you need to know my tribe?" But Tobit[a] said, "I want to be sure, brother, whose son you are and what your name is." [13] He replied, "I am Azariah, the son of the great Hananiah, one of your relatives."

14 Then Tobit said to him, "Welcome! God save you, brother. Do not feel bitter toward me, brother, because I wanted to be sure about your ancestry. It turns out that you are a kinsman, and of good and noble lineage. For I knew Hananiah and Nathan,[b] the two sons of Shemeliah,[c] and they used to go with me to Jerusalem and worshiped with me there, and were not led astray. Your kindred are good people; you come of good stock. Hearty welcome!"

15 Then he added, "I will pay you a drachma a day as wages, as well as expenses for yourself and my son. So go with my son, [16] and[d] I will add something to your wages." Raphael[e] answered, "I will go with him; so do not fear. We shall leave in good health and return to you in good health, because the way is safe." [17] So Tobit[a] said to him, "Blessings be upon you, brother."

Then he called his son and said to him, "Son, prepare supplies for the journey and set out with your brother. May God in heaven bring you safely there and return you in good health to me; and may his angel, my son, accompany you both for your safety."

Before he went out to start his journey, he kissed his father and mother. Tobit then said to him, "Have a safe journey."

18 But his mother[f] began to weep, and said to Tobit, "Why is it that you have sent my child away? Is he not the staff of our hand as he goes in and out before us? [19] Do not heap money upon money, but let it be a ransom for our child. [20] For the life that is

a Gk he   b Other ancient authorities read *Jathan* or *Nathaniah*   c Other ancient authorities read *Shemaiah*   d Other ancient authorities add *when you return safely*   e Gk He   f Other ancient authorities add *Anna*

perceives himself as among the dead. The reference to divine healing recollects Raphael's name (see 3.17n.). **13:** *Azariah* is Hebrew for "God has helped"; *Hananiah* means "God has had mercy." **14:** Reference to the righteous sons of *Shemeliah* belies Tobit's claim (1.5–6) that he alone was faithful. **17:** Tobit's prayer for angelic accompaniment (also 5.22) is already answered. See also Gen 24.40: Tobias's journey will resemble earlier quests for brides, although he does not yet know this.

**5.18–6.1a: Anna's lament.** The couple alternate between practical observations and theological reflection. They will display similar attitudes as their wait continues (10.1–7). **19:** *Ransom* likely suggests the given to us by the Lord is enough for us." [21] Tobit[a] said to her, "Do not worry; our child will leave in good health and return to us in good health. Your eyes will see him on the day when he returns to you in good health. Say no more! Do not fear for them, my sister. [22] For a good angel will accompany him; his journey will be successful, and he will come back in good health." 

6 [1] So she stopped weeping.

The young man went out and the angel went with him; [2] and the dog came out with him and went along with them. So they both journeyed along, and when the first night overtook them they camped by the Tigris river. [3] Then the young man went down to wash his feet in the Tigris river. Suddenly a large fish leaped up from the water and tried to swallow the young man's foot, and he cried out. [4] But the angel said to the young man, "Catch hold of the fish and hang on to it!" So the young man grasped the fish and drew it up on the land. [5] Then the angel said to him, "Cut open the fish and take out its gall, heart, and liver. Keep them with you, but throw away the intestines. For its gall, heart, and liver are useful as medicine." [6] So after cutting open the fish the young man gathered together the gall, heart, and liver; then he roasted and ate some of the fish, and kept some to be salted.

The two continued on their way together until they were near Media.[b] [7] Then the young man questioned the angel and said to him, "Brother Azariah, what medicinal value is there in the fish's heart and liver, and in the gall?" [8] He replied, "As for the fish's heart and liver, you must burn them to make a smoke in the presence of a man or woman afflicted by a demon or evil spirit, and every affliction will flee away and never remain with that person any longer. [9] And as for the gall, anoint a person's eyes where white films have appeared on them; blow upon them, upon the white films, and the eyes[c] will be healed."

10 When he entered Media and already was approaching Ecbatana,[d] [11] Raphael said to the young man, "Brother Tobias." "Here I am," he answered. Then Raphael[e] said to him, "We must stay this night in the home of Raguel. He is your relative, and he has a daughter named Sarah. [12] He has no male heir and no daughter except Sarah only, and you, as next of kin to her, have before all other men a hereditary claim on her. Also it is right for you to inherit her

a Gk He    b Other ancient authorities read *Ecbatana*
c Gk *they*    d Other ancient authorities read *Rages*
e Gk *he*

view that Gabael should keep the funds as though they were ransom for Tobias. **22:** *A good angel* does accompany Tobias, although Tobit does not know this.

**6.1b–9: Dangerous journey.** Still disguised, Raphael will protect Tobias from dangerous fish and provide instruction for protection against lecherous demons. **2:** The *dog* (see 11.4) adds an intimate touch and may suggest Odysseus's faithful pet (*Odyssey* 17.289–327). The Tigris is far west of Nineveh; the geography remains fanciful. **3:** Like the dog, the *large fish* remains problematic: Is this a reversal of the Jonah story (Jon 1.7), wherein a large fish swallows someone attempting to escape Nineveh? Is the reference to a crocodile? The humorous element is unmistakable. In medieval art, Tobias's victory over the fish presages Jesus' defeat of Satan. **5:** Raphael's instructions are consistent with ancient medical texts that provide instructions for the use of fish organs. **6:** No reference is made to the angel consuming food. **8:** *To make a smoke,* or to fumigate, was a standard means for healing and exorcising demons; one suspects the smell of week-old fish guts would easily drive away a demon or evil spirit. **9:** Anointing a person's eyes with a fish gall is prescribed for curing blindness in ancient Assyrian and Egyptian medical texts.

**6.10–18: Prenuptial instructions.** Raphael now reveals to Tobias the additional purpose of their journey; knowing Sarah's past luck with marriages, Tobias is understandably reluctant but quickly warms to the prospect of marrying her. **12:** *No male heir,* although Israelite inheritance laws were patrilineal, brotherless daughters could inherit if they married within the tribe (Num 27.1–11; 36.1–13). *Next of kin* refers to levirate law (3.14–15n.); by marrying Sarah, Tobias will thus obtain Raguel's estate. **13:**

father's possessions. Moreover, the girl is sensible, brave, and very beautiful, and her father is a good man." ¹³He continued, "You have every right to take her in marriage. So listen to me, brother; tonight I will speak to her father about the girl, so that we may take her to be your bride. When we return from Rages we will celebrate her marriage. For I know that Raguel can by no means keep her from you or promise her to another man without incurring the penalty of death according to the decree of the book of Moses. Indeed he knows that you, rather than any other man, are entitled to marry his daughter. So now listen to me, brother, and tonight we shall speak concerning the girl and arrange her engagement to you. And when we return from Rages we will take her and bring her back with us to your house."

14 Then Tobias said in answer to Raphael, "Brother Azariah, I have heard that she already has been married to seven husbands and that they died in the bridal chamber. On the night when they went in to her, they would die. I have heard people saying that it was a demon that killed them. ¹⁵It does not harm her, but it kills anyone who desires to approach her. So now, since I am the only son my father has, I am afraid that I may die and bring my father's and mother's life down to their grave, grieving for me—and they have no other son to bury them."

16 But Raphael[a] said to him, "Do you not remember your father's orders when he commanded you to take a wife from your father's house? Now listen to me, brother, and say no more about this demon. Take her. I know that this very night she will be given to you in marriage. ¹⁷When you enter the bridal chamber, take some of the fish's liver and heart, and put them on the embers of the incense. An odor will be given off; ¹⁸the demon will smell it and flee, and will never be seen near her any more. Now when you are about to go to bed with her, both of you must first stand up and pray, imploring the Lord of heaven that mercy and safety may be granted to you. Do not be afraid, for she was set apart for you before the world was made. You will save her, and she will go with you. I presume that you will have children by her, and they will be as brothers to you. Now say no more!" When Tobias heard the words of Raphael and learned that she was his kinswoman,[b] related through his father's lineage, he loved her very much, and his heart was drawn to her.

7 Now when they[c] entered Ecbatana, Tobias[a] said to him, "Brother Azariah, take me straight to our brother Raguel." So he took him to Raguel's house, where they found him sitting beside the courtyard door. They greeted him first, and he replied, "Joyous greetings, brothers; welcome and good health!" Then he brought them into his house. ²He said to his wife Edna, "How much the young man resembles my kinsman Tobit!" ³Then Edna questioned them, saying, "Where are you from, brothers?" They answered, "We belong to the descendants of Naphtali who are exiles in Nineveh." ⁴She said to them, "Do you know our kinsman Tobit?" And they replied, "Yes, we know him." Then she asked them, "Is he[d] in good health?" ⁵They replied, "He is alive and in good health." And Tobias added, "He is my father!" ⁶At

a Gk *he*   b Gk *sister*   c Other ancient authorities read *he*   d Other ancient authorities add *alive and*

*Penalty of death,* perhaps an exaggerated reference to Num 36.6–8. **14–15:** Tobias's hesitancy increases the tension in the plot; his fear is not primarily for his own life, but for the grief his death will cause his parents (see 3.10). **16:** Raphael eases Tobias's fear by repeating his concern for the parents, but changing his focus. **17:** On fumigating as an exorcism technique, see 6.8n. **18:** Raphael's advice, coupled with the announcement that the match was made in heaven and that Sarah is his relative, both calms Tobias's fears and prompts his love.

**7.1–16: Tobit and Sarah marry.** Raguel and Edna's welcome repeats the theme of family connections. **3:** Edna asks the more pertinent questions. **5:** Tobias does not mention his father's illness. **7:** Raguel's that Raguel jumped up and kissed him and wept. [7] He also spoke to him as follows, "Blessings on you, my child, son of a good and noble father![a] O most miserable of calamities that such an upright and beneficent man has become blind!" He then embraced his kinsman Tobias and wept. [8] His wife Edna also wept for him, and their daughter Sarah likewise wept. [9] Then Raguel[b] slaughtered a ram from the flock and received them very warmly.

When they had bathed and washed themselves and had reclined to dine, Tobias said to Raphael, "Brother Azariah, ask Raguel to give me my kinswoman[c] Sarah." [10] But Raguel overheard it and said to the lad, "Eat and drink, and be merry tonight. For no one except you, brother, has the right to marry my daughter Sarah. Likewise I am not at liberty to give her to any other man than yourself, because you are my nearest relative. But let me explain to you the true situation more fully, my child. [11] I have given her to seven men of our kinsmen, and all died on the night when they went in to her. But now, my child, eat and drink, and the Lord will act on behalf of you both." But Tobias said, "I will neither eat nor drink anything until you settle the things that pertain to me." So Raguel said, "I will do so. She is given to you in accordance with the decree in the book of Moses, and it has been decreed from heaven that she be given to you. Take your kinswoman;[c] from now on you are her brother and she is your sister. She is given to you from today and forever. May the Lord of heaven, my child, guide and prosper you both this night and grant you mercy and peace." [12] Then Raguel summoned his

daughter Sarah. When she came to him he took her by the hand and gave her to Tobias,[d] saying, "Take her to be your wife in accordance with the law and decree written in the book of Moses. Take her and bring her safely to your father. And may the God of heaven prosper your journey with his peace." [13] Then he called her mother and told her to bring writing material; and he wrote out a copy of a marriage contract, to the effect that he gave her to him as wife according to the decree of the law of Moses. [14] Then they began to eat and drink.

[15] Raguel called his wife Edna and said to her, "Sister, get the other room ready, and take her there." [16] So she went and made the bed in the room as he had told her, and brought Sarah[e] there. She wept for her daughter.[e] Then, wiping away the tears,[f] she said to her, "Take courage, my daughter; the Lord of heaven grant you joy[g] in place of your sorrow. Take courage, my daughter." Then she went out.

**8** When they had finished eating and drinking they wanted to retire; so they took the young man and brought him into the bedroom. [2] Then Tobias remembered the words of Raphael, and he took the fish's liver and heart out of the bag where he had them and put them on the embers of the incense. [3] The odor of the fish so repelled the demon that he fled to the remotest parts[b] of Egypt. But Raphael followed

a Other ancient authorities add *When he heard that Tobit had lost his sight, he was stricken with grief and wept. Then he said,* b Gk *he* c Gk *sister* d Gk *him* e Gk *her* f Other ancient authorities read *the tears of her daughter* g Other ancient authorities read *favor* h Or *fled through the air to the parts*

knowledge of Tobit's blindness is unexplained. **10–11:** The juxtaposition of death threats and joyous feasting is humorous; not every groom would appreciate Sarah's *true situation.* **12,15:** The *decree* is Num 36.8; Raguel repeats the idea (6.18) that Sarah is Tobias's divinely appointed wife. **12:** *Raguel summoned his daughter,* because neither she nor her mother participated in the original conversation about her fate; the match was arranged by the men. **13:** The Jewish marriage *contract* (Heb "ketubah," "writing") protects the wife's financial interests; this is the first recorded reference to this well-known practice. **16:** Edna's emotions encompass both fear and hope; she exhorts her daughter to courage, as Raphael had exhorted Tobias (6.18).

**8.1–9a: Asmodeus is exorcised.** Raphael's advice proves sound as the demon is exorcised and the couple offer a prayer of thanksgiving. **3:** *Bound,* since binding restrains demons (see *1 Enoch* 10.4). **4–5:**

him, and at once bound him there hand and foot.

4 When the parents[a] had gone out and shut the door of the room, Tobias got out of bed and said to Sarah,[b] "Sister, get up, and let us pray and implore our Lord that he grant us mercy and safety." 5 So she got up, and they began to pray and implore that they might be kept safe. Tobias[c] began by saying,

"Blessed are you, O God of our
        ancestors,
    and blessed is your name in all
        generations forever.
Let the heavens and the whole
        creation bless you forever.
6 You made Adam, and for him you
        made his wife Eve
    as a helper and support.
From the two of them the human
        race has sprung.
You said, 'It is not good that the man
        should be alone;
    let us make a helper for him like
        himself.'
7 I now am taking this kinswoman of
        mine,
    not because of lust,
    but with sincerity.
Grant that she and I may find mercy
    and that we may grow old
        together."

8 And they both said, "Amen, Amen." 9 Then they went to sleep for the night.

But Raguel arose and called his servants to him, and they went and dug a grave, 10 for he said, "It is possible that he will die and we will become an object of ridicule and derision." 11 When they had finished digging the grave, Raguel went into his house and called his wife, 12 saying, "Send one of the maids and have her go in to see if he is alive. But if he is dead, let us bury him without anyone knowing it." 13 So they sent the maid, lit a lamp, and opened the door; and she went in and found them sound asleep together. 14 Then the maid came out and informed them that he was alive and that nothing was wrong. 15 So they blessed the God of heaven, and Raguel[a] said,

"Blessed are you, O God, with every
        pure blessing;
    let all your chosen ones bless you.[d]
    Let them bless you forever.
16 Blessed are you because you have
        made me glad.
    It has not turned out as I expected,
    but you have dealt with us
        according to your great mercy.
17 Blessed are you because you had
        compassion
    on two only children.
Be merciful to them, O Master, and
        keep them safe;
    bring their lives to fulfillment
    in happiness and mercy."

18 Then he ordered his servants to fill in the grave before daybreak.

a Gk they   b Gk her   c Gk He   d Other ancient authorities lack this line

The couple's praying contrasts with both Raguel's gravedigging (8.9–11) and the descriptions of ardent love-making found in non-Jewish Hellenistic romances. **5–7:** Prayers are frequently attributed to characters in Second Temple Jewish literature (Jdt 9; Add Esth; Sus; Song of Thr). **5:** *God of our ancestors,* see Ex 3.13, Deut 4.1. **6:** *Adam* and *Eve,* one of the earliest biblical references to these figures outside Genesis. In the Septuagint, Eve is mentioned by name only here and in Gen 3.20; 4.1. *You said,* introducing a quotation of Gen 2.18. **7:** *Not because of lust,* chastity becomes a popular motif in Jewish-Hellenistic literature. **8:** *Amen, Amen* are Sarah's only words aside from her prayer (3.11–15).

**8.9b–18: Raguel's fears are assuaged. 9–10:** Raguel's morbid planning contrasts with Tobias's piety; unlike Tobit, Raguel prepares a grave before finding a corpse. **10:** *Ridicule and derision,* Raguel fears for his reputation, not his daughter's happiness or his son-in-law's life; Sarah had already become an object of derision (3.7–9). **12:** *Without anyone knowing* ignores the presence of Azariah/Raphael, as well as the maids and the servants. **15–17:** The prayer continues Raguel's somewhat wry perspective: He praises God for his own good fortune before mentioning the mercy extended to the couple.

19 After this he asked his wife to bake many loaves of bread; and he went out to the herd and brought two steers and four rams and ordered them to be slaughtered. So they began to make preparations. 20 Then he called for Tobias and swore on oath to him in these words:[a] "You shall not leave here for fourteen days, but shall stay here eating and drinking with me; and you shall cheer up my daughter, who has been depressed. 21 Take at once half of what I own and return in safety to your father; the other half will be yours when my wife and I die. Take courage, my child. I am your father and Edna is your mother, and we belong to you as well as to your wife[b] now and forever. Take courage, my child."

9 Then Tobias called Raphael and said to him, 2 "Brother Azariah, take four servants and two camels with you and travel to Rages. Go to the home of Gabael, give him the bond, get the money, and then bring him with you to the wedding celebration. 4 For you know that my father must be counting the days, and if I delay even one day I will upset him very much. 3 You are witness to the oath Raguel has sworn, and I cannot violate his oath."[c] 5 So Raphael with the four servants and two camels went to Rages in Media and stayed with Gabael. Raphael[d] gave him the bond and informed him that Tobit's son Tobias had married and was inviting him to the wedding celebration. So Gabael[e] got up and counted out to him the money bags, with their seals intact; then they loaded them on the camels.[f] 6 In the morning they both got up early and went to the wedding celebration. When they came into Raguel's house they found Tobias reclining at table. He sprang up and greeted Gabael,[g] who wept and blessed him with the words, "Good and noble son of a father good and noble, upright and generous! May the Lord grant the blessing of heaven to you and your wife, and to your wife's father and mother. Blessed be God, for I see in Tobias the very image of my cousin Tobit."

10 Now, day by day, Tobit kept counting how many days Tobias[e] would need for going and for returning. And when the days had passed and his son did not appear, 2 he said, "Is it possible that he has been detained? Or that Gabael has died, and there is no one to give him the money?" 3 And he began to worry. 4 His wife Anna said, "My child has perished and is no longer among the living." And she began to weep and mourn for her son, saying, 5 "Woe to me, my child, the light of my eyes, that I let you make the journey." 6 But Tobit kept saying to her, "Be quiet and stop worrying, my dear;[b] he is all right. Probably something unexpected has happened there. The man who went with him is trustworthy and is one of our own kin. Do not grieve for him, my dear;[b] he will soon be

a Other ancient authorities read *Tobias and said to him*   b Gk *sister*   c In other ancient authorities verse 3 precedes verse 4   d Gk *He*   e Gk *he*   f Other ancient authorities lack *on the camels*   g Gk *him*

**8.19–9.6:** The wedding celebrated and tasks fulfilled. **20:** *Depressed* either because of past deaths or the prospect of leaving her home. **21:** *Take courage* is what Edna advised Sarah (7.16), but under much different circumstances. The language of *father* and *mother* together with promises of inheritance suggest an adoption formula (see 10.12). **9.1:** Tobias now commands Raphael to action; no longer the youth, he has become an adult. **4:** *I will upset him,* as demonstrated in 10.1–3. **6:** Gabael's blessing indicates that the two families are now regarded as one. His reception of Tobias parallels the welcome granted by Edna and Raguel (7.1–8).

**10.1–7a:** Anxiety at home. The concerns of Tobit and Anna contrast with the celebration in Media and confirm Tobias's own worries (9.4). **1:** *And when the days had passed,* since the two-week wedding celebration, unknown to Tobit and Anna, extended the time of Tobias's absence long past what was required for the journey. **5:** *Light of my eyes,* perhaps a glance at Tobit's blindness, recalls his words to her in 5.21. *Let you make the journey,* Anna suggests she had the power to prevent it (see her initial concern in 5.18–19 and Tobit's command for her silence on the matter in 5.21). **6:** In comforting Anna, Tobit masks his own fears. **7:** Unlike 5.21, here Anna does not heed Tobit's commands.

here." 7 She answered him, "Be quiet yourself! Stop trying to deceive me! My child has perished." She would rush out every day and watch the road her son had taken, and would heed no one.[a] When the sun had set she would go in and mourn and weep all night long, getting no sleep at all.

Now when the fourteen days of the wedding celebration had ended that Raguel had sworn to observe for his daughter, Tobias came to him and said, "Send me back, for I know that my father and mother do not believe that they will see me again. So I beg of you, father, to let me go so that I may return to my own father. I have already explained to you how I left him." 8 But Raguel said to Tobias, "Stay, my child, stay with me; I will send messengers to your father Tobit and they will inform him about you." 9 But he said, "No! I beg you to send me back to my father." 10 So Raguel promptly gave Tobias his wife Sarah, as well as half of all his property: male and female slaves, oxen and sheep, donkeys and camels, clothing, money, and household goods. 11 Then he saw them safely off; he embraced Tobias[b] and said, "Farewell, my child; have a safe journey. The Lord of heaven prosper you and your wife Sarah, and may I see children of yours before I die." 12 Then he kissed his daughter Sarah and said to her, "My daughter, honor your father-in-law and your mother-in-law,[c] since from now on they are as much your parents as those who gave you birth. Go in peace, daughter, and may I hear a good report about you as long as I live." Then he bade them farewell and let them go. Then

Edna said to Tobias, "My child and dear brother, the Lord of heaven bring you back safely, and may I live long enough to see children of you and of my daughter Sarah before I die. In the sight of the Lord I entrust my daughter to you; do nothing to grieve her all the days of your life. Go in peace, my child. From now on I am your mother and Sarah is your beloved wife.[d] May we all prosper together all the days of our lives." Then she kissed them both and saw them safely off. 13 Tobias parted from Raguel with happiness and joy, praising the Lord of heaven and earth, King over all, because he had made his journey a success. Finally, he blessed Raguel and his wife Edna, and said, "I have been commanded by the Lord to honor you all the days of my life."[e]

11 When they came near to Kaserin, which is opposite Nineveh, Raphael said, 2 "You are aware of how we left your father. 3 Let us run ahead of your wife and prepare the house while they are still on the way." 4 As they went on together Raphael[f] said to him, "Have the gall ready." And the dog[g] went along behind them.

5 Meanwhile Anna sat looking intently down the road by which her son would come. 6 When she caught sight of him coming, she said to his father, "Look, your son

a Other ancient authorities read *and she would eat nothing*  b Gk *him*  c Other ancient authorities lack parts of *Then . . . mother-in-law*  d Gk *sister*  e Lat: Meaning of Gk uncertain  f Gk *he*  g Codex Sinaiticus reads *And the Lord*

**10.7b–13: Return to Nineveh.** The couple's leave-taking is much less fraught with worry—and advice—than the parallel scene of 5.17–22. Verse 7b confirms the parental worry of 10.1–7a. **8:** Raguel desires that his new son remain with him, but filial duty prompts Tobit to leave. **10:** Sarah's substantial dowry is part of the inheritance Tobias will receive (6.12). **12:** *Honor your father-in-law and your mother-in-law* extends the Decalogue's commandment (see 4.3n.). *Child and dear brother* intensifies the familial connection; more than just a marriage, the couple's relationship is the merging of two families. *To see children*, this prayer will be granted, as Raphael had already remarked to Tobias (6.18). *Do nothing to grieve her*, the mother is vigilant for her daughter's happiness; the reader may recall the grief Tobit's insults brought Anna (2.11–14). **13:** Tobit confirms his bond with his in-laws; Sarah remains silent.

**11.1–6: Tobias returns. 3:** *Let us run ahead* may indicate Raphael's concern to avoid Sarah's company; unlike Asmodeus, he will not be tempted. **4:** *The dog*, see 6.2n. **6:** Anna, ever watchful (see 10.7), brings the good news to Tobit.

is coming, and the man who went with him!"

7 Raphael said to Tobias, before he had approached his father, "I know that his eyes will be opened. 8 Smear the gall of the fish on his eyes; the medicine will make the white films shrink and peel off from his eyes, and your father will regain his sight and see the light."

9 Then Anna ran up to her son and threw her arms around him, saying, "Now that I have seen you, my child, I am ready to die." And she wept. 10 Then Tobit got up and came stumbling out through the courtyard door. Tobias went up to him, 11 with the gall of the fish in his hand, and holding him firmly, he blew into his eyes, saying, "Take courage, father." With this he applied the medicine on his eyes, 12 and it made them smart.*a* 13 Next, with both his hands he peeled off the white films from the corners of his eyes. Then Tobit*b* saw his son and*c* threw his arms around him, 14 and he wept and said to him, "I see you, my son, the light of my eyes!" Then he said,

"Blessed be God,
and blessed be his great name,
and blessed be all his holy angels.
May his holy name be blessed*d*
throughout all the ages.
15 Though he afflicted me,
he has had mercy upon me.*e*
Now I see my son Tobias!"

So Tobit went in rejoicing and praising God at the top of his voice. Tobias reported to his father that his journey had been successful, that he had brought the money,

that he had married Raguel's daughter Sarah, and that she was, indeed, on her way there, very near to the gate of Nineveh.

16 Then Tobit, rejoicing and praising God, went out to meet his daughter-in-law at the gate of Nineveh. When the people of Nineveh saw him coming, walking along in full vigor and with no one leading him, they were amazed. 17 Before them all, Tobit acknowledged that God had been merciful to him and had restored his sight. When Tobit met Sarah the wife of his son Tobias, he blessed her saying, "Come in, my daughter, and welcome. Blessed be your God who has brought you to us, my daughter. Blessed be your father and your mother, blessed be my son Tobias, and blessed be you, my daughter. Come in now to your home, and welcome, with blessing and joy. Come in, my daughter." So on that day there was rejoicing among all the Jews who were in Nineveh. 18 Ahikar and his nephew Nadab were also present to share Tobit's joy. With merriment they celebrated Tobias's wedding feast for seven days, and many gifts were given to him.*f*

12 When the wedding celebration was ended, Tobit called his son Tobias and said to him, "My child, see to paying the wages of the man who went with you, and give him a bonus as well." 2 He replied,

*a* Lat: Meaning of Gk uncertain   *b* Gk he   *c* Other ancient authorities lack *saw his son and*   *d* Codex Sinaiticus reads *May his great name be upon us and blessed be all the angels*   *e* Lat: Gk lacks this line   *f* Other ancient authorities lack parts of this sentence

**11.7–18: Tobit is healed. 8:** *Gall,* a bitter digestive juice, bile, was recognized as having medicinal properties. **11–13:** See Acts 9.18; the magic properties of the gall work, though physicians' attempts were not successful (2.10). **14:** *Light of my eyes,* fulfilling v. 8, has both metaphoric and literal implications. **14–15:** Tobit's doxology resembles those of Tobias (8.5–7) and Raguel (8.15–17). *Holy angels* is ironic, since Raphael has not revealed his identity. *Afflicted* (lit., scourged) and *had mercy,* conventional terms for divine punishment and reconciliation upon the community's repentance, are applied to Israel in 13.2,5 (see 2 Macc 6.12–16). **16:** *Amazement* is the standard reaction to a miraculous healing. **17:** *My daughter,* a repeated phrase, echoes the familial language of Raguel and Edna; Tobit greets the daughter-in-law for whom he had prayed (4.12–13).
**12.1–22: Raphael's revelations.** Bringing the major plot events to a conclusion, Raphael explains his role in testing Tobit and exhorts Tobit and his son to good deeds and piety. **2:** *How much shall I pay him?* The fee had already been determined (5.15–16). *Half of the possessions* is one-quarter of Raguel's estate plus half the loan. The generosity is consistent with Tobit's insistence on almsgiving. **6:** *Privately,* since

"Father, how much shall I pay him? It would do no harm to give him half of the possessions brought back with me. ³For he has led me back to you safely, he cured my wife, he brought the money back with me, and he healed you. How much extra shall I give him as a bonus?" ⁴Tobit said, "He deserves, my child, to receive half of all that he brought back." ⁵So Tobias[a] called him and said, "Take for your wages half of all that you brought back, and farewell."

6 Then Raphael[a] called the two of them privately and said to them, "Bless God and acknowledge him in the presence of all the living for the good things he has done for you. Bless and sing praise to his name. With fitting honor declare to all people the deeds[b] of God. Do not be slow to acknowledge him. ⁷It is good to conceal the secret of a king, but to acknowledge and reveal the works of God, and with fitting honor to acknowledge him. Do good and evil will not overtake you. ⁸Prayer with fasting[c] is good, but better than both is almsgiving with righteousness. A little with righteousness is better than wealth with wrongdoing.[d] It is better to give alms than to lay up gold. ⁹For almsgiving saves from death and purges away every sin. Those who give alms will enjoy a full life, ¹⁰but those who commit sin and do wrong are their own worst enemies.

11 "I will now declare the whole truth to you and will conceal nothing from you. Already I have declared it to you when I said, 'It is good to conceal the secret of a king, but to reveal with due honor the works of God.' ¹²So now when you and Sarah prayed, it was I who brought and read[e] the record of your prayer before the glory of the Lord, and likewise whenever you would bury the dead. ¹³And that time when you did not hesitate to get up and leave your dinner to go and bury the dead, ¹⁴I was sent to you to test you. And at the same time God sent me to heal you and Sarah your daughter-in-law. ¹⁵I am Raphael, one of the seven angels who stand ready and enter before the glory of the Lord."

16 The two of them were shaken; they fell face down, for they were afraid. ¹⁷But he said to them, "Do not be afraid; peace be with you. Bless God forevermore. ¹⁸As for me, when I was with you, I was not acting on my own will, but by the will of God. Bless him each and every day; sing his praises. ¹⁹Although you were watching me, I really did not eat or drink anything—but what you saw was a vision. ²⁰So now get up from the ground,[f] and acknowledge God. See, I am ascending to him who sent me. Write down all these things that have happened to you." And he ascended. ²¹Then they stood up, and could see him no more. ²²They kept blessing God and singing his praises, and they acknowledged God for these marvelous deeds of his, when an angel of God had appeared to them.

a Gk he   b Gk words; other ancient authorities read words of the deeds   c Codex Sinaiticus with sincerity   d Lat   e Lat: Gk lacks and read   f Other ancient authorities read now bless the Lord on earth

Raphael continues to avoid women (11.3n). *Declare to all people* expresses a universalistic impulse (13.3–4,11; 1.6–7). **7:** *Secret of a king* anticipates Raphael's revelation in v. 11 and recollects Tobit's position at court (1.13–14); indeed, Tobit reveals no court secrets. *To acknowledge,* as Tobit had done in 11.17. **7b–10:** Proverbial sayings continue the emphasis on charitable deeds (4.6–11); for *fasting,* which becomes more important in the postexilic period, see 1 Macc 3.44–48; Esth 4.1–3,15; Mt 6.16–18. **12–13:** The angelic task of conveying prayers and good deeds is mentioned in other Second Temple Jewish literature, such as *1 Enoch*. **14:** *To test* indicates that Tobit's blindness and his subsequent trials resulted from God's active effort (Gen 22.1–22; Job 1–2); unmentioned is whether Sarah's trials were also tests. **15:** *Seven angels* do not appear in earlier biblical material; Daniel mentions Gabriel (8.16; 9.21; cf. Lk 1.19,26) and Michael (Dan 10.13,21; 12.1; cf. Jude 9; Rev 12.7). **16–17:** Fear and prostration are standard reactions to epiphanies (Dan 10.1–12), as is the response, *Do not be afraid*. **19:** *I really did not eat* reflects the traditional view that angels do not require food (Judg 13.16). **20–21:** Jesus' ascension in Acts 1.9 (cf. Jn 16.5) shares several motifs with this scene.

# 13

Then Tobit[a] said:
"Blessed be God who lives forever,
because his kingdom[b] lasts
throughout all ages.
2 For he afflicts, and he shows mercy;
he leads down to Hades in the
lowest regions of the earth,
and he brings up from the great
abyss,[c]
and there is nothing that can escape
his hand.
3 Acknowledge him before the nations,
O children of Israel;
for he has scattered you among
them.
4 He has shown you his greatness
even there.
Exalt him in the presence of every
living being,
because he is our Lord and he is
our God;
he is our Father and he is God
forever.
5 He will afflict[d] you for your
iniquities,
but he will again show mercy on all
of you.
He will gather you from all the
nations
among whom you have been
scattered.
6 If you turn to him with all your heart
and with all your soul,
to do what is true before him,
then he will turn to you
and will no longer hide his face
from you.
So now see what he has done for you;
acknowledge him at the top of your
voice.

Bless the Lord of righteousness,
and exalt the King of the ages.[e]
In the land of my exile I acknowledge
him,
and show his power and majesty to
a nation of sinners:
'Turn back, you sinners, and do what
is right before him;
perhaps he may look with favor
upon you and show you
mercy.'
7 As for me, I exalt my God,
and my soul rejoices in the King of
heaven.
8 Let all people speak of his majesty,
and acknowledge him in Jerusalem.
9 O Jerusalem, the holy city,
he afflicted[f] you for the deeds of
your hands,[g]
but will again have mercy on the
children of the righteous.
10 Acknowledge the Lord, for he is
good,[h]
and bless the King of the ages,
so that his tent[i] may be rebuilt in
you in joy.
May he cheer all those within you
who are captives,
and love all those within you who
are distressed,
to all generations forever.

a Gk *he*   b Other ancient authorities read *forever,
and his kingdom*   c Gk *from destruction*   d Other
ancient authorities read *He afflicted*   e The lacuna in
codex Sinaiticus, verses 6b to 10a, is filled in from
other ancient authorities   f Other ancient authorities
read *will afflict*   g Other ancient authorities read
*your children*   h Other ancient authorities read *Lord
worthily*   i Or *tabernacle*

**13.1–14.1: Tobit's hymn.** The hymn expands upon 11.14–15; the vocabulary evokes Psalms 92–118,
and the form may indicate liturgical models in use in the early Second Temple period. **2:** *Afflicts* and
*shows mercy* (also v. 5), see 11.15n.; Tobit's (and Sarah's) trials encapsulate the difficulties of exile. Tobit
repeats the Deuteronomic view that sin leads to punishment, and repentance to redemption (Deut 28–33;
cf. Wis 12.22). Some interpreters see in *brings up from the great abyss* belief in resurrection; others associate
the references with sickness and recovery, or exile and return; see Deut 32.39; 1 Sam 2.6; Wis 16.13–15;
2 Macc 7.35. **5:** The in-gathering of the exiles, a popular theme in Second Temple Jewish literature,
becomes in Jewish tradition a sign of the messianic age (14.7; Sir 36.11; Bar 4.21–5.9). **6:** *Heart* and *soul*
are to be inclined toward God (Deut 6.5). **8–17:** A celebration of *Jerusalem*, a focus with which the book
began (1.4–10); now Tobit speaks of Jerusalem's glory rather than its destruction. **11:** *Many nations will*

11 A bright light will shine to all the
        ends of the earth;
    many nations will come to you
        from far away,
    the inhabitants of the remotest parts
        of the earth to your holy name,
    bearing gifts in their hands for the
        King of heaven.
    Generation after generation will give
        joyful praise in you;
    the name of the chosen city will
        endure forever.
12 Cursed are all who speak a harsh
        word against you;
    cursed are all who conquer you
        and pull down your walls,
    all who overthrow your towers
        and set your homes on fire.
    But blessed forever will be all who
        revere you.*a*
13 Go, then, and rejoice over the
        children of the righteous,
    for they will be gathered together
        and will praise the Lord of the
        ages.
14 Happy are those who love you,
        and happy are those who rejoice in
        your prosperity.
    Happy also are all people who grieve
        with you
    because of your afflictions;
    for they will rejoice with you
        and witness all your glory forever.
15 My soul blesses*b* the Lord, the great
        King!
16 For Jerusalem will be built*c* as his
        house for all ages.
    How happy I will be if a remnant of
        my descendants should survive
    to see your glory and acknowledge
        the King of heaven.

The gates of Jerusalem will be built
        with sapphire and emerald,
    and all your walls with precious
        stones.
    The towers of Jerusalem will be built
        with gold,
    and their battlements with pure
        gold.
    The streets of Jerusalem will be paved
        with ruby and with stones of
        Ophir.
17 The gates of Jerusalem will sing
        hymns of joy,
    and all her houses will cry,
        'Hallelujah!
    Blessed be the God of Israel!'
    and the blessed will bless the holy
        name forever and ever."

14 So ended Tobit's words of praise.
2 Tobit*d* died in peace when he
was one hundred twelve years old, and was
buried with great honor in Nineveh. He
was sixty-two*e* years old when he lost his
eyesight, and after regaining it he lived in
prosperity, giving alms and continually
blessing God and acknowledging God's
majesty.

3 When he was about to die, he called
his son Tobias and the seven sons of Tobias*f* and gave this command: "My son, take
your children 4 and hurry off to Media, for
I believe the word of God that Nahum
spoke about Nineveh, that all these things
will take place and overtake Assyria and
Nineveh. Indeed, everything that was spoken by the prophets of Israel, whom God

a Other ancient authorities read *who build you up*
b Or *O my soul, bless*   c Other ancient authorities
add *for a city*   d Gk *He*   e Other ancient
authorities read *fifty-eight*   f Lat: Gk lacks *and the
seven sons of Tobias*

come is another sign of the messianic age (Zech 14.16). **12:** *Who conquer you* is anachronistic for Tobit's
ostensible date; the reference shows knowledge of Nebuchadnezzar's attack on Jerusalem in 586 BCE.
**16–17:** For similar views of Jerusalem's restoration, see Isa 54.11–14; Rev 21.9–27.
**14.2–11a: Tobit's testament.** Tobit's second testament (4.1–13n.) confirms his earlier insistence that
piety will ultimately be rewarded. **2:** *Giving alms* and *blessing God* are the two major exhortations made
throughout the volume. **3:** *Seven sons*, Edna's wish for grandchildren is granted (10.12). **4–7:** Unlike the
first testament (ch 4), this one opens with predictions of the future; Tobit's comments are among the
earliest claims that events are predetermined (see Dan 10–12). *Nahum* (v. 4) predicted the destruction of
*Assyria and Nineveh*; Babylon conquered Nineveh in 612 BCE (see v. 15; 13.12n.). **5–7:** With the restora-

sent, will occur. None of all their words will fail, but all will come true at their appointed times. So it will be safer in Media than in Assyria and Babylon. For I know and believe that whatever God has said will be fulfilled and will come true; not a single word of the prophecies will fail. All of our kindred, inhabitants of the land of Israel, will be scattered and taken as captives from the good land; and the whole land of Israel will be desolate, even Samaria and Jerusalem will be desolate. And the temple of God in it will be burned to the ground, and it will be desolate for a while.*

5 "But God will again have mercy on them, and God will bring them back into the land of Israel; and they will rebuild the temple of God, but not like the first one until the period when the times of fulfillment shall come. After this they all will return from their exile and will rebuild Jerusalem in splendor; and in it the temple of God will be rebuilt, just as the prophets of Israel have said concerning it. 6 Then the nations in the whole world will all be converted and worship God in truth. They will all abandon their idols, which deceitfully have led them into their error; 7 and in righteousness they will praise the eternal God. All the Israelites who are saved in those days and are truly mindful of God will be gathered together; they will go to Jerusalem and live in safety forever in the land of Abraham, and it will be given over to them. Those who sincerely love God will rejoice, but those who commit sin and injustice will vanish from all the earth. 8,9 So now, my children, I command you, serve God faithfully and do what is pleasing in his sight. Your children are also to be commanded to do what is right and to give alms, and to be mindful of God and to bless his name at

all times with sincerity and with all their strength. So now, my son, leave Nineveh; do not remain here. 10 On whatever day you bury your mother beside me, do not stay overnight within the confines of the city. For I see that there is much wickedness within it, and that much deceit is practiced within it, while the people are without shame. See, my son, what Nadab did to Ahikar who had reared him. Was he not, while still alive, brought down into the earth? For God repaid him to his face for this shameful treatment. Ahikar came out into the light, but Nadab went into the eternal darkness, because he tried to kill Ahikar. Because he gave alms, Ahikar[b] escaped the fatal trap that Nadab had set for him, but Nadab fell into it himself, and was destroyed. 11 So now, my children, see what almsgiving accomplishes, and what injustice does—it brings death! But now my breath fails me."

Then they laid him on his bed, and he died; and he received an honorable funeral. 12 When Tobias's mother died, he buried her beside his father. Then he and his wife and children[c] returned to Media and settled in Ecbatana with Raguel his father-in-law. 13 He treated his parents-in-law[d] with great respect in their old age, and buried them in Ecbatana of Media. He inherited both the property of Raguel and that of his father Tobit. 14 He died highly respected at the age of one hundred seventeen[e] years. 15 Before he died he heard[f] of the destruction of Nineveh, and he saw its prisoners

a Lat: Other ancient authorities read *of God will be in distress and will be burned for a while*  b Gk *he*; other ancient authorities read *Manasses*  c Codex Sinaiticus lacks *and children*  d Gk *them*  e Other authorities read other numbers  f Codex Sinaiticus reads *saw and heard*

tion that began with the edict of Cyrus of Persia in 539 BCE, the hymn shifts to a vision of the splendid future of a renewed Jerusalem, glorified temple, return of the exiles (13.5n.), conversion of the Gentiles, and elimination of sin. **10**: Recognizing that Anna will outlive him, Tobit insists that his son provide for her in life and in death; reference to burial, now after a long life, contrasts positively with Tobit's interring of unburied corpses. *Nadab did to Ahikar*, see 1.21–22n.

**14.11b–15: Tobit and Anna die.** Tobias is obedient to his father's command (14.10) and fulfills his filial duty also by burying his in-laws. Of all the main characters, only Sarah's fate is left undeveloped in being led into Media, those whom King Cy-axares[a] of Media had taken captive. Tobi-as[b] praised God for all he had done to the people of Nineveh and Assyria; before he died he rejoiced over Nineveh, and he blessed the Lord God forever and ever. Amen.[c]

a Cn: Codex Sinaiticus *Ahikar*; other ancient authorities read *Nebuchadnezzar and Ahasuerus*
b Gk *He*    c Other ancient authorities lack *Amen*

the final chapter. **15:** Reference to the destruction of Nineveh suggests that Tobit's other predictions (14.4–7) will also come to pass. Appropriately, the book ends with praise to God.

# JUDITH

꙳ ꙳

Judith, perhaps more than any other biblical book, consistently reverses the reader's expectations. The potent Assyrian army, able to defeat mighty nations both east and west, is routed by the tiny Israelite town of Bethulia. Judith, a Jewish widow, so beguiles Holofernes, the invincible head of the Assyrian army, and all his servants and soldiers that she is able to assassinate him in the middle of his camp and sneak away without being caught. The book's characters and scenes resonate with irony, humor, wordplay, suspense, and the unexpected. The story's characters are vividly drawn and take on lives of their own. Judith is an especially compelling figure. She is morally ambiguous: Although pious, faithful, and religiously observant, she lies, seduces, and murders. She is introduced as a traditionally ideal Jewish woman in many aspects: beautiful, well-connected, devoted to God and her late husband; yet it is she, and not the male rulers of Bethulia, who acts to save the town and rallies the people to her cause. She has often been viewed as a model for human liberation, and her courage and complexity have fascinated artists, writers, and composers for centuries.

The book of Judith is a well-crafted work of fiction, an example of the ancient Jewish novel in the Greco-Roman period. Its tone is exaggerated throughout; it contains historical inaccuracies so great that they strike a reader as absurd; and many of the geographical sites, including the principal scene of the action (the town of Bethulia), are unknown. Religion is a primary concern in the book. The plot's central conflict revolves around the question of whether true power lies with Israel's God or with the military might of a foreign ruler. The work evidences traditional religious practices, including prayer, fasting, and observation of dietary laws.

The unity of plot and detail suggests that the book of Judith is almost certainly the work of a single anonymous author. Because the story reflects Assyrian, Babylonian, Persian, and Hellenistic persons and practices, it is difficult to know when the book was originally composed. Most scholars agree that it was written at some point during the Hasmonean dynasty (165–37 BCE). As *1 Clement* mentions Judith in the first century CE, it is clear that the book was completed and well known by this time. The geographical setting of the story in Palestine, along with its emphasis upon worship in Jerusalem, may suggest that it was composed by a Palestinian Jew.

The figure of Judith and her mode of operation have been variously compared to the biblical characters of Jael and Deborah (Judg 4.4–5.31), Moses, Esther, Abraham, Delilah (Judg 16), and Woman Wisdom (Prov 8). Yet she also may have been fashioned after the real-life persons Judas Maccabeus (hence her name "Judith") or the popular queen Salome Alexandra. It is probably best to view Judith as a fabricated character, a composite of the traits and activities of many other figures from the Bible and from history.

Although the character after whom the book is named does not appear until ch 8, the first seven chapters establish the narrative themes that undergird the entire story: fear, deceit, hearing, blessing, and the proper recipient of worship. Contrasts such as weakness and strength, innocence and guilt, courage and timidity, and godliness and ungodliness should be noted. False appearances and misunderstandings occur regularly; for instance, the Assyrian army only seems strong. Judith's lies are often interpreted as wisdom, and the success of her mission is achieved by means of cosmetic adornment.

The book is divided into two main parts, each with a chiastic structure and thematic repetition. The first part (1.1–7.32), which narrates the Assyrian campaign and revenge against western nations, begins with Nebuchadnezzar's campaign against Arphaxad (1.1–16), his commissioning of Holofernes to attack disobedient vassals (2.1–13), and Holofernes's attack (2.14–7.32). In Holofernes's campaign, the people of other nations surrender (2.14–3.10), and consequently Israel is afraid and Joakim prepares for war (4.1–15). After advising Holofernes, Achior is expelled (5.1–6.11). Then the pattern reverses itself: Achior is received into Bethulia and advises the Israelites (6.12–21); when Holofernes prepares for war, Israel is afraid (7.1–5); and in the campaign against Bethulia, the people wish to surrender (7.6–32). In the second part Judith accomplishes her victory over the Assyrians (8.1–16.25). Judith is introduced (8.1–8) and plans to save Israel (8.9–10.8). Judith and her servant leave Bethulia (10.9–10), and Judith's stratagem succeeds: She overcomes Holofernes (10.11–13.10a). Then the pattern in part two reverses itself: Judith and her servant return to Bethulia (13.10b–11), Judith plans to destroy Israel's enemy (13.12–16.20), and the narrative concludes with a summary of Judith's remaining life (16.21–25).

1 It was the twelfth year of the reign of Nebuchadnezzar, who ruled over the Assyrians in the great city of Nineveh. In those days Arphaxad ruled over the Medes in Ecbatana. 2 He built walls around Ecbatana with hewn stones three cubits thick and six cubits long; he made the walls seventy cubits high and fifty cubits wide. 3 At its gates he raised towers one hundred cubits high and sixty cubits wide at the foundations. 4 He made its gates seventy cubits high and forty cubits wide to allow his armies to march out in force and his infantry to form their ranks. 5 Then King Nebuchadnezzar made war against King Arphaxad in the great plain that is on the borders of Ragau. 6 There rallied to him all the people of the hill country and all those who lived along the Euphrates, the Tigris, and the Hydaspes, and, on the plain, Arioch, king of the Elymeans. Thus, many nations joined the forces of the Chaldeans.[a]

7 Then Nebuchadnezzar, king of the Assyrians, sent messengers to all who lived in Persia and to all who lived in the west, those who lived in Cilicia and Damascus, Lebanon and Antilebanon, and all who lived along the seacoast, 8 and those among the nations of Carmel and Gilead, and Upper Galilee and the great plain of Esdrae-

a Syr: Gk Cheleoudites

1.1–6: Nebuchadnezzar is introduced. He declares war on Arphaxad, the king of Media. 1: Nebuchadnezzar (605–562 BCE) was the second and best-known ruler of the Neo-Babylonian empire (not over the Assyrians), ruling from Babylon (not Nineveh, the Assyrian capital that had been destroyed in 612). He destroyed Jerusalem in 586 and deported the Jews into Babylonian exile (2 Kings 24–25). The author of the book of Judith instead presents him as flourishing after the exile (4.3; 5.19). Some scholars believe that the historical inaccuracies of the book are deliberate attempts to present this story unquestionably as fiction. Arphaxad is unknown, as are many persons and places in this book. (Only those historically identifiable will be described in these notes.) Ecbatana, in the northwest part of modern Iran, was the capital of the empire of the Medes (Ezra 6.2; Tob 3.7). 2: A cubit was about 45 cm (18 in) long. 5: Ragau, the Median region where Arphaxad is killed (v. 15), is about 300 km (185 mi) northeast of Ecbatana, near modern Teheran. 6: Euphrates, Tigris, the principal rivers of Mesopotamia. Hydaspes, a river in India, but here evidently placed in Mesopotamia. Elymeans, possibly the inhabitants of Elyma, a Persian district. Chaldeans, Neo-Babylonians (see v. 1n.).

1.7–11: The Persians and the western nations disregard Nebuchadnezzar's pleas for assistance. 7–10: The nations listed correspond to modern Iran, Syria, southern Turkey, Lebanon, Israel, Palestine, Jordan, and Egypt. 8: Esdraelon, formerly Jezreel (Judg 6.33), the great plain cutting across Palestine just north of Mt. Carmel. 9: Samaria, the region between the plain of Esdraelon and Judea. 11: Afraid, fear (of lon, 9and all who were in Samaria and its towns, and beyond the Jordan as far as Jerusalem and Bethany and Chelous and Kadesh and the river of Egypt, and Tahpanhes and Raamses and the whole land of Goshen, 10even beyond Tanis and Memphis, and all who lived in Egypt as far as the borders of Ethiopia. 11But all who lived in the whole region disregarded the summons of Nebuchadnezzar, king of the Assyrians, and refused to join him in the war; for they were not afraid of him, but regarded him as only one man.ᵃ So they sent back his messengers empty-handed and in disgrace.

12 Then Nebuchadnezzar became very angry with this whole region, and swore by his throne and kingdom that he would take revenge on the whole territory of Cilicia and Damascus and Syria, that he would kill with his sword also all the inhabitants of the land of Moab, and the people of Ammon, and all Judea, and every one in Egypt, as far as the coasts of the two seas.

13 In the seventeenth year he led his forces against King Arphaxad and defeated him in battle, overthrowing the whole army of Arphaxad and all his cavalry and all his chariots. 14Thus he took possession of his towns and came to Ecbatana, captured its towers, plundered its markets, and turned its glory into disgrace. 15He captured Arphaxad in the mountains of Ragau and struck him down with his spears, thus destroying him once and for all. 16Then he returned to Nineveh, he and all his combined forces, a vast body of troops; and there he and his forces rested and feasted for one hundred twenty days.

2 In the eighteenth year, on the twenty-second day of the first month, there was talk in the palace of Nebuchadnezzar, king of the Assyrians, about carrying out his revenge on the whole region, just as he had said. 2He summoned all his ministers and all his nobles and set before them his secret plan and recounted fully, with his own lips, all the wickedness of the region.ᵇ 3They decided that every one who had not obeyed his command should be destroyed.

4 When he had completed his plan, Nebuchadnezzar, king of the Assyrians, called Holofernes, the chief general of his army, second only to himself, and said to him, 5"Thus says the Great King, the lord of the whole earth: Leave my presence and take with you men confident in their strength, one hundred twenty thousand foot soldiers and twelve thousand cavalry. 6March out against all the land to the west, because they disobeyed my orders. 7Tell them to prepare earth and water, for I am coming against them in my anger, and will cover the whole face of the earth with the feet of my troops, to whom I will hand them over to be plundered. 8Their wounded shall fill their ravines and gullies, and the swelling river shall be filled with their dead. 9I will lead them away captive to the ends of the whole earth. 10You shall go and seize all their territory for me in advance. They must yield themselves to you, and you shall hold them for me until the day of their punishment. 11But to those who resist show no mercy, but hand them over to slaughter and plunder throughout your whole region. 12For as I live, and by the power of my kingdom, what I have spoken I will accomplish by my own hand. 13And you—take

ᵃ Or a man   ᵇ Meaning of Gk uncertain

enemies or of God) is a frequent motif (2.28; 4.2; 5.23; 7.4; 8.8; 11.17; 14.3,7,19; 15.2; 16.10,15,16).
**1.12–16:** Nebuchadnezzar vows revenge upon the western nations and alone defeats Arphaxad. **12:** *The two seas* possibly denotes the Red and the Mediterranean.
**2.1–13:** Nebuchadnezzar commissions Holofernes to lead a punitive expedition against the disobedient nations. **1:** *The eighteenth year,* 587 BCE, when the siege of Jerusalem occurred (see Jer 52.29). The *whole region,* the very large geographical territory ranging west of Persia as far as Egypt, is frequently mentioned throughout chs 1–2. The domain of the historical Nebuchadnezzar was never this extended. **2:** Though Nebuchadnezzar tells others *his secret plan* before acting upon it, Judith later does not reveal hers (8.34). **7:** It was a Persian practice to demand *earth and water* from foreign states as a sign of submission (Herodotus 6.48). **12:** *My own hand,* Judith also will later emphasize instrumentality through her hand,

care not to transgress any of your lord's commands, but carry them out exactly as I have ordered you; do it without delay."

14 So Holofernes left the presence of his lord, and summoned all the commanders, generals, and officers of the Assyrian army. [15] He mustered the picked troops by divisions as his lord had ordered him to do, one hundred twenty thousand of them, together with twelve thousand archers on horseback, [16] and he organized them as a great army is marshaled for a campaign. [17] He took along a vast number of camels and donkeys and mules for transport, and innumerable sheep and oxen and goats for food; [18] also ample rations for everyone, and a huge amount of gold and silver from the royal palace.

19 Then he set out with his whole army, to go ahead of King Nebuchadnezzar and to cover the whole face of the earth to the west with their chariots and cavalry and picked foot soldiers. [20] Along with them went a mixed crowd like a swarm of locusts, like the dust[a] of the earth—a multitude that could not be counted.

21 They marched for three days from Nineveh to the plain of Bectileth, and camped opposite Bectileth near the mountain that is to the north of Upper Cilicia. [22] From there Holofernes[b] took his whole army, the infantry, cavalry, and chariots, and went up into the hill country. [23] He ravaged Put and Lud, and plundered all the Rassisites and the Ishmaelites on the border of the desert, south of the country of the Chelleans. [24] Then he followed[c] the Eu-

phrates and passed through Mesopotamia and destroyed all the fortified towns along the brook Abron, as far as the sea. [25] He also seized the territory of Cilicia, and killed everyone who resisted him. Then he came to the southern borders of Japheth, facing Arabia. [26] He surrounded all the Midianites, and burned their tents and plundered their sheepfolds. [27] Then he went down into the plain of Damascus during the wheat harvest, and burned all their fields and destroyed their flocks and herds and sacked their towns and ravaged their lands and put all their young men to the sword.

28 So fear and dread of him fell upon all the people who lived along the seacoast, at Sidon and Tyre, and those who lived in Sur and Ocina and all who lived in Jamnia. Those who lived in Azotus and Ascalon feared him greatly.

3 They therefore sent messengers to him to sue for peace in these words: [2] "We, the servants of Nebuchadnezzar, the Great King, lie prostrate before you. Do with us whatever you will. [3] See, our buildings and all our land and all our wheat fields and our flocks and herds and all our encampments[d] lie before you; do with them as you please. [4] Our towns and their inhabitants are also your slaves; come and deal with them as you see fit."

5 The men came to Holofernes and told him all this. [6] Then he went down to the

---

a Gk sand   b Gk he   c Or crossed   d Gk all the sheepfolds of our tents

---

echoing the figure of Moses (Ex 14.21). **13:** *Carry them out exactly as I have ordered you*, in actuality, Holofernes does not precisely follow Nebuchadnezzar's commands (see 3.8n.).

**2.14–27:** Holofernes musters an enormous army, attacking and defeating the western nations. **21:** *Upper Cilicia*, in southeastern Asia Minor, is 650 km (400 mi) from Nineveh, a distance far too great to travel on foot in *three days*. **23:** *Ishmaelites*, Arabs (Gen 16.11–12). **24:** The geography here is confused. The natural line of march would be directly south from Cilicia to Damascus. **26:** *Midianites*, a population inhabiting the southern Transjordan area, often presented as nomads (Gen 37.28; Judg 6.1–6). **27:** *Damascus*, the capital of Syria.

**2.28–3.4:** The peoples of the seacoast become afraid and surrender. **28:** *Sidon*, a city on the Phoenician coast. *Tyre*, another Phoenician city, originally an island off the coast, and therefore difficult to capture. *Jamnia*, just north of *Azotus* (Ashdod) and *Ascalon* (Ashkelon), two of the five principal ancient Philistine cities on the Mediterranean coast of Palestine.

**3.5–9:** Despite the peoples' submission, Holofernes destroys their religious sites. **8:** In the instructions seacoast with his army and stationed garrisons in the fortified towns and took picked men from them as auxiliaries. 7 These people and all in the countryside welcomed him with garlands and dances and tambourines. 8 Yet he demolished all their shrines[a] and cut down their sacred groves; for he had been commissioned to destroy all the gods of the land, so that all nations should worship Nebuchadnezzar alone, and that all their dialects and tribes should call upon him as a god.

9 Then he came toward Esdraelon, near Dothan, facing the great ridge of Judea; 10 he camped between Geba and Scythopolis, and remained for a whole month in order to collect all the supplies for his army.

4 When the Israelites living in Judea heard of everything that Holofernes, the general of Nebuchadnezzar, the king of the Assyrians, had done to the nations, and how he had plundered and destroyed all their temples, 2 they were therefore greatly terrified at his approach; they were alarmed both for Jerusalem and for the temple of the Lord their God. 3 For they had only recently returned from exile, and all the people of Judea had just now gathered together, and the sacred vessels and the altar and the temple had been consecrated after their profanation. 4 So they sent word to every district of Samaria, and to Kona, Bethhoron, Belmain, and Jericho, and to Choba and Aesora, and the valley of Salem. 5 They immediately seized all the high hilltops and fortified the villages on them and stored up food in preparation for war—since their fields had recently been harvested.

6 The high priest, Joakim, who was in Jerusalem at the time, wrote to the people of Bethulia and Betomesthaim, which faces Esdraelon opposite the plain near Dothan, 7 ordering them to seize the mountain passes, since by them Judea could be invaded; and it would be easy to stop any who tried to enter, for the approach was narrow, wide enough for only two at a time to pass.

8 So the Israelites did as they had been ordered by the high priest Joakim and the senate of the whole people of Israel, in session at Jerusalem. 9 And every man of Israel cried out to God with great fervor, and they humbled themselves with much fasting. 10 They and their wives and their children and their cattle and every resident alien and hired laborer and purchased slave—they all put sackcloth around their waists. 11 And all the Israelite men, women, and children living at Jerusalem prostrated themselves before the temple and put ashes on their heads and spread out their sackcloth before the Lord. 12 They even draped the altar with sackcloth and cried out in unison, praying fervently to the God of Israel not to allow their infants to be carried off and their

a Syr: Gk *borders*

quoted in 2.5–13, Nebuchadnezzar had said nothing about *destroying all the gods of the land* and enforcing worship of himself. **9:** *Esdraelon,* see 1.8n. *Dothan,* a short distance south of the plain of Esdraelon. **10:** *Scythopolis* (Beth-shan), the only city identified by its Greek name in the book, is located near the junction of Esdraelon and the Jordan Valley.

**4.1–15: The Israelites become afraid, prepare for battle, and pray. 1:** The scene shifts to Judea to the south. *Heard,* hearing or demanding to be heard is a theme throughout the book (see 8.1,9,11,32; 9.4,12; 14.1,19; 15.1). **2:** *They were alarmed both for Jerusalem and for the temple,* Holofernes's campaign for religious unity renders a threat to the Israelites' religious integrity as well as their national security. **3:** The statement that they had only recently returned from exile is anachronistic, as it was Nebuchadnezzar who took the Israelites into exile (see 1.1n.). The return did not occur until some fifty years later under the Persian king Cyrus (Ezra 1.1–3). **4:** *Samaria,* see 1.9n. *Beth-horon,* 18 km (11 m) north-northwest of Jerusalem. *Jericho,* in the Jordan Valley, 24 km (15 mi) northeast of Jerusalem. The other places cannot be identified. **6:** The name of the high priest, *Joakim,* is possibly derived from Neh 12.26. *Bethulia* is unknown from other sources. **8:** *Senate,* another anachronism. This governing council in Jerusalem originated during the Hellenistic period. **9–12:** *Fasting, sackcloth,* and *ashes,* traditionally used in mourning and penitence. For *cattle* in sackcloth see Jon 3.7–8. **14:** *The daily burnt offerings* were the wives to be taken as booty, and the towns they had inherited to be destroyed, and the sanctuary to be profaned and desecrated to the malicious joy of the Gentiles.

13 The Lord heard their prayers and had regard for their distress; for the people fasted many days throughout Judea and in Jerusalem before the sanctuary of the Lord Almighty. 14 The high priest Joakim and all the priests who stood before the Lord and ministered to the Lord, with sackcloth around their loins, offered the daily burnt offerings, the votive offerings, and freewill offerings of the people. 15 With ashes on their turbans, they cried out to the Lord with all their might to look with favor on the whole house of Israel.

5 It was reported to Holofernes, the general of the Assyrian army, that the people of Israel had prepared for war and had closed the mountain passes and fortified all the high hilltops and set up barricades in the plains. 2 In great anger he called together all the princes of Moab and the commanders of Ammon and all the governors of the coastland, 3 and said to them, "Tell me, you Canaanites, what people is this that lives in the hill country? What towns do they inhabit? How large is their army, and in what does their power and strength consist? Who rules over them as king and leads their army? 4 And why have they alone, of all who live in the west, refused to come out and meet me?"

5 Then Achior, the leader of all the Am-

monites, said to him, "May my lord please listen to a report from the mouth of your servant, and I will tell you the truth about this people that lives in the mountain district near you. No falsehood shall come from your servant's mouth. 6 These people are descended from the Chaldeans. 7 At one time they lived in Mesopotamia, because they did not wish to follow the gods of their ancestors who were in Chaldea. 8 Since they had abandoned the ways of their ancestors, and worshiped the God of heaven, the God they had come to know, their ancestors[a] drove them out from the presence of their gods. So they fled to Mesopotamia, and lived there for a long time. 9 Then their God commanded them to leave the place where they were living and go to the land of Canaan. There they settled, and grew very prosperous in gold and silver and very much livestock. 10 When a famine spread over the land of Canaan they went down to Egypt and lived there as long as they had food. There they became so great a multitude that their race could not be counted. 11 So the king of Egypt became hostile to them; he exploited them and forced them to make bricks. 12 They cried out to their God, and he afflicted the whole land of Egypt with incurable plagues. So the Egyptians drove them out of their sight. 13 Then God dried up the Red Sea before them, 14 and he led them by the way of Sinai and Kadesh-

a Gk they

prescribed sacrifices (Ex 29.38–42); the *votive* and *freewill offerings* were presented voluntarily as occasion required (Lev 22.18–30).

**5.1–4**: Holofernes questions the unique character of the Israelites. **1**: The scene shifts to the Assyrian camp outside Bethulia. **2**: *Moab*, the region directly east of the Dead Sea; *Ammon,* north of Moab. Both nations were traditional enemies of Israel (Judg 3.12–30; 2 Sam 10–12).

**5.5–22**: Achior instructs Holofernes by outlining the history of the Israelites. **5–21**: The historical summary runs from Abraham until the return from exile. **6–9**: The migration of Abraham and the prosperity of his descendants (Gen 11.27–37.1). **6**: *Chaldeans,* Abraham came from Ur of the Chaldees (Gen 11.27–31), in southern Babylonia. It is characteristic of Greek and Roman ethnography to begin by noting the origins of a people. **7**: Early Jewish tradition ascribes the migration of Abraham's family to a desire to escape the influence of polytheism (*Jubilees* 11.16–12.7; Josephus, *Ant.* 1.134–157). *Mesopotamia* here is the region in northern Syria around Haran (Gen 11.31). **8**: *The God of heaven,* a popular title during the Persian period and later (Ezra 1.2; Tob 10.11). Various characters use similar terminology in reference to God, which helps to unify the book (see 6.19; 9.12; 11.17; 13.18). **10–13**: The descent into Egypt and the Exodus (Gen 37–Ex 18). **14**: *Sinai,* Ex 19–Num 10. *Kadesh-barnea,* Num 20.1.

barnea. They drove out all the people of the desert, [15] and took up residence in the land of the Amorites, and by their might destroyed all the inhabitants of Heshbon; and crossing over the Jordan they took possession of all the hill country. [16] They drove out before them the Canaanites, the Perizzites, the Jebusites, the Shechemites, and all the Gergesites, and lived there a long time.

[17] "As long as they did not sin against their God they prospered, for the God who hates iniquity is with them. [18] But when they departed from the way he had prescribed for them, they were utterly defeated in many battles and were led away captive to a foreign land. The temple of their God was razed to the ground, and their towns were occupied by their enemies. [19] But now they have returned to their God, and have come back from the places where they were scattered, and have occupied Jerusalem, where their sanctuary is, and have settled in the hill country, because it was uninhabited.

[20] "So now, my master and lord, if there is any oversight in this people and they sin against their God and we find out their offense, then we can go up and defeat them. [21] But if they are not a guilty nation, then let my lord pass them by; for their Lord and God will defend them, and we shall become the laughingstock of the whole world."

[22] When Achior had finished saying these things, all the people standing around the tent began to complain; Holofernes' officers and all the inhabitants of the seacoast and Moab insisted that he should be cut to pieces. [23] They said, "We are not afraid of the Israelites; they are a people with no strength or power for making war. [24] Therefore let us go ahead, Lord Holofernes, and your vast army will swallow them up."

**6** When the disturbance made by the people outside the council had died down, Holofernes, the commander of the Assyrian army, said to Achior[a] in the presence of all the foreign contingents:

[2] "Who are you, Achior and you mercenaries of Ephraim, to prophesy among us as you have done today and tell us not to make war against the people of Israel because their God will defend them? What god is there except Nebuchadnezzar? He will send his forces and destroy them from the face of the earth. Their God will not save them; [3] we the king's[b] servants will destroy them as one man. They cannot resist the might of our cavalry. [4] We will overwhelm them;[c] their mountains will be drunk with their blood, and their fields will be full of their dead. Not even their footprints will survive our attack; they will utterly perish. So says King Nebuchadnezzar, lord of the whole earth. For he has spoken; none of his words shall be in vain.

[5] "As for you, Achior, you Ammonite mercenary, you have said these words in a moment of perversity; you shall not see my face again from this day until I take revenge on this race that came out of Egypt. [6] Then at my return the sword of my army and the spear[d] of my servants shall pierce your sides, and you shall fall among their wounded. [7] Now my slaves are going to take you back into the hill country and put you in one of the towns beside the passes. [8] You will not die until you perish along with them. [9] If you really hope in your heart that they will not be taken, then do not

a Other ancient authorities add *and to all the Moabites*    b Gk *his*    c Other ancient authorities add *with it*    d Lat Syr: Gk *people*

**15–16:** The conquests in Transjordan and Canaan (Num 20–Josh 11). For similar lists see Gen 15.19–21; Deut 7.1; Josh 11.3. **15:** *Amorites . . . Heshbon,* Num 21.21–32. **16:** *Shechemites,* Judith's ancestor Simeon (9.2) avenged the rape of his sister Dinah by Shechem (Gen 34). **17–18:** The perspective of Deuteronomy (28.1–14). **19:** The return from exile (Ezra 1–3).

**6.1–13: Holofernes denounces Achior and ejects him from the camp. 2–4:** Holofernes again asserts the divine sovereignty of Nebuchadnezzar; see 3.8. **5:** That Achior *shall not see* [Holofernes's] *face again* anticipates 14.6. **11:** *Springs,* in Palestine many towns were built near springs for their water supply.

look downcast! I have spoken, and none of my words shall fail to come true."

10 Then Holofernes ordered his slaves, who waited on him in his tent, to seize Achior and take him away to Bethulia and hand him over to the Israelites. 11 So the slaves took him and led him out of the camp into the plain, and from the plain they went up into the hill country and came to the springs below Bethulia. 12 When the men of the town saw them,*a* they seized their weapons and ran out of the town to the top of the hill, and all the slingers kept them from coming up by throwing stones at them. 13 So having taken shelter below the hill, they bound Achior and left him lying at the foot of the hill, and returned to their master.

14 Then the Israelites came down from their town and found him; they untied him and brought him into Bethulia and placed him before the magistrates of their town, 15 who in those days were Uzziah son of Micah, of the tribe of Simeon, and Chabris son of Gothoniel, and Charmis son of Melchiel. 16 They called together all the elders of the town, and all their young men and women ran to the assembly. They set Achior in the midst of all their people, and Uzziah questioned him about what had happened. 17 He answered and told them what had taken place at the council of Holofernes, and all that he had said in the presence of the Assyrian leaders, and all that Holofernes had boasted he would do against the house of Israel. 18 Then the people fell down and worshiped God, and cried out:

19 "O Lord God of heaven, see their arrogance, and have pity on our people in their humiliation, and look kindly today on the faces of those who are consecrated to you."

20 Then they reassured Achior, and praised him highly. 21 Uzziah took him from the assembly to his own house and gave a banquet for the elders; and all that night they called on the God of Israel for help.

7 The next day Holofernes ordered his whole army, and all the allies who had joined him, to break camp and move against Bethulia, and to seize the passes up into the hill country and make war on the Israelites. 2 So all their warriors marched off that day; their fighting forces numbered one hundred seventy thousand infantry and twelve thousand cavalry, not counting the baggage and the foot soldiers handling it, a very great multitude. 3 They encamped in the valley near Bethulia, beside the spring, and they spread out in breadth over Dothan as far as Balbaim and in length from Bethulia to Cyamon, which faces Esdraelon.

4 When the Israelites saw their vast numbers, they were greatly terrified and said to one another, "They will now strip clean the whole land; neither the high mountains nor the valleys nor the hills will bear their weight." 5 Yet they all seized their weapons, and when they had kindled fires on their towers, they remained on guard all that night.

6 On the second day Holofernes led out all his cavalry in full view of the Israelites in Bethulia. 7 He reconnoitered the ap-

*a* Other ancient authorities add *on the top of the hill*

**6.14–21:** The Israelites find and rescue Achior, bringing him into Bethulia. **14:** The perspective shifts from that of the Assyrians to that of the Israelites. **15:** *Simeon*, the tribe of Simeon was given an allotment within the tribal territory of Judah in southern Canaan (Josh 19.1–9). During the Divided Monarchy it seems to have been considered as one of the northern tribes (1 Kings 12.20–23). Judith is also of this lineage, of which she is proud (9.2). **19,21:** Again the Israelites pray to their God (4.12).

**7.1–5:** The Assyrians begin war preparations; the Israelites are again frightened and prepare to fight. **1:** The scene shifts to the Assyrian camp, then quickly back to Bethulia (v. 4). **1–3:** The line of march is south from Esdraelon. **2:** *One hundred seventy thousand infantry*, the troops have grown from 120,000 (1.16; 2.5,15), perhaps because of the uncountable multitude traveling along (2.20). **3:** *Dothan, Esdraelon*, see 3.9n.

**7.6–18:** Holofernes, on the advice of his leaders, decides to seize Bethulia's water supply. **8:** *Edomites,* proaches to their town, and visited the springs that supplied their water; he seized them and set guards of soldiers over them, and then returned to his army.

8 Then all the chieftains of the Edomites and all the leaders of the Moabites and the commanders of the coastland came to him and said, 9 "Listen to what we have to say, my lord, and your army will suffer no losses. 10 This people, the Israelites, do not rely on their spears but on the height of the mountains where they live, for it is not easy to reach the tops of their mountains. 11 Therefore, my lord, do not fight against them in regular formation, and not a man of your army will fall. 12 Remain in your camp, and keep all the men in your forces with you; let your servants take possession of the spring of water that flows from the foot of the mountain, 13 for this is where all the people of Bethulia get their water. So thirst will destroy them, and they will surrender their town. Meanwhile, we and our people will go up to the tops of the nearby mountains and camp there to keep watch to see that no one gets out of the town. 14 They and their wives and children will waste away with famine, and before the sword reaches them they will be strewn about in the streets where they live. 15 Thus you will pay them back with evil, because they rebelled and did not receive you peaceably."

16 These words pleased Holofernes and all his attendants, and he gave orders to do as they had said. 17 So the army of the Ammonites moved forward, together with five thousand Assyrians, and they encamped in the valley and seized the water supply and the springs of the Israelites. 18 And the Edomites and Ammonites went up and encamped in the hill country opposite Dothan; and they sent some of their men to-

ward the south and the east, toward Egrebeh, which is near Chusi beside the Wadi Mochmur. The rest of the Assyrian army encamped in the plain, and covered the whole face of the land. Their tents and supply trains spread out in great number, and they formed a vast multitude.

19 The Israelites then cried out to the Lord their God, for their courage failed, because all their enemies had surrounded them, and there was no way of escape from them. 20 The whole Assyrian army, their infantry, chariots, and cavalry, surrounded them for thirty-four days, until all the water containers of every inhabitant of Bethulia were empty; 21 their cisterns were going dry, and on no day did they have enough water to drink, for their drinking water was rationed. 22 Their children were listless, and the women and young men fainted from thirst and were collapsing in the streets of the town and in the gateways; they no longer had any strength.

23 Then all the people, the young men, the women, and the children, gathered around Uzziah and the rulers of the town and cried out with a loud voice, and said before all the elders, 24 "Let God judge between you and us! You have done us a great injury in not making peace with the Assyrians. 25 For now we have no one to help us; God has sold us into their hands, to be strewn before them in thirst and exhaustion. 26 Now summon them and surrender the whole town as booty to the army of Holofernes and to all his forces. 27 For it would be better for us to be captured by them.[a] We shall indeed become slaves, but our lives will be spared, and we shall not witness our little ones dying before our eyes, and our wives and children drawing

a Other ancient authorities add *than to die of thirst*

located southeast of the Dead Sea; Edom was a traditional enemy of Israel (Ob 18; 1 Macc 5.1–5). **13:** *No one gets out of the town:* This part of the plan fails, for Judith and her servant are able to leave the mountain without difficulty (10.10). **18:** *Egrebeh, Chusi,* and the valley of *Mochmur* are most likely sites in the neighborhood of Shechem.

**7.19–28:** Driven to desperation, the citizens of Bethulia urge the leaders to surrender. **22:** The events occur just as their enemies had predicted (v. 14). **23:** *Uzziah,* 6.15. **25:** Though the readers have been told that God has heard the people's prayers (4.13), the Israelites themselves do not know of God's attention.

their last breath. 28 We call to witness against you heaven and earth and our God, the Lord of our ancestors, who punishes us for our sins and the sins of our ancestors; do today the things that we have described!"

29 Then great and general lamentation arose throughout the assembly, and they cried out to the Lord God with a loud voice. 30 But Uzziah said to them, "Courage, my brothers and sisters!*a* Let us hold out for five days more; by that time the Lord our God will turn his mercy to us again, for he will not forsake us utterly. 31 But if these days pass by, and no help comes for us, I will do as you say."

32 Then he dismissed the people to their various posts, and they went up on the walls and towers of their town. The women and children he sent home. In the town they were in great misery.

8 Now in those days Judith heard about these things: she was the daughter of Merari son of Ox son of Joseph son of Oziel son of Elkiah son of Ananias son of Gideon son of Raphain son of Ahitub son of Elijah son of Hilkiah son of Eliab son of Nathanael son of Salamiel son of Sarasadai son of Israel. 2 Her husband Manasseh, who belonged to her tribe and family, had died during the barley harvest. 3 For as he stood overseeing those who were binding sheaves in the field, he was overcome by the burning heat, and took to his bed and died

in his town Bethulia. So they buried him with his ancestors in the field between Dothan and Balamon. 4 Judith remained as a widow for three years and four months 5 at home where she set up a tent for herself on the roof of her house. She put sackcloth around her waist and dressed in widow's clothing. 6 She fasted all the days of her widowhood, except the day before the sabbath and the sabbath itself, the day before the new moon and the day of the new moon, and the festivals and days of rejoicing of the house of Israel. 7 She was beautiful in appearance, and was very lovely to behold. Her husband Manasseh had left her gold and silver, men and women slaves, livestock, and fields; and she maintained this estate. 8 No one spoke ill of her, for she feared God with great devotion.

9 When Judith heard the harsh words spoken by the people against the ruler, because they were faint for lack of water, and when she heard all that Uzziah said to them, and how he promised them under oath to surrender the town to the Assyrians after five days, 10 she sent her maid, who was in charge of all she possessed, to summon Uzziah and*b* Chabris and Charmis, the elders of her town. 11 They came to her, and she said to them:

"Listen to me, rulers of the people of Be-

a *Gk Courage, brothers*    b *Other ancient authorities lack* Uzziah and *(see verses 28 and 35)*

**28:** *Our sins and the sins of our ancestors,* the Israelites blame themselves for their predicament; cf. Judith's interpretation in 8.18,27.

**7.29–32: Uzziah advises instead a delay of five days. 29:** Again, the Israelites pray (4.12; 6.19–21). Judith will also pray *with a loud voice* (9.1; 13.14).

**8.1–8: Judith is introduced. 1:** The word *Judith* is the grammatically feminine form of the word "Jew" or "Judean." Her name reflects how she functions as a representative of the Jewish community as a whole. Like "Israel," it is a name both of a people and of a significant individual within its rank. Judith's genealogy is the longest attributed to any woman in the Bible. **2–3:** Judith's husband *Manasseh* died of sunstroke (cf. 2 Kings 4.18–20). *To her tribe and family,* it is unconventional in the Bible to identify a man by his relationship to a woman. **6:** Judith's rigorous fasting is suspended only for those days when it was forbidden to fast. **7:** *Beautiful . . . very lovely to behold,* significant women in the Bible are often described as being beautiful (Sarah, Rebekah, Bathsheba, Esther). **8:** Judith has the respect and approval of the Israelite community (see 8.28–29; 13.18–20; 15.9–12; 16.21) on account of her piety.

**8.9–27: Judith upbraids the Bethulian leaders. 10–11:** Judith's *maid,* despite being unnamed, is an important character. Since she has great responsibility, being *in charge of all she possessed,* the elders do her bidding without question. **12:** Judith argues that the rulers are in error *to put God to the test* (see Deut thulia! What you have said to the people today is not right; you have even sworn and pronounced this oath between God and you, promising to surrender the town to our enemies unless the Lord turns and helps us within so many days. 12 Who are you to put God to the test today, and to set yourselves up in the place of[a] God in human affairs? 13 You are putting the Lord Almighty to the test, but you will never learn anything! 14 You cannot plumb the depths of the human heart or understand the workings of the human mind; how do you expect to search out God, who made all these things, and find out his mind or comprehend his thought? No, my brothers, do not anger the Lord our God. 15 For if he does not choose to help us within these five days, he has power to protect us within any time he pleases, or even to destroy us in the presence of our enemies. 16 Do not try to bind the purposes of the Lord our God; for God is not like a human being, to be threatened, or like a mere mortal, to be won over by pleading. 17 Therefore, while we wait for his deliverance, let us call upon him to help us, and he will hear our voice, if it pleases him.

18 "For never in our generation, nor in these present days, has there been any tribe or family or people or town of ours that worships gods made with hands, as was done in days gone by. 19 That was why our ancestors were handed over to the sword and to pillage, and so they suffered a great catastrophe before our enemies. 20 But we know no other god but him, and so we hope that he will not disdain us or any of our nation. 21 For if we are captured, all Judea will be captured and our sanctuary will be plundered; and he will make us pay for its desecration with our blood. 22 The

slaughter of our kindred and the captivity of the land and the desolation of our inheritance—all this he will bring on our heads among the Gentiles, wherever we serve as slaves; and we shall be an offense and a disgrace in the eyes of those who acquire us. 23 For our slavery will not bring us into favor, but the Lord our God will turn it to dishonor.

24 "Therefore, my brothers, let us set an example for our kindred, for their lives depend upon us, and the sanctuary—both the temple and the altar—rests upon us. 25 In spite of everything let us give thanks to the Lord our God, who is putting us to the test as he did our ancestors. 26 Remember what he did with Abraham, and how he tested Isaac, and what happened to Jacob in Syrian Mesopotamia, while he was tending the sheep of Laban, his mother's brother. 27 For he has not tried us with fire, as he did them, to search their hearts, nor has he taken vengeance on us; but the Lord scourges those who are close to him in order to admonish them."

28 Then Uzziah said to her, "All that you have said was spoken out of a true heart, and there is no one who can deny your words. 29 Today is not the first time your wisdom has been shown, but from the beginning of your life all the people have recognized your understanding, for your heart's disposition is right. 30 But the people were so thirsty that they compelled us to do for them what we have promised, and made us take an oath that we cannot break. 31 Now since you are a God-fearing woman, pray for us, so that the Lord may send us rain to fill our cisterns. Then we will no longer feel faint from thirst."

a Or above

6.16). **15–17:** Judith holds that God has complete freedom and sovereignty, with no obligation to heed the people's pleas. **25–27:** In Judith's mind the present calamities are occurring because God is testing the people, not, as they think, because of their own sinfulness (7.28). *Abraham,* Gen 22; *Jacob,* Gen 29.9–30.

**8.28–36:** The leaders acknowledge Judith's wisdom and she vows to deliver the city. **29:** *Wisdom, understanding,* speaking what is *right,* Judith reflects aspects of Woman Wisdom (Prov 8.6). The areas in which Judith demonstrates herself knowledgeable suggest that she may have been formally educated. Despite long recognizing Judith's wisdom and exemplary character, Uzziah did not think to solicit her advice during the crisis. **30:** *The people were so thirsty . . . ,* Uzziah states that his hand was forced. **33:**

32 Then Judith said to them, "Listen to me. I am about to do something that will go down through all generations of our descendants. 33 Stand at the town gate tonight so that I may go out with my maid; and within the days after which you have promised to surrender the town to our enemies, the Lord will deliver Israel by my hand. 34 Only, do not try to find out what I am doing; for I will not tell you until I have finished what I am about to do."

35 Uzziah and the rulers said to her, "Go in peace, and may the Lord God go before you, to take vengeance on our enemies." 36 So they returned from the tent and went to their posts.

9 Then Judith prostrated herself, put ashes on her head, and uncovered the sackcloth she was wearing. At the very time when the evening incense was being offered in the house of God in Jerusalem, Judith cried out to the Lord with a loud voice, and said,

2 "O Lord God of my ancestor Simeon, to whom you gave a sword to take revenge on those strangers who had torn off a virgin's clothing[a] to defile her, and exposed her thighs to put her to shame, and polluted her womb to disgrace her; for you said, 'It shall not be done'—yet they did it; 3 so you gave up their rulers to be killed, and their bed, which was ashamed of the deceit they had practiced, was stained with blood, and you struck down slaves along with princes, and princes on their thrones. 4 You gave up their wives for booty and their daughters to captivity, and all their booty to be divided among your beloved children who burned with zeal for you and abhorred the pollution of their blood and called on you for help. O God, my God, hear me also, a widow.

5 "For you have done these things and those that went before and those that followed. You have designed the things that are now, and those that are to come. What you had in mind has happened; 6 the things you decided on presented themselves and said, 'Here we are!' For all your ways are prepared in advance, and your judgment is with foreknowledge.

7 "Here now are the Assyrians, a greatly increased force, priding themselves in their horses and riders, boasting in the strength of their foot soldiers, and trusting in shield and spear, in bow and sling. They do not know that you are the Lord who crushes wars; the Lord is your name. 8 Break their strength by your might, and bring down their power in your anger; for they intend to defile your sanctuary, and to pollute the tabernacle where your glorious name resides, and to break off the horns[b] of your altar with the sword. 9 Look at their pride, and send your wrath upon their heads. Give to me, a widow, the strong hand to do what I plan. 10 By the deceit of my lips strike down the slave with the prince and the prince with his servant; crush their arrogance by the hand of a woman.

11 "For your strength does not depend on numbers, nor your might on the powerful. But you are the God of the lowly, helper of the oppressed, upholder of the weak,

a Cn: Gk *loosed her womb*    b Syr: Gk *horn*

Judith promises that God will act through her. *Within the days after which you have promised,* ironically, Judith also tests God by swearing that *the Lord* will work within the people's time frame. She implicitly refutes the complete freedom she earlier attributed to God (vv. 16–17). **34:** Judith's secret plan; see 2.2n.

**9.1–14: Judith prays. 1:** *Evening incense,* Ex 30.8; Ps 141.2. It may have become customary to offer prayer regularly at this time of day. **2:** *My ancestor Simeon,* he and his brother Levi, sons of Jacob, avenged the rape of their sister Dinah by means of deception (Gen 34). **4:** God's special care for the *widow* is an important biblical theme (Deut 10.18; Ps 146.9). **5–6:** Judith describes God as having absolute foreknowledge and control of history (Isa 44.6–8). **8:** *Horns,* see 1 Kings 1.50n. **10–13:** *By the deceit of my lips, my deceitful words,* Judith announces that she plans to perform her strategy through subterfuge and asks for God's blessing. Deceit is a common mode of operation for trickster figures (Rebekah, Jacob, Tamar, Abraham). *By the hand of a woman,* biblical tradition holds it to be particularly ignominious to be destroyed by a woman (Judg 9.53–54).

protector of the forsaken, savior of those without hope. [12]Please, please, God of my father, God of the heritage of Israel, Lord of heaven and earth, Creator of the waters, King of all your creation, hear my prayer! [13]Make my deceitful words bring wound and bruise on those who have planned cruel things against your covenant, and against your sacred house, and against Mount Zion, and against the house your children possess. [14]Let your whole nation and every tribe know and understand that you are God, the God of all power and might, and that there is no other who protects the people of Israel but you alone!"

10 When Judith[a] had stopped crying out to the God of Israel, and had ended all these words, [2]she rose from where she lay prostrate. She called her maid and went down into the house where she lived on sabbaths and on her festal days. [3]She removed the sackcloth she had been wearing, took off her widow's garments, bathed her body with water, and anointed herself with precious ointment. She combed her hair, put on a tiara, and dressed herself in the festive attire that she used to wear while her husband Manasseh was living. [4]She put sandals on her feet, and put on her anklets, bracelets, rings, earrings, and all her other jewelry. Thus she made herself very beautiful, to entice the eyes of all the men who might see her. [5]She gave her maid a skin of wine and a flask of oil, and filled a bag with roasted grain, dried fig cakes, and fine bread;[b] then she wrapped up all her dishes and gave them to her to carry.

[6]Then they went out to the town gate of Bethulia and found Uzziah standing there with the elders of the town, Chabris and Charmis. [7]When they saw her transformed in appearance and dressed differently, they were very greatly astounded at her beauty and said to her, [8]"May the God of our ancestors grant you favor and fulfill your plans, so that the people of Israel may glory and Jerusalem may be exalted." She bowed down to God.

[9]Then she said to them, "Order the gate of the town to be opened for me so that I may go out and accomplish the things you have just said to me." So they ordered the young men to open the gate for her, as she requested. [10]When they had done this, Judith went out, accompanied by her maid. The men of the town watched her until she had gone down the mountain and passed through the valley, where they lost sight of her.

[11]As the women[c] were going straight on through the valley, an Assyrian patrol met her [12]and took her into custody. They asked her, "To what people do you belong, and where are you coming from, and where are you going?" She replied, "I am a daughter of the Hebrews, but I am fleeing from them, for they are about to be handed over to you to be devoured. [13]I am on my way to see Holofernes the commander of your army, to give him a true report; I will show him a way by which he can go and capture all the hill country without losing one of his men, captured or slain."

a Gk she    b Other ancient authorities add *and cheese*
c Gk they

**10.1–5: Judith bathes and dresses in preparation for her mission. 3:** As does Esther, Judith prepares for her dangerous task by donning special clothing (Esth 5.1). *Bathed her body with water,* unlike the rest of Bethulia, Judith does not lack for water. **5:** *Dishes,* for cooking her food in accordance with Jewish dietary laws.

**10.6–10: The elders bless Judith and she and her servant leave Bethulia. 7:** The town leaders display their approval of her attempt. *Greatly astounded at her beauty,* the elders are the first of a series of men to be amazed at Judith's beautified appearance and wisdom (see 10.14,19,23; 11.21,23; 12.13; 16.9). **8:** *She bowed down to God,* Judith performs prayer and other acts of piety throughout her mission.

**10.11–23: The two women are captured by the Assyrians and brought to Holofernes. 11:** A shift in point of view, from seeing the action through the eyes of the Bethulians as they watch the women depart (v. 10) to the perspective of the *Assyrian patrol* who meet them as they come into the enemy camp. **12:** *I am fleeing from them,* Judith begins the deception she promised (see 9.10–13n.). **14:** *Heard her words,*

14 When the men heard her words, and observed her face—she was in their eyes marvelously beautiful—they said to her, 15 "You have saved your life by hurrying down to see our lord. Go at once to his tent; some of us will escort you and hand you over to him. 16 When you stand before him, have no fear in your heart, but tell him what you have just said, and he will treat you well."

17 They chose from their number a hundred men to accompany her and her maid, and they brought them to the tent of Holofernes. 18 There was great excitement in the whole camp, for her arrival was reported from tent to tent. They came and gathered around her as she stood outside the tent of Holofernes, waiting until they told him about her. 19 They marveled at her beauty and admired the Israelites, judging them by her. They said to one another, "Who can despise these people, who have women like this among them? It is not wise to leave one of their men alive, for if we let them go they will be able to beguile the whole world!"

20 Then the guards of Holofernes and all his servants came out and led her into the tent. 21 Holofernes was resting on his bed under a canopy that was woven with purple and gold, emeralds and other precious stones. 22 When they told him of her, he came to the front of the tent, with silver lamps carried before him. 23 When Judith came into the presence of Holofernes[a] and his servants, they all marveled at the beauty of her face. She prostrated herself and did obeisance to him, but his slaves raised her up.

11 Then Holofernes said to her, "Take courage, woman, and do not be afraid in your heart, for I have never hurt anyone who chose to serve Nebuchadnezzar, king of all the earth. 2 Even now, if your people who live in the hill country had not slighted me, I would never have lifted my spear against them. They have brought this on themselves. 3 But now tell me why you have fled from them and have come over to us. In any event, you have come to safety. Take courage! You will live tonight and ever after. 4 No one will hurt you. Rather, all will treat you well, as they do the servants of my lord King Nebuchadnezzar."

5 Judith answered him, "Accept the words of your slave, and let your servant speak in your presence. I will say nothing false to my lord this night. 6 If you follow out the words of your servant, God will accomplish something through you, and my lord will not fail to achieve his purposes. 7 By the life of Nebuchadnezzar, king of the whole earth, and by the power of him who has sent you to direct every living being! Not only do human beings serve him because of you, but also the animals of the field and the cattle and the birds of the air will live, because of your power, under Nebuchadnezzar and all his house. 8 For we have heard of your wisdom and skill, and

a Gk him

observed her face, the Assyrians are convinced by both Judith's rhetoric and her beauty. 17: A hundred men, surely more than would be needed for an escort. 18: Whole camp, the entire camp is thrown into disarray at Judith's presence. 19: The Assyrians' overreaction is one of the humorous moments of the story.

11.1–4: Holofernes welcomes Judith. 1: I have never hurt anyone who chose to serve Nebuchadnezzar, a false statement (see 3.2–8).

11.5–23: Judith's explanation of her departure commends her to Holofernes and his advisors. 5–19: Judith's speech is a masterwork of double meanings. Every verse contains an equivocation, half-truth, or deliberate misrepresentation. 5: Nothing false, Judith's opening statement echoes Achior's (5.5). 5–6: My lord, by this designation does Judith refer to God or Holofernes? 6: The idea that Israel's God can work through non-Israelite leaders and armies is fairly common in the Bible (Isa 10.5; Jer 25.9). 7: The description of Nebuchadnezzar's power over human beings ... animals of the field ... cattle ... birds echoes Dan 2.38. See also Jer 27.6; 28.14. Here, however, Judith cleverly adapts the praise of Nebuchadnezzar to flatter Holofernes. 9: Achior's speech, see 5.5–21. 11: Sin has overtaken them, Judith earlier it is reported throughout the whole world that you alone are the best in the whole kingdom, the most informed and the most astounding in military strategy.

9 "Now as for Achior's speech in your council, we have heard his words, for the people of Bethulia spared him and he told them all he had said to you. [10] Therefore, lord and master, do not disregard what he said, but keep it in your mind, for it is true. Indeed our nation cannot be punished, nor can the sword prevail against them, unless they sin against their God.

11 "But now, in order that my lord may not be defeated and his purpose frustrated, death will fall upon them, for a sin has overtaken them by which they are about to provoke their God to anger when they do what is wrong. [12] Since their food supply is exhausted and their water has almost given out, they have planned to kill their livestock and have determined to use all that God by his laws has forbidden them to eat. [13] They have decided to consume the first fruits of the grain and the tithes of the wine and oil, which they had consecrated and set aside for the priests who minister in the presence of our God in Jerusalem—things it is not lawful for any of the people even to touch with their hands. [14] Since even the people in Jerusalem have been doing this, they have sent messengers there in order to bring back permission from the council of the elders. [15] When the response reaches them and they act upon it, on that very day they will be handed over to you to be destroyed.

16 "So when I, your slave, learned all this, I fled from them. God has sent me to accomplish with you things that will astonish the whole world wherever people shall hear about them. [17] Your servant is indeed

God-fearing and serves the God of heaven night and day. So, my lord, I will remain with you; but every night your servant will go out into the valley and pray to God. He will tell me when they have committed their sins. [18] Then I will come and tell you, so that you may go out with your whole army, and not one of them will be able to withstand you. [19] Then I will lead you through Judea, until you come to Jerusalem; there I will set your throne.[a] You will drive them like sheep that have no shepherd, and no dog will so much as growl at you. For this was told me to give me foreknowledge; it was announced to me, and I was sent to tell you."

20 Her words pleased Holofernes and all his servants. They marveled at her wisdom and said, [21] "No other woman from one end of the earth to the other looks so beautiful or speaks so wisely!" [22] Then Holofernes said to her, "God has done well to send you ahead of the people, to strengthen our hands and bring destruction on those who have despised my lord. [23] You are not only beautiful in appearance, but wise in speech. If you do as you have said, your God shall be my God, and you shall live in the palace of King Nebuchadnezzar and be renowned throughout the whole world."

12 Then he commanded them to bring her in where his silver dinnerware was kept, and ordered them to set a table for her with some of his own delicacies, and with some of his own wine to drink. [2] But Judith said, "I cannot partake of them, or it will be an offense; but I will have enough with the things I brought with me." [3] Holofernes said to her, "If your supply runs out,

a Or *chariot*

asserted that the Israelites' crisis was not caused by their own sin (see 8.25–27n.). **13:** *First fruits,* Ex 23.19; *tithes,* Lev 27.30. **16:** *Things that will astonish the whole world,* indeed such is the case, though not in the way that Holofernes anticipates. **17:** *Every night your servant will go out into the valley and pray,* Judith is establishing a pretense by which she will ultimately be able to escape the Assyrian camp (13.3,10). **23:** *Your God shall be my God,* in light of his earlier insistence that Nebuchadnezzar alone is God (3.8; 6.2), it is doubtful that Holofernes is sincere in this statement (see Ruth 1.16–17).

**12.1–9: Judith establishes a pattern of leaving the camp for prayer. 2:** Judith, like Daniel, is careful to maintain Jewish dietary conventions even when living in a foreign environment (Dan 1.8–19). **4:** *Before* where can we get you more of the same? For none of your people are here with us." ⁴Judith replied, "As surely as you live, my lord, your servant will not use up the supplies I have with me before the Lord carries out by my hand what he has determined."

5 Then the servants of Holofernes brought her into the tent, and she slept until midnight. Toward the morning watch she got up ⁶and sent this message to Holofernes: "Let my lord now give orders to allow your servant to go out and pray." ⁷So Holofernes commanded his guards not to hinder her. She remained in the camp three days. She went out each night to the valley of Bethulia, and bathed at the spring in the camp.ᵃ ⁸After bathing, she prayed the Lord God of Israel to direct her way for the triumph of hisᵇ people. ⁹Then she returned purified and stayed in the tent until she ate her food toward evening.

10 On the fourth day Holofernes held a banquet for his personal attendants only, and did not invite any of his officers. ¹¹He said to Bagoas, the eunuch who had charge of his personal affairs, "Go and persuade the Hebrew woman who is in your care to join us and to eat and drink with us. ¹²For it would be a disgrace if we let such a woman go without having intercourse with her. If we do not seduce her, she will laugh at us."

13 So Bagoas left the presence of Holofernes, and approached her and said, "Let this pretty girl not hesitate to come to my lord to be honored in his presence, and to enjoy drinking wine with us, and to become today like one of the Assyrian women who serve in the palace of Nebuchadnezzar." ¹⁴Judith replied, "Who am I to refuse my lord? Whatever pleases him I will do at once, and it will be a joy to me until the day of my death." ¹⁵So she proceeded to dress herself in all her woman's finery. Her maid went ahead and spread for her on the ground before Holofernes the lambskins she had received from Bagoas for her daily use in reclining.

16 Then Judith came in and lay down. Holofernes' heart was ravished with her and his passion was aroused, for he had been waiting for an opportunity to seduce her from the day he first saw her. ¹⁷So Holofernes said to her, "Have a drink and be merry with us!" ¹⁸Judith said, "I will gladly drink, my lord, because today is the greatest day in my whole life." ¹⁹Then she took what her maid had prepared and ate and drank before him. ²⁰Holofernes was greatly pleased with her, and drank a great quantity of wine, much more than he had ever drunk in any one day since he was born.

13 When evening came, his slaves quickly withdrew. Bagoas closed the tent from outside and shut out the attendants from his master's presence. They went to bed, for they all were weary because the banquet had lasted so long. ²But Judith was left alone in the tent, with Holofernes stretched out on his bed, for he was dead drunk.

3 Now Judith had told her maid to stand

a Other ancient authorities lack in the camp
b Other ancient authorities read her

the Lord carries out by my hand, foreshadows the murder. 8: To direct her way, Judith's praying is not for the purpose she declared to Holofernes (11.17).

12.10–20: Holofernes invites Judith to a banquet. 11: Bagoas is a well-known Persian name. In ancient Near Eastern society eunuchs were often in charge of the women (Esth 2.14), frequently attaining positions of considerable responsibility (Dan 1.3). 12: A comical statement, to think it offensive to a woman not to be sexually harassed. 14: Who am I to refuse my lord? Whatever pleases him I will do, is masterful irony; Bagoas thinks that Judith is referring to Holofernes as her lord, but the reader can understand it to be God. 16: His passion was aroused, for he had been waiting for an opportunity to seduce her, Holofernes's purpose for inviting Judith to his banquet now is revealed. Paralleling Judith's deception, he has the intention to mislead her. 18: Today is the greatest day in my whole life, Holofernes would hear this statement as honoring him.

13.1–10a: Judith, alone with Holofernes, decapitates him. 4–7: It is ironic that Holofernes is killed, outside the bedchamber and to wait for her to come out, as she did on the other days; for she said she would be going out for her prayers. She had said the same thing to Bagoas. [4]So everyone went out, and no one, either small or great, was left in the bedchamber. Then Judith, standing beside his bed, said in her heart, "O Lord God of all might, look in this hour on the work of my hands for the exaltation of Jerusalem. [5]Now indeed is the time to help your heritage and to carry out my design to destroy the enemies who have risen up against us."

6 She went up to the bedpost near Holofernes' head, and took down his sword that hung there. [7]She came close to his bed, took hold of the hair of his head, and said, "Give me strength today, O Lord God of Israel!" [8]Then she struck his neck twice with all her might, and cut off his head. [9]Next she rolled his body off the bed and pulled down the canopy from the posts. Soon afterward she went out and gave Holofernes' head to her maid, [10]who placed it in her food bag.

Then the two of them went out together, as they were accustomed to do for prayer. They passed through the camp, circled around the valley, and went up the mountain to Bethulia, and came to its gates. [11]From a distance Judith called out to the sentries at the gates, "Open, open the gate! God, our God, is with us, still showing his power in Israel and his strength against our enemies, as he has done today!"

12 When the people of her town heard her voice, they hurried down to the town gate and summoned the elders of the town.

[13]They all ran together, both small and great, for it seemed unbelievable that she had returned. They opened the gate and welcomed them. Then they lit a fire to give light, and gathered around them. [14]Then she said to them with a loud voice, "Praise God, O praise him! Praise God, who has not withdrawn his mercy from the house of Israel, but has destroyed our enemies by my hand this very night!"

15 Then she pulled the head out of the bag and showed it to them, and said, "See here, the head of Holofernes, the commander of the Assyrian army, and here is the canopy beneath which he lay in his drunken stupor. The Lord has struck him down by the hand of a woman. [16]As the Lord lives, who has protected me in the way I went, I swear that it was my face that seduced him to his destruction, and that he committed no sin with me, to defile and shame me."

17 All the people were greatly astonished. They bowed down and worshiped God, and said with one accord, "Blessed are you our God, who have this day humiliated the enemies of your people."

18 Then Uzziah said to her, "O daughter, you are blessed by the Most High God above all other women on earth; and blessed be the Lord God, who created the heavens and the earth, who has guided you to cut off the head of the leader of our enemies. [19]Your praise[a] will never depart from the hearts of those who remember the power of God. [20]May God grant this to be

a Other ancient authorities read hope

---

with his own sword, by the very person he expected to violate. As Judith prays twice (vv. 4–5,7) so she strikes his neck twice. **10a:** That Judith's food bag is ready and available shows the detail with which she has planned her scheme.

**13.10b–20: Judith flees the enemy camp and returns to Bethulia. 10b:** As they were accustomed to do for prayer, the women's established action of leaving the camp during the middle of the night now serves to permit them to leave without arousing suspicion (11.17; 12.7). **11:** God, our God is with us, in contrast to the Israelites' fears that God had deserted them (7.25). **13:** It seemed unbelievable that she had returned, highlights the danger in which Judith had placed herself and her servant. **15:** The head of Holofernes, the canopy, Judith exhibits them as a trophy; it now becomes clear why she needed to take them (v. 9). By the hand of a woman, see 9.10n. **18:** You are blessed ... above all other women, as Judith's mode of murder greatly resembles that of Jael, so do others' assessments of her (see Judg 5.24).

a perpetual honor to you, and may he reward you with blessings, because you risked your own life when our nation was brought low, and you averted our ruin, walking in the straight path before our God." And all the people said, "Amen. Amen."

14 Then Judith said to them, "Listen to me, my friends. Take this head and hang it upon the parapet of your wall. 2 As soon as day breaks and the sun rises on the earth, each of you take up your weapons, and let every able-bodied man go out of the town; set a captain over them, as if you were going down to the plain against the Assyrian outpost; only do not go down. 3 Then they will seize their arms and go into the camp and rouse the officers of the Assyrian army. They will rush into the tent of Holofernes and will not find him. Then panic will come over them, and they will flee before you. 4 Then you and all who live within the borders of Israel will pursue them and cut them down in their tracks. 5 But before you do all this, bring Achior the Ammonite to me so that he may see and recognize the man who despised the house of Israel and sent him to us as if to his death."

6 So they summoned Achior from the house of Uzziah. When he came and saw the head of Holofernes in the hand of one of the men in the assembly of the people, he fell down on his face in a faint. 7 When they raised him up he threw himself at Judith's feet, and did obeisance to her, and said, "Blessed are you in every tent of Judah! In every nation those who hear your name will be alarmed. 8 Now tell me what you have done during these days."

So Judith told him in the presence of the people all that she had done, from the day she left until the moment she began speaking to them. 9 When she had finished, the people raised a great shout and made a joyful noise in their town. 10 When Achior saw all that the God of Israel had done, he believed firmly in God. So he was circumcised, and joined the house of Israel, remaining so to this day.

11 As soon as it was dawn they hung the head of Holofernes on the wall. Then they all took their weapons, and they went out in companies to the mountain passes. 12 When the Assyrians saw them they sent word to their commanders, who then went to the generals and the captains and to all their other officers. 13 They came to Holofernes' tent and said to the steward in charge of all his personal affairs, "Wake up our lord, for the slaves have been so bold as to come down against us to give battle, to their utter destruction."

14 So Bagoas went in and knocked at the entry of the tent, for he supposed that he was sleeping with Judith. 15 But when no one answered, he opened it and went into the bedchamber and found him sprawled on the floor dead, with his head missing. 16 He cried out with a loud voice and wept and groaned and shouted, and tore his clothes. 17 Then he went to the tent where Judith had stayed, and when he did not find her, he rushed out to the people and shouted, 18 "The slaves have tricked us! One Hebrew woman has brought disgrace on

14.1–5: Judith directs the Israelites' military strategy. 1–4: Judith concocts a strategy that, respecting the physically weakened state of the Israelites (7.22), requires little effort on their part. Israel will be on the offensive, not the defensive.

14.6–10: Achior identifies the head of Holofernes and converts. 6: *He came and saw the head,* Achior sees Holofernes again, though not precisely in the fashion predicted by Holofernes (6.5). *He fell down on his face in a faint,* that Achior faints at merely the sight of the severed head makes Judith's courage appear all the greater. 7: *Blessed are you,* see 13.18n. 10: *He was circumcised, and joined the house of Israel,* Deut 23.3 prohibits Ammonites and Moabites from converting. Ruth is another exception.

14.11–19: The enemy discovers Holofernes's death. 11–15: The Assyrians respond just as Judith had predicted. 16–19: *They . . . were greatly dismayed, and their loud cries and shouts rose up throughout the camp,* the Assyrians react much like the Israelites did upon hearing of Holofernes's advance (4.1–12).

the house of King Nebuchadnezzar. Look, Holofernes is lying on the ground, and his head is missing!"

19 When the leaders of the Assyrian army heard this, they tore their tunics and were greatly dismayed, and their loud cries and shouts rose up throughout the camp.

15 When the men in the tents heard it, they were amazed at what had happened. 2 Overcome with fear and trembling, they did not wait for one another, but with one impulse all rushed out and fled by every path across the plain and through the hill country. 3 Those who had camped in the hills around Bethulia also took to flight. Then the Israelites, everyone that was a soldier, rushed out upon them. 4 Uzziah sent men to Betomasthaim[a] and Choba and Kola, and to all the frontiers of Israel, to tell what had taken place and to urge all to rush out upon the enemy to destroy them. 5 When the Israelites heard it, with one accord they fell upon the enemy,[b] and cut them down as far as Choba. Those in Jerusalem and all the hill country also came, for they were told what had happened in the camp of the enemy. The men in Gilead and in Galilee outflanked them with great slaughter, even beyond Damascus and its borders. 6 The rest of the people of Bethulia fell upon the Assyrian camp and plundered it, acquiring great riches. 7 And the Israelites, when they returned from the slaughter, took possession of what remained. Even the villages and towns in the hill country and in the plain got a great amount of booty, since there was a vast quantity of it.

8 Then the high priest Joakim and the elders of the Israelites who lived in Jerusalem came to witness the good things that the Lord had done for Israel, and to see Judith and to wish her well. 9 When they met her, they all blessed her with one accord and said to her, "You are the glory of Jerusalem, you are the great boast of Israel, you are the great pride of our nation! 10 You have done all this with your own hand; you have done great good to Israel, and God is well pleased with it. May the Almighty Lord bless you forever!" And all the people said, "Amen."

11 All the people plundered the camp for thirty days. They gave Judith the tent of Holofernes and all his silver dinnerware, his beds, his bowls, and all his furniture. She took them and loaded her mules and hitched up her carts and piled the things on them.

12 All the women of Israel gathered to see her, and blessed her, and some of them performed a dance in her honor. She took ivy-wreathed wands in her hands and distributed them to the women who were with her; 13 and she and those who were with her crowned themselves with olive wreaths. She went before all the people in the dance, leading all the women, while all the men of Israel followed, bearing their arms and wearing garlands and singing hymns.

14 Judith began this thanksgiving before all Israel, and all the people loudly sang this

a Other ancient authorities add and Bebai
b Gk them

**15.1–7: The Assyrians flee in panic; the Israelites follow and lay waste to them. 2:** In a reversal, the Assyrians now experience the same *fear and trembling* they caused to the other nations (2.28). **3:** *Those who had camped in the hills,* the Edomites and Ammonites (7.18). **5:** *Gilead,* situated in the northern part of Transjordan, and *Galilee,* in the north of Palestine, lay on either flank of the enemy's northeastward flight to *Damascus* and back toward Assyria.

**15.8–13: Judith is honored and leads in triumph to Jerusalem. 8–10:** *The high priest Joakim and the elders* travel from *Jerusalem* to see Judith with their own eyes. They speak very highly of her. **12:** *All the women . . . performed a dance,* women often danced and led victory songs (Ex 15.20–21; 1 Sam 18.6–7; Judg 11.34). **13:** Wearing *olive wreaths,* a Greek custom. The destination of the procession is the Temple in Jerusalem (16.18).

**15.14–16.17: Judith and the people sing a thanksgiving psalm.** This victory hymn shares similarities with the songs of Moses (Ex 15) and Deborah (Judg 5). The fact that portions of it appear in the first person (vv. 1–4, 11–17) and other portions in the third person (vv. 5–10) suggests that it may have been

# 16

song of praise. ¹ And Judith said,
Begin a song to my God with
tambourines,
sing to my Lord with cymbals.
Raise to him a new psalm;ᵃ
exalt him, and call upon his name.
² For the Lord is a God who crushes
wars;
he sets up his camp among his
people;
he delivered me from the hands of
my pursuers.
³ The Assyrian came down from the
mountains of the north;
he came with myriads of his
warriors;
their numbers blocked up the wadis,
and their cavalry covered the hills.
⁴ He boasted that he would burn up
my territory,
and kill my young men with the
sword,
and dash my infants to the ground,
and seize my children as booty,
and take my virgins as spoil.

⁵ But the Lord Almighty has foiled
them
by the hand of a woman.ᵇ
⁶ For their mighty one did not fall by
the hands of the young men,
nor did the sons of the Titans strike
him down,
nor did tall giants set upon him;
but Judith daughter of Merari
with the beauty of her countenance
undid him.

⁷ For she put away her widow's
clothing
to exalt the oppressed in Israel.
She anointed her face with perfume;
⁸ she fastened her hair with a tiara
and put on a linen gown to beguile
him.

⁹ Her sandal ravished his eyes,
her beauty captivated his mind,
and the sword severed his neck!
¹⁰ The Persians trembled at her
boldness,
the Medes were daunted at her
daring.

¹¹ Then my oppressed people shouted;
my weak people cried out,ᶜ and
the enemyᵈ trembled;
they lifted up their voices, and the
enemyᵈ were turned back.
¹² Sons of slave-girls pierced them
through
and wounded them like the children
of fugitives;
they perished before the army of
my Lord.

¹³ I will sing to my God a new song:
O Lord, you are great and glorious,
wonderful in strength, invincible.
¹⁴ Let all your creatures serve you,
for you spoke, and they were
made.
You sent forth your spirit,ᵉ and it
formed them;ᶠ
there is none that can resist your
voice.
¹⁵ For the mountains shall be shaken to
their foundations with the
waters;
before your glance the rocks shall
melt like wax.
But to those who fear you
you show mercy.
¹⁶ For every sacrifice as a fragrant
offering is a small thing,

a Other ancient authorities read *a psalm and praise*
b Other ancient authorities add *he has confounded them*   c Other ancient authorities read *feared*
d Gk *they*   e Or *breath*   f Other ancient authorities read *they were created*

sung responsively between Judith and the people. **16:1–2:** *Begin a song,* a call to praise. *A new psalm,* Ps 96.1; 98.1. **3–12:** Description of the victory. **6:** *Sons of the Titans* alludes to Greek mythology, but may be an attempt to render a comparable allusion in Hebrew, "the Rephaim" (Deut 3.11); see also Gen 6.4. **13–16:** A general hymn of praise; as others had marveled at Judith, now she marvels at the power of God.

and the fat of all whole burnt
offerings to you is a very little
thing;
but whoever fears the Lord is great
forever.

17 Woe to the nations that rise up
against my people!
The Lord Almighty will take
vengeance on them in the day
of judgment;
he will send fire and worms into their
flesh;
they shall weep in pain forever.

18 When they arrived at Jerusalem, they worshiped God. As soon as the people were purified, they offered their burnt offerings, their freewill offerings, and their gifts. 19 Judith also dedicated to God all the possessions of Holofernes, which the people had given her; and the canopy that she had taken for herself from his bedchamber she gave as a votive offering. 20 For three months the people continued feasting in Jerusalem before the sanctuary, and Judith remained with them.

21 After this they all returned home to their own inheritances. Judith went to Bethulia, and remained on her estate. For the rest of her life she was honored throughout the whole country. 22 Many desired to marry her, but she gave herself to no man all the days of her life after her husband Manasseh died and was gathered to his people. 23 She became more and more famous, and grew old in her husband's house, reaching the age of one hundred five. She set her maid free. She died in Bethulia, and they buried her in the cave of her husband Manasseh; 24 and the house of Israel mourned her for seven days. Before she died she distributed her property to all those who were next of kin to her husband Manasseh, and to her own nearest kindred. 25 No one ever again spread terror among the Israelites during the lifetime of Judith, or for a long time after her death.

---

13: *A new song,* Ps 33.3; 149.1; Isa 42.10. **14:** See Ps 104.30. **15:** See Ps 97.5. **17:** Concluding anathema on Israel's enemies.

**16.18–20: The procession arrives in Jerusalem. 19:** Judith dedicates to the Temple all the plundered articles that the people had given to her (15.11).

**16.21–25: Judith's subsequent life.** This report shares similar elements to Judith's introduction (8.1–8). **24:** *Seven days,* the customary period of mourning the dead (1 Sam 31.13; Sir 22.12). She *distributed her property,* according to Mosaic law (Num 27.11).

NOTE. The deuterocanonical portions of the Book of Esther are several additional passages found in the Greek translation of the Hebrew Book of Esther, a translation that differs also in other respects from the Hebrew text (the latter is translated in the NRSV Old Testament). The disordered chapter numbers come from the displacement of the additions to the end of the canonical Book of Esther by Jerome in his Latin translation and from the subsequent division of the Bible into chapters by Stephen Langton, who numbered the additions consecutively as though they formed a direct continuation of the Hebrew text. So that the additions may be read in their proper context, the whole of the Greek version is here translated, though certain familiar names are given according to their Hebrew rather than their Greek form; for example, Mordecai and Vashti instead of Mardocheus and Astin. The order followed is that of the Greek text, but the chapter and verse numbers conform to those of the King James or Authorized Version. The additions, conveniently indicated by the letters A—F, are located as follows: A, before 1.1; B, after 3.13; C and D, after 4.17; E, after 8.12; F, after 10.3.

# ESTHER
## (The Greek Version Containing the Additional Chapters)

The Greek version of Esther is a translation of the canonical Hebrew book of Esther (i.e., the one included in the "Hebrew Scriptures" portion of this Bible). The translation was made for Greek-speaking Jews in the second or first century BCE.

The translator—very likely the Lysimachus of Jerusalem mentioned in 11.1—produced a systematic but relatively free translation of the Hebrew. Besides numerous small but often significant omissions and additions, the Greek version includes six extra sections that have no counterparts in the Hebrew. These additional sections are clearly intrusive and secondary, for they contradict the Hebrew at a number of points. While they sometimes make the characters and events more vivid or dramatic, their main purpose is to transform the comparatively subtle and enigmatic Hebrew story of Esther into a more conventional tale of divine intervention and exemplary Jewish piety.

The Additions to the book of Esther comprise 107 verses. Their contents are as follows:

- Addition A: Mordecai's dream (11.2–12) and his discovery of a plot against the king (12.1–6)
- Addition B: The royal edict dictated by Haman, decreeing the extermination of the Jews (13.1–7)
- Addition C: The prayers of Mordecai (13.8–18) and Esther (14.1–19)
- Addition D: Esther's appearing unsummoned, before the king (15.4–19)
- Addition E: The royal edict dictated by Mordecai, counteracting the edict sent by Haman (16.1–24)
- Addition F: The interpretation of Mordecai's dream (10.4–13) and the colophon (an inscription at the end of a manuscript) to the Greek version (1.11)

Although there is no mention of God in the Hebrew narrative, in the Greek version the terms "Lord" or "God" appear more than fifty times. Most of these occurrences are in the Additions, but occasionally the Greek translation inserts references to God into verses that correspond to the canonical Hebrew text (see 2.20; 4.8; 6.13).

The additions provide their authors with an opportunity to express their own particular theological views. Additions A and F introduce apocalyptic motifs to emphasize God's providential care for the people Israel in a universally hostile world. Addition C attests to the efficacy of prayer and expresses Queen Esther's abhorrence at being married to a Gentile, her loathing of all things worldly and courtly, and her strict observance of Jewish dietary laws—none of which is so much as hinted at in the Hebrew. Thanks largely to Addition D, the climax of the Greek version is reached when God miraculously changes to gentleness the king's "fierce anger" at Esther's unannounced entrance. Taken together, the six additions deemphasize the establishment of Purim and express a deep distrust of Gentiles.

Besides giving the story a more explicitly religious character, the additions create new emphases. A and F, which frame the story, graft onto it a new apocalyptic perspective of cosmic struggle between good and evil. The juxtaposition of C's extensive praise of God, with similar terms and phrases applied to Ahasuerus in D, makes explicit the Greek version's intent to contrast the capricious earthly king with God the trustworthy heavenly king. Similarly, the royal decrees in B and E highlight the theme of human commandments versus the law of Moses to which Esther also alludes when she prays in C.

Originally, A, C, D, and F were probably composed in either Hebrew or Aramaic (both Semitic languages) and, if so, were already part of that particular Semitic text used by the Greek translator. The florid rhetorical phraseology of B and E indicates that they must originally have been composed in Greek, perhaps in Alexandria, a sophisticated Greek-Jewish center.

The additions were not composed at the same time. The latest possible date for B, C, D, and E is 93 CE, when the historian Josephus paraphrased them in his *Jewish Antiquities*. The colophon's location (11.1) immediately after F suggests that A as well as F were part of the Semitic text at the time that Lysimachus made his Greek translation in the late second or first century BCE.

## ADDITION A

**11** [a] 2 In the second year of the reign of Artaxerxes the Great, on the first day of Nisan, Mordecai son of Jair son of Shimei[b] son of Kish, of the tribe of Benjamin, had a dream. 3 He was a Jew living in the city of Susa, a great man, serving in the court of the king. 4 He was one of the captives whom King Nebuchadnezzar of Babylon had brought from Jerusalem with King Jeconiah of Judea. And this was his dream: 5 Noises[c] and confusion, thunders and earthquake, tumult on the earth! 6 Then two great dragons came forward, both

*a* Chapters 11.2—12.6 correspond to chapter A 1-17 in some translations.    *b* Gk *Semeios*    *c* Or *Voices*

**11.2–12: Mordecai's prophetic dream of impending danger to the Jews. 2:** *Artaxerxes*, a mistranslation of the Heb "Ahasuerus," that is, Xerxes I (486–465 BCE); the *second year* would be 485. *Nisan*, March-April, the first month of the new year. Thus, the dream comes on New Year's Day. All the month names in Esther are Babylonian. *Mordecai's* name derives from the name of the Babylonian god, Marduk. His genealogy connecting him with King Saul (1 Sam 9.1; 2 Sam 16.5–18) is repeated in 2.5. **3:** *Jew* (Heb "yehudi"), originally meaning someone from the kingdom of Judah (2 Kings 16.6), is used here in its usual later sense of an adherent of Judaism. *Susa*, westernmost of the three capital cities of the Achaemenid Persian Empire in northwestern Iran. In contrast to Hebrew Esther, Mordecai is already an important royal official. **4:** Mordecai would be well over 100 years old by 484 BCE if he, along with Judah's last king Jeconiah (Jehoiachin), had been exiled by Nebuchadnezzar in 597 (2 Kings 24). **5–11:** Persecution and the subsequent salvation of the Jews, described in apocalyptic terms. **5:** The language of cosmic chaos is typical of apocalyptic texts (see Isa 24.17–20; Dan 12.1,4). **6:** *Two great dragons*, Mordecai and Haman (see 10.7). God defeated the chaos dragon (a sea monster) at the time of creation (Ps 74.13; 89.10; Isa ready to fight, and they roared terribly. [7] At their roaring every nation prepared for war, to fight against the righteous nation. [8] It was a day of darkness and gloom, of tribulation and distress, affliction and great tumult on the earth! [9] And the whole righteous nation was troubled; they feared the evils that threatened them,[a] and were ready to perish. [10] Then they cried out to God; and at their outcry, as though from a tiny spring, there came a great river, with abundant water; [11] light came, and the sun rose, and the lowly were exalted and devoured those held in honor.

12 Mordecai saw in this dream what God had determined to do, and after he awoke he had it on his mind, seeking all day to understand it in every detail.

12 Now Mordecai took his rest in the courtyard with Gabatha and Tharra, the two eunuchs of the king who kept watch in the courtyard. [2] He overheard their conversation and inquired into their purposes, and learned that they were preparing to lay hands on King Artaxerxes; and he informed the king concerning them. [3] Then the king examined the two eunuchs, and after they had confessed it, they were led away to execution. [4] The king made a permanent record of these things, and Mordecai wrote an account of them. [5] And the king ordered Mordecai to serve in the court, and rewarded him for these things. [6] But Haman son of Hammedatha, a Bougean, who was in great honor with the king, determined to injure Mordecai and his people because of the two eunuchs of the king.

END OF ADDITION A

1 It was after this that the following things happened in the days of Artaxerxes, the same Artaxerxes who ruled over one hundred twenty-seven provinces from India to Ethiopia.[b] [2] In those days, when King Artaxerxes was enthroned in the city of Susa, [3] in the third year of his reign, he gave a banquet for his Friends and other persons of various nations, the Persians and Median nobles, and the governors of the provinces. [4] After this, when he had displayed to them the riches of his kingdom and the splendor of his bountiful celebration during the course of one hundred eighty days, [5] at the end of the festivity[c] the king gave a drinking party for the

*a* Gk *their own evils*   *b* Other ancient authorities lack *to Ethiopia*   *c* Gk *marriage feast*

27.1; 51.9–10; Job 26.12–13); imagery from this primordial battle reappears in apocalyptic literature (Dan 7; Rev 12.3; 13.2; 20.2). Two dragons (see 2 Esd 6.49–52), one good, one evil, are unusual and may reflect Persian influence. **7:** *Righteous nation,* the Jews (see Dan 7.27). Unlike the Heb, Gk Esther perceives the entire Gentile (non-Jewish) world as a danger to the Jews. **10:** *Cried out,* Ex 3.7; Jdt 3.9; 4.3; 6.6. *Tiny spring* and *great river* refer to Esther (10.6). **11:** *Light* and morning, symbolizing joy, salvation, and new life (Ps 30.5; 46.5; 112.4; Isa 33.2). *Lowly were exalted,* 1 Sam 2.4–9. One *held in honor* is Haman (12.6). **12:** In contrast to the Heb, all the events in Gk Esther are foreordained by God, although Mordecai does not yet fully understand the dream's symbolism (10.4–9).

**12.1–6: Mordecai saves the king's life.** It is unclear whether this conspiracy is the same as the one in Esth 2.19–23 of the Heb text or an earlier one. **5:** The king *rewarded* Mordecai immediately (in contrast to 6.1–3). **6:** The Gk text suggests (in contrast to the Heb) that Haman took part in the eunuchs' foiled plot and thus provides a motivation for both Mordecai's and Haman's subsequent actions. *Bougean,* in 3.1 "Bougean" is an attempt to translate the Heb word "Agagite" which connects Haman to the Amalekite king, Agag, Saul's vanquished enemy (see 1 Sam 15.8). Mordecai and Haman share an ancestral enmity (Ex 17.8–16; Num 24.7).

**1.1–12: Artaxerxes's banquet. 1:** *Ethiopia* (Heb "Cush"), in the Bible this term refers to the territory of modern Sudan and modern Ethiopia. **3:** Greek writers mention fabulous feasts given by Persian kings. Ahasuerus's *banquet* is the first of numerous banquets that occur at key points in the story (1.5,9; 2.18; 3.15; 5.7; 7.1; 9.17,19,22). *Friends,* a special class of courtiers. **5:** *Festivity,* or *marriage feast* (see note *c*), which would clarify the behavior of the king and Vashti (see 1.11). *Six days,* 1.10 (and Heb 1.5,10) people of various nations who lived in the city. This was held for six days in the courtyard of the royal palace, 6which was adorned with curtains of fine linen and cotton, held by cords of purple linen attached to gold and silver blocks on pillars of marble and other stones. Gold and silver couches were placed on a mosaic floor of emerald, mother-of-pearl, and marble. There were coverings of gauze, embroidered in various colors, with roses arranged around them. 7The cups were of gold and silver, and a miniature cup was displayed, made of ruby, worth thirty thousand talents. There was abundant sweet wine, such as the king himself drank. 8The drinking was not according to a fixed rule; but the king wished to have it so, and he commanded his stewards to comply with his pleasure and with that of the guests.

9 Meanwhile, Queen Vashti[a] gave a drinking party for the women in the palace where King Artaxerxes was.

10 On the seventh day, when the king was in good humor, he told Haman, Bazan, Tharra, Boraze, Zatholtha, Abataza, and Tharaba, the seven eunuchs who served King Artaxerxes, 11to escort the queen to him in order to proclaim her as queen and to place the diadem on her head, and to have her display her beauty to all the governors and the people of various nations, for she was indeed a beautiful woman. 12But Queen Vashti[a] refused to obey him and would not come with the eunuchs. This of-fended the king and he became furious. 13He said to his Friends, "This is how Vashti[a] has answered me.[b] Give therefore your ruling and judgment on this matter." 14Arkesaeus, Sarsathaeus, and Malesear, then the governors of the Persians and Medes who were closest to the king—Arkesaeus, Sarsathaeus, and Malesear, who sat beside him in the chief seats—came to him 15and told him what must be done to Queen Vashti[a] for not obeying the order that the king had sent her by the eunuchs. 16Then Muchaeus said to the king and the governors, "Queen Vashti[a] has insulted not only the king but also all the king's governors and officials" 17(for he had reported to them what the queen had said and how she had defied the king). "And just as she defied King Artaxerxes, 18so now the other ladies who are wives of the Persian and Median governors, on hearing what she has said to the king, will likewise dare to insult their husbands. 19If therefore it pleases the king, let him issue a royal decree, inscribed in accordance with the laws of the Medes and Persians so that it may not be altered, that the queen may no longer come into his presence; but let the king give her royal rank to a woman better than she. 20Let whatever law the king enacts be proclaimed in his kingdom, and thus all women will give honor to their husbands, rich and poor alike." 21This speech

a Gk Astin    b Gk Astin has said thus and so

says the party lasted seven days. **6–7:** The description is more extravagant than in the Heb version. **9:** There are no ancient references to *Vashti;* Xerxes I's queen was Amestris (Herodotus 7.61). Although in 5.5 women and men of the Persian court banquet together, *Queen Vashti gave a drinking party for the women* emphasizes the separate worlds of king and queen, a factor in Esther's later bravery. It also sets the scene for a quasi-comic contest of the sexes.

**1.10–22: The fall of Vashti and the king's first edict. 11:** *Proclaim her as queen,* in contrast to the Heb, Vashti is summoned for her official coronation as well as for display. **12:** An inversion of Vashti's disobedience occurs when Esther, Vashti's replacement, dares to enter unbidden into his presence (4.11,16; 15). **13–14:** Three *governors* rather than the seven sages named in the Heb. **16–18:** The fear of a feminine insurrection against patriarchal order lies just below the surface of many ancient myths and legends. Contrary to Muchaeus's dire imaginings, the real threat to the king and Persia will come in the form of a conspiracy by two palace bodyguards (2.21). **19:** There is no historical evidence that the *laws of the Medes and Persians* were unalterable (Esth 8.8; Dan 6.9,13). The phrase sets up a tension in the narrative between rigid legalism and the requirements of true justice. **20:** By issuing an absurdly unenforceable decree, the king only succeeds in drawing attention to his own inability to rule his wife.

pleased the king and the governors, and the king did as Muchaeus had recommended. 22 The king sent the decree into all his kingdom, to every province in its own language, so that in every house respect would be shown to every husband.

2 After these things, the king's anger abated, and he no longer was concerned about Vashti[a] or remembered what he had said and how he had condemned her. 2 Then the king's servants said, "Let beautiful and virtuous girls be sought out for the king. 3 The king shall appoint officers in all the provinces of his kingdom, and they shall select beautiful young virgins to be brought to the harem in Susa, the capital. Let them be entrusted to the king's eunuch who is in charge of the women, and let ointments and whatever else they need be given them. 4 And the woman who pleases the king shall be queen instead of Vashti."[a] This pleased the king, and he did so.

5 Now there was a Jew in Susa the capital whose name was Mordecai son of Jair son of Shimei[b] son of Kish, of the tribe of Benjamin; 6 he had been taken captive from Jerusalem among those whom King Nebuchadnezzar of Babylon had captured. 7 And he had a foster child, the daughter of his father's brother, Aminadab, and her name

was Esther. When her parents died, he brought her up to womanhood as his own. The girl was beautiful in appearance. 8 So, when the decree of the king was proclaimed, and many girls were gathered in Susa the capital in custody of Gai, Esther also was brought to Gai, who had custody of the women. 9 The girl pleased him and won his favor, and he quickly provided her with ointments and her portion of food,[c] as well as seven maids chosen from the palace; he treated her and her maids with special favor in the harem. 10 Now Esther had not disclosed her people or country, for Mordecai had commanded her not to make it known. 11 And every day Mordecai walked in the courtyard of the harem, to see what would happen to Esther.

12 Now the period after which a girl was to go to the king was twelve months. During this time the days of beautification are completed—six months while they are anointing themselves with oil of myrrh, and six months with spices and ointments for women. 13 Then she goes in to the king; she is handed to the person appointed, and goes with him from the harem to the king's palace. 14 In the evening she enters and in the morning she departs to the second har-

a Gk Astin    b Gk Semeios    c Gk lacks of food

22: The first of several decrees in the book (see 2.8; 3.12; 13; 8.9–11; 9.20–22,29–32). Aramaic was the official *language* of Persian diplomacy, but the historical record attests to Persian imperial pronouncements issued in the *languages* of subject peoples (see Ezra 6.3–5).

2.1–18: Esther becomes the new queen. 2: Consistent with its concern for moral rectitude, the Gk version adds that the winning *girl* (Heb "virgin") must be *virtuous* as well as *beautiful*. 3: Perhaps custom required the king to marry a *virgin* (see 1 Kings 1.1–14; Lev 21.13), or it may be a convention of historical romance. In fact, Persian kings could only marry women from certain noble Persian families.

2.5–7: Mordecai and Esther. 5–6: For a second time, the Gk introduces Mordecai (see 11.2–4n.). 7: The name *Esther* derives from Ishtar, the Babylonian goddess of love and war (Marduk and Ishtar were cousins), or from the Persian word for "star," or both. The Gk fails to mention Esther's Hebrew name, Hadassah. *Aminadab*, in the Heb (2.15) Esther's father is named Abihail. 8: By beginning the book (11.2–12) with Mordecai's prophetic dream, the Gk version presents Esther's presence as part of a divine plan (see 10.4–6). Here, as in the Heb, there is no suggestion of coercion when Esther *was brought* to the palace. This is contradicted later in one of the Gk additions to Esther (14.15–18). 9: In winning the *favor* of Gai (a foreshadowing of 2.15,17; 5.8; 7.3), Esther resembles Joseph in the house of Potiphar (Gen 39.2–6) and Daniel at the Babylonian court (Dan 1.9). 10: Esther's silence about her Jewish identity (reiterated in v. 20) is a narrative ploy to heighten suspense and to demonstrate her obedience to Mordecai.

2.12–18: Esther becomes queen. 14: The impossibility of seeing the king again unless *summoned by* em, where Gai the king's eunuch is in charge of the women; and she does not go in to the king again unless she is summoned by name.

15 When the time was fulfilled for Esther daughter of Aminadab, the brother of Mordecai's father, to go in to the king, she neglected none of the things that Gai, the eunuch in charge of the women, had commanded. Now Esther found favor in the eyes of all who saw her. 16 So Esther went in to King Artaxerxes in the twelfth month, which is Adar, in the seventh year of his reign. 17 And the king loved Esther and she found favor beyond all the other virgins, so he put on her the queen's diadem. 18 Then the king gave a banquet lasting seven days for all his Friends and the officers to celebrate his marriage to Esther; and he granted a remission of taxes to those who were under his rule.

19 Meanwhile Mordecai was serving in the courtyard. 20 Esther had not disclosed her country—such were the instructions of Mordecai; but she was to fear God and keep his laws, just as she had done when she was with him. So Esther did not change her mode of life.

21 Now the king's eunuchs, who were chief bodyguards, were angry because of Mordecai's advancement, and they plotted to kill King Artaxerxes. 22 The matter became known to Mordecai, and he warned Esther, who in turn revealed the plot to the king. 23 He investigated the two eunuchs and hanged them. Then the king ordered a memorandum to be deposited in the royal library in praise of the goodwill shown by Mordecai.

3 After these events King Artaxerxes promoted Haman son of Hammedatha, a Bougean, advancing him and granting him precedence over all the king's[a] Friends. 2 So all who were at court used to do obeisance to Haman,[b] for so the king had commanded to be done. Mordecai, however, did not do obeisance. 3 Then the king's courtiers said to Mordecai, "Mordecai, why do you disobey the king's command?" 4 Day after day they spoke to him, but he would not listen to them. Then they informed Haman that Mordecai was resisting the king's command. Mordecai had told them that he was a Jew. 5 So when Haman learned that Mordecai was not doing obeisance to him, he became furiously angry, 6 and plotted to destroy all the Jews under Artaxerxes' rule.

7 In the twelfth year of King Artaxerxes Haman[c] came to a decision by casting lots,

a Gk all his    b Gk him    c Gk he

name foreshadows Esther's dilemma in 4.11–16 and 15.1–16 when she must violate this law to save her people (1.12n.,19n.). 16: Adar, March-April. The Heb gives a different month, Tebeth (December-January). 17: Esther is given the diadem with which Vashti was to be crowned (1.11). 18: Another plot-marking banquet (see 1.3n.), clearly a marriage feast (unlike the Heb), foreshadows the two dinners Esther gives later (5.5; 6.14–7.1) and the feast of Purim (9.22). Remission of taxes, the Gk correctly interprets the Hebrew term, "holiday," in economic terms.

2.19–23: Mordecai and Esther save the king's life. This may be a second version of the plot in 12.1–6 or a different episode altogether. 20: Mode of life, there is no hint of this in the Heb, where Esther is a Jew more by ethnicity than religious faith or observance. 21: The Heb does not explain that the conspirators were motivated specifically by jealousy of Mordecai (see Dan 6.3–5). 23: Hanged, impaled, not strangulation with a rope. The verse foreshadows the gallows Haman prepares for Mordecai (5.14) only to die upon it himself (7.9–10; 9.13–14).

3.1–13: Haman plots to annihilate the Jews. 1: Bougean, see 12.6n. Haman's unexplained promotion contrasts ironically with Mordecai's unrewarded service. 2: V. 4 cites Mordecai's Jewishness to justify his refusal to do obeisance to Haman. Although Jews may bow in obeisance to other people (Gen 23.7; 27.29; 1 Kings 1.31), in the added prayer in 13.14 Mordecai asserts that one should give homage only to God. 4: Day after day, reminiscent of Gen 39.10, in which Joseph resists Potiphar's wife just as Mordecai resists the courtiers' entreaties. Both men suffer false accusation, then vindication and promotion. 7: The Hebrew word for lot, "pur" (pl. "purim"), is borrowed from Babylonian. Haman resorts to this common form taking the days and the months one by one, to fix on one day to destroy the whole race of Mordecai. The lot fell on the fourteenth*a* day of the month of Adar.

8 Then Haman*b* said to King Artaxerxes, "There is a certain nation scattered among the other nations in all your kingdom; their laws are different from those of every other nation, and they do not keep the laws of the king. It is not expedient for the king to tolerate them. 9 If it pleases the king, let it be decreed that they are to be destroyed, and I will pay ten thousand talents of silver into the king's treasury." 10 So the king took off his signet ring and gave it to Haman to seal the decree*c* that was to be written against the Jews. 11 The king told Haman, "Keep the money, and do whatever you want with that nation."

12 So on the thirteenth day of the first month the king's secretaries were summoned, and in accordance with Haman's instructions they wrote in the name of King Artaxerxes to the magistrates and the governors in every province from India to Ethiopia. There were one hundred twenty-seven provinces in all, and the governors were addressed each in his own language. 13 Instructions were sent by couriers throughout all the empire of Artaxerxes to destroy the Jewish people on a given day of the twelfth month, which is Adar, and to plunder their goods.

following to the governors of the hundred twenty-seven provinces from India to Ethiopia and to the officials under them:

2 "Having become ruler of many nations and master of the whole world (not elated with presumption of authority but always acting reasonably and with kindness), I have determined to settle the lives of my subjects in lasting tranquility and, in order to make my kingdom peaceable and open to travel throughout all its extent, to restore the peace desired by all people.

3 "When I asked my counselors how this might be accomplished, Haman—who excels among us in sound judgment, and is distinguished for his unchanging goodwill and steadfast fidelity, and has attained the second place in the kingdom— 4 pointed out to us that among all the nations in the world there is scattered a certain hostile people, who have laws contrary to those of every nation and continually disregard the ordinances of kings, so that the unifying of the kingdom that we honorably intend cannot be brought about. 5 We understand that this people, and it alone, stands constantly in opposition to every nation, perversely following a strange manner of life and laws, and is ill-disposed to our government, doing all the harm they can so that our kingdom may not attain stability.

6 "Therefore we have decreed that those indicated to you in the letters written by Haman, who is in charge of affairs and is

### ADDITION B

**13**
*d* This is a copy of the letter: "The Great King, Artaxerxes, writes the

*a* Other ancient witnesses read *thirteenth*; see 8.12
*b* Gk *he*   *c* Gk lacks *the decree*   *d* Chapter 13.1-7 corresponds to chapter B 1-7 in some translations.

of magic (Herodotus 3.128), employed also in ancient Israel (1 Sam 14.42; cf. Acts 1.26), to determine the date. *Adar,* February-March. Instead of the *fourteenth day,* 8.12 of the Gk and the Heb rightly have "the thirteenth." **8:** Haman's insidious manipulation of the pliable king (see 1.16–20; Job 2.1–6) begins with the truth: The Jews were indeed *scattered* (Zech 7.14) and, like other subject peoples in the Persian Empire, their *laws* were different (Deut 4.5–6). **9:** *Ten thousand talents of silver,* an astronomical sum, hundreds of millions of U.S. dollars. **10:** The king's *signet ring* gave Haman unlimited power to sign documents in the king's name (8.2,8; Gen 41.41–42). **12:** *In his own language,* see 1.22n. **13:** *Couriers,* the Persian Empire's communication system was renowned in the ancient world (Herodotus 8.98). *A given day,* the thirteenth (see 8.12 of the Gk and Heb). *Adar,* February-March.

**13.1–7:** The text of the king's letter authorizing the slaughter of the Jews. This addition to the Gk version of Esther was composed in Greek, not Hebrew. The same author composed 16.1–24, the text of the edict that neutralizes Haman's order to slaughter the Jews. **6:** *Fourteenth day,* a correction of the Gk's our second father, shall all—wives and children included—be utterly destroyed by the swords of their enemies, without pity or restraint, on the fourteenth day of the twelfth month, Adar, of this present year, [7] so that those who have long been hostile and remain so may in a single day go down in violence to Hades, and leave our government completely secure and untroubled hereafter."

END OF ADDITION B

3 [14] Copies of the document were posted in every province, and all the nations were ordered to be prepared for that day. [15] The matter was expedited also in Susa. And while the king and Haman caroused together, the city of Susa[a] was thrown into confusion.

4 When Mordecai learned of all that had been done, he tore his clothes, put on sackcloth, and sprinkled himself with ashes; then he rushed through the street of the city, shouting loudly: "An innocent nation is being destroyed!" [2] He got as far as the king's gate, and there he stopped, because no one was allowed to enter the courtyard clothed in sackcloth and ashes. [3] And in every province where the king's proclamation had been posted there was a loud cry of mourning and lamentation among the Jews, and they put on sackcloth and ashes. [4] When the queen's[b] maids and eunuchs came and told her, she was deeply troubled by what she heard had happened, and sent some clothes to Mordecai to put on instead of sackcloth; but he would not consent. [5] Then Esther summoned Hachratheus, the eunuch who attended her, and

ordered him to get accurate information for her from Mordecai.[c]

[7] So Mordecai told him what had happened and how Haman had promised to pay ten thousand talents into the royal treasury to bring about the destruction of the Jews. [8] He also gave him a copy of what had been posted in Susa for their destruction, to show to Esther; and he told him to charge her to go in to the king and plead for his favor in behalf of the people. "Remember," he said, "the days when you were an ordinary person, being brought up under my care—for Haman, who stands next to the king, has spoken against us and demands our death. Call upon the Lord; then speak to the king in our behalf, and save us from death."

[9] Hachratheus went in and told Esther all these things. [10] And she said to him, "Go to Mordecai and say, [11] 'All nations of the empire know that if any man or woman goes to the king inside the inner court without being called, there is no escape for that person. Only the one to whom the king stretches out the golden scepter is safe—and it is now thirty days since I was called to go to the king.'"

[12] When Hachratheus delivered her entire message to Mordecai, [13] Mordecai told him to go back and say to her, "Esther, do not say to yourself that you alone among all the Jews will escape alive. [14] For if you keep quiet at such a time as this, help and protection will come to the Jews from another quarter, but you and your father's

---

*a* Gk *the city*  *b* Gk *When her*  *c* Other ancient witnesses add [6] *So Hachratheus went out to Mordecai in the street of the city opposite the city gate.*

"thirteenth"; see (Heb) 3.13; 8.12; 9.1; (Gk) 16.20; 8.12. *Adar*, February-March. **7:** *Hades,* the underworld (Heb "Sheol").

**3.14–15:** Haman and the king celebrate the publication of the decree.

**4.1–17:** Mordecai persuades Queen Esther to risk her life and save her people. **1:** *Sackcloth* and *ashes* and torn clothing were traditional signs of mourning and repentance (2 Sam 3.31; Job 42.6; Dan 9.3; Jon 3.6). **2:** No one rendered ritually unclean by mourning could *enter the courtyard.* **4:** Esther has kept her Jewish identity a secret (see 2.10n.,20n.) and is unaware of the edict. **11:** Like other biblical heroes called upon to save their people (Ex 3.11; 4.10; 10.28; Judg 6.15; Jer 1.6), Esther initially objects. **14:** *From another quarter,* divine providence (see 10.4–5). *Who knows?* often precedes an expression of hope for divine mercy (2 Sam 12.22; Joel 2.14; Jon 3.9). **16–17:** Resolving to act *contrary to the law* (see 4.11) family will perish. Yet, who knows whether it was not for such a time as this that you were made queen?" [15] Then Esther gave the messenger this answer to take back to Mordecai: [16] "Go and gather all the Jews who are in Susa and fast on my behalf; for three days and nights do not eat or drink, and my maids and I will also go without food. After that I will go to the king, contrary to the law, even if I must die." [17] So Mordecai went away and did what Esther had told him to do.

### ADDITION C

**13** [8][a] Then Mordecai[b] prayed to the Lord, calling to remembrance all the works of the Lord.

[9] He said, "O Lord, Lord, you rule as King over all things, for the universe is in your power and there is no one who can oppose you when it is your will to save Israel, [10] for you have made heaven and earth and every wonderful thing under heaven. [11] You are Lord of all, and there is no one who can resist you, the Lord. [12] You know all things; you know, O Lord, that it was not in insolence or pride or for any love of glory that I did this, and refused to bow down to this proud Haman; [13] for I would have been willing to kiss the soles of his feet to save Israel! [14] But I did this so that I might not set human glory above the glory of God, and I will not bow down to anyone but you, who are my Lord; and I will not do these things in pride. [15] And now, O Lord God and King, God of Abraham, spare your people; for the eyes of our

foes are upon us[c] to annihilate us, and they desire to destroy the inheritance that has been yours from the beginning. [16] Do not neglect your portion, which you redeemed for yourself out of the land of Egypt. [17] Hear my prayer, and have mercy upon your inheritance; turn our mourning into feasting that we may live and sing praise to your name, O Lord; do not destroy the lips[d] of those who praise you."

[18] And all Israel cried out mightily, for their death was before their eyes.

**14** Then Queen Esther, seized with deadly anxiety, fled to the Lord. [2] She took off her splendid apparel and put on the garments of distress and mourning, and instead of costly perfumes she covered her head with ashes and dung, and she utterly humbled her body; every part that she loved to adorn she covered with her tangled hair. [3] She prayed to the Lord God of Israel, and said: "O my Lord, you only are our king; help me, who am alone and have no helper but you, [4] for my danger is in my hand. [5] Ever since I was born I have heard in the tribe of my family that you, O Lord, took Israel out of all the nations, and our ancestors from among all their forebears, for an everlasting inheritance, and that you did for them all that you promised. [6] And now we have sinned before you, and you have handed us over to our enemies [7] because we glorified their gods. You are righteous, O Lord! [8] And now they are not sat-

---

*a* Chapters 13.8—15.16 correspond to chapters C 1-30 and D 1-16 in some translations.   *b* Gk *he*   *c* Gk *for they are eying us*   *d* Gk *mouth*

---

on behalf of her people (see 1.19n.), Esther takes charge. Communal or individual fasting was a rite of repentance believed to influence the deity (Lev 16.29–31; Judg 20.26; 2 Sam 12.16; 1 Kings 21.27; Jon 3.5,8; Ezra 8.21–23; Joel 1.14; 2.12,15; 1 Macc 3.47).

**13.8–14.19:** The prayers of Mordecai and Esther give the book an explicitly religious tone. Both contain themes common to national laments (Neh 9; Dan 9). **12–14:** Mordecai justifies his refusal to bow to Haman (3.2) on religious grounds (see Dan 3.12,16–18; 6.10–13; 2 Macc 7.2), disclaiming any pride on his own part (see 14.15–18). **16:** Mordecai is confident in the God who liberated the Israelites, God's *portion* (Deut 32.9) from enslavement in *Egypt* (Ex 1–14).

**14.1–19: Esther humbly petitions God.** Her prayer (see especially Jdt 9) resembles Mordecai's in its sincere, if conventional, piety and its concern for religious self-justification. **2:** Humble *garments,* filth, and disarray are appropriate to penitential prayer (2 Kings 19.1; Neh 1.4; Dan 9.3–4; Jdt 9.1). **8:** *Bitter slavery* interprets the exile and Diaspora in terms evocative of the bondage in Egypt (Ex 1–15). **9:** *Your* isfied that we are in bitter slavery, but they have covenanted with their idols [9] to abolish what your mouth has ordained, and to destroy your inheritance, to stop the mouths of those who praise you and to quench your altar and the glory of your house, [10] to open the mouths of the nations for the praise of vain idols, and to magnify forever a mortal king.

[11] "O Lord, do not surrender your scepter to what has no being; and do not let them laugh at our downfall; but turn their plan against them, and make an example of him who began this against us. [12] Remember, O Lord; make yourself known in this time of our affliction, and give me courage, O King of the gods and Master of all dominion! [13] Put eloquent speech in my mouth before the lion, and turn his heart to hate the man who is fighting against us, so that there may be an end of him and those who agree with him. [14] But save us by your hand, and help me, who am alone and have no helper but you, O Lord. [15] You have knowledge of all things, and you know that I hate the splendor of the wicked and abhor the bed of the uncircumcised and of any alien. [16] You know my necessity—that I abhor the sign of my proud position, which is upon my head on days when I appear in public. I abhor it like a filthy rag, and I do not wear it on the days when I am at leisure. [17] And your servant has not eaten at Haman's table, and I have not honored the king's feast or drunk the wine of libations. [18] Your servant has had no joy since the day that I was brought here until now, except in you, O Lord God of Abraham. [19] O God, whose might is over all, hear the voice of the despairing, and save us from the hands of evildoers. And save me from my fear!"

END OF ADDITION C

ADDITION D

15 On the third day, when she ended her prayer, she took off the garments in which she had worshiped, and arrayed herself in splendid attire. [2] Then, majestically adorned, after invoking the aid of the all-seeing God and Savior, she took two maids with her; [3] on one she leaned gently for support, [4] while the other followed, carrying her train. [5] She was radiant with perfect beauty, and she looked happy, as if beloved, but her heart was frozen with fear. [6] When she had gone through all the doors, she stood before the king. He was seated on his royal throne, clothed in the full array of his majesty, all covered with gold and precious stones. He was most terrifying.

7 Lifting his face, flushed with splendor, he looked at her in fierce anger. The queen faltered, and turned pale and faint, and collapsed on the head of the maid who went in

---

altar and *your house* refer to the ruined Temple in Jerusalem (2 Macc 14.33; 3 Macc 5.43), a subject ignored in the Heb. **13:** *Eloquent speech*, in 15.5 it is her beauty on which she initially relies. *Lion*, Ahasuerus. God will begin the process of *turning* the king's *heart* by changing the king's wrathful spirit to gentleness (15.7–8) when Esther approaches him. **15:** *Abhor the bed of the uncircumcised*, the Jewish prohibition of mixed marriage (Deut 7.3–4; Ezra 10.2; Neh 13.23–27). *Wicked, uncircumcised, alien*, non-Jews. Unlike the Heb, Gk Esther takes a negative view of Gentiles. **16:** The *sign* upon Esther's *head* is the crown which she abhors as *a filthy rag* (literally, a rag soaked in menstrual blood; see Lev 15.19–24; Isa 64.6). Contrast Deut 6.9. **17:** Esther observes the Jewish dietary laws (Lev 11; see Jdt 12.1–2).

**15.1–16: Esther approaches the king.** This chapter expands upon 5.1–2 in the Heb, heightening the suspense with added details and, consistent with the Gk version's theological perspective, crediting God's intervention for Esther's success. **1:** Like an epic hero arming for battle (see *Iliad* 19.338–9; 360–391; 1 Sam 17.5–7,38–39) Esther adorns herself (see Jdt. 10.3; 12.15) for her "assault" on the king (see 4.11). **7:** Esther's appearance infuriates the king (see 4.11). Esther, terrified and weakened by fasting, cannot withstand his wrath (see 1.12; 7.7,10; Prov 19.12; 20.2) and *collapses* (see 7.8). This episode, absent in the Heb, portrays an Esther undone by feminine weakness and incapable of fulfilling her mission on her own (see 4.15). The narrative assigns the credit for the salvation of the Jews primarily to God (see v. 8).

front of her. ⁸Then God changed the spirit of the king to gentleness, and in alarm he sprang from his throne and took her in his arms until she came to herself. He comforted her with soothing words, and said to her, ⁹"What is it, Esther? I am your husband.ª Take courage; ¹⁰You shall not die, for our law applies only to our subjects.ᵇ Come near."

11 Then he raised the golden scepter and touched her neck with it; ¹²he embraced her, and said, "Speak to me." ¹³She said to him, "I saw you, my lord, like an angel of God, and my heart was shaken with fear at your glory. ¹⁴For you are wonderful, my lord, and your countenance is full of grace." ¹⁵And while she was speaking, she fainted and fell. ¹⁶Then the king was agitated, and all his servants tried to comfort her.

END OF ADDITION D

5 ᶜ³The king said to her, "What do you wish, Esther? What is your request? It shall be given you, even to half of my kingdom." ⁴And Esther said, "Today is a special day for me. If it pleases the king, let him and Haman come to the dinner that I shall prepare today." ⁵Then the king said, "Bring Haman quickly, so that we may do as Esther desires." So they both came to the dinner that Esther had spoken about. ⁶While they were drinking wine, the king said to Esther, "What is it, Queen Esther? It

shall be granted you." ⁷She said, "My petition and request is: ⁸if I have found favor in the sight of the king, let the king and Haman come to the dinner that I shall prepare them, and tomorrow I will do as I have done today."

9 So Haman went out from the king joyful and glad of heart. But when he saw Mordecai the Jew in the courtyard, he was filled with anger. ¹⁰Nevertheless, he went home and summoned his friends and his wife Zosara. ¹¹And he told them about his riches and the honor that the king had bestowed on him, and how he had advanced him to be the first in the kingdom. ¹²And Haman said, "The queen did not invite anyone to the dinner with the king except me; and I am invited again tomorrow. ¹³But these things give me no pleasure as long as I see Mordecai the Jew in the courtyard." ¹⁴His wife Zosara and his friends said to him, "Let a gallows be made, fifty cubits high, and in the morning tell the king to have Mordecai hanged on it. Then, go merrily with the king to the dinner." This advice pleased Haman, and so the gallows was prepared.

6 That night the Lord took sleep from the king, so he gave orders to his secretary to bring the book of daily records,

a Gk brother   b Meaning of Gk uncertain
c In Greek, Chapter D replaces verses 1 and 2 in Hebrew.

**8:** The dramatic climax of Gk Esther. *God changed the spirit of the king,* see v. 7n.; the human king must yield to the divine king. **9:** Husband, Gk "brother," a metaphorical expression of endearment found in Egyptian and Israelite love poetry (see "sister" in Song 4.9–10; 5.1–2). **13:** *Like an angel of God,* see 2 Sam 14.17,20. The phrase (not present in the Heb) implies wisdom and absence of evil intent (1 Sam 29.9; 2 Sam 19.27). **15:** See v. 7n.

**5.3–8: Esther invites the king and Haman to dinner. 3:** *Half of my kingdom* is customary hyperbole (7.2). **4:** Esther frames her request in the most self-effacing terms. *Dinner,* see 1.3n. Food is a frequent motif in stories of women confronting powerful men (Judg 5.25; Jdt 10.5; 12.1,17–20).

**5.9–14: Haman's happiness is spoiled. 11–12:** Haman's boasting sets him up as an arrogant fool ripe for catastrophe (Prov 11.28; 13.3; 16.5,18; 27.1; 29.20). **14:** *Zosara* is an exemplary son-bearing wife (9.7–10) whose loyal advice her husband follows. *Gallows,* (also 9.13–14) see 2.23n. *Fifty cubits,* ca. 22m (72 ft), an exaggerated height. Only *the king* can order an execution.

**6.1–13: Mordecai's triumph.** The episode is a masterpiece of ironic narrative. **1:** *The Lord took sleep from the king,* unlike the Heb, the Gk explains events of the story in terms of divine intention (11.1–12; 10.4–12; 4.14n.) and intervention (15.1–16). The sleepless king is a traditional folktale motif (Dan 6.18; 3 Esdras 3.3). **3:** Herodotus (8.85,90) notes that Persian kings kept records of courtiers' noble deeds. *You* and to read to him. 2He found the words written about Mordecai, how he had told the king about the two royal eunuchs who were on guard and sought to lay hands on King Artaxerxes. 3The king said, "What honor or dignity did we bestow on Mordecai?" The king's servants said, "You have not done anything for him." 4While the king was inquiring about the goodwill shown by Mordecai, Haman was in the courtyard. The king asked, "Who is in the courtyard?" Now Haman had come to speak to the king about hanging Mordecai on the gallows that he had prepared. 5The servants of the king answered, "Haman is standing in the courtyard." And the king said, "Summon him." 6Then the king said to Haman, "What shall I do for the person whom I wish to honor?" And Haman said to himself, "Whom would the king wish to honor more than me?" 7So he said to the king, "For a person whom the king wishes to honor, 8let the king's servants bring out the fine linen robe that the king has worn, and the horse on which the king rides, 9and let both be given to one of the king's honored Friends, and let him robe the person whom the king loves and mount him on the horse, and let it be proclaimed through the open square of the city, saying, 'Thus shall it be done to everyone whom the king honors.'" 10Then the king said to Haman, "You have made an excellent suggestion! Do just as you have said for Mordecai the Jew, who is on duty in the courtyard. And let nothing be omitted from what you have proposed." 11So Haman got the robe and the horse; he put the robe on Mordecai and made him ride through the open square of the city, proclaiming, "Thus shall it be done to everyone whom the king wishes to honor." 12Then Mordecai returned to the courtyard, and Haman hurried back to his house, mourning and with his head covered. 13Haman told his wife Zosara and his friends what had befallen him. His friends and his wife said to him, "If Mordecai is of the Jewish people, and you have begun to be humiliated before him, you will surely fall. You will not be able to defend yourself, because the living God is with him."

14 While they were still talking, the eunuchs arrived and hurriedly brought Haman to the banquet that Esther had prepared. 7 1So the king and Haman went in to drink with the queen. 2And the second day, as they were drinking wine, the king said, "What is it, Queen Esther? What is your petition and what is your request? It shall be granted to you, even to half of my kingdom." 3She answered and said, "If I have found favor with the king, let my life be granted me at my petition, and my people at my request. 4For we have been sold, I and my people, to be destroyed, plundered, and made slaves—we and our children—male and female slaves. This has come to my knowledge. Our antagonist brings shame on[a] the king's court." 5Then the king said, "Who is the person that would dare to do this thing?" 6Esther said, "Our enemy is this

a Gk is not worthy of

have not done anything for him, in contrast to the king's rewarding Mordecai for reporting the first plot (see 12.5). **6:** The king's omission of the name of his honoree parallels the way Haman concealed the identity of the people he intended to annihilate (3.8). **8:** A robe and horse were gestures of favor and honor (Gen 37.3; 41.42; 1 Sam 18.4; 1 Kings 1.33). **12:** Haman covered his head as a sign of grief (2 Sam 15.30; 19.4; Jer 14.4; Ezek 24.17). **13:** Because the living God is with him (lacking in Heb), an example of Gentile wisdom, Zosara and Haman's friends make explicit the story's theme of divine retribution and Jewish triumph (11.1–12; 15.1–16; 6.1; 10.4–12; 4.14n.; Josh 2.9–14; Jdt 5.20–21; 3 Macc 3.8–10,31).

**6.14–7.10:** Esther's second banquet and Haman's fall. **2:** Half of my kingdom, see 5.3n. **4:** Sold, Probably a reference to Haman's bribe in 3.11; 4.7 (note the metaphorical use of the verb in Deut 32.30; Judg 2.14; 3.6; 4.2,9; 10.7). Shame on the king's court, perhaps the king would be shamed if his queen were dishonored. **6:** Haman, the enemy of Queen Esther and the Jews, is denounced as the king's enemy, too. Like Esther as she approached the king in 15.5, now Haman is terrified in the presence of the king and queen. **7:** Again like Esther (7.3–4), Haman begs for his life. **8:** Following common custom (8.3; 1 Sam evil man Haman!" At this, Haman was ter-rified in the presence of the king and queen.

7 The king rose from the banquet and went into the garden, and Haman began to beg for his life from the queen, for he saw that he was in serious trouble. 8 When the king returned from the garden, Haman had thrown himself on the couch, pleading with the queen. The king said, "Will he dare even assault my wife in my own house?" Haman, when he heard, turned away his face. 9 Then Bugathan, one of the eunuchs, said to the king, "Look, Haman has even prepared a gallows for Mordecai, who gave information of concern to the king; it is standing at Haman's house, a gallows fifty cubits high." So the king said, "Let Haman be hanged on that." 10 So Haman was hanged on the gallows he had prepared for Mordecai. With that the anger of the king abated.

8 On that very day King Artaxerxes granted to Esther all the property of the persecutor[a] Haman. Mordecai was summoned by the king, for Esther had told the king[b] that he was related to her. 2 The king took the ring that had been taken from Haman, and gave it to Mordecai; and Esther set Mordecai over everything that had been Haman's.

3 Then she spoke once again to the king and, falling at his feet, she asked him to avert all the evil that Haman had planned against the Jews. 4 The king extended his golden scepter to Esther, and she rose and stood before the king. 5 Esther said, "If it pleases you, and if I have found favor, let an order be sent rescinding the letters that Haman wrote and sent to destroy the Jews in your kingdom. 6 How can I look on the ruin of my people? How can I be safe if my ancestral nation[c] is destroyed?" 7 The king said to Esther, "Now that I[d] have granted all of Haman's property to you and have hanged him on a tree because he acted against the Jews, what else do you request? 8 Write in my name what you think best and seal it with my ring; for whatever is written at the king's command and sealed with my ring cannot be contravened."

9 The secretaries were summoned on the twenty-third day of the first month, that is, Nisan, in the same year; and all that he commanded with respect to the Jews was given in writing to the administrators and governors of the provinces from India to Ethiopia, one hundred twenty-seven prov-inces, to each province in its own language. 10 The edict was written[e] with the king's authority and sealed with his ring, and sent out by couriers. 11 He ordered the Jews in every city to observe their own laws, to de-fend themselves, and to act as they wished against their opponents and enemies 12 on a certain day, the thirteenth of the twelfth month, which is Adar, throughout all the kingdom of Artaxerxes.

a Gk slanderer    b Gk him    c Gk country
d Gk If I    e Gk It was written

25.23,24; 2 Kings 4.27; Mk 7.25), Haman tries to supplicate the queen by falling at her feet (a reversal of 15.7). His gesture contrasts with Mordecai's in 3.2. *Assault my wife*, Ahasuerus misinterprets Ha-man's gesture as a sexual assault, an unpardonable affront to both male and royal honor and as such, a capital offense (see 2 Sam 16.20–22; 1 Kings 2.13–25). 9–10: *Bugathan*, Heb "Harbona." *Gallows*, see 2.23n. Poetic justice prevails (cf. Prov 26.27).

8.1–12: The king shows favor to Esther, Mordecai, and the Jews. The chapter overflows with reversals (see 1 Sam 2.1–10). 2: Haman's position as grand vizier (3.10) becomes Mordecai's with the transfer of the king's signet *ring*. 4: *Scepter*: 4.11; 14.11n.; 15.11. 5: *That Haman wrote*, Esther diplomatically dissociates the king from the royal edict condemning the Jews. 8: The king's earlier edict *cannot be contravened* (1.19n.), but a new edict can neutralize the former's intent. 9: The verse follows the same general structure as 3.12–13 (see 2.19–21) while reversing their effect. *First month . . . Nisan* (March-April), Heb "third month . . . Sivan (May-June)." 11: This explicit permission for the *Jews . . . to observe their own laws* (see 3.8n.; 13.4–5), which is a distinctly religious concern, is lacking in the Heb. 12: The date of the intended extermination (3.7,13) becomes a day of triumph and relates to the Purim festival (see 9.21).

ADDITION E

**16** [a] The following is a copy of this letter:

"The Great King, Artaxerxes, to the governors of the provinces from India to Ethiopia, one hundred twenty-seven provinces, and to those who are loyal to our government, greetings.

2 "Many people, the more they are honored with the most generous kindness of their benefactors, the more proud do they become, 3 and not only seek to injure our subjects, but in their inability to stand prosperity, they even undertake to scheme against their own benefactors. 4 They not only take away thankfulness from others, but, carried away by the boasts of those who know nothing of goodness, they even assume that they will escape the evil-hating justice of God, who always sees everything. 5 And often many of those who are set in places of authority have been made in part responsible for the shedding of innocent blood, and have been involved in irremediable calamities, by the persuasion of friends who have been entrusted with the administration of public affairs, 6 when these persons by the false trickery of their evil natures beguile the sincere goodwill of their sovereigns.

7 "What has been wickedly accomplished through the pestilent behavior of those who exercise authority unworthily can be seen, not so much from the more ancient records that we hand on, as from investigation of matters close at hand.[b] 8 In the future we will take care to render our kingdom quiet and peaceable for all, 9 by changing our methods and always judging what comes before our eyes with more equitable consideration. 10 For Haman son of Hammedatha, a Macedonian (really an alien to the Persian blood, and quite devoid of our kindliness), having become our guest, 11 enjoyed so fully the goodwill that we have for every nation that he was called our father and was continually bowed down to by all as the person second to the royal throne. 12 But, unable to restrain his arrogance, he undertook to deprive us of our kingdom and our life,[c] 13 and with intricate craft and deceit asked for the destruction of Mordecai, our savior and perpetual benefactor, and of Esther, the blameless partner of our kingdom, together with their whole nation. 14 He thought that by these methods he would catch us undefended and would transfer the kingdom of the Persians to the Macedonians.

15 "But we find that the Jews, who were consigned to annihilation by this thrice-accursed man, are not evildoers, but are governed by most righteous laws 16 and are children of the living God, most high, most mighty,[d] who has directed the kingdom both for us and for our ancestors in the most excellent order.

17 "You will therefore do well not to put in execution the letters sent by Haman son of Hammedatha, 18 since he, the one who did these things, has been hanged at the gate of Susa with all his household—for God, who rules over all things, has speedily inflicted on him the punishment that he deserved.

a Chapter 16.1-24 corresponds to chapter E 1-24 in some translations. b Gk *matters beside* (your) *feet* c Gk *our spirit* d Gk *greatest*

**16.1–24:** The king's second letter denounces Haman, praises Mordecai and Esther, and directs his subjects to help the Jews. This addition to the Gk version of Esther is a counterpoint to 13.1–7. Both were composed in Gk probably by the same author. The Gentile king refers in the most positive terms to the Jews and their God (Ex 9.27; 18.10–11; Num 22–24; 2 Kings 5.15; Dan 2.47; 3.29; 4.1–3,34–37; 6.26–27; Jdt 5.5–21). **2:** *Benefactors,* a reference to Ahasuerus. **10:** Haman is actually a *Macedonian* scheming to overthrow Persian rule (v. 14; see 12.6), a plot twist not found in the Heb. This may be an allusion to the conquest of Persia by the Macedonian Alexander the Great in 333 BCE. **11:** *Our father,* 13.6. *Second to the royal throne,* 13.3 (2 Chr 28.7; 1 Esd 3.7). **15–16:** The king commends the Jews and their laws (Torah) and confesses his indebtedness to their God (see Ezra 1.2; 7.23–28). **17:** See 8.5n. **18:** The edict's reference to the death of Haman's family contradicts 7.9 and 9.7–10,13–14. **19:** *Their own*

19 "Therefore post a copy of this letter publicly in every place, and permit the Jews to live under their own laws. 20 And give them reinforcements, so that on the thirteenth day of the twelfth month, Adar, on that very day, they may defend themselves against those who attack them at the time of oppression. 21 For God, who rules over all things, has made this day to be a joy for his chosen people instead of a day of destruction for them.

22 "Therefore you shall observe this with all good cheer as a notable day among your commemorative festivals, 23 so that both now and hereafter it may represent deliverance for you*a* and the loyal Persians, but that it may be a reminder of destruction for those who plot against us.

24 "Every city and country, without exception, that does not act accordingly shall be destroyed in wrath with spear and fire. It shall be made not only impassable for human beings, but also most hateful to wild animals and birds for all time.

END OF ADDITION E

8 13 "Let copies of the decree be posted conspicuously in all the kingdom, and let all the Jews be ready on that day to fight against their enemies."

14 So the messengers on horseback set out with all speed to perform what the king had commanded; and the decree was published also in Susa. 15 Mordecai went out dressed in the royal robe and wearing a gold crown and a turban of purple linen. The people in Susa rejoiced on seeing him. 16 And the Jews had light and gladness 17 in every city and province wherever the decree was published; wherever the proclamation was made, the Jews had joy and gladness, a banquet and a holiday. And many of the Gentiles were circumcised and became Jews out of fear of the Jews.

9 Now on the thirteenth day of the twelfth month, which is Adar, the decree written by the king arrived. 2 On that same day the enemies of the Jews perished; no one resisted, because they feared them. 3 The chief provincial governors, the princes, and the royal secretaries were paying honor to the Jews, because fear of Mordecai weighed upon them. 4 The king's decree required that Mordecai's name be held in honor throughout the kingdom.*b* 6 Now in the city of Susa the Jews killed five hundred people, 7 including Pharsannestain, Delphon, Phasga, 8 Pharadatha, Barea, Sarbacha, 9 Marmasima, Aruphaeus, Arsaeus, Zabutheus, 10 the ten sons of Haman son of Hammedatha, the Bougean, the enemy of the Jews—and they indulged*c* themselves in plunder.

11 That very day the number of those killed in Susa was reported to the king. 12 The king said to Esther, "In Susa, the capital, the Jews have destroyed five hundred people. What do you suppose they have done in the surrounding countryside? Whatever more you ask will be done for you." 13 And Esther said to the king, "Let

a Other ancient authorities read *for us*    b Meaning of Gk uncertain. Some ancient authorities add verse 5, *So the Jews struck down all their enemies with the sword, killing and destroying them, and they did as they pleased to those who hated them.*    c Other ancient authorities read *did not indulge*

laws (absent in the Heb), see vv. 15–16; 8.11. **21:** *Chosen people,* 1 Kings 3.8; 1 Chr 16.13; Ps 105.6; Isa 43.20 (cf. Esth 13.15–17; 14.5). **22–23:** These verses, addressed to all the king's subjects, may hint at the non-Jewish origin of the Purim festival.

**8.13–17:** Dispatch and posting of the king's decree. **14:** See 3.13n. **17:** *Gentiles were circumcised and became Jews,* the Gk here interprets literally the ambiguous wording of the Heb.

**9.1–19:** The Jews triumph over their enemies. **2:** *No one resisted,* contradicts the Heb ("no one could withstand them"), and vv. 11,16. **10:** The death of *the ten sons of Haman* agrees with the Heb but contradicts 16.18 (see note). *Indulged themselves in plunder,* contradicted by both the Heb and 9.15–16. **12–15:** Notice of the extra day for observing the king's edict is probably included to explain why the Jews of Susa celebrated Purim on the fifteenth of Adar and country Jews on the fourteenth (see 9.18–19). *Plunder,* see v. 10n. **16:** *Destroyed fifteen thousand,* Heb "seventy-five thousand." **18–19:** Differences in the Jews be allowed to do the same tomorrow. Also, hang up the bodies of Haman's ten sons." [14] So he permitted this to be done, and handed over to the Jews of the city the bodies of Haman's sons to hang up. [15] The Jews who were in Susa gathered on the fourteenth and killed three hundred people, but took no plunder.

[16] Now the other Jews in the kingdom gathered to defend themselves, and got relief from their enemies. They destroyed fifteen thousand of them, but did not engage in plunder. [17] On the fourteenth day they rested and made that same day a day of rest, celebrating it with joy and gladness. [18] The Jews who were in Susa, the capital, came together also on the fourteenth, but did not rest. They celebrated the fifteenth with joy and gladness. [19] On this account then the Jews who are scattered around the country outside Susa keep the fourteenth of Adar as a joyful holiday, and send presents of food to one another, while those who live in the large cities keep the fifteenth day of Adar as their joyful holiday, also sending presents to one another.

[20] Mordecai recorded these things in a book, and sent it to the Jews in the kingdom of Artaxerxes both near and far, [21] telling them that they should keep the fourteenth and fifteenth days of Adar, [22] for on these days the Jews got relief from their enemies. The whole month (namely, Adar), in which their condition had been changed from sorrow into gladness and from a time of distress to a holiday, was to be celebrated as a time for feasting[a] and gladness and for sending presents of food to their friends and to the poor.

[23] So the Jews accepted what Mordecai had written to them [24]—how Haman son of Hammedatha, the Macedonian,[b] fought against them, how he made a decree and cast lots[c] to destroy them, [25] and how he went in to the king, telling him to hang Mordecai; but the wicked plot he had devised against the Jews came back upon himself, and he and his sons were hanged. [26] Therefore these days were called "Purim," because of the lots (for in their language this is the word that means "lots"). And so, because of what was written in this letter, and because of what they had experienced in this affair and what had befallen them, Mordecai established this festival,[d] [27] and the Jews took upon themselves, upon their descendants, and upon all who would join them, to observe it without fail.[e] These days of Purim should be a memorial and kept from generation to generation, in every city, family, and country. [28] These days of Purim were to be observed for all time, and the commemoration of them was never to cease among their descendants.

[29] Then Queen Esther daughter of Aminadab along with Mordecai the Jew wrote down what they had done, and gave full authority to the letter about Purim.[f] [31] And Mordecai and Queen Esther established this decision on their own responsibility, pledging their own well-being to the plan.[e] [32] Esther established it by a decree forever, and it was written for a memorial.

a Gk of weddings   b Other ancient witnesses read the Bougean   c Gk a lot   d Gk he established (it)   e Meaning of Gk uncertain   f Verse 30 in Heb is lacking in Gk: *Letters were sent to all the Jews, to the one hundred twenty-seven provinces of the kingdom of Ahasuerus, in words of peace and truth.*

Purim dates are explained (see 9.12–15n.). Jews today continue to observe Purim with feasting and *presents of food.*

**9.20–32: The inauguration of the feast of Purim.** The emphasis upon the written word, a particular concern in postexilic Judaism, was probably intended to legitimize a festival not mentioned in the Torah (cf. the origin of Hanukkah: 1 Macc 4.56–59; 2 Macc 1.1–2.28; 10.1–8). **21:** See 9.12–15n. **22:** Purim commemorates not the day of the Jews' military triumph but the day they obtained their *relief. Sorrow into gladness,* see Isa 61.3; Jer 31.13. **24–26:** This plot summary, which does not mention Esther, differs slightly from the book of Esther. The festival came to be called "*Purim*" for the lot, *pur* (plural, *purim*), which Haman cast (see 3.7n.). **32:** *Esther established it,* Queen Esther is the only woman in the Bible credited with authorizing a religious observance.

# 10

The king levied a tax upon his kingdom both by land and sea. ²And as for his power and bravery, and the wealth and glory of his kingdom, they were recorded in the annals of the kings of the Persians and the Medes. ³Mordecai acted with authority on behalf of King Artaxerxes and was great in the kingdom, as well as honored by the Jews. His way of life was such as to make him beloved to his whole nation.

## ADDITION F

4ᵃAnd Mordecai said, "These things have come from God; ⁵for I remember the dream that I had concerning these matters, and none of them has failed to be fulfilled. ⁶There was the little spring that became a river, and there was light and sun and abundant water—the river is Esther, whom the king married and made queen. ⁷The two dragons are Haman and myself. ⁸The nations are those that gathered to destroy the name of the Jews. ⁹And my nation, this is Israel, who cried out to God and was saved. The Lord has saved his people; the Lord has rescued us from all these evils; God has done great signs and wonders, wonders that have never happened among the nations. ¹⁰For this purpose he made two lots, one for the people of God and one for all the nations, ¹¹and these two lots came to the hour and moment and day of decision before God and among all the nations. ¹²And God remembered his people and vindicated his inheritance. ¹³So they will observe these days in the month of Adar, on the fourteenth and fifteenthᵇ of that month, with an assembly and joy and gladness before God, from generation to generation forever among his people Israel."

# 11

¹In the fourth year of the reign of Ptolemy and Cleopatra, Dositheus, who said that he was a priest and a Levite,ᶜ and his son Ptolemy brought to Egyptᵈ the preceding Letter about Purim, which they said was authentic and had been translated by Lysimachus son of Ptolemy, one of the residents of Jerusalem.

### END OF ADDITION F

a Chapter 10.4-13 and 11.1 correspond to chapter F 1-11 in some translations.  b Other ancient authorities lack *and fifteenth*  c Or *priest, and Levitas*  d Cn: Gk *brought in*

**10.1–3: The greatness of Ahasuerus and Mordecai. 2:** A standard formula for historical reports in Kings and Chronicles (1 Kings 14.19,29; 2 Chr 25.26; 32.32).

**10.4–11.1: Epilogue: Mordecai's dream explained.** This addition rounds out the Gk version of Esther with an explanation of Mordecai's dream with which the book began (11.2–12n.). **4:** *These things have come from God,* the theme of Gk Esther (11.12; 4.14; 15.8; 6.1,13; 16.4; see Ps 118.23). **6:** *Light and sun,* 11.11n., 8.16. **8:** *Name,* in ancient times, the essence of one's identity resided largely in one's name. **9:** *Cried out,* see 11.10n. **10:** *Two lots,* not mentioned in 11.2–12. This verse may represent an alternative derivation for Purim. It assumes a different context for the "lots" that give Purim its name (9.23; 3.7n.), understanding them as symbols of destiny (Dan 12.13; Isa 17.14; Jer 13.25). A similar concept appears in the Dead Sea Scrolls (*Manual of Discipline* 2.2,5; 3.1–4.26). **13:** See 9.20–22.

**11.1: The Colophon to Gk Esther** provides a probable date reference for the Gk translation. *Ptolemy and Cleopatra,* because three kings of Egypt named Ptolemy married women named Cleopatra, the *fourth year* could be 114–13, 78–77, or 49–48 BCE. *Dositheus,* a common Hellenistic name (2 Macc 12.19,35; 3 Macc 1.3); presumably a copyist, he affirms the text's authenticity and his own religious authority. *Letter about Purim,* probably the entire book of Esther. *Lysimachus,* a Greek name (cf. 2 Macc 4.29), very likely the translator of Heb Esther into Gk.

# THE WISDOM OF SOLOMON

v v

The Wisdom of Solomon was written as a message of encouragement and exhortation for Jews living somewhere in the Diaspora (the Jewish communities outside the land of Israel) during the Greco-Roman era. Immersed in a cosmopolitan, pagan culture, one that generally viewed Judaism with suspicion if not contempt, many Jews felt hard-pressed to remain loyal to the basic principles and practices of their faith. This book simultaneously affirms the basis of that faith and critiques those who oppose it, in the interests of promoting adherence to Jewish traditions in changing, difficult circumstances.

Although the author claims to be King Solomon (with parts of ch 9 based on his prayer for wisdom in 1 Kings 3.6–9), this ascription has been recognized as a literary fiction since ancient times. Instead, the author is an anonymous Hellenistic Jew writing sometime in the late first century BCE or early first century CE. The book's bitter polemic against Egyptian religion (see, for instance, ch 12) suggests Alexandria as a location, and anti-Jewish uprisings in that city may provide part of the background for the author's reflections.

Composed in Greek, this book is among the most Hellenized works of the Apocrypha; that is, it reflects extensive interaction with Greek literary and philosophical conventions (see, for example, the use of the standard list of cardinal virtues in 8.7). The author's intention, however, is not to promote the achievements of Greek culture, but to appropriate them, so as to prove the excellence of Judaism in categories relevant to his readers' multicultural environment. As for its literary genre, many modern critics describe the Wisdom of Solomon as a form of didactic exhortation that demonstrates the superiority of a particular way of life or school of philosophy (in this case, Judaism) over its competitors and detractors. (This is technically called "protreptic discourse.") So, for example, while the author can describe wisdom as an emanation of divine power that pervades the entire world, he contends that it comes to most perfect expression in God's revelation to Israel, and depicts it in terms familiar from the personified Wisdom (Gk, "Sophia") of biblical texts like Proverbs 8, Job 28, Sirach 24, and Baruch 3–4. Above all, the author is concerned to portray wisdom as the guiding force of divine providence, saving righteous Israelites and punishing their wicked adversaries. In conjunction with this aim, the book also asserts the significance of Jewish faith in terms of the ultimate benefits it confers. Thus persecutors, sinners, and idolaters face divine retribution in the afterlife, while the faithful will "live forever" (5.15). This emphasis on immortality represents one of the book's distinctive features, as well as something of a new development in Jewish thought (see 3.4n.).

The book consists of three major sections. The first, chs 1–6, contrasts the lives of the just and the wicked, dramatizing the eschatological destinies of the two groups. The section begins and ends with exhortation to seek wisdom and righteousness (1.1–15; 6.1–25). The next section, chs 7–10, celebrates the figure of divine Sophia. The author's persona as Solomon emerges most clearly here, as the king describes wisdom and his pursuit of her. The third section, chs 11–19, adopts the approach of historical comparison, presenting an elaborate system of contrasts based largely on Exodus 7–14. A series of digressions in 11.17–15.19 explains why God's judgment manifested itself differently in dealing with the Egyptians and the Israelites. This adaptation of the Exodus story is meant to complement the arguments of the first two sections, providing biblical examples of the righteous and the unrighteous, and demonstrating how the power of divine wisdom operates in human history.

The book is included among the deuterocanonical books of the Roman Catholic and Eastern Orthodox churches, but is considered one of the Apocrypha by Protestant churches.

1 Love righteousness, you rulers of the earth,
think of the Lord in goodness
and seek him with sincerity of heart;
2 because he is found by those who do
not put him to the test,
and manifests himself to those who
do not distrust him.
3 For perverse thoughts separate people
from God,
and when his power is tested, it
exposes the foolish;
4 because wisdom will not enter a
deceitful soul,
or dwell in a body enslaved to sin.
5 For a holy and disciplined spirit will
flee from deceit,
and will leave foolish thoughts
behind,
and will be ashamed at the approach
of unrighteousness.

6 For wisdom is a kindly spirit,
but will not free blasphemers from
the guilt of their words;
because God is witness of their
inmost feelings,
and a true observer of their hearts,
and a hearer of their tongues.
7 Because the spirit of the Lord has
filled the world,

and that which holds all things
together knows what is said,
8 therefore those who utter unrighteous
things will not escape notice,
and justice, when it punishes, will not
pass them by.
9 For inquiry will be made into the
counsels of the ungodly,
and a report of their words will come
to the Lord,
to convict them of their lawless deeds;
10 because a jealous ear hears all things,
and the sound of grumbling does not
go unheard.
11 Beware then of useless grumbling,
and keep your tongue from slander;
because no secret word is without
result,[a]
and a lying mouth destroys the soul.

12 Do not invite death by the error of
your life,
or bring on destruction by the works
of your hands;
13 because God did not make death,
and he does not delight in the death
of the living.
14 For he created all things so that they
might exist;

a Or will go unpunished

**1.1–6.25: A discourse contrasting the righteous and the wicked**, their ways, their reasoning about life, and their destinies. Elements of the section are familiar from popular stories about the persecution and vindication of a just Israelite living in a foreign land (such as Gen 37–50; Esth 1–8; Dan 1–6).
**1.1–15: Prologue.** Wisdom and righteousness lead to immortality. **1:** The address to Gentile rulers is part of the book's literary fiction (cf. 6.1); the intended readers are Jews governed by such rulers. *With sincerity of heart*, see 6.17; 1 Chr 29.17; Tob 14.7–9. **6:** *A kindly spirit*, literally "a philanthropic spirit," i.e., loving humankind (cf. 7.22–23; 12.19; 15.1). **7:** See 12.1n. **10–11:** *Grumbling*, referring especially to Israel's faithless complaints against God in Ex 15–17; Num 11; 14; 16; 20–21. **11:** *Tongue*, counsel on the vices of human speech is ubiquitous in wisdom literature (see Prov 2.12; 4.24; 6.12; 10.11,18–19,31–32; 12.6; 26.28; Sir 9.18; 19.15–16; 20.24–26; 26.5–6; 28.12–26; Jas 3.1–12). **14:** *Hades*, the abode of the dead in Greek tradition; comparable to Hebrew "Sheol." **15:** Immortality is not

the generative forces[a] of the world
  are wholesome,
and there is no destructive poison in
  them,
and the dominion[b] of Hades is not
  on earth.
15 For righteousness is immortal.

16 But the ungodly by their words and
  deeds summoned death;[c]
considering him a friend, they pined
  away
and made a covenant with him,
because they are fit to belong to his
  company.

2 For they reasoned unsoundly, saying
  to themselves,
"Short and sorrowful is our life,
and there is no remedy when a life
  comes to its end,
and no one has been known to return
  from Hades.
2 For we were born by mere chance,
and hereafter we shall be as though
  we had never been,
for the breath in our nostrils is
  smoke,
and reason is a spark kindled by the
  beating of our hearts;
3 when it is extinguished, the body will
  turn to ashes,
and the spirit will dissolve like empty
  air.
4 Our name will be forgotten in time,
and no one will remember our works;
our life will pass away like the traces
  of a cloud,
and be scattered like mist
that is chased by the rays of the sun
and overcome by its heat.

5 For our allotted time is the passing of
  a shadow,
and there is no return from our death,
because it is sealed up and no one
  turns back.

6 "Come, therefore, let us enjoy the
  good things that exist,
and make use of the creation to the
  full as in youth.
7 Let us take our fill of costly wine and
  perfumes,
and let no flower of spring pass us
  by.
8 Let us crown ourselves with rosebuds
  before they wither.
9 Let none of us fail to share in our
  revelry;
everywhere let us leave signs of
  enjoyment,
because this is our portion, and this
  our lot.
10 Let us oppress the righteous poor
  man;
let us not spare the widow
or regard the gray hairs of the aged.
11 But let our might be our law of right,
for what is weak proves itself to be
  useless.

12 "Let us lie in wait for the righteous
  man,
because he is inconvenient to us and
  opposes our actions;
he reproaches us for sins against the
  law,
and accuses us of sins against our
  training.

a Or the creatures     b Or palace     c Gk him

an innate condition of the soul but God's gift to the righteous (see Philo, *On the Confusion of Tongues*
149). **1.16–2.24: The deluded reasoning of the ungodly.** The passage's style resembles that of the Greco-Roman diatribe, which often included argumentative exchanges with a fictional adversary. Here the ungodly are made to explain their actions and motives *to themselves* (2.1–20). **1.16:** For the *covenant* with *death*, cf. Isa 28.15. **2.1–5:** This view of death is reflected also in Job 7.9–10; 14.1–2; Eccl 2.14,16,24; 3.12,19; 6.12; 9.2,7–9. **1:** *Hades*, see 1.14n. **6–9:** In the reasoning of the ungodly, the threat of death warrants sensuality (see Isa 22.13). In Eccl 9.7 enjoyment of pleasure is recommended as a proper response to life under the shadow of death. **10–20:** The wicked are misled by an irrational antipathy for the righteous and the weak, persecuting those who call *God* their *father*. **13:** *Knowledge of God*, a gift

13 He professes to have knowledge of
    God,
and calls himself a child[a] of the
    Lord.
14 He became to us a reproof of our
    thoughts;
15 the very sight of him is a burden to
    us,
because his manner of life is unlike
    that of others,
and his ways are strange.
16 We are considered by him as
    something base,
and he avoids our ways as unclean;
he calls the last end of the righteous
    happy,
and boasts that God is his father.
17 Let us see if his words are true,
and let us test what will happen at
    the end of his life;
18 for if the righteous man is God's
    child, he will help him,
and will deliver him from the hand of
    his adversaries.
19 Let us test him with insult and
    torture,
so that we may find out how gentle
    he is,
and make trial of his forbearance.
20 Let us condemn him to a shameful
    death,
for, according to what he says, he will
    be protected."

21 Thus they reasoned, but they were led
    astray,

for their wickedness blinded them,
22 and they did not know the secret
    purposes of God,
nor hoped for the wages of holiness,
nor discerned the prize for blameless
    souls;
23 for God created us for incorruption,
and made us in the image of his own
    eternity,[b]
24 but through the devil's envy death
    entered the world,
and those who belong to his company
    experience it.

3 But the souls of the righteous are in
    the hand of God,
and no torment will ever touch them.
2 In the eyes of the foolish they seemed
    to have died,
and their departure was thought to be
    a disaster,
3 and their going from us to be their
    destruction;
but they are at peace.
4 For though in the sight of others they
    were punished,
their hope is full of immortality.
5 Having been disciplined a little, they
    will receive great good,
because God tested them and found
    them worthy of himself;
6 like gold in the furnace he tried them,
and like a sacrificial burnt offering he
    accepted them.

*a* Or *servant*    *b* Other ancient authorities read *nature*

of wisdom illuminating the path to immortality (6.22; 7.12,17; 8.4,9; 10.10; 15.2–3; 18.6). Conversely, the wicked refuse to know God (2.22; 12.27; 13.1,9; 14.22; 15.11; 16.16). **17:** Cf. Gen 37.20. **21–24:** The author's assessment: The ungodly show themselves to be ignorant of God's *secret purposes* (6.22; 7.21–22). **23:** *Incorruption*, i.e., immortality, explaining the ultimate purpose of human existence (see 3.4n.; 1 Cor 15.42–54; 1 Pet 1.4,23; Philo, *Questions on Genesis* 1.16). **24:** *Devil's envy*, referring to the temptation story of Gen 3.1–24 (see 6.23; 2 Enoch 31.3–6).

**3.1–9: The reward of the righteous.** The affliction of *the righteous* may seem to be punishment, but is in reality divine testing; after death they are forever at peace with God, sharing in God's rule. **1:** *Souls*, the author repeatedly emphasizes the primacy of the soul in constituting human identity (1.4,11; 2.22; 3.13; 4.14; 7.27; 8.19; 9.15; 10.16; 15.8,11). **4:** The emphasis on *immortality* rather than bodily resurrection reflects Greek influence (1.15; 2.23; 4.1; 6.18–19; 8.13,17; 12.1; 15.3; 2 Esd 2.45; 7.13,96; 8.54; 4 Macc 9.22n.). **5:** Wisdom writers in particular deemed this sort of divine discipline essential to the life of faith; see 11.8–10; 12.20–22; 16.3–6,11; 18.20; Deut 8.5; Job 5.17; Prov 3.11–12; Sir 2.1–5; 4.17; 18.13–14; 32.14; 2 Macc 6.12–16; 7.33. **7–8:** In their vindication, the righteous *will shine forth* (cf. Ps

7 In the time of their visitation they will
  shine forth,
and will run like sparks through the
  stubble.
8 They will govern nations and rule
  over peoples,
and the Lord will reign over them
  forever.
9 Those who trust in him will
  understand truth,
and the faithful will abide with him in
  love,
because grace and mercy are upon his
  holy ones,
and he watches over his elect.*

10 But the ungodly will be punished as
  their reasoning deserves,
those who disregarded the righteous*b*
and rebelled against the Lord;
11 for those who despise wisdom and
  instruction are miserable.
Their hope is vain, their labors are
  unprofitable,
and their works are useless.
12 Their wives are foolish, and their
  children evil;
13 their offspring are accursed.
  For blessed is the barren woman who
  is undefiled,
who has not entered into a sinful
  union;
she will have fruit when God
  examines souls.
14 Blessed also is the eunuch whose
  hands have done no lawless
  deed,

and who has not devised wicked
  things against the Lord;
for special favor will be shown him
  for his faithfulness,
and a place of great delight in the
  temple of the Lord.
15 For the fruit of good labors is
  renowned,
and the root of understanding does
  not fail.
16 But children of adulterers will not
  come to maturity,
and the offspring of an unlawful
  union will perish.
17 Even if they live long they will be
  held of no account,
and finally their old age will be
  without honor.
18 If they die young, they will have no
  hope
and no consolation on the day of
  judgment.
19 For the end of an unrighteous
  generation is grievous.

4 Better than this is childlessness with
  virtue,
for in the memory of virtue*c* is
  immortality,
because it is known both by God and
  by mortals.
2 When it is present, people imitate*d* it,

a Text of this line uncertain; omitted by some ancient
authorities. Compare 4.15   b Or *what is right*
c Gk *it*   d Other ancient authorities read *honor*

37.6; Dan 12.3; Zech 9.16; 2 Esd 7.97) and *govern nations* (see Dan 7.14). **9:** *Watches over his elect,* see
4.15; Ps 1.6; 145.20; Sir 46.14; 2 Macc 7.6.
  **3.10–4.6: Rewards and punishments.** Virtue, not long life or many children, is the sign of God's favor.
**3.10:** *The ungodly will be punished,* a major theme of the book. **12–13:** Since children were considered
a blessing in the ancient world (e.g., Ps 127.3–5; 128.3–4), the author shows how the apparent good
fortune of the ungodly in having children is illusory. See also 3.16–19; 4.3–6; cf. Sir 16.1–4; 23.24–25;
41.5–9. In contrast, barrenness, which was often thought to indicate divine displeasure (Gen 30.23) if not
sin (*1 Enoch* 98.5), may be the condition of the morally pure. **14:** Although Deut 23.1 excluded eunuchs
from the cultic assembly, this author assures the virtuous eunuch a place in *the temple of the Lord,*
referring perhaps to the heavenly temple; cf. Isa 56.4–5. **16:** See Sir 23.23–25. **18:** *The day of judgment,*
cf. Jdt 16.17; 2 Esd 7.38. **4.1:** *The memory of virtue,* God's remembrance of the virtuous is their guaran-
tee of eternal life (cf. 8.13; Ps 112.6; Prov 10.7; Sir 44.8–15; 2 Esd 12.47). Conversely, the memory of
the wicked will perish (4.19; see 2.4; Eccl 9.5). **2:** On the *contest* for virtue, see 4 Macc 17.11–16n. **3–5:**

and they long for it when it has
    gone;
throughout all time it marches,
    crowned in triumph,
victor in the contest for prizes that
    are undefiled.
3 But the prolific brood of the ungodly
    will be of no use,
and none of their illegitimate
    seedlings will strike a deep root
or take a firm hold.
4 For even if they put forth boughs for
    a while,
standing insecurely they will be
    shaken by the wind,
and by the violence of the winds they
    will be uprooted.
5 The branches will be broken off
    before they come to maturity,
and their fruit will be useless,
not ripe enough to eat, and good for
    nothing.
6 For children born of unlawful unions
are witnesses of evil against their
    parents when God examines
    them.*a*
7 But the righteous, though they die
    early, will be at rest.
8 For old age is not honored for length
    of time,
or measured by number of years;
9 but understanding is gray hair for
    anyone,
and a blameless life is ripe old age.

10 There were some who pleased God
    and were loved by him,
and while living among sinners were
    taken up.

11 They were caught up so that evil
    might not change their
    understanding
or guile deceive their souls.
12 For the fascination of wickedness
    obscures what is good,
and roving desire perverts the
    innocent mind.
13 Being perfected in a short time, they
    fulfilled long years;
14 for their souls were pleasing to the
    Lord,
therefore he took them quickly from
    the midst of wickedness.
15 Yet the peoples saw and did not
    understand,
or take such a thing to heart,
that God's grace and mercy are with
    his elect,
and that he watches over his holy
    ones.

16 The righteous who have died will
    condemn the ungodly who are
    living,
and youth that is quickly perfected*b*
    will condemn the prolonged
    old age of the unrighteous.
17 For they will see the end of the wise,
and will not understand what the
    Lord purposed for them,
and for what he kept them safe.
18 The unrighteous*c* will see, and will
    have contempt for them,
but the Lord will laugh them to
    scorn.

*a Gk at their examination    b Or ended    c Gk They*

For the imagery, cf. Job 15.32–34; Ps 1.3–4; Ezek 17.9; 31.10–14; Dan 4.14; Sir 23.25. **6:** *Witnesses . . . against their parents,* see 4.20.

**4.7–19: The blessedness of the righteous despite early death. 7–9:** In contrast to the traditional association of old age with wisdom (Job 15.7–10), *understanding,* not *length of time,* is the true measure of righteousness (see 4.15; Philo, *On Abraham* 271). **10:** An allusion to Enoch who was *taken up* in this manner (Gen 5.24; cf. Sir 44.16). *Genesis Rabbah* 25.1 also claims that the purpose of Enoch's removal was to preserve his character. **12:** *Roving desire,* see 15.5–6; Eccl 6.9; 11.9; Sir 18.30–19.3; Jas 1.14–15. **14–15,17:** Premature death is interpreted not as a curse (cf. Ps 109.8–9) but as a sign of God's favor. These verses may be based on Isa 57.1–2. **17:** *They will see,* answering 2.17 (cf. 5.2). **18a:** *The Lord will laugh,* cf. Ps 2.4; Prov 1.26. **18b–19:** These threats are familiar from prophetic announcements of judgment (Isa 13.6–16; 24.17–23; 66.24; Jer 15.7–9). **19:** *Memory,* see 4.1n.

After this they will become
  dishonored corpses,
and an outrage among the dead
  forever;
19 because he will dash them speechless
  to the ground,
and shake them from the foundations;
they will be left utterly dry and
  barren,
and they will suffer anguish,
and the memory of them will perish.

20 They will come with dread when their
  sins are reckoned up,
and their lawless deeds will convict
  them to their face.

5 Then the righteous will stand with
  great confidence
in the presence of those who have
  oppressed them
and those who make light of their
  labors.
2 When the unrighteous[a] see them,
  they will be shaken with
  dreadful fear,
and they will be amazed at the
  unexpected salvation of the
  righteous.
3 They will speak to one another in
  repentance,
and in anguish of spirit they will
  groan, and say,
4 "These are persons whom we once
  held in derision
and made a byword of reproach—
  fools that we were!
We thought that their lives were
  madness
and that their end was without
  honor.
5 Why have they been numbered
  among the children of God?

And why is their lot among the
  saints?
6 So it was we who strayed from the
  way of truth,
and the light of righteousness did not
  shine on us,
and the sun did not rise upon us.
7 We took our fill of the paths of
  lawlessness and destruction,
and we journeyed through trackless
  deserts,
but the way of the Lord we have not
  known.
8 What has our arrogance profited us?
And what good has our boasted
  wealth brought us?

9 "All those things have vanished like a
  shadow,
and like a rumor that passes by;
10 like a ship that sails through the
  billowy water,
and when it has passed no trace can
  be found,
no track of its keel in the waves;
11 or as, when a bird flies through the
  air,
no evidence of its passage is found;
the light air, lashed by the beat of its
  pinions
and pierced by the force of its rushing
  flight,
is traversed by the movement of its
  wings,
and afterward no sign of its coming is
  found there;
12 or as, when an arrow is shot at a
  target,
the air, thus divided, comes together
  at once,

a Gk they

**4.20–5.23: The final judgment.** In contrast to their arrogant speech of 2.1–20, *the unrighteous* now speak with remorse and self-condemnation (5.4–13). **4.20–5.8:** The reaction of *the unrighteous* to *the righteous* parallels the so-called servant song of Isa 52.13–53.12, which describes the astonishing restoration of Israel after terrible affliction. **20:** See Isa 59.12; Jer 2.19. **5.5:** *Among the children of God . . . among the saints,* the righteous are to be counted in the heavenly court, with the angelic host; cf. Dan 12.2–3; *1 Enoch* 39.1–5; 104.2,6. **6–8:** The wicked's confession of guilt (compare Isa 59.2–3, 7–10). **6:** *The light . . . did not shine,* see 17.2–21. **9–14:** The ephemeral existence of *the ungodly,* cf. Isa 40.6–8; Hos 13.3; 2 Esd 7.61; Jas 4.14. **10–11:** *A ship . . . a bird,* perhaps adapting the riddle of Prov 30.18–19.

so that no one knows its pathway.

13 So we also, as soon as we were born,
      ceased to be,
   and we had no sign of virtue to
      show,
   but were consumed in our
      wickedness."
14 Because the hope of the ungodly is
      like thistledown<sup>a</sup> carried by
      the wind,
   and like a light frost<sup>b</sup> driven away by
      a storm;
   it is dispersed like smoke before the
      wind,
   and it passes like the remembrance of
      a guest who stays but a day.

15 But the righteous live forever,
   and their reward is with the Lord;
   the Most High takes care of them.
16 Therefore they will receive a glorious
      crown
   and a beautiful diadem from the hand
      of the Lord,
   because with his right hand he will
      cover them,
   and with his arm he will shield them.
17 The Lord<sup>c</sup> will take his zeal as his
      whole armor,
   and will arm all creation to repel<sup>d</sup>
      his enemies;
18 he will put on righteousness as a
      breastplate,
   and wear impartial justice as a
      helmet;
19 he will take holiness as an invincible
      shield,
20 and sharpen stern wrath for a sword,

and creation will join with him to
      fight against his frenzied foes.
21 Shafts of lightning will fly with true
      aim,
   and will leap from the clouds to the
      target, as from a well-drawn
      bow,
22 and hailstones full of wrath will be
      hurled as from a catapult;
   the water of the sea will rage against
      them,
   and rivers will relentlessly overwhelm
      them;
23 a mighty wind will rise against them,
   and like a tempest it will winnow
      them away.
   Lawlessness will lay waste the whole
      earth,
   and evildoing will overturn the
      thrones of rulers.

6 Listen therefore, O kings, and
      understand;
   learn, O judges of the ends of the
      earth.
 2 Give ear, you that rule over
      multitudes,
   and boast of many nations.
 3 For your dominion was given you
      from the Lord,
   and your sovereignty from the Most
      High;
   he will search out your works and
      inquire into your plans.

a Other ancient authorities read *dust*    b Other
ancient authorities read *spider's web*    c Gk *He*
d Or *punish*

**15–21:** *The righteous* will receive a royal *reward* while God's *enemies* will be defeated in battle. **16:** *Glorious crown . . . beautiful diadem,* cf. Isa 62.3. **17–20:** The imagery of God putting on various attributes as divine armor derives from Isa 59.17; on the divine warrior, see 18.15; Ps 7.12–13; Eph 6.13–17. **17:** *Will arm all creation,* see 5.20–23; 19.6; Sir 39.28–31. **21–22:** *Lightning . . . hailstones . . . water,* cf. 16.15–29.

   **6.1–25: Exhortation to seek wisdom,** emphasizing both the necessity and the ease of the quest. Some of the passage's themes are familiar from philosophical treatises on kingship (e.g., Plutarch, *To an Uneducated Ruler*), which generally stressed the need for rulers to be wise and benevolent (cf. 12.15–18n.). Kingship is also an important theme in another book attributed to Solomon, Proverbs (e.g., 16.10–19; 20.26–28; 25.1–7; 29.4,12–14; 30.21–31). **1:** The fictional address to *kings* and *judges* indicates the gravity of the appeal (see 1.1n.; 6.9). **3:** Political authority is granted by God (Prov 8.15–16; Jer 27.5–7; Dan 2.37–38; 4.17; Sir 10.4–5; Rom 13.1–7). **4–6:** For God's judgment against *the mighty,*

4 Because as servants of his kingdom
> you did not rule rightly,
or keep the law,
or walk according to the purpose of
> God,
5 he will come upon you terribly and
> swiftly,
because severe judgment falls on those
> in high places.
6 For the lowliest may be pardoned in
> mercy,
but the mighty will be mightily
> tested.
7 For the Lord of all will not stand in
> awe of anyone,
or show deference to greatness;
because he himself made both small
> and great,
and he takes thought for all alike.
8 But a strict inquiry is in store for the
> mighty.
9 To you then, O monarchs, my words
> are directed,
so that you may learn wisdom and
> not transgress.
10 For they will be made holy who
> observe holy things in holiness,
and those who have been taught them
> will find a defense.
11 Therefore set your desire on my
> words;
long for them, and you will be
> instructed.

12 Wisdom is radiant and unfading,
and she is easily discerned by those
> who love her,
and is found by those who seek her.
13 She hastens to make herself known to
> those who desire her.
14 One who rises early to seek her will
> have no difficulty,
for she will be found sitting at the
> gate.

15 To fix one's thought on her is perfect
> understanding,
and one who is vigilant on her
> account will soon be free from
> care,
16 because she goes about seeking those
> worthy of her,
and she graciously appears to them in
> their paths,
and meets them in every thought.

17 The beginning of wisdom[a] is the
> most sincere desire for
> instruction,
and concern for instruction is love of
> her,
18 and love of her is the keeping of her
> laws,
and giving heed to her laws is
> assurance of immortality,
19 and immortality brings one near to
> God;
20 so the desire for wisdom leads to a
> kingdom.

21 Therefore if you delight in thrones
> and scepters, O monarchs over
> the peoples,
honor wisdom, so that you may reign
> forever.
22 I will tell you what wisdom is and
> how she came to be,
and I will hide no secrets from you,
but I will trace her course from the
> beginning of creation,
and make knowledge of her clear,
and I will not pass by the truth;
23 nor will I travel in the company of
> sickly envy,
for envy[b] does not associate with
> wisdom.

a Gk *Her beginning*    b Gk *this*

cf. 1 Sam 2.3–5; Job 12.17–25; 34.24–30; Ps 2; Isa 2.11–17; Jer 25.15–29; Ezek 21.25–27; Sir 10.8–18.
**7:** *Small and great,* cf. Job 34.19. **12–16:** *Wisdom* is personified as a desirable woman, as in Prov 8.1–21;
see 7.22b–8.1n. **14:** *The gate,* the place in a city where legal and commercial transactions were carried
out (Deut 22.15,24; Prov 22.22; Isa 29.21; Amos 5.10–12,15); cf. Prov 1.20–21. **17–21:** This kind of
chain argument, or "sorites," was a common rhetorical device in ancient literature (see Rom 5.3–4; 2 Pet
1.5–7). **22:** *The beginning of creation,* cf. 8.4–6; 9.9; Prov 3.19–20; 8.22–31; Sir 24.4–6, 9.

24 The multitude of the wise is the
    salvation of the world,
  and a sensible king is the stability of
    any people.
25 Therefore be instructed by my words,
    and you will profit.

7 I also am mortal, like everyone
    else,
  a descendant of the first-formed
    child of earth;
  and in the womb of a mother I was
    molded into flesh,
2 within the period of ten months,
    compacted with blood,
  from the seed of a man and the
    pleasure of marriage.
3 And when I was born, I began to
    breathe the common air,
  and fell upon the kindred earth;
  my first sound was a cry, as is true of
    all.
4 I was nursed with care in swaddling
    cloths.
5 For no king has had a different
    beginning of existence;
6 there is for all one entrance into life,
    and one way out.
7 Therefore I prayed, and understanding
    was given me;
  I called on God, and the spirit of
    wisdom came to me.
8 I preferred her to scepters and
    thrones,

and I accounted wealth as nothing in
    comparison with her.
9 Neither did I liken to her any
    priceless gem,
  because all gold is but a little sand in
    her sight,
  and silver will be accounted as clay
    before her.
10 I loved her more than health and
    beauty,
  and I chose to have her rather than
    light,
  because her radiance never ceases.
11 All good things came to me along
    with her,
  and in her hands uncounted wealth.
12 I rejoiced in them all, because wisdom
    leads them;
  but I did not know that she was their
    mother.
13 I learned without guile and I impart
    without grudging;
  I do not hide her wealth,
14 for it is an unfailing treasure for
    mortals;
  those who get it obtain friendship
    with God,
  commended for the gifts that come
    from instruction.

15 May God grant me to speak with
    judgment,
  and to have thoughts worthy of what
    I have received;

**7.1–10.21: King Solomon and the quest for wisdom.** The presentation of wisdom in the preceding passage segues to a largely autobiographical section in which the author, in the guise of Solomon, extols the power of divine Sophia (wisdom) and shows how to acquire her.

**7.1–8.20: Solomon's speech** concentrates on wisdom's many attributes and benefits, describing her as mortals' greatest desire. **7.1–6:** King Solomon does not claim divinity (as many ancient monarchs did), but begins his pursuit of wisdom *like everyone else*. Insofar as the goal of Jewish religion is to live wisely and to rule with God (see 3.8–9; 4.16; 5.16; 6.20; 9.3; 10.2), Solomon is a model for the readers to emulate, the ideal sage and ruler. **1–2:** This description is based on ancient assumptions about pregnancy (cf. Job 10.9–11; Ps 139.13–16). **1:** *Child of earth,* see Gen 2.7; Sir 17.1; 1 Cor 15.47. **2:** *Ten months,* i.e., lunar months of four weeks, for a total of forty weeks of gestation. **6:** Cf. Sir 40.1. **7–14:** Solomon desires wisdom above all else since she is the source of *all good things.* **7,11:** Cf. 1 Kings 3.5–15. **8–9:** Cf. Job 28.15–19; Prov. 2.4; 3.14–16. **11–12:** *Wisdom* is further personified as the *mother* of all external goods (see 6.12–16n.; 7.22; 8.5–6). **14:** Abraham in particular was known for his *friendship with God* (2 Chr 20.7; Isa 41.8; Jas 2.23); see also 7.27; 8.18; Job 29.4; Ps 25.14; Jer 3.4. **15–22a:** Divine wisdom is presented in scientific and philosophical terms; this sort of encyclopedic knowledge was a common

for he is the guide even of wisdom
and the corrector of the wise.

16 For both we and our words are in his
     hand,
   as are all understanding and skill in
     crafts.

17 For it is he who gave me unerring
     knowledge of what exists,
   to know the structure of the world
     and the activity of the
     elements;

18 the beginning and end and middle of
     times,
   the alternations of the solstices and
     the changes of the seasons,

19 the cycles of the year and the
     constellations of the stars,

20 the natures of animals and the
     tempers of wild animals,
   the powers of spirits*a* and the
     thoughts of human beings,
   the varieties of plants and the virtues
     of roots;

21 I learned both what is secret and
     what is manifest,

22 for wisdom, the fashioner of all
     things, taught me.

There is in her a spirit that is
     intelligent, holy,
unique, manifold, subtle,
mobile, clear, unpolluted,
distinct, invulnerable, loving the good,
     keen,
irresistible, 23 beneficent, humane,
steadfast, sure, free from anxiety,
all-powerful, overseeing all,
and penetrating through all
     spirits

that are intelligent, pure, and
     altogether subtle.

24 For wisdom is more mobile than any
     motion;
   because of her pureness she pervades
     and penetrates all things.

25 For she is a breath of the power of
     God,
   and a pure emanation of the glory of
     the Almighty;
   therefore nothing defiled gains
     entrance into her.

26 For she is a reflection of eternal light,
   a spotless mirror of the working of
     God,
   and an image of his goodness.

27 Although she is but one, she can do
     all things,
   and while remaining in herself, she
     renews all things;
   in every generation she passes into
     holy souls
   and makes them friends of God, and
     prophets;

28 for God loves nothing so much as the
     person who lives with wisdom.

29 She is more beautiful than the sun,
   and excels every constellation of the
     stars.
   Compared with the light she is found
     to be superior,

30 for it is succeeded by the night,
   but against wisdom evil does not
     prevail.

8 She reaches mightily from one end of
     the earth to the other,
   and she orders all things well.

*a Or winds*

interest of ancient wisdom literature. **17:** *The elements,* see 19.18; Col 2.8,20. **18–19:** Compare Job 38.31–33. **20:** See 1 Kings 4.33.

   **7.22b–8.1:** The divine essence and activity of wisdom. **22b–23:** As Philo observes (*Allegorical Interpretation* 1.43), wisdom has many names and appellations. Most of the twenty-one (the product of three and seven, numbers signifying completeness and perfection) epithets here have parallels in Greek philosophy (cf. Pseudo-Aristotle, *On the Cosmos* 400B–401B); a similar litany of attributes, glorifying the deity, is used in the *Apocalypse of Abraham* 17.8–15. **25–26:** The description of wisdom as a pure *emanation* or effluence of God reflects the influence of philosophical concepts (e.g., Cicero, *The Nature of the Gods* 2.79; cf. Sir 1.9; 24.23–33). **25:** *Breath,* see 11.20; Sir 24.3. **26:** *Mirror,* cf. 2 Cor 3.18; Philo, *Questions on Genesis* 1.57. Heb 1.3 similarly uses the image of Christ as the reflection of God's glory. **30:** *Succeeded by the night,* cf. Isa 60.19–21.

2 I loved her and sought her from my
        youth;
  I desired to take her for my bride,
  and became enamored of her beauty.
3 She glorifies her noble birth by living
        with God,
  and the Lord of all loves her.
4 For she is an initiate in the knowledge
        of God,
  and an associate in his works.
5 If riches are a desirable possession in
        life,
  what is richer than wisdom, the active
        cause of all things?
6 And if understanding is effective,
  who more than she is fashioner of
        what exists?
7 And if anyone loves righteousness,
  her labors are virtues;
  for she teaches self-control and
        prudence,
  justice and courage;
  nothing in life is more profitable for
        mortals than these.
8 And if anyone longs for wide
        experience,
  she knows the things of old, and
        infers the things to come;
  she understands turns of speech and
        the solutions of riddles;
  she has foreknowledge of signs and
        wonders
  and of the outcome of seasons and
        times.
9 Therefore I determined to take her to
        live with me,
  knowing that she would give me good
        counsel
  and encouragement in cares and grief.
10 Because of her I shall have glory
        among the multitudes
  and honor in the presence of the
        elders, though I am young.
11 I shall be found keen in judgment,

and in the sight of rulers I shall be
        admired.
12 When I am silent they will wait for
        me,
  and when I speak they will give
        heed;
  if I speak at greater length,
  they will put their hands on their
        mouths.
13 Because of her I shall have
        immortality,
  and leave an everlasting remembrance
        to those who come after me.
14 I shall govern peoples,
  and nations will be subject to me;
15 dread monarchs will be afraid of me
        when they hear of me;
  among the people I shall show myself
        capable, and courageous in
        war.
16 When I enter my house, I shall find
        rest with her;
  for companionship with her has no
        bitterness,
  and life with her has no pain, but
        gladness and joy.
17 When I considered these things
        inwardly,
  and pondered in my heart
  that in kinship with wisdom there is
        immortality,
18 and in friendship with her, pure
        delight,
  and in the labors of her hands,
        unfailing wealth,
  and in the experience of her company,
        understanding,
  and renown in sharing her words,
  I went about seeking how to get her
        for myself.
19 As a child I was naturally gifted,
  and a good soul fell to my lot;
20 or rather, being good, I entered an
        undefiled body.

**8.2–20:** **The many benefits of a relationship with wisdom** include virtue, knowledge, glory, and power.
**8.2:** *Loved,* see 6.12–16n.; 8.9; Prov 7.4; Sir 15.2. **4–6:** On wisdom's agency in creation, see Prov
8.22–31. **7:** The standard list of cardinal virtues (*self-control, prudence, justice, courage*) is familiar from
Platonic and Stoic writings (see 4 Macc 1.2–4n.). **8:** *Turns of speech,* 1.11n.; Prov 1.5–6; 12.6,16,21,23;
Sir 4.23–24; 21.7,16; 27.6. **10–12:** Cf. Job 29.7–11,21–23; Sir 15.4–6. **15–16:** *Rest,* see Sir 6.28. **17:** See
3.4n. **19–20:** The Platonic view of the soul as preexistent is reflected here, as in other Hellenistic Jewish

21 But I perceived that I would not
possess wisdom unless God
gave her to me—
and it was a mark of insight to know
whose gift she was—
so I appealed to the Lord and
implored him,
and with my whole heart I said:

9 "O God of my ancestors and Lord of
mercy,
who have made all things by your
word,

2 and by your wisdom have formed
humankind
to have dominion over the creatures
you have made,

3 and rule the world in holiness and
righteousness,
and pronounce judgment in
uprightness of soul,

4 give me the wisdom that sits by your
throne,
and do not reject me from among
your servants.

5 For I am your servant[a] the son of
your serving girl,
a man who is weak and short-lived,
with little understanding of judgment
and laws;

6 for even one who is perfect among
human beings
will be regarded as nothing without
the wisdom that comes from
you.

7 You have chosen me to be king of
your people
and to be judge over your sons and
daughters.

8 You have given command to build a
temple on your holy mountain,

and an altar in the city of your
habitation,
a copy of the holy tent that you
prepared from the beginning.

9 With you is wisdom, she who knows
your works
and was present when you made the
world;
she understands what is pleasing in
your sight
and what is right according to your
commandments.

10 Send her forth from the holy heavens,
and from the throne of your glory
send her,
that she may labor at my side,
and that I may learn what is pleasing
to you.

11 For she knows and understands all
things,
and she will guide me wisely in my
actions
and guard me with her glory.

12 Then my works will be acceptable,
and I shall judge your people justly,
and shall be worthy of the throne[b] of
my father.

13 For who can learn the counsel of
God?
Or who can discern what the Lord
wills?

14 For the reasoning of mortals is
worthless,
and our designs are likely to fail;

15 for a perishable body weighs down
the soul,
and this earthy tent burdens the
thoughtful[c] mind.

a Gk *slave*    b Gk *thrones*    c Or *anxious*

writings (compare Philo, *On the Giants* 6–14). The author may be referring also to Hellenistic theories
about the transmigration of souls, a belief attributed by Josephus to the Pharisees (*War* 2.8.14).
**8.21–9.18**: Solomon's prayer for wisdom (1 Kings 3.6–9; 2 Chr 1.8–10). After an introduction (8.21),
the prayer consists of an address to God (9.1–3), two parallel petitions (9.4–9,10–12), and a meditation
on humankind's insignificance before God (9.13–18). **8.21**: *Whose gift she was,* see 7.7,14; 9.4,17; Sir
1.10; 24.8; Bar 3.29–37. **9.2**: *Dominion,* see 10.2; Gen 1.26,28; Ps 8.6; Sir 17.2–4. **4**: *Wisdom . . . sits
by your throne,* see 9.10; 18.15; Prov 8.30; Sir 24.4; *1 Enoch* 84.3. **5**: *Your servant,* see Ps 86.16; 116.16.
**8**: That the earthly temple on Mount Zion was only a *copy* of a heavenly archetype may be an interpretation of Ex 25.9,40; 26.30 (cf. Heb 8.2–5; Rev 11.19; *1 Enoch* 14.10–20). **9**: See 8.4–6. **12**: *My father,*
David. **13**: Compare Isa 40.12–14; Sir 1.2–6; Bar 3.29–31. **15**: That the *body weighs down the soul* was

16 We can hardly guess at what is on
　　earth,
　and what is at hand we find with
　　labor;
　but who has traced out what is in the
　　heavens?
17 Who has learned your counsel,
　unless you have given wisdom
　and sent your holy spirit from on
　　high?
18 And thus the paths of those on earth
　　were set right,
　and people were taught what pleases
　　you,
　and were saved by wisdom."

10 Wisdom[a] protected the
　first-formed father of the
　world, when he alone had been
　created;
she delivered him from his
　transgression,
2 and gave him strength to rule all
　things.
3 But when an unrighteous man
　　departed from her in his anger,
he perished because in rage he killed
　his brother.
4 When the earth was flooded because
　of him, wisdom again saved it,
steering the righteous man by a paltry
　piece of wood.
5 Wisdom[a] also, when the nations in
　　wicked agreement had been put
　to confusion,
recognized the righteous man and
　preserved him blameless before
　God,

and kept him strong in the face of his
　compassion for his child.
6 Wisdom[a] rescued a righteous man
　when the ungodly were
　perishing;
he escaped the fire that descended on
　the Five Cities.[b]
7 Evidence of their wickedness still
　remains:
a continually smoking wasteland,
plants bearing fruit that does not
　ripen,
and a pillar of salt standing as a
　monument to an unbelieving
　soul.
8 For because they passed wisdom by,
they not only were hindered from
　recognizing the good,
but also left for humankind a
　reminder of their folly,
so that their failures could never go
　unnoticed.
9 Wisdom rescued from troubles those
　who served her.
10 When a righteous man fled from his
　　brother's wrath,
she guided him on straight paths;
she showed him the kingdom of God,
and gave him knowledge of holy
　things;
she prospered him in his labors,
and increased the fruit of his toil.
11 When his oppressors were covetous,
she stood by him and made him rich.
12 She protected him from his enemies,

*a* Gk *She*　　*b* Or *on Pentapolis*

a common philosophical belief (see Plato, *Phaedo* 81C). **18:** *Saved by wisdom,* the attribution of a saving role to wisdom is one of the book's distinctive features; here as elsewhere activities usually reserved for God are assigned to wisdom.

**10.1–21: Historical illustrations of wisdom's saving and punishing power.** The author presents seven righteous heroes as evidence of wisdom's providential ordering of Israelite history, each contrasted with some unrighteous villain; personal names are avoided in favor of generic categories. A comparable listing of biblical figures is used in Sir 44.1–50.21, cf. Heb 11.4–38. **1–2:** Adam (Gen 1.26–5.5). **3:** Cain and Abel (Gen 4.1–16). **4:** *Because of him,* Cain's crime is interpreted by the author as the cause of the Flood. *The righteous man,* Noah (Gen 5.28–9.29). **5:** Abraham (Gen 11.26–25.10). *The nations,* referring to the Tower of Babel story (Gen 11.1–9). *Compassion for his child,* cf. Gen 22.1–19. **6–8:** Lot (Gen 19.1–29).

and kept him safe from those who lay
    in wait for him;
in his arduous contest she gave him
    the victory,
so that he might learn that godliness
    is more powerful than anything
    else.

13 When a righteous man was sold,
    wisdom*a* did not desert him,
but delivered him from sin.
She descended with him into the
    dungeon,
14 and when he was in prison she did
    not leave him,
until she brought him the scepter of a
    kingdom
and authority over his masters.
Those who accused him she showed
    to be false,
and she gave him everlasting honor.

15 A holy people and blameless race
wisdom delivered from a nation of
    oppressors.
16 She entered the soul of a servant of
    the Lord,
and withstood dread kings with
    wonders and signs.
17 She gave to holy people the reward of
    their labors;
she guided them along a marvelous
    way,
and became a shelter to them by day,
and a starry flame through the night.
18 She brought them over the Red Sea,
and led them through deep waters;
19 but she drowned their enemies,

and cast them up from the depth of
    the sea.
20 Therefore the righteous plundered the
    ungodly;
they sang hymns, O Lord, to your
    holy name,
and praised with one accord your
    defending hand;
21 for wisdom opened the mouths of
    those who were mute,
and made the tongues of infants
    speak clearly.

11 Wisdom*b* prospered their works
    by the hand of a holy prophet.
2 They journeyed through an
    uninhabited wilderness,
and pitched their tents in untrodden
    places.
3 They withstood their enemies and
    fought off their foes.
4 When they were thirsty, they called
    upon you,
and water was given them out of
    flinty rock,
and from hard stone a remedy for
    their thirst.
5 For through the very things by which
    their enemies were punished,
they themselves received benefit in
    their need.
6 Instead of the fountain of an
    ever-flowing river,
stirred up and defiled with blood
7 in rebuke for the decree to kill the
    infants,

*a* Gk *she*    *b* Gk *She*

---

**9–12:** Jacob (Gen 27–33). **10:** *The kingdom of God,* see Gen 28.12,17,22. **12:** *Arduous contest,* Gen 32.22–32; Hos 12.3–4. **13–14:** Joseph (Gen 37–50). **15–21:** Moses (Ex 1–17).

**11.1–19.21: A historical meditation contrasting God's dealings with the Israelites and the Egyptians.** The presentation of Moses in the preceding passage leads without a break into an elaborate comparison (Gk, "synkrisis") consisting of seven historical contrasts, supplemented by a digression in 11.17–15.19. Although based on the events of Ex 7–14, the author's interpretation is apologetic in nature, underscoring the Egyptians' culpability while omitting reference to any of Israel's failures (see 1.10–11n.).

**11.1–16: The first contrast:** the plague of the Nile and water from the rock; God gives the Israelites drink while the Egyptians thirst. **1–3:** Without making specific references, the author establishes the historical setting for what follows, the Israelites' struggle in the *wilderness.* **4,6–8:** See Ex 7.14–25; 17.1–7; Num 20.2–13. **5:** The principle behind all the contrasts: God uses the same means for aiding Israel and punishing her *enemies* (see 11.13; 16.24; 18.8). **8–10:** The righteous must also experience

you gave them abundant water
    unexpectedly,
8 showing by their thirst at that time
how you punished their enemies.
9 For when they were tried, though
    they were being disciplined in
    mercy,
they learned how the ungodly were
    tormented when judged in
    wrath.
10 For you tested them as a parent[a]
    does in warning,
but you examined the ungodly[b] as a
    stern king does in
    condemnation.
11 Whether absent or present, they were
    equally distressed,
12 for a twofold grief possessed them,
and a groaning at the memory of
    what had occurred.
13 For when they heard that through
    their own punishments
the righteous[c] had received benefit,
    they perceived it was the
    Lord's doing.
14 For though they had mockingly
    rejected him who long before
    had been cast out and exposed,
at the end of the events they marveled
    at him,
when they felt thirst in a different
    way from the righteous.

15 In return for their foolish and wicked
    thoughts,
which led them astray to worship
    irrational serpents and
    worthless animals,
you sent upon them a multitude of
    irrational creatures to punish
    them,

16 so that they might learn that one is
    punished by the very things by
    which one sins.
17 For your all-powerful hand,
    which created the world out of
    formless matter,
did not lack the means to send upon
    them a multitude of bears, or
    bold lions,
18 or newly-created unknown beasts full
    of rage,
or such as breathe out fiery breath,
or belch forth a thick pall of smoke,
or flash terrible sparks from their
    eyes;
19 not only could the harm they did
    destroy people,[d]
but the mere sight of them could kill
    by fright.
20 Even apart from these, people[e] could
    fall at a single breath
when pursued by justice
and scattered by the breath of your
    power.
But you have arranged all things by
    measure and number and
    weight.

21 For it is always in your power to
    show great strength,
and who can withstand the might of
    your arm?
22 Because the whole world before you
    is like a speck that tips the
    scales,
and like a drop of morning dew that
    falls on the ground.

a Gk *a father*    b Gk *those*    c Gk *they*
d Gk *them*

God's punishment, though not as a matter of condemnation but of compassionate testing and discipline (see 3.5n.). **15–16:** Here and elsewhere (e.g., 12.23,27; 16.1) the author assumes the principle of retribution in kind, as stated in Ex 21.23–25; Lev 24.18–20; Deut 19.19–21 (cf. Ps 7.15–16; 2 Macc 4.38; 5.10; 13.8).

**11.17–15.19: A series of digressions** explains how and why God judges the nations, contrasting the results of true worship (Jewish monotheism) and false worship (idolatry).

**11.17–12.2: God exercises power and mercy in judgment** so as to free all creation from wickedness. **11.17:** *Formless matter,* a concept of Greek philosophy (see Plato, *Timaeus* 50D–E), here describing the chaos of Gen 1.2. **18–19:** Cf. Job 41.12–21. **21:** See 12.12n. **23:** *Merciful to all,* see 12.13,16,18; 15.1;

23 But you are merciful to all, for you
    can do all things,
and you overlook people's sins, so
    that they may repent.
24 For you love all things that exist,
    and detest none of the things that you
        have made,
for you would not have made
    anything if you had hated it.
25 How would anything have endured if
    you had not willed it?
Or how would anything not called
    forth by you have been
    preserved?
26 You spare all things, for they are
    yours, O Lord, you who love
    the living.

**12** For your immortal spirit is in all
    things.
2 Therefore you correct little by little
    those who trespass,
and you remind and warn them of
    the things through which
    they sin,
so that they may be freed from
    wickedness and put their trust
    in you, O Lord.

3 Those who lived long ago in your
    holy land
4 you hated for their detestable
    practices,
their works of sorcery and unholy
    rites,
5 their merciless slaughter<sup>a</sup> of children,
and their sacrificial feasting on human
    flesh and blood.
These initiates from the midst of a
    heathen cult,<sup>b</sup>

6 these parents who murder helpless
    lives,
you willed to destroy by the hands of
    our ancestors,
7 so that the land most precious of all
    to you
might receive a worthy colony of the
    servants<sup>c</sup> of God.
8 But even these you spared, since they
    were but mortals,
and sent wasps<sup>d</sup> as forerunners of
    your army
to destroy them little by little,
9 though you were not unable to give
    the ungodly into the hands of
    the righteous in battle,
or to destroy them at one blow by
    dread wild animals or your
    stern word.
10 But judging them little by little you
    gave them an opportunity to
    repent,
though you were not unaware that
    their origin<sup>e</sup> was evil
and their wickedness inborn,
and that their way of thinking would
    never change.
11 For they were an accursed race from
    the beginning,
and it was not through fear of anyone
    that you left them unpunished
    for their sins.

12 For who will say, "What have you
    done?"
or will resist your judgment?

a Gk *slaughterers*   b Meaning of Gk uncertain
c Or *children*   d Or *hornets*   e Or *nature*

Sir 16.11–14; 18.11–14; 2 Esd 8.45. **12.1:** *Your . . . spirit is in all things,* see 1.7; 15.11; cf. Gen 6.3; Ps 104.30; Jdt 16.14. **2:** *You remind . . . them,* see 16.6, 11n.

    **12.3–11: Divine judgment of the ancient Canaanites,** a common theme of Jewish apologetic (see *Jubilees* 10.27–34; 22.20–22), gives an illustration of the preceding argument; although hating their *wickedness,* God showed forbearance in destroying them. **5:** Compare Lev 20.2–5. **8:** *Wasps,* see Ex 23.28. **10:** *Little by little,* see 12.2,8; Ex 23.28–30. *Their origin was evil* (see text note e) cf. Sir 33.10–15. **11:** *An accursed race,* see the curse placed on Canaan in Gen 9.25–27.

    **12.12–27: Divine righteousness and forbearance.** God gives opportunity for *repentance* (v. 19; see also 11.23; 12.10) but condemns the obstinate. **12–14:** The affirmation of divine providence, making use of legal terminology. **12:** For similar rhetorical questions, see 9.13; 11.21; Job 9.12,19; Ps 76.7; Isa 40.13–14. **13:** *Any god besides you,* see Deut 32.39; cf. Ex 20.3. **15–18:** The portrayal of God's universal

Who will accuse you for the
destruction of nations that you
made?
Or who will come before you to
plead as an advocate for the
unrighteous?
13 For neither is there any god besides
you, whose care is for all
people,ᵃ
to whom you should prove that you
have not judged unjustly;
14 nor can any king or monarch
confront you about those
whom you have punished.
15 You are righteous and you rule all
things righteously,
deeming it alien to your power
to condemn anyone who does not
deserve to be punished.
16 For your strength is the source of
righteousness,
and your sovereignty over all causes
you to spare all.
17 For you show your strength when
people doubt the completeness
of your power,
and you rebuke any insolence among
those who know it.ᵇ
18 Although you are sovereign in
strength, you judge with
mildness,
and with great forbearance you
govern us;
for you have power to act whenever
you choose.

19 Through such works you have taught
your people
that the righteous must be kind,
and you have filled your children
with good hope,
because you give repentance for
sins.

20 For if you punished with such great
care and indulgenceᶜ
the enemies of your servantsᵈ and
those deserving of death,
granting them time and opportunity
to give up their wickedness,
21 with what strictness you have judged
your children,
to whose ancestors you gave oaths
and covenants full of good
promises!
22 So while chastening us you scourge
our enemies ten thousand times
more,
so that, when we judge, we may
meditate upon your goodness,
and when we are judged, we may
expect mercy.

23 Therefore those who lived
unrighteously, in a life of folly,
you tormented through their own
abominations.
24 For they went far astray on the paths
of error,
accepting as gods those animals that
even their enemiesᵉ despised;
they were deceived like foolish
infants.
25 Therefore, as though to children who
cannot reason,
you sent your judgment to mock
them.
26 But those who have not heeded the
warning of mild rebukes
will experience the deserved judgment
of God.
27 For when in their suffering they
became incensed

a Or *all things*   b Meaning of Gk uncertain
c Other ancient authorities lack *and indulgence*; others
read *and entreaty*   d Or *children*   e Gk *they*

power and *forbearance* shares themes used to describe the ideal ruler in philosophical treatises on kingship
(see 6.1–25n.). **17**: *You rebuke any insolence,* see Ps 119.21; Isa 13.11; Jer 48.28–33; Sir 35.22–26; Bar
4.34; 3 Macc 2.3,21. **19–22**: Divine judgment is a model of *goodness* and *mercy* for God's children.
**20–21**: If repentance is available to the wicked, it is all the more available to the heirs of God's *promises.*
**23–27**: Condemnation of animal worshipers (see 11.15–16; 13.14; 15.18–19); divine judgment forces
them to recognize *the true God.* On their refusal *to know* God, see 2.13n. **25**: *To mock them,* cf. Ex 10.2;
Isa 66.4.

at those creatures that they had
    thought to be gods, being
    punished by means of them,
they saw and recognized as the true
    God the one whom they had
    before refused to know.
Therefore the utmost condemnation
    came upon them.

**13** For all people who were ignorant
    of God were foolish by nature;
and they were unable from the good
    things that are seen to know
    the one who exists,
nor did they recognize the artisan
    while paying heed to his
    works;
2 but they supposed that either fire or
    wind or swift air,
or the circle of the stars, or turbulent
    water,
or the luminaries of heaven were the
    gods that rule the world.
3 If through delight in the beauty of
    these things people assumed
    them to be gods,
let them know how much better than
    these is their Lord,
for the author of beauty created
    them.
4 And if people[a] were amazed at their
    power and working,
let them perceive from them
how much more powerful is the one
    who formed them.
5 For from the greatness and beauty of
    created things
comes a corresponding perception of
    their Creator.

6 Yet these people are little to be
    blamed,
for perhaps they go astray
while seeking God and desiring to
    find him.
7 For while they live among his works,
    they keep searching,
and they trust in what they see,
    because the things that are seen
    are beautiful.
8 Yet again, not even they are to be
    excused;
9 for if they had the power to know so
    much
that they could investigate the world,
how did they fail to find sooner the
    Lord of these things?

10 But miserable, with their hopes set on
    dead things, are those
who give the name "gods" to the
    works of human hands,
gold and silver fashioned with skill,
and likenesses of animals,
or a useless stone, the work of an
    ancient hand.
11 A skilled woodcutter may saw down
    a tree easy to handle
and skillfully strip off all its bark,
and then with pleasing workmanship
make a useful vessel that serves life's
    needs,
12 and burn the cast-off pieces of his
    work
to prepare his food, and eat his fill.
13 But a cast-off piece from among
    them, useful for nothing,

a Gk *they*

**13.1–15.19: The folly of false worship.** The author attacks, with increasing vehemence, the worship of nature, idols, and animals. **13.1–9: Critique of nature worship.** While the search for God in *good things that are seen* is understandable (vv. 6–7), it fails to find the *Creator* (v. 5) and *Lord* (v. 9); cf. Rom 1.18–23; Philo, *The Decalogue 52–55.* **2:** *Gods that rule the world,* such "astral piety" was common in antiquity (cf. 2 Kings 17.16; 23.4; Job 31.26–28; Gal 4.3,8–9; Col 2.8; Cicero, *The Nature of the Gods 2.15*). **6:** *Seeking God,* cf. Philo, *On Abraham 124–30;* Acts 17.26–27. **9:** In Hellenistic speculation, *world* (Gk, "aion") could represent a mystical concept, the personification of a kind of world-soul, as in Plato's *Timaeus 37D.* **13.10–14.11: Polemic against idolatry.** Cf. Ps 115.3–8; 135.15–18; Isa 40.18–20; 44.9–20; Jer 10.1–16; Letter of Jeremiah. **13.10–16:** A sarcastic description of how idol "gods" are created from discarded wood (see 15.7–19). **13:** *In the likeness of a human being,* cf. 14.19; Deut 4.16. **13.17–14.2:**

a stick crooked and full of knots,
he takes and carves with care in his
leisure,
and shapes it with skill gained in
idleness;[a]
he forms it in the likeness of a human
being,

14 or makes it like some worthless
animal,
giving it a coat of red paint and
coloring its surface red
and covering every blemish in it with
paint;

15 then he makes a suitable niche
for it,
and sets it in the wall, and fastens
it there with iron.

16 He takes thought for it, so that it
may not fall,
because he knows that it cannot help
itself,
for it is only an image and has need
of help.

17 When he prays about possessions and
his marriage and children,
he is not ashamed to address a lifeless
thing.

18 For health he appeals to a thing that
is weak;
for life he prays to a thing that is
dead;
for aid he entreats a thing that is
utterly inexperienced;
for a prosperous journey, a thing that
cannot take a step;

19 for money-making and work and
success with his hands
he asks strength of a thing whose
hands have no strength.

14 Again, one preparing to sail and
about to voyage over raging
waves

calls upon a piece of wood more
fragile than the ship that
carries him.

2 For it was desire for gain that
planned that vessel,
and wisdom was the artisan who built
it;

3 but it is your providence, O Father,
that steers its course,
because you have given it a path in
the sea,
and a safe way through the waves,

4 showing that you can save from every
danger,
so that even a person who lacks skill
may put to sea.

5 It is your will that works of your
wisdom should not be without
effect;
therefore people trust their lives even
to the smallest piece of wood,
and passing through the billows on a
raft they come safely to land.

6 For even in the beginning, when
arrogant giants were perishing,
the hope of the world took refuge on
a raft,
and guided by your hand left to the
world the seed of a new
generation.

7 For blessed is the wood by which
righteousness comes.

8 But the idol made with hands is
accursed, and so is the one
who made it—
he for having made it, and the
perishable thing because it was
named a god.

9 For equally hateful to God are the
ungodly and their ungodliness;

a Other ancient authorities read *with intelligent skill*

The ironically ineffective prayer of the idolater contrasts with that of Solomon in 9.1–18. **14.3–11:** Safety and salvation come from God, not idols. **3:** *Providence*, see 17.2; 4 Macc 9.24n. O *Father*, compare Isa 63.16; Tob 13.4; Sir 23.1; 3 Macc 6.3; Mt 6.9; Mk 14.36; Rom 8.14–15; Gal 4.6. **6:** *Arrogant giants*, see Gen 6.1–4 (cf. Sir 16.7; Bar 3.26–28; 3 Macc 2.4). *A raft*, Noah's ark (Gen 6.5–9.29). **8–11:** The author's premise is that one takes on the status of what one worships; in this case both idols and idolaters are *accursed* by God. **11:** *Visitation*, the occasion of God's judgment; see 3.7; Sir 16.18; Lk 19.44.

10 for what was done will be punished
together with the one who did
it.
11 Therefore there will be a visitation
also upon the heathen idols,
because, though part of what God
created, they became an
abomination,
snares for human souls
and a trap for the feet of the
foolish.

12 For the idea of making idols was the
beginning of fornication,
and the invention of them was the
corruption of life;
13 for they did not exist from the
beginning,
nor will they last forever.
14 For through human vanity they
entered the world,
and therefore their speedy end has
been planned.

15 For a father, consumed with grief at
an untimely bereavement,
made an image of his child, who had
been suddenly taken from him;
he now honored as a god what was
once a dead human being,
and handed on to his dependents
secret rites and initiations.
16 Then the ungodly custom, grown
strong with time, was kept as a
law,
and at the command of monarchs
carved images were worshiped.
17 When people could not honor
monarchs[a] in their presence,
since they lived at a distance,
they imagined their appearance far
away,

and made a visible image of the king
whom they honored,
so that by their zeal they might flatter
the absent one as though
present.

18 Then the ambition of the artisan
impelled
even those who did not know the
king to intensify their worship.
19 For he, perhaps wishing to please his
ruler,
skillfully forced the likeness to take
more beautiful form,
20 and the multitude, attracted by the
charm of his work,
now regarded as an object of worship
the one whom shortly before
they had honored as a human
being.
21 And this became a hidden trap for
humankind,
because people, in bondage to
misfortune or to royal
authority,
bestowed on objects of stone or wood
the name that ought not to be
shared.

22 Then it was not enough for them to
err about the knowledge of
God,
but though living in great strife due to
ignorance,
they call such great evils peace.
23 For whether they kill children in their
initiations, or celebrate secret
mysteries,
or hold frenzied revels with strange
customs,

a Gk them

Abomination, a common term for idolatry (see 12.23; 2 Chr 34.33; Ezra 9.1,11,14; Jer 2.7–8; Ezek 8.6–17; 18.12–13; Mal 2.11; 1 Macc 1.43–49).

14.12–21: Idols are the invention of human vanity. Because they are a corruption of God's plan, they will be destroyed. 12: Fornication, the prophets sometimes spoke of idolatry metaphorically as sexual collusion (Jer 3.1–3; Ezek 16.28–41; Hos 2.2–15). 17–20: The Greek writer Euhemerus (ca. 300 BCE) argued that the gods were nothing more than human kings who became deified after death.

14.22–31: The repercussions of idolatry include strife, murder, adultery, and perjury. 23: Cf. 11.7; 12.4–5. 25: Similar crimes are enumerated in Jer 7.9; Hos 4.2; Rom 1.29–31. 27: Cf. 14.12. 29: They

24 they no longer keep either their lives
        or their marriages pure,
    but they either treacherously kill one
        another, or grieve one another
        by adultery,
25 and all is a raging riot of blood and
        murder, theft and deceit,
        corruption, faithlessness,
        tumult, perjury,
26 confusion over what is good,
        forgetfulness of favors,
    defiling of souls, sexual perversion,
    disorder in marriages, adultery, and
        debauchery.
27 For the worship of idols not to be
        named
    is the beginning and cause and end of
        every evil.
28 For their worshipers[a] either rave in
        exultation,
    or prophesy lies, or live unrighteously,
        or readily commit perjury;
29 for because they trust in lifeless idols
    they swear wicked oaths and expect
        to suffer no harm.
30 But just penalties will overtake them
        on two counts:
    because they thought wrongly about
        God in devoting themselves to
        idols,
    and because in deceit they swore
        unrighteously through
        contempt for holiness.
31 For it is not the power of the things
        by which people swear,[b]
    but the just penalty for those who sin,
    that always pursues the transgression
        of the unrighteous.

15 But you, our God, are kind and
        true,
    patient, and ruling all things[c] in
        mercy.

2 For even if we sin we are yours,
        knowing your power;
    but we will not sin, because we know
        that you acknowledge us as
        yours.
3 For to know you is complete
        righteousness,
    and to know your power is the root
        of immortality.
4 For neither has the evil intent of
        human art misled us,
    nor the fruitless toil of painters,
    a figure stained with varied colors,
5 whose appearance arouses yearning in
        fools,
    so that they desire[d] the lifeless form
        of a dead image.
6 Lovers of evil things and fit for such
        objects of hope[e]
    are those who either make or desire
        or worship them.

7 A potter kneads the soft earth
    and laboriously molds each vessel for
        our service,
    fashioning out of the same clay
    both the vessels that serve clean
        uses
    and those for contrary uses, making
        all alike;
    but which shall be the use of each of
        them
    the worker in clay decides.
8 With misspent toil, these workers
        form a futile god from the
        same clay—
    these mortals who were made of earth
        a short time before

a Gk they    b Or of the oaths people swear
c Or ruling the universe    d Gk and he desires
e Gk such hopes

swear wicked oaths, for the seriousness with which false oaths were regarded, see Hos 10.4; Sir 23.11; 41.19; 1 Macc 7.18; 1 Esd 1.48.
**15.1–6: The benefits of true worship** include *righteousness* and *immortality*. **1–2:** Allusion to Ex 34.6–9 makes it clear that the author associates authentic worship with the Sinai covenant. **5–6:** *Desire*, cf. 4.12; 6.11,13,17,20; 8.2; 13.6; 15.19.
**15.7–19: The fabrication of idols** (cf. 13.10–16). Such work is both *futile* and sinful. **7:** Cf. Jer 18.4; Sir 33.13. **8:** That *souls are borrowed* was a philosophical conception (cf. 15.16). **11:** *A living spirit*, see

and after a little while go to the earth
  from which all mortals are
  taken,
when the time comes to return the
  souls that were borrowed.
9 But the workers are not concerned
  that mortals are destined to die
or that their life is brief,
but they compete with workers in
  gold and silver,
and imitate workers in copper;
and they count it a glorious thing to
  mold counterfeit gods.
10 Their heart is ashes, their hope is
  cheaper than dirt,
and their lives are of less worth than
  clay,
11 because they failed to know the one
  who formed them
and inspired them with active souls
and breathed a living spirit into them.
12 But they considered our existence an
  idle game,
and life a festival held for profit,
for they say one must get money
  however one can, even by base
  means.
13 For these persons, more than all
  others, know that they sin
when they make from earthy matter
  fragile vessels and carved
  images.
14 But most foolish, and more miserable
  than an infant,
are all the enemies who oppressed
  your people.
15 For they thought that all their
  heathen idols were gods,
though these have neither the use of
  their eyes to see with,

nor nostrils with which to draw
  breath,
nor ears with which to hear,
nor fingers to feel with,
and their feet are of no use for
  walking.
16 For a human being made them,
and one whose spirit is borrowed
  formed them;
for none can form gods that are like
  themselves.
17 People are mortal, and what they
  make with lawless hands is
  dead;
for they are better than the objects
  they worship,
since*a* they have life, but the idols*b*
  never had.

18 Moreover, they worship even the
  most hateful animals,
which are worse than all others when
  judged by their lack of
  intelligence;
19 and even as animals they are not so
  beautiful in appearance that
  one would desire them,
but they have escaped both the praise
  of God and his blessing.

16 Therefore those people*c* were
  deservedly punished through
  such creatures,
and were tormented by a multitude of
  animals.
2 Instead of this punishment you
  showed kindness to your
  people,
and you prepared quails to eat,

*a* Other ancient authorities read *of which*    *b* Gk *but
they*    *c* Gk *they*

12.1n. **12**: The image of *life* as a *game* or *festival* was common in ancient literature, e.g., Isa 22.12–13;
Mt 11.16–17; Epictetus, *Discourses* 2.14.23–29. **14**: *Most foolish* are the Egyptians who *oppressed* the
Israelites. **18–19**: Egyptian animal worship was denounced by Romans as well as Jews, e.g., Juvenal,
*Satire* 15.1–11; cf. Philo, *The Decalogue* 76–80. **19**: *They have escaped . . . blessing*, referring perhaps
to Gen 3.14–15 (cf. Wis 11.15; 16.5,10).
  **16.1–4: The second contrast**: the plague of small animals and the sending of the quail (Ex 8.1–15; Num
11). **1**: The author returns to the series of contrasts with a summarizing statement that gives justification
for God's actions against the Egyptians: They deserved to be *punished* through the very *creatures* they
worshiped. **4**: *It was . . . shown*, throughout the section the author assumes that both the Israelites and

a delicacy to satisfy the desire of
appetite;

3 in order that those people, when they
desired food,
might lose the least remnant of
appetite[a]
because of the odious creatures sent
to them,
while your people,[b] after suffering
want a short time,
might partake of delicacies.

4 For it was necessary that upon those
oppressors inescapable want
should come,
while to these others it was merely
shown how their enemies were
being tormented.

5 For when the terrible rage of wild
animals came upon your
people[c]
and they were being destroyed by the
bites of writhing serpents,
your wrath did not continue to the
end;

6 they were troubled for a little while as
a warning,
and received a symbol of deliverance
to remind them of your law's
command.

7 For the one who turned toward it was
saved, not by the thing that
was beheld,
but by you, the Savior of all.

8 And by this also you convinced our
enemies
that it is you who deliver from every
evil.

9 For they were killed by the bites of
locusts and flies,

and no healing was found for them,
because they deserved to be punished
by such things.

10 But your children were not conquered
even by the fangs of venomous
serpents,
for your mercy came to their help and
healed them.

11 To remind them of your oracles they
were bitten,
and then were quickly delivered,
so that they would not fall into deep
forgetfulness
and become unresponsive[d] to your
kindness.

12 For neither herb nor poultice cured
them,
but it was your word, O Lord, that
heals all people.

13 For you have power over life and
death;
you lead mortals down to the gates of
Hades and back again.

14 A person in wickedness kills another,
but cannot bring back the departed
spirit,
or set free the imprisoned soul.

15 To escape from your hand is
impossible;

16 for the ungodly, refusing to know
you,
were flogged by the strength of your
arm,
pursued by unusual rains and hail and
relentless storms,
and utterly consumed by fire.

a Gk *loathed the necessary appetite*   b Gk *they*
c Gk *them*   d Meaning of Gk uncertain

the Egyptians know what happens to the other side (cf. 11.13–14; 16.8,22; 18.1).
   **16.5–14: The third contrast:** the plague of insects and the bronze serpent (Ex 8.20–32; 10.1–20; Num
21.6–9). The *bites* are a warning to the Israelites but death to the Egyptians. **6–7:** *Symbol of deliverance,*
cf. 2 Kings 18.4; Philo, *Allegorical Interpretation* 2.79–81. **11:** *To remind them,* see 12.2; cf. Deut
7.17–19; 8.2; 9.7. **13:** *Down to . . . Hades and back again,* see 1.14n.; 2.1; 17.14; Sir 48.5; 2 Esd 4.7;
Song of Thr 1.66.
   **16.15–29: The fourth contrast:** the plague of storms and the rain of manna (Ex 9.13–26; 16.1–36).
God destroys the Egyptians' *crops* while giving the Israelites miraculous sustenance. **15:** *To escape from
your hand,* cf. 1.8; Tob 13.2; 2 Macc 7.31. **17:** *Water . . . fire,* referring to the hail and lightning of Ex

17 For—most incredible of all—in water,
    which quenches all things,
the fire had still greater effect,
for the universe defends the righteous.
18 At one time the flame was restrained,
    so that it might not consume the
    creatures sent against the
    ungodly,
but that seeing this they might know
that they were being pursued by the
    judgment of God;
19 and at another time even in the midst
    of water it burned more
    intensely than fire,
to destroy the crops of the
    unrighteous land.
20 Instead of these things you gave your
    people food of angels,
and without their toil you supplied
    them from heaven with bread
    ready to eat,
providing every pleasure and suited to
    every taste.
21 For your sustenance manifested your
    sweetness toward your
    children;
and the bread, ministering[a] to the
    desire of the one who took it,
was changed to suit everyone's liking.
22 Snow and ice withstood fire without
    melting,
so that they might know that the
    crops of their enemies
were being destroyed by the fire that
    blazed in the hail
and flashed in the showers of rain;
23 whereas the fire,[b] in order that the
    righteous might be fed,
even forgot its native power.

24 For creation, serving you who made
    it,
exerts itself to punish the unrighteous,
and in kindness relaxes on behalf of
    those who trust in you.
25 Therefore at that time also, changed
    into all forms,
it served your all-nourishing bounty,
according to the desire of those who
    had need,[c]
26 so that your children, whom you
    loved, O Lord, might learn
that it is not the production of crops
    that feeds humankind
but that your word sustains those
    who trust in you.
27 For what was not destroyed by
    fire
was melted when simply warmed
    by a fleeting ray of the sun,
28 to make it known that one must rise
    before the sun to give you
    thanks,
and must pray to you at the dawning
    of the light;
29 for the hope of an ungrateful person
    will melt like wintry frost,
and flow away like waste water.

17 Great are your judgments and
    hard to describe;
therefore uninstructed souls have gone
    astray.
2 For when lawless people supposed
    that they held the holy nation
    in their power,

a Gk and it, ministering    b Gk this    c Or who
made supplication

---

9.23–24. **18:** *So that it might not consume,* cf. 19.21. *The creatures,* the animals and insects of 16.1–14;
apparently the author assumes that the plagues occurred at one time. **20:** *Food of angels,* cf. Ps 78.24–25.
**21:** *Changed to suit everyone's liking,* a tradition also reflected in 6 *Yoma* 75a and *Mekilta* on Ex 16.23.
**24:** *Creation,* since it was fashioned in accordance with wisdom, inherently assists providence, functioning
as an instrument of both condemnation and blessing; see 8.4–6n.; 19.18–21n. (cf. Josh 10.11–14; Judg
5.20–21). **26:** Cf. Deut 8.3. **28:** *Rise before the sun,* cf. Ps 119.147; Sir 39.5. **29:** *Hope . . . will melt,*
cf. 5.14; Job 14.19.

    **17.1–18.4: The fifth contrast:** the plague of darkness and the pillar of fire (Ex 10.21–28; 13.21–22;
14.24–25). This passage, the longest of the contrasts, is notable for its unusual, poetic language and its
psychologically informed exposition of torment. **17.2–21:** The description of the Egyptians' *terror* is
reminiscent of the "descent into Hades" genre, of which Book 6 of Virgil's *Aeneid* was a popular

they themselves lay as captives of
    darkness and prisoners of long
    night,
shut in under their roofs, exiles from
    eternal providence.
3 For thinking that in their secret sins
    they were unobserved
behind a dark curtain of forgetfulness,
they were scattered, terribly<sup>a</sup>
    alarmed,
and appalled by specters.
4 For not even the inner chamber that
    held them protected them from
    fear,
but terrifying sounds rang out around
    them,
and dismal phantoms with gloomy
    faces appeared.
5 And no power of fire was able to give
    light,
nor did the brilliant flames of the
    stars
avail to illumine that hateful night.
6 Nothing was shining through to
    them
except a dreadful, self-kindled fire,
and in terror they deemed the things
    that they saw
to be worse than that unseen
    appearance.
7 The delusions of their magic art lay
    humbled,
and their boasted wisdom was
    scornfully rebuked.
8 For those who promised to drive off
    the fears and disorders of a
    sick soul
were sick themselves with ridiculous
    fear.
9 For even if nothing disturbing
    frightened them,
yet, scared by the passing of wild
    animals and the hissing of
    snakes
10 they perished in trembling fear,

refusing to look even at the air,
    though it nowhere could be
    avoided.
11 For wickedness is a cowardly thing,
    condemned by its own
    testimony;<sup>b</sup>
distressed by conscience, it has always
    exaggerated<sup>c</sup> the difficulties.
12 For fear is nothing but a giving up of
    the helps that come from
    reason;
13 and hope, defeated by this inward
    weakness,
prefers ignorance of what causes the
    torment.
14 But throughout the night, which was
    really powerless
and which came upon them from the
    recesses of powerless Hades,
they all slept the same sleep,
15 and now were driven by monstrous
    specters,
and now were paralyzed by their
    souls' surrender;
for sudden and unexpected fear
    overwhelmed them.
16 And whoever was there fell down,
and thus was kept shut up in a prison
    not made of iron;
17 for whether they were farmers or
    shepherds
or workers who toiled in the
    wilderness,
they were seized, and endured the
    inescapable fate;
for with one chain of darkness they
    all were bound.
18 Whether there came a whistling wind,
or a melodious sound of birds in
    wide-spreading branches,

---

a Other ancient authorities read *unobserved, they were
darkened behind a dark curtain of forgetfulness,
terribly*   b Meaning of Gk uncertain   c Other
ancient authorities read *anticipated*

example. **3**: *A dark curtain of forgetfulness*, those who thought their sins were hidden are themselves
concealed in darkness (cf. 16.11). **7**: See Ex 7.11,22; 8.7,18; 9.11. **11**: *Conscience*, a common topic in
moral literature (e.g., 1 Tim 4.2; Titus 1.15; T. Reuben 4.3; Philo, *The Worse Attacks the Better* 22–26).
**14**: *Powerless Hades*, see 1.14n.; cf. Ps 88.10–12; Eccl 9.10; Isa 14.9–11. *Sleep*, the divine penalty
includes nightmares (cf. 18.17–19; Job 7.14; Dan 4.5; Sir 40.5–7). **18–19**: They experience *terror* even

or the rhythm of violently rushing
water,

19 or the harsh crash of rocks hurled
down,
or the unseen running of leaping
animals,
or the sound of the most savage
roaring beasts,
or an echo thrown back from a
hollow of the mountains,
it paralyzed them with terror.

20 For the whole world was illumined
with brilliant light,
and went about its work unhindered,

21 while over those people alone heavy
night was spread,
an image of the darkness that was
destined to receive them;
but still heavier than darkness were
they to themselves.

18 But for your holy ones there was
very great light.
Their enemies[a] heard their voices but
did not see their forms,
and counted them happy for not
having suffered,

2 and were thankful that your holy
ones,[b] though previously
wronged, were doing them no
injury;
and they begged their pardon for
having been at variance with
them.[b]

3 Therefore you provided a flaming
pillar of fire
as a guide for your people's[c]
unknown journey,
and a harmless sun for their glorious
wandering.

4 For their enemies[d] deserved to be
deprived of light and
imprisoned in darkness,
those who had kept your children
imprisoned,
through whom the imperishable light
of the law was to be given to
the world.

5 When they had resolved to kill the
infants of your holy ones,
and one child had been abandoned
and rescued,
you in punishment took away a
multitude of their children;
and you destroyed them all together
by a mighty flood.

6 That night was made known
beforehand to our ancestors,
so that they might rejoice in sure
knowledge of the oaths in
which they trusted.

7 The deliverance of the righteous and
the destruction of their enemies
were expected by your people.

8 For by the same means by which you
punished our enemies
you called us to yourself and glorified
us.

9 For in secret the holy children of
good people offered sacrifices,
and with one accord agreed to the
divine law,
so that the saints would share alike
the same things,
both blessings and dangers;
and already they were singing the
praises of the ancestors.[e]

10 But the discordant cry of their
enemies echoed back,

a Gk *They*   b Meaning of Gk uncertain
c Gk *their*   d Gk *those persons*   e Other ancient
authorities read *dangers, the ancestors already leading
the songs of praise*

at ordinary sounds (cf. 17.4; Lev 26.36–37; Job 15.20–21). **18.2:** This verse, the meaning of which is
unclear, may be referring to Ex 12.31–33. **3:** See Ex 13.21–22; 14.24. **4:** *The law was to be given to the
world,* cf. Isa 2.2–3; 42.6; 49.6; 2 Esd 7.20–24; 14.20–22.
   **18.5–25:** The sixth contrast: death of the Egyptian firstborn and Israel's rescue (Ex 11.1–12.32; Ps
105.23). Plotting to kill the Israelites' children, the Egyptians instead lose their own. **5:** *One child,* Moses
(Ex 1.15–2.10). **6–9:** A poetic description of the first Passover (Ex 12.1–28). **9:** *Already they were singing,*
cf. 2 Chr 30.21. **13:** *God's child,* cf. 5.5; Ex 4.22–23; Jer 31.9; Hos 11.1. **15:** *A stern warrior,*

and their piteous lament for their
children was spread abroad.
11 The slave was punished with the same
penalty as the master,
and the commoner suffered the same
loss as the king;
12 and they all together, by the one
form*a* of death,
had corpses too many to count.
For the living were not sufficient even
to bury them,
since in one instant their most valued
children had been destroyed.
13 For though they had disbelieved
everything because of their
magic arts,
yet, when their firstborn were
destroyed, they acknowledged
your people to be God's child.
14 For while gentle silence enveloped all
things,
and night in its swift course was now
half gone,
15 your all-powerful word leaped from
heaven, from the royal throne,
into the midst of the land that was
doomed,
a stern warrior
16 carrying the sharp sword of your
authentic command,
and stood and filled all things with
death,
and touched heaven while standing on
the earth.
17 Then at once apparitions in dreadful
dreams greatly troubled them,
and unexpected fears assailed them;
18 and one here and another there,
hurled down half dead,
made known why they were dying;
19 for the dreams that disturbed them
forewarned them of this,
so that they might not perish without
knowing why they suffered.

20 The experience of death touched also
the righteous,
and a plague came upon the
multitude in the desert,
but the wrath did not long continue.
21 For a blameless man was quick to act
as their champion;
he brought forward the shield of his
ministry,
prayer and propitiation by incense;
he withstood the anger and put an
end to the disaster,
showing that he was your servant.
22 He conquered the wrath*b* not by
strength of body,
not by force of arms,
but by his word he subdued the
avenger,
appealing to the oaths and covenants
given to our ancestors.
23 For when the dead had already fallen
on one another in heaps,
he intervened and held back the
wrath,
and cut off its way to the living.
24 For on his long robe the whole world
was depicted,
and the glories of the ancestors were
engraved on the four rows of
stones,
and your majesty was on the diadem
upon his head.
25 To these the destroyer yielded, these
he*c* feared;
for merely to test the wrath was
enough.

19 But the ungodly were assailed to
the end by pitiless anger,
for God*d* knew in advance even their
future actions:

*a* Gk *name*   *b* Cn: Gk *multitude*   *c* Other ancient
authorities read *they*   *d* Gk *he*

cf. 5.17–20n. **17–19**: Cf. 17.14n. **20–25**: *A blameless man*, in Num 16.41–50, Aaron makes atonement
for the Israelites' rebellion against God by burning *incense*, ending *a plague* that killed 14,700 people. **22**:
*The avenger*, cf. Ps 99.8; 1 Thess 4.6. **24**: See Ex 28.15–38. On the symbolism of the high priest's
vestments, cf. Josephus, *Jewish Antiquities* 3.7.7.
   **19.1–21**: **The seventh contrast**: death and salvation at the Red Sea (Ex 14.1–31). **4**: *Made them forget*,

2 how, though they themselves had
    permitted[a] your people to
    depart
and hastily sent them out,
they would change their minds and
    pursue them.
3 For while they were still engaged in
    mourning,
and were lamenting at the graves of
    their dead,
they reached another foolish decision,
and pursued as fugitives those whom
    they had begged and compelled
    to leave.
4 For the fate they deserved drew them
    on to this end,
and made them forget what had
    happened,
in order that they might fill up the
    punishment that their torments
    still lacked,
5 and that your people might
    experience[b] an incredible
    journey,
but they themselves might meet a
    strange death.

6 For the whole creation in its nature
    was fashioned anew,
complying with your commands,
so that your children[c] might be kept
    unharmed.
7 The cloud was seen overshadowing
    the camp,
and dry land emerging where water
    had stood before,
an unhindered way out of the Red
    Sea,
and a grassy plain out of the raging
    waves,
8 where those protected by your hand
    passed through as one nation,
after gazing on marvelous wonders.
9 For they ranged like horses,
and leaped like lambs,
praising you, O Lord, who delivered
    them.

10 For they still recalled the events of
    their sojourn,
how instead of producing animals the
    earth brought forth gnats,
and instead of fish the river spewed
    out vast numbers of frogs.
11 Afterward they saw also a new kind[d]
    of birds,
when desire led them to ask for
    luxurious food;
12 for, to give them relief, quails came
    up from the sea.

13 The punishments did not come upon
    the sinners
without prior signs in the violence of
    thunder,
for they justly suffered because of
    their wicked acts;
for they practiced a more bitter
    hatred of strangers.
14 Others had refused to receive
    strangers when they came to
    them,
but these made slaves of guests who
    were their benefactors.
15 And not only so—but, while
    punishment of some sort will
    come upon the former
for having received strangers with
    hostility,
16 the latter, having first received them
    with festal celebrations,
afterward afflicted with terrible
    sufferings
those who had already shared the
    same rights.
17 They were stricken also with loss of
    sight—
just as were those at the door of the
    righteous man—
when, surrounded by yawning
    darkness,

*a* Other ancient authorities read *had changed their
minds to permit*    *b* Other ancient authorities read
*accomplish*    *c* Or *servants*    *d* Or *production*

cf. 4.1n.; 17.3n.; 5.14. *Fill up the punishment,* cf. Dan 8.23; 2 Macc 6.14. **6:** See 19.18–21n. **7:** *Cloud,*
Ex 13.21–22. **10:** Ex 8.1–19. **11–12:** See 16.1–4; cf. Num 11.31–32. **14:** *Others,* those of Sodom (Gen
19.1–11). *These,* the Egyptians. *Guests,* see Gen 45.16–20. **17:** Gen 19.11; Ex 14.20. **18–21:** In the

all of them tried to find the way
    through their own doors.

18 For the elements changed[a] places
    with one another,
as on a harp the notes vary the nature
    of the rhythm,
while each note remains the same.[b]
This may be clearly inferred from the
    sight of what took place.
19 For land animals were transformed
    into water creatures,
and creatures that swim moved over
    to the land.
20 Fire even in water retained its normal
    power,
and water forgot its fire-quenching
    nature.

21 Flames, on the contrary, failed to
    consume
the flesh of perishable creatures that
    walked among them,
nor did they melt[c] the crystalline,
    quick-melting kind of heavenly
    food.

22 For in everything, O Lord, you have
    exalted and glorified your
    people,
and you have not neglected to help
    them at all times and in all
    places.

a Gk *changing*    b Meaning of Gk uncertain
c Cn: Gk *nor could be melted*

plagues and at the Red Sea nature *changed* its customary actions so as to effect God's purpose (16.24; 19.6). That the material elements could be transformed in various ways was an assumption of ancient physics, e.g., Cicero, *The Nature of the Gods* 3.39.92.

**19.22:** **The concluding doxology** gives the point of the historical survey: God's unceasing *help* for Israel.

# Ecclesiasticus, or the Wisdom of Jesus, Son of SIRACH

The names by which this book is known reflect something of its origin and history. Sirach is the name of the author, Jesus son of Eleazar son of Sirach (50.27), in Hebrew, Yeshua ben El-azar ben Sira. Although the book was highly regarded in rabbinic literature and even cited in the Talmud, it did not achieve canonical status. The early Christian church, however, did consider it canonical. Although originally it was titled "The Wisdom of Jesus son of Sirach" in Greek and Old Latin manuscripts, many manuscripts of the Latin Vulgate referred to it as "Ecclesiasticus," that is, "the Church's book." The Protestant reformers, in keeping with their practice of conforming the Christian Old Testament to the books deemed canonical in the Hebrew scriptures, relegated it to the Apocrypha.

Because the book was not canonical in Judaism, the original Hebrew text was lost to the western world from about 400 to 1900; the book survived in Greek, Latin, Syriac, and other translations. Since about 1900 fragmentary copies of the Hebrew, dating from antiquity to the Middle Ages, have been discovered in various places: Qumran, Masada, and the Geniza (i.e., storage room) of a medieval Cairo synagogue. In this way two-thirds of the Hebrew text has been recovered. The translation here is one of a critically established text, using both Hebrew and other witnesses to the original. The reader will occasionally find a slightly different verse numbering from that in traditional renderings, since the NRSV follows the numbering of the critical text edited by J. Ziegler.

Ben Sira composed his work in Jerusalem sometime before 180 BCE (see his description in 50.1–24 of Simon II, high priest from 219–196). Thus he wrote before the persecution of the Jews by Antiochus IV Ephiphanes and the ensuing Maccabean revolt (168–164). Sometime after 132 (see the Prologue) his grandson translated the original Hebrew into Greek. The grandson rightly stresses Ben Sira's profound knowledge of Hebrew traditions (designated in the Prologue as "the Law and the Prophets and the other books"—already the three-fold division of the Hebrew Bible was in formation).

Like the book of Proverbs, Sirach stresses characteristic wisdom teachings: prudent speech, wealth and poverty, honesty, diligence, choice of friends, sin and death, retribution, and wisdom itself. Unlike Proverbs 10ff., individual proverbs are not set apart, but are incorporated into smooth-flowing poems of some length (often 22 lines in accordance with the number of letters of the Hebrew alphabet). The doctrine is surprisingly traditional, almost as if Job and Ecclesiastes had never been written. Ben Sira is not unaware of the problem of suffering (2.1–6; 11.14; 40.1–10), but he firmly believes in the justice of divine retribution. God will reward all according to their deserts (15.11–16.23). There is no intimation of a future life with God in the Hebrew text as one begins to find in some Jewish literature of the Hellenistic age (e.g., 2 Macc 7.9; Wis 5.15–16); rather, all go to Sheol, the traditional abode of the dead (14.12–19; 38.16–23). This is the usual view of the Hebrew Bible, where immortality is understood only in terms of one's progeny and good name (44.13–15).

The earlier biblical wisdom literature lacks reference to Israel's sacred history and covenantal traditions. Sirach, in contrast, reprises biblical history in the "Hymn in Honor of Our Ancestors" (chs

44–49), and clearly identifies the figure of Wisdom with the Torah or law (24.23). Unlike earlier wisdom writings, Sirach is immersed in the environment of Jerusalem Temple worship and sacrifice (35.1–12; 50.1–24). Nevertheless, the book belongs definitely to the genre of wisdom literature, with its stress on the lessons of experience and on the "fear of the Lord" (1.11–30; 25.10–11; 40.25–27).

Ben Sira describes his profession as a "scribe," or scholar of the sacred writings (39.1–11) and invites students to his school (51.23). The work's original addressees were young men preparing for leading adult roles in the Jewish community. This is evident in many aspects of the book, including its treatment of women. The vivid portrayal of Wisdom as a sublime woman, sometimes with erotic overtones (e.g., 14.20–27; 15.2; and especially the Hebrew version of 51.13–30), seems particularly designed to capture the imagination of Ben Sira's young male students. Ben Sira's teachings about actual women are androcentric at best, as in his advice concerning marriage (26.13–18; 36.26–31); at times he expresses an untempered misogyny (e.g., 42.13–14).

Sirach's teachings are not arranged in a logical sequence. Reading straight through the book from beginning to end, therefore, is not necessarily the best approach. Good places to start reading Sirach are the two pivotal poems on personified Wisdom (1.1–30; 24.1–34; each introduces a major collection of instructional material) and the hymn of praise to Israel's ancestors (44.1–49.16).

The book consists of three major blocks of teaching: 1.1–23.27; 24.1–42.14; and 42.15–50.24. In its current form these are preceded by the Prologue and followed by concluding comments and additions (50.25–51.30). Each of the first two collections begins with a poem in praise of Wisdom (1.1–30; 24.1–34); the third collection consists entirely of hymns of praise, of the creator (42.15–43.33), of Israel's ancestors (44.1–49.16), and of the high priest Simon (50.1–24).

## THE PROLOGUE

Many great teachings have been given to us through the Law and the Prophets and the others*a* that followed them, and for these we should praise Israel for instruction and wisdom. Now, those who read the scriptures must not only themselves understand them, but must also as lovers of learning be able through the spoken and written word to help the outsiders. So my grandfather Jesus, who had devoted himself especially to the reading of the Law and the Prophets and the other books of our ancestors, and had acquired considerable proficiency in them, was himself also led to write something pertaining to instruction and wisdom, so that by becoming familiar

also with his book*b* those who love learning might make even greater progress in living according to the law.

You are invited therefore to read it with goodwill and attention, and to be indulgent in cases where, despite our diligent labor in translating, we may seem to have rendered some phrases imperfectly. For what was originally expressed in Hebrew does not have exactly the same sense when translated into another language. Not only this book, but even the Law itself, the Prophecies, and the rest of the books differ not a little when read in the original.

When I came to Egypt in the thirty-eighth year of the reign of Euergetes and

*a* Or *other books*   *b* Gk *with these things*

**Prologue:** Ben Sira's translator (his grandson) explains his reasons for rendering the original Hebrew work into Greek. This prologue contains the earliest reference to a three-fold division of the Hebrew Bible: *the Law and the Prophets and the other books* (cf. Luke 24.44). *Jesus* is the Greek form of the author's Hebrew name, probably "Yeshua" (50.27). Arriving in Egypt in the *thirty-eighth year of* Ptolemy VII Physkon *Euergetes* II (132 BCE), the translator found a ready audience for his grandfather's teaching in the well-established Jewish community there and completed his translation probably sometime after Euergetes's death in 117 BCE.

stayed for some time, I found opportunity for no little instruction.[a] It seemed highly necessary that I should myself devote some diligence and labor to the translation of this book. During that time I have applied my skill day and night to complete and publish the book for those living abroad who wished to gain learning and are disposed to live according to the law.

1 All wisdom is from the Lord,
  and with him it remains forever.
2 The sand of the sea, the drops of rain,
  and the days of eternity—who can count them?
3 The height of heaven, the breadth of the earth,
  the abyss, and wisdom[b]—who can search them out?
4 Wisdom was created before all other things,
  and prudent understanding from eternity.[c]
6 The root of wisdom—to whom has it been revealed?
  Her subtleties—who knows them?[d]
8 There is but one who is wise, greatly to be feared,
  seated upon his throne—the Lord.
9 It is he who created her;
  he saw her and took her measure;
  he poured her out upon all his works,
10 upon all the living according to his gift;
  he lavished her upon those who love him.[e]
11 The fear of the Lord is glory and exultation,
  and gladness and a crown of rejoicing.
12 The fear of the Lord delights the heart,
  and gives gladness and joy and long life.[f]
13 Those who fear the Lord will have a happy end;
  on the day of their death they will be blessed.
14 To fear the Lord is the beginning of wisdom;
  she is created with the faithful in the womb.
15 She made[g] among human beings an eternal foundation,
  and among their descendants she will abide faithfully.
16 To fear the Lord is fullness of wisdom;

a Other ancient authorities read I found a copy affording no little instruction   b Other ancient authorities read the depth of the abyss   c Other ancient authorities add as verse 5, The source of wisdom is God's word in the highest heaven, and her ways are the eternal commandments.   d Other ancient authorities add as verse 7, The knowledge of wisdom—to whom was it manifested? And her abundant experience—who has understood it?   e Other ancient authorities add Love of the Lord is glorious wisdom; to those to whom he appears he apportions her, that they may see him.   f Other ancient authorities add The fear of the Lord is a gift from the Lord; also for love he makes firm paths.   g Gk made as a nest

**1.1–10: Wisdom, God's unfathomable gift** (cf. 24.1–12; Job 28; Prov 8.22–31). Wisdom is personified as a feminine figure, created by God and graciously bestowed upon humanity. **1:** *From the Lord*, a divine origin (24.3; Prov 2.6; 8.22–23; Job 12.13; Wis 7.25–26). **2–3:** Divine Wisdom is as incalculable as the limits of the cosmos (cf. 18.4–7). **4:** *Created before all other things*, Prov 8.22–31. **6–10:** Wisdom belongs to God alone (Job 28); yet God has *lavished her* upon *all the living*, i.e., both Jews and Gentiles, and particularly upon *those who love him*: Israel (1.26; 24.7–12).

**1.11–30: Wisdom as fear of the Lord.** A programmatic statement of Sirach's central theme: the inseparability of wisdom and piety. **12:** *Long life* (Deut 6.2), a frequent wisdom topic (cf. v. 20; Prov 3.16). **13:** *On the day of their death*, no afterlife is envisioned here, simply the *blessed* state of a pious life at its end (cf. 11.26–28). **14:** *The beginning of wisdom*, cf. Prov 1.7; 9.10; Job 28.28; Ps 111.10. *With the faithful in the womb*, a prophetic motif (49.7; Jer 1.5; Isa 44.2,24; 49.1,5; see also Ps 139.13). **15:** *Among human beings*, cf. 24.8–12; Prov 8.31. **20:** Wisdom as a flourishing tree of life (24.13–14,16–17; Prov 3.18). **22:**

she inebriates mortals with her
fruits;

17 she fills their*a* whole house with
desirable goods,
and their*a* storehouses with her
produce.

18 The fear of the Lord is the crown of
wisdom,
making peace and perfect health to
flourish.*b*

19 She rained down knowledge and
discerning comprehension,
and she heightened the glory of
those who held her fast.

20 To fear the Lord is the root of
wisdom,
and her branches are long life.*c*

22 Unjust anger cannot be justified,
for anger tips the scale to one's
ruin.

23 Those who are patient stay calm until
the right moment,
and then cheerfulness comes back
to them.

24 They hold back their words until the
right moment;
then the lips of many tell of their
good sense.

25 In the treasuries of wisdom are wise
sayings,
but godliness is an abomination to
a sinner.

26 If you desire wisdom, keep the
commandments,
and the Lord will lavish her upon
you.

27 For the fear of the Lord is wisdom
and discipline,
fidelity and humility are his delight.

28 Do not disobey the fear of the Lord;

do not approach him with a
divided mind.

29 Do not be a hypocrite before others,
and keep watch over your lips.

30 Do not exalt yourself, or you may fall
and bring dishonor upon yourself.
The Lord will reveal your secrets
and overthrow you before the
whole congregation,
because you did not come in the fear
of the Lord,
and your heart was full of deceit.

2 My child, when you come to serve
the Lord,
prepare yourself for testing.*d*

2 Set your heart right and be steadfast,
and do not be impetuous in time of
calamity.

3 Cling to him and do not depart,
so that your last days may be
prosperous.

4 Accept whatever befalls you,
and in times of humiliation be
patient.

5 For gold is tested in the fire,
and those found acceptable, in the
furnace of humiliation.*e*

6 Trust in him, and he will help you;
make your ways straight, and hope
in him.

7 You who fear the Lord, wait for his
mercy;
do not stray, or else you may fall.

*a* Other ancient authorities read *her*   *b* Other ancient
authorities add *Both are gifts of God for peace; glory
opens out for those who love him. He saw her and
took her measure.*   *c* Other ancient authorities add
as verse 21, *The fear of the Lord drives away sins; and
where it abides, it will turn away all anger.*
*d* Or *trials*   *e* Other ancient authorities add *in
sickness and poverty put your trust in him*

The danger of yielding to *anger* (27.30; 28.3–11; Prov 10.18; 12.16; 29.22). **26:** *Keep the commandments,* wisdom is equated with the law of Moses (24.23). **30:** *Dishonor,* an intense concern in Sirach
(3.2–11; 4.21; 7.7; 10.19–11.6; 41.17–42.8). *Congregation* (Gk "synagoge") refers chiefly to the community gathered in public assembly (4.7; 23.24; 41.18; cf. Prov 5.12–14).
 **2.1–18: Trust in God. 1:** *My child,* the sage's typical address to a student (Prov 1.8,10,15; 4.10).
*Testing by God is a common theme in Sirach and elsewhere in the Bible (4.17; 6.20–21; 44.20; Gen 22.1;
Ex 16.4; Judg 2.22; Job 7.18; Isa 48.10). **5:** *Tested in the fire,* cf. Prov 17.3; Wis 3.6. **9:** *Lasting joy* (cf. Isa

8 You who fear the Lord, trust in him,
  and your reward will not be lost.
9 You who fear the Lord, hope for
    good things,
  for lasting joy and mercy.*a*
10 Consider the generations of old and
    see:
  has anyone trusted in the Lord and
    been disappointed?
  Or has anyone persevered in the fear
    of the Lord*b* and been
    forsaken?
  Or has anyone called upon him and
    been neglected?
11 For the Lord is compassionate and
    merciful;
  he forgives sins and saves in time of
    distress.

12 Woe to timid hearts and to slack
    hands,
  and to the sinner who walks a
    double path!
13 Woe to the fainthearted who have no
    trust!
  Therefore they will have no shelter.
14 Woe to you who have lost your
    nerve!
  What will you do when the Lord's
    reckoning comes?

15 Those who fear the Lord do not
    disobey his words,
  and those who love him keep his
    ways.
16 Those who fear the Lord seek to
    please him,
  and those who love him are filled
    with his law.
17 Those who fear the Lord prepare
    their hearts,
  and humble themselves before him.
18 Let us fall into the hands of the Lord,

but not into the hands of mortals;
  for equal to his majesty is his mercy,
    and equal to his name are his
    works.*c*

3 Listen to me your father, O children;
  act accordingly, that you may be
    kept in safety.
2 For the Lord honors a father above
    his children,
  and he confirms a mother's right
    over her children.
3 Those who honor their father atone
    for sins,
4 and those who respect their mother
    are like those who lay up
    treasure.
5 Those who honor their father will
    have joy in their own children,
  and when they pray they will be
    heard.
6 Those who respect their father will
    have long life,
  and those who honor*d* their
    mother obey the Lord;
7 they will serve their parents as their
    masters.*e*
8 Honor your father by word and deed,
    that his blessing may come upon
    you.
9 For a father's blessing strengthens the
    houses of the children,
  but a mother's curse uproots their
    foundations.
10 Do not glorify yourself by
    dishonoring your father,

a Other ancient authorities add *For his reward is an
everlasting gift with joy.*   b Gk *of him*   c Syr: Gk
lacks this line   d Heb: Other ancient authorities read
*comfort*   e In other ancient authorities this line is
preceded by *Those who fear the Lord honor their
father,*

35.10; 51.11; 61.7) in this life, not in the next. **10–11:** Israel's history (chs 44–50) shows the efficacy of
trust in God, who is *compassionate and merciful* (Ex 34.6–7; Ps 103.8–9; Jon 4.2). **18:** 2 Sam 24.14;
1 Chr 21.13.
  **3.1–16: Honor of parents** (Ex 20.12; Lev 19.3; Deut 5.16). The father is head of household (7.23–26;
22.3–5; 26.1–27; 36.29), but respect for the mother is also emphasized here (vv. 2,4,6,9,11,16; cf. Prov
1.8; 4.3; 6.20). **3:** Like other observance of the law, keeping of the commandment to honor one's parents
(Ex 20.12) atones *for sins* (cf. vv.14–15). **14:** *Kindness,* literally "righteousness," understood as atoning

for your father's dishonor is no
glory to you.
11 The glory of one's father is one's own
glory,
and it is a disgrace for children not
to respect their mother.

12 My child, help your father in his old
age,
and do not grieve him as long as he
lives;
13 even if his mind fails, be patient with
him;
because you have all your faculties
do not despise him.
14 For kindness to a father will not be
forgotten,
and will be credited to you against
your sins;
15 in the day of your distress it will be
remembered in your favor;
like frost in fair weather, your sins
will melt away.
16 Whoever forsakes a father is like a
blasphemer,
and whoever angers a mother is
cursed by the Lord.

17 My child, perform your tasks with
humility;*a*
then you will be loved by those
whom God accepts.
18 The greater you are, the more you
must humble yourself;
so you will find favor in the sight
of the Lord.*b*
20 For great is the might of the Lord;
but by the humble he is glorified.
21 Neither seek what is too difficult for
you,
nor investigate what is beyond your
power.

22 Reflect upon what you have been
commanded,
for what is hidden is not your
concern.
23 Do not meddle in matters that are
beyond you,
for more than you can understand
has been shown you.
24 For their conceit has led many astray,
and wrong opinion has impaired
their judgment.

25 Without eyes there is no light;
without knowledge there is no
wisdom.*c*
26 A stubborn mind will fare badly at
the end,
and whoever loves danger will
perish in it.
27 A stubborn mind will be burdened by
troubles,
and the sinner adds sin to sins.
28 When calamity befalls the proud,
there is no healing,
for an evil plant has taken root in
him.
29 The mind of the intelligent
appreciates proverbs,
and an attentive ear is the desire of
the wise.

30 As water extinguishes a blazing fire,
so almsgiving atones for sin.
31 Those who repay favors give thought
to the future;
when they fall they will find
support.

*a* Heb: Gk *meekness*    *b* Other ancient authorities
add as verse 19, *Many are lofty and renowned, but to
the humble he reveals his secrets.*    *c* Heb: Other
ancient authorities lack verse 25

acts of mercy, of which almsgiving was a chief example (3.30–4.10; 7.10,32; 29.8–13; Tob 14.10–11).
**3.17–24: Humility.** A frequent topic in wisdom instruction (7.16–17; 10.28; Prov 11.2; 15.33; 18.12;
22.4); this passage emphasizes intellectual humility (vv. 21–24). **21–24:** Ben Sira urges meditation on
*what you have been commanded,* Jewish law and tradition, rather than philosophical or mystical speculation. **21:** Cf. Ps 131; Eccl 7.24.
**3.25–29: Stubbornness.** A person of *stubborn mind* (literally "heavy heart," cf. Ex 7.14) will suffer
*calamity* (cf. Prov 28.14).
**3.30–4.10: Care for the poor.** A fundamental obligation (cf. Deut 15.7–11). **30:** *Almsgiving,* see 3.14n.

**4** My child, do not cheat the poor of
their living,
and do not keep needy eyes
waiting.
2 Do not grieve the hungry,
or anger one in need.
3 Do not add to the troubles of the
desperate,
or delay giving to the needy.
4 Do not reject a suppliant in distress,
or turn your face away from the
poor.
5 Do not avert your eye from the
needy,
and give no one reason to curse
you;
6 for if in bitterness of soul some
should curse you,
their Creator will hear their prayer.

7 Endear yourself to the congregation;
bow your head low to the great.
8 Give a hearing to the poor,
and return their greeting politely.
9 Rescue the oppressed from the
oppressor;
and do not be hesitant in giving a
verdict.
10 Be a father to orphans,
and be like a husband to their
mother;
you will then be like a son of the
Most High,
and he will love you more than
does your mother.

11 Wisdom teaches[a] her children
and gives help to those who seek
her.
12 Whoever loves her loves life,
and those who seek her from early
morning are filled with joy.

13 Whoever holds her fast inherits glory,
and the Lord blesses the place she[b]
enters.
14 Those who serve her minister to the
Holy One;
the Lord loves those who love her.
15 Those who obey her will judge the
nations,
and all who listen to her will live
secure.
16 If they remain faithful, they will
inherit her;
their descendants will also obtain
her.
17 For at first she will walk with them
on tortuous paths;
she will bring fear and dread upon
them,
and will torment them by her
discipline
until she trusts them,[c]
and she will test them with her
ordinances.
18 Then she will come straight back to
them again and gladden them,
and will reveal her secrets to them.
19 If they go astray she will forsake
them,
and hand them over to their ruin.

20 Watch for the opportune time, and
beware of evil,
and do not be ashamed to be
yourself.
21 For there is a shame that leads to sin,
and there is a shame that is glory
and favor.
22 Do not show partiality, to your own
harm,

a Heb Syr: Gk *exalts*   b Or *he*   c Or *until they
remain faithful in their heart*

4.1: Cf. 29.8. 4: Tob 4.7. 6: Ex 22.23; Deut 15.9. 9–10: Cf. 34.24–27. Orphans and widows were likely
to be poor and defenseless (Ex 22.21–23). For God as *father to orphans*, see Ps 68.5.
    4.11–19: Wisdom's rewards and trials. Personified Wisdom (1.9–10; 24.1–34) loves her followers, but
also tests them. 14: *Minister to the Holy One*, like priests at the altar in Temple worship, those who serve
Wisdom serve God, and God will love *those who love her* (Prov 8.17). 15: The wise *will judge the nations*,
cf. Prov 8.15–16; Wis 3.8. 17–18: Cf. 6.20–21; 44.20; Prov 3.11–12.
    4.20–31: On reticence, true and false. 21: On appropriate and inappropriate shame, see 20.22–23;
41.14–42.8. 23–24: Proper and timely speech is a major concern of wisdom literature (1.23; 20.7,20;

or deference, to your downfall.

23 Do not refrain from speaking at the
   proper moment,[a]
   and do not hide your wisdom.[b]
24 For wisdom becomes known through
   speech,
   and education through the words of
   the tongue.
25 Never speak against the truth,
   but be ashamed of your ignorance.
26 Do not be ashamed to confess your
   sins,
   and do not try to stop the current
   of a river.
27 Do not subject yourself to a fool,
   or show partiality to a ruler.
28 Fight to the death for truth,
   and the Lord God will fight for
   you.

29 Do not be reckless in your speech,
   or sluggish and remiss in your
   deeds.
30 Do not be like a lion in your home,
   or suspicious of your servants.
31 Do not let your hand be stretched out
   to receive
   and closed when it is time to give.

5 Do not rely on your wealth,
   or say, "I have enough."
2 Do not follow your inclination and
   strength
   in pursuing the desires of your
   heart.
3 Do not say, "Who can have power
   over me?"
   for the Lord will surely punish
   you.

4 Do not say, "I sinned, yet what has
   happened to me?"
   for the Lord is slow to anger.

5 Do not be so confident of
   forgiveness[c]
   that you add sin to sin.
6 Do not say, "His mercy is great,
   he will forgive[d] the multitude of
   my sins,"
   for both mercy and wrath are with
   him,
   and his anger will rest on sinners.
7 Do not delay to turn back to the
   Lord,
   and do not postpone it from day to
   day;
   for suddenly the wrath of the Lord
   will come upon you,
   and at the time of punishment you
   will perish.
8 Do not depend on dishonest wealth,
   for it will not benefit you on the
   day of calamity.

9 Do not winnow in every wind,
   or follow every path.[e]
10 Stand firm for what you know,
   and let your speech be consistent.
11 Be quick to hear,
   but deliberate in answering.
12 If you know what to say, answer your
   neighbor;
   but if not, put your hand over your
   mouth.

13 Honor and dishonor come from
   speaking,
   and the tongue of mortals may be
   their downfall.
14 Do not be called double-tongued[f]

a Heb: Gk *at a time of salvation*   b So some Gk Mss
and Heb Syr Lat: Other Gk Mss lack *and do not hide
your wisdom*   c Heb: Gk *atonement*   d Heb: Gk
*he (or it) will atone for*   e Gk adds *so it is with the
double-tongued sinner* (see 6.1)   f Heb: Gk *a
slanderer*

Prov 13.3; 25.11). **26:** It is as futile to hide one's sins from God as to try to stop a river from flowing.
**30:** *A lion,* wild, relentless, destructive. **31:** *Hand,* Deut 15.7–8; Prov 11.24–25.
   **5.1–8: Against presumption,** especially the ethical complacency that results from false reliance on
*wealth* (vv. 1,8). **4:** *Slow to anger,* Ex 34.6. **6:** The Lord is a God of both *mercy and wrath,* cf. 16.11–12.
   **5.9–6.4: Honesty and self-control. 5.9:** A condemnation of duplicity. **12:** *Hand . . . mouth,* to keep
silence (Job 21.5; Prov 30.32; Wis 8.12). **13:** The use and abuse of the *tongue* is a frequent topic (19.6–17;

and do not lay traps with your
  tongue;
for shame comes to the thief,
  and severe condemnation to the
    double-tongued.
15 In great and small matters cause no
  harm,[a]

6 ¹and do not become an enemy
    instead of a friend;
for a bad name incurs shame and
  reproach;
  so it is with the double-tongued
    sinner.

2 Do not fall into the grip of passion,[b]
  or you may be torn apart as by a
    bull.[c]
3 Your leaves will be devoured and
    your fruit destroyed,
  and you will be left like a withered
    tree.
4 Evil passion destroys those who have
    it,
  and makes them the laughingstock
    of their enemies.

5 Pleasant speech multiplies friends,
  and a gracious tongue multiplies
    courtesies.
6 Let those who are friendly with you
    be many,
  but let your advisers be one in a
    thousand.
7 When you gain friends, gain them
    through testing,
  and do not trust them hastily.
8 For there are friends who are such
    when it suits them,
  but they will not stand by you in
    time of trouble.
9 And there are friends who change
    into enemies,
  and tell of the quarrel to your
    disgrace.

10 And there are friends who sit at your
    table,
  but they will not stand by you in
    time of trouble.
11 When you are prosperous, they
    become your second self,
  and lord it over your servants;
12 but if you are brought low, they turn
    against you,
  and hide themselves from you.
13 Keep away from your enemies,
  and be on guard with your friends.

14 Faithful friends are a sturdy shelter:
  whoever finds one has found a
    treasure.
15 Faithful friends are beyond price;
  no amount can balance their worth.
16 Faithful friends are life-saving
    medicine;
  and those who fear the Lord will
    find them.
17 Those who fear the Lord direct their
    friendship aright,
  for as they are, so are their
    neighbors also.

18 My child, from your youth choose
    discipline,
  and when you have gray hair you
    will still find wisdom.
19 Come to her like one who plows and
    sows,
  and wait for her good harvest.
  For when you cultivate her you will
    toil but little,
  and soon you will eat of her
    produce.
20 She seems very harsh to the
    undisciplined;
  fools cannot remain with her.

a Heb Syr: Gk *be ignorant*   b Heb: Meaning of Gk
uncertain   c Meaning of Gk uncertain

20.16–20; 22.27–23.15; 28.12–26). **6.2–4:** Sexual misconduct appears to be the chief concern here
(cf. 18.30–19.3). **3:** Cf. Ps 1.3.

  **6.5–17:** True and false friendship (cf. 11.29–34; 12.8–12; 22.19–26; 37.1–6; Prov 27.5–6). Just as
Wisdom tests her followers (4.17; 6.21), friends are to be gained *through testing* (vv. 5–12). True friends
are a *treasure,* a gift from God (vv. 13–17).

  **6.18–37:** Wisdom's discipline. **18:** *My child,* see 2.1n. **22:** *Like her name,* there is a word play on

21 She will be like a heavy stone to test
    them,
  and they will not delay in casting
    her aside.
22 For wisdom is like her name;
  she is not readily perceived by
    many.

23 Listen, my child, and accept my
    judgment;
  do not reject my counsel.
24 Put your feet into her fetters,
  and your neck into her collar.
25 Bend your shoulders and carry her,
  and do not fret under her bonds.
26 Come to her with all your soul,
  and keep her ways with all your
    might.
27 Search out and seek, and she will
    become known to you;
  and when you get hold of her, do
    not let her go.
28 For at last you will find the rest she
    gives,
  and she will be changed into joy for
    you.
29 Then her fetters will become for you
    a strong defense,
  and her collar a glorious robe.
30 Her yoke*a* is a golden ornament,
  and her bonds a purple cord.
31 You will wear her like a glorious
    robe,
  and put her on like a splendid
    crown.*b*

32 If you are willing, my child, you can
    be disciplined,
  and if you apply yourself you will
    become clever.
33 If you love to listen you will gain
    knowledge,

and if you pay attention you will
    become wise.
34 Stand in the company of the elders.
  Who is wise? Attach yourself to
    such a one.
35 Be ready to listen to every godly
    discourse,
  and let no wise proverbs escape
    you.
36 If you see an intelligent person, rise
    early to visit him;
  let your foot wear out his doorstep.
37 Reflect on the statutes of the Lord,
  and meditate at all times on his
    commandments.
  It is he who will give insight to*c* your
    mind,
  and your desire for wisdom will be
    granted.

7 Do no evil, and evil will never
    overtake you.
2 Stay away from wrong, and it will
    turn away from you.
3 Do*d* not sow in the furrows of
    injustice,
  and you will not reap a sevenfold
    crop.

4 Do not seek from the Lord high
    office,
  or the seat of honor from the king.
5 Do not assert your righteousness
    before the Lord,
  or display your wisdom before the
    king.
6 Do not seek to become a judge,
  or you may be unable to root out
    injustice;

*a* Heb: Gk *Upon her*   *b* Heb: Gk *crown of gladness*
*c* Heb: Gk *will confirm*   *d* Gk *My child, do*

Hebrew "musar," *discipline* (v. 18), which can also suggest the meaning "withdrawn," hence *not readily perceived by many.* **26:** *All your soul, and . . . all your might,* cf. Deut 6.5. **30–31:** *Her yoke,* cf. 51.26. *Purple cord,* cf. Num 15.38–40. Although wisdom is often likened to an ornament (e.g., Prov 1.9; 3.22; 4.8–9), here the language evokes ritual garments like those of the high priest (50.11). **32–37:** The seeker of Wisdom should attend closely to the wise (vv. 32–36) and to the law (v. 37; cf. 15.1; 19.20; 23.27; 24.23; see also Josh 1.8; Ps 1.2).
  **7.1–17: Ethical conduct.** A sequence mostly composed as negative admonitions ("Do not . . ."; see Prov

you may be partial to the powerful,
and so mar your integrity.

7 Commit no offense against the public,
and do not disgrace yourself among
the people.

8 Do not commit a sin twice;
not even for one will you go
unpunished.

9 Do not say, "He will consider the
great number of my gifts,
and when I make an offering to the
Most High God, he will accept
it."

10 Do not grow weary when you pray;
do not neglect to give alms.

11 Do not ridicule a person who is
embittered in spirit,
for there is One who humbles and
exalts.

12 Do not devise[a] a lie against your
brother,
or do the same to a friend.

13 Refuse to utter any lie,
for it is a habit that results in no
good.

14 Do not babble in the assembly of the
elders,
and do not repeat yourself when
you pray.

15 Do not hate hard labor
or farm work, which was created
by the Most High.

16 Do not enroll in the ranks of sinners;
remember that retribution does not
delay.

17 Humble yourself to the utmost,
for the punishment of the ungodly
is fire and worms.[b]

18 Do not exchange a friend for money,

or a real brother for the gold of
Ophir.

19 Do not dismiss[c] a wise and good
wife,
for her charm is worth more than
gold.

20 Do not abuse slaves who work
faithfully,
or hired laborers who devote
themselves to their task.

21 Let your soul love intelligent slaves;[d]
do not withhold from them their
freedom.

22 Do you have cattle? Look after them;
if they are profitable to you, keep
them.

23 Do you have children? Discipline
them,
and make them obedient[e] from
their youth.

24 Do you have daughters? Be concerned
for their chastity,[f]
and do not show yourself too
indulgent with them.

25 Give a daughter in marriage, and you
complete a great task;
but give her to a sensible man.

26 Do you have a wife who pleases
you?[g] Do not divorce her;
but do not trust yourself to one
whom you detest.

27 With all your heart honor your
father,
and do not forget the birth pangs
of your mother.

a Heb: Gk plow   b Heb for the expectation of
mortals is worms   c Heb: Gk deprive yourself of
d Heb Love a wise slave as yourself   e Gk bend their
necks   f Gk body   g Heb Syr lack who pleases you

3.1–4; 22.22–29). **11:** See 1 Sam 2.7. **14:** Cf. Eccl 5.2. **15:** *Hard labor,* cf. 38.24–39.11. *Created,* see Gen 2.15. **17:** *Worms,* the Hebrew text mentions only the corruption in the grave that awaits all flesh. The later Greek version adds an image of fiery punishment after death (cf. Isa 66.24).

**7.18–28: Authority in the household.** Addressing the male head of household, Ben Sira commends prudent management of *wife, slaves, cattle,* and *children,* especially *daughters* (for wife, slaves, and animals as property, cf. Ex 20.17; Deut 5.21). **18:** *Ophir,* in southern Arabia, or possibly east Africa, was famous for its gold (1 Kings 9.28). **21:** *Freedom,* see Ex 21.2; Deut 15.12–15. **22–26:** On *daughters,* cf. 22.3–5; 42.9–13; and on wives, 9.1; 25.1,8,13–26; 26.1–18; 36.26–31. **27–28:** Cf. 3.1–16.

28 Remember that it was of your
    parents[a] you were born;
  how can you repay what they have
    given to you?
29 With all your soul fear the Lord,
    and revere his priests.
30 With all your might love your Maker,
    and do not neglect his ministers.
31 Fear the Lord and honor the priest,
    and give him his portion, as you
      have been commanded:
  the first fruits, the guilt offering, the
    gift of the shoulders,
  the sacrifice of sanctification, and
    the first fruits of the holy
    things.

32 Stretch out your hand to the poor,
    so that your blessing may be
      complete.
33 Give graciously to all the living;
    do not withhold kindness even
      from the dead.
34 Do not avoid those who weep,
    but mourn with those who mourn.
35 Do not hesitate to visit the sick,
    because for such deeds you will be
      loved.
36 In all you do, remember the end of
    your life,
    and then you will never sin.

8 Do not contend with the powerful,
    or you may fall into their hands.
 2 Do not quarrel with the rich,
    in case their resources outweigh
      yours;
  for gold has ruined many,
    and has perverted the minds of
      kings.
 3 Do not argue with the loud of mouth,
    and do not heap wood on their fire.

4 Do not make fun of one who is
    ill-bred,
    or your ancestors may be insulted.
5 Do not reproach one who is turning
    away from sin;
  remember that we all deserve
    punishment.
6 Do not disdain one who is old,
    for some of us are also growing
      old.
7 Do not rejoice over anyone's death;
    remember that we must all die.

8 Do not slight the discourse of the
    sages,
  but busy yourself with their
    maxims;
  because from them you will learn
    discipline
    and how to serve princes.
9 Do not ignore the discourse of the
    aged,
  for they themselves learned from
    their parents;[b]
  from them you learn how to
    understand
    and to give an answer when the
      need arises.

10 Do not kindle the coals of sinners,
    or you may be burned in their
      flaming fire.
11 Do not let the insolent bring you to
    your feet,
    or they may lie in ambush against
      your words.
12 Do not lend to one who is stronger
    than you;
  but if you do lend anything, count
    it as a loss.

a Gk *them*   b Or *ancestors*

**7.29–36:** Obligations to priests and to the poor. **31:** For the priestly *portion*, see Ex 29.27; Lev 7.31–34; Num 18.8–20; Deut 18.3. In contrast to Proverbs, which seldom makes reference to ritual practice (Prov 3.9), Ben Sira includes such observance as a part of wisdom literature. **33:** *Kindness*, here perhaps support for the bereaved is meant (cf. v. 34), or provision for an honorable burial (Tob 1.17). **36:** *The end of your life*, cf. 1.13; 28.6.

**8.1–19:** Caution in relationships. **3:** *Fire*, a common image for quarreling (cf. v. 10; 28.8–11; Prov 26.21). **8–9:** See Prov 1.8; 13.1,14; 15.5. **12–13:** Ben Sira is cautious about loans and surety, but not

13 Do not give surety beyond your
    means;
    but if you give surety, be prepared
        to pay.

14 Do not go to law against a judge,
    for the decision will favor him
        because of his standing.
15 Do not go traveling with the reckless,
    or they will be burdensome to you;
    for they will act as they please,
    and through their folly you will
        perish with them.
16 Do not pick a fight with the
        quick-tempered,
    and do not journey with them
        through lonely country,
    because bloodshed means nothing to
        them,
    and where no help is at hand, they
        will strike you down.
17 Do not consult with fools,
    for they cannot keep a secret.
18 In the presence of strangers do
        nothing that is to be kept secret,
    for you do not know what they will
        divulge.*a*
19 Do not reveal your thoughts to
        anyone,
    or you may drive away your
        happiness.*b*

9 Do not be jealous of the wife of your
        bosom,
    or you will teach her an evil lesson
        to your own hurt.
2 Do not give yourself to a woman
    and let her trample down your
        strength.
3 Do not go near a loose woman,

    or you will fall into her snares.
4 Do not dally with a singing girl,
    or you will be caught by her tricks.
5 Do not look intently at a virgin,
    or you may stumble and incur
        penalties for her.
6 Do not give yourself to prostitutes,
    or you may lose your inheritance.
7 Do not look around in the streets of a
        city,
    or wander about in its deserted
        sections.
8 Turn away your eyes from a shapely
        woman,
    and do not gaze at beauty
        belonging to another;
    many have been seduced by a
        woman's beauty,
    and by it passion is kindled like a
        fire.
9 Never dine with another man's wife,
    or revel with her at wine;
    or your heart may turn aside to her,
    and in blood*c* you may be plunged
        into destruction.

10 Do not abandon old friends,
    for new ones cannot equal them.
    A new friend is like new wine;
    when it has aged, you can drink it
        with pleasure.

11 Do not envy the success of sinners,
    for you do not know what their
        end will be like.
12 Do not delight in what pleases the
        ungodly;

*a* Or *it will bring forth*    *b* Heb: Gk *and let him not
return a favor to you*    *c* Heb: Gk *by your spirit*

opposed to them (29.1–7), in contrast to Prov 6.1–5; 11.15. **18:** The Hebrew evokes the danger of easy
confidences with a word play on the terms *strangers*, "zar," and *secret*, "raz."

**9.1–9: Warnings about women.** Ben Sira expresses anxiety, from a patently male perspective, concerning women of all sorts: from a man's own wife to the wife of another, unfamiliar women, singing girls,
virgins, prostitutes, and women of beauty; cf. Job 31.1–12. **3:** *Loose*, literally, "strange" woman (Heb
"zarah"; see Prov 2.16; 5.3; 5.20; 7.5; 22.14; 23.27). **4:** *Singing girl*, presumed to be a prostitute (cf. Isa
23.15–16). **6:** *Lose your inheritance*, cf. Prov 29.3. **7:** *In the streets of a city*, cf. Prov 7.7–10. **9:** *Destruction*, alluding to the death penalty for adultery (see Lev 20.10; Deut 22.22; Prov 7.19–27).

**9.10–16: Friends and associates. 13:** *Power to kill*, belongs to kings and rulers (cf. Prov 16.14).
*Walking on the city battlements*, exposed to attack.

remember that they will not be held
guiltless all their lives.

13 Keep far from those who have power
to kill,
and you will not be haunted by the
fear of death.
But if you approach them, make no
misstep,
or they may rob you of your life.
Know that you are stepping among
snares,
and that you are walking on the
city battlements.

14 As much as you can, aim to know
your neighbors,
and consult with the wise.
15 Let your conversation be with
intelligent people,
and let all your discussion be about
the law of the Most High.
16 Let the righteous be your dinner
companions,
and let your glory be in the fear of
the Lord.

17 A work is praised for the skill of the
artisan;
so a people's leader is proved wise
by his words.
18 The loud of mouth are feared in their
city,
and the one who is reckless in
speech is hated.
10 A wise magistrate educates his
people,
and the rule of an intelligent person
is well ordered.
2 As the people's judge is, so are his
officials;
as the ruler of the city is, so are all
its inhabitants.

3 An undisciplined king ruins his
people,
but a city becomes fit to live in
through the understanding of
its rulers.
4 The government of the earth is in the
hand of the Lord,
and over it he will raise up the
right leader for the time.
5 Human success is in the hand of the
Lord,
and it is he who confers honor
upon the lawgiver.[a]

6 Do not get angry with your neighbor
for every injury,
and do not resort to acts of
insolence.
7 Arrogance is hateful to the Lord and
to mortals,
and injustice is outrageous to both.
8 Sovereignty passes from nation to
nation
on account of injustice and
insolence and wealth.[b]
9 How can dust and ashes be proud?
Even in life the human body
decays.[c]
10 A long illness baffles the physician;[d]
the king of today will die
tomorrow.
11 For when one is dead
he inherits maggots and vermin[e]
and worms.
12 The beginning of human pride is to
forsake the Lord;

a Heb: Gk *scribe*   b Other ancient authorities add
here or after verse 9a, *Nothing is more wicked than
one who loves money, for such a person puts his own
soul up for sale.*   c Heb: Meaning of Gk uncertain
d Heb Lat: Meaning of Gk uncertain   e Heb: Gk
*wild animals*

**9.17–10.5: Concerning rulers.** Perhaps an indirect critique of the Ptolemaic and Seleucid rulers of the
day. Comment on wise and foolish rulers, however, is a traditional wisdom topic. See Prov 25.4–5;
28.2–3,16; 29.4,12,14.
**10.6–18: Concerning arrogance and pride.** Like 9.17–10.5, this section probably has implications for
rulers contemporary to the author, but several verses apply to ordinary people (vv. 6–7,12,18). **9:** *Dust
and ashes,* Gen 18.27; Job 30.19; 42.6. *The human body decays,* cf. Eccl 12.1–7. **14–15:** Cf. 1 Sam
2.4–8.

the heart has withdrawn from its
Maker.

13 For the beginning of pride is sin,
and the one who clings to it pours
out abominations.
Therefore the Lord brings upon them
unheard-of calamities,
and destroys them completely.

14 The Lord overthrows the thrones of
rulers,
and enthrones the lowly in their
place.

15 The Lord plucks up the roots of the
nations,[a]
and plants the humble in their
place.

16 The Lord lays waste the lands of the
nations,
and destroys them to the
foundations of the earth.

17 He removes some of them and
destroys them,
and erases the memory of them
from the earth.

18 Pride was not created for human
beings,
or violent anger for those born of
women.

19 Whose offspring are worthy of
honor?
Human offspring.
Whose offspring are worthy of
honor?
Those who fear the Lord.
Whose offspring are unworthy of
honor?
Human offspring.
Whose offspring are unworthy of
honor?
Those who break the
commandments.

20 Among family members their leader is
worthy of honor,
but those who fear the Lord are
worthy of honor in his eyes.[b]

22 The rich, and the eminent, and the
poor—
their glory is the fear of the Lord.

23 It is not right to despise one who is
intelligent but poor,
and it is not proper to honor one
who is sinful.

24 The prince and the judge and the
ruler are honored,
but none of them is greater than
the one who fears the Lord.

25 Free citizens will serve a wise servant,
and an intelligent person will not
complain.

26 Do not make a display of your
wisdom when you do your
work,
and do not boast when you are in
need.

27 Better is the worker who has goods in
plenty
than the boaster who lacks bread.

28 My child, honor yourself with
humility,
and give yourself the esteem you
deserve.

29 Who will acquit those who
condemn[c] themselves?
And who will honor those who
dishonor themselves?[d]

30 The poor are honored for their
knowledge,
while the rich are honored for their
wealth.

31 One who is honored in poverty, how
much more in wealth!
And one dishonored in wealth, how
much more in poverty!

a Other ancient authorities read *proud nations*
b Other ancient authorities add as verse 21, *The fear
of the Lord is the beginning of acceptance; obduracy
and pride are the beginning of rejection.*   c Heb: Gk
*sin against*   d Heb Lat: Gk *their own life*

**10.19–11.6: True honor. 19:** *Human offspring,* giving the same answer to opposite questions is a form
of riddle, designed to provoke reflection. *Fear,* i.e., respect for *the Lord* is a central virtue in wisdom (see
Prov 1.7; 9.10; Job 28.28). **23:** Cf. Eccl 9.15–16. **28:** Genuine *honor* is compatible with *humility.* **30–31:**

**11** The wisdom of the humble lifts
their heads high,
and seats them among the great.
2 Do not praise individuals for their
good looks,
or loathe anyone because of
appearance alone.
3 The bee is small among flying
creatures,
but what it produces is the best of
sweet things.
4 Do not boast about wearing fine
clothes,
and do not exalt yourself when you
are honored;
for the works of the Lord are
wonderful,
and his works are concealed from
humankind.
5 Many kings have had to sit on the
ground,
but one who was never thought of
has worn a crown.
6 Many rulers have been utterly
disgraced,
and the honored have been handed
over to others.
7 Do not find fault before you
investigate;
examine first, and then criticize.
8 Do not answer before you listen,
and do not interrupt when another
is speaking.
9 Do not argue about a matter that
does not concern you,
and do not sit with sinners when
they judge a case.

10 My child, do not busy yourself with
many matters;
if you multiply activities, you will
not be held blameless.
If you pursue, you will not overtake,
and by fleeing you will not escape.
11 There are those who work and
struggle and hurry,
but are so much the more in want.
12 There are others who are slow and
need help,
who lack strength and abound in
poverty;
but the eyes of the Lord look kindly
upon them;
he lifts them out of their lowly
condition
13 and raises up their heads
to the amazement of the many.

14 Good things and bad, life and death,
poverty and wealth, come from the
Lord.*a*
17 The Lord's gift remains with the
devout,
and his favor brings lasting success.
18 One becomes rich through diligence
and self-denial,
and the reward allotted to him is
this:
19 when he says, "I have found rest,
and now I shall feast on my
goods!"
he does not know how long it will be
until he leaves them to others and
dies.
20 Stand by your agreement and attend
to it,
and grow old in your work.
21 Do not wonder at the works of a
sinner,

a Other ancient authorities add as verses 15 and 16,
15 *Wisdom, understanding, and knowledge of the law
come from the Lord; affection and the ways of good
works come from him.* 16 *Error and darkness were
created with sinners; evil grows old with those who
take pride in malice.*

*Wealth* does make a difference, even for the wise. **11.3:** See Prov 6.6–8; 30.15–19,24–31 for similar
analogies between human conduct and animal behavior. **6:** *Handed over,* in defeat as war captives.
**11.7–9: Against hasty and rash actions** (cf. 5.11–12; Prov 18.13). **11.10–19: Do not strive for material security** (cf. Prov 13.11; 20.21; 23.4–5; Eccl 5.10–12). **12–13:**
See 10.14–15. **14:** Cf. Job 2.10. **19:** *Leaves them to others and dies,* cf. Ps 49.7–12; Eccl 2.18–22; 6.1–2.
**11.20–28: Retribution. 20–26:** God's reward or punishment occurs in this life, down to the very end.

but trust in the Lord and keep at
   your job;
for it is easy in the sight of the Lord
   to make the poor rich suddenly, in
      an instant.

22 The blessing of the Lord is[a] the
      reward of the pious,
   and quickly God causes his blessing
      to flourish.

23 Do not say, "What do I need,
   and what further benefit can be
      mine?"

24 Do not say, "I have enough,
   and what harm can come to me
      now?"

25 In the day of prosperity, adversity is
      forgotten,
   and in the day of adversity,
      prosperity is not remembered.

26 For it is easy for the Lord on the day
      of death
   to reward individuals according to
      their conduct.

27 An hour's misery makes one forget
      past delights,
   and at the close of one's life one's
      deeds are revealed.

28 Call no one happy before his death;
   by how he ends, a person becomes
      known.[b]

29 Do not invite everyone into your
      home,
   for many are the tricks of the
      crafty.

30 Like a decoy partridge in a cage, so is
      the mind of the proud,
   and like spies they observe your
      weakness;[c]

31 for they lie in wait, turning good into
      evil,
   and to worthy actions they attach
      blame.

32 From a spark many coals are kindled,
   and a sinner lies in wait to shed
      blood.

33 Beware of scoundrels, for they devise
      evil,
   and they may ruin your reputation
      forever.

34 Receive strangers into your home and
      they will stir up trouble for
      you,
   and will make you a stranger to
      your own family.

12 If you do good, know to whom
      you do it,
   and you will be thanked for your
      good deeds.

2 Do good to the devout, and you will
      be repaid—
   if not by them, certainly by the
      Most High.

3 No good comes to one who persists
      in evil
   or to one who does not give alms.

4 Give to the devout, but do not help
      the sinner.

5 Do good to the humble, but do not
      give to the ungodly;
   hold back their bread, and do not
      give it to them,
   for by means of it they might
      subdue you;
   then you will receive twice as much
      evil
   for all the good you have done to
      them.

6 For the Most High also hates sinners
   and will inflict punishment on the
      ungodly.[d]

a Heb: Gk *is in*    b Heb: Gk *and through his children
a person becomes known*    c Heb: Gk *downfall*
d Other ancient authorities add *and he is keeping them
for the day of their punishment*

**27–28:** The *close of one's life* is a final test (cf. 1.13; 7.36; 28.6; Eccl 7.1). Reward comes not in an
afterlife, but as *a person becomes known* in the memory of those who live on.
   **11.29–12.18: Choosing companions. 29–34:** Great caution is urged concerning those invited into the
*home*. **12.1–7:** While the advice given here is positive, it is also self-serving and at odds with the generous
spirit found elsewhere in Sirach (e.g., 18.15–18; 29.8–13). The contrast between the *sinners* and the
*devout* is sharply drawn. As sinner, the *ungodly* one deserves rejection by God (12.6, "hate" is not a mere
emotion). **8–18:** A warning against false friends (cf. 6.5–17).

7 Give to the one who is good, but do
   not help the sinner.
8 A friend is not known[a] in prosperity,
   nor is an enemy hidden in
   adversity.
9 One's enemies are friendly[b] when
   one prospers,
   but in adversity even one's friend
   disappears.
10 Never trust your enemy,
   for like corrosion in copper, so is
   his wickedness.
11 Even if he humbles himself and walks
   bowed down,
   take care to be on your guard
   against him.
   Be to him like one who polishes a
   mirror,
   to be sure it does not become
   completely tarnished.
12 Do not put him next to you,
   or he may overthrow you and take
   your place.
   Do not let him sit at your right hand,
   or else he may try to take your
   own seat,
   and at last you will realize the truth
   of my words,
   and be stung by what I have said.

13 Who pities a snake charmer when he
   is bitten,
   or all those who go near wild
   animals?
14 So no one pities a person who
   associates with a sinner
   and becomes involved in the other's
   sins.
15 He stands by you for a while,
   but if you falter, he will not be
   there.
16 An enemy speaks sweetly with his
   lips,
   but in his heart he plans to throw
   you into a pit;
   an enemy may have tears in his eyes,
   but if he finds an opportunity he
   will never have enough of your
   blood.
17 If evil comes upon you, you will find
   him there ahead of you;
   pretending to help, he will trip you
   up.
18 Then he will shake his head, and clap
   his hands,
   and whisper much, and show his
   true face.

13 Whoever touches pitch gets dirty,
   and whoever associates with a
   proud person becomes like
   him.
2 Do not lift a weight too heavy for you,
   or associate with one mightier and
   richer than you.
   How can the clay pot associate with
   the iron kettle?
   The pot will strike against it and be
   smashed.
3 A rich person does wrong, and even
   adds insults;
   a poor person suffers wrong, and
   must add apologies.
4 A rich person[c] will exploit you if
   you can be of use to him,
   but if you are in need he will
   abandon you.
5 If you own something, he will live
   with you;
   he will drain your resources
   without a qualm.
6 When he needs you he will deceive
   you,
   and will smile at you and
   encourage you;
   he will speak to you kindly and
   say, "What do you need?"
7 He will embarrass you with his
   delicacies,

a Other ancient authorities read *punished*    b Heb:
Gk *grieved*    c Gk *He*

13.1–13: **Warnings about associates.** Unequal matches, especially between rich and poor, will be costly
to the weaker party. **1:** A vivid picture of taint by association. **3:** *Poor . . . must add apologies,* cf. Prov
18.23. **4:** Cf. Prov 14.20; Eccl 9.16. **9:** *Influential person,* one of noble social rank, possessing wealth and
power. **10:** *Do not be forward,* cf. Prov 25.6–7; Lk 14.7–11.

until he has drained you two or
three times,
and finally he will laugh at you.
Should he see you afterwards, he will
pass you by
and shake his head at you.

8 Take care not to be led astray
and humiliated when you are
enjoying yourself.*a*
9 When an influential person invites
you, be reserved,
and he will invite you more
insistently.
10 Do not be forward, or you may be
rebuffed;
do not stand aloof, or you will be
forgotten.
11 Do not try to treat him as an equal,
or trust his lengthy conversations;
for he will test you by prolonged talk,
and while he smiles he will be
examining you.
12 Cruel are those who do not keep your
secrets;
they will not spare you harm or
imprisonment.
13 Be on your guard and very careful,
for you are walking about with
your own downfall.*b*

15 Every creature loves its like,
and every person the neighbor.
16 All living beings associate with their
own kind,
and people stick close to those like
themselves.
17 What does a wolf have in common
with a lamb?
No more has a sinner with the
devout.
18 What peace is there between a hyena
and a dog?
And what peace between the rich
and the poor?

19 Wild asses in the wilderness are the
prey of lions;
likewise the poor are feeding
grounds for the rich.
20 Humility is an abomination to the
proud;
likewise the poor are an
abomination to the rich.
21 When the rich person totters, he is
supported by friends,
but when the humble*c* falls, he is
pushed away even by friends.
22 If the rich person slips, many come to
the rescue;
he speaks unseemly words, but they
justify him.
If the humble person slips, they even
criticize him;
he talks sense, but is not given a
hearing.
23 The rich person speaks and all are
silent;
they extol to the clouds what he
says.
The poor person speaks and they say,
"Who is this fellow?"
And should he stumble, they even
push him down.
24 Riches are good if they are free from
sin;
poverty is evil only in the opinion
of the ungodly.

25 The heart changes the countenance,
either for good or for evil.*d*
26 The sign of a happy heart is a
cheerful face,

a Other ancient authorities read *in your folly*
b Other ancient authorities add as verse 14, *When you
hear these things in your sleep, wake up! During all
your life love the Lord, and call on him for your
salvation.* c Other ancient authorities read *poor*
d Other ancient authorities add *and a glad heart
makes a cheerful countenance*

**13.15–23: Rich and poor.** "Like loves like," and the poor suffer at the hands of the rich. **17:** *Wolf . . .
lamb,* cf. Isa 11.6. **18:** *A hyena and a dog* are natural enemies; the hyena was the stronger and more rapa-
cious of the two. **19:** For *lions* as symbols of the wicked and the powerful, cf. Ps 35.17; 58.6.
**13.24–14.2: Wealth and conscience. 24:** Cf. 31.8. **25–26:** The *countenance* reveals the inner disposition (cf. Prov 15.13; Eccl 8.1). **14.1–2:** A clear conscience, not wealth, makes one *happy*.

but to devise proverbs requires
    painful thinking.

**14** Happy are those who do not
    blunder with their lips,
and need not suffer remorse for
    sin.

2 Happy are those whose hearts do not
    condemn them,
and who have not given up their
    hope.

3 Riches are inappropriate for a
    small-minded person;
and of what use is wealth to a
    miser?

4 What he denies himself he collects for
    others;
and others will live in luxury on his
    goods.

5 If one is mean to himself, to whom
    will he be generous?
He will not enjoy his own riches.

6 No one is worse than one who is
    grudging to himself;
this is the punishment for his
    meanness.

7 If ever he does good, it is by mistake;
and in the end he reveals his
    meanness.

8 The miser is an evil person;
he turns away and disregards people.

9 The eye of the greedy person is not
    satisfied with his share;
greedy injustice withers the soul.

10 A miser begrudges bread,
and it is lacking at his table.

11 My child, treat yourself well,
    according to your means,
and present worthy offerings to the
    Lord.

12 Remember that death does not tarry,
and the decree[a] of Hades has not
    been shown to you.

13 Do good to friends before you die,
and reach out and give to them as
    much as you can.

14 Do not deprive yourself of a day's
    enjoyment;
do not let your share of desired
    good pass by you.

15 Will you not leave the fruit of your
    labors to another,
and what you acquired by toil to be
    divided by lot?

16 Give, and take, and indulge yourself,
because in Hades one cannot look
    for luxury.

17 All living beings become old like a
    garment,
for the decree[b] from of old is,
    "You must die!"

18 Like abundant leaves on a spreading
    tree
that sheds some and puts forth
    others,
so are the generations of flesh and
    blood:
one dies and another is born.

19 Every work decays and ceases to exist,
and the one who made it will pass
    away with it.

20 Happy is the person who meditates
    on[c] wisdom
and reasons intelligently,

21 who[d] reflects in his heart on her
    ways
and ponders her secrets,

a Heb Syr: Gk *covenant*    b Heb: Gk *covenant*
c Other ancient authorities read *dies in*    d The
structure adopted in verses 21-27 follows the Heb

**14.3–19: The proper use of wealth. 3–10:** A description of the *miser* and his fate; cf. Prov 11.24–25.
**11–19:** In contrast to vv. 3–10, riches are to be used generously because there will be no opportunity after
death (vv. 12,16), which is inevitable (vv. 17–19). **12:** *Hades,* in Greek the abode of the dead, called
"Sheol" in Hebrew. **14:** Cf. Eccl 9.7. **15:** *Divided by lot,* cf. Ps 22.18. **17:** *Decree from of old,* Gen 2.17;
3.3,19. **18–19:** Cf. Eccl 1.2–4; *Iliad* 6.146–49.

**14.20–15.10: The search for Wisdom and her blessings. 20–27:** The fervent seeker of wisdom is compared to a man passionately pursuing a woman. This erotic language (cf. 15.2) is designed to capture the
imagination of Ben Sira's young male students. **20:** Cf. 6.37; Ps 1.2. **23:** *Peers through her windows,* cf.
Song 2.9. **24:** *Camps near her house,* see Prov 8.34. **26:** *Under her boughs,* wisdom as a life-giving

22 pursuing her like a hunter,
    and lying in wait on her
      paths;
23 who peers through her windows
    and listens at her doors;
24 who camps near her house
    and fastens his tent peg to her
      walls;
25 who pitches his tent near
      her,
    and so occupies an excellent
      lodging place;
26 who places his children under her
      shelter,
    and lodges under her boughs;
27 who is sheltered by her from the
      heat,
    and dwells in the midst of her
      glory.

15 Whoever fears the Lord will do
    this,
    and whoever holds to the law will
      obtain wisdom.*a*
2 She will come to meet him like a
      mother,
    and like a young bride she will
      welcome him.
3 She will feed him with the bread of
      learning,
    and give him the water of wisdom
      to drink.
4 He will lean on her and not fall,
    and he will rely on her and not be
      put to shame.
5 She will exalt him above his
      neighbors,
    and will open his mouth in the
      midst of the assembly.

6 He will find gladness and a crown of
      rejoicing,
    and will inherit an everlasting
      name.
7 The foolish will not obtain her,
    and sinners will not see her.
8 She is far from arrogance,
    and liars will never think of her.
9 Praise is unseemly on the lips of a
      sinner,
    for it has not been sent from the
      Lord.
10 For in wisdom must praise be
      uttered,
    and the Lord will make it prosper.

11 Do not say, "It was the Lord's doing
      that I fell away";
    for he does not do*b* what he
      hates.
12 Do not say, "It was he who led me
      astray";
    for he has no need of the sinful.
13 The Lord hates all abominations;
    such things are not loved by those
      who fear him.
14 It was he who created humankind in
      the beginning,
    and he left them in the power of
      their own free choice.
15 If you choose, you can keep the
      commandments,
    and to act faithfully is a matter of
      your own choice.
16 He has placed before you fire and
      water;

*a* Gk *her*    *b* Heb: Gk *you ought not to do*

tree (1.20; 24.13–17; Prov 3.18). **15.1–10:** Wisdom's response to those who seek her, and hold to the *law* (v. 1; cf. 1.11–30; 6.32–37; 24.23). **2:** Wisdom receives the faithful student with the tenderness of a *mother* (cf. Isa 49.15; 66.13; Wis 7.12), and the ardor of a *young bride* (cf. Prov 5.18; 7.4; Song 4.9,12; 5.1–2; Wis 8.2). **3:** *Bread* and *water*, cf. 1.16; 24.19–21; Prov 9.1–5; Isa 55.1–2.

　　**15.11–20: Human responsibility. 11–13:** God cannot be blamed for human sinfulness. **14–17:** Ben Sira does not advance a consistent doctrine of "free will" (contrast v. 14b with 23.19–20 and 33.13); but here he argues against divine responsibility for sin by emphasizing human *free choice* ("yetser" in v. 14b). The Hebrew word is a technical term, sometimes used in a good sense (Isa 26.3; 1 Chr 29.18), but usually it refers to an evil tendency or inclination toward sin (Gen 6.5; 8.21; cf. 2 Esd 4.30–31). In postbiblical times the doctrine arose of a good and an evil "yetser" that every person possesses (cf. 37.3). **16:** *Fire and*

stretch out your hand for whichever
you choose.
17 Before each person are life and death,
and whichever one chooses will be
given.
18 For great is the wisdom of the Lord;
he is mighty in power and sees
everything;
19 his eyes are on those who fear him,
and he knows every human action.
20 He has not commanded anyone to be
wicked,
and he has not given anyone
permission to sin.

16 Do not desire a multitude of
worthless[a] children,
and do not rejoice in ungodly
offspring.
2 If they multiply, do not rejoice in
them,
unless the fear of the Lord is in
them.
3 Do not trust in their survival,
or rely on their numbers;[b]
for one can be better than a
thousand,
and to die childless is better than to
have ungodly children.
4 For through one intelligent person a
city can be filled with people,
but through a clan of outlaws it
becomes desolate.

5 Many such things my eye has seen,
and my ear has heard things more
striking than these.
6 In an assembly of sinners a fire is
kindled,
and in a disobedient nation wrath
blazes up.

7 He did not forgive the ancient giants
who revolted in their might.
8 He did not spare the neighbors of
Lot,
whom he loathed on account of
their arrogance.
9 He showed no pity on the doomed
nation,
on those dispossessed because of
their sins;[c]
10 or on the six hundred thousand foot
soldiers
who assembled in their
stubbornness.[d]
11 Even if there were only one
stiff-necked person,
it would be a wonder if he
remained unpunished.
For mercy and wrath are with the
Lord;[e]
he is mighty to forgive—but he also
pours out wrath.
12 Great as is his mercy, so also is his
chastisement;
he judges a person according to his
or her deeds.
13 The sinner will not escape with
plunder,
and the patience of the godly will
not be frustrated.
14 He makes room for every act of
mercy;

a Heb: Gk *unprofitable*   b Other ancient authorities
add *For you will groan in untimely mourning, and will
know of their sudden end.*   c Other ancient
authorities add *All these things he did to the
hard-hearted nations, and by the multitude of his holy
ones he was not appeased.*   d Other ancient
authorities add *Chastising, showing mercy, striking,
healing, the Lord persisted in mercy and discipline.*
e Gk *him*

*water,* represent opposite extremes. *Fire* here has no eschatological significance. **17:** Deut 30.19; Jer 21.8.
**18–20:** The divine attributes mentioned here reaffirm the point of 14.11–13.
   **16.1–23: The certainty of punishment for sin. 1–4:** Ben Sira counters the notion that children are a sure
sign of blessing (Prov 17.6; Ps 127.3–5) with the observation that sinful offspring will result in woe
(cf. 40.15–16; 41.5–13). **6–8:** The author refers to the fate of Korah, Dathan, and Abiram (v. 6;
cf. 45.18–19; Num 16), *the ancient giants* of Gen 6.4, and the people of Sodom (v. 8; Ezek 16.49–50;
Gen 19). **9:** *Doomed nation,* the Canaanites (see Lev 18.3; 24–25). **10:** The *six hundred thousand* are the
Israelites in the desert (cf. 46.8; Ex 12.37; Num 14.38). **11:** *Mercy and wrath,* 5.6. **12–14:** God rewards
*every act of mercy* and punishes wrongdoing (cf. 11.26; 29.11–12). **17–23:** Despite the immensity of

everyone receives in accordance
  with his or her deeds.[a]

17 Do not say, "I am hidden from the
    Lord,
  and who from on high has me in
    mind?
  Among so many people I am
    unknown,
  for what am I in a boundless
    creation?
18 Lo, heaven and the highest heaven,
  the abyss and the earth, tremble at
    his visitation![b]
19 The very mountains and the
    foundations of the earth
  quiver and quake when he looks
    upon them.
20 But no human mind can grasp this,
  and who can comprehend his
    ways?
21 Like a tempest that no one can see,
  so most of his works are
    concealed.[c]
22 Who is to announce his acts of
    justice?
  Or who can await them? For his
    decree[d] is far off."[e]
23 Such are the thoughts of one devoid
    of understanding;
  a senseless and misguided person
    thinks foolishly.

24 Listen to me, my child, and acquire
    knowledge,
  and pay close attention to my
    words.
25 I will impart discipline precisely[f]
  and declare knowledge accurately.

26 When the Lord created[g] his works
    from the beginning,

and, in making them, determined
  their boundaries,
27 he arranged his works in an eternal
    order,
  and their dominion[h] for all
    generations.
  They neither hunger nor grow weary,
  and they do not abandon their
    tasks.
28 They do not crowd one another,
  and they never disobey his word.
29 Then the Lord looked upon the earth,
  and filled it with his good things.
30 With all kinds of living beings he
    covered its surface,
  and into it they must return.

17 The Lord created human beings
    out of earth,
  and makes them return to it again.
2 He gave them a fixed number of days,
  but granted them authority over
    everything on the earth.[i]
3 He endowed them with strength like
    his own,[j]
  and made them in his own image.
4 He put the fear of them[k] in all living
    beings,

a Other ancient authorities add [15]The Lord hardened
Pharaoh so that he did not recognize him, in order
that his works might be known under heaven. [16]His
mercy is manifest to the whole of creation, and he
divided his light and darkness with a plumb line.
b Other ancient authorities add The whole world past
and present is in his will.   c Meaning of Gk
uncertain: Heb Syr If I sin, no eye can see me, and if I
am disloyal all in secret, who is to know?   d Heb the
decree: Gk the covenant   e Other ancient authorities
add and a scrutiny for all comes at the end   f Gk by
weight   g Heb: Gk judged   h Or elements
i Lat: Gk it   j Lat: Gk proper to them
k Syr: Gk him

God's *boundless creation*, one should not think it is possible to escape God's attention (cf. 15.19;
17.15–24; Ps 139.7–18; Am 9.2–3). **18–19:** See Judg 5.4–5; Ps 104.32. **22:** Cf. Deut 30.11–14. Verse 23
pronounces judgment on the ideas expressed in vv.17–22.
  **16.24–17.14: God's wisdom in creation. 26:** *From the beginning,* Gen 1.1; Prov 8.22–23. *Their
boundaries,* Ps 104.9. **27b–28:** Apparently referring to the heavenly bodies; cf. Ps 104.19. **29:** *Good
things,* Gen 1.4,10,12, etc.; Ps 104.24,28. **30:** *They must return,* cf. 17.1; 40.11; Gen 3.19. **17.1–14:** The
creation of *human beings* culminates in God's gifts of the *law, covenant,* and *commandment* (vv. 11–14).
**1:** Gen 3.19. **2:** Gen 1.28. **3:** Gen 1.26. **4:** Gen 1.28; 9.2. **7:** Cf. Gen 2.17; 3.5,22. **11:** *The law of life,*

and gave them dominion over
  beasts and birds.*a*

6 Discretion and tongue and eyes,
    ears and a mind for thinking he
    gave them.
7 He filled them with knowledge and
    understanding,
  and showed them good and evil.
8 He put the fear of him into*b* their
    hearts
  to show them the majesty of his
    works.*c*
10 And they will praise his holy name,
9   to proclaim the grandeur of his
    works.
11 He bestowed knowledge upon them,
  and allotted to them the law of
    life.*d*
12 He established with them an eternal
    covenant,
  and revealed to them his decrees.
13 Their eyes saw his glorious majesty,
  and their ears heard the glory of his
    voice.
14 He said to them, "Beware of all evil."
  And he gave commandment to each
    of them concerning the
    neighbor.
15 Their ways are always known to him;
  they will not be hid from his eyes.*e*
17 He appointed a ruler for every nation,
  but Israel is the Lord's own
    portion.*f*
19 All their works are as clear as the sun
    before him,
  and his eyes are ever upon their
    ways.
20 Their iniquities are not hidden from
    him,
  and all their sins are before the
    Lord.*g*
22 One's almsgiving is like a signet ring
    with the Lord,*h*

and he will keep a person's
  kindness like the apple of his
  eye.*i*
23 Afterward he will rise up and repay
    them,
  and he will bring their recompense
    on their heads.
24 Yet to those who repent he grants a
    return,
  and he encourages those who are
    losing hope.

25 Turn back to the Lord and forsake
    your sins;
  pray in his presence and lessen your
    offense.
26 Return to the Most High and turn
    away from iniquity,*j*
  and hate intensely what he abhors.
27 Who will sing praises to the Most
    High in Hades
  in place of the living who give
    thanks?

a Other ancient authorities add as verse 5, *They
obtained the use of the five faculties of the Lord; as
sixth he distributed to them the gift of mind, and as
seventh, reason, the interpreter of one's faculties.*
b Other ancient authorities read *He set his eye upon*
c Other ancient authorities add *and he gave them to
boast of his marvels forever*    d Other ancient
authorities add *so that they may know that they who
are alive now are mortal*    e Other ancient authorities
add 16*Their ways from youth tend toward evil, and
they are unable to make for themselves hearts of flesh
in place of their stony hearts.* 17*For in the division of
the nations of the whole earth, he appointed*    f Other
ancient authorities add as verse 18, *whom, being his
firstborn, he brings up with discipline, and allotting to
him the light of his love, he does not neglect him.*
g Other ancient authorities add as verse 21, *But the
Lord, who is gracious and knows how they are
formed, has neither left them nor abandoned them, but
has spared them.*    h Gk *him*    i Other ancient
authorities add *apportioning repentance to his sons
and daughters*    j Other ancient authorities add *for he
will lead you out of darkness to the light of health.*

the laws of the covenant, Deut 30.15–20. **12–13**: *Established . . . saw,* on Mt. Sinai; Ex 19. **14**: *The
neighbor,* Ex 20.13–17; Lev 19.18; Deut 5.17–21.
  **17.15–24**: *The divine judge.* God requites the good and the sinful actions of all. **17**: *Lord's own
portion,* see Deut 32.8–9. **22**: *Signet ring* (Jer 22.24; Hag 2.23) and *apple of his eye* (Deut 32.1) both
indicate a close, even affectionate connection. **23**: See Ps 7.16; Jer 23.19; Ezek 22.31; Joel 4.4,7; cf. Prov
25.22. **24**: *A return,* to God's favor.
  **17.25–32**: *A call for repentance.* **27–28**: There is no worship of God in *Hades* (Sheol, the abode of the

28 From the dead, as from one who does
not exist, thanksgiving has
ceased;
those who are alive and well sing
the Lord's praises.
29 How great is the mercy of the Lord,
and his forgiveness for those who
return to him!
30 For not everything is within human
capability,
since human beings are not
immortal.
31 What is brighter than the sun? Yet it
can be eclipsed.
So flesh and blood devise evil.
32 He marshals the host of the height of
heaven;
but all human beings are dust and
ashes.

18 He who lives forever created the
whole universe;
2 the Lord alone is just.[a]
4 To none has he given power to
proclaim his works;
and who can search out his mighty
deeds?
5 Who can measure his majestic power?
And who can fully recount his
mercies?
6 It is not possible to diminish or
increase them,
nor is it possible to fathom the
wonders of the Lord.
7 When human beings have finished,
they are just beginning,
and when they stop, they are still
perplexed.
8 What are human beings, and of what
use are they?
What is good in them, and what is
evil?

9 The number of days in their life is
great if they reach one hundred
years.[b]
10 Like a drop of water from the sea
and a grain of sand,
so are a few years among the days
of eternity.
11 That is why the Lord is patient with
them
and pours out his mercy upon
them.
12 He sees and recognizes that their end
is miserable;
therefore he grants them forgiveness
all the more.
13 The compassion of human beings is
for their neighbors,
but the compassion of the Lord is
for every living thing.
He rebukes and trains and teaches
them,
and turns them back, as a shepherd
his flock.
14 He has compassion on those who
accept his discipline
and who are eager for his precepts.
15 My child, do not mix reproach with
your good deeds,
or spoil your gift by harsh words.
16 Does not the dew give relief from the
scorching heat?
So a word is better than a gift.
17 Indeed, does not a word surpass a
good gift?

a Other ancient authorities add *and there is no other
beside him;* 3*he steers the world with the span of his
hand, and all things obey his will; for he is king of all
things by his power, separating among them the holy
things from the profane.* b Other ancient authorities
add *but the death of each one is beyond the
calculation of all*

dead; cf. Ps 6.5; 30.9; 88.10–12; 115.17–18; Isa 38.18–19; Bar 2.17), but by repentance one can be *alive,*
and *sing the Lord's praises.* **31:** If the *sun* can suffer an eclipse, a mere human can also fail. **32:** Cf. Job
4.17–21; 25.2–6. *Dust and ashes,* see 10.9n.
**18.1–14: In praise of God's majesty and mercy.** Although the Lord is beyond comprehension (vv. 1–7),
and humans are weak and short-lived (vv. 8–10), God is *patient* and merciful to them (vv. 11–14). **8:**
*What are human beings?* (Ps 8.4). **9:** Cf. Ps 90.10. **11:** Wis 15.1. **13:** *Shepherd,* Ps 80.1; Isa 40.11.
**18.15–19.19: Advice for living. 15–18:** On *gracious* giving. True generosity adds kind words to
almsgiving. **19–21:** Be prepared: *Examine* and *humble* yourself. **22–26:** Caution in making vows. See

Both are to be found in a gracious
person.

18 A fool is ungracious and abusive,
and the gift of a grudging giver
makes the eyes dim.

19 Before you speak, learn;
and before you fall ill, take care of
your health.

20 Before judgment comes, examine
yourself;
and at the time of scrutiny you will
find forgiveness.

21 Before falling ill, humble yourself;
and when you have sinned, repent.

22 Let nothing hinder you from paying a
vow promptly,
and do not wait until death to be
released from it.

23 Before making a vow, prepare
yourself;
do not be like one who puts the
Lord to the test.

24 Think of his wrath on the day of
death,
and of the moment of vengeance
when he turns away his face.

25 In the time of plenty think of the time
of hunger;
in days of wealth think of poverty
and need.

26 From morning to evening conditions
change;
all things move swiftly before the
Lord.

27 One who is wise is cautious in
everything;
when sin is all around, one guards
against wrongdoing.

28 Every intelligent person knows
wisdom,
and praises the one who finds her.

29 Those who are skilled in words
become wise themselves,
and pour forth apt proverbs.ᵃ

### SELF-CONTROLᵇ

30 Do not follow your base desires,
but restrain your appetites.

31 If you allow your soul to take
pleasure in base desire,
it will make you the laughingstock
of your enemies.

32 Do not revel in great luxury,
or you may become impoverished
by its expense.

33 Do not become a beggar by feasting
with borrowed money,
when you have nothing in your
purse.ᶜ

19 The one who does thisᵈ will not
become rich;
one who despises small things will
fail little by little.

2 Wine and women lead intelligent men
astray,
and the man who consorts with
prostitutes is reckless.

3 Decay and worms will take possession
of him,
and the reckless person will be
snatched away.

4 One who trusts others too quickly has
a shallow mind,
and one who sins does wrong to
himself.

5 One who rejoices in wickednessᵉ will
be condemned,ᶠ

6 but one who hates gossip has less
evil.

7 Never repeat a conversation,
and you will lose nothing at all.

---

a Other ancient authorities add *Better is confidence in
the one Lord than clinging with a dead heart to a dead
one.*   b This heading is included in the Gk text.
c Other ancient authorities add *for you will be plotting
against your own life*   d Heb: Gk *A worker who is a
drunkard*   e Other ancient authorities read *heart*
f Other ancient authorities add *but one who
withstands pleasures crowns his life.* ⁶*One who
controls the tongue will live without strife,*

---

Prov 20.25; Eccl 5.4–5. **23**: *Test*, cf. Ex 17.2; Deut 6.16. **27–29**: How to recognize the *wise*. **18.30–19.3**:
On self-control. This advice is tailored especially to Ben Sira's students, young men who might have both
the freedom and inclination to self-indulgence. **19.2**: Cf. Prov 20.1; 31.3–5. **4–17**: Warnings against
imprudent speech. Discretion is the rule, *unless* by keeping silent *it would be a sin* (v. 8; cf. Lev 5.1).

8 With friend or foe do not report it,
  and unless it would be a sin for
      you, do not reveal it;
9 for someone may have heard you and
      watched you,
  and in time will hate you.
10 Have you heard something? Let it die
      with you.
  Be brave, it will not make you burst!
11 Having heard something, the fool
      suffers birth pangs
  like a woman in labor with a child.
12 Like an arrow stuck in a person's
      thigh,
  so is gossip inside a fool.

13 Question a friend; perhaps he did not
      do it;
  or if he did, so that he may not do
      it again.
14 Question a neighbor; perhaps he did
      not say it;
  or if he said it, so that he may not
      repeat it.
15 Question a friend, for often it is
      slander;
  so do not believe everything you
      hear.
16 A person may make a slip without
      intending it.
  Who has not sinned with his
      tongue?
17 Question your neighbor before you
      threaten him;
  and let the law of the Most High
      take its course.*a*

20 The whole of wisdom is fear of the
      Lord,
  and in all wisdom there is the
      fulfillment of the law.*b*
22 The knowledge of wickedness is not
      wisdom,

nor is there prudence in the counsel
    of sinners.
23 There is a cleverness that is
      detestable,
  and there is a fool who merely
      lacks wisdom.
24 Better are the God-fearing who lack
      understanding
  than the highly intelligent who
      transgress the law.
25 There is a cleverness that is exact but
      unjust,
  and there are people who abuse
      favors to gain a verdict.
26 There is the villain bowed down in
      mourning,
  but inwardly he is full of deceit.
27 He hides his face and pretends not to
      hear,
  but when no one notices, he will
      take advantage of you.
28 Even if lack of strength keeps him
      from sinning,
  he will nevertheless do evil when he
      finds the opportunity.
29 A person is known by his appearance,
  and a sensible person is known
      when first met, face to face.
30 A person's attire and hearty laughter,
  and the way he walks, show what
      he is.

20 There is a rebuke that is untimely,
  and there is the person who is
      wise enough to keep silent.

*a* Other ancient authorities add *and do not be angry.* [18]*The fear of the Lord is the beginning of acceptance, and wisdom obtains his love.* [19]*The knowledge of the Lord's commandments is life-giving discipline; and those who do what is pleasing to him enjoy the fruit of the tree of immortality.* *b* Other ancient authorities add *and the knowledge of his omnipotence.* [21]*When a slave says to his master, "I will not act as you wish," even if later he does it, he angers the one who supports him.*

**18–19:** These verses are found in the translators' note to 19.17. They are a later addition; the reference to *immortality* is inconsistent with the views of the book elsewhere.
  **19.20–30: Wisdom and cleverness contrasted.** True *wisdom is fear of the Lord* (see Prov 1.7) and *fulfillment of the law* (v. 20); mere *cleverness* enables the *intelligent* to *transgress the law* and commit injustice. **26–30:** Appearances can be both deceiving and revealing.
  **20.1–8: Speech and silence. 4:** One can no more be compelled to do what is *right* than can a *eunuch* engage in sexual intercourse. **5–6:** Prov 17.27–28. **7:** *The right moment,* Prov 15.23; 25.11.

2 How much better it is to rebuke than
    to fume!
3 And the one who admits his fault will
    be kept from failure.
4 Like a eunuch lusting to violate a girl
    is the person who does right under
    compulsion.
5 Some people keep silent and are
    thought to be wise,
  while others are detested for being
    talkative.
6 Some people keep silent because they
    have nothing to say,
  while others keep silent because
    they know when to speak.
7 The wise remain silent until the right
    moment,
  but a boasting fool misses the right
    moment.
8 Whoever talks too much is detested,
  and whoever pretends to authority
    is hated.*a*

9 There may be good fortune for a
    person in adversity,
  and a windfall may result in a loss.
10 There is the gift that profits you
    nothing,
  and the gift to be paid back double.
11 There are losses for the sake of glory,
  and there are some who have raised
    their heads from humble
    circumstances.
12 Some buy much for little,
  but pay for it seven times over.
13 The wise make themselves beloved by
    only few words,*b*
  but the courtesies of fools are
    wasted.
14 A fool's gift will profit you nothing,*c*
  for he looks for recompense
    sevenfold.*d*
15 He gives little and upbraids much;
  he opens his mouth like a town
    crier.

Today he lends and tomorrow he asks
    it back;
  such a one is hateful to God and
    humans.*e*
16 The fool says, "I have no friends,
  and I get no thanks for my good
    deeds.
  Those who eat my bread are
    evil-tongued."
17 How many will ridicule him, and how
    often!*f*

18 A slip on the pavement is better than
    a slip of the tongue;
  the downfall of the wicked will
    occur just as speedily.
19 A coarse person is like an
    inappropriate story,
  continually on the lips of the
    ignorant.
20 A proverb from a fool's lips will be
    rejected,
  for he does not tell it at the proper
    time.

21 One may be prevented from sinning
    by poverty;
  so when he rests he feels no
    remorse.
22 One may lose his life through shame,
  or lose it because of human
    respect.*g*
23 Another out of shame makes promises
    to a friend,

---

*a* Other ancient authorities add *How good it is to show repentance when you are reproved, for so you will escape deliberate sin!*  *b* Heb: Gk *by words*  *c* Other ancient authorities add *so it is with the envious who give under compulsion*  *d* Syr: Gk *he has many eyes instead of one*  *e* Other ancient authorities lack *to God and humans*  *f* Other ancient authorities add *for he has not honestly received what he has, and what he does not have is unimportant to him*  *g* Other ancient authorities read *his foolish look*

**20.9–17: Paradoxical appearances** are instructive to the wise.
**20.18–20: Inappropriate speech** brings undesirable results.
**20.21–26: Shameful circumstances. 21:** Paradoxically, *poverty* may keep one from more shameful *sinning*. **23:** The *promises* are either insincere or impossible. **24–26:** Lying has its costs (7.13; 25.2; Prov 6.16–19; 12.22; Ps 5.6).

and so makes an enemy for
    nothing.

24 A lie is an ugly blot on a person;
    it is continually on the lips of the
        ignorant.
25 A thief is preferable to a habitual liar,
    but the lot of both is ruin.
26 A liar's way leads to disgrace,
    and his shame is ever with him.

PROVERBIAL SAYINGS *a*

27 The wise person advances himself by
        his words,
    and one who is sensible pleases the
        great.
28 Those who cultivate the soil heap up
        their harvest,
    and those who please the great
        atone for injustice.
29 Favors and gifts blind the eyes of the
        wise;
    like a muzzle on the mouth they
        stop reproofs.
30 Hidden wisdom and unseen treasure,
    of what value is either?
31 Better are those who hide their folly
    than those who hide their
        wisdom.*b*

21 Have you sinned, my child? Do so
        no more,
    but ask forgiveness for your past
        sins.
2 Flee from sin as from a snake;
    for if you approach sin, it will bite
        you.
    Its teeth are lion's teeth,
    and can destroy human lives.
3 All lawlessness is like a two-edged
        sword;

there is no healing for the wound it
    inflicts.

4 Panic and insolence will waste away
        riches;
    thus the house of the proud will be
        laid waste.*c*
5 The prayer of the poor goes from
        their lips to the ears of God,*d*
    and his judgment comes speedily.
6 Those who hate reproof walk in the
        sinner's steps,
    but those who fear the Lord repent
        in their heart.
7 The mighty in speech are widely
        known;
    when they slip, the sensible person
        knows it.
8 Whoever builds his house with other
        people's money
    is like one who gathers stones for
        his burial mound.*e*
9 An assembly of the wicked is like a
        bundle of tow,
    and their end is a blazing fire.
10 The way of sinners is paved with
        smooth stones,
    but at its end is the pit of Hades.
11 Whoever keeps the law controls his
        thoughts,
    and the fulfillment of the fear of
        the Lord is wisdom.

*a* This heading is included in the Gk text.    *b* Other
ancient authorities add 32*Unwearied endurance in
seeking the Lord is better than a masterless charioteer
of one's own life.*    *c* Other ancient authorities read
*uprooted*    *d* Gk *his ears*    *e* Other ancient
authorities read *for the winter*

**20.27–31: Wise counsel. 29:** *Gifts* or bribes compromise one's capacity to speak the truth (cf. Prov
15.27; 17.23).

**21.1–10: Warnings against sin. 2–3:** *Sin* is as subtle as a *snake* (Gen 3.1–5), strong as a lion (27.10;
Joel 1.6), and deadly as a *two-edged sword* (Prov 5.4). **5:** Cf. 35.17–21. **7:** An ironic comment on the
*mighty* talker, who is unaware of his errors. **8:** *Other people's money,* ill-gotten gain leads to destruction.
**9:** *Tow,* fibers. The image of *fire* refers to disaster in this world, not punishment in an afterlife (cf. 16.6).
**10:** *Hades,* Sheol, the abode of the dead (see 17.27n.).

**21.11–28: A series of contrasts between the wise and fools. 11:** See Prov 1.7. **13–14:** The contrast is

12 The one who is not clever cannot be
taught,
but there is a cleverness that
increases bitterness.
13 The knowledge of the wise will
increase like a flood,
and their counsel like a life-giving
spring.
14 The mind[a] of a fool is like a broken
jar;
it can hold no knowledge.

15 When an intelligent person hears a
wise saying,
he praises it and adds to it;
when a fool[b] hears it, he laughs at[c]
it
and throws it behind his back.
16 A fool's chatter is like a burden on a
journey,
but delight is found in the speech of
the intelligent.
17 The utterance of a sensible person is
sought in the assembly,
and they ponder his words in their
minds.
18 Like a house in ruins is wisdom to a
fool,
and to the ignorant, knowledge is
talk that has no meaning.
19 To a senseless person education is
fetters on his feet,
and like manacles on his right
hand.
20 A fool raises his voice when he
laughs,
but the wise[d] smile quietly.
21 To the sensible person education is
like a golden ornament,
and like a bracelet on the right
arm.

22 The foot of a fool rushes into a house,
but an experienced person waits
respectfully outside.
23 A boor peers into the house from the
door,
but a cultivated person remains
outside.
24 It is ill-mannered for a person to
listen at a door;
the discreet would be grieved by the
disgrace.

25 The lips of babblers speak of what is
not their concern,[e]
but the words of the prudent are
weighed in the balance.
26 The mind of fools is in their mouth,
but the mouth of the wise is in[f]
their mind.
27 When an ungodly person curses an
adversary,[g]
he curses himself.
28 A whisperer degrades himself
and is hated in his neighborhood.

22 The idler is like a filthy stone,
and every one hisses at his
disgrace.
2 The idler is like the filth of dunghills;
anyone that picks it up will shake it
off his hand.

3 It is a disgrace to be the father of an
undisciplined son,
and the birth of a daughter is a
loss.

a Syr Lat: Gk *entrails*    b Syr: Gk *reveler*    c Syr: Gk
*dislikes*    d Syr Lat: Gk *clever*    e Other ancient
authorities read *of strangers speak of these things*
f Other ancient authorities omit *in*    g Or *curses
Satan*

between a *spring* and a *broken jar* (or cistern, Jer 2.13), which holds no water. All the comparisons that
follow are in favor of the wise: increasing wisdom (v. 15), giving *delight* (v. 16), a *golden ornament*
(v. 21), courtesy (vv. 22–24), careful *words* (vv. 25–26). **27:** *Curses himself*, in the sense that the curse
recoils upon him.

**22.1–2: On laziness.** The language is intended to convey disgust. *Filthy stone . . . dunghills*, the ancients
apparently used small stones to clean themselves after eliminating.

**22.3–6: On children.** In Ben Sira's era, women and children were subordinate to the male head of

4 A sensible daughter obtains a
   husband of her own,
   but one who acts shamefully is a
   grief to her father.
5 An impudent daughter disgraces
   father and husband,
   and is despised by both.
6 Like music in time of mourning is
   ill-timed conversation,
   but a thrashing and discipline are at
   all times wisdom.ᵃ

9 Whoever teaches a fool is like one
   who glues potsherds together,
   or who rouses a sleeper from deep
   slumber.
10 Whoever tells a story to a fool tells it
   to a drowsy man;
   and at the end he will say, "What
   is it?"
11 Weep for the dead, for he has left the
   light behind;
   and weep for the fool, for he has
   left intelligence behind.
   Weep less bitterly for the dead, for he
   is at rest;
   but the life of the fool is worse
   than death.
12 Mourning for the dead lasts seven
   days,
   but for the foolish or the ungodly it
   lasts all the days of their lives.

13 Do not talk much with a senseless
   person
   or visit an unintelligent person.ᵇ
   Stay clear of him, or you may have
   trouble,

and be spattered when he shakes
   himself off.
   Avoid him and you will find rest,
   and you will never be wearied by
   his lack of sense.
14 What is heavier than lead?
   And what is its name except
   "Fool"?
15 Sand, salt, and a piece of iron
   are easier to bear than a stupid
   person.

16 A wooden beam firmly bonded into a
   building
   is not loosened by an earthquake;
   so the mind firmly resolved after due
   reflection
   will not be afraid in a crisis.
17 A mind settled on an intelligent
   thought
   is like stucco decoration that makes
   a wall smooth.
18 Fencesᶜ set on a high place
   will not stand firm against the
   wind;
   so a timid mind with a fool's resolve
   will not stand firm against any fear.

19 One who pricks the eye brings tears,
   and one who pricks the heart
   makes clear its feelings.

a Other ancient authorities add ⁷Children who are brought up in a good life, conceal the lowly birth of their parents. ⁸Children who are disdainfully and boorishly haughty stain the nobility of their kindred. b Other ancient authorities add For being without sense he will despise everything about you   c Other ancient authorities read Pebbles

household, whose honor depended on controlling them effectively. Female children were typically regarded as a greater liability than sons, hence the misogynistic statement that *the birth of a daughter is a loss* (v. 3; on daughters cf. 7.24–25; 42.9–13). **6:** *Thrashing,* physical punishment was a common form of discipline in antiquity (cf. 30.1–13; Prov 13.24; 23.13–14). **7–8:** Translated in the marginal notes, these verses are not considered part of the original composition.
**22.9–18: On fools. 9:** *Glues potsherds,* tries to reassemble broken pottery, a futile effort. **11–12:** One can *weep for the fool* more than for *the dead. Seven days* was the usual period of mourning (Gen 50.10). **13:** *Shakes himself off,* as would an animal, to remove filth. **14–15:** The fool is difficult *to bear* (cf. 21.16; Prov 27.3). **16–18:** The resilient *mind* of the wise is contrasted with the weak *resolve* of the fool.
**22.19–26: Preserving friendship. 19:** An observation about close relationships: Like the *eye,* the *heart*

20 One who throws a stone at birds
        scares them away,
    and one who reviles a friend
        destroys a friendship.
21 Even if you draw your sword against
        a friend,
    do not despair, for there is a way
        back.
22 If you open your mouth against your
        friend,
    do not worry, for reconciliation is
        possible.
    But as for reviling, arrogance,
        disclosure of secrets, or a
        treacherous blow—
    in these cases any friend will take
        to flight.

23 Gain the trust of your neighbor in his
        poverty,
    so that you may rejoice with him in
        his prosperity.
    Stand by him in time of distress,
    so that you may share with him in
        his inheritance.ᵃ
24 The vapor and smoke of the furnace
        precede the fire;
    so insults precede bloodshed.
25 I am not ashamed to shelter a friend,
    and I will not hide from him.
26 But if harm should come to me
        because of him,
    whoever hears of it will beware of
        him.

27 Who will set a guard over my mouth,
    and an effective seal upon my lips,
    so that I may not fall because of
        them,
    and my tongue may not destroy
        me?

23 O Lord, Father and Master of my
        life,
    do not abandon me to their designs,
    and do not let me fall because of
        them!
2 Who will set whips over my thoughts,
    and the discipline of wisdom over
        my mind,
    so as not to spare me in my errors,
    and not overlook myᵇ sins?
3 Otherwise my mistakes may be
        multiplied,
    and my sins may abound,
    and I may fall before my adversaries,
    and my enemy may rejoice over
        me.ᶜ
4 O Lord, Father and God of my life,
    do not give me haughty eyes,
5 and remove evil desire from me.
6 Let neither gluttony nor lust
        overcome me,
    and do not give me over to
        shameless passion.

DISCIPLINE OF THE TONGUE ᵈ

7 Listen, my children, to instruction
        concerning the mouth;
    the one who observes it will never
        be caught.
8 Sinners are overtaken through their
        lips;
    by them the reviler and the
        arrogant are tripped up.
9 Do not accustom your mouth to
        oaths,

a Other ancient authorities add *For one should not
always despise restricted circumstances, or admire a
rich person who is stupid.*   b Gk *their*   c Other
ancient authorities add *From them the hope of your
mercy is remote*   d This heading is included in the
Gk text.

is sensitive and will express its hurt *feelings*. **20–22:** The things that destroy friendship (cf. 27.16–21;
42.1; Prov 11.13; 20.19; 25.9). **23–26:** Friendship through good and bad circumstances.

**22.27–23.6: A prayer for self-control**, stressing the dual concerns of sins of the *tongue* (22.27–23.1,
treated further in 23.7–15) and sins of *passion*, especially sexual offenses (23.2–6, discussed also in
23.16–26). **27:** *Guard over my mouth*, cf. Ps 141.3; Prov 21.23. **23.1,4:** *Father*, cf. 51.10.

**23.7–15: Sinful speech.** Warnings against the casual use of *oaths* (vv. 9–11; Ex 20.7; Lev 5.4; 19.12;
Deut 5.11), against blasphemy (v. 12; cf. Lev 24.11–16), and against *coarse* and *abusive language*
(vv.13–15). **14:** *Curse . . . birth*, see Job 3.3–10; Jer 20.14–18.

nor habitually utter the name of the
Holy One;
10 for as a servant who is constantly
under scrutiny
will not lack bruises,
so also the person who always swears
and utters the Name
will never be cleansed[a] from sin.
11 The one who swears many oaths is
full of iniquity,
and the scourge will not leave his
house.
If he swears in error, his sin remains
on him,
and if he disregards it, he sins
doubly;
if he swears a false oath, he will not
be justified,
for his house will be filled with
calamities.

12 There is a manner of speaking
comparable to death;[b]
may it never be found in the
inheritance of Jacob!
Such conduct will be far from the
godly,
and they will not wallow in sins.
13 Do not accustom your mouth to
coarse, foul language,
for it involves sinful speech.
14 Remember your father and mother
when you sit among the great,
or you may forget yourself in their
presence,
and behave like a fool through bad
habit;
then you will wish that you had never
been born,
and you will curse the day of your
birth.
15 Those who are accustomed to using
abusive language

will never become disciplined as
long as they live.

16 Two kinds of individuals multiply
sins,
and a third incurs wrath.
Hot passion that blazes like a fire
will not be quenched until it burns
itself out;
one who commits fornication with his
near of kin
will never cease until the fire burns
him up.
17 To a fornicator all bread is sweet;
he will never weary until he dies.
18 The one who sins against his marriage
bed
says to himself, "Who can see me?
Darkness surrounds me, the walls
hide me,
and no one sees me. Why should I
worry?
The Most High will not remember
sins."
19 His fear is confined to human eyes
and he does not realize that the
eyes of the Lord
are ten thousand times brighter
than the sun;
they look upon every aspect of human
behavior
and see into hidden corners.
20 Before the universe was created, it
was known to him,
and so it is since its completion.
21 This man will be punished in the
streets of the city,
and where he least suspects it, he
will be seized.

a Syr *be free*  b Other ancient authorities read
*clothed about with death*

**23.16–27: Sexual misconduct. 16–17:** This numerical saying (a frequently used literary device, especially in wisdom literature; see Job 5.19; Prov 30.15–19,21–29) singles out three kinds of offenders: the licentious, the incestuous, and the adulterer. **17:** *All bread is sweet,* a reference to the deceptive pleasure of adulterous relations (cf. Prov 9.17). **18–21:** The adulterer's self-delusion. **20:** God knows the people's misdeeds even before creation. **21:** According to Lev 20.10 and Deut 22.22–27, the punishment was death; here it is not specified. **22–26:** The fate of a woman guilty of adultery. **23:** *Disobeyed the law,* see

22 So it is with a woman who leaves her
husband
    and presents him with an heir by
    another man.
23 For first of all, she has disobeyed the
law of the Most High;
    second, she has committed an
    offense against her husband;
    and third, through her fornication she
    has committed adultery
    and brought forth children by
    another man.
24 She herself will be brought before the
assembly,
    and her punishment will extend to
    her children.
25 Her children will not take root,
    and her branches will not bear
    fruit.
26 She will leave behind an accursed
memory
    and her disgrace will never be
    blotted out.
27 Those who survive her will recognize
    that nothing is better than the fear
    of the Lord,
    and nothing sweeter than to heed the
    commandments of the Lord.*a*

THE PRAISE OF WISDOM *b*

24 Wisdom praises herself,
    and tells of her glory in the midst
    of her people.

2 In the assembly of the Most High she
opens her mouth,
    and in the presence of his hosts she
    tells of her glory:
3 "I came forth from the mouth of the
Most High,
    and covered the earth like a mist.
4 I dwelt in the highest heavens,
    and my throne was in a pillar of
    cloud.
5 Alone I compassed the vault of
heaven
    and traversed the depths of the
    abyss.
6 Over waves of the sea, over all the
earth,
    and over every people and nation I
    have held sway.*c*
7 Among all these I sought a resting
place;
    in whose territory should I abide?

8 "Then the Creator of all things gave
me a command,
    and my Creator chose the place for
    my tent.
He said, 'Make your dwelling in
    Jacob,

*a* Other ancient authorities add as verse 28, *It is a
great honor to follow God, and to be received by him
is long life.* *b* This heading is included in the Gk
text. *c* Other ancient authorities read *I have
acquired a possession*

Ex 20.14, which, however, is explicitly addressed to a male. **24:** *To her children,* cf. Wis 3.16–19; 4.3–6.
**25:** Cf. Hos 9.16. **27:** A conclusion reprising Ben Sira's emphasis on *fear of the Lord* (see Prov 1.7) and
*the commandments.*
  **24.1–34:** Praise of Wisdom (cf. 1.1–20; 4.11–19; 6.18–37; 14.20–15.10; Job 28; Prov 8.22–31; Wis
7–10; Bar 3.9–4.4). Vividly personified as a female figure with divine attributes, Wisdom recounts her
divine origin (vv. 1–7), her relationship with Israel (vv. 8–12), and her beauty and desirability
(vv. 13–17). Following an invitation to her listeners (vv. 19–22), she is closely identified with the Torah
(vv. 23–29). A first-person reflection by Ben Sira on the transforming power of wisdom instruction
concludes the chapter (vv. 30–34). **1–2:** Introduction of Wisdom, speaking to *her people* (Israel,
cf. 1.10n.) and to the *assembly of the Most High* (the heavenly council, cf. Ps 82.1,6–7) concerning her
glory. Such speeches, recounting the speaker's virtues, are characteristic of the Egyptian goddess Isis. **3:**
*From the mouth of the Most High,* cf. Gen 1.1–3; Ps 33.6; Prov 2.6; Wis 9.1–2. **4:** *Pillar of cloud,* cf. Ex
13.21–22; 33.9–10. **5–7:** The theme of wisdom's abode or resting place is taken up also in Job 28; Bar
3.14–37; 1 Enoch 42. For the cosmic reach of wisdom, see Prov 8.27–29; Job 38.16; Wis 8.1. **8–12:**
Obeying the divine command to make her *dwelling in Jacob* (cf. Deut 12.5; Bar 3.36), eternal Wisdom
(v. 9; cf. Prov 8.22–23) ministers to the Lord in the *holy tent* (the tabernacle, Ex 25.8–9) and is estab-

and in Israel receive your
inheritance.'

9 Before the ages, in the beginning, he
created me,
and for all the ages I shall not cease
to be.
10 In the holy tent I ministered before
him,
and so I was established in Zion.
11 Thus in the beloved city he gave me a
resting place,
and in Jerusalem was my domain.
12 I took root in an honored people,
in the portion of the Lord, his
heritage.

13 "I grew tall like a cedar in Lebanon,
and like a cypress on the heights of
Hermon.
14 I grew tall like a palm tree in
En-gedi,[a]
and like rosebushes in Jericho;
like a fair olive tree in the field,
and like a plane tree beside water[b]
I grew tall.
15 Like cassia and camel's thorn I gave
forth perfume,
and like choice myrrh I spread my
fragrance,
like galbanum, onycha, and stacte,
and like the odor of incense in the
tent.
16 Like a terebinth I spread out my
branches,
and my branches are glorious and
graceful.
17 Like the vine I bud forth delights,
and my blossoms become glorious
and abundant fruit.[c]

19 "Come to me, you who desire me,
and eat your fill of my fruits.
20 For the memory of me is sweeter than
honey,
and the possession of me sweeter
than the honeycomb.
21 Those who eat of me will hunger for
more,
and those who drink of me will
thirst for more.
22 Whoever obeys me will not be put to
shame,
and those who work with me will
not sin."

23 All this is the book of the covenant of
the Most High God,
the law that Moses commanded us
as an inheritance for the
congregations of Jacob.[d]
25 It overflows, like the Pishon, with
wisdom,
and like the Tigris at the time of
the first fruits.
26 It runs over, like the Euphrates, with
understanding,
and like the Jordan at harvest time.
27 It pours forth instruction like the
Nile,[e]

a Other ancient authorities read *on the beaches*
b Other ancient authorities omit *beside water*
c Other ancient authorities add as verse 18, *I am the
mother of beautiful love, of fear, of knowledge, and of
holy hope; being eternal, I am given to all my children,
to those who are named by him.* d Other ancient
authorities add as verse 24, *"Do not cease to be strong
in the Lord, cling to him so that he may strengthen
you; the Lord Almighty alone is God, and besides him
there is no savior."* e Syr: Gk It makes instruction
*shine forth like light*

lished in the Temple in Jerusalem (*Zion*) (vv. 10–12). **13–17:** Her splendor is lavishly compared to trees,
plants, and exotic aromatics. **13:** *Hermon,* the highest mountain in the Levant, located northeast of Israel.
**14:** *En-gedi,* an oasis on the west shore of the Dead Sea, 48 km (30 mi) south of *Jericho.* Both towns had
luxuriant vegetation. **15:** The choice substances are used in the *perfume* and *incense* of Jerusalem Temple
worship (see Ex 30.23–38). **18:** See 22.7–8n. **19–22:** Wisdom concludes her speech with an invitation to
her unusual meal, which offers unending delight and keeps from sin. **19:** *Come to me,* cf. 51.23–30; Prov
9.5; in Christian literature a similar saying is attributed to Jesus (Mt 11.28–30). **21:** In Christian scriptures
cf. Jn 6.35. **23–29:** Sirach identifies Wisdom with the Torah (1.26; 6.32–37; 15.1; 19.20; 23.27). **23:**
*Book of the covenant,* cf. Ex 24.7; *law that Moses commanded us,* cf. Deut 4.5–8; 33.4; Bar 4.1. **24:** See
22.7–8n. **25–27:** The inexhaustible bounty of Wisdom and the Mosaic Torah is like that of the four rivers
of Eden (*Pishon, Tigris, Euphrates, Gihon,* Gen 2.10–14) plus the *Jordan* and the *Nile.* **28:** Just as the

like the Gihon at the time of
vintage.
28 The first man did not know wisdom[a]
fully,
nor will the last one fathom her.
29 For her thoughts are more abundant
than the sea,
and her counsel deeper than the
great abyss.

30 As for me, I was like a canal from a
river,
like a water channel into a garden.
31 I said, "I will water my garden
and drench my flower-beds."
And lo, my canal became a river,
and my river a sea.
32 I will again make instruction shine
forth like the dawn,
and I will make it clear from far
away.
33 I will again pour out teaching like
prophecy,
and leave it to all future
generations.
34 Observe that I have not labored for
myself alone,
but for all who seek wisdom.[a]

25 I take pleasure in three things,
and they are beautiful in the sight
of God and of mortals:[b]
agreement among brothers and sisters,
friendship among neighbors,
and a wife and a husband who live
in harmony.
2 I hate three kinds of people,
and I loathe their manner of life:
a pauper who boasts, a rich person
who lies,

and an old fool who commits
adultery.

3 If you gathered nothing in your
youth,
how can you find anything in your
old age?
4 How attractive is sound judgment in
the gray-haired,
and for the aged to possess good
counsel!
5 How attractive is wisdom in the aged,
and understanding and counsel in
the venerable!
6 Rich experience is the crown of the
aged,
and their boast is the fear of the
Lord.

7 I can think of nine whom I would call
blessed,
and a tenth my tongue proclaims:
a man who can rejoice in his children;
a man who lives to see the downfall
of his foes.
8 Happy the man who lives with a
sensible wife,
and the one who does not plow
with ox and ass together.[c]
Happy is the one who does not sin
with the tongue,
and the one who has not served an
inferior.
9 Happy is the one who finds a
friend,[d]

a Gk *her*    b Syr Lat: Gk *In three things I was
beautiful and I stood in beauty before the Lord and
mortals.*    c Heb Syr: Gk lacks *and the one who does
not plow with ox and ass together*    d Lat Syr: Gk
*good sense*

*first man* (Adam) did not know her (since the Torah was given first to Moses), so the *last one* will never
exhaust such profound wisdom. **30–34:** Ben Sira describes how in channeling this wisdom in his book,
he has become indeed a *river*, a veritable *sea* whose *instruction* (comparable to *prophecy*) reaches *all
future generations.*
    **25.1–2:** Numerical sayings (see 23.16–17n.) about social harmony (v.1) and ill-fitting conduct (v. 2).
In v. 1 the Greek text reads "brothers" ("adelphon").
    **25.3–6:** Wisdom and maturity.
    **25.7–11:** A numerical saying of ten blessings. **8:** To *plow with ox and ass* is prohibited (Deut 22.10).
Here the phrase seems to refer to polygamous relations with incompatible wives (cf. 26.6; 37.11; Judg
14.18).

and the one who speaks to attentive
    listeners.
10 How great is the one who finds
    wisdom!
    But none is superior to the one who
    fears the Lord.
11 Fear of the Lord surpasses everything;
    to whom can we compare the one
    who has it?[a]
13 Any wound, but not a wound of the
    heart!
    Any wickedness, but not the
    wickedness of a woman!
14 Any suffering, but not suffering from
    those who hate!
    And any vengeance, but not the
    vengeance of enemies!
15 There is no venom[b] worse than a
    snake's venom,[b]
    and no anger worse than a
    woman's[c] wrath.
16 I would rather live with a lion and a
    dragon
    than live with an evil woman.
17 A woman's wickedness changes her
    appearance,
    and darkens her face like that of a
    bear.
18 Her husband sits[d] among the
    neighbors,
    and he cannot help sighing[e]
    bitterly.
19 Any iniquity is small compared to a
    woman's iniquity;
    may a sinner's lot befall her!
20 A sandy ascent for the feet of the
    aged—

such is a garrulous wife to a quiet
    husband.
21 Do not be ensnared by a woman's
    beauty,
    and do not desire a woman for her
    possessions.[f]
22 There is wrath and impudence and
    great disgrace
    when a wife supports her husband.
23 Dejected mind, gloomy face,
    and wounded heart come from an
    evil wife.
    Drooping hands and weak knees
    come from the wife who does not
    make her husband happy.
24 From a woman sin had its beginning,
    and because of her we all die.
25 Allow no outlet to water,
    and no boldness of speech to an
    evil wife.
26 If she does not go as you direct,
    separate her from yourself.

26 Happy is the husband of a good
    wife;
    the number of his days will be
    doubled.
2 A loyal wife brings joy to her
    husband,
    and he will complete his years in
    peace.
3 A good wife is a great blessing;

a Other ancient authorities add as verse 12, *The fear
of the Lord is the beginning of love for him, and faith
is the beginning of clinging to him.*    b Syr: Gk *head*
c Other ancient authorities read *an enemy's*
d Heb Syr: Gk *loses heart*    e Other ancient
authorities read *and listening he sighs*    f Heb Syr:
Other Gk authorities read *for her beauty*

**25.13–26.27: Sayings, from a distinctly male point of view, about desirable and undesirable women.**
Ben Sira uses strong language in his denunciations of various types of people (e.g., 22.1–2; 25.2; 27.24).
His pronouncements against women, however, are among the worst; they would appear to compromise
his teaching against the use of abusive language (23.15; cf. 26.12,22).

**25.13–26: Woeful women and bad wives.** Ben Sira means to caution his young male students about
their choices in marriage (cf. 36.26–31; Prov 21.19; 25.24; 27.15; Eccl 7.26). **13–19:** *Wickedness of a
woman . . . a woman's iniquity,* cf. 42.14n. **16:** Prov 21.19; 25.24; 27.15. **22:** *Supports her husband,*
economically. Ben Sira views a man's financial dependence on his wife as disgraceful (cf. v. 21b). **24:**
*From a woman sin,* an interpretation of the Adam and Eve story that exceeds Gen 3 in placing blame
upon the woman (cf. 2 Cor 11.3; 1 Tim 2.14). **26:** *Separate her,* refers to divorce (Deut 24.1).

**26.1–4: The good wife** is counted as a *great blessing* (v. 3); cf. Prov 31.

she will be granted among the
  blessings of the man who fears
  the Lord.
4 Whether rich or poor, his heart is
    content,
  and at all times his face is cheerful.
5 Of three things my heart is frightened,
    and of a fourth I am in great fear:[a]
  Slander in the city, the gathering of a
    mob,
  and false accusation—all these are
    worse than death.
6 But it is heartache and sorrow when a
    wife is jealous of a rival,
  and a tongue-lashing makes it
    known to all.
7 A bad wife is a chafing yoke;
  taking hold of her is like grasping a
    scorpion.
8 A drunken wife arouses great anger;
  she cannot hide her shame.
9 The haughty stare betrays an unchaste
    wife;
  her eyelids give her away.

10 Keep strict watch over a headstrong
    daughter,
  or else, when she finds liberty, she
    will make use of it.
11 Be on guard against her impudent
    eye,
  and do not be surprised if she sins
    against you.
12 As a thirsty traveler opens his mouth
  and drinks from any water near
    him,
  so she will sit in front of every tent
    peg
  and open her quiver to the arrow.

13 A wife's charm delights her husband,

and her skill puts flesh on his
    bones.
14 A silent wife is a gift from the
    Lord,
  and nothing is so precious as her
    self-discipline.
15 A modest wife adds charm to charm,
  and no scales can weigh the value
    of her chastity.
16 Like the sun rising in the heights of
    the Lord,
  so is the beauty of a good wife in
    her well-ordered home.
17 Like the shining lamp on the holy
    lampstand,
  so is a beautiful face on a stately
    figure.
18 Like golden pillars on silver bases,
  so are shapely legs and steadfast
    feet.

_____

Other ancient authorities add
    verses 19–27:

19 *My child, keep sound the bloom of*
    *your youth,*
  *and do not give your strength to*
    *strangers.*
20 *Seek a fertile field within the whole*
    *plain,*
  *and sow it with your own seed,*
    *trusting in your fine stock.*
21 *So your offspring will prosper,*
  *and, having confidence in their*
    *good descent, will grow great.*
22 *A prostitute is regarded as spittle,*
  *and a married woman as a tower of*
    *death to her lovers.*

a Syr: Meaning of Gk uncertain

**26.5–12: More objectionable women. 5–6:** In numerical proverbs (see 23.16–17n.) the last element is
the climax. **6:** *Jealous of a rival,* probably referring to enmity among wives in a polygamous household.
**10:** *Headstrong daughter,* here probably referring to an insubordinate wife (but cf. 42.11). **12:** Indirect
reference to illicit sexual intercourse.
  **26.13–18: Praise of the good wife. 13:** *Her skill,* cf. Prov 31.10–31. **17–18:** Cf. Song 4.1–7.
  **26.19–27: Further teaching concerning women.** These verses are present in Greek and Syriac manuscripts, but not in Hebrew. Praise for women who are pious, modest, deferential, and quiet (vv. 23–27);
and graphic reproach of those who do not submit to the authority of the household (vv. 22,25). **20:** An
agricultural metaphor for reproduction.

23 A godless wife is given as a portion to
    a lawless man,
  but a pious wife is given to the
    man who fears the Lord.
24 A shameless woman constantly acts
    disgracefully,
  but a modest daughter will even be
    embarrassed before her
    husband.
25 A headstrong wife is regarded as a dog,
  but one who has a sense of shame
    will fear the Lord.
26 A wife honoring her husband will
    seem wise to all,
  but if she dishonors him in her
    pride she will be known to all
    as ungodly.
  Happy is the husband of a good
    wife;
  for the number of his years will be
    doubled.
27 A loud-voiced and garrulous wife is
    like a trumpet sounding the
    charge,
  and every person like this lives in
    the anarchy of war.

---

28 At two things my heart is grieved,
  and because of a third anger comes
    over me:
  a warrior in want through poverty,
  intelligent men who are treated
    contemptuously,
  and a man who turns back from
    righteousness to sin—
  the Lord will prepare him for the
    sword!

29 A merchant can hardly keep from
    wrongdoing,
  nor is a tradesman innocent of sin.

27 Many have committed sin for
    gain,[a]
  and those who seek to get rich will
    avert their eyes.

2 As a stake is driven firmly into a
    fissure between stones,
  so sin is wedged in between selling
    and buying.
3 If a person is not steadfast in the fear
    of the Lord,
  his house will be quickly
    overthrown.
4 When a sieve is shaken, the refuse
    appears;
  so do a person's faults when he
    speaks.
5 The kiln tests the potter's vessels;
  so the test of a person is in his
    conversation.
6 Its fruit discloses the cultivation of a
    tree;
  so a person's speech discloses the
    cultivation of his mind.
7 Do not praise anyone before he
    speaks,
  for this is the way people are
    tested.

8 If you pursue justice, you will attain it
  and wear it like a glorious robe.
9 Birds roost with their own kind,
  so honesty comes home to those
    who practice it.
10 A lion lies in wait for prey;
  so does sin for evildoers.

11 The conversation of the godly is
    always wise,
  but the fool changes like the moon.
12 Among stupid people limit your time,
  but among thoughtful people linger
    on.
13 The talk of fools is offensive,
  and their laughter is wantonly
    sinful.
14 Their cursing and swearing make
    one's hair stand on end,

a Other ancient authorities read a trifle

**26.28–27.15: Tests of character. 28:** The Greek reading, *warrior*, apparently misconstrues a Hebrew expression for "wealthy man." For the form of the saying, see 23.16–17n. **26.29–27.3:** Corrupt commerce, cf. Prov 11.1; 20.10,14. **4–7:** Speech reveals character. **8–10:** The reward of honesty. **11–15:** Various kinds of talk.

and their quarrels make others stop
their ears.

15 The strife of the proud leads to
bloodshed,
and their abuse is grievous to hear.

16 Whoever betrays secrets destroys
confidence,
and will never find a congenial
friend.

17 Love your friend and keep faith with
him;
but if you betray his secrets, do not
follow after him.

18 For as a person destroys his enemy,
so you have destroyed the
friendship of your neighbor.

19 And as you allow a bird to escape
from your hand,
so you have let your neighbor go,
and will not catch him again.

20 Do not go after him, for he is too far
off,
and has escaped like a gazelle from
a snare.

21 For a wound may be bandaged,
and there is reconciliation after
abuse,
but whoever has betrayed secrets is
without hope.

22 Whoever winks the eye plots mischief,
and those who know him will keep
their distance.

23 In your presence his mouth is all
sweetness,
and he admires your words;
but later he will twist his speech
and with your own words he will
trip you up.

24 I have hated many things, but him
above all;
even the Lord hates him.

25 Whoever throws a stone straight up
throws it on his own head,
and a treacherous blow opens up
many wounds.

26 Whoever digs a pit will fall into
it,
and whoever sets a snare will be
caught in it.

27 If a person does evil, it will roll back
upon him,
and he will not know where it
came from.

28 Mockery and abuse issue from the
proud,
but vengeance lies in wait for them
like a lion.

29 Those who rejoice in the fall of the
godly will be caught in a snare,
and pain will consume them before
their death.

30 Anger and wrath, these also are
abominations,
yet a sinner holds on to them.

28 The vengeful will face the Lord's
vengeance,
for he keeps a strict account of[a]
their sins.

2 Forgive your neighbor the wrong he
has done,
and then your sins will be pardoned
when you pray.

3 Does anyone harbor anger against
another,
and expect healing from the Lord?

4 If one has no mercy toward another
like himself,
can he then seek pardon for his
own sins?

5 If a mere mortal harbors wrath,
who will make an atoning sacrifice
for his sins?

6 Remember the end of your life, and
set enmity aside;
remember corruption and death,
and be true to the
commandments.

a Other ancient authorities read *for he firmly
establishes*

27.16–28.26: Damaged relationships. 16–21: Against disclosing secrets (cf. Prov 20.19; 25.8–10). 21:
*Without hope*, of reconciliation (cf. 22.22). 22–27: Against hypocrisy. 22: *Winks*, with insincerity
(cf. Prov 6.13; 10.10). 25–27: Evil cause and effect (cf. Ps 7.14–16; 9.15–16; Prov 26.27; Eccl 10.8).

7 Remember the commandments, and
   do not be angry with your
   neighbor;
   remember the covenant of the Most
   High, and overlook faults.

8 Refrain from strife, and your sins will
   be fewer;
   for the hot-tempered kindle strife,
9 and the sinner disrupts friendships
   and sows discord among those who
   are at peace.
10 In proportion to the fuel, so will the
   fire burn,
   and in proportion to the obstinacy,
   so will strife increase;[a]
   in proportion to a person's strength
   will be his anger,
   and in proportion to his wealth he
   will increase his wrath.
11 A hasty quarrel kindles a fire,
   and a hasty dispute sheds blood.
12 If you blow on a spark, it will glow;
   if you spit on it, it will be put out;
   yet both come out of your mouth.

13 Curse the gossips and the
   double-tongued,
   for they destroy the peace of many.
14 Slander[b] has shaken many,
   and scattered them from nation to
   nation;
   it has destroyed strong cities,
   and overturned the houses of the
   great.
15 Slander[b] has driven virtuous women
   from their homes,
   and deprived them of the fruit of
   their toil.
16 Those who pay heed to slander[c] will
   not find rest,
   nor will they settle down in
   peace.
17 The blow of a whip raises a welt,

but a blow of the tongue crushes
   the bones.
18 Many have fallen by the edge of the
   sword,
   but not as many as have fallen
   because of the tongue.
19 Happy is the one who is protected
   from it,
   who has not been exposed to its
   anger,
   who has not borne its yoke,
   and has not been bound with its
   fetters.
20 For its yoke is a yoke of iron,
   and its fetters are fetters of bronze;
21 its death is an evil death,
   and Hades is preferable to it.
22 It has no power over the godly;
   they will not be burned in its flame.
23 Those who forsake the Lord will fall
   into its power;
   it will burn among them and will
   not be put out.
   It will be sent out against them like a
   lion;
   like a leopard it will mangle them.
24a As you fence in your property with
   thorns,
25b so make a door and a bolt for your
   mouth.
24b As you lock up your silver and gold,
25a so make balances and scales for
   your words.
26 Take care not to err with your
   tongue,[d]
   and fall victim to one lying in wait.

29 The merciful lend to their
   neighbors;
   by holding out a helping hand they
   keep the commandments.

a Other ancient authorities read *burn*   b Gk *A third
tongue*   c Gk *it*   d Gk *with it*

27.28–28.7: *Vengeance* is ultimately *the Lord's; to forgive* others is required of the faithful (cf. 8.5). **7:**
Cf. Lev 19.18. **8–26:** Quarreling and slander. **10–12:** Cf. Prov 26.20–21. **17–18:** Cf. Prov 15.4; 25.15.
**21:** *Hades* (Sheol, the abode of the dead) is *preferable* to the living *death* inflicted by the *evil* tongue.
**24–25:** One should guard one's *words* as carefully as prized possessions.
   **29.1–20:** Loans, alms, surety. **1–7:** Loans were given without charging interest (Ex 22.25; Lev
25.35–37; Neh 5.10–11), but interest was permitted if one loaned to non-Jews (Deut 23.20–21). **3:** If a

2 Lend to your neighbor in his time of
        need;
    repay your neighbor when a loan
        falls due.
3 Keep your promise and be honest
        with him,
    and on every occasion you will find
        what you need.
4 Many regard a loan as a windfall,
    and cause trouble to those who
        help them.
5 One kisses another's hands until he
        gets a loan,
    and is deferential in speaking of his
        neighbor's money;
    but at the time for repayment he
        delays,
    and pays back with empty
        promises,
    and finds fault with the time.
6 If he can pay, his creditor[a] will
        hardly get back half,
    and will regard that as a windfall.
    If he cannot pay, the borrower[a] has
        robbed the other of his money,
    and he has needlessly made him an
        enemy;
    he will repay him with curses and
        reproaches,
    and instead of glory will repay him
        with dishonor.
7 Many refuse to lend, not because of
        meanness,
    but from fear[b] of being defrauded
        needlessly.

8 Nevertheless, be patient with someone
        in humble circumstances,
    and do not keep him waiting for
        your alms.
9 Help the poor for the
        commandment's sake,
    and in their need do not send them
        away empty-handed.
10 Lose your silver for the sake of a
        brother or a friend,

and do not let it rust under a stone
        and be lost.
11 Lay up your treasure according to the
        commandments of the Most
        High,
    and it will profit you more than
        gold.
12 Store up almsgiving in your treasury,
    and it will rescue you from every
        disaster;
13 better than a stout shield and a sturdy
        spear,
    it will fight for you against the
        enemy.

14 A good person will be surety for his
        neighbor,
    but the one who has lost all sense
        of shame will fail him.
15 Do not forget the kindness of your
        guarantor,
    for he has given his life for you.
16 A sinner wastes the property of his
        guarantor,
17     and the ungrateful person abandons
        his rescuer.
18 Being surety has ruined many who
        were prosperous,
    and has tossed them about like
        waves of the sea;
    it has driven the influential into
        exile,
    and they have wandered among
        foreign nations.
19 The sinner comes to grief through
        surety;
    his pursuit of gain involves him in
        lawsuits.
20 Assist your neighbor to the best of
        your ability,
    but be careful not to fall yourself.

a Gk *he*    b Other ancient authorities read *many
refuse to lend, therefore, because of such meanness;
they are afraid*

loan is repaid on time, one can count on receiving a future loan. **8–13:** As regards the poor, almsgiving
is a duty (cf. 3.30–4.10). **9:** *For the commandment's sake,* Deut 15.7–11. **10:** *Silver,* money. **14–20:** The
dangers in guaranteeing a loan for another. Ben Sira urges support of those in need, but also advises
caution (cf. 8.12–13; Prov 6.1–5; 11.15; 17.18; 20.16; 22.26).

21 The necessities of life are water,
    bread, and clothing,
  and also a house to assure privacy.
22 Better is the life of the poor under
    their own crude roof
  than sumptuous food in the house
    of others.
23 Be content with little or much,
  and you will hear no reproach for
    being a guest.[a]
24 It is a miserable life to go from house
    to house;
  as a guest you should not open
    your mouth;
25 you will play the host and provide
    drink without being thanked,
  and besides this you will hear rude
    words like these:
26 "Come here, stranger, prepare the
    table;
  let me eat what you have there."
27 "Be off, stranger, for an honored
    guest is here;
  my brother has come for a visit,
    and I need the guest-room."
28 It is hard for a sensible person to bear
  scolding about lodging[b] and the
    insults of the moneylender.

CONCERNING CHILDREN[c]

30 He who loves his son will whip
    him often,
  so that he may rejoice at the way
    he turns out.
2 He who disciplines his son will profit
    by him,
  and will boast of him among
    acquaintances.
3 He who teaches his son will make his
    enemies envious,
  and will glory in him among his
    friends.

4 When the father dies he will not seem
    to be dead,
  for he has left behind him one like
    himself,
5 whom in his life he looked upon with
    joy
  and at death, without grief.
6 He has left behind him an avenger
    against his enemies,
  and one to repay the kindness of
    his friends.

7 Whoever spoils his son will bind up
    his wounds,
  and will suffer heartache at every
    cry.
8 An unbroken horse turns out
    stubborn,
  and an unchecked son turns out
    headstrong.
9 Pamper a child, and he will terrorize
    you;
  play with him, and he will grieve
    you.
10 Do not laugh with him, or you will
    have sorrow with him,
  and in the end you will gnash your
    teeth.
11 Give him no freedom in his youth,
  and do not ignore his errors.
12 Bow down his neck in his youth,[d]
    and beat his sides while he is young,
  or else he will become stubborn and
    disobey you,
  and you will have sorrow of soul
    from him.[e]

a Lat: Gk *reproach from your family*; other ancient
authorities lack this line    b Or *scolding from the
household*    c This heading is included in the Gk text.
d Other ancient authorities lack this line and the
preceding line    e Other ancient authorities lack this
line

**29.21–28: Frugality. 21:** Compare the longer list of necessities in 39.26. **23–28:** Live within your
means and preserve your independence. **25:** *Play the host*, the freeloading guest will be pressed into service
at the table.
**30.1–13: Training of children. 1:** Physical punishment was taken for granted in Ben Sira's era (cf. 22.6;
Prov 13.24; 19.18; 23.13–14; 29.15). **4:** The child is the image of the *father* (see Tob 9.6). **6:** *Avenger*, a
vindicator of the father's honor (cf. Ps 127.5). **7–13:** Lack of discipline brings sorrow and shame (cf. Deut
21.18–21).

13 Discipline your son and make his
   yoke heavy,[a]
   so that you may not be offended by
   his shamelessness.

14 Better off poor, healthy, and fit
   than rich and afflicted in body.
15 Health and fitness are better than any
   gold,
   and a robust body than countless
   riches.
16 There is no wealth better than health
   of body,
   and no gladness above joy of heart.
17 Death is better than a life of misery,
   and eternal sleep[b] than chronic
   sickness.

### CONCERNING FOODS[c]

18 Good things poured out upon a
   mouth that is closed
   are like offerings of food placed
   upon a grave.
19 Of what use to an idol is a sacrifice?
   For it can neither eat nor smell.
   So is the one punished by the Lord;
20 he sees with his eyes and groans
   as a eunuch groans when
   embracing a girl.[d]

21 Do not give yourself over to sorrow,
   and do not distress yourself
   deliberately.
22 A joyful heart is life itself,
   and rejoicing lengthens one's life
   span.
23 Indulge yourself[e] and take comfort,
   and remove sorrow far from you,
   for sorrow has destroyed many,
   and no advantage ever comes from
   it.
24 Jealousy and anger shorten life,
   and anxiety brings on premature
   old age.

25 Those who are cheerful and merry at
   table
   will benefit from their food.

31 Wakefulness over wealth wastes
   away one's flesh,
   and anxiety about it drives away
   sleep.
2 Wakeful anxiety prevents slumber,
   and a severe illness carries off
   sleep.[f]
3 The rich person toils to amass a
   fortune,
   and when he rests he fills himself
   with his dainties.
4 The poor person toils to make a
   meager living,
   and if ever he rests he becomes
   needy.

5 One who loves gold will not be
   justified;
   one who pursues money will be led
   astray[g] by it.
6 Many have come to ruin because of
   gold,
   and their destruction has met them
   face to face.
7 It is a stumbling block to those who
   are avid for it,
   and every fool will be taken captive
   by it.
8 Blessed is the rich person who is
   found blameless,
   and who does not go after gold.

a Heb: Gk *take pains with him*    b Other ancient
authorities lack *eternal sleep*    c This heading is
included in the Gk text; other ancient authorities place
the heading before verse 16    d Other ancient
authorities add *So is the person who does right under
compulsion*    e Other ancient authorities read *Beguile
yourself*    f Other ancient authorities read *sleep
carries off a severe illness*    g Heb Syr: Gk *pursues
destruction will be filled*

**30.14–25:** On health and the enjoyment of life. **17:** *Death is better,* cf. Job 3.11,13,17; Eccl 4.1–2; Tob
3.6,10,13. **18–20:** The deceased in the *grave* (Tob 4.17), the inanimate *idol* (Deut 4.28; Isa 44.9–11), and
the *eunuch* (20.4a), are, like the ill person, unable to enjoy the pleasures of life. **21–23:** Cf. Eccl 2.24; 9.7;
11.9–10.
   **31.1–11:** On wealth. **1–4:** Cf. Prov 30.8–9; Eccl 5.10. **5–11:** The rhetorical questions in vv. 9–10
imply that few rich people are also just (cf. 13.24; Prov 28.20).

9 Who is he, that we may praise
     him?
  For he has done wonders among
     his people.
10 Who has been tested by it and been
     found perfect?
  Let it be for him a ground for
     boasting.
  Who has had the power to transgress
     and did not transgress,
  and to do evil and did not do it?
11 His prosperity will be established,[a]
  and the assembly will proclaim his
     acts of charity.

12 Are you seated at the table of the
     great?[b]
  Do not be greedy at it,
  and do not say, "How much food
     there is here!"
13 Remember that a greedy eye is a bad
     thing.
  What has been created more greedy
     than the eye?
  Therefore it sheds tears for any
     reason.
14 Do not reach out your hand for
     everything you see,
  and do not crowd your neighbor[c]
     at the dish.
15 Judge your neighbor's feelings by
     your own,
  and in every matter be thoughtful.
16 Eat what is set before you like a well
     brought-up person,[d]
  and do not chew greedily, or you
     will give offense.
17 Be the first to stop, as befits good
     manners,
  and do not be insatiable, or you
     will give offense.
18 If you are seated among many
     persons,
  do not help yourself[e] before they do.

19 How ample a little is for a
     well-disciplined person!

  He does not breathe heavily when
     in bed.
20 Healthy sleep depends on moderate
     eating;
  he rises early, and feels fit.
  The distress of sleeplessness and of
     nausea
  and colic are with the glutton.
21 If you are overstuffed with food,
  get up to vomit, and you will have
     relief.
22 Listen to me, my child, and do not
     disregard me,
  and in the end you will appreciate
     my words.
  In everything you do be moderate,[f]
  and no sickness will overtake you.
23 People bless the one who is liberal
     with food,
  and their testimony to his
     generosity is trustworthy.
24 The city complains of the one who is
     stingy with food,
  and their testimony to his stinginess
     is accurate.

25 Do not try to prove your strength by
     wine-drinking,
  for wine has destroyed many.
26 As the furnace tests the work of the
     smith,[g]
  so wine tests hearts when the
     insolent quarrel.
27 Wine is very life to human beings
  if taken in moderation.
  What is life to one who is without
     wine?
  It has been created to make people
     happy.
28 Wine drunk at the proper time and in
     moderation

a Other ancient authorities add because of this
b Heb Syr: Gk at a great table    c Gk him
d Heb: Gk like a human being    e Gk reach out your
hand   f Heb Syr: Gk industrious   g Heb: Gk tests
the hardening of steel by dipping

**31.12–32.13:** Temperance in eating and drinking. **12:** *Table of the great,* cf. Prov 23.1–3. **13–18:** Ben
Sira stresses politeness and kindness when eating with others. **20–21:** The point is to avoid excess in the
first place (cf. 37.29–31). **25–31:** Excessive *wine-drinking* is harmful (vv. 25–26,29–30; cf. Prov 20.1;

is rejoicing of heart and gladness of
soul.

29 Wine drunk to excess leads to
bitterness of spirit,
to quarrels and stumbling.

30 Drunkenness increases the anger of a
fool to his own hurt,
reducing his strength and adding
wounds.

31 Do not reprove your neighbor at a
banquet of wine,
and do not despise him in his
merrymaking;
speak no word of reproach to him,
and do not distress him by making
demands of him.

32 If they make you master of the
feast, do not exalt yourself;
be among them as one of their
number.
Take care of them first and then sit
down;

2 when you have fulfilled all your
duties, take your place,
so that you may be merry along with
them
and receive a wreath for your
excellent leadership.

3 Speak, you who are older, for it is
your right,
but with accurate knowledge, and
do not interrupt the music.

4 Where there is entertainment, do not
pour out talk;
do not display your cleverness at
the wrong time.

5 A ruby seal in a setting of gold
is a concert of music at a banquet
of wine.

6 A seal of emerald in a rich setting of
gold
is the melody of music with good
wine.

7 Speak, you who are young, if you are
obliged to,
but no more than twice, and only if
asked.

8 Be brief; say much in few words;
be as one who knows and can still
hold his tongue.

9 Among the great do not act as their
equal;
and when another is speaking, do
not babble.

10 Lightning travels ahead of the
thunder,
and approval goes before one who
is modest.

11 Leave in good time and do not be the
last;
go home quickly and do not linger.

12 Amuse yourself there to your heart's
content,
but do not sin through proud
speech.

13 But above all bless your Maker,
who fills you with his good gifts.

14 The one who seeks God[a] will accept
his discipline,
and those who rise early to seek
him[b] will find favor.

15 The one who seeks the law will be
filled with it,
but the hypocrite will stumble at it.

16 Those who fear the Lord will form
true judgments,
and they will kindle righteous deeds
like a light.

17 The sinner will shun reproof,
and will find a decision according
to his liking.

a Heb: Gk who fears the Lord    b Other ancient
authorities lack to seek him

23.29–35; 31.4–5), yet *in moderation* wine is one of the good things of life (vv. 27–28; cf. Ps 104.15).
**32.1–13: Banquet etiquette. 1–2:** The *master of the feast* cared for the needs of those at the table (cf. Esth
1.8; 2 Macc 2.27). **3–10:** Directions to the *older* people and the *young*. **11–13:** These words are meant
for all.
    **32.14–33.6: The God-fearing person contrasted with the sinner. 14:** *Discipline* (Heb "musar") is a
frequent topic (see 1.27; 4.17; 6.18,22; 21.19,21; 22.6; 23.2,7; 26.14; 42.5,8; 50.27). *Rise early,* for

18 A sensible person will not overlook a
thoughtful suggestion;
an insolent[a] and proud person will
not be deterred by fear.[b]

19 Do nothing without deliberation,
but when you have acted, do not
regret it.

20 Do not go on a path full of hazards,
and do not stumble at an obstacle
twice.[c]

21 Do not be overconfident on a
smooth[d] road,

22 and give good heed to your
paths.[e]

23 Guard[f] yourself in every act,
for this is the keeping of the
commandments.

24 The one who keeps the law preserves
himself,[g]
and the one who trusts the Lord
will not suffer loss.

33 No evil will befall the one who
fears the Lord,
but in trials such a one will be
rescued again and again.

2 The wise will not hate the law,
but the one who is hypocritical
about it is like a boat in a
storm.

3 The sensible person will trust in the
law;
for such a one the law is as
dependable as a divine oracle.

4 Prepare what to say, and then you
will be listened to;
draw upon your training, and give
your answer.

5 The heart of a fool is like a cart
wheel,
and his thoughts like a turning
axle.

6 A mocking friend is like a stallion
that neighs no matter who the rider
is.

7 Why is one day more important than
another,
when all the daylight in the year is
from the sun?

8 By the Lord's wisdom they were
distinguished,
and he appointed the different
seasons and festivals.

9 Some days he exalted and hallowed,
and some he made ordinary days.

10 All human beings come from the
ground,
and humankind[h] was created out
of the dust.

11 In the fullness of his knowledge the
Lord distinguished them
and appointed their different ways.

12 Some he blessed and exalted,
and some he made holy and
brought near to himself;
but some he cursed and brought low,
and turned them out of their place.

13 Like clay in the hand of the potter,

a Heb: Gk *alien*   b Meaning of Gk uncertain. Other
ancient authorities add *and after acting, with him,
without deliberation*   c Heb: Gk *stumble on stony
ground*   d Or *an unexplored*   e Heb Syr: Gk *and
beware of your children*   f Heb Syr: Gk *Trust*
g Heb: Gk *who believes the law heeds the
commandments*   h Heb: Gk *Adam*

prayer, cf. 39.5. **17:** *A decision*, i.e. an interpretation (of the law). **33.1:** Cf. Wis 10.1–21. **2:** Hebrew, "He
that hates the law is not wise, and is tossed about like a boat in a storm." **3:** *Divine oracle*, the Urim and
Thummim, see 45.10; Ex 28.30; Num 27.21; 1 Sam 14.41–42.

**33.7–15: Divinely ordained opposites in creation.** Corresponding to wise (righteous) and foolish (sinner) are the polarities to be found in life, such as holy days and *ordinary days* (v. 9), the blessed and the
cursed (v. 12). **8–9:** Cf. Gen 1.14; 2.3; Deut 16.1–15. **10:** See Gen 2.7; 3.19. **12:** Perhaps the reference
is to the election of Israel (Gen 12.2–3; Ex 32.13) and the dispossession of the Canaanites (Gen 6.25–27;
12.6–7; Ex 33.1–3). **13:** *Clay . . . potter*, a common biblical image (Isa 29.16; 45.9; 64.8; Jer 18.1–12;
Wis 15.7–8) that suggests divine determinism, although elsewhere Ben Sira emphasizes human responsibility (15.11–20).

to be molded as he pleases,
so all are in the hand of their Maker,
  to be given whatever he decides.

14 Good is the opposite of evil,
  and life the opposite of death;
  so the sinner is the opposite of the
    godly.
15 Look at all the works of the Most
    High;
  they come in pairs, one the
    opposite of the other.

16 Now I was the last to keep vigil;
  I was like a gleaner following the
    grape-pickers;
17 by the blessing of the Lord I arrived
    first,
  and like a grape-picker I filled my
    wine press.
18 Consider that I have not labored for
    myself alone,
  but for all who seek instruction.
19 Hear me, you who are great among
    the people,
  and you leaders of the
    congregation, pay heed!

20 To son or wife, to brother or friend,
  do not give power over yourself, as
    long as you live;
  and do not give your property to
    another,
  in case you change your mind and
    must ask for it.
21 While you are still alive and have
    breath in you,
  do not let anyone take your place.
22 For it is better that your children
    should ask from you
  than that you should look to the
    hand of your children.

23 Excel in all that you do;
  bring no stain upon your honor.
24 At the time when you end the days of
    your life,
  in the hour of death, distribute
    your inheritance.

25 Fodder and a stick and burdens for a
    donkey;
  bread and discipline and work for a
    slave.
26 Set your slave to work, and you will
    find rest;
  leave his hands idle, and he will
    seek liberty.
27 Yoke and thong will bow the neck,
  and for a wicked slave there are
    racks and tortures.
28 Put him to work, in order that he
    may not be idle,
29 for idleness teaches much evil.
30 Set him to work, as is fitting for him,
  and if he does not obey, make his
    fetters heavy.
  Do not be overbearing toward
    anyone,
  and do nothing unjust.

31 If you have but one slave, treat him
    like yourself,
  because you have bought him with
    blood.
  If you have but one slave, treat him
    like a brother,
  for you will need him as you need
    your life.
32 If you ill-treat him, and he leaves you
    and runs away,
33 which way will you go to seek him?

34 The senseless have vain and false
    hopes,

---

**33.16–19:** The author's qualifications (see 24.30–34; 39.12–13; 51.13–28). **16:** *Keep vigil,* Ben Sira aligns himself with the prophets (cf. 24.33; Ezek 3.17; 33.7; Hab 2.1). **18:** Cf. 24.34.

**33.20–33:** On property and slaves. **20–33:** One should preserve financial independence up to the end of life. **25–33:** Ben Sira takes the institution of slavery for granted (cf. 7.20–21). His advice to *do nothing unjust* presupposes the limited rights of a slave as defined in the law codes (Ex 21.2–6,20–21,26–27; Lev 25.46; Deut 15.12–18). **32:** *If . . . he . . . runs away,* the law forbids the return of an escaped slave to the owner (Deut 23.15–16).

**34.1–8:** The vanity of dreams and omens (Deut 13.2–5; 18.9–14; Eccl 5.7; Jer 29.8). **2:** *Pursues the* and dreams give wings to fools.

2 As one who catches at a shadow and
pursues the wind,
so is anyone who believes in[a]
dreams.

3 What is seen in dreams is but a
reflection,
the likeness of a face looking at
itself.

4 From an unclean thing what can be
clean?
And from something false what can
be true?

5 Divinations and omens and dreams
are unreal,
and like a woman in labor, the
mind has fantasies.

6 Unless they are sent by intervention
from the Most High,
pay no attention to them.

7 For dreams have deceived many,
and those who put their hope in
them have perished.

8 Without such deceptions the law will
be fulfilled,
and wisdom is complete in the
mouth of the faithful.

9 An educated[b] person knows many
things,
and one with much experience
knows what he is talking
about.

10 An inexperienced person knows few
things,

11 but he that has traveled acquires
much cleverness.

12 I have seen many things in my travels,
and I understand more than I can
express.

13 I have often been in danger of death,
but have escaped because of these
experiences.

14 The spirit of those who fear the Lord
will live,

15 for their hope is in him who saves
them.

16 Those who fear the Lord will not be
timid,
or play the coward, for he is their
hope.

17 Happy is the soul that fears the Lord!

18 To whom does he look? And who
is his support?

19 The eyes of the Lord are on those
who love him,
a mighty shield and strong support,
a shelter from scorching wind and a
shade from noonday sun,
a guard against stumbling and a
help against falling.

20 He lifts up the soul and makes the
eyes sparkle;
he gives health and life and
blessing.

21 If one sacrifices ill-gotten goods, the
offering is blemished;[c]

22 the gifts[d] of the lawless are not
acceptable.

23 The Most High is not pleased with
the offerings of the ungodly,
nor for a multitude of sacrifices
does he forgive sins.

24 Like one who kills a son before his
father's eyes
is the person who offers a sacrifice
from the property of the poor.

25 The bread of the needy is the life of
the poor;
whoever deprives them of it is a
murderer.

a Syr: Gk *pays heed to*   b Other ancient authorities
read *A traveled*   c Other ancient authorities read *is
made in mockery*   d Other ancient authorities read
*mockeries*

*wind*, cf. Hos 12.1; Eccl 1.14. **3**: *Dreams* have no reality; they are a reflection of one's concerns. **4**: Cf. Job
14.4. **6**: Allowance is made for God-given dreams (Gen 37.5–10; Judg 7.13–15; Job 33.15–18).
**34.9–13**: Learning from experience. On the significance of *travels*, cf. 39.4; 51.13.
**34.14–20**: The blessings of those who fear God. **19**: *Eyes of the Lord*, Ps 34.15. *Shelter*, Ps 61.2–4;
91.1–4; Isa 25.4. The *scorching wind* is the well-known sirocco in spring and autumn.
**34.21–31**: Unacceptable sacrifices (cf. 1 Sam 15.22; Ps 51.16–19; Prov 15.8; 21.3; Hos 6.6; Am
5.21–24; Mt 23.23). **21**: *Blemished*, cf. Lev 22.18–25. **26–27**: Cf. Lev 19.13. **28**: *One builds*, i.e., the

26 To take away a neighbor's living is to
    commit murder;
27   to deprive an employee of wages is
    to shed blood.

28 When one builds and another tears
    down,
    what do they gain but hard work?
29 When one prays and another curses,
    to whose voice will the Lord listen?
30 If one washes after touching a corpse,
    and touches it again,
    what has been gained by washing?
31 So if one fasts for his sins,
    and goes again and does the same
    things,
    who will listen to his prayer?
    And what has he gained by
    humbling himself?

35 The one who keeps the law makes
    many offerings;
2   one who heeds the commandments
    makes an offering of
    well-being.
3 The one who returns a kindness offers
    choice flour,
4   and one who gives alms sacrifices a
    thank offering.
5 To keep from wickedness is pleasing
    to the Lord,
    and to forsake unrighteousness is
    an atonement.
6 Do not appear before the Lord
    empty-handed,
7   for all that you offer is in
    fulfillment of the
    commandment.
8 The offering of the righteous enriches
    the altar,

and its pleasing odor rises before
    the Most High.
9 The sacrifice of the righteous is
    acceptable,
    and it will never be forgotten.
10 Be generous when you worship the
    Lord,
    and do not stint the first fruits of
    your hands.
11 With every gift show a cheerful face,
    and dedicate your tithe with
    gladness.
12 Give to the Most High as he has
    given to you,
    and as generously as you can
    afford.
13 For the Lord is the one who repays,
    and he will repay you sevenfold.
14 Do not offer him a bribe, for he will
    not accept it;
15   and do not rely on a dishonest
    sacrifice;
    for the Lord is the judge,
    and with him there is no partiality.
16 He will not show partiality to the
    poor;
    but he will listen to the prayer of
    one who is wronged.
17 He will not ignore the supplication of
    the orphan,
    or the widow when she pours out
    her complaint.
18 Do not the tears of the widow run
    down her cheek
19   as she cries out against the one who
    causes them to fall?
20 The one whose service is pleasing to
    the Lord will be accepted,
    and his prayer will reach to the
    clouds.

poor person victimized by the rich, who *tears down;* both of them lose. **29:** The rich person *prays* hypocritically and incurs the curse of the poor; it is clear that the Lord will listen to the *voice* of the poor (4.5–6; 35.17–21). **30:** *Touching a corpse* makes one impure (Num 19.11).

**35.1–13: Acceptable sacrifices** (cf. Isa 1.11–18; Mic 6.6–8; Tob 1.6–8). Ethical obedience, especially almsgiving, is as worthy as *many offerings* (vv. 1–5). Yet it is equally important to give tithes and offerings *before the Lord* (i.e., at the Temple), *generously* and with *a cheerful face* (vv. 6–13).

**35.14–26: A warning against exploitation of the poor. 15:** *Dishonest sacrifice,* one made possible by injustice (34.21). *No partiality,* Deut 10.17; 2 Chr 19.7; Job 34.19; Wis 6.7. **17–18:** Because the *orphan* and the *widow* are especially powerless, God will defend them (cf. 4.9–10; Ps 68.5; Prov 23.10–11).

21 The prayer of the humble pierces the
   clouds,
      and it will not rest until it reaches
      its goal;
   it will not desist until the Most High
      responds
22 and does justice for the righteous,
      and executes judgment.
   Indeed, the Lord will not delay,
      and like a warrior[a] will not be
      patient
   until he crushes the loins of the
      unmerciful
23 and repays vengeance on the
      nations;
   until he destroys the multitude of the
      insolent,
      and breaks the scepters of the
      unrighteous;
24 until he repays mortals according to
      their deeds,
      and the works of all according to
      their thoughts;
25 until he judges the case of his people
      and makes them rejoice in his
      mercy.
26 His mercy is as welcome in time of
      distress
      as clouds of rain in time of
      drought.

36 Have mercy upon us, O God[b] of
   all,
2    and put all the nations in fear of
      you.
3 Lift up your hand against foreign
      nations
      and let them see your might.
4 As you have used us to show your
      holiness to them,
   so use them to show your glory to
      us.

5 Then they will know,[c] as we have
   known,
      that there is no God but you,
      O Lord.
6 Give new signs, and work other
      wonders;
7 make your hand and right arm
      glorious.
8 Rouse your anger and pour out your
      wrath;
9 destroy the adversary and wipe out
      the enemy.
10 Hasten the day, and remember the
      appointed time,[d]
      and let people recount your mighty
      deeds.
11 Let survivors be consumed in the fiery
      wrath,
      and may those who harm your
      people meet destruction.
12 Crush the heads of hostile rulers
      who say, "There is no one but
      ourselves."
13 Gather all the tribes of Jacob,[e]
16      and give them their inheritance, as
      at the beginning.
17 Have mercy, O Lord, on the people
      called by your name,
      on Israel, whom you have named[f]
      your firstborn,
18 Have pity on the city of your
      sanctuary,[g]
      Jerusalem, the place of your
      dwelling.[h]

a Heb: Gk *and with them*    b Heb: Gk *O Master, the
God*    c Heb: Gk *And let them know you*    d Other
ancient authorities read *remember your oath*
e Owing to a dislocation in the Greek Mss of Sirach,
the verse numbers 14 and 15 are not used in
chapter 36, though no text is missing.    f Other
ancient authorities read *you have likened to*    g Or *on
your holy city*    h Heb: Gk *your rest*

**22–26:** This serves as an introduction to the prayer in 36.1–19; Ben Sira has in mind the oppression of
the chosen people by foreign oppressors. **36.1–22: A prayer for the deliverance and restoration of Israel**(cf. Ps 44.2–9; 2 Macc 1.24–29). **1:** *God
of all*, not just of Israel (cf. 50.22). **2:** *All the nations*, especially meant are the Seleucid rulers, who had
power over Palestine after 198 BCE. **4:** As God demonstrated *holiness* by vindicating Israel in exile (Ezek
20.41; 28.25), so now let God display *glory* by subduing the Gentiles. **6–7:** *Signs, wonders, hand and
right arm*, allusions to the events of the Exodus (Ex 11.9–10; 15.6; Deut 4.34; 7.19; Neh 9.10). **10:** *The*

19 Fill Zion with your majesty,[a]
    and your temple[b] with your glory.
20 Bear witness to those whom you
        created in the beginning,
    and fulfill the prophecies spoken in
        your name.
21 Reward those who wait for you
    and let your prophets be found
        trustworthy.
22 Hear, O Lord, the prayer of your
        servants, according to your
        goodwill toward[c] your people,
    and all who are on the earth will
        know
    that you are the Lord, the God of
        the ages.

23 The stomach will take any food,
    yet one food is better than another.
24 As the palate tastes the kinds of
        game,
    so an intelligent mind detects false
        words.
25 A perverse mind will cause grief,
    but a person with experience will
        pay him back.
26 A woman will accept any man as a
        husband,
    but one girl is preferable to
        another.
27 A woman's beauty lights up a man's
        face,
    and there is nothing he desires
        more.
28 If kindness and humility mark her
        speech,
    her husband is more fortunate than
        other men.
29 He who acquires a wife gets his best
        possession,[d]

a helper fit for him and a pillar of
    support.[e]
30 Where there is no fence, the property
        will be plundered;
    and where there is no wife, a man
        will become a fugitive and a
        wanderer.[f]
31 For who will trust a nimble robber
        that skips from city to city?
    So who will trust a man that has no
        nest,
    but lodges wherever night overtakes
        him?

37 Every friend says, "I too am a
        friend";
    but some friends are friends only in
        name.
2 Is it not a sorrow like that for death
        itself
    when a dear friend turns into an
        enemy?
3 O inclination to evil, why were you
        formed
    to cover the land with deceit?
4 Some companions rejoice in the
        happiness of a friend,
    but in time of trouble they are
        against him.
5 Some companions help a friend for
        their stomachs' sake,
    yet in battle they will carry his shield.
6 Do not forget a friend during the
        battle,[g]

a Heb Syr: Gk the celebration of your wondrous deeds
b Heb Syr: Gk Lat people   c Heb and two Gk
witnesses: Lat and most Gk witnesses read according
to the blessing of Aaron for   d Heb: Gk enters upon
a possession   e Heb: Gk rest   f Heb: Gk wander
about and sigh   g Heb: Gk in your heart

appointed time, the awaited deliverance from domination by foreign rulers. **18:** See Ps 132.13–14. **19:**
Cf. 1 Kings 8.11; Ps 26.8; 63.2; 102.16.
    **36.23–37.31: Concerning discrimination. 23–25:** Three sayings, drawing a parallel between the
trained palate and the discriminating mind, introduce a larger unit of loosely gathered sayings on prudent
choices.
    **36.26–31: On choices in marriage** (cf. 26.13–18). **26:** *Will accept any man,* the woman effectively has
no choice, as marriages are arranged by the father (cf. 7.25). **29:** *A helper fit for him,* Gen 2.18. **30:** *A
fugitive and a wanderer,* like Cain (Gen 4.12,14).
    **37.1–6: False friends** (cf. 6.7–13). **3:** *Inclination to evil,* the evil "yetser" (see 15.14n.). **4:** *Happiness,*
arising from feasting (see v. 5). **5:** *Carry his shield,* defend him from attack (cf. Ps 35.2).

and do not be unmindful of him
when you distribute your
spoils.[a]

7 All counselors praise the counsel they
give,
but some give counsel in their own
interest.
8 Be wary of a counselor,
and learn first what is his interest,
for he will take thought for himself.
He may cast the lot against you
9 and tell you, "Your way is good,"
and then stand aside to see what
happens to you.
10 Do not consult the one who regards
you with suspicion;
hide your intentions from those
who are jealous of you.
11 Do not consult with a woman about
her rival
or with a coward about war,
with a merchant about business
or with a buyer about selling,
with a miser about generosity[b]
or with the merciless about
kindness,
with an idler about any work
or with a seasonal laborer about
completing his work,
with a lazy servant about a big task—
pay no attention to any advice they
give.
12 But associate with a godly person
whom you know to be a keeper of
the commandments,
who is like-minded with yourself,
and who will grieve with you if you
fail.
13 And heed[c] the counsel of your own
heart,
for no one is more faithful to you
than it is.
14 For our own mind sometimes keeps
us better informed

than seven sentinels sitting high on
a watchtower.
15 But above all pray to the Most High
that he may direct your way in
truth.

16 Discussion is the beginning of every
work,
and counsel precedes every
undertaking.
17 The mind is the root of all conduct;
18 it sprouts four branches,[d]
good and evil, life and death;
and it is the tongue that continually
rules them.
19 Some people may be clever enough to
teach many,
and yet be useless to themselves.
20 A skillful speaker may be hated;
he will be destitute of all food,
21 for the Lord has withheld the gift of
charm,
since he is lacking in all wisdom.
22 If a person is wise to his own
advantage,
the fruits of his good sense will be
praiseworthy.[e]
23 A wise person instructs his own
people,
and the fruits of his good sense will
endure.
24 A wise person will have praise heaped
upon him,
and all who see him will call him
happy.
25 The days of a person's life are
numbered,
but the days of Israel are without
number.

---

a Heb: Gk *him in your wealth*    b Heb: Gk *gratitude*
c Heb: Gk *establish*    d Heb: Gk *As a clue to changes
of heart four kinds of destiny appear*    e Other
ancient witnesses read *trustworthy*

**37.7–15: On taking counsel.** Avoid self-interested and biased advisers (vv. 7–11). Inquire instead of pious individuals, take your own counsel, and seek divine guidance (vv. 12–15). **11:** *Her rival,* another wife (see 26.6n.).

**37.16–26: Enduring wisdom. 16–21:** Wisdom and speech. **22–26:** Recognition accorded to the wise. **25:** Cf. 2 Macc 14.15.

26 One who is wise among his people
  will inherit honor,[a]
  and his name will live forever.

27 My child, test yourself while you live;
  see what is bad for you and do not
    give in to it.
28 For not everything is good for
    everyone,
  and no one enjoys everything.
29 Do not be greedy for every delicacy,
  and do not eat without restraint;
30 for overeating brings sickness,
  and gluttony leads to nausea.
31 Many have died of gluttony,
  but the one who guards against it
    prolongs his life.

38 Honor physicians for their
    services,
  for the Lord created them;
2 for their gift of healing comes from
    the Most High,
  and they are rewarded by the
    king.
3 The skill of physicians makes them
    distinguished,
  and in the presence of the great
    they are admired.
4 The Lord created medicines out of the
    earth,
  and the sensible will not despise
    them.
5 Was not water made sweet with a
    tree
  in order that its[b] power might be
    known?
6 And he gave skill to human beings
  that he[c] might be glorified in his
    marvelous works.
7 By them the physician[d] heals and
    takes away pain;

8 the pharmacist makes a mixture
    from them.
  God's[e] works will never be finished;
  and from him health[f] spreads over
    all the earth.

9 My child, when you are ill, do not
    delay,
  but pray to the Lord, and he will
    heal you.
10 Give up your faults and direct your
    hands rightly,
  and cleanse your heart from all sin.
11 Offer a sweet-smelling sacrifice, and a
    memorial portion of choice
    flour,
  and pour oil on your offering, as
    much as you can afford.[g]
12 Then give the physician his place, for
    the Lord created him;
  do not let him leave you, for you
    need him.
13 There may come a time when
    recovery lies in the hands of
    physicians,[h]
14 for they too pray to the Lord
  that he grant them success in
    diagnosis[i]
  and in healing, for the sake of
    preserving life.
15 He who sins against his Maker,
  will be defiant toward the
    physician.[j]

16 My child, let your tears fall for the
    dead,

a Other ancient authorities read *confidence*   b Or *his*
c Or *they*   d Heb: Gk *he*   e Gk *His*   f Or *peace*
g Heb: Lat lacks *as much as you can afford*; Meaning
of Gk uncertain   h Gk *in their hands*   i Heb: Gk
*rest*   j Heb: Gk *may he fall into the hands of the
physician*

37.27–31: **Temperance** (cf. 31.12–31). The concluding words about illness anticipate the following
passage on physicians.
  38.1–15: **Concerning physicians. 5:** *Water made sweet,* see Ex 15.23–25. **9–15:** Ben Sira upholds the
traditional view that illness results from sin (cf. Deut 28.21–22,27–28; Prov 3.7–8). Only after prayer
and sacrifice (see Lev 2.1–3), therefore, should the ill person *give the physician his place* (cf. 2 Chr 16.12).
  38.16–23: **On mourning and grief** (cf. 22.11–12). Ben Sira stresses the obligation to provide proper
*burial* and *mourning* of the dead (vv. 16–17; cf. Tob 1.17–18; 4.3–4; 6.15; 12.12; 14.12–13), yet he
counsels against extreme *grief,* which may itself *result in death* (vv. 18–23).

and as one in great pain begin the
    lament.
Lay out the body with due ceremony,
    and do not neglect the burial.
17 Let your weeping be bitter and your
    wailing fervent;
    make your mourning worthy of the
        departed,
    for one day, or two, to avoid
        criticism;
    then be comforted for your grief.
18 For grief may result in death,
    and a sorrowful heart saps one's
        strength.
19 When a person is taken away, sorrow
    is over;
    but the life of the poor weighs
        down the heart.
20 Do not give your heart to grief;
    drive it away, and remember your
        own end.
21 Do not forget, there is no coming
    back;
    you do the dead*a* no good, and
        you injure yourself.
22 Remember his*b* fate, for yours is like
    it;
    yesterday it was his,*c* and today it
        is yours.
23 When the dead is at rest, let his
    remembrance rest too,
    and be comforted for him when his
        spirit has departed.

24 The wisdom of the scribe depends on
    the opportunity of leisure;
    only the one who has little business
        can become wise.
25 How can one become wise who
    handles the plow,
    and who glories in the shaft of a
        goad,
    who drives oxen and is occupied with
        their work,
    and whose talk is about bulls?
26 He sets his heart on plowing furrows,

and he is careful about fodder for
    the heifers.
27 So it is with every artisan and master
    artisan
    who labors by night as well as by
        day;
    those who cut the signets of seals,
    each is diligent in making a great
        variety;
    they set their heart on painting a
        lifelike image,
    and they are careful to finish their
        work.
28 So it is with the smith, sitting by the
    anvil,
    intent on his iron-work;
    the breath of the fire melts his flesh,
    and he struggles with the heat of
        the furnace;
    the sound of the hammer deafens his
        ears,*d*
    and his eyes are on the pattern of
        the object.
    He sets his heart on finishing his
        handiwork,
    and he is careful to complete its
        decoration.
29 So it is with the potter sitting at his
    work
    and turning the wheel with his feet;
    he is always deeply concerned over
        his products,
    and he produces them in quantity.
30 He molds the clay with his arm
    and makes it pliable with his feet;
    he sets his heart to finish the glazing,
    and he takes care in firing*e* the
        kiln.

31 All these rely on their hands,
    and all are skillful in their own
        work.

*a* Gk *him*    *b* Heb: Gk *my*    *c* Heb: Gk *mine*
*d* Cn: Gk *renews his ear*    *e* Cn: Gk *cleaning*

**38.24–34a: Skilled workers contrasted with the scribe. 24:** The learned *scribe* is devoted to study rather
than a manual trade (but cf. 7.15,22). **25–30:** Ben Sira respects the farmer and the seal-maker, the *smith*
and the *potter,* and he describes their work with admiration. **31–34a:** Although *they maintain the fabric
of the world,* artisans are not found in the *public assembly,* the *courts,* or *among the rulers.*

32 Without them no city can be
      inhabited,
   and wherever they live, they will
      not go hungry.<sup>a</sup>
   Yet they are not sought out for the
      council of the people,<sup>b</sup>
33    nor do they attain eminence in the
      public assembly.
   They do not sit in the judge's seat,
      nor do they understand the
      decisions of the courts;
   they cannot expound discipline or
      judgment,
   and they are not found among the
      rulers.<sup>c</sup>
34 But they maintain the fabric of the
      world,
   and their concern is for<sup>d</sup> the
      exercise of their trade.

   How different the one who devotes
      himself
   to the study of the law of the Most
      High!

**39** He seeks out the wisdom of all the
      ancients,
   and is concerned with prophecies;
2 he preserves the sayings of the famous
   and penetrates the subtleties of
      parables;
3 he seeks out the hidden meanings of
      proverbs
   and is at home with the obscurities
      of parables.
4 He serves among the great
   and appears before rulers;
   he travels in foreign lands
   and learns what is good and evil in
      the human lot.
5 He sets his heart to rise early
   to seek the Lord who made him,
   and to petition the Most High;

   he opens his mouth in prayer
   and asks pardon for his sins.
6 If the great Lord is willing,
   he will be filled with the spirit of
      understanding;
   he will pour forth words of wisdom
      of his own
   and give thanks to the Lord in
      prayer.
7 The Lord<sup>e</sup> will direct his counsel and
      knowledge,
   as he meditates on his mysteries.
8 He will show the wisdom of what he
      has learned,
   and will glory in the law of the
      Lord's covenant.
9 Many will praise his understanding;
   it will never be blotted out.
   His memory will not disappear,
   and his name will live through all
      generations.
10 Nations will speak of his wisdom,
   and the congregation will proclaim
      his praise.
11 If he lives long, he will leave a name
      greater than a thousand,
   and if he goes to rest, it is enough<sup>f</sup>
      for him.

12 I have more on my mind to express;
   I am full like the full moon.
13 Listen to me, my faithful children,
      and blossom
   like a rose growing by a stream of
      water.
14 Send out fragrance like incense,
   and put forth blossoms like a lily.

a Syr: Gk *and people can neither live nor walk there*
b Most ancient authorities lack this line   c Cn: Gk
*among parables*   d Syr: Gk *prayer is in*   e Gk *He
himself*   f Cn: Meaning of Gk uncertain

**38.34b–39.11: Praise of the scribe.** The highest vocation is that of the scribe, who is concerned with the *law, wisdom* (i.e., the Writings), and *prophecies;* this reflects the threefold division of the Hebrew Bible (39.1–3; see also the Prologue by Ben Sira's grandson). **34b:** Cf. Ezra 7.6,10. **39.2–3:** Cf. Prov 1.5–6; 25.1. **9:** *His memory* and *name will live,* cf. 37.26; 44.10–15. **11:** *Greater than a thousand,* cf. Job 9.3; 33.23; Eccl 7.28.

**39.12–35: A hymn of praise** about the goodness and purposefulness of creation (vv. 16,21,33–35; cf. 16.26–29). Both *good* and *bad* things are used by God for the divine purpose (vv. 25–31; cf. 33.7–15).

Scatter the fragrance, and sing a
hymn of praise;
bless the Lord for all his works.
15 Ascribe majesty to his name
and give thanks to him with praise,
with songs on your lips, and with
harps;
this is what you shall say in
thanksgiving:

16 "All the works of the Lord are very
good,
and whatever he commands will be
done at the appointed time.
17 No one can say, 'What is this?' or
'Why is that?'—
for at the appointed time all such
questions will be answered.
At his word the waters stood in a
heap,
and the reservoirs of water at the
word of his mouth.
18 When he commands, his every
purpose is fulfilled,
and none can limit his saving
power.
19 The works of all are before him,
and nothing can be hidden from his
eyes.
20 From the beginning to the end of time
he can see everything,
and nothing is too marvelous for
him.
21 No one can say, 'What is this?' or
'Why is that?'—
for everything has been created for
its own purpose.

22 "His blessing covers the dry land like
a river,
and drenches it like a flood.
23 But his wrath drives out the nations,
as when he turned a watered land
into salt.
24 To the faithful his ways are straight,
but full of pitfalls for the wicked.

25 From the beginning good things were
created for the good,
but for sinners good things and
bad.[a]
26 The basic necessities of human life
are water and fire and iron and salt
and wheat flour and milk and honey,
the blood of the grape and oil and
clothing.
27 All these are good for the godly,
but for sinners they turn into evils.

28 "There are winds created for
vengeance,
and in their anger they can dislodge
mountains;[b]
on the day of reckoning they will
pour out their strength
and calm the anger of their Maker.
29 Fire and hail and famine and
pestilence,
all these have been created for
vengeance;
30 the fangs of wild animals and
scorpions and vipers,
and the sword that punishes the
ungodly with destruction.
31 They take delight in doing his
bidding,
always ready for his service on
earth;
and when their time comes they
never disobey his command."

32 So from the beginning I have been
convinced of all this
and have thought it out and left it
in writing:
33 All the works of the Lord are good,
and he will supply every need in its
time.
34 No one can say, "This is not as good
as that,"

a Heb Lat: Gk *sinners bad things*    b Heb Syr: Gk
*can scourge mightily*

16: *Very good,* Gen 1.4,10,12,18,21,25,31. **17**: *The appointed time,* cf. vv. 16,34; Eccl 3.11. *Waters stood in a heap,* cf. Gen 1.9–10; Ex 15.8. **23**: *He turned a watered land into salt;* cf. Gen 19.24–26; Ps 107.34. **26**: *The basic necessities,* cf. 29.21.

for everything proves good in its
  appointed time.
35 So now sing praise with all your heart
  and voice,
  and bless the name of the Lord.

40 Hard work was created for
  everyone,
  and a heavy yoke is laid on the
  children of Adam,
from the day they come forth from
  their mother's womb
until the day they return to*a* the
  mother of all the living.*b*
2 Perplexities and fear of heart are
  theirs,
  and anxious thought of the day of
  their death.
3 From the one who sits on a splendid
  throne
  to the one who grovels in dust and
  ashes,
4 from the one who wears purple and a
  crown
  to the one who is clothed in burlap,
5 there is anger and envy and trouble
  and unrest,
  and fear of death, and fury and
  strife.
And when one rests upon his bed,
  his sleep at night confuses his
  mind.
6 He gets little or no rest;
  he struggles in his sleep as he did
  by day.*c*
He is troubled by the visions of his
  mind
  like one who has escaped from the
  battlefield.
7 At the moment he reaches safety he
  wakes up,
  astonished that his fears were
  groundless.
8 To all creatures, human and animal,
  but to sinners seven times more,

9 come death and bloodshed and strife
  and sword,
  calamities and famine and ruin and
  plague.
10 All these were created for the wicked,
  and on their account the flood
  came.
11 All that is of earth returns to earth,
  and what is from above returns
  above.*d*
12 All bribery and injustice will be
  blotted out,
  but good faith will last forever.
13 The wealth of the unjust will dry up
  like a river,
  and crash like a loud clap of
  thunder in a storm.
14 As a generous person has cause to
  rejoice,
  so lawbreakers will utterly fail.
15 The children of the ungodly put out
  few branches;
  they are unhealthy roots on sheer
  rock.
16 The reeds by any water or river bank
  are plucked up before any grass;
17 but kindness is like a garden of
  blessings,
  and almsgiving endures forever.

18 Wealth and wages make life sweet,*e*
  but better than either is finding a
  treasure.
19 Children and the building of a city
  establish one's name,
  but better than either is the one
  who finds wisdom.
Cattle and orchards make one
  prosperous;*f*

*a* Other Gk and Lat authorities read *are buried in*
*b* Heb: Gk *of all*   *c* Arm: Meaning of Gk uncertain
*d* Heb Syr: Gk Lat *from the waters returns to the sea*
*e* Heb: Gk *Life is sweet for the self-reliant worker*
*f* Heb Syr: Gk lacks *but better . . . prosperous*

**40.1–41.13: Reflections on the human condition,** its miseries (40.1–17; 40.28–41.13) and its joys (40.18–27). **1:** *Hard work was created,* Gen 3.17–19. *Their mother's womb,* cf. Job 1.21; Eccl 5.15. **5–7:** On troubled sleep and dreams, cf. 34.1–8; Eccl 2.23; Job 7.4. **10:** *The flood* is the deluge of the Noah story, Gen 6–8. **11:** *Returns to the earth,* cf. v. 1; 16.30–17.1; Gen 3.19. *What is from above,* the life-breath of God (Gen 2.7; Eccl 12.7). **15:** Job 18.16. **18–27:** The culmination of the ten "better" sayings

but a blameless wife is accounted
better than either.

20 Wine and music gladden the heart,
but the love of friends*a* is better
than either.

21 The flute and the harp make sweet
melody,
but a pleasant voice is better than
either.

22 The eye desires grace and beauty,
but the green shoots of grain more
than either.

23 A friend or companion is always
welcome,
but a sensible wife*b* is better than
either.

24 Kindred and helpers are for a time of
trouble,
but almsgiving rescues better than
either.

25 Gold and silver make one stand firm,
but good counsel is esteemed more
than either.

26 Riches and strength build up
confidence,
but the fear of the Lord is better
than either.
There is no want in the fear of the
Lord,
and with it there is no need to seek
for help.

27 The fear of the Lord is like a garden
of blessing,
and covers a person better than any
glory.

28 My child, do not lead the life of a
beggar;
it is better to die than to beg.

29 When one looks to the table of
another,
one's way of life cannot be
considered a life.
One loses self-respect with another
person's food,

but one who is intelligent and well
instructed guards against that.

30 In the mouth of the shameless begging
is sweet,
but it kindles a fire inside him.

41 O death, how bitter is the thought
of you
to the one at peace among
possessions,
who has nothing to worry about and
is prosperous in everything,
and still is vigorous enough to
enjoy food!

2 O death, how welcome is your
sentence
to one who is needy and failing in
strength,
worn down by age and anxious about
everything;
to one who is contrary, and has
lost all patience!

3 Do not fear death's decree for you;
remember those who went before
you and those who will come
after.

4 This is the Lord's decree for all flesh;
why then should you reject the will
of the Most High?
Whether life lasts for ten years or a
hundred or a thousand,
there are no questions asked in
Hades.

5 The children of sinners are
abominable children,
and they frequent the haunts of the
ungodly.

6 The inheritance of the children of
sinners will perish,
and on their offspring will be a
perpetual disgrace.

*a* Heb: Gk *wisdom*    *b* Heb Compare Syr: Gk *wife
with her husband*

is *fear of the Lord* (see 1.11–30). **28–30:** On the shamefulness of begging, cf. 29.24–28; 30.17. **41.3–4:**
Ben Sira advises a realistic acceptance of death (cf. 14.11–19; 17.25–28; 38.16–23). *Hades* (Sheol), the
abode of the dead. **5–13:** A contrast between the fate of the virtuous and the wicked. For the *offspring*
of the ungodly as a *perpetual disgrace* (v. 6), cf. Wis 3.12–13,16–19; 4.3–6. On the value of a *good name*
(v. 13), cf. Prov 22.1; Eccl 7.1.

7 Children will blame an ungodly
          father,
    for they suffer disgrace because of
          him.
8 Woe to you, the ungodly,
    who have forsaken the law of the
          Most High God!
9 If you have children, calamity will be
          theirs;
    you will beget them only for
          groaning.
    When you stumble, there is lasting
          joy;*a*
    and when you die, a curse is your
          lot.
10 Whatever comes from earth returns to
          earth;
    so the ungodly go from curse to
          destruction.

11 The human body is a fleeting thing,
    but a virtuous name will never be
          blotted out.*b*
12 Have regard for your name, since it
          will outlive you
    longer than a thousand hoards of
          gold.
13 The days of a good life are numbered,
    but a good name lasts forever.

14 My children, be true to your training
          and be at peace;
    hidden wisdom and unseen treasure—
    of what value is either?
15 Better are those who hide their folly
    than those who hide their wisdom.
16 Therefore show respect for my words;
    for it is not good to feel shame in
          every circumstance,
    nor is every kind of abashment to
          be approved.*c*

17 Be ashamed of sexual immorality,
          before your father or mother;
    and of a lie, before a prince or a
          ruler;

18 of a crime, before a judge or
          magistrate;
    and of a breach of the law, before
          the congregation and the
          people;
    of unjust dealing, before your partner
          or your friend;
19 and of theft, in the place where you
          live.
    Be ashamed of breaking an oath or
          agreement,*d*
    and of leaning on your elbow at
          meals;
    of surliness in receiving or giving,
20 and of silence, before those who
          greet you;
    of looking at a prostitute,
21 and of rejecting the appeal of a
          relative;
    of taking away someone's portion or
          gift,
    and of gazing at another man's
          wife;
22 of meddling with his servant-girl—
    and do not approach her bed;
    of abusive words, before friends—
    and do not be insulting after
          making a gift.

42 Be ashamed of repeating what you
          hear,
    and of betraying secrets.
    Then you will show proper shame,
    and will find favor with everyone.

    Of the following things do not be
          ashamed,
    and do not sin to save face:
2 Do not be ashamed of the law of the
          Most High and his covenant,
    and of rendering judgment to
          acquit the ungodly;

*a* Heb: Meaning of Gk uncertain  *b* Heb: Gk *People
grieve over the death of the body, but the bad name of
sinners will be blotted out*  *c* Heb: Gk *and not
everything is confidently esteemed by everyone*
*d* Heb: Gk *before the truth of God and the covenant*

**41.14–42.8: A poem on shame, true and false.** After an introduction (41.14–16), Ben Sira identifies
behaviors that properly bring shame (sexual misconduct, dishonesty, rudeness, 41.17–42.1a) and those
of which a man ought not to be ashamed (fidelity to the law, fair trade, controlling one's household, and
issuing reproof; 42.1b–8).

3 of keeping accounts with a partner or
     with traveling companions,
  and of dividing the inheritance of
     friends;
4 of accuracy with scales and weights,
     and of acquiring much or little;
5 of profit from dealing with
     merchants,
  and of frequent disciplining of
     children,
  and of drawing blood from the
     back of a wicked slave.
6 Where there is an untrustworthy wife,
     a seal is a good thing;
  and where there are many hands,
     lock things up.
7 When you make a deposit, be sure it
     is counted and weighed,
  and when you give or receive, put it
     all in writing.
8 Do not be ashamed to correct the
     stupid or foolish
  or the aged who are guilty of
     sexual immorality.
  Then you will show your sound
     training,
  and will be approved by all.

9 A daughter is a secret anxiety to her
     father,
  and worry over her robs him of
     sleep;
  when she is young, for fear she may
     not marry,
  or if married, for fear she may be
     disliked;
10 while a virgin, for fear she may be
     seduced
  and become pregnant in her father's
     house;

or having a husband, for fear she may
     go astray,
  or, though married, for fear she
     may be barren.
11 Keep strict watch over a headstrong
     daughter,
  or she may make you a
     laughingstock to your enemies,
  a byword in the city and the assembly
     of[a] the people,
  and put you to shame in public
     gatherings.[b]
See that there is no lattice in her
     room,
  no spot that overlooks the
     approaches to the house.[c]
12 Do not let her parade her beauty
     before any man,
  or spend her time among married
     women;[a]
13 for from garments comes the moth,
  and from a woman comes woman's
     wickedness.
14 Better is the wickedness of a man
     than a woman who does good;
  it is woman who brings shame and
     disgrace.

15 I will now call to mind the works of
     the Lord,
  and will declare what I have seen.
  By the word of the Lord his works
     are made;
  and all his creatures do his will.[d]
16 The sun looks down on everything
     with its light,

a Heb: Meaning of Gk uncertain    b Heb: Gk to
shame before the great multitude    c Heb: Gk lacks
See . . . house    d Syr Compare Heb: most Gk
witnesses lack and all . . . will

**42.9–14: A man's anxiety over daughters** (cf. 7.24–25; 22.3–6). **9–10:** *Worry over her,* fathers were
responsible for marriage arrangements, in which a high premium was placed on young women's virginity
and fertility (cf. 22.3b–5; Deut 22.13–29). **11–12:** *Headstrong daughter,* a man who failed to control the
women of his household was subject to great *shame.* Consequently, the daily lives of unmarried daughters
were severely restricted. **13:** *From a woman comes woman's wickedness.* Ben Sira here glosses over the
inevitable aspect of male complicity in the undesirable outcomes mentioned above (vv. 9–11). **14:** *Better
is the wickedness of a man.* Absurd at face value, the intemperance of this statement cannot be attributed
simply to hyperbole. It expresses a real, and lamentable, misogyny (cf. 25.13,19).

**42.15–43.33: In praise of God and the wonders of creation. 15:** The *works of the Lord* include the
whole of the universe. For creation *by the word,* cf. Gen 1.1–31; Ps 33.6; Jdt 16.14; Wis 9.1. **17:** *Holy*

and the work of the Lord is full of
his glory.

17 The Lord has not empowered even his
holy ones
to recount all his marvelous works,
which the Lord the Almighty has
established
so that the universe may stand firm
in his glory.

18 He searches out the abyss and the
human heart;
he understands their innermost
secrets.
For the Most High knows all that
may be known;
he sees from of old the things that
are to come.[a]

19 He discloses what has been and what
is to be,
and he reveals the traces of hidden
things.

20 No thought escapes him,
and nothing is hidden from him.

21 He has set in order the splendors of
his wisdom;
he is from all eternity one and the
same.
Nothing can be added or taken away,
and he needs no one to be his
counselor.

22 How desirable are all his works,
and how sparkling they are to
see![b]

23 All these things live and remain
forever;
each creature is preserved to meet a
particular need.[c]

24 All things come in pairs, one opposite
the other,
and he has made nothing
incomplete.

25 Each supplements the virtues of the
other.
Who could ever tire of seeing his
glory?

43 The pride of the higher realms is
the clear vault of the sky,
as glorious to behold as the sight of
the heavens.

2 The sun, when it appears, proclaims
as it rises
what a marvelous instrument it is,
the work of the Most High.

3 At noon it parches the land,
and who can withstand its burning
heat?

4 A man tending[d] a furnace works in
burning heat,
but three times as hot is the sun
scorching the mountains;
it breathes out fiery vapors,
and its bright rays blind the eyes.

5 Great is the Lord who made it;
at his orders it hurries on its
course.

6 It is the moon that marks the
changing seasons,[e]
governing the times, their
everlasting sign.

7 From the moon comes the sign for
festal days,
a light that wanes when it
completes its course.

8 The new moon, as its name suggests,
renews itself;[f]

a Heb: Gk *he sees the sign(s) of the age*    b Meaning
of Gk uncertain    c Heb: Gk *forever for every need,
and all are obedient*    d Other ancient authorities
read *blowing upon*    e Heb: Meaning of Gk uncertain
f Heb: Gk *The month is named after the moon*

ones, the members of the heavenly court, or angels, as in Job 5.1; 15.15; Ps 89.8. Even they are unable
adequately to declare God's *marvelous works*. **18–21:** The divine omniscience extends to the *abyss* and
its chaotic forces, and to the *human heart* (see Prov 15.11), to past and future (v. 19; cf. Isa 48.3–6),
because God is *from all eternity one and the same* (v. 21), and *needs no . . . counselor* (see Isa 40.13). **22–25:**
The beauty and splendor of God's *works* are increased by their purposefulness (v. 23), and their symmetry
(vv. 24–25; cf. 33.15). **43.1–26:** Cf. Job 38.1–38; Ps 104. The splendor of natural phenomena spans
from the heavens (*sky, sun* [cf. Ps 19.4–6], *moon* [Ps 104.19], *stars*, and *rainbow*, vv. 1–11), to the earth
(*snow, wind, frost, ice* and *dew*, vv. 13–22), to the depths of the *sea* (vv. 23–25; cf. Ps 104.24–26;
107.23–24). **27:** *He is the all*, in the sense that all creation reveals the divine presence (cf. Wis 1.7).

how marvelous it is in this change,
a beacon to the hosts on high,
  shining in the vault of the heavens!

9 The glory of the stars is the beauty of
    heaven,
  a glittering array in the heights of
    the Lord.
10 On the orders of the Holy One they
    stand in their appointed places;
  they never relax in their watches.
11 Look at the rainbow, and praise him
    who made it;
  it is exceedingly beautiful in its
    brightness.
12 It encircles the sky with its glorious
    arc;
  the hands of the Most High have
    stretched it out.

13 By his command he sends the driving
    snow
  and speeds the lightnings of his
    judgment.
14 Therefore the storehouses are opened,
  and the clouds fly out like birds.
15 In his majesty he gives the clouds
    their strength,
  and the hailstones are broken in
    pieces.
17a The voice of his thunder rebukes the
    earth;
16   when he appears, the mountains
    shake.
  At his will the south wind blows;
17b   so do the storm from the north and
    the whirlwind.
  He scatters the snow like birds flying
    down,
  and its descent is like locusts
    alighting.
18 The eye is dazzled by the beauty of its
    whiteness,
  and the mind is amazed as it falls.
19 He pours frost over the earth like salt,
  and icicles form like pointed thorns.
20 The cold north wind blows,
  and ice freezes on the water;
  it settles on every pool of water,
  and the water puts it on like a
    breastplate.

21 He consumes the mountains and
    burns up the wilderness,
  and withers the tender grass like
    fire.
22 A mist quickly heals all things;
  the falling dew gives refreshment
    from the heat.

23 By his plan he stilled the deep
  and planted islands in it.
24 Those who sail the sea tell of its
    dangers,
  and we marvel at what we hear.
25 In it are strange and marvelous
    creatures,
  all kinds of living things, and huge
    sea-monsters.
26 Because of him each of his messengers
    succeeds,
  and by his word all things hold
    together.

27 We could say more but could never
    say enough;
  let the final word be: "He is the
    all."
28 Where can we find the strength to
    praise him?
  For he is greater than all his works.
29 Awesome is the Lord and very great,
  and marvelous is his power.
30 Glorify the Lord and exalt him as
    much as you can,
  for he surpasses even that.
  When you exalt him, summon all
    your strength,
  and do not grow weary, for you
    cannot praise him enough.
31 Who has seen him and can describe
    him?
  Or who can extol him as he is?
32 Many things greater than these lie
    hidden,
  for I[a] have seen but few of his
    works.
33 For the Lord has made all things,
  and to the godly he has given
    wisdom.

a Heb: Gk we

HYMN IN HONOR
OF OUR ANCESTORS [a]

**44** Let us now sing the praises of
famous men,
our ancestors in their generations.

2 The Lord apportioned to them [b] great
glory,
his majesty from the beginning.

3 There were those who ruled in their
kingdoms,
and made a name for themselves by
their valor;
those who gave counsel because they
were intelligent;
those who spoke in prophetic
oracles;

4 those who led the people by their
counsels
and by their knowledge of the
people's lore;
they were wise in their words of
instruction;

5 those who composed musical tunes,
or put verses in writing;

6 rich men endowed with resources,
living peacefully in their homes—

7 all these were honored in their
generations,
and were the pride of their times.

8 Some of them have left behind a
name,
so that others declare their praise.

9 But of others there is no memory;
they have perished as though they
had never existed;
they have become as though they had
never been born,

they and their children after them.

10 But these also were godly men,
whose righteous deeds have not
been forgotten;

11 their wealth will remain with their
descendants,
and their inheritance with their
children's children. [c]

12 Their descendants stand by the
covenants;
their children also, for their sake.

13 Their offspring will continue forever,
and their glory will never be blotted
out.

14 Their bodies are buried in peace,
but their name lives on generation
after generation.

15 The assembly declares [d] their wisdom,
and the congregation proclaims
their praise.

16 Enoch pleased the Lord and was
taken up,
an example of repentance to all
generations.

17 Noah was found perfect and
righteous;
in the time of wrath he kept the
race alive; [e]
therefore a remnant was left on the
earth
when the flood came.

*a* This title is included in the Gk text.  *b* Heb: Gk
*created*  *c* Heb Compare Lat Syr: Meaning of Gk
uncertain  *d* Heb: Gk *Peoples declare*  *e* Heb: Gk
*was taken in exchange*

**44.1–50.24: In praise of Israel's ancestors.** Ben Sira celebrates the covenant with the patriarchs and
Israel by recounting the great figures of Israel's history (44.1–49.16), culminating in the high priest
Simon II (50.1–24).

**44.1–15: Introduction. 1:** *Famous men,* Hebrew and Syriac, "men of piety." **3–7:** Ben Sira lists the
classes of people (numbering twelve in the Hebrew text), who were *the pride of their times* and will be
exemplified in the names to follow. **9–10:** Some good people have left no memorial, but they will not be
forgotten.

**44.16: Enoch.** Burgeoning interest in the figure of *Enoch* (Gen 5.4; Wis 4.10; Heb 11.5; *1 Enoch*)
during the Hellenistic era may be the reason his name heads the list (although it is lacking in several
ancient witnesses to the text), and closes it in 49.14.

**44.17–45.26: Seven covenantal figures: Noah** (44.17–18), **Abraham** (44.19–21), **Isaac** (44.22), **Jacob/Israel** (44.23a), **Moses** (44.23b–45.5), **Aaron** (45.6–22), and **Phinehas** (45.23–24).

**44.17–18: Noah. 17:** *Righteous,* cf. Gen 6.9; 7.1. **18:** *Everlasting covenants,* cf. Gen 9.8–17.

18 Everlasting covenants were made with
  him
  that all flesh should never again be
  blotted out by a flood.

19 Abraham was the great father of a
  multitude of nations,
  and no one has been found like him
  in glory.

20 He kept the law of the Most High,
  and entered into a covenant with
  him;
  he certified the covenant in his flesh,
  and when he was tested he proved
  faithful.

21 Therefore the Lord[a] assured him
  with an oath
  that the nations would be blessed
  through his offspring;
  that he would make him as numerous
  as the dust of the earth,
  and exalt his offspring like the
  stars,
  and give them an inheritance from sea
  to sea
  and from the Euphrates[b] to the
  ends of the earth.

22 To Isaac also he gave the same
  assurance
  for the sake of his father Abraham.
  The blessing of all people and the
  covenant

23 he made to rest on the head of
  Jacob;
  he acknowledged him with his
  blessings,
  and gave him his inheritance;
  he divided his portions,

and distributed them among twelve
  tribes.

From his descendants the Lord[a]
  brought forth a godly man,
  who found favor in the sight of all

**45** 1 and was beloved by God and
  people,
  Moses, whose memory is blessed.

2 He made him equal in glory to the
  holy ones,
  and made him great, to the terror
  of his enemies.

3 By his words he performed swift
  miracles;[c]
  the Lord[a] glorified him in the
  presence of kings.
  He gave him commandments for his
  people,
  and revealed to him his glory.

4 For his faithfulness and meekness he
  consecrated him,
  choosing him out of all humankind.

5 He allowed him to hear his voice,
  and led him into the dark cloud,
  and gave him the commandments face
  to face,
  the law of life and knowledge,
  so that he might teach Jacob the
  covenant,
  and Israel his decrees.

6 He exalted Aaron, a holy man like
  Moses[d]

a Gk he    b Syr: Heb Gk River    c Heb: Gk caused
signs to cease    d Gk him

**44.19–23a: Abraham, Isaac, and Jacob/Israel. 19:** *Father of a multitude of nations,* Gen 17.4–8. **20:** *Kept the law,* Gen 26.5; *certified the covenant in his flesh,* by circumcision (Gen 17.9–14,23–27); *when he was tested,* in the binding of Isaac (Gen 22.1–14). **21:** *Oath,* Gen 15.18–21; 22.15–18. **22:** *Isaac,* Gen 17.19; 26.3–5; 28.3–4. **23:** *Jacob,* Gen 27.27–29; 28.13–15; *his inheritance* is the promised land (Gen 28.4).

**44.23b–45.5: Moses. 45.3:** *Miracles,* the plagues leading up to the Exodus (Ex 7.1–11.10; 12.29–32); *commandments,* the Decalogue (Ex 20.1–17; Deut 5.1–33); *glory,* Ex 33.18–23. **4:** On Moses' *meekness,* see Num 12.3. **5:** *Dark cloud,* Ex 20.21; 24.18; *face to face,* Num 12.8; *that he might teach,* Deut 4.1.

**45.6–25: Aaron and Phinehas.** The glorification of Aaron reflects the ascendancy of the high priesthood in Ben Sira's day. Much more space is given to him and Phinehas (and then to Simeon the high priest in ch 50) than to Moses. **6:** *His brother,* of the tribe of Levi, Ex 4.14. **7:** *Everlasting covenant,* of priesthood who was his brother, of the tribe of Levi.

7 He made an everlasting covenant with him,
    and gave him the priesthood of the people.
He blessed him with stateliness,
    and put a glorious robe on him.
8 He clothed him in perfect splendor,
    and strengthened him with the symbols of authority,
    the linen undergarments, the long robe, and the ephod.
9 And he encircled him with pomegranates,
    with many golden bells all around,
to send forth a sound as he walked,
    to make their ringing heard in the temple
    as a reminder to his people;
10 with the sacred vestment, of gold and violet
    and purple, the work of an embroiderer;
with the oracle of judgment, Urim and Thummim;
11    with twisted crimson, the work of an artisan;
with precious stones engraved like seals,
    in a setting of gold, the work of a jeweler,
to commemorate in engraved letters
    each of the tribes of Israel;
12 with a gold crown upon his turban,
    inscribed like a seal with "Holiness,"
a distinction to be prized, the work of an expert,
    a delight to the eyes, richly adorned.
13 Before him such beautiful things did not exist.
    No outsider ever put them on,

but only his sons
    and his descendants in perpetuity.
14 His sacrifices shall be wholly burned
    twice every day continually.
15 Moses ordained him,
    and anointed him with holy oil;
it was an everlasting covenant for him
    and for his descendants as long as the heavens endure,
to minister to the Lord[a] and serve as priest
    and bless his people in his name.
16 He chose him out of all the living
    to offer sacrifice to the Lord,
incense and a pleasing odor as a memorial portion,
    to make atonement for the[b] people.
17 In his commandments he gave him authority and statutes and[c] judgments,
    to teach Jacob the testimonies,
    and to enlighten Israel with his law.
18 Outsiders conspired against him,
    and envied him in the wilderness,
Dathan and Abiram and their followers
    and the company of Korah, in wrath and anger.
19 The Lord saw it and was not pleased,
    and in the heat of his anger they were destroyed;
he performed wonders against them
    to consume them in flaming fire.
20 He added glory to Aaron
    and gave him a heritage;
he allotted to him the best of the first fruits,
    and prepared bread of first fruits in abundance;
21 for they eat the sacrifices of the Lord,

a Gk *him*   b Other ancient authorities read *his* or *your*   c Heb: Gk *authority in covenants of*

(cf. vv. 13,15; Ex 28.1–4; 29.9; 40.15). **8:** *Perfect splendor,* for the details of the priestly vestments, which are elaborated upon in vv. 8–13, see Ex 28–29; cf. Sir 50.5–11. **10:** *Urim and Thummim,* cf. Ex 28.30; Num 27.21; 1 Sam 14.41–42. **14:** See Lev 6.8–15; Num 28.3–4. **15:** *Moses ordained . . . and anointed him,* Ex 28.41; Lev 8.1–30; *bless his people,* cf. Num 6.22–27; *everlasting covenant,* see Lev 24.8–9; Num 18.19. **17:** For the priestly *authority . . . to teach,* see Lev 10.11; Deut 33.10; Mal 2.7. **18:** *Dathan . . . company of Korah,* Num 16.1–33. **21:** *Eat the sacrifices,* Num 18.8–19. **22:** See Num 18.20; Deut

which he gave to him and his
descendants.

22 But in the land of the people he has
no inheritance,
and he has no portion among the
people;
for the Lord[a] himself is his[b]
portion and inheritance.

23 Phinehas son of Eleazar ranks third in
glory
for being zealous in the fear of the
Lord,
and standing firm, when the people
turned away,
in the noble courage of his soul;
and he made atonement for
Israel.

24 Therefore a covenant of friendship
was established with him,
that he should be leader of the
sanctuary and of his people,
that he and his descendants should
have
the dignity of the priesthood
forever.

25 Just as a covenant was established
with David
son of Jesse of the tribe of Judah,
that the king's heritage passes only
from son to son,
so the heritage of Aaron is for his
descendants alone.

26 And now bless the Lord
who has crowned you with glory.[c]
May the Lord[a] grant you wisdom of
mind
to judge his people with justice,
so that their prosperity may not
vanish,
and that their glory may endure
through all their generations.

46 Joshua son of Nun was mighty in
war,
and was the successor of Moses in
the prophetic office.
He became, as his name implies,
a great savior of God's[d] elect,
to take vengeance on the enemies that
rose against them,
so that he might give Israel its
inheritance.

2 How glorious he was when he lifted
his hands
and brandished his sword against
the cities!

3 Who before him ever stood so firm?
For he waged the wars of the Lord.

4 Was it not through him that the sun
stood still
and one day became as long as
two?

5 He called upon the Most High, the
Mighty One,
when enemies pressed him on every
side,
and the great Lord answered him
with hailstones of mighty power.

6 He overwhelmed that nation in battle,
and on the slope he destroyed his
opponents,
so that the nations might know his
armament,
that he was fighting in the sight of
the Lord;
for he was a devoted follower of
the Mighty One.

7 And in the days of Moses he proved
his loyalty,
he and Caleb son of Jephunneh:
they opposed the congregation,[e]

a Gk he    b Other ancient authorities read your
c Heb: Gk lacks And . . . glory    d Gk his    e Other
ancient authorities read the enemy

12.12. 23: *Phinehas,* Num 25.10–13; Ps 106.30; 1 Macc 2.54. 24–25: *The covenant with Phinehas, like
the covenant . . . with David* (2 Sam 7; Ps 89.19–37) was both dynastic and eternal.
    45.26: *A prayer for high priests. You* refers to Simon, son of Onias (see 50.1n.) and his successors.
    46.1–20: *Joshua* (vv. 1–7), **Caleb** (vv. 7–10), **the judges** (vv. 11–12), **and Samuel** (vv. 13–20). 1: *Succes-
sor of Moses,* Deut 34.9; Josh 1.1,5; 3.7; *his name* means "The Lord is salvation." 2–8: The conquest of
the promised land; see Josh 6–11. 4: *Sun stood still,* Josh 10.12–14. 5: *Hailstones,* Josh 10.11. 7: *Proved
his loyalty,* see Num 14.6–10; cf. 1 Macc 2.55–56. 8: *Two alone . . . of six hundred thousand,* Ex 12.37;

restrained the people from sin,
and stilled their wicked grumbling.
8 And these two alone were spared
out of six hundred thousand
infantry,
to lead the people*a* into their
inheritance,
the land flowing with milk and
honey.
9 The Lord gave Caleb strength,
which remained with him in his old
age,
so that he went up to the hill country,
and his children obtained it for an
inheritance,
10 so that all the Israelites might see
how good it is to follow the Lord.

11 The judges also, with their respective
names,
whose hearts did not fall into
idolatry
and who did not turn away from the
Lord—
may their memory be blessed!
12 May their bones send forth new life
from where they lie,
and may the names of those who
have been honored
live again in their children!

13 Samuel was beloved by his Lord;
a prophet of the Lord, he
established the kingdom
and anointed rulers over his
people.
14 By the law of the Lord he judged
the congregation,
and the Lord watched over Jacob.
15 By his faithfulness he was proved to
be a prophet,
and by his words he became known
as a trustworthy seer.

16 He called upon the Lord, the Mighty
One,
when his enemies pressed him on
every side,
and he offered in sacrifice a
suckling lamb.
17 Then the Lord thundered from
heaven,
and made his voice heard with a
mighty sound;
18 he subdued the leaders of the enemy*b*
and all the rulers of the Philistines.
19 Before the time of his eternal sleep,
Samuel*c* bore witness before the
Lord and his anointed:
"No property, not so much as a pair
of shoes,
have I taken from anyone!"
And no one accused him.
20 Even after he had fallen asleep, he
prophesied
and made known to the king his
death,
and lifted up his voice from the
ground
in prophecy, to blot out the
wickedness of the people.

47 After him Nathan rose up
to prophesy in the days of David.
2 As the fat is set apart from the
offering of well-being,
so David was set apart from the
Israelites.
3 He played with lions as though they
were young goats,
and with bears as though they were
lambs of the flock.
4 In his youth did he not kill a giant,

*a* Gk *them*    *b* Heb: Gk *leaders of the people of Tyre*
*c* Gk *he*

Num 11.21; 14.38; 26.65. **9:** For Caleb's *inheritance*, see Josh 14.6–14. **12:** *Bones send forth new life* (cf. 49.10), the meaning is to be interpreted in the light of the last line of the verse. **13–14:** *Anointed rulers,* 1 Sam 10.1; 16.13. *Judged,* 1 Sam 7.3–17. **15:** *Prophet,* 1 Sam 3.19–20. **16–18:** See 1 Sam 7.9–11. **19:** *Bore witness,* 1 Sam 12.3. **20:** *Lifted up his voice from the ground,* 1 Sam 28.8–19.

**47.1–22: Nathan** (v. 1), **David** (vv. 2–11), **and Solomon** (vv. 12–22). **1:** See 2 Sam 7.2–3; 12.1; 1 Chr 17.1. **2:** *The fat,* the portion reserved for sacrifice (Lev 3.3–5). *David* was likewise *set apart* as the Lord's choice (1 Sam 16.1–12). **3:** *Played with lions,* 1 Sam 17.34–36. **4:** *Kill a giant,* Goliath (1 Sam 17.49–51).

and take away the people's
disgrace,
when he whirled the stone in the sling
and struck down the boasting
Goliath?
5 For he called on the Lord, the Most
High,
and he gave strength to his right
arm
to strike down a mighty warrior,
and to exalt the power[a] of his
people.
6 So they glorified him for the tens of
thousands he conquered,
and praised him for the blessings
bestowed by the Lord,
when the glorious diadem was
given to him.
7 For he wiped out his enemies on
every side,
and annihilated his adversaries the
Philistines;
he crushed their power[a] to our
own day.
8 In all that he did he gave thanks
to the Holy One, the Most High,
proclaiming his glory;
he sang praise with all his heart,
and he loved his Maker.
9 He placed singers before the altar,
to make sweet melody with their
voices.[b]
10 He gave beauty to the festivals,
and arranged their times
throughout the year,[c]
while they praised God's[d] holy name,
and the sanctuary resounded from
early morning.
11 The Lord took away his sins,
and exalted his power[a] forever;
he gave him a covenant of kingship
and a glorious throne in Israel.

12 After him a wise son rose up
who because of him lived in
security:[e]
13 Solomon reigned in an age of peace,
because God made all his borders
tranquil,
so that he might build a house in his
name
and provide a sanctuary to stand
forever.
14 How wise you were when you were
young!
You overflowed like the Nile[f] with
understanding.
15 Your influence spread throughout the
earth,
and you filled it with proverbs
having deep meaning.
16 Your fame reached to far-off islands,
and you were loved for your
peaceful reign.
17 Your songs, proverbs, and parables,
and the answers you gave
astounded the nations.
18 In the name of the Lord God,
who is called the God of Israel,
you gathered gold like tin
and amassed silver like lead.
19 But you brought in women to lie at
your side,
and through your body you were
brought into subjection.
20 You stained your honor,
and defiled your family line,
so that you brought wrath upon your
children,
and they were grieved[g] at your folly,
21 because the sovereignty was divided

a Gk *born*    b Other ancient authorities add *and
daily they sing his praises*    c Gk *to completion*
d Gk *his*    e Heb: Gk *in a broad place*    f Heb: Gk *a
river*    g Other ancient authorities read *I was grieved*

6: *Tens of thousands*, 1 Sam 18.7. 8–10: For David as founder of worship in the Jerusalem Temple, see
1 Chr 16.4; 23.1–6,24–32. 11: *His sins*, 2 Sam 11.1–12.25; *covenant of kingship*, cf. 45.25; 47.22;
2 Sam 7.12–16; Ps 89.28–37. 13: According to 1 Kings 4.3–5, David could not build the Temple because
he was engaged in warfare, but when *peace* was established, Solomon was able to carry out the building
of the Temple (1 Kings 5–8). 14–18: On Solomon's wisdom and wealth, see 1 Kings 3.12–13; 4.21–34;
10.14–27. *Proverbs*, see Prov 1.1; 10.1. 19: *Women*, 1 Kings 11.1–11. 21: The *divided* kingdoms of Israel
(or *Ephraim*) and Judah, 1 Kings 12.15–20. 22: *Or . . . perish*, Hebrew "He will let none of his words
fall to the ground." *Root*, see Isa 11.10.

and a rebel kingdom arose out of
  Ephraim.
22 But the Lord will never give up his
  mercy,
  or cause any of his works to perish;
  he will never blot out the descendants
  of his chosen one,
  or destroy the family line of him
  who loved him.
  So he gave a remnant to Jacob,
  and to David a root from his own
  family.

23 Solomon rested with his ancestors,
  and left behind him one of his sons,
  broad in*a* folly and lacking in sense,
  Rehoboam, whose policy drove the
  people to revolt.
  Then Jeroboam son of Nebat led
  Israel into sin
  and started Ephraim on its sinful
  ways.
24 Their sins increased more and more,
  until they were exiled from their
  land.
25 For they sought out every kind of
  wickedness,
  until vengeance came upon them.

48 Then Elijah arose, a prophet like
  fire,
  and his word burned like a torch.
2 He brought a famine upon them,
  and by his zeal he made them few
  in number.
3 By the word of the Lord he shut up
  the heavens,
  and also three times brought down
  fire.
4 How glorious you were, Elijah, in
  your wondrous deeds!

Whose glory is equal to yours?
5 You raised a corpse from death
  and from Hades, by the word of
  the Most High.
6 You sent kings down to destruction,
  and famous men, from their
  sickbeds.
7 You heard rebuke at Sinai
  and judgments of vengeance at
  Horeb.
8 You anointed kings to inflict
  retribution,
  and prophets to succeed you.*b*
9 You were taken up by a whirlwind of
  fire,
  in a chariot with horses of fire.
10 At the appointed time, it is written,
  you are destined*c*
  to calm the wrath of God before it
  breaks out in fury,
  to turn the hearts of parents to their
  children,
  and to restore the tribes of Jacob.
11 Happy are those who saw you
  and were adorned*d* with your love!
  For we also shall surely live.*e*

12 When Elijah was enveloped in the
  whirlwind,
  Elisha was filled with his spirit.
  He performed twice as many signs,
  and marvels with every utterance of
  his mouth.*f*
  Never in his lifetime did he tremble
  before any ruler,

a Heb (with a play on the name Rehoboam) Syr: Gk
*the people's*   b Heb: Gk *him*   c Heb: Gk *are for
reproofs*   d Other ancient authorities read *and have
died*   e Text and meaning of Gk uncertain
f Heb: Gk lacks *He performed . . . mouth*

**47.23–48.16: Kings and prophets.** Solomon's son, *Rehoboam,* and *Jeroboam* in the Northern Kingdom
are mentioned briefly (47.23–25), while the deeds of *Elijah* (48.1–11) and *Elisha* (48.12–14) are described in detail. **23:** On *Rehoboam,* see 1 Kings 11.43–12.19; for *Jeroboam,* 1 Kings 12.28–30. **24:** See
2 Kings 17.6–8, 18.
  **48.1–11: Elijah. 1:** 1 Kings 17.1. *Torch,* Heb "furnace." **3:** 1 Kings 18.38; 2 Kings 1.10–12. **5:** 1 Kings
17.21–22. **6:** 2 Kings 1.16. **7:** 1 Kings 19.8. **8:** 1 Kings 19.15–16. **9:** 2 Kings 2.11. **10:** *It is written,* in
Mal 4.5–6.
  **48.12–16: Elisha. 12:** *Filled with his spirit,* 2 Kings 2.9,13. **13:** *His body prophesied,* 2 Kings
13.20–21. **15:** 2 Kings 18.11–12.

nor could anyone intimidate him at
all.

13 Nothing was too hard for him,
and when he was dead, his body
prophesied.
14 In his life he did wonders,
and in death his deeds were
marvelous.

15 Despite all this the people did not
repent,
nor did they forsake their sins,
until they were carried off as plunder
from their land,
and were scattered over all the
earth.
The people were left very few in
number,
but with a ruler from the house of
David.
16 Some of them did what was right,
but others sinned more and more.

17 Hezekiah fortified his city,
and brought water into its midst;
he tunneled the rock with iron tools,
and built cisterns for the water.
18 In his days Sennacherib invaded the
country;
he sent his commander[a] and
departed;
he shook his fist against Zion,
and made great boasts in his
arrogance.
19 Then their hearts were shaken and
their hands trembled,
and they were in anguish, like
women in labor.
20 But they called upon the Lord who is
merciful,
spreading out their hands toward
him.

The Holy One quickly heard them
from heaven,
and delivered them through Isaiah.
21 The Lord[b] struck down the camp of
the Assyrians,
and his angel wiped them out.
22 For Hezekiah did what was pleasing
to the Lord,
and he kept firmly to the ways of
his ancestor David,
as he was commanded by the prophet
Isaiah,
who was great and trustworthy in
his visions.
23 In Isaiah's[c] days the sun went
backward,
and he prolonged the life of the
king.
24 By his dauntless spirit he saw the
future,
and comforted the mourners in
Zion.
25 He revealed what was to occur to the
end of time,
and the hidden things before they
happened.

49 The name[d] of Josiah is like
blended incense
prepared by the skill of the
perfumer;
his memory[e] is as sweet as honey to
every mouth,
and like music at a banquet of
wine.
2 He did what was right by reforming
the people,

a Other ancient authorities add *from Lachish*
b Gk *He*      c Gk *his*      d Heb: Gk *memory*
e Heb: Gk *it*

48.17–49.13: Rulers and prophets in the kingdom of Judah.
48.17–22: Hezekiah. 17: *Fortified his city*, 2 Kings 20.20. 18: 2 Kings 18.13,17; Isa 36.1. 20: 2 Kings
19.15–20. 21: 2 Kings 19.35; Isa 37.36; 1 Macc 7.41. 22: 2 Kings 18.3.
48.23–25: Isaiah. 23: *Sun went backward*, 2 Kings 20.10–11; Isa 38.8. 24–25: Cf. Isa 40.1–2; Isa
42.9.
49.1–10: Josiah (vv. 1–3), Jeremiah (vv. 4–7), Ezekiel (v. 8), Job (v. 9), and the Twelve Prophets
(v. 10). 2–3: 2 Kings 23.3, 25. 4: *All of them were great sinners*, the narratives of the kings in 1–2 Kings

and removing the wicked
abominations.
3 He kept his heart fixed on the Lord;
in lawless times he made godliness
prevail.

4 Except for David and Hezekiah and
Josiah,
all of them were great sinners,
for they abandoned the law of the
Most High;
the kings of Judah came to an end.
5 They[a] gave their power to others,
and their glory to a foreign nation,
6 who set fire to the chosen city of the
sanctuary,
and made its streets desolate,
as Jeremiah had foretold.[b]
7 For they had mistreated him,
who even in the womb had been
consecrated a prophet,
to pluck up and ruin and destroy,
and likewise to build and to
plant.
8 It was Ezekiel who saw the vision of
glory,
which God[c] showed him above the
chariot of the cherubim.
9 For God[d] also mentioned Job
who held fast to all the ways of
justice.[e]
10 May the bones of the Twelve
Prophets
send forth new life from where they
lie,
for they comforted the people of
Jacob

and delivered them with confident
hope.

11 How shall we magnify Zerubbabel?
He was like a signet ring on the
right hand,
12 and so was Jeshua son of Jozadak;
in their days they built the house
and raised a temple[f] holy to the
Lord,
destined for everlasting glory.
13 The memory of Nehemiah also is
lasting;
he raised our fallen walls,
and set up gates and bars,
and rebuilt our ruined houses.

14 Few have[g] ever been created on earth
like Enoch,
for he was taken up from the earth.
15 Nor was anyone ever born like
Joseph;[h]
even his bones were cared for.
16 Shem and Seth and Enosh were
honored,[i]
but above every other created living
being was Adam.

50 The leader of his brothers and the
pride of his people[j]

a Heb He   b Gk by the hand of Jeremiah
c Gk He   d Gk he   e Heb Compare Syr: Meaning
of Gk uncertain   f Other ancient authorities read
people   g Heb Syr: Gk No one has   h Heb Syr: Gk
adds the leader of his brothers, the support of the
people   i Heb: Gk Shem and Seth were honored by
people   j Heb Syr: Gk lacks this line. Compare 49.15

customarily included an evaluation (e.g., 2 Kings 12.2–3; 13.6). Only David, Hezekiah, and Josiah receive
complete approbation. **5–7:** 2 Chr 36.17–19; Jer 1.5–10; 39.8. **8:** Ezek 1.3–15; 13.11; 38.9,16,22. **9:**
Ezek 14.14–20. **10:** *The Twelve Prophets* probably constituted a corpus of writings by the time of Ben
Sira; *bones*, see 46.12n.
**49.11–13: Leaders of the restoration:** Zerubbabel (v. 11), Jeshua (v. 12), and Nehemiah (v. 13). Ezra
is notably absent. **11:** *Zerubbabel*, Ezra 3.2; *like a signet ring*, Hag 2.23. **12:** *Jeshua*, Ezra 3.2; Hag 1.12;
2.2; Zech 3.1. **13:** *Nehemiah . . . raised our fallen walls*, Neh 7.1.
**49.14–16: Conclusion of the historical review.** The mention of *Enoch* (see 44.16) and *Joseph* along
with *Shem, Seth*, and *Enosh* leads back to Adam. **14:** *Taken up*, Gen 5.24; Wis 4.10–14; Heb 11.5. **15:**
*Even his bones*, Gen 50.25–26. **16:** Gen 5.3,32.
**50.1–24: Simon, son of Onias. 1:** Simon II "the Just," was high priest ca. 219–196 BCE (Josephus,
*Ant*.12.4.10). *Onias* is the Greek form of Johanan. *The house*, of God. **11:** *Glorious robe*, Ex 28.2–43;

was the high priest, Simon son of
Onias,
who in his life repaired the house,
and in his time fortified the
temple.

2 He laid the foundations for the high
double walls,
the high retaining walls for the
temple enclosure.

3 In his days a water cistern was dug,*a*
a reservoir like the sea in
circumference.

4 He considered how to save his people
from ruin,
and fortified the city against siege.

5 How glorious he was, surrounded by
the people,
as he came out of the house of the
curtain.

6 Like the morning star among the
clouds,
like the full moon at the festal
season;*a*

7 like the sun shining on the temple of
the Most High,
like the rainbow gleaming in
splendid clouds;

8 like roses in the days of first fruits,
like lilies by a spring of water,
like a green shoot on Lebanon on a
summer day;

9 like fire and incense in the censer,
like a vessel of hammered gold
studded with all kinds of precious
stones;

10 like an olive tree laden with fruit,
and like a cypress towering in the
clouds.

11 When he put on his glorious robe
and clothed himself in perfect
splendor,
when he went up to the holy altar,
he made the court of the sanctuary
glorious.

12 When he received the portions from
the hands of the priests,
as he stood by the hearth of the
altar
with a garland of brothers around
him,

he was like a young cedar on
Lebanon
surrounded by the trunks of palm
trees.

13 All the sons of Aaron in their
splendor
held the Lord's offering in their
hands
before the whole congregation of
Israel.

14 Finishing the service at the altars,*b*
and arranging the offering to the
Most High, the Almighty,

15 he held out his hand for the cup
and poured a drink offering of the
blood of the grape;
he poured it out at the foot of the
altar,
a pleasing odor to the Most High,
the king of all.

16 Then the sons of Aaron shouted;
they blew their trumpets of
hammered metal;
they sounded a mighty fanfare
as a reminder before the Most
High.

17 Then all the people together quickly
fell to the ground on their faces
to worship their Lord,
the Almighty, God Most High.

18 Then the singers praised him with
their voices
in sweet and full-toned melody.*c*

19 And the people of the Lord Most
High offered
their prayers before the Merciful
One,
until the order of worship of the Lord
was ended,
and they completed his ritual.

20 Then Simon*d* came down and raised
his hands
over the whole congregation of
Israelites,
to pronounce the blessing of the Lord
with his lips,

*a* Heb: Meaning of Gk uncertain   *b* Other ancient
authorities read *altar*   *c* Other ancient authorities
read *in sweet melody throughout the house*   *d* Gk *he*

and to glory in his name;
21 and they bowed down in worship a
second time,
to receive the blessing from the
Most High.

22 And now bless the God of all,
who everywhere works great
wonders,
who fosters our growth from birth,
and deals with us according to his
mercy.
23 May he give us[a] gladness of heart,
and may there be peace in our[b]
days
in Israel, as in the days of old.
24 May he entrust to us his mercy,
and may he deliver us in our[c] days!

25 Two nations my soul detests,
and the third is not even a
people:
26 Those who live in Seir,[d] and the
Philistines,
and the foolish people that live in
Shechem.

27 Instruction in understanding and
knowledge
I have written in this book,
Jesus son of Eleazar son of Sirach[e] of
Jerusalem,
whose mind poured forth wisdom.
28 Happy are those who concern
themselves with these things,
and those who lay them to heart
will become wise.
29 For if they put them into practice,
they will be equal to anything,

for the fear[f] of the Lord is their
path.

PRAYER OF JESUS SON OF SIRACH[g]
51 I give you thanks, O Lord and
King,
and praise you, O God my Savior.
I give thanks to your name,
2 for you have been my protector and
helper
and have delivered me from
destruction
and from the trap laid by a
slanderous tongue,
from lips that fabricate lies.
In the face of my adversaries
you have been my helper 3 and
delivered me,
in the greatness of your mercy and
of your name,
from grinding teeth about to devour me,
from the hand of those seeking my
life,
from the many troubles I endured,
4 from choking fire on every side,
and from the midst of fire that I
had not kindled,
5 from the deep belly of Hades,
from an unclean tongue and lying
words—
6 the slander of an unrighteous
tongue to the king.

a Other ancient authorities read *you*    b Other
ancient authorities read *your*    c Other ancient
authorities read *his*    d Heb Compare Lat: Gk *on the
mountain of Samaria*    e Heb: Meaning of Gk
uncertain    f Heb: Other ancient authorities read *light*
g This title is included in the Gk text.

39.1–31. 16: *Trumpets,* Num 10.2; 31.6. 18: *Singers,* 2 Chr 29.26–30. 20: *The blessing,* namely Num
6.24–27. *His name,* only the high priest (and only once a year, on the Day of Atonement) could utter the
ineffable name, YHWH. 22–24: A concluding benediction. 24: Hebrew, "May his love abide upon
Simeon, and may he keep in him the covenant of Phinehas; may one never be cut off from him; and as
for his offspring, (may it be) as the days of heaven."

50.25–26: An invective against Idumeans (*Seir*), pagans or Hellenists (*Philistines*), and Samaritans
(*Shechem*).

50.27–29: A postscript, probably the author's original ending; he gives his full name and recommends
*this book.* 27: *Jesus son of Eleazar son of Sirach,* in Hebrew, the name would probably be "Yeshua ben
El-azar ben Sira."

51.1–30: Appendices. 1–12: A psalm of thanksgiving for deliverance (cf. Ps 18.1–19). 5: *Hades,* see

My soul drew near to death,
and my life was on the brink of
Hades below.
7 They surrounded me on every
side,
and there was no one to help
me;
I looked for human assistance,
and there was none.
8 Then I remembered your mercy,
O Lord,
and your kindness[a] from of old,
for you rescue those who wait for
you
and save them from the hand of
their enemies.
9 And I sent up my prayer from the
earth,
and begged for rescue from death.
10 I cried out, "Lord, you are my
Father;[b]
do not forsake me in the days of
trouble,
when there is no help against the
proud.
11 I will praise your name continually,
and will sing hymns of
thanksgiving."
My prayer was heard,
12     for you saved me from destruction
and rescued me in time of trouble.
For this reason I thank you and praise
you,
and I bless the name of the Lord.

---

Heb adds:

*Give thanks to the LORD, for he is
good,
for his steadfast love endures forever;*

*Give thanks to the God of praises,
for his steadfast love endures forever;*

*Give thanks to the guardian of Israel,
for his steadfast love endures forever;*

*Give thanks to him who formed all
things,
for his steadfast love endures forever;*

*Give thanks to the redeemer of Israel,
for his steadfast love endures forever;*

*Give thanks to him who gathers the
dispersed of Israel,
for his steadfast love endures forever;*

*Give thanks to him who rebuilt his
city and his sanctuary,
for his steadfast love endures forever;*

*Give thanks to him who makes a
horn to sprout for the house of
David,
for his steadfast love endures forever;*

*Give thanks to him who has chosen
the sons of Zadok to be priests,
for his steadfast love endures forever;*

*Give thanks to the shield of Abraham,
for his steadfast love endures forever;*

*Give thanks to the rock of Isaac,
for his steadfast love endures forever;*

*Give thanks to the mighty one of
Jacob,
for his steadfast love endures forever;*

*Give thanks to him who has chosen
Zion,
for his steadfast love endures forever;*

*Give thanks to the King of the kings
of kings,
for his steadfast love endures forever;*

a Other ancient authorities read *work*  b Heb: Gk
*the Father of my lord*

14.12n. **10:** *Father,* see 23.1,4. After v. 12 the Hebrew text adds a litany of praise comparable to Ps 136.
Absent from the Greek and Syriac versions, this section is probably a later addition composed by an
author other than Ben Sira.

*He has raised up a horn for his people,*
*praise for all his loyal ones.*

*For the children of Israel, the people*
*close to him.*
*Praise the LORD!*

_____

13 While I was still young, before I went
on my travels,
I sought wisdom openly in my
prayer.
14 Before the temple I asked for her,
and I will search for her until the
end.

15 From the first blossom to the ripening
grape
my heart delighted in her;
my foot walked on the straight path;
from my youth I followed her steps.

16 I inclined my ear a little and received
her,
and I found for myself much
instruction.
17 I made progress in her;
to him who gives wisdom I will
give glory.

18 For I resolved to live according to
wisdom,*a*
and I was zealous for the good,
and I shall never be disappointed.
19 My soul grappled with wisdom,*a*
and in my conduct I was strict;*b*

I spread out my hands to the heavens,
and lamented my ignorance of her.
20 I directed my soul to her,
and in purity I found her.

With her I gained understanding from
the first;
therefore I will never be forsaken.

21 My heart was stirred to seek her;
therefore I have gained a prize
possession.
22 The Lord gave me my tongue as a
reward,
and I will praise him with it.

23 Draw near to me, you who are
uneducated,
and lodge in the house of
instruction.
24 Why do you say you are lacking in
these things,*c*
and why do you endure such great
thirst?
25 I opened my mouth and said,
Acquire wisdom*d* for yourselves
without money.

26 Put your neck under her*e* yoke,
and let your souls receive
instruction;
it is to be found close by.

27 See with your own eyes that I have
labored but little
and found for myself much
serenity.
28 Hear but a little of my instruction,
and through me you will acquire
silver and gold.*f*

29 May your soul rejoice in God's*g*
mercy,
and may you never be ashamed to
praise him.
30 Do your work in good time,
and in his own time God*h* will give
you your reward.

a Gk *her*   b Meaning of Gk uncertain
c Cn Compare Heb Syr: Meaning of Gk uncertain
d Heb: Gk lacks *wisdom*   e Heb: other ancient
authorities read *the*   f Syr Compare Heb: Gk *Get
instruction with a large sum of silver, and you will
gain by it much gold.*   g Gk *his*   h Gk *he*

**51.13–30:** An acrostic poem about the author's love for Wisdom. Vv. 13–20a have been preserved
in a psalms scroll from Qumran (11QPsᵃ). **13:** *Travels,* cf. 34.11; 39.4. **23:** Wisdom's invitation
(cf. 14.20–27; Prov 9.1–6). *House of instruction,* likely refers to a school, or a formal educational setting
maintained by the sages of the Hellenistic period. **26:** *Yoke,* cf. 6.23–31; in the New Testament Mt
11.29–30 applies this image to Jesus.

# BARUCH

❧ ❧

The book of Baruch was probably written sometime between 200 and 60 BCE; it is set, however, during the Babylonian exile of the early sixth century BCE and attributed to Jeremiah's friend and secretary, Baruch son of Neriah (Jer 32.12; 36.4; 43.3; 45.1). Although Jeremiah and Baruch both are reported (Jer 43.1–7) to have been taken to Egypt in 582, a tradition developed later, which is reflected in the book of Baruch and other Jewish sources (*Seder Olam Rabbah 26; Midrash Rabbah Song 5.5; Babylonian Talmud Megillah 16b*), that Baruch went to Babylon. The number of historical errors in the introduction (1.1–14) makes it unlikely that the book was written by Baruch or near the time of the exile. Although few clues to the date of the composition exist, allusions to Sir 24 (ca. 180) and Dan 9 (ca. 165) imply a date not earlier than the middle of the second century BCE.

Most of Baruch is made up of pastiches of biblical passages copied or paraphrased (e.g., Dan 9; Job 28; Isa 40–66). This mosaic technique was popular in the late Second Temple period. Authors recombined texts in new ways both as a means of interpreting canonical literature and as a means of creating new literary entities.

Baruch falls into two main sections, each of which consists of two parts. The first section, in prose, includes an introduction (1.1–14) and a corporate confession of sin (1.15–3.8) for Jews in Jerusalem to recite at the altar there, along with appropriate sacrifices, on various festival days and seasons. The idea of a letter or scroll written in Babylon to be read aloud in Jerusalem is derived from the exchange of letters recorded in Jer 29 and the scroll of Jeremiah's oracles penned by Baruch and read before King Jehoiakim in 605 BCE (Jer 36). The corporate confession is modeled on Dan 9.4–19 (cf. Ezra 9.6–15; Neh 9.6–37).

The second section consists of two poems. The first (3.9–4.4) is a paean of praise of Wisdom. Drawing on Job 28 and Sir 24, it describes Wisdom as elusive but also as the Torah, God's precious gift to Israel. The second contains an address by Jerusalem to the people of Israel (4.5–29) and a rhetorical address to Jerusalem (4.30–5.9), inspired no doubt by Isa 51.17–52.10; 54; and 60–62.

The text on which the following translation is based is the Greek Septuagint; ancient Syriac, Latin, Coptic, Ethiopic, Arabic, and Armenian versions based on the Greek also exist. The prose section (1.1–3.8) has long been viewed as a translation of a lost Hebrew original; recent research indicates that the poetic sections also derive from Hebrew originals.

Each of the major sections of the book has distinctive stylistic aspects that may indicate different authors. For instance, different names for God are used in the confession ("Lord"), in the wisdom poem ("God"), and in the Zion poem ("the Everlasting"). Judgment as to whether Baruch is the product of a single author or of an editor who compiled already existing materials is complicated by the heavy dependence of the confession and the poems on various scriptural models, since this dependence may account for much of the variation in style and theological perspective.

The book of Baruch would have well served Jewish communities in Judah and the Diaspora during the Seleucid and later eras of suffering and repression, since it deals with theological themes of particular interest to Jews at that time: the confession of corporate sin in the context of biblical history, the Torah as the gift of divine wisdom, and the restoration of Zion. There is no evidence, however, that any Jewish community afforded Baruch canonical status. In Christianity it is included among the deuterocanonical books of the Roman Catholic and Eastern Orthodox churches, but is listed in the Apocrypha by Protestant churches.

1 These are the words of the book that Baruch son of Neriah son of Mahseiah son of Zedekiah son of Hasadiah son of Hilkiah wrote in Babylon, 2 in the fifth year, on the seventh day of the month, at the time when the Chaldeans took Jerusalem and burned it with fire.

3 Baruch read the words of this book to Jeconiah son of Jehoiakim, king of Judah, and to all the people who came to hear the book, 4 and to the nobles and the princes, and to the elders, and to all the people, small and great, all who lived in Babylon by the river Sud.

5 Then they wept, and fasted, and prayed before the Lord; 6 they collected as much money as each could give, 7 and sent it to Jerusalem to the high priest[a] Jehoiakim son of Hilkiah son of Shallum, and to the priests, and to all the people who were present with him in Jerusalem. 8 At the same time, on the tenth day of Sivan, Baruch[b] took the vessels of the house of the Lord, which had been carried away from the temple, to return them to the land of Judah—the silver vessels that Zedekiah son of Josiah, king of Judah, had made, 9 after King Nebuchadnezzar of Babylon had carried away from Jerusalem Jeconiah and the princes and the prisoners and the nobles and the people of the land, and brought them to Babylon.

10 They said: Here we send you money; so buy with the money burnt offerings and sin offerings and incense, and prepare a grain offering, and offer them on the altar of the Lord our God; 11 and pray for the life of King Nebuchadnezzar of Babylon, and for the life of his son Belshazzar, so that their days on earth may be like the days of heaven. 12 The Lord will give us strength, and light to our eyes; we shall live under the protection[c] of King Nebuchadnezzar of Babylon, and under the protection of his son Belshazzar, and we shall serve them many days and find favor in their sight. 13 Pray also for us to the Lord our God, for we have sinned against the Lord our God, and to this day the anger of the Lord and his wrath have not turned away from us. 14 And you shall read aloud this scroll that we are sending you, to make your confession in the house of the Lord on the days of the festivals and at appointed seasons.

15 And you shall say: The Lord our God is in the right, but there is open shame on us

a Gk the priest   b Gk he   c Gk in the shadow

1.1–14: Historical introduction. 1–2: Authorship and date. 1: Baruch, Jeremiah's secretary (Jer 32.12). 2: Fifth year, after the fall of Jerusalem in 586 BCE (2 Kings 25.8–12). 3–4: The book is read before the king and the other exiles (cf. Jer 36.10). 3: Jeconiah, also called Jehoiachin (2 Kings 24.15; Jer 24.1). 4: Sud, unknown. 5–14: A gift of money, the temple vessels, and the book are sent to Jerusalem. 5: The word Lord occurs only in the first part of the book (1.1–3.8). 6: They collected, see Ezra 1. 7: The high priest Jehoiakim, otherwise unknown. 8: Sivan, the third month (May-June), presumably ten months after the events recorded in vv. 1–4. For a more reliable account of the return of the gold and silver vessels under the Persian king Cyrus, see Ezra 1.7–11. 9: Jer 24.1; 2 Kings 24.10–16. 10–14: The cover letter sent along with the "book" that begins in v. 15. For the continuation of offerings in the ruins of the Temple, see Jer 41.5. 11: Jer 29.7. Belshazzar was actually the son of Nabonidus. The same error is made in Dan 5. Like the days of heaven, without end (Deut 11.21).

1.15–3.8: Confession of sin, first for the Jerusalem community (1.15–2.5), and then for the exiles (2.6–3.8); compare 1.15–16 and 2.6. This section is based largely on Dan 9.4–15 with supplementation from Lev 26, Deut 28, and portions of the book of Jeremiah. 1.15–2.5: Disobedience brought the judgment of exile. 15–18: A refrain based on Dan 9.7–10 and echoed in 2.6–10 marking the division between the two halves of this confession. 15: Ezra 9.7 and, especially, Dan 9.7, repeated in 2.6. 18: Dan today, on the people of Judah, on the inhabitants of Jerusalem, 16 and on our kings, our rulers, our priests, our prophets, and our ancestors, 17 because we have sinned before the Lord. 18 We have disobeyed him, and have not heeded the voice of the Lord our God, to walk in the statutes of the Lord that he set before us. 19 From the time when the Lord brought our ancestors out of the land of Egypt until today, we have been disobedient to the Lord our God, and we have been negligent, in not heeding his voice. 20 So to this day there have clung to us the calamities and the curse that the Lord declared through his servant Moses at the time when he brought our ancestors out of the land of Egypt to give to us a land flowing with milk and honey. 21 We did not listen to the voice of the Lord our God in all the words of the prophets whom he sent to us, 22 but all of us followed the intent of our own wicked hearts by serving other gods and doing what is evil in the sight of the Lord our God.

2 So the Lord carried out the threat he spoke against us: against our judges who ruled Israel, and against our kings and our rulers and the people of Israel and Judah. 2 Under the whole heaven there has not been done the like of what he has done in Jerusalem, in accordance with the threats that were*a* written in the law of Moses. 3 Some of us ate the flesh of their sons and others the flesh of their daughters. 4 He made them subject to all the kingdoms around us, to be an object of scorn and a desolation among all the surrounding peoples, where the Lord has scattered them. 5 They were brought down and not raised up, because our nation*b* sinned against the Lord our God, in not heeding his voice.

6 The Lord our God is in the right, but there is open shame on us and our ancestors this very day. 7 All those calamities with which the Lord threatened us have come upon us. 8 Yet we have not entreated the favor of the Lord by turning away, each of us, from the thoughts of our wicked hearts. 9 And the Lord has kept the calamities ready, and the Lord has brought them upon us, for the Lord is just in all the works that he has commanded us to do. 10 Yet we have not obeyed his voice, to walk in the statutes of the Lord that he set before us.

11 And now, O Lord God of Israel, who brought your people out of the land of Egypt with a mighty hand and with signs and wonders and with great power and outstretched arm, and made yourself a name that continues to this day, 12 we have sinned, we have been ungodly, we have done wrong, O Lord our God, against all your ordinances. 13 Let your anger turn away from us, for we are left, few in number, among the nations where you have scattered us. 14 Hear, O Lord, our prayer and our supplication, and for your own sake deliver us, and grant us favor in the sight of those who have carried us into exile; 15 so that all the earth may know that you are the Lord our God, for Israel and his descendants are called by your name.

16 O Lord, look down from your holy dwelling, and consider us. Incline your ear, O Lord, and hear; 17 open your eyes, O Lord, and see, for the dead who are in Hades, whose spirit has been taken from their bodies, will not ascribe glory or justice to the Lord; 18 but the person who is deeply grieved, who walks bowed and feeble, with failing eyes and famished soul, will declare your glory and righteousness, O Lord.

19 For it is not because of any righteous deeds of our ancestors or our kings that we bring before you our prayer for mercy, O Lord our God. 20 For you have sent your anger and your wrath upon us, as you declared by your servants the prophets, say-

a Gk *in accordance with what is*   b Gk *because we*

9.10, repeated in 2.10. **20:** Deut 28; Jer 11.3–5. **21:** Jer 7.25–26; Dan 9.5. **2.1–2:** Dan 9.12–13. **3:** Lev 26.29; Deut 28.53; Jer 19.9; Lam 4.10. **5:** Deut 28.13. **6–10:** Confession of guilt. **7–9:** Dan 9.12–14. **11–26:** Supplication and confession. **11–14:** Dan 9.15–17. **12:** Cf. Ps 106.6 and 1 Kings 8.47. **13:** Deut 4.27; Jer 42.2. **16:** Deut 26.15. **17:** Ps 6.5; 30.9; Isa 38.18; Sir 17.27–28. *Hades,* Sheol, the underworld where all the dead go. **18:** Deut 28.65–66. **21:** Jer 27.11–12. **23:** Jer 7.34. **25:** Jer 36.30. **26:** Jer 7.14.

ing: 21 Thus says the Lord: Bend your shoulders and serve the king of Babylon, and you will remain in the land that I gave to your ancestors. 22 But if you will not obey the voice of the Lord and will not serve the king of Babylon, 23 I will make to cease from the towns of Judah and from the region around Jerusalem the voice of mirth and the voice of gladness, the voice of the bridegroom and the voice of the bride, and the whole land will be a desolation without inhabitants.

24 But we did not obey your voice, to serve the king of Babylon; and you have carried out your threats, which you spoke by your servants the prophets, that the bones of our kings and the bones of our ancestors would be brought out of their resting place; 25 and indeed they have been thrown out to the heat of day and the frost of night. They perished in great misery, by famine and sword and pestilence. 26 And the house that is called by your name you have made as it is today, because of the wickedness of the house of Israel and the house of Judah.

27 Yet you have dealt with us, O Lord our God, in all your kindness and in all your great compassion, 28 as you spoke by your servant Moses on the day when you commanded him to write your law in the presence of the people of Israel, saying, 29 "If you will not obey my voice, this very great multitude will surely turn into a small number among the nations, where I will scatter them. 30 For I know that they will not obey me, for they are a stiff-necked people. But in the land of their exile they will come to themselves 31 and know that I am the Lord their God. I will give them a heart that obeys and ears that hear; 32 they

will praise me in the land of their exile, and will remember my name 33 and turn from their stubbornness and their wicked deeds; for they will remember the ways of their ancestors, who sinned before the Lord. 34 I will bring them again into the land that I swore to give to their ancestors, to Abraham, Isaac, and Jacob, and they will rule over it; and I will increase them, and they will not be diminished. 35 I will make an everlasting covenant with them to be their God and they shall be my people; and I will never again remove my people Israel from the land that I have given them."

3 O Lord Almighty, God of Israel, the soul in anguish and the wearied spirit cry out to you. 2 Hear, O Lord, and have mercy, for we have sinned before you. 3 For you are enthroned forever, and we are perishing forever. 4 O Lord Almighty, God of Israel, hear now the prayer of the people[a] of Israel, the children of those who sinned before you, who did not heed the voice of the Lord their God, so that calamities have clung to us. 5 Do not remember the iniquities of our ancestors, but in this crisis remember your power and your name. 6 For you are the Lord our God, and it is you, O Lord, whom we will praise. 7 For you have put the fear of you in our hearts so that we would call upon your name; and we will praise you in our exile, for we have put away from our hearts all the iniquity of our ancestors who sinned against you. 8 See, we are today in our exile where you have scattered us, to be reproached and cursed and punished for all the iniquities of our ancestors, who forsook the Lord our God.

a Gk dead

27–35: Repentance and restoration under an everlasting covenant. No passage in the Hebrew Bible corresponds exactly to the words attributed to Moses. The speech is a pastiche of phrases largely from Jeremiah and Deuteronomy. 28–29: Deut 28.58,62. 30: 1 Kings 8.47. 31: Jer 24.7. 33: Deut 9.6. 34: Lev 26.42; Deut 6.10; Jer 32.37. 35: Jer 32.38–40; Ezek 36.26–29; Am 9.15. 3.1–8: Impassioned plea of repentant exiles. 4: The Greek *dead* (see textual note *a*) probably represents the translator's confusion of two very similar Hebrew roots, one meaning "dead" and the other "men." As it stands, the Greek must be understood as implying that the Israelites in exile were as though "dead" (vv. 10–11; Isa 59.10b; Lam 3.6). 7: Jer 32.40b. 8: The ancestors' sins (2.33; 3.4–5) are visited on later generations (Ex 34.7; Lam 5.7; cf. Jer 31.29 and Ezek 18.2–32).

9 Hear the commandments of life,
O Israel;
give ear, and learn wisdom!
10 Why is it, O Israel, why is it that you
are in the land of your
enemies,
that you are growing old in a
foreign country,
that you are defiled with the dead,
11 that you are counted among those
in Hades?
12 You have forsaken the fountain of
wisdom.
13 If you had walked in the way of God,
you would be living in peace
forever.
14 Learn where there is wisdom,
where there is strength,
where there is understanding,
so that you may at the same time
discern
where there is length of days, and
life,
where there is light for the eyes,
and peace.

15 Who has found her place?
And who has entered her
storehouses?
16 Where are the rulers of the nations,
and those who lorded it over the
animals on earth;
17 those who made sport of the birds of
the air,
and who hoarded up silver and
gold
in which people trust,
and there is no end to their getting;

18 those who schemed to get silver, and
were anxious,
but there is no trace of their works?
19 They have vanished and gone down
to Hades,
and others have arisen in their
place.
20 Later generations have seen the light
of day,
and have lived upon the earth;
but they have not learned the way to
knowledge,
nor understood her paths,
nor laid hold of her.
21 Their descendants have strayed far
from her*a* way.
22 She has not been heard of in Canaan,
or seen in Teman;
23 the descendants of Hagar, who seek
for understanding on the earth,
the merchants of Merran and
Teman,
the story-tellers and the seekers for
understanding,
have not learned the way to wisdom,
or given thought to her paths.
24 O Israel, how great is the house of
God,
how vast the territory that he
possesses!
25 It is great and has no bounds;
it is high and immeasurable.
26 The giants were born there, who were
famous of old,

*a Other ancient authorities read their*

**3.9–4.4: Wisdom, found by God, was given to Israel as the Torah. 3.9–14:** Introduction to the poem. **9:** *The commandments of life,* see Deut 30.15–20. **10:** This verse links the otherwise unrelated poem on wisdom to the confession. Israel's punishment (1.15–3.8) resulted from her abandonment of wisdom, to be praised now without further reference to the exile. *Growing old,* the exile has been long (contrast 1.2). **11:** Ps 28.1; 88.4. *Hades,* see 2.17n. **12:** Prov 18.4; Jer 2.13. **14:** Prov 3.16; 8.14. **15–28:** The Gentile rulers of the world and the mighty have not found wisdom. **15:** Job 28.12. **16b–17a:** Jer 27.6; Dan 2.38; Jdt 11.7. **19:** The transience of human effort and accomplishment is contrasted with wisdom that brings life (4.1). **22:** *Canaan,* wisdom is attributed to the Phoenician (Canaanite) cities of Tyre and Sidon (Ezek 28.3–5; Zech 9.2). *Teman,* in Edom, was reputed for its wisdom (Jer 49.7; Ob 8–9). **23:** *Descendants of Hagar,* see Gen 25.12–15. *Merran,* perhaps a corruption that arose in the Hebrew text for "Midian," in northern Arabia; see Gen 37.28; Isa 60.6. **24:** *House of God,* the created world. **26:** *Giants,* ancient demigods whose origin is described in Gen 6.1–4; see Wis 14.6; *1 Enoch 7.* **28:** Sir 16.7. **29–37:** God found Wisdom and

great in stature, expert in war.
27 God did not choose them,
    or give them the way to knowledge;
28 so they perished because they had no
        wisdom,
    they perished through their folly.

29 Who has gone up into heaven, and
        taken her,
    and brought her down from the
        clouds?
30 Who has gone over the sea, and
        found her,
    and will buy her for pure gold?
31 No one knows the way to her,
    or is concerned about the path to
        her.
32 But the one who knows all things
        knows her,
    he found her by his understanding.
    The one who prepared the earth for
        all time
    filled it with four-footed creatures;
33 the one who sends forth the light, and
        it goes;
    he called it, and it obeyed him,
        trembling;
34 the stars shone in their watches, and
        were glad;
    he called them, and they said,
        "Here we are!"
    They shone with gladness for him
        who made them.
35 This is our God;
    no other can be compared to him.
36 He found the whole way to
        knowledge,
    and gave her to his servant Jacob

and to Israel, whom he loved.
37 Afterward she appeared on earth
    and lived with humankind.

4 She is the book of the commandments
        of God,
    the law that endures forever.
    All who hold her fast will live,
    and those who forsake her will die.
2 Turn, O Jacob, and take her;
    walk toward the shining of her
        light.
3 Do not give your glory to another,
    or your advantages to an alien
        people.
4 Happy are we, O Israel,
    for we know what is pleasing to
        God.

5 Take courage, my people,
    who perpetuate Israel's name!
6 It was not for destruction
    that you were sold to the nations,
    but you were handed over to your
        enemies
    because you angered God.
7 For you provoked the one who made
        you
    by sacrificing to demons and not to
        God.
8 You forgot the everlasting God, who
        brought you up,
    and you grieved Jerusalem, who
        reared you.
9 For she saw the wrath that came
        upon you from God,
    and she said:
    Listen, you neighbors of Zion,

gave her to Israel (Sir 24.1–12). **29–30:** Deut 30.12–13; cf. Job 28.13–14; Prov 30.3–4. **32–34:** Job 28.23–26; Prov 8.22–31. **33:** *Light*, Gen 1.3; Job 38.35. **34:** *Stars . . . were glad*, Job 38.7. **36:** Sir 24.8. **37:** The notion of Wisdom living among humankind is attested in Prov 8.1–4,31; Wis 9.10; Sir 24.11–12; later, early Christian commentators took this as an allusion to the incarnation. **4.1–3:** The identification of Wisdom with the law (Torah), as in Sir 24.23, softens the implicit mythological character of Wisdom in 3.37 and in Job 28; Prov 8; Sir 24.1–22. **1:** Sir 24.23. **2:** Isa 60.3.

**4.5–5.9: Poem of comfort and restoration. 4.5–20:** Israel provoked God, and Zion now mourns for her captive children. **5:** *Take courage, my people*, a refrain repeated in vv. 21,27,30, inspired by Isa 40.1 (cf. Deut 31.6). **6:** Isa 50.1b; 52.3. **7:** *Demons*, Deut 32.16–17; Ps 106.37. **8:** *The everlasting God*, Isa 9.6; 40.28. **9b–16:** Jerusalem speaks to her *neighbors* (i.e., neighboring cities). **9:** Lam 1.12. **10:** Isa 60.4; Lam 4.2. **12:** *Widow*, Isa 54.4; Lam 1.1 On the bereavement of mother Jerusalem, see Isa 49.20–21. **13:** Jer

God has brought great sorrow
    upon me;
10 for I have seen the exile of my sons
    and daughters,
    which the Everlasting brought upon
      them.
11 With joy I nurtured them,
    but I sent them away with weeping
    and sorrow.
12 Let no one rejoice over me, a widow
    and bereaved of many;
    I was left desolate because of the sins
      of my children,
    because they turned away from the
      law of God.
13 They had no regard for his statutes;
    they did not walk in the ways of
      God's commandments,
    or tread the paths his righteousness
      showed them.
14 Let the neighbors of Zion come;
    remember the capture of my sons
      and daughters,
    which the Everlasting brought upon
      them.
15 For he brought a distant nation
    against them,
    a nation ruthless and of a strange
      language,
    which had no respect for the aged
    and no pity for a child.
16 They led away the widow's beloved
      sons,
    and bereaved the lonely woman of
      her daughters.
17 But I, how can I help you?
18 For he who brought these calamities
    upon you
    will deliver you from the hand of
      your enemies.
19 Go, my children, go;
    for I have been left desolate.
20 I have taken off the robe of peace

and put on sackcloth for my
    supplication;
    I will cry to the Everlasting all my
    days.
21 Take courage, my children, cry to
    God,
    and he will deliver you from the
      power and hand of the enemy.
22 For I have put my hope in the
    Everlasting to save you,
    and joy has come to me from the
      Holy One,
    because of the mercy that will soon
      come to you
    from your everlasting savior.[a]
23 For I sent you out with sorrow and
    weeping,
    but God will give you back to me
      with joy and gladness forever.
24 For as the neighbors of Zion have
    now seen your capture,
    so they soon will see your salvation
      by God,
    which will come to you with great
      glory
    and with the splendor of the
      Everlasting.
25 My children, endure with patience the
    wrath that has come upon you
    from God.
    Your enemy has overtaken you,
    but you will soon see their
      destruction
    and will tread upon their necks.
26 My pampered children have traveled
    rough roads;
    they were taken away like a flock
      carried off by the enemy.

27 Take courage, my children, and cry to
    God,

a Or *from the Everlasting, your savior*

4.10. **15**: Deut 28.49–50; Isa 28.11; 33.19. **17–29**: *Jerusalem encourages her exiled children.* **20**: Isa 52.1. *Robe of peace*, garment worn in time of prosperity. *Sackcloth*, garb of mourning and penitence; see Isa 3.24; Dan 9.3. **23**: Ps 126.6; Isa 35.10; 51.11; Jer 31.12–13. **24**: Isa 60.1–3. **25**: Deut 33.29; cf. Isa 51.23. *The wrath* is only temporary (Isa 54.7–8). **4.30–5.9**: *Jerusalem encouraged.* **30**: *The one who named you*, see 5.4n. *Comfort*, see Isa 51.3. **31–35**: As in 4.6, etc., the enemies of Jerusalem are unnamed.

for you will be remembered by the
one who brought this upon
you.

28 For just as you were disposed to go
astray from God,
return with tenfold zeal to seek him.

29 For the one who brought these
calamities upon you
will bring you everlasting joy with
your salvation.

30 Take courage, O Jerusalem,
for the one who named you will
comfort you.

31 Wretched will be those who
mistreated you
and who rejoiced at your fall.

32 Wretched will be the cities that your
children served as slaves;
wretched will be the city that
received your offspring.

33 For just as she rejoiced at your fall
and was glad for your ruin,
so she will be grieved at her own
desolation.

34 I will take away her pride in her great
population,
and her insolence will be turned to
grief.

35 For fire will come upon her from the
Everlasting for many days,
and for a long time she will be
inhabited by demons.

36 Look toward the east, O Jerusalem,
and see the joy that is coming to
you from God.

37 Look, your children are coming,
whom you sent away;
they are coming, gathered from east
and west,
at the word of the Holy One,
rejoicing in the glory of God.

5 Take off the garment of your sorrow
and affliction, O Jerusalem,
and put on forever the beauty of
the glory from God.

2 Put on the robe of the righteousness
that comes from God;
put on your head the diadem of the
glory of the Everlasting;

3 for God will show your splendor
everywhere under heaven.

4 For God will give you evermore the
name,
"Righteous Peace, Godly Glory."

5 Arise, O Jerusalem, stand upon the
height;
look toward the east,
and see your children gathered from
west and east
at the word of the Holy One,
rejoicing that God has remembered
them.

6 For they went out from you on
foot,
led away by their enemies;
but God will bring them back to
you,
carried in glory, as on a royal
throne.

7 For God has ordered that every high
mountain and the everlasting
hills be made low
and the valleys filled up, to make
level ground,
so that Israel may walk safely in
the glory of God.

8 The woods and every fragrant tree
have shaded Israel at God's
command.

9 For God will lead Israel with joy,
in the light of his glory,
with the mercy and righteousness
that come from him.

Elsewhere both Edom (see Ps 137.7; Isa 34; 63.1–6; Ob 8–14) and Babylon (Ps 137.8; Isa 13; 47) are
singled out. Contrast the attitude toward Babylon in 1.11–12. **35**: *Fire*, Jer 51.58. *Demons*, Isa 13.21. **35**:
Isa 40.9–11. **37**: Isa 43.5. **5.1–9**: Glorification of Jerusalem and return of the exiles. Compare *Psalms of
Solomon* 11. **1–2**: Cf. 4.20; see Isa 52.1; 61.3,10. **4**: Giving a new name signifies a change in status. Renaming
Jerusalem is a frequent prophetic theme; see Isa 1.26; 60.14; 62.2–4; Jer 33.16; Ezek 48.35. *Righteous
Peace*, Isa 32.17; 60.17. **5**: Isa 40.9; 43.5; 49.18; 51.17; 60.4. **6**: Isa 49.22; 66.20. **7**: Isa 40.4–5; 42.16. **8**:
Isa 41.19.

# THE LETTER OF JEREMIAH

These seventy-three verses purport to be a letter composed by Jeremiah for those about to be taken into exile from Judah to Babylonia in 597 BCE by Nebuchadnezzar's forces. It was undoubtedly inspired by Jeremiah's letter (Jer 29.1–23) to those taken hostage in 597, a decade before the final defeat of Judah and the destruction of Jerusalem. The Letter of Jeremiah is an impassioned sermon against idol worship and polytheism based on Jer 10, and particularly Jer 10.11: "The gods who did not make the heavens and the earth shall perish from the earth and from under the heavens." The Letter is also influenced, however, by other biblical polemics against idol worship (Ps 115.4–8; 135.15–18; Isa 40.18–20; 41.6–7; 44.9–20; 46.1–7; etc.). The body of the letter is composed of a series of ten warnings to Jews, who might be attracted to idol worship, to recognize and be wary of idolatry. Each part ends on a common refrain, with variations, insisting that idols are not gods nor to be confused with the one, true God (vv. 16,23,29,40,44,52,56,65,69,72).

Although all surviving manuscripts of the letter are in Greek, including one fragment from Cave 7 at Qumran, the Letter was probably composed originally in Hebrew or Aramaic. Most scholars date the Letter to the Hellenistic period. The reference in v. 3 to an exile lasting seven generations (280 years) has been taken as a clue to the date of composition of the letter (317 BCE), but the reference to seven generations is probably symbolic. The allusion to the Letter in 2 Macc 2.1–3 would indicate a date no later than the second century BCE.

The Letter has different placements in various manuscripts and versions of the Bible. It stands as a discrete work between Lamentations and Ezekiel in two major Greek Septuagint manuscripts (fourth-century Vaticanus and fifth-century Alexandrinus), in the Milan Syriac Hexapla, and in Arabic. In other Greek and Syriac manuscripts, and in the Latin version, it appears as the sixth chapter of Baruch. Since it is, however, clearly independent of Baruch, the New Revised Standard Version treats it as a separate book. This pseudepigraphical work was written for a Jewish audience, perhaps in Palestine. It is not included in either the Jewish or the Protestant canons, but is one of the deutero-canonical books of the Roman Catholic and Orthodox churches.

6 [a]A copy of a letter that Jeremiah sent to those who were to be taken to Babylon as exiles by the king of the Babylonians, to give them the message that God had commanded him.

2 Because of the sins that you have committed before God, you will be taken to Babylon as exiles by Nebuchadnezzar, king of the Babylonians. 3 Therefore when you have come to Babylon you will remain there for many years, for a long time, up to

[a] The King James Version (like the Latin Vulgate) prints The Letter of Jeremiah as Chapter 6 of the Book of Baruch, and the chapter and verse numbers are here retained. In the Greek Septuagint, the Letter is separated from Baruch by the Book of Lamentations.

**6.1–7: Historical introduction. 1:** The exile of 597 BCE (2 Kings 24.10–17). *Copy of a letter,* according to Jer 29.1, Jeremiah sent a letter to the exiles in Babylon. What follows is an independent work, not a version of the letter in Jer 29, and not conforming to the genre of letters known from antiquity. *King of the Babylonians,* but "king of Babylon" in the book of Jeremiah (Jer 20.4; 21.2; etc.). **3:** *Seven generations,* contrast seventy years in Jer 29.10, forty years in Ezek 4.6, seventy weeks of years in Dan 9.24. **4:**

seven generations; after that I will bring you away from there in peace. 4 Now in Babylon you will see gods made of silver and gold and wood, which people carry on their shoulders, and which cause the heathen to fear. 5 So beware of becoming at all like the foreigners or of letting fear for these gods[a] possess you 6 when you see the multitude before and behind them worshiping them. But say in your heart, "It is you, O Lord, whom we must worship." 7 For my angel is with you, and he is watching over your lives.

8 Their tongues are smoothed by the carpenter, and they themselves are overlaid with gold and silver; but they are false and cannot speak. 9 People[b] take gold and make crowns for the heads of their gods, as they might for a girl who loves ornaments. 10 Sometimes the priests secretly take gold and silver from their gods and spend it on themselves, 11 or even give some of it to the prostitutes on the terrace. They deck their gods[c] out with garments like human beings—these gods of silver and gold and wood 12 that cannot save themselves from rust and corrosion. When they have been dressed in purple robes, 13 their faces are wiped because of the dust from the temple, which is thick upon them. 14 One of them holds a scepter, like a district judge, but is unable to destroy anyone who offends it. 15 Another has a dagger in its right hand, and an ax, but cannot defend itself from war and robbers. 16 From this it is evident that they are not gods; so do not fear them.

17 For just as someone's dish is useless when it is broken, 18 so are their gods when they have been set up in the temples. Their eyes are full of the dust raised by the feet of those who enter. And just as the gates are shut on every side against anyone who has offended a king, as though under sentence of death, so the priests make their temples secure with doors and locks and bars, in order that they may not be plundered by robbers. 19 They light more lamps for them than they light for themselves, though their gods[d] can see none of them. 20 They are[e] just like a beam of the temple, but their hearts, it is said, are eaten away when crawling creatures from the earth devour them and their robes. They do not notice 21 when their faces have been blackened by the smoke of the temple. 22 Bats, swallows, and birds alight on their bodies and heads; and so do cats. 23 From this you will know that they are not gods; so do not fear them.

24 As for the gold that they wear for beauty—it[f] will not shine unless someone wipes off the tarnish; for even when they were being cast, they did not feel it. 25 They are bought without regard to cost, but there is no breath in them. 26 Having no feet, they are carried on the shoulders of others, revealing to humankind their worthlessness. And those who serve them are put to shame 27 because, if any of these

a Gk for them   b Gk They   c Gk them
d Gk they   e Gk It is   f Lat Syr: Gk they

*Silver and gold,* overlaid on wood (v. 55; Isa 40.19; Jer 10.3–4). *Which people carry on their shoulders,* perhaps an allusion to the Babylonian New Year procession; see Isa 46.7; Jer 10.5. **5**: *Like the foreigners,* Jer 10.2. **7**: *My angel,* Ex 23.23; 32.34; Ps 91.11–12; etc.

**6.8–73: Condemnation of idolatry. 8–16: Idols are decked out like people. 8**: *Carpenter,* Isa 40.20; 44.13; Jer 10.3–4. *Cannot speak,* Ps 115.4–5; 135.15–16. **11**: *Prostitutes,* women sometimes earned money to pay vows by prostituting themselves near temples. **12**: *Purple robes,* a symbol of authority (Jer 10.9). **15**: See vv. 48–49,57. *Dagger,* the Hebrew word behind the Greek could also mean "sword." Ancient deities are often depicted bearing scepters, swords, daggers, and battle-axes.

**6.17–23: Uselessness and helplessness of idols. 17**: *Dish . . . broken,* a common image for uselessness (Isa 30.14; Jer 19.11; 22.28). **18**: See v. 57. *Gates,* the idols are locked up, just as one locks up prisoners (Jer 32.2). **19**: Ps 115.5. *Lamps* have been found in excavated temples. **22**: This is the earliest Jewish reference to *cats,* which were first domesticated in Egypt.

**6.24–29: Idols are unable to feel or move. 25**: *No breath,* Ps 135.17; Jer 10.14; Hab 2.19. **26**: Isa 46.1, 7; Jer 10.5b. **27**: *Cannot move,* Isa 46.7; Jer 10.4. *Tipped over,* 1 Sam 5.3. *Gifts for the dead,* Ps 106.28;

gods falls[a] to the ground, they themselves must pick it up. If anyone sets it upright, it cannot move itself; and if it is tipped over, it cannot straighten itself. Gifts are placed before them just as before the dead. 28 The priests sell the sacrifices that are offered to these gods[b] and use the money themselves. Likewise their wives preserve some of the meat[c] with salt, but give none to the poor or helpless. 29 Sacrifices to them may even be touched by women in their periods or at childbirth. Since you know by these things that they are not gods, do not fear them.

30 For how can they be called gods? Women serve meals for gods of silver and gold and wood; 31 and in their temples the priests sit with their clothes torn, their heads and beards shaved, and their heads uncovered. 32 They howl and shout before their gods as some do at a funeral banquet. 33 The priests take some of the clothing of their gods[d] to clothe their wives and children. 34 Whether one does evil to them or good, they will not be able to repay it. They cannot set up a king or depose one. 35 Likewise they are not able to give either wealth or money; if one makes a vow to them and does not keep it, they will not require it. 36 They cannot save anyone from death or rescue the weak from the strong. 37 They cannot restore sight to the blind; they cannot rescue one who is in distress. 38 They cannot take pity on a widow or do good to an orphan. 39 These things that are made of wood and overlaid with gold and silver are like stones from the mountain, and those who serve them will be put to shame. 40 Why then must anyone think that they are gods, or call them gods?

Besides, even the Chaldeans themselves dishonor them; for when they see someone who cannot speak, they bring Bel and pray that the mute may speak, as though Bel[e] were able to understand! 41 Yet they themselves cannot perceive this and abandon them, for they have no sense. 42 And the women, with cords around them, sit along the passageways, burning bran for incense. 43 When one of them is led off by one of the passers-by and is taken to bed by him, she derides the woman next to her, because she was not as attractive as herself and her cord was not broken. 44 Whatever is done for these idols[f] is false. Why then must anyone think that they are gods, or call them gods?

45 They are made by carpenters and goldsmiths; they can be nothing but what the artisans wish them to be. 46 Those who make them will certainly not live very long themselves; 47 how then can the things that are made by them be gods? They have left only lies and reproach for those who come after. 48 For when war or calamity comes upon them, the priests consult together as to where they can hide themselves and their gods.[f] 49 How then can one fail to see that these are not gods, for they cannot save themselves from war or calamity? 50 Since

a Gk *if they fall*   b Gk *to them*   c Gk *of them*
d Gk *some of their clothing*   e Gk *he*   f Gk *them*

Sir 30.18–19. **29:** According to biblical law (Lev 12.2–5; 15.19–24), during and immediately after menstruation and childbirth women were unclean, i.e., not permitted to participate in acts of worship.

**6.30–40a: Idols cannot repay good or evil, or help worshipers. 30:** *Women,* there were only male ministrants in the Jewish temple. Thus the custom of women's service is treated as lacking dignity. **31–32:** Ritual lamentations for dying gods (such as Tammuz, Ezek 8.14; cf. Lev 21.5,10; Ezek 24.17). *Funeral banquet,* Jer 16.5,7. These practices, too, which were alien to Israelite worship, are considered unseemly. **34b:** See v. 53; cf. Job 12.18; Dan 2.21. **35b:** Cf. Deut 23.21. **36:** On the contrary, the Lord can do this (Deut 32.39; 1 Sam 2.6; Ps 49.15). **37:** Cf. Ps 146.8. **38:** Deut 10.18; Ps 146.9. **39:** Hab 2.19.

**6.40b–44: The Chaldeans dishonor their own idols. 40b:** *Chaldeans* may refer here to a class of professional diviners (Dan 2.2) rather than to the Babylonians in general. *Bel* ("Lord"), the title of the Babylonian god Marduk (Isa 46.1; Bel 1.3). **43:** A similar Babylonian practice is described by Herodotus (1.199).

**6.45–52: Idols are but the work of human hands. 45:** Isa 40.19; Jer 10.9. **47:** The makers of idols bequeath lies and reproach, not real gods, to posterity. **50:** *Afterward,* when the veneer has been exposed for what it is. *False,* a fraud.

they are made of wood and overlaid with gold and silver, it will afterward be known that they are false. ⁵¹It will be manifest to all the nations and kings that they are not gods but the work of human hands, and that there is no work of God in them. ⁵²Who then can fail to know that they are not gods?ᵃ

53 For they cannot set up a king over a country or give rain to people. ⁵⁴They cannot judge their own cause or deliver one who is wronged, for they have no power; ⁵⁵they are like crows between heaven and earth. When fire breaks out in a temple of wooden gods overlaid with gold or silver, their priests will flee and escape, but the godsᵇ will be burned up like timbers. ⁵⁶Besides, they can offer no resistance to king or enemy. Why then must anyone admit or think that they are gods?

57 Gods made of wood and overlaid with silver and gold are unable to save themselves from thieves or robbers. ⁵⁸Anyone who can will strip them of their gold and silver and of the robes they wear, and go off with this booty, and they will not be able to help themselves. ⁵⁹So it is better to be a king who shows his courage, or a household utensil that serves its owner's need, than to be these false gods; better even the door of a house that protects its contents, than these false gods; better also a wooden pillar in a palace, than these false gods.

60 For sun and moon and stars are bright, and when sent to do a service, they are obedient. ⁶¹So also the lightning, when it flashes, is widely seen; and the wind likewise blows in every land. ⁶²When God commands the clouds to go over the whole world, they carry out his command. ⁶³And the fire sent from above to consume mountains and woods does what it is ordered. But these idolsᶜ are not to be compared with them in appearance or power. ⁶⁴Therefore one must not think that they are gods, nor call them gods, for they are not able either to decide a case or to do good to anyone. ⁶⁵Since you know then that they are not gods, do not fear them.

66 They can neither curse nor bless kings; ⁶⁷they cannot show signs in the heavens for the nations, or shine like the sun or give light like the moon. ⁶⁸The wild animals are better than they are, for they can flee to shelter and help themselves. ⁶⁹So we have no evidence whatever that they are gods; therefore do not fear them.

70 Like a scarecrow in a cucumber bed, which guards nothing, so are their gods of wood, overlaid with gold and silver. ⁷¹In the same way, their gods of wood, overlaid with gold and silver, are like a thornbush in a garden on which every bird perches; or like a corpse thrown out in the darkness. ⁷²From the purple and linenᵈ that rot upon them you will know that they are not gods; and they will finally be consumed themselves, and be a reproach in the land. ⁷³Better, therefore, is someone upright who has no idols; such a person will be far above reproach.

a Meaning of Gk uncertain   b Gk *they*   c Gk *these things*   d Cn: Gk *marble*, Syr *silk*

**6.53–56: The impotence of idols. 53:** *Set up a king,* see v. 34b and note. *Give rain,* Deut 11.14; 28.12; Ps 147.8; Jer 14.22. **55:** *Crows,* the original Hebrew may have read "clouds"; the metaphor is unclear.

**6.57–65: Idols are helpless, useless, and not to be compared with celestial phenomena. 59:** *Utensil,* see v. 17. **61:** Ps 97.4. **64:** *Decide a case,* the true God does this (Ex 18.19; Ps 43.1; Isa 41.21).

**6.66–69: The helplessness of idols. 66:** Jer 10.5; for the idiom see Num 22.6. **67:** *Signs,* portents (Jer 10.2; Joel 2.30).

**6.70–73: Idols are compared with a scarecrow, thornbush, and corpse. 70:** *Scarecrow,* Jer 10.5. This expression does not occur in the Greek of Jer 10.5, again suggesting that the Letter depends on the Hebrew. **71:** *Thornbush,* an ordinary, useless shrub (see Judg 9.14–15). *A corpse thrown out,* Jer 14.16; 22.19; Isa 34.3. **72:** The Greek text ("marble," see textual note d) is a misinterpretation of the Hebrew homonym "shesh," which means both "linen" and "alabaster" ("marble").

# THE ADDITIONS TO DANIEL

GREEK MANUSCRIPTS of both the Septuagint and the Theodotion versions of the book of Daniel add three Additions to the twelve original Hebrew and Aramaic chapters: "The Prayer of Azariah and the Song of the Three Jews," "Susanna," and "Bel and the Dragon." Behind the Greek may lie Hebrew or Aramaic originals, although no such versions of the three stories have been found even among the Dead Sea Scrolls, and there is no indisputable Talmudic reference to them. Like the folktales in Dan 1–6, the Additions in all probability originated prior to the Maccabean revolt in the mid-second century BCE; they may have been originally composed as early as the Persian period (fifth-fourth century BCE). Scholars debate the place of composition: a Semitic (Hebrew or Aramaic) original would strengthen the argument for an origin in Israel or the Eastern Diaspora; a Greek original would suggest a provenance in Alexandria. The Additions, which do not cite each other, likely circulated independently and only later, perhaps ca. 100 BCE when the book of Daniel was translated into Greek, were they added to the Danielic corpus. The first independent citations of the Additions date from the church fathers of the second century CE.

The Prayer of Azariah and the Song of the Three Jews are found in all Greek versions between Dan 3.23 and 3.24. The Septuagint locates the other two Additions at the end of the book of Daniel, after 12.13; Theodotion's version places Susanna at the opening of the book of Daniel, and Bel and the Dragon at the conclusion of ch 6. Other ancient versions follow Theodotion's order. The NRSV follows Theodotion's text but places the Additions by themselves in the Apocrypha rather than integrating them into the text.

# THE PRAYER OF AZARIAH
## and the Song of the Three Jews

❧ ❧

The Prayer of Azariah (vv. 1–22) and the Song of the Three Jews (vv. 28–68), along with a brief prose paragraph (vv. 23–27) concerning the fate of the three in Nebuchadnezzar's furnace, are placed by ancient manuscripts between Dan 3.23 and 3.24. Likely composed independently in the second or first century BCE, the Prayer and Song (with the exception of the end of the Song) may have originally had no connection to the book of Daniel. They appear as numbers 7 and 8 of the fifteen "Odes" added to the Psalter in a few manuscripts of the Septuagint, a placement that complements the resemblance of these Additions to Ps 148 in terms of theme and Ps 136 in terms of structure. Their placement in Dan 3 gives their general emphasis on hope for deliverance, national repentance, and divine faithfulness a poignant focus as the three Jews face death in Babylonian exile.

Similar prayers and hymns are a hallmark of Second Temple Jewish texts, and they are found in such works as Judith, Tobit, and Baruch, as well as in Dan 9 and among the scrolls discovered at Qumran (the Dead Sea Scrolls); they may represent early forms of synagogue liturgies. The Additions to Daniel are, in particular, comparable to the Additions to Esther: In both, prose narrative is supplemented with prayer and song that emphasize the piety of the main characters. The Prayer of Azariah resembles other postexilic works highlighting divine righteousness, the failure of the covenant community to remain faithful, assertion of divine mercy, and appeal for mercy (Ps 106; Ezra 9.6–15; Neh 1.5–11; Bar 1.15–3.8; and some Qumran texts). The Song of the Three Jews has allusions to numerous psalmic and prophetic passages in its exhortations to the heavens (vv. 36–41), nature (vv. 42–51), earth and its creatures (vv. 52–59), and humanity (vv. 60–68). Unlike the book of Daniel and the Prayer of Azariah, however, it does not suggest a period of persecution or a time when the Temple was either destroyed or profaned.

Whether the Prayer and Song were initially written in Hebrew or Aramaic or even Greek remains debated; their place of composition does as well, although the Prayer contains several references that correspond to the time of Antiochus IV (175–164 BCE).

(Additions to Daniel, inserted between 3.23 and 3.24)

1 They[a] walked around in the midst of the flames, singing hymns to God and blessing the Lord. 2 Then Azariah stood still in the fire and prayed aloud:

3 "Blessed are you, O Lord, God of our ancestors, and worthy of praise;

a That is, Hananiah, Mishael, and Azariah (Dan 2.17), the original names of Shadrach, Meshach, and Abednego (Dan 1.6-7)

1–22 The prayer of Azariah. 1: *They* refers to Daniel's three friends, Shadrach, Meshach, and Abednego, as named in Dan 1.6–7; 3.22–23. 2: *Azariah*, named Abednego by Nebuchadnezzar (Dan 1.7); the Babylonian names do not appear in these Additions. 5: *True judgments*, Neh 9.33; Lam 1.18; Tobit, and

and glorious is your name forever!

4 For you are just in all you have done;
  all your works are true and your
    ways right,
  and all your judgments are true.

5 You have executed true judgments in
    all you have brought upon us
  and upon Jerusalem, the holy city
    of our ancestors;
  by a true judgment you have
    brought all this upon us
  because of our sins.

6 For we have sinned and broken your
    law in turning away from you;
  in all matters we have sinned
    grievously.

7 We have not obeyed your
    commandments,
  we have not kept them or done
  what you have commanded us
  for our own good.

8 So all that you have brought upon us,
  and all that you have done to us,
  you have done by a true judgment.

9 You have handed us over to our
    enemies, lawless and hateful
    rebels,
  and to an unjust king, the most
    wicked in all the world.

10 And now we cannot open our
    mouths;
  we, your servants who worship
    you, have become a shame and
    a reproach.

11 For your name's sake do not give us
    up forever,

and do not annul your covenant.

12 Do not withdraw your mercy from
    us,
  for the sake of Abraham your beloved
  and for the sake of your servant
    Isaac
  and Israel your holy one,

13 to whom you promised
  to multiply their descendants like
    the stars of heaven
  and like the sand on the shore of
    the sea.

14 For we, O Lord, have become fewer
    than any other nation,
  and are brought low this day in all
    the world because of our sins.

15 In our day we have no ruler, or
    prophet, or leader,
  no burnt offering, or sacrifice, or
    oblation, or incense,
  no place to make an offering before
    you and to find mercy.

16 Yet with a contrite heart and a
    humble spirit may we be
    accepted,

17 as though it were with burnt
    offerings of rams and bulls,
  or with tens of thousands of fat
    lambs;
  such may our sacrifice be in your
    sight today,
  and may we unreservedly follow
    you,*a*

*a* Meaning of Gk uncertain

other texts attribute the Babylonian exile to the community's sin. **6–8:** The confession of sin resembles Dan 9.5,15; Ezra 9.6; Neh 9.26. **9:** The *unjust king* in the context of the book of Daniel is Nebuchadnezzar (Dan 3.19), but the vague reference makes the statement applicable to other tyrants, such as Antiochus IV Epiphanes (see 1 Macc 1 and notes to Dan 10–12); *rebels* may refer to Jews who supported Antiochus and the Hellenization of Jerusalem (1 Macc 1.11–15,41–60). **10:** *Shame and a reproach*, see Dan 9.12. **11:** *Covenant*, see Gen 15.18; 17.7–8. **12:** *Abraham* is identified as beloved of God in Isa 41.8; 2 Chr 20.7; Jas 2.23, as well as the Qur'an (4.125). *Isaac* is called *servant* in Gen 24.14. *Holy one* is more typically used for heavenly beings (Dan 4.10,20; 8.13). **13:** On the promise, see Gen 15.5; 22.17; Ex 32.13; Jer 33.22. **15:** No *leader*, when read in the context of Dan 3, may refer to Nebuchadnezzar's blinding and exiling the Judean king (2 Kings 24.15); the lament is more generally expressed in Lam 2.9; Hos 3.4. No *prophet* is exaggerated for the Babylonian context, but it may fit the later postexilic period, such as the time of Antiochus IV (see Zech 13.3–6). No *burnt offering*, cessation of proper sacrifices occurred both when Nebuchadnezzar destroyed the Temple and when Antiochus IV profaned it. **16:** Contrition and humility substitute for sacrifice (1 Sam 15.22; Ps 51.16–17; 141.2; Hos 6.6); the context

for no shame will come to those
who trust in you.

18 And now with all our heart we follow
you;
we fear you and seek your
presence.

19 Do not put us to shame,
but deal with us in your
patience
and in your abundant mercy.

20 Deliver us in accordance with your
marvelous works,
and bring glory to your name,
O Lord.

21 Let all who do harm to your servants
be put to shame;
let them be disgraced and deprived
of all power,
and let their strength be broken.

22 Let them know that you alone are the
Lord God,
glorious over the whole world."

23 Now the king's servants who threw
them in kept stoking the furnace with
naphtha, pitch, tow, and brushwood.
24 And the flames poured out above the furnace forty-nine cubits, 25 and spread out
and burned those Chaldeans who were
caught near the furnace. 26 But the angel
of the Lord came down into the furnace
to be with Azariah and his companions,
and drove the fiery flame out of the furnace, 27 and made the inside of the furnace

as though a moist wind were whistling
through it. The fire did not touch them at
all and caused them no pain or distress.

28 Then the three with one voice praised
and glorified and blessed God in the furnace:

29 "Blessed are you, O Lord, God of our
ancestors,
and to be praised and highly
exalted forever;

30 And blessed is your glorious, holy
name,
and to be highly praised and highly
exalted forever.

31 Blessed are you in the temple of your
holy glory,
and to be extolled and highly
glorified forever.

32 Blessed are you who look into the
depths from your throne on
the cherubim,
and to be praised and highly
exalted forever.

33 Blessed are you on the throne of your
kingdom,
and to be extolled and highly
exalted forever.

34 Blessed are you in the firmament of
heaven,
and to be sung and glorified
forever.

35 "Bless the Lord, all you works of the
Lord;

of the prayer, the impending martyrdom of the three, makes the point acute. **21:** *Put to shame,* in the context of the book of Daniel, anticipates Nebuchadnezzar's madness in Dan 4 (see Sir 36.9 on the hope for the enemy's demise).

**23–27: Protection in the furnace. 23:** *Naphtha* is a type of petroleum (see 2 Macc 1.20–22,30–36). **24:** *Forty-nine cubits* is 22 m (71 ft); the multiple of seven suggests Dan 3.19, in which Nebuchadnezzar orders the furnace heated to seven times its usual temperature. **25:** *Burned those Chaldeans* is noted in Dan 3.22; the king's agents die from the flames. **26:** The protecting *angel* is an increasingly common figure in Second Temple literature (Tobit; Sus 44–45 in the Old Greek; *1 Enoch*); this verse makes the angelic presence, implicit in the reference to a "fourth man" in Dan 3, explicit. **27:** The verse is evoked in 3 Macc 6.6.

**28–34: Song of thanksgiving. 29:** The song begins with direct address to God. Vv. 29–30 resemble Tob 8.5. **31:** *Temple* may refer to the heavenly, not the Jerusalem, sanctuary, as in Ps 11.4; Hab 2.20. **32:** *Cherubim* are winged creatures who serve as the divine throne (Ex 25.18–20; 2 Sam 6.2; 22.11; Ps 18.10).

**35–66: The litany of praise. 30:** *Glorious, holy name,* see Ps 29.2; 66.2; 79.9; etc. **31:** *Temple of your . . . glory* may indicate the heavenly temple, or that the earthly one is functioning. **35:** The song shifts to exhortations to creation and thereby recalls both the refrain of Ps 136 and the exhortations of Ps 148.

sing praise to him and highly exalt
 him forever.

36 Bless the Lord, you heavens;
 sing praise to him and highly exalt
  him forever.

37 Bless the Lord, you angels of the
  Lord;
 sing praise to him and highly exalt
  him forever.

38 Bless the Lord, all you waters above
  the heavens;
 sing praise to him and highly exalt
  him forever.

39 Bless the Lord, all you powers of the
  Lord;
 sing praise to him and highly exalt
  him forever.

40 Bless the Lord, sun and moon;
 sing praise to him and highly exalt
  him forever.

41 Bless the Lord, stars of heaven;
 sing praise to him and highly exalt
  him forever.

42 "Bless the Lord, all rain and
  dew;
 sing praise to him and highly exalt
  him forever.

43 Bless the Lord, all you winds;
 sing praise to him and highly exalt
  him forever.

44 Bless the Lord, fire and heat;
 sing praise to him and highly exalt
  him forever.

45 Bless the Lord, winter cold and
  summer heat;
 sing praise to him and highly exalt
  him forever.

46 Bless the Lord, dews and falling
  snow;
 sing praise to him and highly exalt
  him forever.

47 Bless the Lord, nights and days;
 sing praise to him and highly exalt
  him forever.

48 Bless the Lord, light and darkness;
 sing praise to him and highly exalt
  him forever.

49 Bless the Lord, ice and cold;
 sing praise to him and highly exalt
  him forever.

50 Bless the Lord, frosts and snows;
 sing praise to him and highly exalt
  him forever.

51 Bless the Lord, lightnings and clouds;
 sing praise to him and highly exalt
  him forever.

52 "Let the earth bless the Lord;
 let it sing praise to him and highly
  exalt him forever.

53 Bless the Lord, mountains and hills;
 sing praise to him and highly exalt
  him forever.

54 Bless the Lord, all that grows in the
  ground;
 sing praise to him and highly exalt
  him forever.

55 Bless the Lord, seas and rivers;
 sing praise to him and highly exalt
  him forever.

56 Bless the Lord, you springs;
 sing praise to him and highly exalt
  him forever.

57 Bless the Lord, you whales and all
  that swim in the waters;
 sing praise to him and highly exalt
  him forever.

58 Bless the Lord, all birds of the air;
 sing praise to him and highly exalt
  him forever.

59 Bless the Lord, all wild animals and
  cattle;
 sing praise to him and highly exalt
  him forever.

60 "Bless the Lord, all people on earth;
 sing praise to him and highly exalt
  him forever.

61 Bless the Lord, O Israel;
 sing praise to him and highly exalt
  him forever.

62 Bless the Lord, you priests of the
  Lord;
 sing praise to him and highly exalt
  him forever.

**38:** *Waters above,* see Gen 1.7; Ps 148.4. **39:** *Powers* suggests the heavenly host (see Ps 148.2–3). **57:** *Whales,* or sea monsters, suggest Leviathan (Isa 27.1; Ps 104.26; Job 41). **62:** *Priests* may imply a Temple

63 Bless the Lord, you servants of the
Lord;
sing praise to him and highly exalt
him forever.
64 Bless the Lord, spirits and souls of the
righteous;
sing praise to him and highly exalt
him forever.
65 Bless the Lord, you who are holy and
humble in heart;
sing praise to him and highly exalt
him forever.

66 "Bless the Lord, Hananiah, Azariah,
and Mishael;
sing praise to him and highly exalt
him forever.

For he has rescued us from Hades
and saved us from the power[a]
of death,
and delivered us from the midst of
the burning fiery furnace;
from the midst of the fire he has
delivered us.
67 Give thanks to the Lord, for he is
good,
for his mercy endures forever.
68 All who worship the Lord, bless the
God of gods,
sing praise to him and give thanks
to him,
for his mercy endures forever."

a Gk hand

setting for the Song's original performance. **63:** *Servants* could, given biblical literature's use of parallelism, refer to priests or other Temple functionaries. **66:** The friends are identified by their Hebrew names, as in Dan 1.6; 1 Macc 2.59. *Hananiah* means "Yahweh is gracious"; *Azariah* is "Yahweh has helped" (in the book of Tobit, this is the name the disguised angel Raphael assumes); and *Mishael* is "who is like God?" *Hades,* the abode of the dead in Greek, equivalent to Hebrew Sheol (Ps 16.10).

# SUSANNA

❧ ❧

Often called the first detective story, this Addition to the book of Daniel appears in two different forms and locations in the early textual traditions. The Septuagint (and the Vulgate) locate it after Dan 13; Theodotion, the version followed in this as well as most modern translations, locates the story at the beginning of the book of Daniel, since Sus 45 describes Daniel as a "young man." Perhaps composed as early as the Persian period (fifth-fourth century BCE), Susanna's tale was added to the Danielic literature probably ca. 100 BCE. The story may originally not have been about Daniel, and the naming of the rescuing lad Daniel thus a secondary attribute of the story, added when the tale was attached to the other materials concerning Daniel, just as the Prayer of Azariah and the Song of the Three Jews may not have had an original connection to Dan 3. Susanna's setting in peaceful Babylon, in which the enemies are not wicked pagan kings but corrupt Jewish judges, contrasts with threats emphasized in Dan 1–6.

Like Greek Esther, Judith, and Sarah of the book of Tobit, Susanna is beautiful and chaste, and as in those books, prayer and piety are major motifs. Indeed, with the exception of the villainous elders, all the characters—including the narrator—mention God. First cited as having canonical status by the church father Irenaeus of Lyons in the late second century, Susanna's story was also adapted by Samaritan and medieval Jewish (including Falashic) writers.

1 There was a man living in Babylon whose name was Joakim. ²He married the daughter of Hilkiah, named Susanna, a very beautiful woman and one who feared the Lord. ³Her parents were righteous, and had trained their daughter according to the law of Moses. ⁴Joakim was very rich, and had a fine garden adjoining his house; the Jews used to come to him because he was the most honored of them all.

5 That year two elders from the people were appointed as judges. Concerning them the Lord had said: "Wickedness came forth from Babylon, from elders who were judges, who were supposed to govern the people." ⁶These men were frequently at

1–4: **Introduction. 1:** Set in *Babylon*, the story is typically dated during the Babylonian exile (587–538 BCE) because of its connection to Daniel; however, an exact date is never specified. Joakim does not appear to be connected to others with the same name in 2 Kings 24.15; Neh 12.10,12,26; or Jdt 4.6; 15.8. **2:** *Susanna*, the name, which means "lily," appears in Luke 8.3, but not elsewhere in the Jewish or Christian canons. It is attested in Neo-Babylonian sources. *Hilkiah* was a common name in priestly circles (2 Kings 22.4; Neh 12.7; Jer 1.1) and so perhaps suggests that Susanna's father was a priest. Beauty and piety are typically associated with heroines in the Apocrypha (Jdt 8.7–8; Tob 6.12; Esth 2.7,20 [LXX]). **4:** The prosperity of some Jews in Babylon is attested by archaeological findings (see also Jer 29.5–7; 2 Esd 3.1b–2). *Joakim's* honor appears based on wealth. *Garden* (Gk "Paradeisos") describes Eden (Gen 2–3) and the setting of the Song of Solomon (4.13).

5–14: **The elders' plot. 5:** The *year* is not identified. *Elders*, community leaders (Ruth 4; Ezek 8.1; 14.1; 20.1; Jer 29.1). *Wickedness came forth* is unattested in existing prophetic books, but see Jer 23.14–15; the church fathers Origin and Jerome associate the reference with Jer 29.20–23. **8:** *Lust*, in violation of Ex 20.17. **9:** *Heaven* is a circumlocution for God.

Joakim's house, and all who had a case to be tried came to them there.

7 When the people left at noon, Susanna would go into her husband's garden to walk. 8 Every day the two elders used to see her, going in and walking about, and they began to lust for her. 9 They suppressed their consciences and turned away their eyes from looking to Heaven or remembering their duty to administer justice. 10 Both were overwhelmed with passion for her, but they did not tell each other of their distress, 11 for they were ashamed to disclose their lustful desire to seduce her. 12 Day after day they watched eagerly to see her.

13 One day they said to each other, "Let us go home, for it is time for lunch." So they both left and parted from each other. 14 But turning back, they met again; and when each pressed the other for the reason, they confessed their lust. Then together they arranged for a time when they could find her alone.

15 Once, while they were watching for an opportune day, she went in as before with only two maids, and wished to bathe in the garden, for it was a hot day. 16 No one was there except the two elders, who had hidden themselves and were watching her. 17 She said to her maids, "Bring me olive oil and ointments, and shut the garden doors so that I can bathe." 18 They did as she told them: they shut the doors of the garden and went out by the side doors to bring what they had been commanded; they did not see the elders, because they were hiding.

19 When the maids had gone out, the two elders got up and ran to her. 20 They said, "Look, the garden doors are shut, and no one can see us. We are burning with desire for you; so give your consent, and lie with us. 21 If you refuse, we will testify against you that a young man was with you, and this was why you sent your maids away."

22 Susanna groaned and said, "I am completely trapped. For if I do this, it will mean death for me; if I do not, I cannot escape your hands. 23 I choose not to do it; I will fall into your hands, rather than sin in the sight of the Lord."

24 Then Susanna cried out with a loud voice, and the two elders shouted against her. 25 And one of them ran and opened the garden doors. 26 When the people in the house heard the shouting in the garden, they rushed in at the side door to see what had happened to her. 27 And when the elders told their story, the servants felt very much ashamed, for nothing like this had ever been said about Susanna.

28 The next day, when the people gathered at the house of her husband Joakim, the two elders came, full of their wicked plot to have Susanna put to death. In the

15–21: The attempted rape. 15: Contrary to most artistic depictions, Susanna never actually bathes. *In the garden*, the scene recollects both depictions of luxuriant beauty and physical love in the Song of Solomon and the garden of Eden (Gen 2–3) as a site of temptation. *Bathe* suggests both Bathsheba (2 Sam 11) and observations in Jewish-Hellenistic literature (*Jubilees* 22; *Testament of Reuben* 3) that Reuben sinned with Bilhah after seeing her bathe. *Maids* frequently accompany heroines in the Apocrypha (Jdt, Tob, Add Esth). 17: *Oil and ointments*, compare 2 Sam 12.20; Ruth 3.3; Jdt 10.3. *Shut the garden doors* attests to Susanna's modesty. 20: *Give your consent*, Susanna's choice is adultery or death.

22–27: Susanna's response. 22: *Death*, because adultery was a capital crime (Lev 20.10; Deut 22.21–24; see John 8.4–5). Susanna knows the "law of Moses" (v. 3). 23: *Sin in the sight of the Lord* is the same concern voiced by Joseph in similar circumstances (Gen 39.9). 24: Deut 22.24 legislates that a woman, facing rape, is to cry *out with a loud voice*; again, Susanna shows fidelity to the law. 27: That servants would be ashamed indicates the substantial dishonor adulterous accusations bring to a household. Although the elders (v. 11) and servants feel shame, Susanna is never described in this manner, despite being placed in a situation of public humiliation (vv. 31–32). *Nothing like this*, although carrying an unblemished reputation, Susanna is presumed guilty.

28–41: Accusation. 30: Susanna is accompanied by all her family except Joakim. The Septuagint (LXX)

presence of the people they said, [29] "Send for Susanna daughter of Hilkiah, the wife of Joakim." [30] So they sent for her. And she came with her parents, her children, and all her relatives.

31 Now Susanna was a woman of great refinement and beautiful in appearance. [32] As she was veiled, the scoundrels ordered her to be unveiled, so that they might feast their eyes on her beauty. [33] Those who were with her and all who saw her were weeping.

34 Then the two elders stood up before the people and laid their hands on her head. [35] Through her tears she looked up toward Heaven, for her heart trusted in the Lord. [36] The elders said, "While we were walking in the garden alone, this woman came in with two maids, shut the garden doors, and dismissed the maids. [37] Then a young man, who was hiding there, came to her and lay with her. [38] We were in a corner of the garden, and when we saw this wickedness we ran to them. [39] Although we saw them embracing, we could not hold the man, because he was stronger than we, and he opened the doors and got away. [40] We did, however, seize this woman and asked who the young man was, [41] but she would not tell us. These things we testify."

Because they were elders of the people and judges, the assembly believed them and condemned her to death.

42 Then Susanna cried out with a loud voice, and said, "O eternal God, you know what is secret and are aware of all things before they come to be; [43] you know that these men have given false evidence against me. And now I am to die, though I have done none of the wicked things that they have charged against me!"

44 The Lord heard her cry. [45] Just as she was being led off to execution, God stirred up the holy spirit of a young lad named Daniel, [46] and he shouted with a loud voice, "I want no part in shedding this woman's blood!"

47 All the people turned to him and asked, "What is this you are saying?" [48] Taking his stand among them he said, "Are you such fools, O Israelites, as to condemn a daughter of Israel without examination and without learning the facts? [49] Return to court, for these men have given false evidence against her."

50 So all the people hurried back. And

version notes that Susanna had four children. **31:** *Refinement* and beauty are attributes of (Gk) Esther. **32:** *Veiled* emphasizes her modesty; although the trial occurs in her home, the proceedings are public. To be *unveiled* in public would be humiliating; the LXX describes Susanna as being stripped (see Hos 2.3–10; Ezek 16.37–39). **34:** *Laid their hands* indicates that the elders serve as witnesses (Lev 24.14; see Lev 8.14,18,22; Ex 29.10,15,19 for sacrificial imagery, and Lev 16.21–22 for the scapegoat ritual). The elders planned to lay their hands upon Susanna in order to have sexual intercourse with her; now their gesture seeks to condemn her. Two witnesses are required (Num 35.30; Deut 17.6; 19.15). **41:** *Condemned her* without cross-examination (Deut 19.15–21) or Susanna's own testimony; the "trial" is illegal according to both biblical and later rabbinic regulations.

**42–43: Susanna's prayer.** Like (Gk) Esther (14.3–19), Judith (9.2–14), and Sarah (Tob 2.10–15), as well as Azariah of the Additions to Daniel, Susanna offers personal prayer in a time of distress. **42:** *Know what is secret* is a divine attribute stressed in Dan 2.22. **43:** *Given false evidence*, Susanna's prayer locates God as the (true) judge and jury even as it, again, shows her knowledge of the law (Deut 19.16–21). *Now I am to die* leaves Susanna's request for justice implicit.

**44–49: Daniel responds. 44:** God responds to Susanna's prayer, not to the events that prompted it. **45:** *Young lad* contrasts Daniel with the "elders"; the term indicates a youth of marriageable age (Tob 5.17) and subtly recalls the "young man" the elders claimed was with Susanna (37–39). *Holy spirit* is associated with both prophetic abilities and the possession of wisdom. **46:** *I want no part*, since the community is responsible for justice (Deut 22.20–21; Mt 27.24; Acts 24.26).

**50–63: Susanna's acquittal. 48:** *Examination*, or cross-examination, is mandated by Deut 19.15–20. *Daughter of Israel*, see also v. 57, which describes Susanna as a *daughter of Judah*. **50:** Daniel's status appears miraculously granted. His youth contrasts with his *standing as an elder*, even as his words the rest of the[a] elders said to him, "Come, sit among us and inform us, for God has given you the standing of an elder." 51 Daniel said to them, "Separate them far from each other, and I will examine them."

52 When they were separated from each other, he summoned one of them and said to him, "You old relic of wicked days, your sins have now come home, which you have committed in the past, 53 pronouncing unjust judgments, condemning the innocent and acquitting the guilty, though the Lord said, 'You shall not put an innocent and righteous person to death.' 54 Now then, if you really saw this woman, tell me this: Under what tree did you see them being intimate with each other?" He answered, "Under a mastic tree."[b] 55 And Daniel said, "Very well! This lie has cost you your head, for the angel of God has received the sentence from God and will immediately cut[b] you in two."

56 Then, putting him to one side, he ordered them to bring the other. And he said to him, "You offspring of Canaan and not of Judah, beauty has beguiled you and lust has perverted your heart. 57 This is how you have been treating the daughters of Israel, and they were intimate with you through fear; but a daughter of Judah would not

tolerate your wickedness. 58 Now then, tell me: Under what tree did you catch them being intimate with each other?" He answered, "Under an evergreen oak."[c] 59 Daniel said to him, "Very well! This lie has cost you also your head, for the angel of God is waiting with his sword to split[c] you in two, so as to destroy you both."

60 Then the whole assembly raised a great shout and blessed God, who saves those who hope in him. 61 And they took action against the two elders, because out of their own mouths Daniel had convicted them of bearing false witness; they did to them as they had wickedly planned to do to their neighbor. 62 Acting in accordance with the law of Moses, they put them to death. Thus innocent blood was spared that day.

63 Hilkiah and his wife praised God for their daughter Susanna, and so did her husband Joakim and all her relatives, because she was found innocent of a shameful deed. 64 And from that day onward Daniel had a great reputation among the people.

a Gk lacks rest of the   b The Greek words for mastic tree and cut are similar, thus forming an ironic wordplay   c The Greek words for evergreen oak and split are similar, thus forming an ironic wordplay

contrast with the wicked elders' false witness. 50: Rest of the elders indicates that not all the leaders are wicked. 53: Pronouncing unjust judgments, Daniel accuses the first elder of a pattern of injustice. The citation evokes Ex 23.7. 54–55: A mastic . . . cut, clove . . . cleave provides an English version of the Greek pun. 55: Angels become increasingly common in Jewish Hellenistic literature (including Daniel; see Isa 37.36; Ezek 9). 56–57: The comment compares three nations. Offspring of Canaan suggests the sexual crimes attributed to the indigenous population of the promised land (Lev 18.24–28); daughters of Israel refers to the Northern Kingdom, destroyed by Assyria in 720 (2 Kings 17); daughter of Judah, Susanna is from the Southern Kingdom, whose exile created the Babylonian Jewish community and from whom the Jews trace their descent. 58–59: Evergreen oak, "Yew" and "hew" recreate the Greek pun. 59: Sword recollects Gen 3.24, as Susanna's garden suggests Eden (Gen 2–3). 62: Law of Moses is Deut 19.16–21.

64: Epilogue. If Susanna is placed at the opening of the book of Daniel, Daniel's great reputation is seen to increase in the subsequent stories.

# BEL AND THE DRAGON

Perhaps composed as early as the Persian period (fifth-fourth centuries BCE) as a midrash on Jer 51; these idol parodies which appear as ch 14 of the Greek version of the book of Daniel display the foolishness of pagan worship, divine protection of faithful Jews, and the cleverness of the court favorite, Daniel. In the account of Bel, Daniel demonstrates that the idol is not a god by proving that it does not eat the food set out for it each night; the second story reverses this scenario as Daniel proves the dragon is not divine by feeding it a noxious concoction that kills it. This second story recapitulates the account of Daniel in the lion's den (Dan 6.16–24) and adds to it Daniel's own miraculous feeding by the prophet Habbakuk. Food references culminate at the end, when Daniel's enemies are eaten by the lions into whose den Daniel had been thrown.

1 When King Astyages was laid to rest with his ancestors, Cyrus the Persian succeeded to his kingdom. 2 Daniel was a companion of the king, and was the most honored of all his Friends.

3 Now the Babylonians had an idol called Bel, and every day they provided for it twelve bushels of choice flour and forty sheep and six measures[a] of wine. 4 The king revered it and went every day to worship it. But Daniel worshiped his own God.

So the king said to him, "Why do you not worship Bel?" 5 He answered, "Because I do not revere idols made with hands, but the living God, who created heaven and earth and has dominion over all living creatures."

6 The king said to him, "Do you not think that Bel is a living god? Do you not see how much he eats and drinks every day?" 7 And Daniel laughed, and said, "Do not be deceived, O king, for this thing is only clay inside and bronze outside, and it never ate or drank anything."

8 Then the king was angry and called the priests of Bel[b] and said to them, "If you do not tell me who is eating these provisions, you shall die. 9 But if you prove that Bel is eating them, Daniel shall die, because he has spoken blasphemy against Bel." Daniel said to the king, "Let it be done as you have said."

10 Now there were seventy priests of Bel, besides their wives and children. So the

a A little more than fifty gallons  b Gk his priests

1–2: Daniel in the Persian court. 1: Astyages, last king of Media (585–550 BCE), was defeated by his grandson, Cyrus the Persian (Dan 6.28). 2: Companion of the king, perhaps an official position (1 Macc 2.18), suggests a confidant. Most honored, see Dan 2.48.

3–7: The worship of Bel. 3: Bel, an epithet of Marduk, headed the Babylonian pantheon (Jer 50.2). Ancient Babylonian sources confirm Bel's extensive diet. 4: The king revered it, although ancient sources indicate that in actual practice, the "leftovers" were sent to the king, and their consumption was considered to provide blessings. The king's support for the priests who were consuming the food is therefore ironic. 4: The question indicates the story's original independence from the book of Daniel, although even in Dan 1–6 kings continually require reeducation about Daniel's faith and practices. 7: Laughed (also in 19) indicates Daniel's familiarity with the king; Bel is also ridiculed in Isa 46.1–2.

8–22: Bel's trial. 8: The abruptness of You shall die (Dan 2.5; 3.6; 6.7) is conventional in folktales. 10: Wives and children contrasts Daniel's single status. 11: Prepare the wine by mixing it with water (2 Macc king went with Daniel into the temple of Bel. 11 The priests of Bel said, "See, we are now going outside; you yourself, O king, set out the food and prepare the wine, and shut the door and seal it with your signet. 12 When you return in the morning, if you do not find that Bel has eaten it all, we will die; otherwise Daniel will, who is telling lies about us." 13 They were unconcerned, for beneath the table they had made a hidden entrance, through which they used to go in regularly and consume the provisions. 14 After they had gone out, the king set out the food for Bel. Then Daniel ordered his servants to bring ashes, and they scattered them throughout the whole temple in the presence of the king alone. Then they went out, shut the door and sealed it with the king's signet, and departed. 15 During the night the priests came as usual, with their wives and children, and they ate and drank everything.

16 Early in the morning the king rose and came, and Daniel with him. 17 The king said, "Are the seals unbroken, Daniel?" He answered, "They are unbroken, O king." 18 As soon as the doors were opened, the king looked at the table, and shouted in a loud voice, "You are great, O Bel, and in you there is no deceit at all!"

19 But Daniel laughed and restrained the king from going in. "Look at the floor," he said, "and notice whose footprints these are." 20 The king said, "I see the footprints of men and women and children."

21 Then the king was enraged, and he arrested the priests and their wives and children. They showed him the secret doors through which they used to enter to consume what was on the table. 22 Therefore the king put them to death, and gave Bel over to Daniel, who destroyed it and its temple.

23 Now in that place[a] there was a great dragon, which the Babylonians revered. 24 The king said to Daniel, "You cannot deny that this is a living god; so worship him." 25 Daniel said, "I worship the Lord my God, for he is the living God. 26 But give me permission, O king, and I will kill the dragon without sword or club." The king said, "I give you permission."

27 Then Daniel took pitch, fat, and hair, and boiled them together and made cakes, which he fed to the dragon. The dragon ate them, and burst open. Then Daniel said, "See what you have been worshiping!"

28 When the Babylonians heard about it, they were very indignant and conspired against the king, saying, "The king has become a Jew; he has destroyed Bel, and killed the dragon, and slaughtered the priests." 29 Going to the king, they said,

a Other ancient authorities lack *in that place*

15.39) or spices (Isa 5.22; Song 8.2). **14:** *Ordered his servants,* unlike Dan 1–6, where Daniel relies on divine revelation and aid, here as well as in Susanna he succeeds by his wits. **22:** *Put them to death* echoes the punishment of the wicked elders (Sus 62; see Dan 2.12; 6.24). Bel's idol and *temple* were, according to the Greek historian Herodotus and other ancient sources, destroyed by the Persian king Xerxes in 479 BCE, who melted the temple's 6 m (18 ft) high statue of Bel into 363 kg (800 lb) of gold bullion. Daniel's action responds to Babylon's destruction of the Jerusalem Temple.

**23–27: The destruction of the dragon. 23:** *Great dragon,* dragons or snakes could symbolize the divine in ancient Near Eastern and Mediterranean cultures (Num 21.8–9; 2 Kings 18.4), but there is no independent evidence of Babylonian snake worship. **24:** *Living god* contrasts the delegitimation of the idol Bel, for the snake is clearly alive. **25:** Daniel resists apostasy, a special concern for Jews in the Diaspora and during the persecution of Antiochus IV Epiphanes. **27:** The snake eats and dies, unlike Bel who is proven false because he cannot eat; within the Danielic corpus, this detail offers subtle comparisons. Daniel and his friends prosper by restricting their diet (Dan 1); Belshazzar falls because of his blasphemous feasting (Dan 5).

**28–42: Daniel in the lion pit. 28:** *Become a Jew* anticipates v. 41, where the king affirms Daniel's God; he does not, however, convert. **29:** The death threat repeats the punishment of Bel's priests and their

"Hand Daniel over to us, or else we will kill you and your household." 30 The king saw that they were pressing him hard, and under compulsion he handed Daniel over to them.

31 They threw Daniel into the lions' den, and he was there for six days. 32 There were seven lions in the den, and every day they had been given two human bodies and two sheep; but now they were given nothing, so that they would devour Daniel.

33 Now the prophet Habakkuk was in Judea; he had made a stew and had broken bread into a bowl, and was going into the field to take it to the reapers. 34 But the angel of the Lord said to Habakkuk, "Take the food that you have to Babylon, to Daniel, in the lions' den." 35 Habakkuk said, "Sir, I have never seen Babylon, and I know nothing about the den." 36 Then the angel of the Lord took him by the crown of his head and carried him by his hair; with the speed of the wind[a] he set him down in Babylon, right over the den.

37 Then Habakkuk shouted, "Daniel, Daniel! Take the food that God has sent you." 38 Daniel said, "You have remembered me, O God, and have not forsaken those who love you." 39 So Daniel got up and ate. And the angel of God immediately returned Habakkuk to his own place.

40 On the seventh day the king came to mourn for Daniel. When he came to the den he looked in, and there sat Daniel! 41 The king shouted with a loud voice, "You are great, O Lord, the God of Daniel, and there is no other besides you!" 42 Then he pulled Daniel[b] out, and threw into the den those who had attempted his destruction, and they were instantly eaten before his eyes.

a Or *by the power of his spirit*   b Gk *him*

families. **30:** The king's reluctance resembles that of Darius (Dan 6). **31:** *Lions' den*, see Dan 6.16–24, where Daniel spends one night, not six. Daniel destroyed Babylon's animal god; now the Babylonians anticipate that animals will destroy him. **32:** The description continues the author's interest in dietary matters, but only in this case will concerns for eating be connected to the miraculous. **33:** *Habbakuk* prophesied ca. 612–597 BCE, well before the events recounted here could have occurred. **34:** Angels appear in the book of Daniel as protectors as well as apocalyptic revealers and interpreters. *The food* is part of the tale's humor: The lions, not Daniel, have the greater problem with hunger. **36:** *By his hair*, see Ezek 8.3. **40:** Unlike the earlier episode, no explanation for the result of the test is given. **41:** *You are great* replaces the king's praise of Bel in v. 18. **42:** References to food reach their conclusion as Daniel's accusers are consumed.

# 1 MACCABEES

༒ ༒

Set in the tumultuous years of 175–143 BCE, 1 Maccabees narrates the history of the revolt against Seleucid rule in Judea led by Judas Maccabeus and his brothers. Although the book opens with a brief historical summary of events leading up to the revolt, a word of background on the religious situation will be helpful to the reader. Judea had known a long period of relative peace and prosperity, first under Alexander the Great (332–323), then under the Ptolemies, the successors to Alexander's rule in Egypt (323–198). As a result of Alexander's rule, Hellenism, a mixture of Greek and Semitic cultures, had dominated all the countries of the eastern Mediterranean basin. The book of Sirach and the translation of the Hebrew Scriptures into Greek (the Septuagint) demonstrate the influence of Greek ideas on Judaism during the fourth and third centuries. By the second century, however, when Judea came under the control of the Seleucids, the successors to Alexander's rule in Mesopotamia and Syria, Jews were divided over the problem of accommodating to Gentile culture. The upper classes in Jerusalem, the Hellenizers, had long adopted Greek ways, while the poorer people of the rural areas tended to cling to the customs of their ancestors. The conflict among Judeans is evident at the beginning of 1 Maccabees (1.11–15) and is present throughout the book.

In this situation of complex religious, economic, and political tensions, the actions of the Seleucid ruler Antiochus IV were a match in a tinderbox. Motivated perhaps by a political desire to remove Jewish religious law as a source of conflict and potential rebellion within Judea, Antiochus tried to eradicate the distinctive identity of the Jews. By plundering the Temple and outlawing religious practices, however, Antiochus instead sparked the first Jewish war of independence as well as the first Jewish martyrdoms. The first chapters of 1 Maccabees describe this edict and its immediate consequences. Jews were prohibited from making daily offerings in the Temple, keeping the sabbath, and circumcising their sons, and were required to make sacrifices to other gods. Those who obeyed the Torah rather than the king were publicly put to death, and those who withdrew to the wilderness were slaughtered on the sabbath, when they would not fight.

Into this crisis the author introduces the priestly family of Mattathias and his sons Judas (whose epithet Maccabeus, "the hammer," gives rise to the name Maccabees), Jonathan, and Simon as the deliverers of Judea. Fearing that the Seleucids would kill all observant Jews and that the Hellenizers would destroy Judaism, Judas Maccabeus and his men mounted a campaign of armed resistance against both enemies. Using a combination of guerrilla warfare and diplomacy, they succeeded in recovering and purifying the Temple after Antiochus had defiled it, fortifying Jerusalem and securing a measure of independence for Judea. The book is organized into sections that recount the history of each hero: Mattathias (ch 2); Judas Maccabeus (3.1–9.22); Jonathan (9.23–12.53); Simon (13.1–15.41), and John (16.1–24). By the end of the book three generations of Mattathias's family had fought for Judea's independence from the Seleucids and had established a ruling dynasty (called Hasmonean after their ancestor, see 2.1n.) that would remain in power until the Roman occupation in 63 BCE.

First Maccabees is written in the straightforward style of historical narrative filled with realistic detail. Scholars consider it the most reliable historical resource for the study of the Maccabean revolt. The author used both Jerusalem archives and Seleucid annals as sources; diplomatic correspondence and royal edicts are cited fourteen times in the book. Oral traditions of Jewish history probably supplemented written sources. Following the conventions of both biblical and Hellenistic historiography, the author placed eloquent speeches on the lips of major characters at critical points in the narrative. These compositions provide the reader with clues to some of the important religious themes in the book. The author used the Jewish scriptures as a literary model and constant backdrop for his story. The book is organized in the manner of the historical books of the Hebrew Bible, which tend to mark periods in Israel's history by the deaths of divinely appointed deliverers (Josh 1.1; Judg 1.1; 2 Sam 1.17; 1 Kings 11.41–43). In 1 Maccabees the reader is clearly guided by refrains signaling the peaceful passing of leadership from one member of the Hasmonean family to the next (2.69–70; 9.19–22; 13.25–30). There are no accounts of miraculous interventions, but the author believes that God was working through the Maccabees, as he did through the deliverers in Israel (5.62; cf. Judg 2.16; 6.14).

Frequent allusions to Israel's history and the use of biblical vocabulary guide the reader to see Mattathias and his sons as heirs of biblical heroes. Mattathias is portrayed in language that evokes the stories of Phineas (2.23–26; Num 25.6–9) and Jacob (2.49–70; Gen 49), while Judas is likened to Jonathan son of Saul (3.16–22; 1 Sam 14.6) and to Solomon (4.52–58; 1 Kings 8). Even a simple phrase like "he tore down their altars" (5.68) evokes the story of Gideon (Judg 6.25) and the commands of Moses (Deut 7.5; 12.3). The use of anachronistic terms like "Philistines" and "Israel" link the Maccabean battles with the times of Joshua and David. The most overt guide for the reader is the set of ten poetic pieces scattered throughout the narrative. Their vocabulary and style evoke the poetry of ancient Israel, especially the Psalms, and their allusions often bring to mind the destruction of Jerusalem by the Babylonians in 586 BCE. Like the poetry in the narratives of the Hebrew Bible (for example, Ex 15; 1 Sam 2; 2 Sam 1; 2 Sam 22), they provide the reader with theological commentary on the action of the story. In short, the author has woven scriptural allusions into the history of the Maccabean revolt.

The work was written between the rule of John Hyrcanus I, introduced at the end of the book (134–104 BCE), and Pompey's conquest of Rome in 63 BCE. Josephus used it as a source when he began his *Jewish Antiquities* in about 75 CE. The earliest extant manuscripts are from the fourth and fifth centuries CE in Greek and Latin. Scholars since the time of Jerome have noticed that the Greek of 1 Maccabees reads like a translation from Hebrew, almost certainly the book's original language.

1 After Alexander son of Philip, the Macedonian, who came from the land of Kittim, had defeated[a] King Darius of the Persians and the Medes, he succeeded him as king. (He had previously become king of Greece.) 2 He fought many battles, conquered strongholds, and put to death the kings of the earth. 3 He advanced to the ends of the earth, and plundered many nations. When the earth became quiet before him, he was exalted, and his heart was lifted up. 4 He gathered a very strong army and ruled over countries, nations, and princes, and they became tributary to him.

5 After this he fell sick and perceived that he was dying. 6 So he summoned his

a Gk adds *and he defeated*

**1.1–10: Introduction.** A summary of history from Alexander to Antiochus IV, setting the stage for the story that follows. For a fuller version, see Dan 11.1–28. **1:** *Alexander* the Great (356–323 BCE), son of Philip of Macedon, who had conquered *Kittim* (Greece), swept through Asia Minor and *defeated King Darius* III at Issus (333 BCE) and at Gaugamela (331). **3:** After taking Egypt, Mesopotamia, and Persia *he advanced to the ends of the earth* (to Bactria and India). *He was exalted*, i.e., he was deified; such pride in rulers is castigated in Isa 2.5–22; *and his heart was lifted up* is a biblical idiom for pride (2 Chr 26.16, Ezek 28.2). **4:** He planned a universal empire dominated by Greek culture. **5:** *He fell sick* in Babylon. **6:**

most honored officers, who had been brought up with him from youth, and divided his kingdom among them while he was still alive. 7 And after Alexander had reigned twelve years, he died.

8 Then his officers began to rule, each in his own place. 9 They all put on crowns after his death, and so did their descendants after them for many years; and they caused many evils on the earth.

10 From them came forth a sinful root, Antiochus Epiphanes, son of King Antiochus; he had been a hostage in Rome. He began to reign in the one hundred thirty-seventh year of the kingdom of the Greeks.*a*

11 In those days certain renegades came out from Israel and misled many, saying, "Let us go and make a covenant with the Gentiles around us, for since we separated from them many disasters have come upon us." 12 This proposal pleased them, 13 and some of the people eagerly went to the king, who authorized them to observe the ordinances of the Gentiles. 14 So they built a gymnasium in Jerusalem, according to Gentile custom, 15 and removed the marks of circumcision, and abandoned the holy covenant. They joined with the Gentiles and sold themselves to do evil.

16 When Antiochus saw that his kingdom was established, he determined to become king of the land of Egypt, in order that he might reign over both kingdoms. 17 So he invaded Egypt with a strong force, with chariots and elephants and cavalry and with a large fleet. 18 He engaged King Ptolemy of Egypt in battle, and Ptolemy turned and fled before him, and many were wounded and fell. 19 They captured the fortified cities in the land of Egypt, and he plundered the land of Egypt.

20 After subduing Egypt, Antiochus returned in the one hundred forty-third year.*b* He went up against Israel and came to Jerusalem with a strong force. 21 He ar-

*a* 175 B.C.    *b* 169 B.C.

A complex history of power struggles lies behind this statement. **8–9:** By 275 three dynasties were established: the Antigonids of Macedonia, the Ptolemies of Egypt, and the Seleucids of Syria. **9:** *Crowns,* lit. "diadems"; these were strips of white cloth decorated on the edges. **10:** *Sinful root,* cf. Isa 11.10; Dan 11.7. *Antiochus IV,* who took the name *Epiphanes* ("god manifest"), reigned 175–164; he was *son of King Antiochus III* the Great (223–187), who had wrested Palestine from Egypt at the battle of Paneas in 198 but lost most of Asia Minor to Rome at Magnesia in 190. Because of this defeat the son *had been a hostage in Rome. One hundred thirty-seventh year* of the Seleucid era; reckoning of this era varied in different places; dates given in the notes (*b, c,* etc.) are approximate.

**1.11–15: Conflicts over Hellenization.** Greek culture had become a part of life in Judea, but now enthusiasts introduced customs that compromised Jewish religious observance (2 Macc 4.11–17). **11:** *Certain renegades,* led by Jason, whom Antiochus appointed high priest in place of his brother Onias III (2 Macc 4.7). *Renegades,* lit. "lawless ones," those who compromised the law of Moses. The term is used throughout 1 Maccabees to describe Jews who did not support the Hasmoneans. Making a *covenant with the Gentiles* was expressly forbidden (Ex 34.11–16; Deut 7.1–6) because of the danger of being led into idolatry. *Disasters,* loss of business and prestige because relations with Syria had deteriorated, cf. Jer 44.15–23. **14:** *A gymnasium,* the center of political and cultural education, as well as sports (2 Macc 4.9–10). **15:** *Removed the marks of circumcision* by a surgical procedure (epispasm), since Greek athletics were performed in the nude.

**1.16–40: Antiochus invades Egypt and Palestine.** Invasion of Egypt is followed by plundering of the Temple in Jerusalem (2 Macc 5.1,11–26; Dan 11.25–28). **17:** The Syrian army had *elephants,* though the treaty of Apamea with Rome (188 BCE) had forbidden this. **18:** *Ptolemy* VI Philometor reigned 180–145. **20:** *Antiochus returned* because the Roman envoy, Popilius Laenas, threatened him with war if he annexed Egypt; also, news of internal strife in Jerusalem had reached him, and he feared a revolt (2 Macc 5). **20–23:** Although plundering temples was a sacrilegious act, cash-strapped kings often resorted to it. Antiochus may have justified his act because the high priest Menelaus had not paid him promised funds (2 Macc 5.15). **22:** *The bread of the Presence,* twelve loaves of unleavened bread set in the Temple rogantly entered the sanctuary and took the golden altar, the lampstand for the light, and all its utensils. 22 He took also the table for the bread of the Presence, the cups for drink offerings, the bowls, the golden censers, the curtain, the crowns, and the gold decoration on the front of the temple; he stripped it all off. 23 He took the silver and the gold, and the costly vessels; he took also the hidden treasures that he found. 24 Taking them all, he went into his own land.

He shed much blood,
and spoke with great arrogance.

25 Israel mourned deeply in every
community,
26 rulers and elders groaned,
young women and young men became
faint,
the beauty of the women faded.
27 Every bridegroom took up the lament;
she who sat in the bridal chamber
was mourning.
28 Even the land trembled for its
inhabitants,
and all the house of Jacob was
clothed with shame.

29 Two years later the king sent to the cities of Judah a chief collector of tribute, and he came to Jerusalem with a large force. 30 Deceitfully he spoke peaceable words to them, and they believed him; but he suddenly fell upon the city, dealt it a severe blow, and destroyed many people of Israel. 31 He plundered the city, burned it with fire, and tore down its houses and its surrounding walls. 32 They took captive the women and children, and seized the livestock. 33 Then they fortified the city of David with a great strong wall and strong towers, and it became their citadel. 34 They stationed there a sinful people, men who were renegades. These strengthened their position; 35 they stored up arms and food, and collecting the spoils of Jerusalem they stored them there, and became a great menace,

36 for the citadel[a] became an ambush
against the sanctuary,
an evil adversary of Israel at all
times.
37 On every side of the sanctuary they
shed innocent blood;
they even defiled the sanctuary.
38 Because of them the residents of
Jerusalem fled;
she became a dwelling of strangers;
she became strange to her offspring,
and her children forsook her.
39 Her sanctuary became desolate like a
desert;
her feasts were turned into
mourning,
her sabbaths into a reproach,
her honor into contempt.
40 Her dishonor now grew as great as
her glory;
her exaltation was turned into
mourning.

41 Then the king wrote to his whole kingdom that all should be one people,

a Gk it

sanctuary by the priests every sabbath, symbolizing the covenant between God and Israel (Ex 30.25; Lev 24.5–9). **24–28:** Fragment of a contemporary poem. **28:** *The house of Jacob,* Israel, the Jewish people. **29:** *Chief collector of tribute* may be a mistranslation of "chief of the Mysians," mercenary troops from Asia Minor (2 Macc 5.22–26). **33:** *City of David,* a term with several different meanings in the Bible (cf. Isa 22.9 and 1 Kings 11.27 with 2 Sam 5.7,9); the precise location of this fortification within Jerusalem is unknown. The term highlights the author's point that Antiochus is not the true king. The *citadel* remained in Seleucid control until 141 when it was captured by Simon (1 Macc 13.49–52). **34:** *Sinful people,* like "lawless ones," a biblical term used primarily for Israelites who were not faithful to the covenant (Isa 1.4); here it connotes Jews who supported the Seleucids. **36–40:** Lament for Jerusalem; cf. Ps 74; 79; Lamentations.

**1.41–64: Desecration of the Temple.** The first religious persecution of Jews, also recounted in Dan 11.29–39 (cf. 2 Macc 6.1–11). **41–42:** *His whole kingdom,* Syria, Palestine, Mesopotamia, Persia, and parts of Asia Minor. Parallel accounts in 2 Macc 6 and Josephus (*Ant.* 12.5.5) report that the decree was aimed solely at Palestinian Jews and Samaritans. **45:** *Burnt offerings and sacrifices and drink offerings*

42 and that all should give up their particular customs. 43 All the Gentiles accepted the command of the king. Many even from Israel gladly adopted his religion; they sacrificed to idols and profaned the sabbath. 44 And the king sent letters by messengers to Jerusalem and the towns of Judah; he directed them to follow customs strange to the land, 45 to forbid burnt offerings and sacrifices and drink offerings in the sanctuary, to profane sabbaths and festivals, 46 to defile the sanctuary and the priests, 47 to build altars and sacred precincts and shrines for idols, to sacrifice swine and other unclean animals, 48 and to leave their sons uncircumcised. They were to make themselves abominable by everything unclean and profane, 49 so that they would forget the law and change all the ordinances. 50 He added,[a] "And whoever does not obey the command of the king shall die."

51 In such words he wrote to his whole kingdom. He appointed inspectors over all the people and commanded the towns of Judah to offer sacrifice, town by town. 52 Many of the people, everyone who forsook the law, joined them, and they did evil in the land; 53 they drove Israel into hiding in every place of refuge they had.

54 Now on the fifteenth day of Chislev, in the one hundred forty-fifth year,[b] they erected a desolating sacrilege on the altar of burnt offering. They also built altars in the surrounding towns of Judah, 55 and offered incense at the doors of the houses and in the streets. 56 The books of the law that they found they tore to pieces and burned with fire. 57 Anyone found possessing the book of the covenant, or anyone who adhered to the law, was condemned to death by decree of the king. 58 They kept using violence against Israel, against those who were found month after month in the towns. 59 On the twenty-fifth day of the month they offered sacrifice on the altar that was on top of the altar of burnt offering. 60 According to the decree, they put to death the women who had their children circumcised, 61 and their families and those who circumcised them; and they hung the infants from their mothers' necks.

62 But many in Israel stood firm and were resolved in their hearts not to eat unclean food. 63 They chose to die rather than to be defiled by food or to profane the holy covenant; and they did die. 64 Very great wrath came upon Israel.

2 In those days Mattathias son of John son of Simeon, a priest of the family of Joarib, moved from Jerusalem and settled in Modein. 2 He had five sons, John surnamed Gaddi, 3 Simon called Thassi, 4 Judas called Maccabeus, 5 Eleazar called Avaran, and Jonathan called Apphus. 6 He saw

a Gk lacks He added    b 167 B.C.

were offerings of meat, grain, and drink made in the Temple daily to the Lord, commanded in Ex 29.38–42; Num 28.3–8. 47: *Swine and other unclean animals* were not dirty but ritually impure and unacceptable for sacrifice (Lev 11.1–8; 22.17–30). 54: *Chislev,* November/December. The precise meaning of *desolating sacrilege* is unknown; it included an altar to Zeus Olympios (the Greek equivalent of the Syrian god Baal Shamem) and perhaps a stone statue (Dan 11.31; 12.11; 2 Macc 6.2). *Built altars,* thereby violating the commandment in Deut 12.5–28. 59: *Offered sacrifice,* probably of swine (2 Macc 6.4–5). 60–64: 2 Macc 6–7 and 4 Maccabees contain stories of martyrdoms. *Chose to die rather than to be defiled by food,* cf. Dan 3.8–18. *Wrath came upon Israel* is a formula signifying God's justice when the covenant is broken (Num 25.1–4; Neh 13.15–18; Zech 7.8–14; 2 Macc 6.12–16).
**2.1–48: Revolt of Mattathias. 1:** The family of *Mattathias* is known as Hasmoneans from a traditional ancestor Hashmonia, not mentioned in 1 Maccabees but named in Josephus (*Ant.* 12.6.1). The name may be a rendering of Simeon, the grandfather of Mattathias. *Joarib* was first in the list of divisions of priests (1 Chr 24.7; Neh 11.10). *Modein,* in the hills on the road from Beth-horon, about 30 km (18 mi) northwest of Jerusalem. **2–5:** *Simon,* third of the family to rule (chs 13–16). *Maccabeus,* probably from a Hebrew word meaning "hammer." The other surnames are of uncertain derivation. *Jonathan,* successor of Judas (chs 9–12). **7–13:** Poetic lament (cf. 1.36–40); for the portrait of Jerusalem as a beautiful woman

the blasphemies being committed in Judah and Jerusalem, 7and said,

"Alas! Why was I born to see this,
    the ruin of my people, the ruin of
      the holy city,
and to live there when it was given
      over to the enemy,
    the sanctuary given over to aliens?
8 Her temple has become like a person
      without honor;[a]
9   her glorious vessels have been
      carried into exile.
  Her infants have been killed in her
      streets,
    her youths by the sword of the foe.
10 What nation has not inherited her
      palaces[b]
  and has not seized her spoils?
11 All her adornment has been taken
      away;
    no longer free, she has become a
      slave.
12 And see, our holy place, our beauty,
      and our glory have been laid waste;
  the Gentiles have profaned them.
13   Why should we live any longer?"

14 Then Mattathias and his sons tore their clothes, put on sackcloth, and mourned greatly.

15 The king's officers who were enforcing the apostasy came to the town of Modein to make them offer sacrifice. 16Many from Israel came to them; and Mattathias and his sons were assembled. 17Then the king's officers spoke to Mattathias as follows: "You are a leader, honored and great in this town, and supported by sons and brothers. 18Now be the first to come and do what the king commands, as all the Gentiles and the people of Judah and those that are left in Jerusalem have done. Then you and your sons will be numbered among the Friends of the king, and you and your sons will be honored with silver and gold and many gifts."

19 But Mattathias answered and said in a loud voice: "Even if all the nations that live under the rule of the king obey him, and have chosen to obey his commandments, everyone of them abandoning the religion of their ancestors, 20I and my sons and my brothers will continue to live by the covenant of our ancestors. 21Far be it from us to desert the law and the ordinances. 22We will not obey the king's words by turning aside from our religion to the right hand or to the left."

23 When he had finished speaking these words, a Jew came forward in the sight of all to offer sacrifice on the altar in Modein, according to the king's command. 24When Mattathias saw it, he burned with zeal and his heart was stirred. He gave vent to righteous anger; he ran and killed him on the altar. 25At the same time he killed the king's officer who was forcing them to sacrifice, and he tore down the altar. 26Thus he burned with zeal for the law, just as Phinehas did against Zimri son of Salu.

27 Then Mattathias cried out in the town with a loud voice, saying: "Let every one who is zealous for the law and supports the covenant come out with me!" 28Then he and his sons fled to the hills and left all that they had in the town.

29 At that time many who were seeking righteousness and justice went down to the wilderness to live there, 30they, their sons, their wives, and their livestock, because troubles pressed heavily upon them. 31And it was reported to the king's officers, and to the troops in Jerusalem the city of David, that those who had rejected the king's com-

a Meaning of Gk uncertain  b Other ancient authorities read *has not had a part in her kingdom*

dishonored, see Lam 1.1. **14:** *Tore their clothes, put on sackcloth,* signs of mourning (Gen 37.34). **18:** *The Friends of the king* were a special class of courtiers who wore distinctive purple dress and insignia (1 Macc 10.65; 11.27). **23:** Elsewhere in chs 1–13, "Israelite" is used instead of the term *Jew,* which here perhaps means "Judean." **24:** *His heart,* literally "his kidneys," which were considered the seat of emotion. **25:** *He tore down the altar,* see Judg 6.25. **26:** *As Phinehas did,* the whole episode is written to echo Num 25.6–15. Phineas is praised in Sir 45.23–24. **28:** 2 Macc 5.27. **29–31:** In *the wilderness* of Judea they found *hiding places* (Isa 32.16). **37:** 1.63. **41:** The earliest statement of the principle that one may profane mand had gone down to the hiding places in the wilderness. 32 Many pursued them, and overtook them; they encamped opposite them and prepared for battle against them on the sabbath day. 33 They said to them, "Enough of this! Come out and do what the king commands, and you will live." 34 But they said, "We will not come out, nor will we do what the king commands and so profane the sabbath day." 35 Then the enemy[a] quickly attacked them. 36 But they did not answer them or hurl a stone at them or block up their hiding places, 37 for they said, "Let us all die in our innocence; heaven and earth testify for us that you are killing us unjustly." 38 So they attacked them on the sabbath, and they died, with their wives and children and livestock, to the number of a thousand persons.

39 When Mattathias and his friends learned of it, they mourned for them deeply. 40 And all said to their neighbors: "If we all do as our kindred have done and refuse to fight with the Gentiles for our lives and for our ordinances, they will quickly destroy us from the earth." 41 So they made this decision that day: "Let us fight against anyone who comes to attack us on the sabbath day; let us not all die as our kindred died in their hiding places."

42 Then there united with them a company of Hasideans, mighty warriors of Israel, all who offered themselves willingly for the law. 43 And all who became fugitives to escape their troubles joined them and reinforced them. 44 They organized an army, and struck down sinners in their anger and renegades in their wrath; the survivors fled to the Gentiles for safety. 45 And Mattathias and his friends went around and tore down the altars; 46 they forcibly circumcised all the uncircumcised boys that they found within the borders of Israel. 47 They hunted down the arrogant, and the work prospered in their hands. 48 They rescued the law out of the hands of the Gentiles and kings, and they never let the sinner gain the upper hand.

49 Now the days drew near for Mattathias to die, and he said to his sons: "Arrogance and scorn have now become strong; it is a time of ruin and furious anger. 50 Now, my children, show zeal for the law, and give your lives for the covenant of our ancestors.

51 "Remember the deeds of the ancestors, which they did in their generations; and you will receive great honor and an everlasting name. 52 Was not Abraham found faithful when tested, and it was reckoned to him as righteousness? 53 Joseph in the time of his distress kept the commandment, and became lord of Egypt. 54 Phinehas our ancestor, because he was deeply zealous, received the covenant of everlasting priesthood. 55 Joshua, because he fulfilled the command, became a judge in Israel. 56 Caleb, because he testified in the assembly, received an inheritance in the land. 57 David, because he was merciful, inherited the throne of the kingdom forever. 58 Elijah, because of great zeal for the law, was taken up into heaven. 59 Hananiah, Azariah, and Mishael believed and were saved from the flame. 60 Daniel, because of his innocence, was delivered from the mouth of the lions.

61 "And so observe, from generation to generation, that none of those who put their trust in him will lack strength. 62 Do not fear the words of sinners, for their

a Gk they

one sabbath in order to keep all the others. **42:** *Hasideans,* "the pious," a group not concerned for Jewish nationalism but only for the religious law. At first they resisted passively (1.62–63; 2.37), but now turned to violent action (but see 1 Macc 7.12–13).

**2.49–70: Last words of Mattathias.** Mattathias is portrayed like Jacob in Gen 49. **51:** See Sirach 44–50. **52:** *Faithful when tested,* Gen 22.1–18. *Reckoned to him,* Gen 15.6. **53:** *Joseph,* Gen 39.9; 41.41–43; Ps 105.17–22. **54:** *Phinehas,* v. 26n. **55–56:** *Joshua . . . Caleb,* Num 13.1–14.12; 26.65; Josh 1.1–9. **57:** *Merciful,* or perhaps "loyal" (1 Sam 24.16–22; 2 Sam 7.16; 9.1; Ps 89.35–37; 132.11–12). **58:** 1 Kings 17; 2 Kings 2.9–12. **59–60:** Dan 3.8–30; 6.1–24. **62:** See 2 Macc 9.5–12 on the death of

Chs 2–16: Campaigns of the Maccabees and Hasmoneans. See map on following page for sites in the Jerusalem vicinity.

Chs 2–16: The Jerusalem vicinity.

splendor will turn into dung and worms. 63 Today they will be exalted, but tomorrow they will not be found, because they will have returned to the dust, and their plans will have perished. 64 My children, be courageous and grow strong in the law, for by it you will gain honor.

65 "Here is your brother Simeon who, I know, is wise in counsel; always listen to him; he shall be your father. 66 Judas Maccabeus has been a mighty warrior from his youth; he shall command the army for you and fight the battle against the peoples.[a] 67 You shall rally around you all who observe the law, and avenge the wrong done to your people. 68 Pay back the Gentiles in full, and obey the commands of the law."

69 Then he blessed them, and was gathered to his ancestors. 70 He died in the one hundred forty-sixth year[b] and was buried in the tomb of his ancestors at Modein. And all Israel mourned for him with great lamentation.

3 Then his son Judas, who was called Maccabeus, took command in his place. 2 All his brothers and all who had joined his father helped him; they gladly fought for Israel.

3 He extended the glory of his people.
   Like a giant he put on his
      breastplate;
   he bound on his armor of war and
      waged battles,
   protecting the camp by his sword.
4 He was like a lion in his deeds,
   like a lion's cub roaring for prey.
5 He searched out and pursued those
      who broke the law;
   he burned those who troubled his
      people.
6 Lawbreakers shrank back for fear of
      him;
   all the evildoers were confounded;
   and deliverance prospered by his
      hand.
7 He embittered many kings,
   but he made Jacob glad by his
      deeds,
   and his memory is blessed forever.
8 He went through the cities of Judah;
   he destroyed the ungodly out of the
      land;[c]
   thus he turned away wrath from
      Israel.
9 He was renowned to the ends of the
      earth;
   he gathered in those who were
      perishing.
10 Apollonius now gathered together
Gentiles and a large force from Samaria to

a Or of the people   b 166 B.C.   c Gk it

Antiochus IV. 63: Ps 37.10,35–36. 65: *Simeon*, that is, Simon. 69: *Gathered to his ancestors*, buried with his ancestors (Judg 2.10).

3.1–12: Defeat of Apollonius. 3–9: From a contemporary poem. 4: *Like a lion*, 2 Sam 1.23; Hos 5.14. 8: *He turned away wrath*, i.e., God's punishment (2 Macc 7.38). 10: *Apollonius*, according to Josephus (*Ant.* 12.5.5; 7.1), was governor of Samaria. 12: *Took the sword*, as David took Goliath's (1 Sam 17.51,54).

fight against Israel. 11 When Judas learned of it, he went out to meet him, and he defeated and killed him. Many were wounded and fell, and the rest fled. 12 Then they seized their spoils; and Judas took the sword of Apollonius, and used it in battle the rest of his life.

13 When Seron, the commander of the Syrian army, heard that Judas had gathered a large company, including a body of faithful soldiers who stayed with him and went out to battle, 14 he said, "I will make a name for myself and win honor in the kingdom. I will make war on Judas and his companions, who scorn the king's command." 15 Once again a strong army of godless men went up with him to help him, to take vengeance on the Israelites.

16 When he approached the ascent of Beth-horon, Judas went out to meet him with a small company. 17 But when they saw the army coming to meet them, they said to Judas, "How can we, few as we are, fight against so great and so strong a multitude? And we are faint, for we have eaten nothing today." 18 Judas replied, "It is easy for many to be hemmed in by few, for in the sight of Heaven there is no difference between saving by many or by few. 19 It is not on the size of the army that victory in battle depends, but strength comes from Heaven. 20 They come against us in great insolence and lawlessness to destroy us and our wives and our children, and to despoil us; 21 but we fight for our lives and our laws. 22 He himself will crush them before us; as for you, do not be afraid of them."

23 When he finished speaking, he rushed suddenly against Seron and his army, and they were crushed before him. 24 They pursued them[a] down the descent of Beth-horon to the plain; eight hundred of them fell, and the rest fled into the land of the Philistines. 25 Then Judas and his brothers began to be feared, and terror fell on the Gentiles all around them. 26 His fame reached the king, and the Gentiles talked of the battles of Judas.

27 When King Antiochus heard these reports, he was greatly angered; and he sent and gathered all the forces of his kingdom, a very strong army. 28 He opened his coffers and gave a year's pay to his forces, and ordered them to be ready for any need. 29 Then he saw that the money in the treasury was exhausted, and that the revenues from the country were small because of the dissension and disaster that he had caused in the land by abolishing the laws that had existed from the earliest days. 30 He feared that he might not have such funds as he had before for his expenses and for the gifts that he used to give more lavishly than preceding kings. 31 He was greatly perplexed in mind; then he determined to go to Persia and collect the revenues from those regions and raise a large fund.

32 He left Lysias, a distinguished man of royal lineage, in charge of the king's affairs from the river Euphrates to the borders of Egypt. 33 Lysias was also to take care of his son Antiochus until he returned. 34 And he turned over to Lysias[b] half of his forces and the elephants, and gave him orders about all that he wanted done. As for the residents of Judea and Jerusalem, 35 Lysias was to send a force against them to wipe out and destroy the strength of Israel and the remnant of Jerusalem; he was to banish

a Other ancient authorities read *him*   b Gk *him*

3.13–26: Battle of Beth-horon. Judas's first great victory evokes the story of David and Goliath, 1 Sam 17. 16: *The ascent of Beth-horon* was a route from the coastal plain to the Judean highlands. The town is about 20 km (12 mi) northwest of Jerusalem. 18: The word *Heaven* was used to avoid pronouncing God's name (cf. "he himself," v. 22, and see Sus 9). *By many or by few,* 1 Sam 14.6. 24: *Land of the Philistines,* the southern coastal plain.

3.27–4.35: Campaigns of Lysias. Antiochus IV goes to Persia; Judas defeats Lysias at Emmaus and Beth-zur. 3.28: *Any need* implies that Seleucid power was beginning to decline. 30: Antiochus was noted for his extravagance (2 Macc 4.30). 33: *Antiochus* V Eupator, *his son,* was only nine years old; he reigned 164–162 BCE. 36: *Settle aliens,* as the Assyrians had done (2 Kings 17.24). 37: *Antioch,* modern Antakya, the memory of them from the place, 36 settle aliens in all their territory, and distribute their land by lot. 37 Then the king took the remaining half of his forces and left Antioch his capital in the one hundred and forty-seventh year.ᵃ He crossed the Euphrates river and went through the upper provinces.

38 Lysias chose Ptolemy son of Dorymenes, and Nicanor and Gorgias, able men among the Friends of the king, 39 and sent with them forty thousand infantry and seven thousand cavalry to go into the land of Judah and destroy it, as the king had commanded. 40 So they set out with their entire force, and when they arrived they encamped near Emmaus in the plain. 41 When the traders of the region heard what was said to them, they took silver and gold in immense amounts, and fetters,ᵇ and went to the camp to get the Israelites for slaves. And forces from Syria and the land of the Philistines joined with them.

42 Now Judas and his brothers saw that misfortunes had increased and that the forces were encamped in their territory. They also learned what the king had commanded to do to the people to cause their final destruction. 43 But they said to one another, "Let us restore the ruins of our people, and fight for our people and the sanctuary." 44 So the congregation assembled to be ready for battle, and to pray and ask for mercy and compassion.

45 Jerusalem was uninhabited like a
    wilderness;
  not one of her children went in or
    out.
The sanctuary was trampled down,
  and aliens held the citadel;

it was a lodging place for the
    Gentiles.
Joy was taken from Jacob;
  the flute and the harp ceased to
    play.

46 Then they gathered together and went to Mizpah, opposite Jerusalem, because Israel formerly had a place of prayer in Mizpah. 47 They fasted that day, put on sackcloth and sprinkled ashes on their heads, and tore their clothes. 48 And they opened the book of the law to inquire into those matters about which the Gentiles consulted the likenesses of their gods. 49 They also brought the vestments of the priesthood and the first fruits and the tithes, and they stirred up the nazaritesᶜ who had completed their days; 50 and they cried aloud to Heaven, saying,

"What shall we do with these?
  Where shall we take them?
51 Your sanctuary is trampled down and
    profaned,
  and your priests mourn in
    humiliation.
52 Here the Gentiles are assembled
    against us to destroy us;
  you know what they plot against
    us.
53 How will we be able to withstand
    them,
  if you do not help us?"

54 Then they sounded the trumpets and gave a loud shout. 55 After this Judas appointed leaders of the people, in charge of thousands and hundreds and fifties and tens. 56 Those who were building houses, or

ᵃ 165 B.C.    ᵇ Syr: Gk Mss, Vg *slaves*    ᶜ That is *those separated* or *those consecrated*

near the mouth of the Orontes River in Syria, was built by Seleucus I in 300 BCE and expanded by Antiochus IV. *Upper provinces*, Persia. **38:** *Ptolemy*, known as Macron (2 Macc 10.12). *Nicanor*, 2 Macc 8.9. *Gorgias*, 2 Macc 10.14. **40:** *Emmaus* (not the Emmaus of Lk 24.13) was about 24 km (15 mi) west-northwest of Jerusalem. **45:** See 1.36–40; 2.7–13; cf. Ps 74; Isa 24.8. **46:** *Mizpah*, probably Tell en-Nasbeh, 12 km (8 mi) north of Jerusalem; see 1 Sam 7.5–11. **48:** *The book of the law*, the Pentateuch. The translation of the verse is uncertain. **49:** Important religious activities could no longer be performed because of the defilement of the Temple. *Tithes* were ordinarily brought to Jerusalem and there distributed (Neh 10.35–38). *Nazirites*, Num 6.1–21. **50–53:** See v. 45n. **54:** *Trumpets*, to summon the army (Num 10.1–10). **55:** In Moses' day such *leaders* assisted in civic administration (Ex 18.25); here, as in the Essene *War Scroll* from Qumran, they have a military function (2 Macc 8.22–23). **56:** Deut 20.5–8. **58–60:** See were about to be married, or were planting a vineyard, or were fainthearted, he told to go home again, according to the law. [57] Then the army marched out and encamped to the south of Emmaus.

[58] And Judas said, "Arm yourselves and be courageous. Be ready early in the morning to fight with these Gentiles who have assembled against us to destroy us and our sanctuary. [59] It is better for us to die in battle than to see the misfortunes of our nation and of the sanctuary. [60] But as his will in heaven may be, so shall he do."

4 Now Gorgias took five thousand infantry and one thousand picked cavalry, and this division moved out by night [2] to fall upon the camp of the Jews and attack them suddenly. Men from the citadel were his guides. [3] But Judas heard of it, and he and his warriors moved out to attack the king's force in Emmaus [4] while the division was still absent from the camp. [5] When Gorgias entered the camp of Judas by night, he found no one there, so he looked for them in the hills, because he said, "These men are running away from us."

[6] At daybreak Judas appeared in the plain with three thousand men, but they did not have armor and swords such as they desired. [7] And they saw the camp of the Gentiles, strong and fortified, with cavalry all around it; and these men were trained in war. [8] But Judas said to those who were with him, "Do not fear their numbers or be afraid when they charge. [9] Remember how our ancestors were saved at the Red Sea, when Pharaoh with his forces pursued them. [10] And now, let us cry to Heaven, to see whether he will favor us and remember his covenant with our ancestors and crush this army before us today. [11] Then all the Gentiles will know that there is one who redeems and saves Israel."

[12] When the foreigners looked up and saw them coming against them, [13] they went out from their camp to battle. Then the men with Judas blew their trumpets [14] and engaged in battle. The Gentiles were crushed, and fled into the plain, [15] and all those in the rear fell by the sword. They pursued them to Gazara, and to the plains of Idumea, and to Azotus and Jamnia; and three thousand of them fell. [16] Then Judas and his force turned back from pursuing them, [17] and he said to the people, "Do not be greedy for plunder, for there is a battle before us; [18] Gorgias and his force are near us in the hills. But stand now against our enemies and fight them, and afterward seize the plunder boldly."

[19] Just as Judas was finishing this speech, a detachment appeared, coming out of the hills. [20] They saw that their army[a] had been put to flight, and that the Jews[a] were burning the camp, for the smoke that was seen showed what had happened. [21] When they perceived this, they were greatly frightened, and when they also saw the army of Judas drawn up in the plain for battle, [22] they all fled into the land of the Philistines. [23] Then Judas returned to plunder the camp, and they seized a great amount of gold and silver, and cloth dyed blue and sea purple, and great riches. [24] On their return they sang hymns and praises to Heaven—"For he is good, for his mercy endures forever." [25] Thus Israel had a great deliverance that day.

[26] Those of the foreigners who escaped went and reported to Lysias all that had happened. [27] When he heard it, he was perplexed and discouraged, for things had not happened to Israel as he had intended, nor had they turned out as the king had ordered. [28] But the next year he mustered sixty thousand picked infantry and five thou-

*a* Gk *they*

---

2 Sam 10.12. **4.2:** *Men from the citadel,* Jewish refugees opposed to Judas. **9:** Ex 14.21–29. **15:** The pursuit went in all directions. *Gazara,* or Gezer (Josh 21.21; 1 Kings 9.17), was 8 km (5 mi) west of Emmaus. *Idumea* was far to the south. *Azotus,* or Ashdod, and *Jamnia* lay on the coast to the west and southwest. **17–18:** Judas maintained discipline (2 Macc 8.26). **19:** *The hills,* the Judean highland. **24:** *Heaven,* see 3.18n. See Ps 118.1; 136.1. **26–35:** The account in 2 Macc 11.1–12 puts the rout of Lysias after the death of Timothy. **28:** *The next year,* perhaps as late as autumn, 164 BCE. **29:** *Beth-zur,* about

sand cavalry to subdue them. 29 They came into Idumea and encamped at Beth-zur, and Judas met them with ten thousand men.

30 When he saw that their army was strong, he prayed, saying, "Blessed are you, O Savior of Israel, who crushed the attack of the mighty warrior by the hand of your servant David, and gave the camp of the Philistines into the hands of Jonathan son of Saul, and of the man who carried his armor. 31 Hem in this army by the hand of your people Israel, and let them be ashamed of their troops and their cavalry. 32 Fill them with cowardice; melt the boldness of their strength; let them tremble in their destruction. 33 Strike them down with the sword of those who love you, and let all who know your name praise you with hymns."

34 Then both sides attacked, and there fell of the army of Lysias five thousand men; they fell in action.ᵃ 35 When Lysias saw the rout of his troops and observed the boldness that inspired those of Judas, and how ready they were either to live or to die nobly, he withdrew to Antioch and enlisted mercenaries in order to invade Judea again with an even larger army.

36 Then Judas and his brothers said, "See, our enemies are crushed; let us go up to cleanse the sanctuary and dedicate it." 37 So all the army assembled and went up to Mount Zion. 38 There they saw the sanctuary desolate, the altar profaned, and the gates burned. In the courts they saw bushes sprung up as in a thicket, or as on one of the mountains. They saw also the chambers of the priests in ruins. 39 Then they tore their clothes and mourned with great lamentation; they sprinkled themselves with ashes 40 and fell face down on the ground. And when the signal was given with the trumpets, they cried out to Heaven.

41 Then Judas detailed men to fight against those in the citadel until he had cleansed the sanctuary. 42 He chose blameless priests devoted to the law, 43 and they cleansed the sanctuary and removed the defiled stones to an unclean place. 44 They deliberated what to do about the altar of burnt offering, which had been profaned. 45 And they thought it best to tear it down, so that it would not be a lasting shame to them that the Gentiles had defiled it. So they tore down the altar, 46 and stored the stones in a convenient place on the temple hill until a prophet should come to tell what to do with them. 47 Then they took unhewnᵇ stones, as the law directs, and built a new altar like the former one. 48 They also rebuilt the sanctuary and the interior of the temple, and consecrated the courts. 49 They made new holy vessels, and brought the lampstand, the altar of incense, and the table into the temple. 50 Then they offered incense on the altar and lit the lamps on the lampstand, and these gave light in the temple. 51 They placed the bread on the table and hung up the curtains. Thus they finished all the work they had undertaken.

52 Early in the morning on the twenty-fifth day of the ninth month, which is the

a Or and some fell on the opposite side    b Gk whole

25 km (16 mi) south-southeast of Jerusalem on the road to Hebron. Lysias decided to attack Jerusalem from the south. **30–33:** Judas's prayer, which begins as a blessing, is an early example of what becomes a standard form of Jewish prayer. It echoes David's prayer in 1 Chr 29.10. *The mighty warrior,* Goliath (1 Sam 17); *Jonathan . . . the man who carried his armor* (1 Sam 14). **34–35:** The account in 2 Macc 11.6–15 agrees that Judas won the battle, but states that there was a negotiated peace.

**4.36–61: Rededication of the Temple. 38:** *Chambers of the priests* perhaps surrounded the sanctuary on three sides. **41:** *The citadel,* see 1.33n. **46:** The expectation of an authoritative *prophet* who would herald God's intervention was based on Deut 18.18 and Mal 4.5; this was an important belief among some Jewish groups during the Second Temple period. **47:** Ex 20.25; Deut 27.5–6. **49:** The Temple equipment that Antiochus IV had plundered (1 Macc 1.21–24) is properly replaced (Ex 25.27). **50:** *Offered incense . . . lit the lamps,* Ex 30.7–8. **51:** *The bread,* of the Presence, see 1.22n. *Thus they finished,* the words echo Moses' completion of the tabernacle in the wilderness, Ex 40.33. **52–59:** Judas month of Chislev, in the one hundred forty-eighth year,[a] 53 they rose and offered sacrifice, as the law directs, on the new altar of burnt offering that they had built. 54 At the very season and on the very day that the Gentiles had profaned it, it was dedicated with songs and harps and lutes and cymbals. 55 All the people fell on their faces and worshiped and blessed Heaven, who had prospered them. 56 So they celebrated the dedication of the altar for eight days, and joyfully offered burnt offerings; they offered a sacrifice of well-being and a thanksgiving offering. 57 They decorated the front of the temple with golden crowns and small shields; they restored the gates and the chambers for the priests, and fitted them with doors. 58 There was very great joy among the people, and the disgrace brought by the Gentiles was removed.

59 Then Judas and his brothers and all the assembly of Israel determined that every year at that season the days of dedication of the altar should be observed with joy and gladness for eight days, beginning with the twenty-fifth day of the month of Chislev.

60 At that time they fortified Mount Zion with high walls and strong towers all around, to keep the Gentiles from coming and trampling them down as they had done before. 61 Judas[b] stationed a garrison there to guard it; he also fortified Beth-zur to guard it, so that the people might have a stronghold that faced Idumea.

5 When the Gentiles all around heard that the altar had been rebuilt and the sanctuary dedicated as it was before, they became very angry, 2 and they determined to destroy the descendants of Jacob who lived among them. So they began to kill and destroy among the people. 3 But Judas made war on the descendants of Esau in Idumea, at Akrabattene, because they kept lying in wait for Israel. He dealt them a heavy blow and humbled them and despoiled them. 4 He also remembered the wickedness of the sons of Baean, who were a trap and a snare to the people and ambushed them on the highways. 5 They were shut up by him in their[c] towers; and he encamped against them, vowed their complete destruction, and burned with fire their towers and all who were in them. 6 Then he crossed over to attack the Ammonites, where he found a strong band and many people, with Timothy as their leader. 7 He engaged in many battles with them, and they were crushed before him; he struck them down. 8 He also took Jazer and its villages; then he returned to Judea.

9 Now the Gentiles in Gilead gathered together against the Israelites who lived in their territory, and planned to destroy them. But they fled to the stronghold of Dathema, 10 and sent to Judas and his brothers a letter that said, "The Gentiles around us have gathered together to destroy us. 11 They are preparing to come and capture the stronghold to which we have fled, and Timothy is leading their forces. 12 Now then, come and rescue us from their hands, for many of us have fallen, 13 and all our kindred who were in the land of Tob

a 164 B.C.    b Gk He    c Gk her

set the rededication of the Temple exactly three years after its pollution (1.54) and three and a half years after Antiochus's capture of Jerusalem (Dan 7.25; but see 2 Macc 10.3). The Hanukkah ("dedication") festival, celebrated *for eight days* like Solomon's dedication of the first Temple (1 Kings 8.65–66) and Hezekiah's reconsecration (2 Chr 29.17), commemorates this event.

**5.1–68: Judas gathers Jews into Judea.** Judas now attacked Idumea in the south (vv. 3–5,65), Ammon and Gilead east of the Jordan (vv. 6–13,24–51), Galilee in the north (vv. 21–23), and the coastal plain (see Map, p. 208 AP). These events may have occurred after the death of Antiochus IV (6.16). **2:** *Descendants of Jacob,* Israelites or Jews. **3:** *Descendants of Esau,* Edomites or Idumeans, south of the Dead Sea. *Akrabattene,* perhaps on the border between Idumea and Judea. **4:** *Baean,* probably in Transjordan (Num 32.3). **6:** *Ammonites,* a Semitic people east of the Jordan near modern Amman. **8:** *Jazer,* probably located west of Amman (Num 32.3). **9:** *Gilead,* a general term for the region east of the Jordan River (Josh 22.9). *Dathema,* identification uncertain. **13:** *Land of Tob,* identification uncertain; see Judg 11.3; 2 Macc have been killed; the enemy[a] have captured their wives and children and goods, and have destroyed about a thousand persons there."

14 While the letter was still being read, other messengers, with their garments torn, came from Galilee and made a similar report; 15 they said that the people of Ptolemais and Tyre and Sidon, and all Galilee of the Gentiles,[b] had gathered together against them "to annihilate us." 16 When Judas and the people heard these messages, a great assembly was called to determine what they should do for their kindred who were in distress and were being attacked by enemies.[c] 17 Then Judas said to his brother Simon, "Choose your men and go and rescue your kindred in Galilee; Jonathan my brother and I will go to Gilead." 18 But he left Joseph, son of Zechariah, and Azariah, a leader of the people, with the rest of the forces, in Judea to guard it; 19 and he gave them this command, "Take charge of this people, but do not engage in battle with the Gentiles until we return." 20 Then three thousand men were assigned to Simon to go to Galilee, and eight thousand to Judas for Gilead.

21 So Simon went to Galilee and fought many battles against the Gentiles, and the Gentiles were crushed before him. 22 He pursued them to the gate of Ptolemais; as many as three thousand of the Gentiles fell, and he despoiled them. 23 Then he took the Jews[d] of Galilee and Arbatta, with their wives and children, and all they possessed, and led them to Judea with great rejoicing.

24 Judas Maccabeus and his brother Jonathan crossed the Jordan and made three days' journey into the wilderness. 25 They encountered the Nabateans, who met them peaceably and told them all that had happened to their kindred in Gilead:

26 "Many of them have been shut up in Bozrah and Bosor, in Alema and Chaspho, Maked and Carnaim"—all these towns were strong and large— 27 "and some have been shut up in the other towns of Gilead; the enemy[a] are getting ready to attack the strongholds tomorrow and capture and destroy all these people in a single day."

28 Then Judas and his army quickly turned back by the wilderness road to Bozrah; and he took the town, and killed every male by the edge of the sword; then he seized all its spoils and burned it with fire. 29 He left the place at night, and they went all the way to the stronghold of Dathema.[e] 30 At dawn they looked out and saw a large company, which could not be counted, carrying ladders and engines of war to capture the stronghold, and attacking the Jews within.[f] 31 So Judas saw that the battle had begun and that the cry of the town went up to Heaven, with trumpets and loud shouts, 32 and he said to the men of his forces, "Fight today for your kindred!" 33 Then he came up behind them in three companies, who sounded their trumpets and cried aloud in prayer. 34 And when the army of Timothy realized that it was Maccabeus, they fled before him, and he dealt them a heavy blow. As many as eight thousand of them fell that day.

35 Next he turned aside to Maapha,[g] and fought against it and took it; and he killed every male in it, plundered it, and burned it with fire. 36 From there he marched on and took Chaspho, Maked, and Bosor, and the other towns of Gilead.

37 After these things Timothy gathered another army and encamped opposite Ra-

a Gk they   b Gk aliens   c Gk them   d Gk those
e Gk lacks of Dathema. See verse 9   f Gk and they were attacking them   g Other ancient authorities read Alema

12.17. 15: Ptolemais, or Acco (Judg 1.31), north of Haifa on the Mediterranean coast. Tyre and Sidon, farther north in Lebanon. Galilee of the Gentiles, despite a considerable Jewish population, was so called because of the number of Hellenistic cities located there, especially on its borders; see Isa 9.1; Mt 4.15. 23: Arbatta, occurring only here, its location is uncertain. 25: Nabateans, with their capital at Petra, controlled major trade routes in Transjordan. 26: Bozrah, a city in Gilead ca. 105 km (65 mi) south of Damascus. Bosor in Alema (see Deut 4.43), Chaspho, Maked, and Carnaim are also cities in Gilead (v. 36). 35: Maapha, the text is uncertain. 43: Sacred precincts, of Atargatis, a Syrian goddess (2 Macc phon, on the other side of the stream. [38] Judas sent men to spy out the camp, and they reported to him, "All the Gentiles around us have gathered to him; it is a very large force. [39] They also have hired Arabs to help them, and they are encamped across the stream, ready to come and fight against you." And Judas went to meet them.

40 Now as Judas and his army drew near to the stream of water, Timothy said to the officers of his forces, "If he crosses over to us first, we will not be able to resist him, for he will surely defeat us. [41] But if he shows fear and camps on the other side of the river, we will cross over to him and defeat him." [42] When Judas approached the stream of water, he stationed the officers[a] of the army at the stream and gave them this command, "Permit no one to encamp, but make them all enter the battle." [43] Then he crossed over against them first, and the whole army followed him. All the Gentiles were defeated before him, and they threw away their arms and fled into the sacred precincts at Carnaim. [44] But he took the town and burned the sacred precincts with fire, together with all who were in them. Thus Carnaim was conquered; they could stand before Judas no longer.

45 Then Judas gathered together all the Israelites in Gilead, the small and the great, with their wives and children and goods, a very large company, to go to the land of Judah. [46] So they came to Ephron. This was a large and very strong town on the road, and they could not go around it to the right or to the left; they had to go through it. [47] But the people of the town shut them out and blocked up the gates with stones. [48] Judas sent them this friendly message, "Let us pass through your land to get to our land. No one will do you harm; we will simply pass by on foot." But they refused to open to him. [49] Then Judas ordered proclamation to be made to the army that all should encamp where they were. [50] So the men of the forces encamped, and he fought against the town all that day and all the night, and the town was delivered into his hands. [51] He destroyed every male by the edge of the sword, and razed and plundered the town. Then he passed through the town over the bodies of the dead.

52 Then they crossed the Jordan into the large plain before Beth-shan. [53] Judas kept rallying the laggards and encouraging the people all the way until he came to the land of Judah. [54] So they went up to Mount Zion with joy and gladness, and offered burnt offerings, because they had returned in safety; not one of them had fallen.

55 Now while Judas and Jonathan were in Gilead and their[b] brother Simon was in Galilee before Ptolemais, [56] Joseph son of Zechariah, and Azariah, the commanders of the forces, heard of their brave deeds and of the heroic war they had fought. [57] So they said, "Let us also make a name for ourselves; let us go and make war on the Gentiles around us." [58] So they issued orders to the men of the forces that were with them and marched against Jamnia. [59] Gorgias and his men came out of the town to meet them in battle. [60] Then Joseph and Azariah were routed, and were pursued to the borders of Judea; as many as two thousand of the people of Israel fell that day. [61] Thus the people suffered a great rout because, thinking to do a brave deed, they did not listen to Judas and his brothers. [62] But they did not belong to the family of those men through whom deliverance was given to Israel.

63 The man Judas and his brothers were greatly honored in all Israel and among all the Gentiles, wherever their name was heard. [64] People gathered to them and praised them.

*a Or scribes   b Gk his*

12.26). **45–54:** Judas brings Jews of Gilead to Judah. **46:** *Ephron,* 13 km (8 mi) east of the Jordan, opposite Beth-shan (v. 52). **48:** Num 21.21–24. **52:** *The large plain,* between the Jordan and Mt. Gilboa. *Beth-shan,* also called Scythopolis (2 Macc 12.29), about 26 km (16 mi) south of the Sea of Galilee. **58:** *Jamnia,* a city on the coastal plain, north of Azotus (2 Macc 12.8–9). **62:** Only *the family* of the Hasmoneans is regarded as divinely chosen to save Israel. **65:** *Descendants of Esau,* see v. 3n. *Hebron,*

65 Then Judas and his brothers went out and fought the descendants of Esau in the land to the south. He struck Hebron and its villages and tore down its strongholds and burned its towers on all sides. 66 Then he marched off to go into the land of the Philistines, and passed through Marisa.[a] 67 On that day some priests, who wished to do a brave deed, fell in battle, for they went out to battle unwisely. 68 But Judas turned aside to Azotus in the land of the Philistines; he tore down their altars, and the carved images of their gods he burned with fire; he plundered the towns and returned to the land of Judah.

6 King Antiochus was going through the upper provinces when he heard that Elymais in Persia was a city famed for its wealth in silver and gold. 2 Its temple was very rich, containing golden shields, breastplates, and weapons left there by Alexander son of Philip, the Macedonian king who first reigned over the Greeks. 3 So he came and tried to take the city and plunder it, but he could not because his plan had become known to the citizens 4 and they withstood him in battle. So he fled and in great disappointment left there to return to Babylon.

5 Then someone came to him in Persia and reported that the armies that had gone into the land of Judah had been routed; 6 that Lysias had gone first with a strong force, but had turned and fled before the Jews;[b] that the Jews[c] had grown strong from the arms, supplies, and abundant spoils that they had taken from the armies they had cut down; 7 that they had torn down the abomination that he had erected on the altar in Jerusalem; and that they had surrounded the sanctuary with high walls as before, and also Beth-zur, his town.

8 When the king heard this news, he was astounded and badly shaken. He took to his bed and became sick from disappointment, because things had not turned out for him as he had planned. 9 He lay there for many days, because deep disappointment continually gripped him, and he realized that he was dying. 10 So he called all his Friends and said to them, "Sleep has departed from my eyes and I am downhearted with worry. 11 I said to myself, 'To what distress I have come! And into what a great flood I now am plunged! For I was kind and beloved in my power.' 12 But now I remember the wrong I did in Jerusalem. I seized all its vessels of silver and gold, and I sent to destroy the inhabitants of Judah without good reason. 13 I know that it is because of this that these misfortunes have come upon me; here I am, perishing of bitter disappointment in a strange land."

14 Then he called for Philip, one of his Friends, and made him ruler over all his kingdom. 15 He gave him the crown and his robe and the signet, so that he might guide his son Antiochus and bring him up to be king. 16 Thus King Antiochus died there in the one hundred forty-ninth year.[d] 17 When Lysias learned that the king was dead, he set up Antiochus the king's[e] son

a Other ancient authorities read *Samaria*  b Gk *them*  c Gk *they*  d 163 B.C.  e Gk *his*

the original capital of David, 31 km (20 mi) south of Jerusalem (Gen 23.2; 2 Sam 2.11). **66:** *Marisa,* earlier Mareshah, in the hills 29 km (18 mi) southeast of Azotus. **68:** Judas's actions are described in the language of Deut 7.5 and 12.3.

**6.1–17: Death of Antiochus IV and accession of Antiochus V** (2 Macc 9). **1:** *The upper provinces,* Persia and Mesopotamia (3.31–37). *Elymais,* earlier Elam; according to 2 Macc 9.2 the incident occurred in the city of Persepolis. **2:** *Its temple* was that of Nanea (2 Macc 1.13–16), identified with the Greek goddess Artemis. **5:** *In Persia,* perhaps at Ecbatana (2 Macc 9.3). According to Polybius (*History* 31.11) the king took sick and died at Tabae (perhaps Gabae, modern Isfahan). **7:** *The abomination,* statue of a pagan god; see 1.54n. **8–9:** *Deep disappointment,* perhaps insanity; according to 2 Macc 9.5–12 he was stricken with a loathsome physical malady. **10:** *Friends,* i.e., those courtiers holding the rank of Friends of the king (2.18). **12:** *Its vessels,* Dan 5.2. **14–15:** *Philip . . . ruler,* Lysias, satrap in the west, had previously been given this commission (3.32). Consequently, Philip and Lysias became rivals (6.55–56). *The signet,* a symbol of transfer of authority to the regent. **16:** 2 Macc 11.33 implies that Antiochus IV to reign. Lysias[a] had brought him up from boyhood; he named him Eupator.

18 Meanwhile the garrison in the citadel kept hemming Israel in around the sanctuary. They were trying in every way to harm them and strengthen the Gentiles. 19 Judas therefore resolved to destroy them, and assembled all the people to besiege them. 20 They gathered together and besieged the citadel[b] in the one hundred fiftieth year;[c] and he built siege towers and other engines of war. 21 But some of the garrison escaped from the siege and some of the ungodly Israelites joined them. 22 They went to the king and said, "How long will you fail to do justice and to avenge our kindred? 23 We were happy to serve your father, to live by what he said, and to follow his commands. 24 For this reason the sons of our people besieged the citadel[d] and became hostile to us; moreover, they have put to death as many of us as they have caught, and they have seized our inheritances. 25 It is not against us alone that they have stretched out their hands; they have also attacked all the lands on their borders. 26 And see, today they have encamped against the citadel in Jerusalem to take it; they have fortified both the sanctuary and Beth-zur; 27 unless you quickly prevent them, they will do still greater things, and you will not be able to stop them."

28 The king was enraged when he heard this. He assembled all his Friends, the commanders of his forces and those in authority.[e] 29 Mercenary forces also came to him from other kingdoms and from islands of the seas. 30 The number of his forces was one hundred thousand foot soldiers, twenty thousand horsemen, and thirty-two elephants accustomed to war. 31 They came through Idumea and encamped against Beth-zur, and for many days they fought and built engines of war; but the Jews[f] sallied out and burned these with fire, and fought courageously.

32 Then Judas marched away from the citadel and encamped at Beth-zechariah, opposite the camp of the king. 33 Early in the morning the king set out and took his army by a forced march along the road to Beth-zechariah, and his troops made ready for battle and sounded their trumpets. 34 They offered the elephants the juice of grapes and mulberries, to arouse them for battle. 35 They distributed the animals among the phalanxes; with each elephant they stationed a thousand men armed with coats of mail, and with brass helmets on their heads; and five hundred picked horsemen were assigned to each beast. 36 These took their position beforehand wherever the animal was; wherever it went, they went with it, and they never left it. 37 On the elephants[g] were wooden towers, strong and covered; they were fastened on each animal by special harness, and on each were four[h] armed men who fought from there, and also its Indian driver. 38 The rest of the cavalry were stationed on either side, on the two flanks of the army, to harass the enemy while being themselves protected by the phalanxes. 39 When the sun shone on the shields of gold and brass, the hills were

a Gk He  b Gk it  c 162 B.C.  d Meaning of Gk uncertain  e Gk those over the reins  f Gk they  g Gk them  h Cn: Some authorities read thirty; others thirty-two

had died before the restoration of the Temple at Jerusalem. **17:** The word *Eupator* means "of a good father." Antiochus V ruled 164–162 BCE.

**6.18–54: Attack on the citadel and second battle at Beth-zur.** The citadel was equally important to the Syrians and to Judas, for without it the Seleucid monarchy could not maintain sovereignty in Jerusalem. **21:** *Ungodly,* i.e., pro-Greek. **28–30:** Lysias's second campaign is here dated 162 BCE (v. 20), but in 2 Macc 13.1 a year earlier. **31:** Judas had won the first battle at *Beth-zur* (4.29–34) and had fortified it (4.61). **32:** *Beth-zechariah* was 10 km (6 mi) north of Beth-zur and 16 km (10 mi) southwest of Jerusalem. **34–35:** *The juice* may have been to simulate blood; but *elephants* were sometimes given wine to madden them (see 3 Macc 5). Here the animals were used to force an opening in the ranks. *Phalanxes,* the Greek infantry formation, eight to eighteen men deep, highly disciplined and mobile. The Seleucids could muster 20,000 of such infantry. **43:** *Eleazar,* brother of Judas (2.5). **48:** *Mount Zion,* south of the ablaze with them and gleamed like flaming torches.

40 Now a part of the king's army was spread out on the high hills, and some troops were on the plain, and they advanced steadily and in good order. 41 All who heard the noise made by their multitude, by the marching of the multitude and the clanking of their arms, trembled, for the army was very large and strong. 42 But Judas and his army advanced to the battle, and six hundred of the king's army fell. 43 Now Eleazar, called Avaran, saw that one of the animals was equipped with royal armor. It was taller than all the others, and he supposed that the king was on it. 44 So he gave his life to save his people and to win for himself an everlasting name. 45 He courageously ran into the midst of the phalanx to reach it; he killed men right and left, and they parted before him on both sides. 46 He got under the elephant, stabbed it from beneath, and killed it; but it fell to the ground upon him and he died. 47 When the Jews[a] saw the royal might and the fierce attack of the forces, they turned away in flight.

48 The soldiers of the king's army went up to Jerusalem against them, and the king encamped in Judea and at Mount Zion. 49 He made peace with the people of Bethzur, and they evacuated the town because they had no provisions there to withstand a siege, since it was a sabbatical year for the land. 50 So the king took Beth-zur and stationed a guard there to hold it. 51 Then he encamped before the sanctuary for many days. He set up siege towers, engines of war to throw fire and stones, machines to shoot arrows, and catapults. 52 The Jews[a] also made engines of war to match theirs, and fought for many days. 53 But they had no food in storage,[b] because it was the seventh year; those who had found safety in Judea from the Gentiles had consumed the last of the stores. 54 Only a few men were left in the sanctuary; the rest scattered to their own homes, for the famine proved too much for them.

55 Then Lysias heard that Philip, whom King Antiochus while still living had appointed to bring up his son Antiochus to be king, 56 had returned from Persia and Media with the forces that had gone with the king, and that he was trying to seize control of the government. 57 So he quickly gave orders to withdraw, and said to the king, to the commanders of the forces, and to the troops, "Daily we grow weaker, our food supply is scant, the place against which we are fighting is strong, and the affairs of the kingdom press urgently on us. 58 Now then let us come to terms with these people, and make peace with them and with all their nation. 59 Let us agree to let them live by their laws as they did before; for it was on account of their laws that we abolished that they became angry and did all these things."

60 The speech pleased the king and the commanders, and he sent to the Jews[c] an offer of peace, and they accepted it. 61 So the king and the commanders gave them their oath. On these conditions the Jews[a] evacuated the stronghold. 62 But when the king entered Mount Zion and saw what a strong fortress the place was, he broke the oath he had sworn and gave orders to tear down the wall all around. 63 Then he set off

a Gk they     b Other ancient authorities read in the sanctuary     c Gk them

Temple (1.33). **49:** The garrison was promised immunity if it surrendered. Every seventh year the land had to lie fallow (Ex 23.11; Lev 25.3–7). This *sabbatical year* was apparently 162 (v. 20) or possibly a year earlier.

**6.55–63: Lysias makes peace.** The return of Philip caused a diversion; Lysias abandoned the siege and restored Jewish religious rights. **55:** *Philip* had received the symbols of sovereignty (v. 15), though Antiochus IV had previously appointed Lysias. **59:** In effect Lysias rescinds the decree of Antiochus IV (1.41–50). Judea had generally accepted Seleucid rule until Antiochus IV began his persecution, though there was always a faction engaged in intrigue with Egypt. **62:** Judas had also built a citadel on Mount Zion; its wall was now destroyed.

in haste and returned to Antioch. He found Philip in control of the city, but he fought against him, and took the city by force.

7 In the one hundred fifty-first year*a* Demetrius son of Seleucus set out from Rome, sailed with a few men to a town by the sea, and there began to reign. 2 As he was entering the royal palace of his ancestors, the army seized Antiochus and Lysias to bring them to him. 3 But when this act became known to him, he said, "Do not let me see their faces!" 4 So the army killed them, and Demetrius took his seat on the throne of his kingdom.

5 Then there came to him all the renegade and godless men of Israel; they were led by Alcimus, who wanted to be high priest. 6 They brought to the king this accusation against the people: "Judas and his brothers have destroyed all your Friends, and have driven us out of our land. 7 Now then send a man whom you trust; let him go and see all the ruin that Judas*b* has brought on us and on the land of the king, and let him punish them and all who help them."

8 So the king chose Bacchides, one of the king's Friends, governor of the province Beyond the River; he was a great man in the kingdom and was faithful to the king. 9 He sent him, and with him he sent the ungodly Alcimus, whom he made high priest; and he commanded him to take vengeance on the Israelites. 10 So they marched away and came with a large force into the land of Judah; and he sent messengers to Judas and his brothers with peaceable but treacherous words. 11 But they paid no attention to their words, for they saw that they had come with a large force.

12 Then a group of scribes appeared in a body before Alcimus and Bacchides to ask for just terms. 13 The Hasideans were first among the Israelites to seek peace from them, 14 for they said, "A priest of the line of Aaron has come with the army, and he will not harm us." 15 Alcimus*c* spoke peaceable words to them and swore this oath to them, "We will not seek to injure you or your friends." 16 So they trusted him; but he seized sixty of them and killed them in one day, in accordance with the word that was written,

17 "The flesh of your faithful ones and
    their blood
  they poured out all around
    Jerusalem,
  and there was no one to bury
    them."

18 Then the fear and dread of them fell on

*a* 161 B.C.   *b* Gk he   *c* Gk He

**7.1–4: Demetrius I becomes king** (2 Macc 14.1–2). **1:** *Demetrius* I Soter (reigned 162–150 BCE) was *son of Seleucus* IV Philopator, elder brother of Antiochus IV. When Rome demanded hostages (1.10), Antiochus IV was sent to Rome; later, when Seleucus became king, his son Demetrius replaced Antiochus as a hostage. On Antiochus's death, Demetrius unsuccessfully petitioned the senate to be released. Subsequently he escaped from Rome with a small group of men and landed in Tripolis, *a town by the sea* (2 Macc 14.1). **2:** *Antiochus*, that is, Antiochus V Eupator (6.17). **3:** *Do not let me see their faces*, a signal for the murder.

**7.5–25: Alcimus as high priest.** Legitimate high priests were descended from a particular family. Antiochus IV appointed Jason in place of his brother Onias III (2 Macc 4.7); Jason was in turn supplanted by Menelaus (2 Macc 4.23–26), who was put to death about 162 BCE, after having officiated for ten years (2 Macc 13.1–8). Either Onias III or his son Onias IV, the last legitimate claimant, fled to Egypt and established a temple in Heliopolis (near Cairo). *Alcimus* (v. 5), or Jakim (2 Macc 14.3), claimed to be a member of the high-priestly family, but he belonged to the pro-Seleucid faction and was willing to further Demetrius's plans. Whether he supported the cultural Hellenizers is less clear. **8:** *Beyond the River*, the province west of the Euphrates (Ezra 4.11). **12–14:** *The Hasideans* (see 2.42n.), probably the same as the *group of scribes*, had no political ambitions and were content to live under Syrian rule if they were permitted to keep the law of Moses. **17:** Ps 79.2–3. Many ancient peoples regarded an unburied dead body with horror, and leaving foes unburied was a way of showing contempt or committing a further outrage upon them. **19:** *Beth-zaith*, 19 km (12 mi) southeast of Jerusalem.

all the people, for they said, "There is no truth or justice in them, for they have violated the agreement and the oath that they swore."

19 Then Bacchides withdrew from Jerusalem and encamped in Beth-zaith. And he sent and seized many of the men who had deserted to him,[a] and some of the people, and killed them and threw them into a great pit. 20 He placed Alcimus in charge of the country and left with him a force to help him; then Bacchides went back to the king.

21 Alcimus struggled to maintain his high priesthood, 22 and all who were troubling their people joined him. They gained control of the land of Judah and did great damage in Israel. 23 And Judas saw all the wrongs that Alcimus and those with him had done among the Israelites; it was more than the Gentiles had done. 24 So Judas[b] went out into all the surrounding parts of Judea, taking vengeance on those who had deserted and preventing those in the city[c] from going out into the country. 25 When Alcimus saw that Judas and those with him had grown strong, and realized that he could not withstand them, he returned to the king and brought malicious charges against them.

26 Then the king sent Nicanor, one of his honored princes, who hated and detested Israel, and he commanded him to destroy the people. 27 So Nicanor came to Jerusalem with a large force, and treacherously sent to Judas and his brothers this peaceable message, 28 "Let there be no fighting between you and me; I shall come with a few men to see you face to face in peace."

29 So he came to Judas, and they greeted one another peaceably; but the enemy were preparing to kidnap Judas. 30 It became known to Judas that Nicanor[b] had come to him with treacherous intent, and he was afraid of him and would not meet him again. 31 When Nicanor learned that his plan had been disclosed, he went out to meet Judas in battle near Caphar-salama. 32 About five hundred of the army of Nicanor fell, and the rest[d] fled into the city of David.

33 After these events Nicanor went up to Mount Zion. Some of the priests from the sanctuary and some of the elders of the people came out to greet him peaceably and to show him the burnt offering that was being offered for the king. 34 But he mocked them and derided them and defiled them and spoke arrogantly, 35 and in anger he swore this oath, "Unless Judas and his army are delivered into my hands this time, then if I return safely I will burn up this house." And he went out in great anger. 36 At this the priests went in and stood before the altar and the temple; they wept and said,

37 "You chose this house to be called by
　　　your name,
　　and to be for your people a house
　　　of prayer and supplication.
38 Take vengeance on this man and on
　　　his army,
　　and let them fall by the sword;
　　remember their blasphemies,
　　and let them live no longer."

39 Now Nicanor went out from Jerusalem and encamped in Beth-horon, and the Syrian army joined him. 40 Judas encamped in Adasa with three thousand men. Then Judas prayed and said, 41 "When the messengers from the king spoke blasphemy, your angel went out and struck down one hundred eighty-five thousand of the Assyrians.[e] 42 So also crush this army before us today; let the rest learn that Nicanor[b] has

a Or *many of his men who had deserted*　b Gk *he*　c Gk *and they were prevented*　d Gk *they*　e Gk *of them*

7.26–50: **Defeat of Nicanor.** The last of Judas's great victories (2 Macc 14.12–15.36); see Map 10. **26:** According to Josephus (*Ant.* 12.10.4), *Nicanor* was one of the men who had escaped from Rome with Demetrius (see 7.1n.). **31:** *Caphar-salama*, perhaps Khirbet Deir Sellam, about 8 km (5 mi) north of Jerusalem. **33:** Prayers and sacrifices for rulers are also presumed in Ezra 6.10. **37–38:** Compare 1 Kings 8.29,43. **40:** *Adasa*, about 11 km (7 mi) from Beth-horon on the road to Jerusalem. **41:** 2 Kings 19.35.

spoken wickedly against the sanctuary, and judge him according to this wickedness."

43 So the armies met in battle on the thirteenth day of the month of Adar. The army of Nicanor was crushed, and he himself was the first to fall in the battle. 44 When his army saw that Nicanor had fallen, they threw down their arms and fled. 45 The Jews[a] pursued them a day's journey, from Adasa as far as Gazara, and as they followed they kept sounding the battle call on the trumpets. 46 People came out of all the surrounding villages of Judea, and they outflanked the enemy[b] and drove them back to their pursuers,[c] so that they all fell by the sword; not even one of them was left. 47 Then the Jews[a] seized the spoils and the plunder; they cut off Nicanor's head and the right hand that he had so arrogantly stretched out, and brought them and displayed them just outside Jerusalem. 48 The people rejoiced greatly and celebrated that day as a day of great gladness. 49 They decreed that this day should be celebrated each year on the thirteenth day of Adar. 50 So the land of Judah had rest for a few days.

8 Now Judas heard of the fame of the Romans, that they were very strong and were well-disposed toward all who made an alliance with them, that they pledged friendship to those who came to them, 2 and that they were very strong. He had been told of their wars and of the brave deeds that they were doing among the Gauls, how they had defeated them and forced them to pay tribute, 3 and what they had done in the land of Spain to get control of the silver and gold mines there, 4 and how they had gained control of the whole region by their planning and patience, even though the place was far distant from them. They also subdued the kings who came against them from the ends of the earth, until they crushed them and inflicted great disaster on them; the rest paid them tribute every year. 5 They had crushed in battle and conquered Philip, and King Perseus of the Macedonians,[d] and the others who rose up against them. 6 They also had defeated Antiochus the Great, king of Asia, who went to fight against them with one hundred twenty elephants and with cavalry and chariots and a very large army. He was crushed by them; 7 they took him alive and decreed that he and those who would reign after him should pay a heavy tribute and give hostages and surrender some of their best provinces, 8 the countries of India, Media, and Lydia. These they took from him and gave to King Eumenes. 9 The Greeks planned to come and destroy them, 10 but this became known to them, and they sent a general against the Greeks[b] and attacked them. Many of them were wounded and fell, and the Romans[a] took captive their wives and children; they plundered them, conquered the land, tore down their strong-

a Gk they    b Gk them    c Gk these    d Or Kittim

43: *Adar*, roughly March, in 161 BCE (see 2 Macc 15.36). 45: *Gazara*, Gezer (4.15). 47: *Head . . . right hand*, in punishment for blasphemy and for raising his hand against the Temple (2 Macc 15.32). See 1 Sam 17.54; Jdt 14.1,11. 49: 2 Macc 15.36. This festival, which came to be called Nicanor Day, was one of the days on which mourning was prohibited (cf. 13.52). It is no longer observed.

8.1–32: Treaty with Rome. The author of 1 Maccabees emphasizes friendly relations between Rome and the Jews because the Romans checked the ambitions of the Seleucids. After 190 BCE Rome steadily increased its influence in the Near East and Syrian power declined. 1: *The Romans* had made *an alliance* with kings in Asia Minor and Egypt. 2: Two nations of *Gauls* were *defeated*, those of upper Italy in 191, and the Galatians of Asia Minor in 189. 3–4: Rome conquered the Carthaginian colonies of *Spain*, not *the whole region*, in the Second Punic War (218–201). 5: *Philip* V, defeated at Cynosephalae in 197; *Perseus*, his son, the last Macedonian king, beaten at Pydna in 168. 6–8: *Antiochus* III *the Great* (see 1.10n.) was not captured, but had to *give hostages* (7.1). 8: The text contains some errors of fact. Most of *India* was not part of his domain; he kept *Media*, but he surrendered *Lydia* and other parts of Asia Minor. 9–10: *The Greeks*, probably the Achaean league, defeated by the Roman consul Lucius Mummius in 146. 14: *A crown*, Rome had become a republic by the late sixth century BCE, but holders of several holds, and enslaved them to this day. [11] The remaining kingdoms and islands, as many as ever opposed them, they destroyed and enslaved; [12] but with their friends and those who rely on them they have kept friendship. They have subdued kings far and near, and as many as have heard of their fame have feared them. [13] Those whom they wish to help and to make kings, they make kings, and those whom they wish they depose; and they have been greatly exalted. [14] Yet for all this not one of them has put on a crown or worn purple as a mark of pride, [15] but they have built for themselves a senate chamber, and every day three hundred twenty senators constantly deliberate concerning the people, to govern them well. [16] They trust one man each year to rule over them and to control all their land; they all heed the one man, and there is no envy or jealousy among them.

17 So Judas chose Eupolemus son of John son of Accos, and Jason son of Eleazar, and sent them to Rome to establish friendship and alliance, [18] and to free themselves from the yoke; for they saw that the kingdom of the Greeks was enslaving Israel completely. [19] They went to Rome, a very long journey; and they entered the senate chamber and spoke as follows: [20] "Judas, who is also called Maccabeus, and his brothers and the people of the Jews have sent us to you to establish alliance and peace with you, so that we may be enrolled as your allies and friends." [21] The proposal pleased them, [22] and this is a copy of the letter that they wrote in reply, on bronze tablets, and sent to Jerusalem to remain with them there as a memorial of peace and alliance:

23 "May all go well with the Romans and with the nation of the Jews at sea and on land forever, and may sword and enemy be far from them. [24] If war comes first to Rome or to any of their allies in all their dominion, [25] the nation of the Jews shall act as their allies wholeheartedly, as the occasion may indicate to them. [26] To the enemy that makes war they shall not give or supply grain, arms, money, or ships, just as Rome has decided; and they shall keep their obligations without receiving any return. [27] In the same way, if war comes first to the nation of the Jews, the Romans shall willingly act as their allies, as the occasion may indicate to them. [28] And to their enemies there shall not be given grain, arms, money, or ships, just as Rome has decided; and they shall keep these obligations and do so without deceit. [29] Thus on these terms the Romans make a treaty with the Jewish people. [30] If after these terms are in effect both parties shall determine to add or delete anything, they shall do so at their discretion, and any addition or deletion that they may make shall be valid.

31 "Concerning the wrongs that King Demetrius is doing to them, we have written to him as follows, 'Why have you made your yoke heavy on our friends and allies the Jews? [32] If now they appeal again for help against you, we will defend their rights and fight you on sea and on land.'"

9 When Demetrius heard that Nicanor and his army had fallen in battle, he sent Bacchides and Alcimus into the land of

---

offices wore *purple* borders on their garments. **15:** *Every day*, actually senate meetings were held three times a month, and on the festivals. There were about three hundred senators. **16:** *One man*, in reality there were two consuls, and *envy* and *jealousy* were constant. The author idealizes the Romans. **17:** *Eupolemus*, 2 Macc 4.11. *Accos*, a priestly family (1 Chr 24.10; Ezra 2.61). **19:** *A very long journey* emphasizes that this alliance was in accord with the law of Moses; see Deut 20.15; cf. Josh 9.9. **22:** Important documents were often inscribed *on bronze tablets*. **23–30:** The treaty letter begins with the conventional formula and is drawn up as though the two parties were equals, and Judea a sovereign state. **31–32:** This postscript was not part of the treaty, and it is omitted from it by Josephus (*Ant.* 2.10.6); there is no evidence that the Romans helped Judas against Demetrius.

**9.1–22: Death of Judas.** Continual Syrian pressure weakened Judas's forces, which were a guerrilla band facing a highly organized army. Judas decided that it was better to fall in battle than to withdraw. **1:** For the defeat of *Nicanor*, see 7.43–50. *Bacchides*, 7.8. *Alcimus*, see 7.5–25n. **2:** Josephus (*Ant.*

Judah a second time, and with them the right wing of the army. 2 They went by the road that leads to Gilgal and encamped against Mesaloth in Arbela, and they took it and killed many people. 3 In the first month of the one hundred fifty-second year*a* they encamped against Jerusalem; 4 then they marched off and went to Berea with twenty thousand foot soldiers and two thousand cavalry.

5 Now Judas was encamped in Elasa, and with him were three thousand picked men. 6 When they saw the huge number of the enemy forces, they were greatly frightened, and many slipped away from the camp, until no more than eight hundred of them were left.

7 When Judas saw that his army had slipped away and the battle was imminent, he was crushed in spirit, for he had no time to assemble them. 8 He became faint, but he said to those who were left, "Let us get up and go against our enemies. We may have the strength to fight them." 9 But they tried to dissuade him, saying, "We do not have the strength. Let us rather save our own lives now, and let us come back with our kindred and fight them; we are too few." 10 But Judas said, "Far be it from us to do such a thing as to flee from them. If our time has come, let us die bravely for our kindred, and leave no cause to question our honor."

11 Then the army of Bacchides*b* marched out from the camp and took its stand for the encounter. The cavalry was divided into two companies, and the slingers and the archers went ahead of the army, as did all the chief warriors. 12 Bacchides was on the right wing. Flanked by the two companies, the phalanx advanced to the

sound of the trumpets; and the men with Judas also blew their trumpets. 13 The earth was shaken by the noise of the armies, and the battle raged from morning until evening.

14 Judas saw that Bacchides and the strength of his army were on the right; then all the stouthearted men went with him, 15 and they crushed the right wing, and he pursued them as far as Mount Azotus. 16 When those on the left wing saw that the right wing was crushed, they turned and followed close behind Judas and his men. 17 The battle became desperate, and many on both sides were wounded and fell. 18 Judas also fell, and the rest fled.

19 Then Jonathan and Simon took their brother Judas and buried him in the tomb of their ancestors at Modein, 20 and wept for him. All Israel made great lamentation for him; they mourned many days and said,
21 "How is the mighty fallen,
 the savior of Israel!"
22 Now the rest of the acts of Judas, and his wars and the brave deeds that he did, and his greatness, have not been recorded, but they were very many.

23 After the death of Judas, the renegades emerged in all parts of Israel; all the wrongdoers reappeared. 24 In those days a very great famine occurred, and the country went over to their side. 25 Bacchides chose the godless and put them in charge of the country. 26 They made inquiry and searched for the friends of Judas, and brought them to Bacchides, who took vengeance on them and made sport of them. 27 So there was great distress in Israel, such

*a* 160 B.C. *b* Gk lacks *of Bacchides*

12.11.1) says that they started from Antioch, camped at *Arbela* (in Galilee, for which *Gilgal* is probably a scribal error), besieged refugees in the caves, and went on toward Jerusalem. *Mesaloth*, perhaps the Hebrew word for "steps," i.e., ascents to *Arbela*. **3**: These events occurred in the spring of 160 BCE. **4**: *Berea*, perhaps el-Bireh, opposite Ramallah, 16 km (10 mi) north of Jerusalem. **5**: The precise location of *Elasa* has not been identified. **15**: *Azotus* elsewhere is the Greek rendering of Ashdod (4.15; 5.68). *Mount Azotus* here may be an error. **19**: *Modein*, 2.1,70; 13.27–30. **21**: 2 Sam 1.19. **22**: The expression *Now the rest of the acts* imitates the style of the book of Kings (1 Kings 11.41; etc.).

**9.23–73**: Jonathan becomes leader and defeats Bacchides. **23**: *The renegades*, i.e., the pro-Syrian element (see 1.11n.). **25**: *The godless*, i.e., Hellenized Jews. **27**: *Prophets ceased*, Malachi was regarded as had not been since the time that prophets ceased to appear among them.

28 Then all the friends of Judas assembled and said to Jonathan, 29 "Since the death of your brother Judas there has been no one like him to go against our enemies and Bacchides, and to deal with those of our nation who hate us. 30 Now therefore we have chosen you today to take his place as our ruler and leader, to fight our battle." 31 So Jonathan accepted the leadership at that time in place of his brother Judas.

32 When Bacchides learned of this, he tried to kill him. 33 But Jonathan and his brother Simon and all who were with him heard of it, and they fled into the wilderness of Tekoa and camped by the water of the pool of Asphar. 34 Bacchides found this out on the sabbath day, and he with all his army crossed the Jordan.

35 So Jonathan[a] sent his brother as leader of the multitude and begged the Nabateans, who were his friends, for permission to store with them the great amount of baggage that they had. 36 But the family of Jambri from Medeba came out and seized John and all that he had, and left with it.

37 After these things it was reported to Jonathan and his brother Simon, "The family of Jambri are celebrating a great wedding, and are conducting the bride, a daughter of one of the great nobles of Canaan, from Nadabath with a large escort." 38 Remembering how their brother John had been killed, they went up and hid under cover of the mountain. 39 They looked out and saw a tumultuous procession with a great amount of baggage; and the bridegroom came out with his friends and his brothers to meet them with tambourines and musicians and many weapons. 40 Then they rushed on them from the ambush and began killing them. Many were wounded and fell, and the rest fled to the mountain; and the Jews[b] took all their goods. 41 So the wedding was turned into mourning and the voice of their musicians into a funeral dirge. 42 After they had fully avenged the blood of their brother, they returned to the marshes of the Jordan.

43 When Bacchides heard of this, he came with a large force on the sabbath day to the banks of the Jordan. 44 And Jonathan said to those with him, "Let us get up now and fight for our lives, for today things are not as they were before. 45 For look! the battle is in front of us and behind us; the water of the Jordan is on this side and on that, with marsh and thicket; there is no place to turn. 46 Cry out now to Heaven that you may be delivered from the hands of our enemies." 47 So the battle began, and Jonathan stretched out his hand to strike Bacchides, but he eluded him and went to the rear. 48 Then Jonathan and the men with him leaped into the Jordan and swam across to the other side, and the enemy[b] did not cross the Jordan to attack them. 49 And about one thousand of Bacchides' men fell that day.

50 Then Bacchides[a] returned to Jerusa-

a Gk he   b Gk they

as the last prophet; see also 4.46n. **30–31:** *We have chosen you,* Judas was self-appointed, but *Jonathan* was selected by his peers; he became leader about 160 or 159 BCE and high priest in 152 (10.21). **33:** *Tekoa* (Am 1.1), 18 km (11 mi) south of Jerusalem. *The wilderness* reaches from here to the Dead Sea. The precise location of *the pool of Asphar* is uncertain. **34:** This verse is probably a variant of v. 43, and is misplaced here. **35:** *His brother,* John (v. 36; 2.2). *The Nabateans,* see 5.25n. **36:** *Family of Jambri,* evidently a Nabatean tribe. *Medeba,* or Madeba, on the Jordanian plateau 19 km (12 mi) east of the north end of the Dead Sea. **37:** *Nadabath,* location uncertain. **38:** *John . . . killed,* the sequel to v. 36 was the murder of John and all his companions (Josephus, *Ant.* 13.1.2). **43:** *Bacchides* may have chosen the sabbath expecting no opposition (2.32–38). He apparently came from Jerusalem, crossed the Jordan, and camped on the east side; see Map 10. **45:** The Jews were apparently on the east side of the Jordan, between the river and the Syrian forces. **46:** *Heaven,* see 3.18n. **50–53:** Bacchides established forces and garrisons to prevent guerrilla operations. **50:** See Maps, pp. 208 and 209 AP. *Emmaus,* see 3.40n. *Beth-horon,* see 3.16n. *Bethel,* about 19 km (12 mi) north of Jerusalem. *Timnath, Pharathon, and Tephon* cannot be identified lem and built strong cities in Judea: the fortress in Jericho, and Emmaus, and Beth-horon, and Bethel, and Timnath, and[a] Pharathon, and Tephon, with high walls and gates and bars. 51 And he placed garrisons in them to harass Israel. 52 He also fortified the town of Beth-zur, and Gazara, and the citadel, and in them he put troops and stores of food. 53 And he took the sons of the leading men of the land as hostages and put them under guard in the citadel at Jerusalem.

54 In the one hundred and fifty-third year,[b] in the second month, Alcimus gave orders to tear down the wall of the inner court of the sanctuary. He tore down the work of the prophets! 55 But he only began to tear it down, for at that time Alcimus was stricken and his work was hindered; his mouth was stopped and he was paralyzed, so that he could no longer say a word or give commands concerning his house. 56 And Alcimus died at that time in great agony. 57 When Bacchides saw that Alcimus was dead, he returned to the king, and the land of Judah had rest for two years.

58 Then all the lawless plotted and said, "See! Jonathan and his men are living in quiet and confidence. So now let us bring Bacchides back, and he will capture them all in one night." 59 And they went and consulted with him. 60 He started to come with a large force, and secretly sent letters to all his allies in Judea, telling them to seize Jonathan and his men; but they were unable to do it, because their plan became known. 61 And Jonathan's men[c] seized about fifty of the men of the country who were leaders in this treachery, and killed them.

62 Then Jonathan with his men, and Simon, withdrew to Bethbasi in the wilder-

ness; he rebuilt the parts of it that had been demolished, and they fortified it. 63 When Bacchides learned of this, he assembled all his forces, and sent orders to the men of Judea. 64 Then he came and encamped against Bethbasi; he fought against it for many days and made machines of war.

65 But Jonathan left his brother Simon in the town, while he went out into the country; and he went with only a few men. 66 He struck down Odomera and his kindred and the people of Phasiron in their tents. 67 Then he[d] began to attack and went into battle with his forces; and Simon and his men sallied out from the town and set fire to the machines of war. 68 They fought with Bacchides, and he was crushed by them. They pressed him very hard, for his plan and his expedition had been in vain. 69 So he was very angry at the renegades who had counseled him to come into the country, and he killed many of them. Then he decided to go back to his own land.

70 When Jonathan learned of this, he sent ambassadors to him to make peace with him and obtain release of the captives. 71 He agreed, and did as he said; and he swore to Jonathan[e] that he would not try to harm him as long as he lived. 72 He restored to him the captives whom he had taken previously from the land of Judah; then he turned and went back to his own land, and did not come again into their territory. 73 Thus the sword ceased from Israel. Jonathan settled in Michmash and be-

---

a Some authorities omit *and*    b 159 B.C.
c Gk *they*    d Other ancient authorities read *they*
e Gk *him*

---

securely. **52:** *Beth-zur,* see 4.29n. *Gazara,* see 4.15n. **53:** *Citadel,* see 1.33n. **54:** *The wall of the inner court* separated this part from the rest of the Temple mount; non-priests were now to have access to *the sanctuary. The prophets,* perhaps Haggai and Zechariah. **56:** *Alcimus* had been high priest for about two years (7.5). **57:** *He returned,* believing that with the fortresses garrisoned the situation was stable; his departure gave Jonathan a free hand. **61:** *Fifty . . . leaders,* probably the Hellenizers (see v. 25n.). **62:** *Bethbasi,* perhaps Khirbet Beit-Bassa, about 11 km (7 mi) south of Jerusalem. **66:** *Odomera . . . people of Phasiron,* perhaps local supporters of the Syrians. **68:** *He was crushed,* for Simon attacked by surprise and *Bacchides* had depended heavily on the war machines (v. 67). **72:** Josephus says that there was an exchange of prisoners (*Ant.* 13.1.6). **73:** *Thus the sword ceased,* for about seven years, until the events of 10.69.

gan to judge the people; and he destroyed the godless out of Israel.

10 In the one hundred sixtieth year[a] Alexander Epiphanes, son of Antiochus, landed and occupied Ptolemais. They welcomed him, and there he began to reign. 2 When King Demetrius heard of it, he assembled a very large army and marched out to meet him in battle. 3 Demetrius sent Jonathan a letter in peaceable words to honor him; 4 for he said to himself, "Let us act first to make peace with him[b] before he makes peace with Alexander against us, 5 for he will remember all the wrongs that we did to him and to his brothers and his nation." 6 So Demetrius[c] gave him authority to recruit troops, to equip them with arms, and to become his ally; and he commanded that the hostages in the citadel should be released to him.

7 Then Jonathan came to Jerusalem and read the letter in the hearing of all the people and of those in the citadel. 8 They were greatly alarmed when they heard that the king had given him authority to recruit troops. 9 But those in the citadel released the hostages to Jonathan, and he returned them to their parents.

10 And Jonathan took up residence in Jerusalem and began to rebuild and restore the city. 11 He directed those who were doing the work to build the walls and encircle Mount Zion with squared stones, for better fortification; and they did so.

12 Then the foreigners who were in the strongholds that Bacchides had built fled; 13 all of them left their places and went back to their own lands. 14 Only in Beth-zur did some remain who had forsaken the law and the commandments, for it served as a place of refuge.

15 Now King Alexander heard of all the promises that Demetrius had sent to Jonathan, and he heard of the battles that Jonathan[c] and his brothers had fought, of the brave deeds that they had done, and of the troubles that they had endured. 16 So he said, "Shall we find another such man? Come now, we will make him our friend and ally." 17 And he wrote a letter and sent it to him, in the following words:

18 "King Alexander to his brother Jonathan, greetings. 19 We have heard about you, that you are a mighty warrior and worthy to be our friend. 20 And so we have appointed you today to be the high priest of your nation; you are to be called the king's Friend and you are to take our side and keep friendship with us." He also sent him a purple robe and a golden crown.

21 So Jonathan put on the sacred vestments in the seventh month of the one hundred sixtieth year,[a] at the festival of booths,[d] and he recruited troops and equipped them with arms in abundance. 22 When Demetrius heard of these things he was distressed and said, 23 "What is this

a 152 B.C.    b Gk them    c Gk he
d Or tabernacles

---

Michmash, now Mukhmas, about 13 km (8 mi) north of Jerusalem (1 Sam 14.5–23). *To judge the people*, like Samuel (1 Sam 7.6) and those in the book of Judges.

**10.1–21: Alexander Balas appoints Jonathan high priest. 1:** *Alexander* I *Epiphanes*, who came from Ephesus and whose given name was Balas (perhaps originally Baal), posed as the *son of Antiochus* IV. He claimed the kingship from 150 BCE onward, and reigned until about 145. Attalus II of Pergamum and Ptolemy VI persuaded the Roman senate to recognize him. *Ptolemais*, see 5.15n. **6:** *Gave him authority*, as a local prince or governor, but not independence. *The hostages*, 9.53. The Syrians held the citadel at Jerusalem. **11:** Lysias had ordered the wall of the Jewish fortress torn down (6.62). **14:** *Some*, i.e., Hellenized Jews opposed to the Hasmoneans. **18–20:** *Alexander*, hearing of Demetrius's letter, decided to outbid him. Until the time of Antiochus IV, the hereditary high priest had been confirmed but not appointed by the ruler; now Alexander appointed Jonathan and made him one of his *Friends* (see 2.18n.); the Jews had not elected him. **21:** *The sacred vestments*, Ex 28.1–39; 39.1–26. *Booths*, a seven-day festival held in September (Lev 23.33–43), had come to be associated with the hope of victory over the Gentiles (Zech 14.16–19).

**10.22–50: Demetrius's offer to the Jews; his defeat. 25:** The letter addressed *to the nation*, ignoring that we have done? Alexander has gotten ahead of us in forming a friendship with the Jews to strengthen himself. 24 I also will write them words of encouragement and promise them honor and gifts, so that I may have their help." 25 So he sent a message to them in the following words:

"King Demetrius to the nation of the Jews, greetings. 26 Since you have kept your agreement with us and have continued your friendship with us, and have not sided with our enemies, we have heard of it and rejoiced. 27 Now continue still to keep faith with us, and we will repay you with good for what you do for us. 28 We will grant you many immunities and give you gifts.

29 "I now free you and exempt all the Jews from payment of tribute and salt tax and crown levies, 30 and instead of collecting the third of the grain and the half of the fruit of the trees that I should receive, I release them from this day and henceforth. I will not collect them from the land of Judah or from the three districts added to it from Samaria and Galilee, from this day and for all time. 31 Jerusalem and its environs, its tithes and its revenues, shall be holy and free from tax. 32 I release also my control of the citadel in Jerusalem and give it to the high priest, so that he may station in it men of his own choice to guard it. 33 And everyone of the Jews taken as a captive from the land of Judah into any part of my kingdom, I set free without payment; and let all officials cancel also the taxes on their livestock.

34 "All the festivals and sabbaths and new moons and appointed days, and the three days before a festival and the three after a festival—let them all be days of im-

munity and release for all the Jews who are in my kingdom. 35 No one shall have authority to exact anything from them or annoy any of them about any matter.

36 "Let Jews be enrolled in the king's forces to the number of thirty thousand men, and let the maintenance be given them that is due to all the forces of the king. 37 Let some of them be stationed in the great strongholds of the king, and let some of them be put in positions of trust in the kingdom. Let their officers and leaders be of their own number, and let them live by their own laws, just as the king has commanded in the land of Judah.

38 "As for the three districts that have been added to Judea from the country of Samaria, let them be annexed to Judea so that they may be considered to be under one ruler and obey no other authority than the high priest. 39 Ptolemais and the land adjoining it I have given as a gift to the sanctuary in Jerusalem, to meet the necessary expenses of the sanctuary. 40 I also grant fifteen thousand shekels of silver yearly out of the king's revenues from appropriate places. 41 And all the additional funds that the government officials have not paid as they did in the first years,*a* they shall give from now on for the service of the temple.*b* 42 Moreover, the five thousand shekels of silver that my officials*c* have received every year from the income of the services of the temple, this too is canceled, because it belongs to the priests who minister there. 43 And all who take refuge at the temple in Jerusalem, or in any of its pre-

a Meaning of Gk uncertain   b Gk *house*
c Gk *they*

Jonathan. Demetrius thought that he could drive a wedge between leader and people. **29–30:** *All the Jews* in the Seleucid realm, not merely in Judea. *Tribute,* direct taxes proportionate to individual wealth. *Salt tax,* on salt from the marshes and the Dead Sea. *Crown levies,* fixed amounts of money. *The three districts* (11.34) that Alexander the Great had transferred from Samaria to Judea and Antiochus IV had reassigned to Samaria were now restored (v. 38). **32:** *Release* of *control of the citadel* would free Jerusalem from military domination. **34:** *Appointed days,* other public festivals. **36–37:** Opening the army and the civil service to Jews might strengthen their loyalty to the crown. **39:** *Ptolemais* was in the hands of Alexander (v. 1). This was an invitation to the Jews to help Demetrius recapture it. **40:** A *shekel* weighed ca. 8.5 gr (.3 oz). **41:** *The additional funds* were grants once made to the Temple by Ptolemaic and Seleucid kings, but not paid since the time of Antiochus IV. **44–45:** Here Demetrius followed the custom of Persian kings cincts, because they owe money to the king or are in debt, let them be released and receive back all their property in my kingdom. 44 "Let the cost of rebuilding and restoring the structures of the sanctuary be paid from the revenues of the king. 45 And let the cost of rebuilding the walls of Jerusalem and fortifying it all around, and the cost of rebuilding the walls in Judea, also be paid from the revenues of the king."

46 When Jonathan and the people heard these words, they did not believe or accept them, because they remembered the great wrongs that Demetrius[a] had done in Israel and how much he had oppressed them. 47 They favored Alexander, because he had been the first to speak peaceable words to them, and they remained his allies all his days.

48 Now King Alexander assembled large forces and encamped opposite Demetrius. 49 The two kings met in battle, and the army of Demetrius fled, and Alexander[b] pursued him and defeated them. 50 He pressed the battle strongly until the sun set, and on that day Demetrius fell.

51 Then Alexander sent ambassadors to Ptolemy king of Egypt with the following message: 52 "Since I have returned to my kingdom and have taken my seat on the throne of my ancestors, and established my rule—for I crushed Demetrius and gained control of our country; 53 I met him in battle, and he and his army were crushed by us, and we have taken our seat on the throne of his kingdom— 54 now therefore let us establish friendship with one another; give me now your daughter as my wife, and I will become your son-in-law, and will make gifts to you and to her in keeping with your position."

55 Ptolemy the king replied and said, "Happy was the day on which you re-

turned to the land of your ancestors and took your seat on the throne of their kingdom. 56 And now I will do for you as you wrote, but meet me at Ptolemais, so that we may see one another, and I will become your father-in-law, as you have said."

57 So Ptolemy set out from Egypt, he and his daughter Cleopatra, and came to Ptolemais in the one hundred sixty-second year.[c] 58 King Alexander met him, and Ptolemy[d] gave him his daughter Cleopatra in marriage, and celebrated her wedding at Ptolemais with great pomp, as kings do.

59 Then King Alexander wrote to Jonathan to come and meet him. 60 So he went with pomp to Ptolemais and met the two kings; he gave them and their Friends silver and gold and many gifts, and found favor with them. 61 A group of malcontents from Israel, renegades, gathered together against him to accuse him; but the king paid no attention to them. 62 The king gave orders to take off Jonathan's garments and to clothe him in purple, and they did so. 63 The king also seated him at his side; and he said to his officers, "Go out with him into the middle of the city and proclaim that no one is to bring charges against him about any matter, and let no one annoy him for any reason." 64 When his accusers saw the honor that was paid him, in accord with the proclamation, and saw him clothed in purple, they all fled. 65 Thus the king honored him and enrolled him among his chief[d] Friends, and made him general and governor of the province. 66 And Jonathan returned to Jerusalem in peace and gladness.

67 In the one hundred sixty-fifth year[e] Demetrius son of Demetrius came from

---

a Gk he    b Other ancient authorities read *Alexander fled, and Demetrius*    c 150 B.C.    d Gk *first*    e 147 B.C.

---

(Ezra 6.8; 7.20). 47: *Alexander* was also recognized as king by the Jews' allies, the Romans. 50: *Demetrius fell* probably in 150 BCE (v. 57).

**10.51–66: Alexander's relations with Egypt and Judea. 51:** *Ptolemy* VI Philometor (1.18n.). **55:** *Ptolemy* recognized Alexander as legitimate (see 10.1–21n.). **57:** *Cleopatra* III, who later married her uncle, Ptolemy VIII. **65:** *Chief Friends,* see 2.18n. *General and governor,* with military and civil authority.

**10.67–89: Victories of Jonathan. 67:** *Demetrius* II *son of Demetrius* I disputed the throne with Alexan-

Crete to the land of his ancestors. 68 When King Alexander heard of it, he was greatly distressed and returned to Antioch. 69 And Demetrius appointed Apollonius the governor of Coelesyria, and he assembled a large force and encamped against Jamnia. Then he sent the following message to the high priest Jonathan:

70 "You are the only one to rise up against us, and I have fallen into ridicule and disgrace because of you. Why do you assume authority against us in the hill country? 71 If you now have confidence in your forces, come down to the plain to meet us, and let us match strength with each other there, for I have with me the power of the cities. 72 Ask and learn who I am and who the others are that are helping us. People will tell you that you cannot stand before us, for your ancestors were twice put to flight in their own land. 73 And now you will not be able to withstand my cavalry and such an army in the plain, where there is no stone or pebble, or place to flee."

74 When Jonathan heard the words of Apollonius, his spirit was aroused. He chose ten thousand men and set out from Jerusalem, and his brother Simon met him to help him. 75 He encamped before Joppa, but the people of the city closed its gates, for Apollonius had a garrison in Joppa. 76 So they fought against it, and the people of the city became afraid and opened the gates, and Jonathan gained possession of Joppa.

77 When Apollonius heard of it, he mustered three thousand cavalry and a large army, and went to Azotus as though he were going farther. At the same time he advanced into the plain, for he had a large troop of cavalry and put confidence in it. 78 Jonathan[a] pursued him to Azotus, and the armies engaged in battle. 79 Now Apollonius had secretly left a thousand cavalry behind them. 80 Jonathan learned that there was an ambush behind him, for they surrounded his army and shot arrows at his men from early morning until late afternoon. 81 But his men stood fast, as Jonathan had commanded, and the enemy's[b] horses grew tired.

82 Then Simon brought forward his force and engaged the phalanx in battle (for the cavalry was exhausted); they were overwhelmed by him and fled, 83 and the cavalry was dispersed in the plain. They fled to Azotus and entered Beth-dagon, the temple of their idol, for safety. 84 But Jonathan burned Azotus and the surrounding towns and plundered them; and the temple of Dagon, and those who had taken refuge in it, he burned with fire. 85 The number of those who fell by the sword, with those burned alive, came to eight thousand.

86 Then Jonathan left there and encamped against Askalon, and the people of the city came out to meet him with great pomp.

87 He and those with him then returned to Jerusalem with a large amount of booty. 88 When King Alexander heard of these things, he honored Jonathan still more; 89 and he sent to him a golden buckle, such

a Gk he    b Gk their

der and later with Tryphon and Antiochus VI; in 138 BCE he was taken captive by the Parthians. He reigned again from 129 until his death in 125. 69: *Coelesyria,* meaning "hollow Syria," designated the region between the Lebanon and Anti-lebanon mountains. *Jamnia,* 4.15. 72: *Twice put to flight,* referring to 6.54; 9.18; or perhaps to earlier defeats in Israel's history. 74: Jonathan now had forces for more than guerrilla engagements (v. 65). 75: *Joppa,* now Jaffa, a seaport near Jamnia and 58 km (36 mi) northwest of Jerusalem. 77–78: By stationing his army near *Azotus* (Ashdod), south of Joppa, *Apollonius* drew Jonathan's forces out onto the plain, which Apollonius believed favored his own troops (see vv. 71–73). 82: *His force* had been held in reserve and was fresh. *Phalanx,* the infantry. 83: *Beth-dagon,* house of Dagon, the Philistine grain god (Judg 16.23). 86: *Askalon,* earlier Ashkelon, about 16 km (10 mi) south of Azotus. 89: *A golden buckle,* with which the most select of the Friends of the king fastened their purple robes. *Ekron,* northernmost of the original Philistine cities, about 21 km (13 mi) east of Azotus, was given to Jonathan as a personal possession, and its taxes were assigned to him.

as it is the custom to give to the King's Kinsmen. He also gave him Ekron and all its environs as his possession.

11 Then the king of Egypt gathered great forces, like the sand by the seashore, and many ships; and he tried to get possession of Alexander's kingdom by trickery and add it to his own kingdom. [2] He set out for Syria with peaceable words, and the people of the towns opened their gates to him and went to meet him, for King Alexander had commanded them to meet him, since he was Alexander's[a] father-in-law. [3] But when Ptolemy entered the towns he stationed forces as a garrison in each town.

4 When he[b] approached Azotus, they showed him the burnt-out temple of Dagon, and Azotus and its suburbs destroyed, and the corpses lying about, and the charred bodies of those whom Jonathan[c] had burned in the war, for they had piled them in heaps along his route. [5] They also told the king what Jonathan had done, to throw blame on him; but the king kept silent. [6] Jonathan met the king at Joppa with pomp, and they greeted one another and spent the night there. [7] And Jonathan went with the king as far as the river called Eleutherus; then he returned to Jerusalem.

8 So King Ptolemy gained control of the coastal cities as far as Seleucia by the sea, and he kept devising wicked designs against Alexander. [9] He sent envoys to King Demetrius, saying, "Come, let us make a cove-nant with each other, and I will give you in marriage my daughter who was Alexander's wife, and you shall reign over your father's kingdom. [10] I now regret that I gave him my daughter, for he has tried to kill me." [11] He threw blame on Alexander[d] because he coveted his kingdom. [12] So he took his daughter away from him and gave her to Demetrius. He was estranged from Alexander, and their enmity became manifest.

13 Then Ptolemy entered Antioch and put on the crown of Asia. Thus he put two crowns on his head, the crown of Egypt and that of Asia. [14] Now King Alexander was in Cilicia at that time, because the people of that region were in revolt. [15] When Alexander heard of it, he came against him in battle. Ptolemy marched out and met him with a strong force, and put him to flight. [16] So Alexander fled into Arabia to find protection there, and King Ptolemy was triumphant. [17] Zabdiel the Arab cut off the head of Alexander and sent it to Ptolemy. [18] But King Ptolemy died three days later, and his troops in the strongholds were killed by the inhabitants of the strongholds. [19] So Demetrius became king in the one hundred sixty-seventh year.[e]

20 In those days Jonathan assembled the Judeans to attack the citadel in Jerusalem, and he built many engines of war to use against it. [21] But certain renegades who hat-

a Gk *his*   b Other ancient authorities read *they*
c Gk *he*   d Gk *him*   e 145 B.C.

**11.1–19: Invasion of Ptolemy VI and victory of Demetrius II. 1:** In contrast to the motive given here for Ptolemy's actions, Josephus says that Ptolemy came to aid Alexander, his son-in-law, but that Alexander plotted against Ptolemy's life (*Ant.* 13.4.5–6; see v. 10). **5:** *Kept silent,* he had not yet broken with Alexander and was not ready to commit himself. **7:** *Eleutherus,* now Nahr el-Kebir, north of Tripolis. **8:** *Seleucia* in Pieria, the main port for Antioch, near the mouth of the Orontes. **9:** *My daughter,* Cleopatra III (10.57). **13:** According to Josephus, the army proclaimed *Ptolemy* as king, but he persuaded the people of Antioch to support Demetrius. **14:** *Cilicia,* on the south coast of Turkey, always closely related to Syria, and the only section of Asia Minor then part of the Seleucid Empire. **15:** *Ptolemy marched out,* according to Josephus (*Ant.* 13.4.8), with his son-in-law, Demetrius, who had already married Cleopatra. **16:** *Arabia* here includes the desert east of Damascus. **18:** *Ptolemy died* of wounds suffered in the victory over Alexander. **19:** *Demetrius* had claimed to be *king* since 150 BCE (see 10.67n.).

**11.20–37: Agreement between Demetrius II and Jonathan. 20:** Demetrius I had once promised to turn *the citadel* (see 1.33n.) over to the high priest (10.32), but he refused to recognize Jonathan as such because Jonathan had supported Alexander. Now Jonathan resolved to attack the citadel and make Judea independent. **23–24:** Jonathan decided to *continue the siege* so as to negotiate from strength, but his ed their nation went to the king and reported to him that Jonathan was besieging the citadel. 22 When he heard this he was angry, and as soon as he heard it he set out and came to Ptolemais; and he wrote Jonathan not to continue the siege, but to meet him for a conference at Ptolemais as quickly as possible.

23 When Jonathan heard this, he gave orders to continue the siege. He chose some of the elders of Israel and some of the priests, and put himself in danger, 24 for he went to the king at Ptolemais, taking silver and gold and clothing and numerous other gifts. And he won his favor. 25 Although certain renegades of his nation kept making complaints against him, 26 the king treated him as his predecessors had treated him; he exalted him in the presence of all his Friends. 27 He confirmed him in the high priesthood and in as many other honors as he had formerly had, and caused him to be reckoned among his chief[a] Friends. 28 Then Jonathan asked the king to free Judea and the three districts of Samaria[b] from tribute, and promised him three hundred talents. 29 The king consented, and wrote a letter to Jonathan about all these things; its contents were as follows:

30 "King Demetrius to his brother Jonathan and to the nation of the Jews, greetings. 31 This copy of the letter that we wrote concerning you to our kinsman Lasthenes we have written to you also, so that you may know what it says. 32 'King Demetrius to his father Lasthenes, greetings. 33 We have determined to do good to the nation of the Jews, who are our friends and fulfill their obligations to us, because of the goodwill they show toward us. 34 We have confirmed as their possession both the territory of Judea and the three districts of Aphaire-

ma and Lydda and Rathamin; the latter, with all the region bordering them, were added to Judea from Samaria. To all those who offer sacrifice in Jerusalem we have granted release from[c] the royal taxes that the king formerly received from them each year, from the crops of the land and the fruit of the trees. 35 And the other payments henceforth due to us of the tithes, and the taxes due to us, and the salt pits and the crown taxes due to us—from all these we shall grant them release. 36 And not one of these grants shall be canceled from this time on forever. 37 Now therefore take care to make a copy of this, and let it be given to Jonathan and put up in a conspicuous place on the holy mountain.' "

38 When King Demetrius saw that the land was quiet before him and that there was no opposition to him, he dismissed all his troops, all of them to their own homes, except the foreign troops that he had recruited from the islands of the nations. So all the troops who had served under his predecessors hated him. 39 A certain Trypho had formerly been one of Alexander's supporters; he saw that all the troops were grumbling against Demetrius. So he went to Imalkue the Arab, who was bringing up Antiochus, the young son of Alexander, 40 and insistently urged him to hand Antiochus[d] over to him, to become king in place of his father. He also reported to Imalkue[d] what Demetrius had done and told of the hatred that the troops of Demetrius[e] had for him; and he stayed there many days.

41 Now Jonathan sent to King Demetrius the request that he remove the troops of

a Gk first   b Cn: Gk the three districts and Samaria
c Or Samaria, for all those who offer sacrifice in Jerusalem, in place of   d Gk him   e Gk his troops

dangerous visit and gifts showed that he was willing to make terms. **27–29:** Demetrius II confirms many of the privileges and concessions earlier granted by Demetrius I or Alexander Balas (10.6,15–20,65). **30–37:** The letter repeats earlier promises (10.25–45) but says nothing of the citadel. **31:** *Lasthenes,* probably governor of Coelesyria (see 10.69n.). **34:** *The three districts,* 10.30,38. *Aphairema,* probably et-Taiyibeh, 19 km (12 mi) north of Jerusalem, the "Ephraim" of Jn 11.54. *Lydda,* or Lod, 18 km (11 mi) southeast of Jaffa. *Rathamin,* perhaps Ramathaim-zophim (1 Sam 1.1), the "Arimathea" of Mk 15.43, 13 km (8 mi) northeast of Lydda. **37:** *The holy mountain,* i.e., Mt. Zion.

**11.38–52:** Jonathan's aid to Demetrius. **38:** *Demetrius* in overconfidence reduced his army, probably the citadel from Jerusalem, and the troops in the strongholds; for they kept fighting against Israel. ⁴²And Demetrius sent this message back to Jonathan: "Not only will I do these things for you and your nation, but I will confer great honor on you and your nation, if I find an opportunity. ⁴³Now then you will do well to send me men who will help me, for all my troops have revolted." ⁴⁴So Jonathan sent three thousand stalwart men to him at Antioch, and when they came to the king, the king rejoiced at their arrival.

45 Then the people of the city assembled within the city, to the number of a hundred and twenty thousand, and they wanted to kill the king. ⁴⁶But the king fled into the palace. Then the people of the city seized the main streets of the city and began to fight. ⁴⁷So the king called the Jews to his aid, and they all rallied around him and then spread out through the city; and they killed on that day about one hundred thousand. ⁴⁸They set fire to the city and seized a large amount of spoil on that day, and saved the king. ⁴⁹When the people of the city saw that the Jews had gained control of the city as they pleased, their courage failed and they cried out to the king with this entreaty: ⁵⁰"Grant us peace, and make the Jews stop fighting against us and our city." ⁵¹And they threw down their arms and made peace. So the Jews gained glory in the sight of the king and of all the people in his kingdom, and they returned to Jerusalem with a large amount of spoil.

52 So King Demetrius sat on the throne of his kingdom, and the land was quiet before him. ⁵³But he broke his word about all that he had promised; he became estranged from Jonathan and did not repay the favors that Jonathan*a* had done him, but treated him very harshly.

54 After this Trypho returned, and with him the young boy Antiochus who began to reign and put on the crown. ⁵⁵All the troops that Demetrius had discharged gathered around him; they fought against Demetrius,*b* and he fled and was routed. ⁵⁶Trypho captured the elephants*c* and gained control of Antioch. ⁵⁷Then the young Antiochus wrote to Jonathan, saying, "I confirm you in the high priesthood and set you over the four districts and make you one of the king's Friends." ⁵⁸He also sent him gold plates and a table service, and granted him the right to drink from gold cups and dress in purple and wear a gold buckle. ⁵⁹He appointed Jonathan's*d* brother Simon governor from the Ladder of Tyre to the borders of Egypt.

60 Then Jonathan set out and traveled beyond the river and among the towns, and all the army of Syria gathered to him as allies. When he came to Askalon, the people of the city met him and paid him honor. ⁶¹From there he went to Gaza, but the people of Gaza shut him out. So he besieged it and burned its suburbs with fire and plundered them. ⁶²Then the people of Gaza pleaded with Jonathan, and he made peace with them, and took the sons of their rulers as hostages and sent them to Jerusalem. And he passed through the country as far as Damascus.

63 Then Jonathan heard that the officers

a Gk he   b Gk him   c Gk animals   d Gk his

to save money. This made him unpopular. **42–43:** At last Demetrius seemed to agree (cf. v. 53) to evacuate the citadel and other fortresses. **47:** *Jews*, Judeans (see 2.23n.).

**11.53–74: Estrangement of Demetrius and Jonathan. 53:** Josephus says that Demetrius now demanded tribute as before (*Ant.* 13.5.3). **54:** *Antiochus* VI Epiphanes, son of Alexander Balas, reigned nominally from about 145 to 142 BCE. **55:** *All the troops*, v. 38. **57:** *The four districts*, the three of v. 34 and probably Ekron (10.89). **58:** *Gold cups*, cf. 1 Kings 10.21; Esth 1.7. *Gold buckle*, sign of being a Friend of the king (see 2.18n.; 10.89n.). **59:** *The Ladder of Tyre*, the coastline between Ptolemais and Tyre. **60:** *Beyond the river*, i.e., in the Trans-Euphrates province with that name. **61:** *Gaza*, southernmost of the Philistine cities, near the Egyptian border (Judg 16.1). **62:** *Damascus*, outside Jonathan's control, but his influence extended that far. **63:** *Kadesh*, probably Tell Qades in northern Galilee, strategically located of Demetrius had come to Kadesh in Galilee with a large army, intending to remove him from office. 64 He went to meet them, but left his brother Simon in the country. 65 Simon encamped before Beth-zur and fought against it for many days and hemmed it in. 66 Then they asked him to grant them terms of peace, and he did so. He removed them from there, took possession of the town, and set a garrison over it. 67 Jonathan and his army encamped by the waters of Gennesaret. Early in the morning they marched to the plain of Hazor, 68 and there in the plain the army of the foreigners met him; they had set an ambush against him in the mountains, but they themselves met him face to face. 69 Then the men in ambush emerged from their places and joined battle. 70 All the men with Jonathan fled; not one of them was left except Mattathias son of Absalom and Judas son of Chalphi, commanders of the forces of the army. 71 Jonathan tore his clothes, put dust on his head, and prayed. 72 Then he turned back to the battle against the enemy[a] and routed them, and they fled. 73 When his men who were fleeing saw this, they returned to him and joined him in the pursuit as far as Kadesh, to their camp, and there they encamped. 74 As many as three thousand of the foreigners fell that day. And Jonathan returned to Jerusalem.

12 Now when Jonathan saw that the time was favorable for him, he chose men and sent them to Rome to confirm and renew the friendship with them. 2 He also sent letters to the same effect to the Spartans and to other places. 3 So they went to Rome and entered the senate chamber and said, "The high priest Jonathan and the Jewish nation have sent us to renew the former friendship and alliance with them." 4 And the Romans[b] gave them letters to the people in every place, asking them to provide for the envoys[a] safe conduct to the land of Judah.

5 This is a copy of the letter that Jonathan wrote to the Spartans: 6 "The high priest Jonathan, the senate of the nation, the priests, and the rest of the Jewish people to their brothers the Spartans, greetings. 7 Already in time past a letter was sent to the high priest Onias from Arius,[c] who was king among you, stating that you are our brothers, as the appended copy shows. 8 Onias welcomed the envoy with honor, and received the letter, which contained a clear declaration of alliance and friendship. 9 Therefore, though we have no need of these things, since we have as encouragement the holy books that are in our hands, 10 we have undertaken to send to renew our family ties and friendship with you, so that we may not become estranged from you, for considerable time has passed since you sent your letter to us. 11 We therefore remember you constantly on every occasion, both at our festivals and on other appropriate days, at the sacrifices that we offer and in our prayers, as it is right and proper to remember brothers. 12 And we rejoice in your glory. 13 But as for ourselves, many trials and many wars have encircled us; the kings around us have waged war against us. 14 We were unwilling to annoy you and our other allies and friends with these wars, 15 for we have the help that comes from Heaven for our aid, and so we were delivered from our enemies, and our enemies were humbled. 16 We therefore have chosen Numenius son of Antiochus and Antipater son of Jason, and have sent them to Rome to renew our former friendship and alliance

a Gk them    b Gk they    c Vg Compare verse 20: Gk Darius

13 km (8 mi) north of Hazor (v. 67). **65**: *Beth-zur*, see 10.14. **67**: *The waters of Gennesaret*, the Sea of Galilee. **71**: Cf. Josh 7.6–9.

**12.1–23: Alliances with the Romans and Spartans** (cf. ch 8). **2**: *The Spartans* had not joined the Achaean league (8.9–10n.) against Rome. **4**: *The Romans* continued the old alliance (8.17–32) in order to keep Syria weak. **6**: *The senate*, literally, "council of elders." **7**: *Onias* I, high priest ca. 320–290 BCE. *Arius*, king of Sparta 309–265. **21**: *Brothers . . . of the family of Abraham*, cf. v. 7. This assertion has no historical basis, but served the interests of diplomacy.

with them. 17 We have commanded them to go also to you and greet you and deliver to you this letter from us concerning the renewal of our family ties. 18 And now please send us a reply to this."

19 This is a copy of the letter that they sent to Onias: 20 "King Arius of the Spartans, to the high priest Onias, greetings. 21 It has been found in writing concerning the Spartans and the Jews that they are brothers and are of the family of Abraham. 22 And now that we have learned this, please write us concerning your welfare; 23 we on our part write to you that your livestock and your property belong to us, and ours belong to you. We therefore command that our envoys*a* report to you accordingly."

24 Now Jonathan heard that the commanders of Demetrius had returned, with a larger force than before, to wage war against him. 25 So he marched away from Jerusalem and met them in the region of Hamath, for he gave them no opportunity to invade his own country. 26 He sent spies to their camp, and they returned and reported to him that the enemy*a* were being drawn up in formation to attack the Jews*b* by night. 27 So when the sun had set, Jonathan commanded his troops to be alert and to keep their arms at hand so as to be ready all night for battle, and he stationed outposts around the camp. 28 When the enemy heard that Jonathan and his troops were prepared for battle, they were afraid and were terrified at heart; so they kindled fires in their camp and withdrew.*c* 29 But Jonathan and his troops did not know it until morning, for they saw the fires burning. 30 Then Jonathan pursued them, but he did not overtake them, for they had crossed the Eleutherus river. 31 So Jonathan turned aside against the Arabs who are called Zabadeans, and he crushed them and plundered them. 32 Then he broke camp and went to Damascus, and marched through all that region.

33 Simon also went out and marched through the country as far as Askalon and the neighboring strongholds. He turned aside to Joppa and took it by surprise, 34 for he had heard that they were ready to hand over the stronghold to those whom Demetrius had sent. And he stationed a garrison there to guard it.

35 When Jonathan returned he convened the elders of the people and planned with them to build strongholds in Judea, 36 to build the walls of Jerusalem still higher, and to erect a high barrier between the citadel and the city to separate it from the city, in order to isolate it so that its garrison*a* could neither buy nor sell. 37 So they gathered together to rebuild the city; part of the wall on the valley to the east had fallen, and he repaired the section called Chaphenatha. 38 Simon also built Adida in the Shephelah; he fortified it and installed gates with bolts.

39 Then Trypho attempted to become king in Asia and put on the crown, and to raise his hand against King Antiochus. 40 He feared that Jonathan might not permit him to do so, but might make war on him, so he kept seeking to seize and kill him, and he marched out and came to Beth-shan. 41 Jonathan went out to meet him with forty thousand picked warriors, and he came to Beth-shan. 42 When Trypho saw

*a* Gk *they*    *b* Gk *them*    *c* Other ancient authorities omit *and withdrew*

---

**12.24–53: Jonathan captured by Trypho. 24–25:** Jonathan met the Syrians at the border of Judea to prevent an invasion. *Hamath,* on the Orontes, modern Hama in Syria, ca. 175 km (109 mi) north of Damascus. **28:** *Kindled fires,* so that Jonathan would think they were still in camp. **30:** *Eleutherus,* see 11.7n. **31:** *Zabadeans,* perhaps people northwest of Damascus. **33–34:** *Simon* had been appointed governor of the coastal district by Antiochus VI (11.59). **36:** The purpose was to starve out the garrison. **37:** *The valley to the east,* the Kidron (1 Kings 2.37); here the slope was sometimes steep. The location of *Chaphenatha* is unknown. **38:** *Adida,* about 5 km (3 mi) east of Lydda (Ezra 2.33; Neh 7.37). *Shephelah,* the foothill country between the coastal plain and the central highlands. **39:** *Trypho,* see 11.39. *King in Asia,* i.e., the Seleucid Empire. **40:** *Beth-shan,* see 5.52n. **45:** *Ptolemais,* see 5.15n. *The other strong-*

that he had come with a large army, he was afraid to raise his hand against him. [43] So he received him with honor and commended him to all his Friends, and he gave him gifts and commanded his Friends and his troops to obey him as they would himself. [44] Then he said to Jonathan, "Why have you put all these people to so much trouble when we are not at war? [45] Dismiss them now to their homes and choose for yourself a few men to stay with you, and come with me to Ptolemais. I will hand it over to you as well as the other strongholds and the remaining troops and all the officials, and will turn around and go home. For that is why I am here."

[46] Jonathan[a] trusted him and did as he said; he sent away the troops, and they returned to the land of Judah. [47] He kept with himself three thousand men, two thousand of whom he left in Galilee, while one thousand accompanied him. [48] But when Jonathan entered Ptolemais, the people of Ptolemais closed the gates and seized him, and they killed with the sword all who had entered with him.

[49] Then Trypho sent troops and cavalry into Galilee and the Great Plain to destroy all Jonathan's soldiers. [50] But they realized that Jonathan had been seized and had perished along with his men, and they encouraged one another and kept marching in close formation, ready for battle. [51] When their pursuers saw that they would fight for their lives, they turned back. [52] So they all reached the land of Judah safely, and they mourned for Jonathan and his companions and were in great fear; and all Israel mourned deeply. [53] All the nations around them tried to destroy them, for they said, "They have no leader or helper. Now there-

fore let us make war on them and blot out the memory of them from humankind."

13 Simon heard that Trypho had assembled a large army to invade the land of Judah and destroy it, [2] and he saw that the people were trembling with fear. So he went up to Jerusalem, and gathering the people together [3] he encouraged them, saying to them, "You yourselves know what great things my brothers and I and the house of my father have done for the laws and the sanctuary; you know also the wars and the difficulties that my brothers and I have seen. [4] By reason of this all my brothers have perished for the sake of Israel, and I alone am left. [5] And now, far be it from me to spare my life in any time of distress, for I am not better than my brothers. [6] But I will avenge my nation and the sanctuary and your wives and children, for all the nations have gathered together out of hatred to destroy us."

[7] The spirit of the people was rekindled when they heard these words, [8] and they answered in a loud voice, "You are our leader in place of Judas and your brother Jonathan. [9] Fight our battles, and all that you say to us we will do." [10] So he assembled all the warriors and hurried to complete the walls of Jerusalem, and he fortified it on every side. [11] He sent Jonathan son of Absalom to Joppa, and with him a considerable army; he drove out its occupants and remained there.

[12] Then Trypho left Ptolemais with a large army to invade the land of Judah, and Jonathan was with him under guard. [13] Simon encamped in Adida, facing the plain. [14] Trypho learned that Simon had risen up

a Gk he

holds, probably along the coast. **49:** *The Great Plain,* also called Jezreel (Judg 6.33) and Esdraelon (Jdt 1.8; 3.9), extending from Mt. Carmel to the Jordan Valley. **52:** *They mourned,* because of the supposition that Jonathan had been slain; but see 13.23.

**13.1–30: Simon becomes leader; death of Jonathan. 1:** *Simon* (2.3) was governor of the coastal area (11.59). **4:** Eleazar, Judas, and John had died (6.46; 9.18,42), and Simon supposed that Jonathan had been slain. **7–9:** The account of the people's affirmation of Simon as leader, like that of his brother Jonathan (9.28–30), evokes the biblical precedent of the Judges (Judg 11.6–10). **11:** *Jonathan son of Absalom,* perhaps a brother of Mattathias (11.70). **13:** *Adida,* see 12.38n. First here, then farther south, Simon prevents Trypho from entering the hill country and gaining access to Jerusalem. **20:** *Adora,* or in place of his brother Jonathan, and that he was about to join battle with him, so he sent envoys to him and said, 15 "It is for the money that your brother Jonathan owed the royal treasury, in connection with the offices he held, that we are detaining him. 16 Send now one hundred talents of silver and two of his sons as hostages, so that when released he will not revolt against us, and we will release him."

17 Simon knew that they were speaking deceitfully to him, but he sent to get the money and the sons, so that he would not arouse great hostility among the people, who might say, 18 "It was because Simon[a] did not send him the money and the sons, that Jonathan[b] perished." 19 So he sent the sons and the hundred talents, but Trypho[b] broke his word and did not release Jonathan.

20 After this Trypho came to invade the country and destroy it, and he circled around by the way to Adora. But Simon and his army kept marching along opposite him to every place he went. 21 Now the men in the citadel kept sending envoys to Trypho urging him to come to them by way of the wilderness and to send them food. 22 So Trypho got all his cavalry ready to go, but that night a very heavy snow fell, and he did not go because of the snow. He marched off and went into the land of Gilead. 23 When he approached Baskama, he killed Jonathan, and he was buried there. 24 Then Trypho turned and went back to his own land.

25 Simon sent and took the bones of his brother Jonathan, and buried him in Modein, the city of his ancestors. 26 All Israel bewailed him with great lamentation, and mourned for him many days. 27 And Simon built a monument over the tomb of his father and his brothers; he made it high so that it might be seen, with polished stone at the front and back. 28 He also erected seven pyramids, opposite one another, for his father and mother and four brothers. 29 For the pyramids[c] he devised an elaborate setting, erecting about them great columns, and on the columns he put suits of armor for a permanent memorial, and beside the suits of armor he carved ships, so that they could be seen by all who sail the sea. 30 This is the tomb that he built in Modein; it remains to this day.

31 Trypho dealt treacherously with the young King Antiochus; he killed him 32 and became king in his place, putting on the crown of Asia; and he brought great calamity on the land. 33 But Simon built up the strongholds of Judea and walled them all around, with high towers and great walls and gates and bolts, and he stored food in the strongholds. 34 Simon also chose emissaries and sent them to King Demetrius with a request to grant relief to the country, for all that Trypho did was to plunder. 35 King Demetrius sent him a favorable reply to this request, and wrote him a letter as follows, 36 "King Demetrius to Simon, the

a Gk I    b Gk he    c Gk For these

Adoriam (2 Chr 11.9), 8 km (5mi) south-southwest of Hebron (2 Chr 11.9). See v. 13n. 21: *Men in the citadel,* Jews opposed to the Hasmoneans; see 1.33n. They suggested that Trypho approach from the southeast. 22–23: *He marched off,* south of the Dead Sea. *Baskama,* possibly northeast of the Sea of Galilee. *He killed Jonathan,* late in 143 or early in 142 BCE. 25: *Modein,* 2.1; 9.19. 28: *Pyramids,* combining the Greek custom of building a monument with a suit of armor at the victory site with the Israelite custom of burial at the ancestral home. 29: *Carved ships,* symbols claiming domination of the sea, found also on coins of Herod and Archelaus. They were not visible from the sea; *so that they could be seen by all who sail the sea,* they were intended to serve as a warning to potential naval invaders. The Hasmoneans held the seaport of Joppa (13.11; 14.5,34).

**13.31–53: Simon makes Judea independent. 31–32:** *He killed him,* probably in 142 BCE. *Antiochus* VI was about seven years old and had reigned since 145 (11.54). *Became king,* about 142. *Crown of Asia,* see 12.38n. 34: *Demetrius* II (see 10.67n.) now disputed the throne with Trypho. 36–40: The letter, addressed to *the elders and nation* and to *Simon* as head of a priestly state, recognizes sovereignty (cf. v. 42). The weakness of Demetrius II made possible a great diplomatic victory. 42: The new era, high priest and friend of kings, and to the elders and nation of the Jews, greetings. [37] We have received the gold crown and the palm branch that you[a] sent, and we are ready to make a general peace with you and to write to our officials to grant you release from tribute. [38] All the grants that we have made to you remain valid, and let the strongholds that you have built be your possession. [39] We pardon any errors and offenses committed to this day, and cancel the crown tax that you owe; and whatever other tax has been collected in Jerusalem shall be collected no longer. [40] And if any of you are qualified to be enrolled in our bodyguard,[b] let them be enrolled, and let there be peace between us."

[41] In the one hundred seventieth year[c] the yoke of the Gentiles was removed from Israel, [42] and the people began to write in their documents and contracts, "In the first year of Simon the great high priest and commander and leader of the Jews."

[43] In those days Simon[d] encamped against Gazara[e] and surrounded it with troops. He made a siege engine, brought it up to the city, and battered and captured one tower. [44] The men in the siege engine leaped out into the city, and a great tumult arose in the city. [45] The men in the city, with their wives and children, went up on the wall with their clothes torn, and they cried out with a loud voice, asking Simon to make peace with them; [46] they said, "Do not treat us according to our wicked acts but according to your mercy." [47] So Simon reached an agreement with them and stopped fighting against them. But he expelled them from the city and cleansed the houses in which the idols were located, and then entered it with hymns and praise.

[48] He removed all uncleanness from it, and settled in it those who observed the law. He also strengthened its fortifications and built in it a house for himself.

[49] Those who were in the citadel at Jerusalem were prevented from going in and out to buy and sell in the country. So they were very hungry, and many of them perished from famine. [50] Then they cried to Simon to make peace with them, and he did so. But he expelled them from there and cleansed the citadel from its pollutions. [51] On the twenty-third day of the second month, in the one hundred seventy-first year,[f] the Jews[g] entered it with praise and palm branches, and with harps and cymbals and stringed instruments, and with hymns and songs, because a great enemy had been crushed and removed from Israel. [52] Simon[h] decreed that every year they should celebrate this day with rejoicing. He strengthened the fortifications of the temple hill alongside the citadel, and he and his men lived there. [53] Simon saw that his son John had reached manhood, and so he made him commander of all the forces; and he lived at Gazara.

**14** In the one hundred seventy-second year[i] King Demetrius assembled his forces and marched into Media to obtain help, so that he could make war against Trypho. [2] When King Arsaces of Persia and Media heard that Demetrius had invaded his territory, he sent one of his generals to take him alive. [3] The general[h] went and defeated the army of Demetrius, and

---

a The word *you* in verses 37–40 is plural   b Or *court*
c 142 B.C.   d Gk *he*   e Cn: Gk *Gaza*   f 141 B.C.
g Gk *they*   h Gk *He*   i 140 B.C.

---

replacing the Seleucid era, is a mark of sovereignty. **43:** *Gazara,* see 4.5n. *Siege engine,* a tower on wheels (see 6.51–52). **48:** Later Hasmoneans continued the policy of settling Jews in strategic places. **50:** The *citadel* is finally restored to Jewish control (see 1.33n.). **51:** *The second month,* Iyyar, or May. *Palm branches* symbolized victory (2 Macc 10.7). **52:** Cf. 4.59. **53:** *John* Hyrcanus reigned as high priest 135–104.

**14.1–15: Capture of Demetrius II. 1:** *One hundred seventy-second year,* i.e., 140 BCE; other historians date this invasion to 138, the year in which Demetrius was captured. *Media,* lying north of Persia, was still claimed by the Seleucids. **2–3:** According to other sources, *Arsaces* VI Mithradates I (171–138), founder of the Parthian Empire, treated Demetrius kindly and later married him to his sister. **4–15:** A seized him and took him to Arsaces, who put him under guard.

4 The land[a] had rest all the days of
    Simon.
    He sought the good of his nation;
his rule was pleasing to them,
    as was the honor shown him, all
    his days.
5 To crown all his honors he took
    Joppa for a harbor,
    and opened a way to the isles of
    the sea.
6 He extended the borders of his
    nation,
    and gained full control of the
    country.
7 He gathered a host of captives;
    he ruled over Gazara and Beth-zur
    and the citadel,
    and he removed its uncleanness from
    it;
    and there was none to oppose him.
8 They tilled their land in peace;
    the ground gave its increase,
    and the trees of the plains their
    fruit.
9 Old men sat in the streets;
    they all talked together of good
    things,
    and the youths put on splendid
    military attire.
10 He supplied the towns with food,
    and furnished them with the means
    of defense,
    until his renown spread to the ends
    of the earth.
11 He established peace in the land,
    and Israel rejoiced with great joy.
12 All the people sat under their own
    vines and fig trees,

and there was none to make them
    afraid.
13 No one was left in the land to fight
    them,
    and the kings were crushed in those
    days.
14 He gave help to all the humble among
    his people;
    he sought out the law,
    and did away with all the renegades
    and outlaws.
15 He made the sanctuary glorious,
    and added to the vessels of the
    sanctuary.

16 It was heard in Rome, and as far away as Sparta, that Jonathan had died, and they were deeply grieved. 17 When they heard that his brother Simon had become high priest in his stead, and that he was ruling over the country and the towns in it, 18 they wrote to him on bronze tablets to renew with him the friendship and alliance that they had established with his brothers Judas and Jonathan. 19 And these were read before the assembly in Jerusalem.

20 This is a copy of the letter that the Spartans sent:

"The rulers and the city of the Spartans to the high priest Simon and to the elders and the priests and the rest of the Jewish people, our brothers, greetings. 21 The envoys who were sent to our people have told us about your glory and honor, and we rejoiced at their coming. 22 We have recorded what they said in our public decrees, as follows, 'Numenius son of Antiochus and Antipater son of Jason, envoys of the Jews,

a Other ancient authorities add of Judah

contemporary poem of rejoicing, describing the reign of Simon as the fulfillment of biblical prophecies. **4**: 1 Kings 5.5. **5–7**: 11.65; 12.33; 13.41–53. *A harbor*, important for trade connections with the sea (13.11). *The isles of the sea*, Cyprus, Rhodes, and Crete. **8**: Lev 26.3–4; Zech 8.12. **9**: Zech 8.4. **10**: 12.38; 13.33,52. **12**: 1 Kings 4.25; Mic 4.4; Zech 3.10. **13–14**: Isa 11.3–4. **14**: *Sought out*, he studied the Torah to learn God's will, as the kings of Israel had consulted prophets; see Ezra 7.10. *Renegades and outlaws*, see 1.11n.

**14.16–24: Alliances with Rome and Sparta.** Simon was perhaps the first high priest recognized by the Roman senate as ruler of the Jews. **18**: See 8.17–32; 12.1–23. **19**: *The assembly*, the people as a whole. **22**: *Numenius* and *Antipater*, 12.16. **24**: *Weighing one thousand minas*, the equivalent of several hundred kg. An alternate translation is "worth one thousand minas (of silver)."

have come to us to renew their friendship with us. 23 It has pleased our people to receive these men with honor and to put a copy of their words in the public archives, so that the people of the Spartans may have a record of them. And they have sent a copy of this to the high priest Simon.' "

24 After this Simon sent Numenius to Rome with a large gold shield weighing one thousand minas, to confirm the alliance with the Romans.*

25 When the people heard these things they said, "How shall we thank Simon and his sons? 26 For he and his brothers and the house of his father have stood firm; they have fought and repulsed Israel's enemies and established its freedom." 27 So they made a record on bronze tablets and put it on pillars on Mount Zion.

This is a copy of what they wrote: "On the eighteenth day of Elul, in the one hundred seventy-second year,*b* which is the third year of the great high priest Simon, 28 in Asaramel,*c* in the great assembly of the priests and the people and the rulers of the nation and the elders of the country, the following was proclaimed to us:

29 "Since wars often occurred in the country, Simon son of Mattathias, a priest of the sons*d* of Joarib, and his brothers, exposed themselves to danger and resisted the enemies of their nation, in order that their sanctuary and the law might be preserved; and they brought great glory to their nation. 30 Jonathan rallied the*e* nation, became their high priest, and was gathered to his people. 31 When their enemies decided to invade their country and lay hands on their sanctuary, 32 then Simon rose up and fought for his nation. He spent great sums of his own money; he armed the soldiers of his nation and paid them wages. 33 He fortified the towns of Judea, and Beth-zur on the borders of Judea, where formerly the arms of the enemy had been stored, and he placed there a garrison of Jews. 34 He also fortified Joppa, which is by the sea, and Gazara, which is on the borders of Azotus, where the enemy formerly lived. He settled Jews there, and provided in those towns*a* whatever was necessary for their restoration.

35 "The people saw Simon's faithfulness*f* and the glory that he had resolved to win for his nation, and they made him their leader and high priest, because he had done all these things and because of the justice and loyalty that he had maintained toward his nation. He sought in every way to exalt his people. 36 In his days things prospered in his hands, so that the Gentiles were put out of the*e* country, as were also those in the city of David in Jerusalem, who had built themselves a citadel from which they used to sally forth and defile the environs of the sanctuary, doing great damage to its purity. 37 He settled Jews in it and fortified it for the safety of the country and of the city, and built the walls of Jerusalem higher.

38 "In view of these things King Demetrius confirmed him in the high priesthood, 39 made him one of his Friends, and paid him high honors. 40 For he had heard that the Jews were addressed by the Romans as friends and allies and brothers, and that the

---

*a* Gk *them*     *b* 140 B.C.     *c* This word resembles the Hebrew words for *the court of the people of God* or *the prince of the people of God*     *d* Meaning of Gk uncertain     *e* Gk *their*     *f* Other ancient authorities read *conduct*

---

**14.25–49:** Simon elected high priest, military commander, and ruler. The formal document of vv. 27–49 served as a constitution for the new state of Judea. **27–28:** *Bronze tablets*, see 8.22n. *Mount Zion*, 1.33; 4.37. *Elul*, August–September. *Third year*, see 13.42n. *In Asaramel*, the text is questionable. *The great assembly* represented all classes. In theory the high priest held his office by divine appointment, indicated by descent from a particular family. Since there was no legitimate claimant, Simon was legitimized by a process known in ancient Israel; see Ex 19; 2 Kings 23; Ezra 10; Neh 9. **29:** *Sons of Joarib*, see 2.1n. **30:** The decree recognizes in retrospect the office of *Jonathan*, first Hasmonean *high priest*. **32:** Use of *his own money* has not been previously mentioned. **33–34:** 13.43–48; 14.3–7. **35:** The high priest must have moral responsibility along with his powers. **36–37:** 1.34; 4.41,60; 6.18; 13.49–52. **41–43:** The

Romans[a] had received the envoys of Simon with honor.

41 "The Jews and their priests have resolved that Simon should be their leader and high priest forever, until a trustworthy prophet should arise, 42 and that he should be governor over them and that he should take charge of the sanctuary and appoint officials over its tasks and over the country and the weapons and the strongholds, and that he should take charge of the sanctuary, 43 and that he should be obeyed by all, and that all contracts in the country should be written in his name, and that he should be clothed in purple and wear gold.

44 "None of the people or priests shall be permitted to nullify any of these decisions or to oppose what he says, or to convene an assembly in the country without his permission, or to be clothed in purple or put on a gold buckle. 45 Whoever acts contrary to these decisions or rejects any of them shall be liable to punishment."

46 All the people agreed to grant Simon the right to act in accordance with these decisions. 47 So Simon accepted and agreed to be high priest, to be commander and ethnarch of the Jews and priests, and to be protector of them all.[b] 48 And they gave orders to inscribe this decree on bronze tablets, to put them up in a conspicuous place in the precincts of the sanctuary, 49 and to deposit copies of them in the treasury, so that Simon and his sons might have them.

15 Antiochus, son of King Demetrius, sent a letter from the islands of the sea to Simon, the priest and ethnarch of the Jews, and to all the nation; 2 its contents were as follows: "King Antiochus to Simon the high priest and ethnarch and to the nation of the Jews, greetings. 3 Whereas certain scoundrels have gained control of the kingdom of our ancestors, and I intend to lay claim to the kingdom so that I may restore it as it formerly was, and have recruited a host of mercenary troops and have equipped warships, 4 and intend to make a landing in the country so that I may proceed against those who have destroyed our country and those who have devastated many cities in my kingdom, 5 now therefore I confirm to you all the tax remissions that the kings before me have granted you, and a release from all the other payments from which they have released you. 6 I permit you to mint your own coinage as money for your country, 7 and I grant freedom to Jerusalem and the sanctuary. All the weapons that you have prepared and the strongholds that you have built and now hold shall remain yours. 8 Every debt you owe to the royal treasury and any such future debts shall be canceled for you from henceforth and for all time. 9 When we gain control of our kingdom, we will bestow great honor on you and your nation and the temple, so

a Gk they   b Or to preside over them all

office was to be hereditary in Simon's family; the Hasmonean dynasty is here firmly established. Reference to a *trustworthy prophet* would mollify members of Jewish groups, like those at Qumran, who expected an eschatological prophet (see 4.46n.). A similar compromise occurs in Ezra 2.63 and Neh 7.65. *Clothed in purple and wear gold,* borrowing the dress of the Seleucid kings and courtiers. From Alexander Janneus onwards (103–76 BCE), the Hasmoneans assumed the title of king. Little is known about the political role of high priest during the period of the Second Temple. A letter written in 408 BCE from the Jews at Elephantine requesting help from the Judean government is addressed to the high priest and the nobles; thus the power vested in Simon is probably not entirely new. **46–47:** In this social contract, both the people and Simon accept the conditions. *Ethnarch,* a Greek term meaning national leader. **49:** The *treasury* in the Temple served as a national archive.

**15.1–14: Arrival of Antiochus VII. 1:** *Antiochus* VII (known as Sidetes because he was brought up at Side in Pamphylia), younger brother of Demetrius II, reigned 138–129 BCE. After his brother's capture he married Cleopatra III (10.57–58; 11.12). **3:** *Scoundrels,* Trypho and his faction. **5:** He reaffirms his brother's grants (13.39). **6:** *To mint your own coinage* was legal recognition of independence. When the Seleucids permitted subject cities to coin money, it bore the king's name. **7–8:** 13.38–39. **10:** He first that your glory will become manifest in all the earth."

10 In the one hundred seventy-fourth year[a] Antiochus set out and invaded the land of his ancestors. All the troops rallied to him, so that there were only a few with Trypho. 11 Antiochus pursued him, and Trypho[b] came in his flight to Dor, which is by the sea; 12 for he knew that troubles had converged on him, and his troops had deserted him. 13 So Antiochus encamped against Dor, and with him were one hundred twenty thousand warriors and eight thousand cavalry. 14 He surrounded the town, and the ships joined battle from the sea; he pressed the town hard from land and sea, and permitted no one to leave or enter it.

15 Then Numenius and his companions arrived from Rome, with letters to the kings and countries, in which the following was written: 16 "Lucius, consul of the Romans, to King Ptolemy, greetings. 17 The envoys of the Jews have come to us as our friends and allies to renew our ancient friendship and alliance. They had been sent by the high priest Simon and by the Jewish people 18 and have brought a gold shield weighing one thousand minas. 19 We therefore have decided to write to the kings and countries that they should not seek their harm or make war against them and their cities and their country, or make alliance with those who war against them. 20 And it has seemed good to us to accept the shield from them. 21 Therefore if any scoundrels have fled to you from their country, hand them over to the high priest Simon, so that he may punish them according to their law."

22 The consul[c] wrote the same thing to King Demetrius and to Attalus and Ariarathes and Arsaces, 23 and to all the countries, and to Sampsames,[d] and to the Spartans, and to Delos, and to Myndos, and to Sicyon, and to Caria, and to Samos, and to Pamphylia, and to Lycia, and to Halicarnassus, and to Rhodes, and to Phaselis, and to Cos, and to Side, and to Aradus and Gortyna and Cnidus and Cyprus and Cyrene. 24 They also sent a copy of these things to the high priest Simon.

25 King Antiochus besieged Dor for the second time, continually throwing his forces against it and making engines of war; and he shut Trypho up and kept him from going out or in. 26 And Simon sent to Antiochus[e] two thousand picked troops, to fight for him, and silver and gold and a large amount of military equipment. 27 But he refused to receive them, and broke all the agreements he formerly had made with Simon, and became estranged from him. 28 He sent to him Athenobius, one of his Friends, to confer with him, saying, "You hold control of Joppa and Gazara and the citadel in Jerusalem; they are cities of my kingdom. 29 You have devastated their territory, you have done great damage in the land, and you have taken possession of many places in my kingdom. 30 Now then, hand over the cities that you have seized and the tribute money of the places that you have conquered outside the borders of Judea; 31 or else pay me five hundred talents of silver for the destruction that you have caused and five hundred talents more for

a 138 B.C.    b Gk *he*    c Gk *He*    d The name is uncertain    e Gk *him*

landed in Seleucia (11.8), where Cleopatra was living. **11:** *Dor,* on the Mediterranean coast 21 km (13 mi) south of Mt. Carmel. **13:** The numbers are probably exaggerated.

**15.15–24: Renewal of alliance with Rome.** The letter follows logically after 14.24. **16:** If the letter is genuine, this is *Lucius* Calpurnius Piso, consul 140–139 BCE. *Ptolemy* VIII Physcon reigned 170–116. **18:** *Shield,* see 14.24n. **22–23:** *Demetrius* II was still a prisoner in Parthia; the Romans had not recognized Antiochus VII. *Attalus* II, king of Pergamum 159–138; *Ariarathes* V, king of Cappadocia 162–130. *Delos* in the Cyclades and the other localities were free states in Greece, the Greek islands, and Asia Minor. *Cyrene,* capital of Libya.

**15.25–16.10: War with Antiochus VII. 15.27:** Josephus says that Antiochus accepted this aid (*Ant.* 13.7.2). **30:** *Outside . . . Judea,* perhaps the districts of 11.34; but compare v. 8. **31:** *Talents,* see 11.28n.

the tribute money of the cities. Otherwise we will come and make war on you."

32 So Athenobius, the king's Friend, came to Jerusalem, and when he saw the splendor of Simon, and the sideboard with its gold and silver plate, and his great magnificence, he was amazed. When he reported to him the king's message, 33 Simon said to him in reply: "We have neither taken foreign land nor seized foreign property, but only the inheritance of our ancestors, which at one time had been unjustly taken by our enemies. 34 Now that we have the opportunity, we are firmly holding the inheritance of our ancestors. 35 As for Joppa and Gazara, which you demand, they were causing great damage among the people and to our land; for them we will give you one hundred talents."

Athenobius[a] did not answer him a word, 36 but returned in wrath to the king and reported to him these words, and also the splendor of Simon and all that he had seen. And the king was very angry.

37 Meanwhile Trypho embarked on a ship and escaped to Orthosia. 38 Then the king made Cendebeus commander-in-chief of the coastal country, and gave him troops of infantry and cavalry. 39 He commanded him to encamp against Judea, to build up Kedron and fortify its gates, and to make war on the people; but the king pursued Trypho. 40 So Cendebeus came to Jamnia and began to provoke the people and invade Judea and take the people captive and kill them. 41 He built up Kedron and stationed horsemen and troops there, so that they might go out and make raids along the highways of Judea, as the king had ordered him.

**16** John went up from Gazara and reported to his father Simon what Cendebeus had done. 2 And Simon called in his two eldest sons Judas and John, and said to them: "My brothers and I and my father's house have fought the wars of Israel from our youth until this day, and things have prospered in our hands so that we have delivered Israel many times. 3 But now I have grown old, and you by Heaven's[b] mercy are mature in years. Take my place and my brother's, and go out and fight for our nation, and may the help that comes from Heaven be with you."

4 So John[c] chose out of the country twenty thousand warriors and cavalry, and they marched against Cendebeus and camped for the night in Modein. 5 Early in the morning they started out and marched into the plain, where a large force of infantry and cavalry was coming to meet them; and a stream lay between them. 6 Then he and his army lined up against them. He saw that the soldiers were afraid to cross the stream, so he crossed over first; and when his troops saw him, they crossed over after him. 7 Then he divided the army and placed the cavalry in the center of the infantry, for the cavalry of the enemy were very numerous. 8 They sounded the trumpets, and Cendebeus and his army were put to flight; many of them fell wounded and the rest fled into the stronghold. 9 At that time Judas the brother of John was wounded, but John pursued them until Cendebeus[d] reached Kedron, which he had built. 10 They also fled into the towers that were

a Gk He   b Gk his   c Other ancient authorities read he   d Gk he

32: Cf. 1 Kings 10.4. 33: The Hasmoneans claimed that all Palestine had always belonged by right to the Jews. Greek law recognized the right to reclaim ancestral property that had been seized. 35: *Joppa and Gazara,* 12.33; 13.43–48. 37: *Orthosia,* north of Tripolis on the Phoenician coast; from there Trypho went to Apamea in the interior, where he was besieged and slain. 39–40: *Kedron,* location uncertain. The plan was to control the coastal plain and recover Gazara and Joppa. 16.1: *John* Hyrcanus I commanded Gazara (13.53). 2–3: John is the first of the Hasmoneans to rule by right of succession rather than by popular choice (9.22 and 13.7–9). 4: *Cavalry* are now for the first time part of the Judean army. *Modein,* see 2.1. 7: The meaning is unclear. The author may refer to the prevailing Roman tactic of providing each unit of infantry with a unit of cavalry. 8: *The stronghold,* Kedron (15.39). 10: *Azotus,* destroyed by Jonathan (10.84).

in the fields of Azotus, and John[a] burned it with fire, and about two thousand of them fell. He then returned to Judea safely.

11 Now Ptolemy son of Abubus had been appointed governor over the plain of Jericho; he had a large store of silver and gold, 12 for he was son-in-law of the high priest. 13 His heart was lifted up; he determined to get control of the country, and made treacherous plans against Simon and his sons, to do away with them. 14 Now Simon was visiting the towns of the country and attending to their needs, and he went down to Jericho with his sons Mattathias and Judas, in the one hundred seventy-seventh year,[b] in the eleventh month, which is the month of Shebat. 15 The son of Abubus received them treacherously in the little stronghold called Dok, which he had built; he gave them a great banquet, and hid men there. 16 When Simon and his sons were drunk, Ptolemy and his men rose up, took their weapons, rushed in against Simon in the banquet hall and killed him and his two sons, as well as some of his servants. 17 So he committed an act of great treachery and returned evil for good.

18 Then Ptolemy wrote a report about these things and sent it to the king, asking him to send troops to aid him and to turn over to him the towns and the country. 19 He sent other troops to Gazara to do away with John; he sent letters to the captains asking them to come to him so that he might give them silver and gold and gifts; 20 and he sent other troops to take possession of Jerusalem and the temple hill. 21 But someone ran ahead and reported to John at Gazara that his father and brothers had perished, and that "he has sent men to kill you also." 22 When he heard this, he was greatly shocked; he seized the men who came to destroy him and killed them, for he had found out that they were seeking to destroy him.

23 The rest of the acts of John and his wars and the brave deeds that he did, and the building of the walls that he completed, and his achievements, 24 are written in the annals of his high priesthood, from the time that he became high priest after his father.

a Gk he    b 134 B.C.

**16.11–24: Death of Simon and accession of John Hyrcanus I. 11:** *Plain of Jericho,* the region just north of the Dead Sea. **12:** *The high priest,* Simon. **14:** *Shebat,* February–March. **15:** *Dok,* a fortress near Jericho. **18:** *The king,* Antiochus VII. **23:** *John* was high priest 135–104 BCE. When Antiochus later besieged Jerusalem, John was defeated but made peace and accompanied the king on an expedition to Parthia, where Antiochus was killed. Afterward John gained control of most of Palestine and forced the Idumeans to adopt Judaism. Late in his reign the Pharisees turned against him and demanded that he give up the high priesthood. **24:** *The annals* have not survived. The book concludes in a manner similar to the biblical accounts of the kings of Israel (1 Kings 11.41; 2 Kings 10.34; 12.19; 20.20; etc.).

# 2 MACCABEES

❦❦

Second Maccabees narrates the story of the Maccabean revolt. Like 1 Maccabees and the book of Daniel, 2 Maccabees interprets the religious persecution suffered by the Jews under Antiochus Epiphanes from 168 to 164 BCE. Each of the three books offers a different model of faithfulness in response to persecution as well as distinctive theological reflection on the sources of hope in times of crisis. First Maccabees highlights the military activity of the Maccabees and the subsequent establishment of the Hasmonean dynasty, taking the story down to the third generation in 134. Second Maccabees, in contrast, keeps its focus on the fate of the Temple in Jerusalem, ending its story when the Temple is secure in 161.

The literary style is lively, relying on dramatic narration and vivid portrayals of characters to evoke emotions in the reader. Following the style of Greek historiography, the author composes substantive speeches for his characters in order to entertain and instruct the reader. Written in Greek sometime between 124 and 63 BCE, the work skillfully combines Jewish theology with Greek stylistics. The author's introduction (2.19–32), using conventions of Greek literature, highlights his purposes and summarizes what is in store for the reader in the pages ahead. He reveals that his work is an epitome, condensing the five-volume history of Jason of Cyrene. The epitomist tells the reader that his story will be about Judas Maccabeus and his battles to regain the Temple from Antiochus, free Jerusalem, and restore Jewish law to Judea.

Prefixed to the introduction are two letters exhorting the Jews in Egypt to observe the new festival of Hannukah, which had originated in Judea just over forty years earlier (1.1–2.18). The second letter is of particular interest because it includes stories about Jeremiah and Nehemiah not found in the biblical books. Although it is not known how the letters came to be attached to the work of the epitomist, their focus on the purification of the Temple, like the introduction, helps prepare the reader for the story ahead.

The main body of the work (chs 3–15) recounts three successive attacks on the Temple, heroically repelled by brave Jewish fighters who are supported by heavenly warriors. Within this broad framework another, more explicitly theological structure unfolds. The epitomist has adopted the interpretation of history found in the biblical books of Judges, Samuel, and Kings, clearly laid out in Judg 2.6–23. Israel's history is a recurring cycle of blessing, when the people are faithful to the Lord; sin, when they forsake the Law; punishment, when foreign enemies oppress Israel; and deliverance, when they cry out and the Lord shows mercy by intervening to save them. In 2 Maccabees the history of the Temple, reflecting the fortunes of the Jewish people, follows this cycle.

The history begins with the blessings brought by the good priest Onias (ch 3). The dramatic story of the attack on the Temple treasury by Heliodorus and the angelic intervention that saved it highlights the importance of the Temple as the locus of the divine presence when the people are faithful. The sins of the people are ominously introduced in ch 4 with a description of the Hellenization that occurred under Jason, the brother of Onias. The rich details of this chapter provide a useful historical picture of the conflict in Jerusalem over accommodation to Greek culture, as well as the strife over the high priesthood, during the years before the persecutions of Antiochus. Modern historians have been guided by this nuanced account to view the Maccabean revolt as a mix of civil war and rebellion against a foreign tyrant. In chs 3 and 4, as throughout the book, the epitomist shows that the attack of Seleucid kings on Jerusalem was precipitated by the intrigues of Hellenizers in Jerusalem.

The wrenching stories of the persecutions endured when Antiochus IV swept into Jerusalem to quell civil unrest occupy chs 5–8, the centerpiece of the book. So skilled a historian is the epitomist that the reader understands the actions of Antiochus to be both politically inevitable (5.11–14) and theologically predictable (4.16–17; 5.18–20). Antiochus occupied Jerusalem in order to eliminate the religious traditions of the Jews and to force assimilation of Greek ways. His edict prohibited the Jews from keeping the sabbath, observing their laws of purity, and circumcising their sons. Historians believe he was attempting to remove what he saw as the cause of political disturbances in Judea. In this context the author tells the dramatic stories of the first martyrs. The old man Eleazar chooses to die rather than eat pork, which is forbidden by the Torah. Like Socrates before his death, Eleazar delivers an eloquent speech describing his desire to leave a noble example to the young. The longest and most memorable story is the martyrdom of the mother and her seven sons. In the dramatic speeches made as the brothers go one by one to their deaths, the author articulates some of the most profound and influential religious ideas of the book.

These stories of Jewish faithfulness are set in bold relief against the impious deeds of the Hellenizers. As their abandoning the law for Greek culture brought on the desecration of the Temple, so the prayers of the martyrs make possible the next part of the epitomist's story, the purification of the Temple. The book's theology is expressed in the last words of the seventh brother (7.37–38) as he goes willingly to his death "to bring to an end the wrath of the Almighty that has justly fallen on our whole nation." The introduction of Judas Maccabeus is the sign that God has heard the prayer of the martyrs and has seen their faithfulness. The dramatic account of the revolt of Judas Maccabeus, his victory over Antiochus, and his purification of the Temple (8.1–10.9) weaves military history together with the language of theology. Similarly, the graphic account of Antiochus's death in ch 9 is designed to illustrate divine justice and the vindication of the martyrs.

The final section makes use of diplomatic correspondence and historical records to tell the history of Judea from 164 to 161 BCE under the Seleucid kings Antiochus Eupator and Demetrius I. In spite of royal permission for the Jews to live in peace according to their own laws, local rulers of neighboring regions were constantly stirring up conflict. As in earlier parts of the book, the epitomist frequently alludes to Hellenizers as the initiators of the trouble. Woven throughout these detailed historical accounts are the prayers of Judas and the people. For the epitomist the military victories are signs that God hears the prayers of the faithful. The vivid accounts of three heavenly rescues signal to the reader that God was acting through Judas Maccabeus (10.29–31; 12.22; 15.12–16).

A constellation of important theological ideas not found in the Hebrew scriptures but important in Judaism and Christianity appears in 2 Maccabees. Chief among these are the two related ideas of the creation of the world out of nothing ("creatio ex nihilo," 7.28) and the resurrection of the dead (hinted at in Dan 12.2 but explicitly stated in 2 Macc 7). The relation between these two beliefs is clearly articulated in the speeches of the mother and her seven sons (ch 7), which provide the most closely reasoned arguments in the Bible about resurrection of the dead. This story of the mother encouraging her seven sons to die for their faith in certain hope of resurrection, together with the companion story of the aged Eleazer going willingly to his death rather than eat food forbidden by the Torah (ch 6), became models for later authors writing Jewish and Christian martyrologies. The intrinsic link between the ideas of resurrection and martyrdom is evident as well in the story of Razis (13.37–45).

The belief in resurrection gives rise to the practice of praying for the dead. When Judas Maccabeus discovers that his fallen companions are wearing sacred tokens of the idols of Jamnia, he makes a sin offering and prays that their sin might be blotted out (12.39–43a). The epitomist interprets this as a prayer on behalf of the dead, justified by the hope of the resurrection (12.43b–45). Related to the idea of resurrection is the certainty that God's justice will punish the wicked as it rewards the righteous (3.27–28; 9.28; 13.8; 15.32–33), articulated later in the rabbinic principle of measure for measure. The deaths of Andronicus (4.30–38), Menelaus (13.1–8), and Nicanor (15.1–28) are described with explicit reference to divine justice. The story of the death of Antiochus (ch 9), borrowing themes from Isa 14, provides the most dramatic teaching of this principle.

The theological idea that dominates the book is the assurance that the history of Antiochene persecution and the Maccabean revolt reveals God's care for his people and the holy Temple. Through engaging storytelling and instructive speeches by the characters, the author guides the reader to see the events of this history with the eyes of faith.

1 The Jews in Jerusalem and those in the land of Judea,
To their Jewish kindred in Egypt,
Greetings and true peace.

2 May God do good to you, and may he remember his covenant with Abraham and Isaac and Jacob, his faithful servants. 3 May he give you all a heart to worship him and to do his will with a strong heart and a willing spirit. 4 May he open your heart to his law and his commandments, and may he bring peace. 5 May he hear your prayers and be reconciled to you, and may he not forsake you in time of evil. 6 We are now praying for you here.

7 In the reign of Demetrius, in the one hundred sixty-ninth year,[a] we Jews wrote

to you, in the critical distress that came upon us in those years after Jason and his company revolted from the holy land and the kingdom 8 and burned the gate and shed innocent blood. We prayed to the Lord and were heard, and we offered sacrifice and grain offering, and we lit the lamps and set out the loaves. 9 And now see that you keep the festival of booths in the month of Chislev, in the one hundred eighty-eighth year.[b]

10 The people of Jerusalem and of Judea and the senate and Judas,
To Aristobulus, who is of the family of

a 143 B.C.   b 124 B.C.

1.1–9: Letter to the Jews in Egypt. The authorship of these letters is uncertain. The first is addressed to the large Jewish community that had lived in Egypt for centuries (see Jer 44.1). 1: Greek letters usually began with the word *greetings,* and Jewish ones with *peace* (Rom 1.7). 2: Gen 15.18; 26.3; 35.12; Lev 26.27–45. 5: *Time of evil,* perhaps a persecution of Jews by Ptolemy VIII. 7: The previous letter was in the reign of Demetrius II, who was the son of Demetrius I, and whose reign was marked by conflicts over the kingship; he ruled 145–141 BCE and again 129–125. *The critical distress* was the capture and murder of the high priest Jonathan (1 Macc 12.48; 13.23). *Jason and his company,* 4.7–22; 5.5–10. *The kingdom,* rule of the legitimate high priests. 8: *Burned the gate,* 1 Macc 4.38. *Shed innocent blood,* 1 Macc 1.60–61. *We . . . were heard,* i.e., by God, when Simon made Judea independent (1 Macc 13.1–42). 9: *The festival of booths* would properly be kept in September (Lev 23.33–43). This refers to Hanukkah, celebrated on the 25th of *Chislev* (November/December), commemorating Judas Maccabeus's restoration of the Temple (10.1–8; 1 Macc 4.59). Palestinian Jews now wished the Egyptian Jews to observe the feast in 124 BCE, when they wrote.

1.10–2.18: Letter to Aristobulus. The purpose of the letter is to show why the new eight-day festival should be kept, though it had not been prescribed by the law of Moses. Keeping the festival implied accepting that Judas, like Nehemiah, was doing God's will. Nehemiah's rededication of the Temple was a precedent (1.18–36). 10: *The senate,* literally, "council of elders" (see 1 Macc 12.6). A commentary on the Torah by *Aristobulus* is referred to in other ancient sources, but it has not survived. *The anointed priests,* descendants of Zadok (2 Chr 31.10), from whom high priests were chosen. One branch of these came to Egypt with Ptolemy I. The *King,* Ptolemy VI Philometer (180–145 BCE). 11: *Grave dangers,* in the anointed priests, teacher of King Ptolemy, and to the Jews in Egypt,

Greetings and good health.

11 Having been saved by God out of grave dangers we thank him greatly for taking our side against the king,[a] 12 for he drove out those who fought against the holy city. 13 When the leader reached Persia with a force that seemed irresistible, they were cut to pieces in the temple of Nanea by a deception[b] employed by the priests of the goddess[b] Nanea. 14 On the pretext of intending to marry her, Antiochus came to the place together with his Friends, to secure most of its treasures as a dowry. 15 When the priests of the temple of Nanea had set out the treasures and Antiochus had come with a few men inside the wall of the sacred precinct, they closed the temple as soon as he entered it. 16 Opening a secret door in the ceiling, they threw stones and struck down the leader and his men; they dismembered them and cut off their heads and threw them to the people outside. 17 Blessed in every way be our God, who has brought judgment on those who have behaved impiously.

18 Since on the twenty-fifth day of Chislev we shall celebrate the purification of the temple, we thought it necessary to notify you, in order that you also may celebrate the festival of booths and the festival of the fire given when Nehemiah, who built the temple and the altar, offered sacrifices.

19 For when our ancestors were being led captive to Persia, the pious priests of that time took some of the fire of the altar and secretly hid it in the hollow of a dry cistern, where they took such precautions that the place was unknown to anyone. 20 But after many years had passed, when it pleased God, Nehemiah, having been commissioned by the king of Persia, sent the descendants of the priests who had hidden the fire to get it. And when they reported to us that they had not found fire but only a thick liquid, he ordered them to dip it out and bring it. 21 When the materials for the sacrifices were presented, Nehemiah ordered the priests to sprinkle the liquid on the wood and on the things laid upon it. 22 When this had been done and some time had passed, and when the sun, which had been clouded over, shone out, a great fire blazed up, so that all marveled. 23 And while the sacrifice was being consumed, the priests offered prayer—the priests and everyone. Jonathan led, and the rest responded, as did Nehemiah. 24 The prayer was to this effect:

"O Lord, Lord God, Creator of all things, you are awe-inspiring and strong and just and merciful, you alone are king and are kind, 25 you alone are bountiful, you alone are just and almighty and eternal. You rescue Israel from every evil; you chose the ancestors and consecrated them. 26 Accept this sacrifice on behalf of all your people Israel and preserve your portion and make it holy. 27 Gather together our scattered people, set free those who are slaves

---

a Cn: Gk *as those who array themselves against a king*
b Gk lacks *the goddess*

---

the time of king Antiochus IV (4.7). **13:** *The leader,* Antiochus IV, died later; his forces *were cut to pieces* (9.1–4; 1 Macc 6.1–4). *Nanea,* a Syrian goddess (originally Mesopotamian Nana) equated with the Greek goddess Artemis or Aphrodite. **14:** *Marry her,* the goddess, so as to obtain a large *dowry* from the treasures at her temple (cf. 9.2; 1 Macc 6.1–4). The ritual of sacred marriage between a king and the representative of a goddess is well attested in the ancient Near East. *Friends,* a special group in the king's court. **18:** *The festival of booths,* cf. 1 Macc 10.21; 1 Kings 8.2; Neh 8.13–18. *The festival of the fire,* vv. 19–36. Fire and light are associated with Hanukkah; the candles on an eight-branched candlestick (menorah) are lighted successively during the eight-day celebration. A Talmudic tradition tells of a small amount of oil that burned miraculously for a long time until new oil could be consecrated. **19–36:** The legend of the fire is not found elsewhere. **19:** *Persia,* actually Babylonia (2 Kings 24.14), later part of the Persian empire. **20:** *Many years,* from the early sixth to the mid-fifth centuries BCE. *Nehemiah . . . commissioned,* Neh 2.7–8. *Thick liquid,* naphtha or petroleum (v. 36). **22:** 1 Kings 18.33–38. **25:** *You chose,* Gen 18.19; Deut 4.37; Neh 9.7. **26:** *Your portion,* Israel (Deut 32.9). *Holy,* Lev 19.2. **27:** *Gather* among the Gentiles, look on those who are rejected and despised, and let the Gentiles know that you are our God. 28 Punish those who oppress and are insolent with pride. 29 Plant your people in your holy place, as Moses promised."

30 Then the priests sang the hymns. 31 After the materials of the sacrifice had been consumed, Nehemiah ordered that the liquid that was left should be poured on large stones. 32 When this was done, a flame blazed up; but when the light from the altar shone back, it went out. 33 When this matter became known, and it was reported to the king of the Persians that, in the place where the exiled priests had hidden the fire, the liquid had appeared with which Nehemiah and his associates had burned the materials of the sacrifice, 34 the king investigated the matter, and enclosed the place and made it sacred. 35 And with those persons whom the king favored he exchanged many excellent gifts. 36 Nehemiah and his associates called this "nephthar," which means purification, but by most people it is called naphtha.[a]

2 One finds in the records that the prophet Jeremiah ordered those who were being deported to take some of the fire, as has been mentioned, 2 and that the prophet, after giving them the law, instructed those who were being deported not to forget the commandments of the Lord, or to be led astray in their thoughts on seeing the gold and silver statues and their adornment. 3 And with other similar words he exhorted them that the law should not depart from their hearts.

4 It was also in the same document that the prophet, having received an oracle, ordered that the tent and the ark should follow with him, and that he went out to the mountain where Moses had gone up and had seen the inheritance of God. 5 Jeremiah came and found a cave-dwelling, and he brought there the tent and the ark and the altar of incense; then he sealed up the entrance. 6 Some of those who followed him came up intending to mark the way, but could not find it. 7 When Jeremiah learned of it, he rebuked them and declared: "The place shall remain unknown until God gathers his people together again and shows his mercy. 8 Then the Lord will disclose these things, and the glory of the Lord and the cloud will appear, as they were shown in the case of Moses, and as Solomon asked that the place should be specially consecrated."

9 It was also made clear that being possessed of wisdom Solomon[b] offered sacrifice for the dedication and completion of the temple. 10 Just as Moses prayed to the Lord, and fire came down from heaven and consumed the sacrifices, so also Solomon prayed, and the fire came down and consumed the whole burnt offerings. 11 And Moses said, "They were consumed because the sin offering had not been eaten." 12 Likewise Solomon also kept the eight days.

13 The same things are reported in the records and in the memoirs of Nehemiah, and also that he founded a library and col-

a Gk nephthai   b Gk he

together, Ps 147.2; Jer 23.8; Sir 36.3; Bar 5.6. **28:** Punish . . . insolent, 1 Sam 2.3–4. **29:** As Moses promised, Deut 30.5. **34:** Localities where miracles occurred were enclosed as sacred. The Persians considered fire holy. **36:** Nephthar is an otherwise unknown word. **2.1–3:** Although in Jer 40–43 the prophet remains in Judah after the destruction of Jerusalem, early Jewish traditions tell of his going with the exiles and hiding the ark in the earth (Letter of Jeremiah; 2 Bar 6–10; 4 Bar 3.8–20; Lives of the Prophets 2). **4:** Solomon brought the tent to Jerusalem with the ark (1 Kings 8.4); there is no further record of it in the Hebrew Bible. According to Alexander Polyhistor (first century BCE), perhaps from the historian Eupolemus, Jeremiah concealed the ark after the Temple was destroyed in 586 BCE. The mountain, Nebo (Deut 32.49). **8:** The glory and the cloud indicate God's direct presence (Ex 16.10). Solomon, 1 Kings 8.11. **9:** Solomon's wisdom, 1 Kings 3.3–28; 4.29–34. Offered sacrifice, 1 Kings 8.62–64. **10:** Moses prayed, Lev 9.24. Solomon, 2 Chr 7.1. **11:** The meaning is obscure, but see Lev 10.16–19. **12:** Eight days, 1 Kings 8.65; 2 Chr 7.9. **13:** The memoirs of Nehemiah, the biblical book of Nehemiah does lected the books about the kings and prophets, and the writings of David, and letters of kings about votive offerings. [14] In the same way Judas also collected all the books that had been lost on account of the war that had come upon us, and they are in our possession. [15] So if you have need of them, send people to get them for you.

16 Since, therefore, we are about to celebrate the purification, we write to you. Will you therefore please keep the days? [17] It is God who has saved all his people, and has returned the inheritance to all, and the kingship and the priesthood and the consecration, [18] as he promised through the law. We have hope in God that he will soon have mercy on us and will gather us from everywhere under heaven into his holy place, for he has rescued us from great evils and has purified the place.

19 The story of Judas Maccabeus and his brothers, and the purification of the great temple, and the dedication of the altar, [20] and further the wars against Antiochus Epiphanes and his son Eupator, [21] and the appearances that came from heaven to those who fought bravely for Judaism, so that though few in number they seized the whole land and pursued the barbarian hordes, [22] and regained possession of the temple famous throughout the world, and liberated the city, and re-established the laws that were about to be abolished, while the Lord with great kindness became gracious to them— [23] all this, which has been set forth by Jason of Cyrene in five volumes, we shall attempt to condense into a single book. [24] For considering the flood of statistics involved and the difficulty there is for those who wish to enter upon the narratives of history because of the mass of material, [25] we have aimed to please those who wish to read, to make it easy for those who are inclined to memorize, and to profit all readers. [26] For us who have undertaken the toil of abbreviating, it is no light matter but calls for sweat and loss of sleep, [27] just as it is not easy for one who prepares a banquet and seeks the benefit of others. Nevertheless, to secure the gratitude of many we will gladly endure the uncomfortable toil, [28] leaving the responsibility for exact details to the compiler, while devoting our effort to arriving at the outlines of the condensation. [29] For as the master builder of a new house must be concerned with the whole construction, while the one who undertakes its painting and decoration has to consider only what is suitable for its adornment, such in my judgment is the case with us. [30] It is the duty of the original historian to occupy the ground, to discuss matters from every side, and to take trouble with details, [31] but the one who recasts the narrative should be allowed to strive for brevity of expression and to forego exhaustive treatment. [32] At this point therefore let us begin our narrative, without adding any more to what has already been said; for it would be foolish to lengthen the preface while cutting short the history itself.

not contain these references. See Ezra 3.14; 1 Esd 5.46–50. There is no record that *he founded a library,* but the Pentateuch perhaps achieved canonical status in his time, and he may have collected the books of Kings, as well as other writings. *Votive offerings,* made to the Temple (Ezra 7.15–20). **14:** *Judas* Maccabeus may have *collected all the books* remaining after the destruction in the time of Antiochus IV (1 Macc 1.56–57). **16:** 1.18. **17:** *The kingship,* independence; the Hasmoneans were not yet called kings. **18:** 1.27; Deut 30.3.

**2.19–32: The epitomist's preface.** Following the style of Greek and Roman histories, the Preface presents highlights and entices readers (see Thucydides 1.23.1–3; Tacitus, *Histories* 1.2–3). **20–21:** *Appearances* (Gk "epiphaneiai"), true divine manifestations, in contrast to Antiochus's boastful title *Epiphanes,* "god manifest." *Judaism,* first known use of this term for the religion, in contrast to Hellenism (4.13). *Barbarian,* used by the Greeks for all non-Greeks, connotes "one who speaks a foreign language." It can also mean "savage," as in 4.25; 5.22; 10.4; 15.2. **23:** The five-volume work of *Jason of Cyrene* of which 2 Macc is an epitome, or abridgement, is no longer extant. *Cyrene* was in Libya.

3 While the holy city was inhabited in unbroken peace and the laws were strictly observed because of the piety of the high priest Onias and his hatred of wickedness, [2] it came about that the kings themselves honored the place and glorified the temple with the finest presents, [3] even to the extent that King Seleucus of Asia defrayed from his own revenues all the expenses connected with the service of the sacrifices.

[4] But a man named Simon, of the tribe of Benjamin, who had been made captain of the temple, had a disagreement with the high priest about the administration of the city market. [5] Since he could not prevail over Onias, he went to Apollonius of Tarsus,[a] who at that time was governor of Coelesyria and Phoenicia, [6] and reported to him that the treasury in Jerusalem was full of untold sums of money, so that the amount of the funds could not be reckoned, and that they did not belong to the account of the sacrifices, but that it was possible for them to fall under the control of the king. [7] When Apollonius met the king, he told him of the money about which he had been informed. The king[b] chose Heliodorus, who was in charge of his affairs, and sent him with commands to effect the removal of the reported wealth. [8] Heliodorus at once set out on his journey, ostensibly to make a tour of inspection of the cities of Coelesyria and Phoenicia, but in fact to carry out the king's purpose.

[9] When he had arrived at Jerusalem and had been kindly welcomed by the high priest of[c] the city, he told about the disclosure that had been made and stated why he had come, and he inquired whether this really was the situation. [10] The high priest explained that there were some deposits belonging to widows and orphans, [11] and also some money of Hyrcanus son of Tobias, a man of very prominent position, and that it totaled in all four hundred talents of silver and two hundred of gold. To such an extent the impious Simon had misrepresented the facts. [12] And he said that it was utterly impossible that wrong should be done to those people who had trusted in the holiness of the place and in the sanctity and inviolability of the temple that is honored throughout the whole world.

[13] But Heliodorus, because of the orders he had from the king, said that this money must in any case be confiscated for the king's treasury. [14] So he set a day and went in to direct the inspection of these funds.

There was no little distress throughout the whole city. [15] The priests prostrated themselves before the altar in their priestly vestments and called toward heaven upon him who had given the law about deposits,

a Gk *Apollonius son of Tharseas*   b Gk *He*
c Other ancient authorities read *and*

---

**3.1–4.6: Simon's plot against Onias.** A somewhat different account of this is found in 4 Macc 4.1–14. **3.1:** Jerusalem was not *in unbroken peace,* though quieter than in later years. The high priest Onias III, son of Simon the Just (Sir 50.1–21), ruled before 175 BCE. He turned against Syria and collaborated with Egypt, while his cousins, the family of Tobias, to which Simon (v. 4) belonged, were pro-Syrian. **2:** *The kings,* i.e., the Ptolemies of Egypt and Antiochus III the Great (reigned 233–187). **3:** *Seleucus* IV Philopator, son of Antiochus III, reigned 187–175. The events of 3.1–46 were in his reign. He was assassinated by Heliodorus (v. 7). **4:** *Simon,* was probably not from *the tribe of Benjamin.* Since his brother Menelaus was later appointed high priest (4.22–23), the family must have been from the priestly tribe of Levi. Some manuscripts read Bilgah instead of Benjamin. Bilgah was one of the Levitical priestly clans (Neh 12.5,18; 1 Chr 24.14). **5:** *Tarsus,* capital of Cilicia (Acts 9.11), then part of the Seleucid empire. *Coelesyria,* meaning "hollow Syria," originally designated the country between the Lebanon and Anti-lebanon mountains; here it is Palestine and Transjordan, including the coast (see 1 Macc 10.69). *Apollonius* was removed from office at the death of Seleucus IV in 175 BCE. **7:** *Heliodorus,* see v. 3n. **9:** *The high priest,* Onias III. **11:** *Hyrcanus,* actually a grandson of Tobias, was pro-Egyptian. He fled east of the Jordan after 198 BCE and built the fortress now known as Iraq el-Emir. He committed suicide on the accession of Antiochus IV in 175. *Simon had misrepresented the facts* only in part; Onias and Hyrcanus probably that he should keep them safe for those who had deposited them. 16 To see the appearance of the high priest was to be wounded at heart, for his face and the change in his color disclosed the anguish of his soul. 17 For terror and bodily trembling had come over the man, which plainly showed to those who looked at him the pain lodged in his heart. 18 People also hurried out of their houses in crowds to make a general supplication because the holy place was about to be brought into dishonor. 19 Women, girded with sackcloth under their breasts, thronged the streets. Some of the young women who were kept indoors ran together to the gates, and some to the walls, while others peered out of the windows. 20 And holding up their hands to heaven, they all made supplication. 21 There was something pitiable in the prostration of the whole populace and the anxiety of the high priest in his great anguish.

22 While they were calling upon the Almighty Lord that he would keep what had been entrusted safe and secure for those who had entrusted it, 23 Heliodorus went on with what had been decided. 24 But when he arrived at the treasury with his bodyguard, then and there the Sovereign of spirits and of all authority caused so great a manifestation that all who had been so bold as to accompany him were astounded by the power of God, and became faint with terror. 25 For there appeared to them a magnificently caparisoned horse, with a rider of frightening mien; it rushed furiously at Heliodorus and struck at him with its front hoofs. Its rider was seen to have armor and weapons of gold. 26 Two young men also appeared to him, remarkably strong, gloriously beautiful and splendidly dressed, who stood on either side of him and flogged him continuously, inflicting many blows on him. 27 When he suddenly fell to the ground and deep darkness came over him, his men took him up, put him on a stretcher, 28 and carried him away—this man who had just entered the aforesaid treasury with a great retinue and all his bodyguard but was now unable to help himself. They recognized clearly the sovereign power of God.

29 While he lay prostrate, speechless because of the divine intervention and deprived of any hope of recovery, 30 they praised the Lord who had acted marvelously for his own place. And the temple, which a little while before was full of fear and disturbance, was filled with joy and gladness, now that the Almighty Lord had appeared.

31 Some of Heliodorus's friends quickly begged Onias to call upon the Most High to grant life to one who was lying quite at his last breath. 32 So the high priest, fearing that the king might get the notion that some foul play had been perpetrated by the Jews with regard to Heliodorus, offered sacrifice for the man's recovery. 33 While the high priest was making an atonement, the same young men appeared again to Heliodorus dressed in the same clothing, and they stood and said, "Be very grateful to the high priest Onias, since for his sake the Lord has granted you your life. 34 And see that you, who have been flogged by heaven, report to all people the majestic power of God." Having said this they vanished.

35 Then Heliodorus offered sacrifice to the Lord and made very great vows to the Savior of his life, and having bidden Onias farewell, he marched off with his forces to the king. 36 He bore testimony to all concerning the deeds of the supreme God, which he had seen with his own eyes. 37 When the king asked Heliodorus what sort of person would be suitable to send on another mission to Jerusalem, he replied, 38 "If you have any enemy or plotter against your government, send him there, for you will get him back thoroughly flogged, if he survives at all; for there is certainly some

withheld tribute. **15:** *The law about deposits,* see Ex 22.7–8. **18:** Temples, whether pagan or Jewish, were considered inviolate. **19:** *Sackcloth,* a sign of mourning and penitence. Some young women were *kept indoors* until the marriage (Sir 42.9–12). **20:** *Holding up their hands,* the ancient gesture of prayer (1 Kings 8.54; 1 Tim 2.8). **24:** *Manifestation,* see 2.21n. **26:** *Two young men,* angelic figures; cf. 3 Macc power of God about the place. ³⁹For he who has his dwelling in heaven watches over that place himself and brings it aid, and he strikes and destroys those who come to do it injury." ⁴⁰This was the outcome of the episode of Heliodorus and the protection of the treasury.

4 The previously mentioned Simon, who had informed about the money against*a* his own country, slandered Onias, saying that it was he who had incited Heliodorus and had been the real cause of the misfortune. ²He dared to designate as a plotter against the government the man who was the benefactor of the city, the protector of his compatriots, and a zealot for the laws. ³When his hatred progressed to such a degree that even murders were committed by one of Simon's approved agents, ⁴Onias recognized that the rivalry was serious and that Apollonius son of Menestheus,*b* and governor of Coelesyria and Phoenicia, was intensifying the malice of Simon. ⁵So he appealed to the king, not accusing his compatriots but having in view the welfare, both public and private, of all the people. ⁶For he saw that without the king's attention public affairs could not again reach a peaceful settlement, and that Simon would not stop his folly.

7 When Seleucus died and Antiochus, who was called Epiphanes, succeeded to the kingdom, Jason the brother of Onias obtained the high priesthood by corruption, ⁸promising the king at an interview*c* three hundred sixty talents of silver, and from another source of revenue eighty talents. ⁹In addition to this he promised to pay one hundred fifty more if permission were given to establish by his authority a gymnasium and a body of youth for it, and to enroll the people of Jerusalem as citizens of Antioch. ¹⁰When the king assented and Jason*d* came to office, he at once shifted his compatriots over to the Greek way of life.

11 He set aside the existing royal concessions to the Jews, secured through John the father of Eupolemus, who went on the mission to establish friendship and alliance with the Romans; and he destroyed the lawful ways of living and introduced new customs contrary to the law. ¹²He took delight in establishing a gymnasium right under the citadel, and he induced the noblest of the young men to wear the Greek hat. ¹³There was such an extreme of Helleniza-

a Gk *and*  b Vg Compare verse 21: Meaning of Gk uncertain  c Or *by a petition*  d Gk *he*

6.18–19. 31: *The Most High* (Gen 14.18), a title also often used by non-Jews (Dan 3.26). 4.1–6: Intrigues concerning the high priesthood. *Simon* (see 3.4n.) was disturbed because *Onias* and *Heliodorus* were now friends. The latter may already have planned to kill Seleucus IV and wanted the high priest's good will. *Apollonius,* in favor with Seleucus, continued to support Simon. 5: Before Onias arrived in Antioch, Seleucus had already been assassinated by Heliodorus (175 BCE).

4.7–22: Jason as high priest. 7: *Antiochus* IV *Epiphanes,* "god manifest," called Epimanes, "madman," by his enemies, was brother of Seleucus IV, and *succeeded to the kingdom* despite Heliodorus's attempt at revolution. He reigned 175–164 BCE. He had great ability but intense passion and pride (1 Macc 1.1–10). *Jason the brother of Onias* III (3.1), originally named Joshua, took a Greek name; cf. 4 Macc 4.15–26. 8: A talent weighed about 34 kg (75 lb). 9–10: Like Alexander the Great and his successors, Antiochus promoted *the Greek way of life* in order to strengthen his kingdom through cultural unity. *A gymnasium and a body of youth for it,* the gymnasium was the center of political and cultural education, as well as sports. *To enroll the people of Jerusalem as citizens of Antioch,* may mean that prominent Jerusalemites became honorary citizens of the capital city Antioch, in Syria. Alternately, the phrase may mean that Jerusalem itself was legally organized as a Greek-style city named Antioch, with the honors and commercial advantages pertaining to that status. 11: *Royal concessions,* granted by Antiochus III (3.2). The mission of *Eupolemus* (1 Macc 8.17) was later. *Destroyed,* 1 Macc 1.15,44–50. 12: The broad-brimmed *Greek hat* was worn by the god Hermes; headgear often had national or religious significance. *The citadel,* either a fortification just north of the Temple, or perhaps the Temple mount itself. 13: *Hellenization,* Greek religion and culture (see vv. 9–10n.). *No true high priest,* because he got the office tion and increase in the adoption of foreign ways because of the surpassing wickedness of Jason, who was ungodly and no true[a] high priest, 14 that the priests were no longer intent upon their service at the altar. Despising the sanctuary and neglecting the sacrifices, they hurried to take part in the unlawful proceedings in the wrestling arena after the signal for the discus-throwing, 15 disdaining the honors prized by their ancestors and putting the highest value upon Greek forms of prestige. 16 For this reason heavy disaster overtook them, and those whose ways of living they admired and wished to imitate completely became their enemies and punished them. 17 It is no light thing to show irreverence to the divine laws—a fact that later events will make clear.

18 When the quadrennial games were being held at Tyre and the king was present, 19 the vile Jason sent envoys, chosen as being Antiochian citizens from Jerusalem, to carry three hundred silver drachmas for the sacrifice to Hercules. Those who carried the money, however, thought best not to use it for sacrifice, because that was inappropriate, but to expend it for another purpose. 20 So this money was intended by the sender for the sacrifice to Hercules, but by the decision of its carriers it was applied to the construction of triremes.

21 When Apollonius son of Menestheus was sent to Egypt for the coronation[b] of Philometor as king, Antiochus learned that Philometor[c] had become hostile to his government, and he took measures for his own security. Therefore upon arriving at Joppa he proceeded to Jerusalem. 22 He was welcomed magnificently by Jason and the city, and ushered in with a blaze of torches and with shouts. Then he marched his army into Phoenicia.

23 After a period of three years Jason sent Menelaus, the brother of the previously mentioned Simon, to carry the money to the king and to complete the records of essential business. 24 But he, when presented to the king, extolled him with an air of authority, and secured the high priesthood for himself, outbidding Jason by three hundred talents of silver. 25 After receiving the king's orders he returned, possessing no qualification for the high priesthood, but having the hot temper of a cruel tyrant and the rage of a savage wild beast. 26 So Jason, who after supplanting his own brother was supplanted by another man, was driven as a fugitive into the land of Ammon. 27 Although Menelaus continued to hold the office, he did not pay regularly any of the money promised to the king. 28 When Sostratus the captain of the citadel kept requesting payment—for the collection of the revenue was his responsibility—the two of them were summoned by the king on account of this issue. 29 Menelaus left his own brother Lysimachus as deputy in the high priesthood, while Sostratus left Crates, the commander of the Cyprian troops.

30 While such was the state of affairs, it happened that the people of Tarsus and of Mallus revolted because their cities had

a Gk lacks *true*  b Meaning of Gk uncertain  c Gk *he*

by bribery and did not keep the Mosaic law. **16–17:** For the interpretation of disaster as the result of forsaking the Torah, see 1 Kings 17.5–18, 2 Chr 36.11–21; Neh 9. **18:** *Tyre,* an important port north of Palestine (Josh 19.29; 1 Kings 7.13); *quadrennial games* had been held there as early as the time of Alexander the Great. **19:** *Antiochian citizens from Jerusalem,* see vv. 9–10n. A drachma was equivalent to a day's wages for a laborer. *Hercules,* the Greek name of the god Melkart of Tyre. **20:** *Triremes,* war vessels propelled by three benches of rowers. **21:** *Apollonius,* v. 4. *The coronation* of Ptolemy VI *Philometor* occurred about 172 BCE, some time after the death of his mother, Cleopatra I, and he ruled until 145. His advisors abandoned Cleopatra's policy, became *hostile* to Syria, and claimed Palestine. *Joppa,* the port ca. 56 km (35 mi) northwest of Jerusalem. **22:** *Phoenicia,* the coastal plain.

**4.23–50: Menelaus as high priest. 23:** *Menelaus* was high priest from about 172 to 162 BCE, when he was executed (13.3–8) and replaced by Alcimus (14.3–14). **26:** *Land of Ammon,* east of the Jordan, near modern Amman. **29:** *The Cyprian troops* were mercenaries. **30:** *Mallus* was on the Pyramus river east of been given as a present to Antiochis, the king's concubine. 31 So the king went hurriedly to settle the trouble, leaving Andronicus, a man of high rank, to act as his deputy. 32 But Menelaus, thinking he had obtained a suitable opportunity, stole some of the gold vessels of the temple and gave them to Andronicus; other vessels, as it happened, he had sold to Tyre and the neighboring cities. 33 When Onias became fully aware of these acts, he publicly exposed them, having first withdrawn to a place of sanctuary at Daphne near Antioch. 34 Therefore Menelaus, taking Andronicus aside, urged him to kill Onias. Andronicus[a] came to Onias, and resorting to treachery, offered him sworn pledges and gave him his right hand; he persuaded him, though still suspicious, to come out from the place of sanctuary; then, with no regard for justice, he immediately put him out of the way.

35 For this reason not only Jews, but many also of other nations, were grieved and displeased at the unjust murder of the man. 36 When the king returned from the region of Cilicia, the Jews in the city[b] appealed to him with regard to the unreasonable murder of Onias, and the Greeks shared their hatred of the crime. 37 Therefore Antiochus was grieved at heart and filled with pity, and wept because of the moderation and good conduct of the deceased. 38 Inflamed with anger, he immediately stripped off the purple robe from Andronicus, tore off his clothes, and led him around the whole city to that very place where he had committed the outrage against Onias, and there he dispatched the bloodthirsty fellow. The Lord thus repaid him with the punishment he deserved.

39 When many acts of sacrilege had been committed in the city by Lysimachus with the connivance of Menelaus, and when report of them had spread abroad, the populace gathered against Lysimachus, because many of the gold vessels had already been stolen. 40 Since the crowds were becoming aroused and filled with anger, Lysimachus armed about three thousand men and launched an unjust attack, under the leadership of a certain Auranus, a man advanced in years and no less advanced in folly. 41 But when the Jews[c] became aware that Lysimachus was attacking them, some picked up stones, some blocks of wood, and others took handfuls of the ashes that were lying around, and threw them in wild confusion at Lysimachus and his men. 42 As a result, they wounded many of them, and killed some, and put all the rest to flight; the temple robber himself they killed close by the treasury.

43 Charges were brought against Menelaus about this incident. 44 When the king came to Tyre, three men sent by the senate presented the case before him. 45 But Menelaus, already as good as beaten, promised a substantial bribe to Ptolemy son of Dorymenes to win over the king. 46 Therefore Ptolemy, taking the king aside into a colonnade as if for refreshment, induced the king to change his mind. 47 Menelaus, the cause of all the trouble, he acquitted of the charges against him, while he sentenced to death those unfortunate men, who would have been freed uncondemned if they had pleaded even before Scythians. 48 And so those who had spoken for the city and the

a Gk He   b Or in each city   c Gk they

Tarsus (3.5). Hellenistic kings often provided a wife or *concubine* with a regular income by giving her a city. Antiochus, being extravagant (see 1 Macc 3.30), was often in need of money. **32:** *Gave them,* either to pay tribute or as a bribe. **33:** *Daphne,* about 8 km (5 mi) from *Antioch,* had a *place of sanctuary* at a temple of Apollo and Artemis. **35:** *Unjust murder,* he had been lured from a place protected by the gods. **38:** *Stripped off the purple robe,* degrading him before execution. **39:** *The city,* Jerusalem. *Menelaus* was still in Antioch. **42:** *The temple robber,* Lysimachus. **44:** *The senate,* see 1.10n. **45:** *Dorymenes* had fought for Ptolemy IV against Antiochus III; his son *Ptolemy* had been governor of Cyprus and had deserted to Antiochus IV (see 10.12–13n.). **47:** The *Scythians* lived in what is now southern Russia and were proverbial for their brutality (3 Macc 7.5; 4 Macc 10.7).

villages[a] and the holy vessels quickly suffered the unjust penalty. 49 Therefore even the Tyrians, showing their hatred of the crime, provided magnificently for their funeral. 50 But Menelaus, because of the greed of those in power, remained in office, growing in wickedness, having become the chief plotter against his compatriots.

5 About this time Antiochus made his second invasion of Egypt. 2 And it happened that, for almost forty days, there appeared over all the city golden-clad cavalry charging through the air, in companies fully armed with lances and drawn swords— 3 troops of cavalry drawn up, attacks and counterattacks made on this side and on that, brandishing of shields, massing of spears, hurling of missiles, the flash of golden trappings, and armor of all kinds. 4 Therefore everyone prayed that the apparition might prove to have been a good omen.

5 When a false rumor arose that Antiochus was dead, Jason took no fewer than a thousand men and suddenly made an assault on the city. When the troops on the wall had been forced back and at last the city was being taken, Menelaus took refuge in the citadel. 6 But Jason kept relentlessly slaughtering his compatriots, not realizing that success at the cost of one's kindred is the greatest misfortune, but imagining that he was setting up trophies of victory over enemies and not over compatriots. 7 He did not, however, gain control of the govern-

ment; in the end he got only disgrace from his conspiracy, and fled again into the country of the Ammonites. 8 Finally he met a miserable end. Accused[b] before Aretas the ruler of the Arabs, fleeing from city to city, pursued by everyone, hated as a rebel against the laws, and abhorred as the executioner of his country and his compatriots, he was cast ashore in Egypt. 9 There he who had driven many from their own country into exile died in exile, having embarked to go to the Lacedaemonians in hope of finding protection because of their kinship. 10 He who had cast out many to lie unburied had no one to mourn for him; he had no funeral of any sort and no place in the tomb of his ancestors.

11 When news of what had happened reached the king, he took it to mean that Judea was in revolt. So, raging inwardly, he left Egypt and took the city by storm. 12 He commanded his soldiers to cut down relentlessly everyone they met and to kill those who went into their houses. 13 Then there was massacre of young and old, destruction of boys, women, and children, and slaughter of young girls and infants. 14 Within the total of three days eighty thousand were destroyed, forty thousand in hand-to-hand fighting, and as many were sold into slavery as were killed.

15 Not content with this, Antiochus[c] dared to enter the most holy temple in all

a Other ancient authorities read *the people*
b Cn: Gk *Imprisoned*   c Gk *he*

**5.1–27: Antiochus IV desecrates the Temple. 1:** *Second invasion,* Antiochus first invaded Egypt in 170 BCE (Dan 11.28; 1 Macc 1.16–24). Although 1 Macc speaks only of one invasion, Antiochus actually invaded Egypt again in 168. Though he defeated the Egyptians, the Romans forced him to withdraw (Dan 11.29–30). **2–4:** 3.25–26. *The city,* Jerusalem. **5–8:** *Jason* was an Oniad and pro-Egyptian (see 3.1n.). Thinking *that Antiochus was dead,* he planned, with Egyptian help, to recover the high priesthood. He was opposed by *Menelaus* the Tobiad (4.23) and also by the Jews loyal to Judaism; he massacred people of both factions. *Ammonites,* 4.26n. *Aretas* I, king of Nabatean Arabia, south and east of Palestine; his capital was at Petra. **9–10:** Rejected in Egypt, Jason fled to the *Lacedaemonians* in Sparta (1 Macc 12.7). *Unburied,* ancient peoples regarded an unburied dead body with horror, and leaving foes unburied was a way of showing contempt or committing a further outrage upon them (see 1 Macc 7.17; 1 Kings 13.22). **11–14:** So confused was the situation that Antiochus thought all *Judea was in revolt.* He was *raging inwardly* because the Romans had forced him out of Egypt (the Roman envoy, Popilius Laenas, had threatened him with war if he attempted to annex Egypt; see 1 Macc 1.20); both his foreign and his domestic programs were collapsing. **11:** *The city,* Jerusalem. **15–23a:** The Temple had been the world, guided by Menelaus, who had become a traitor both to the laws and to his country. 16 He took the holy vessels with his polluted hands, and swept away with profane hands the votive offerings that other kings had made to enhance the glory and honor of the place. 17 Antiochus was elated in spirit, and did not perceive that the Lord was angered for a little while because of the sins of those who lived in the city, and that this was the reason he was disregarding the holy place. 18 But if it had not happened that they were involved in many sins, this man would have been flogged and turned back from his rash act as soon as he came forward, just as Heliodorus had been, whom King Seleucus sent to inspect the treasury. 19 But the Lord did not choose the nation for the sake of the holy place, but the place for the sake of the nation. 20 Therefore the place itself shared in the misfortunes that befell the nation and afterward participated in its benefits; and what was forsaken in the wrath of the Almighty was restored again in all its glory when the great Lord became reconciled.

21 So Antiochus carried off eighteen hundred talents from the temple, and hurried away to Antioch, thinking in his arrogance that he could sail on the land and walk on the sea, because his mind was elated. 22 He left governors to oppress the people: at Jerusalem, Philip, by birth a Phrygian and in character more barbarous than the man who appointed him; 23 and at Gerizim, Andronicus; and besides these Menelaus, who lorded it over his compatriots worse than the others did. In his malice toward the Jewish citizens,[a] 24 Antiochus[b] sent Apollonius, the captain of the Mysians, with an army of twenty-two thousand, and commanded him to kill all the grown men and to sell the women and boys as slaves. 25 When this man arrived in Jerusalem, he pretended to be peaceably disposed and waited until the holy sabbath day; then, finding the Jews not at work, he ordered his troops to parade under arms. 26 He put to the sword all those who came out to see them, then rushed into the city with his armed warriors and killed great numbers of people.

27 But Judas Maccabeus, with about nine others, got away to the wilderness, and kept himself and his companions alive in the mountains as wild animals do; they continued to live on what grew wild, so that they might not share in the defilement.

6 Not long after this, the king sent an Athenian[c] senator[d] to compel the Jews to forsake the laws of their ancestors and no longer to live by the laws of God; 2 also to pollute the temple in Jerusalem and to call it the temple of Olympian Zeus, and to call the one in Gerizim the temple of Zeus-the-Friend-of-Strangers, as did the people who lived in that place.

3 Harsh and utterly grievous was the onslaught of evil. 4 For the temple was filled with debauchery and reveling by the Gentiles, who dallied with prostitutes and had

a Or worse than the others did in his malice toward the Jewish citizens  b Gk he  c Other ancient authorities read Antiochian  d Or Geron an Athenian

pillaged after the first Egyptian invasion (1 Macc 1.21–28). **15–16:** As a non-Jew Antiochus was forbidden to enter the most holy parts of the Temple. That the high priest Menelaus should conduct him shows how unfit Menelaus was (4.25). **17:** *Angered for a little while*, not permanently (cf. 6.12–16). **18:** *Heliodorus*, ch 3. **21:** *Talents*, see 4.8n. *His arrogance* was to think of himself as a god manifest (see 4.7n.). **22–23:** *Philip*, probably not the later regent (9.29). *Andronicus* (4.31, if this is indeed the same person) was now made governor of *Gerizim* in Samaria. **24–26:** *Antiochus sent Apollonius* about two years after the events of vv. 15–23 (see 1 Macc 1.29). Loyal Jews did not yet fight on the *sabbath* (1 Macc 2.32–41). **27:** *Judas Maccabeus*, the third son of Mattathias, of the Hasmonean family (1 Macc 2.1–28). *The defilement*, 4.11; 1 Macc 1.48,63.

**6.1–6: Campaign against Judaism.** What had been voluntary (4.9–17) was now enforced. This was the first religious persecution of the Jews (see 1 Macc 1.41–64). **2:** *Olympian Zeus* was now identified with the God of Israel and probably with Antiochus. *To pollute the temple*, they set up a statue or pagan altar intercourse with women within the sacred precincts, and besides brought in things for sacrifice that were unfit. ⁵The altar was covered with abominable offerings that were forbidden by the laws. ⁶People could neither keep the sabbath, nor observe the festivals of their ancestors, nor so much as confess themselves to be Jews.

7 On the monthly celebration of the king's birthday, the Jews*ᵃ* were taken, under bitter constraint, to partake of the sacrifices; and when a festival of Dionysus was celebrated, they were compelled to wear wreaths of ivy and to walk in the procession in honor of Dionysus. ⁸At the suggestion of the people of Ptolemais*ᵇ* a decree was issued to the neighboring Greek cities that they should adopt the same policy toward the Jews and make them partake of the sacrifices, ⁹and should kill those who did not choose to change over to Greek customs. One could see, therefore, the misery that had come upon them. ¹⁰For example, two women were brought in for having circumcised their children. They publicly paraded them around the city, with their babies hanging at their breasts, and then hurled them down headlong from the wall. ¹¹Others who had assembled in the caves nearby, in order to observe the seventh day secretly, were betrayed to Philip and were all burned together, because their piety kept them from defending themselves, in view of their regard for that most holy day.

12 Now I urge those who read this book not to be depressed by such calamities, but to recognize that these punishments were designed not to destroy but to discipline our people. ¹³In fact, it is a sign of great kindness not to let the impious alone for long, but to punish them immediately. ¹⁴For in the case of the other nations the Lord waits patiently to punish them until they have reached the full measure of their sins; but he does not deal in this way with us, ¹⁵in order that he may not take vengeance on us afterward when our sins have reached their height. ¹⁶Therefore he never withdraws his mercy from us. Although he disciplines us with calamities, he does not forsake his own people. ¹⁷Let what we have said serve as a reminder; we must go on briefly with the story.

18 Eleazar, one of the scribes in high position, a man now advanced in age and of noble presence, was being forced to open his mouth to eat swine's flesh. ¹⁹But he, welcoming death with honor rather than life with pollution, went up to the rack of his own accord, spitting out the flesh, ²⁰as all ought to go who have the courage to refuse things that it is not right to taste, even for the natural love of life.

21 Those who were in charge of that unlawful sacrifice took the man aside because of their long acquaintance with him, and privately urged him to bring meat of his own providing, proper for him to use, and to pretend that he was eating the flesh of the sacrificial meal that had been com-

*a* Gk *they*   *b* Cn: Gk *suggestion of the Ptolemies (or of Ptolemy)*

(1 Macc 1.54). The Samaritans, heterodox Jews, had built their temple on Mount *Gerizim*. **4**: *Things . . . unfit*, swine (Lev 11.7; 1 Macc 1.47). **6**: 1 Macc 1.45–51.
**6.7–17**: **The first martyrdoms.** Chs 6–7 are the earliest martyrologies, a type of writing popular subsequently in Christianity, designed to encourage the faithful when persecuted. **7**: *Dionysus*, Greek god of wine and the grape harvest; *ivy* was one of his symbols. **8**: *Ptolemais*, modern Acco, a coastal city 16 km (10 mi) north of Mt. Carmel. If the correct reading is *Ptolemies* or *Ptolemy* (as in textual note *b*), see 4.45n. *The same policy toward the Jews* living as citizens of the Antiochene republic. **10**: See 1 Macc 1.60–61. **11**: A different account is given in 1 Macc 2.29–41. *Philip*, see 5.22n. **12–17**: The victories of Israel's enemies are explained as God's corrective punishment, always followed by mercy (compare Isa 54.7–8; Ps 94.12–15).
**6.18–31**: **Martyrdom of Eleazar.** The story is told more elaborately in 4 Macc 5–7. **18**: *Scribes*, scholars learned in the law of Moses, not necessarily priests. *Swine's flesh* is prohibited according to Lev 11.7–8. **23**: *Hades*, the abode of the dead in Greek, referred to as "Sheol" in Hebrew texts. **24–28**:

manded by the king, 22 so that by doing this he might be saved from death, and be treated kindly on account of his old friendship with them. 23 But making a high resolve, worthy of his years and the dignity of his old age and the gray hairs that he had reached with distinction and his excellent life even from childhood, and moreover according to the holy God-given law, he declared himself quickly, telling them to send him to Hades.

24 "Such pretense is not worthy of our time of life," he said, "for many of the young might suppose that Eleazar in his ninetieth year had gone over to an alien religion, 25 and through my pretense, for the sake of living a brief moment longer, they would be led astray because of me, while I defile and disgrace my old age. 26 Even if for the present I would avoid the punishment of mortals, yet whether I live or die I will not escape the hands of the Almighty. 27 Therefore, by bravely giving up my life now, I will show myself worthy of my old age 28 and leave to the young a noble example of how to die a good death willingly and nobly for the revered and holy laws."

When he had said this, he went[a] at once to the rack. 29 Those who a little before had acted toward him with goodwill now changed to ill will, because the words he had uttered were in their opinion sheer madness.[b] 30 When he was about to die under the blows, he groaned aloud and said: "It is clear to the Lord in his holy knowledge that, though I might have been saved from death, I am enduring terrible sufferings in my body under this beating, but in my soul I am glad to suffer these things because I fear him."

31 So in this way he died, leaving in his death an example of nobility and a memorial of courage, not only to the young but to the great body of his nation.

7 It happened also that seven brothers and their mother were arrested and were being compelled by the king, under torture with whips and thongs, to partake of unlawful swine's flesh. 2 One of them, acting as their spokesman, said, "What do you intend to ask and learn from us? For we are ready to die rather than transgress the laws of our ancestors."

3 The king fell into a rage, and gave orders to have pans and caldrons heated. 4 These were heated immediately, and he commanded that the tongue of their spokesman be cut out and that they scalp him and cut off his hands and feet, while the rest of the brothers and the mother looked on. 5 When he was utterly helpless, the king[c] ordered them to take him to the fire, still breathing, and to fry him in a pan. The smoke from the pan spread widely, but the brothers[d] and their mother encouraged one another to die nobly, saying, 6 "The Lord God is watching over us and in truth has compassion on us, as Moses declared in his song that bore witness against the people to their faces, when he said, 'And he will have compassion on his servants.' "[e]

7 After the first brother had died in this way, they brought forward the second for their sport. They tore off the skin of his head with the hair, and asked him, "Will you eat rather than have your body punished limb by limb?" 8 He replied in the language of his ancestors and said to them, "No." Therefore he in turn underwent tortures as the first brother had done. 9 And

a Other ancient authorities read was dragged
b Meaning of Gk uncertain   c Gk he   d Gk they
e Gk slaves

Eleazar's speech resembles the last speech of Socrates in Plato's *Apology*. **30:** *Fear*, revere (Job 28.28; Ps 19.9).

**7.1–42: Martyrdom of seven brothers and their mother.** This story is a turning point in the book. The death of martyrs is both the height of Antiochus's persecution and the beginning of divine deliverance through Judas Maccabeus. The story is the principal subject of 4 Maccabees. **1:** *The king,* Antiochus IV Epiphanes. **6:** Deut 32.36. **8:** *The language of his ancestors,* Hebrew. No, "lo'" in Hebrew. **9:** God is often addressed in postbiblical Jewish prayer as *King of the universe.* The phrase *raise us up to an everlasting* when he was at his last breath, he said, "You accursed wretch, you dismiss us from this present life, but the King of the universe will raise us up to an everlasting renewal of life, because we have died for his laws."

10 After him, the third was the victim of their sport. When it was demanded, he quickly put out his tongue and courageously stretched forth his hands, 11 and said nobly, "I got these from Heaven, and because of his laws I disdain them, and from him I hope to get them back again." 12 As a result the king himself and those with him were astonished at the young man's spirit, for he regarded his sufferings as nothing.

13 After he too had died, they maltreated and tortured the fourth in the same way. 14 When he was near death, he said, "One cannot but choose to die at the hands of mortals and to cherish the hope God gives of being raised again by him. But for you there will be no resurrection to life!"

15 Next they brought forward the fifth and maltreated him. 16 But he looked at the king,*a* and said, "Because you have authority among mortals, though you also are mortal, you do what you please. But do not think that God has forsaken our people. 17 Keep on, and see how his mighty power will torture you and your descendants!"

18 After him they brought forward the sixth. And when he was about to die, he said, "Do not deceive yourself in vain. For we are suffering these things on our own account, because of our sins against our own God. Therefore*b* astounding things have happened. 19 But do not think that you will go unpunished for having tried to fight against God!"

20 The mother was especially admirable and worthy of honorable memory. Although she saw her seven sons perish within a single day, she bore it with good courage because of her hope in the Lord. 21 She encouraged each of them in the language of their ancestors. Filled with a noble spirit, she reinforced her woman's reasoning with a man's courage, and said to them, 22 "I do not know how you came into being in my womb. It was not I who gave you life and breath, nor I who set in order the elements within each of you. 23 Therefore the Creator of the world, who shaped the beginning of humankind and devised the origin of all things, will in his mercy give life and breath back to you again, since you now forget yourselves for the sake of his laws."

24 Antiochus felt that he was being treated with contempt, and he was suspicious of her reproachful tone. The youngest brother being still alive, Antiochus*c* not only appealed to him in words, but promised with oaths that he would make him rich and enviable if he would turn from the ways of his ancestors, and that he would take him for his Friend and entrust him with public affairs. 25 Since the young man would not listen to him at all, the king called the mother to him and urged her to advise the youth to save himself. 26 After much urging on his part, she undertook to persuade her son. 27 But, leaning close to him, she spoke in their native language as follows, deriding the cruel tyrant: "My son, have pity on me. I carried you nine months in my womb, and nursed you for three

*a* Gk *at him*   *b* Lat: Other ancient authorities lack *Therefore*   *c* Gk *he*

*renewal of life* draws on the Greek translation of Dan 12.2, which adds that some would be raised for reproach and eternal shame. **11:** *Heaven,* a circumlocution for God; used also in v. 34. **14:** Antiochus will have *no resurrection to life,* but rather to eternal reproach (see 7.9n.). **17:** Antiochus IV died in misery and his son was murdered (9.5–28). **18–19:** 6.12–16. **22:** The mother's speech appears to combine references to Sir 1.1–3, which it refutes, with technical vocabulary from Greek philosophy (*set in order the elements;* Plato, *Theaetetus* 210e; Aristotle, *Metaphysics* 998a.23). The author argues that resurrection is a mystery analogous to the creation of the world, or of a human being. Just as God caused something to exist that had not existed previously (see v. 28), so God can resurrect a person who has ceased to exist. **23:** A link between creation and redemption is made in Isa 43.1–2,6–7; 44.1–2; 46.3–4. **24:** *Friend,* see 1.14n. **28:** This verse was understood by Origen (185–254 CE) and subsequent Christian years, and have reared you and brought you up to this point in your life, and have taken care of you.[a] 28 I beg you, my child, to look at the heaven and the earth and see everything that is in them, and recognize that God did not make them out of things that existed.[b] And in the same way the human race came into being. 29 Do not fear this butcher, but prove worthy of your brothers. Accept death, so that in God's mercy I may get you back again along with your brothers."

30 While she was still speaking, the young man said, "What are you[c] waiting for? I will not obey the king's command, but I obey the command of the law that was given to our ancestors through Moses. 31 But you,[d] who have contrived all sorts of evil against the Hebrews, will certainly not escape the hands of God. 32 For we are suffering because of our own sins. 33 And if our living Lord is angry for a little while, to rebuke and discipline us, he will again be reconciled with his own servants.[e] 34 But you, unholy wretch, you most defiled of all mortals, do not be elated in vain and puffed up by uncertain hopes, when you raise your hand against the children of heaven. 35 You have not yet escaped the judgment of the almighty, all-seeing God. 36 For our brothers after enduring a brief suffering have drunk[f] of ever-flowing life, under God's covenant; but you, by the judgment of God, will receive just punishment for your arrogance. 37 I, like my brothers, give up body and life for the laws of our ancestors, appealing to God to show mercy soon to our nation and by trials and plagues to make you confess that he alone is God, 38 and through me and my brothers to bring to an end the wrath of the Almighty that has justly fallen on our whole nation."

39 The king fell into a rage, and handled him worse than the others, being exasperated at his scorn. 40 So he died in his integrity, putting his whole trust in the Lord.

41 Last of all, the mother died, after her sons.

42 Let this be enough, then, about the eating of sacrifices and the extreme tortures.

8 Meanwhile Judas, who was also called Maccabeus, and his companions secretly entered the villages and summoned their kindred and enlisted those who had continued in the Jewish faith, and so they gathered about six thousand. 2 They implored the Lord to look upon the people who were oppressed by all; and to have pity on the temple that had been profaned by the godless; 3 to have mercy on the city that was being destroyed and about to be leveled to the ground; to hearken to the blood that cried out to him; 4 to remember also the lawless destruction of the innocent babies and the blasphemies committed against his name; and to show his hatred of evil.

5 As soon as Maccabeus got his army organized, the Gentiles could not withstand him, for the wrath of the Lord had turned to mercy. 6 Coming without warning, he would set fire to towns and villages. He captured strategic positions and put to flight not a few of the enemy. 7 He found the nights most advantageous for such at-

---

a Or have borne the burden of your education
b Or God made them out of things that did not exist
c The Gk here for you is plural  d The Gk here for you is singular  e Gk slaves  f Cn: Gk fallen

---

authors to be a statement of the doctrine that God created the universe out of nothing. **32:** *Suffering because of our own sins* refers not to individual sins, but to the sin of the whole people, forsaking the laws of the Torah for Greek practices. **33:** 5.17; 6.12–16. **34–35:** This theology is developed in Wis 2–5. **36–37:** This prediction is graphically fulfilled in ch 9. **38:** *To bring to an end the wrath of the Almighty,* not by atoning for Israel's sins through their deaths (as in 4 Macc 1.11; 17.20–22), but by increasing the suffering of Israel to such a degree that God would be moved to intervene for them. See Deut 32.36; Judg 2.18; and especially Bar 4.

**8.1–7: Judas begins the revolt.** See 1 Macc 3.1–41. **2–4:** The prayer, referring to the profanation of *the Temple* (5.15–20; 6.1–5), the destruction of *the city* (5.21–26), the destruction of the innocent, and the commission of blasphemy (6.7–7.42), summarizes the account given so far in 2 Macc.

**Chs 8–15: Campaigns of the Maccabees.**

tacks. And talk of his valor spread everywhere.

8 When Philip saw that the man was gaining ground little by little, and that he was pushing ahead with more frequent successes, he wrote to Ptolemy, the governor of Coelesyria and Phoenicia, to come to the aid of the king's government. [9] Then Ptolemy[a] promptly appointed Nicanor son of Patroclus, one of the king's chief[b] Friends, and sent him, in command of no fewer than twenty thousand Gentiles of all nations, to wipe out the whole race of Judea. He associated with him Gorgias, a general and a man of experience in military service. [10] Nicanor determined to make up for the king the tribute due to the Romans, two thousand talents, by selling the captured Jews into slavery. [11] So he immediately sent to the towns on the seacoast, inviting them to buy Jewish slaves and promising to hand over ninety slaves for a talent, not expecting the judgment from the Almighty that was about to overtake him.

12 Word came to Judas concerning Nicanor's invasion; and when he told his companions of the arrival of the army, [13] those who were cowardly and distrustful of God's justice ran off and got away. [14] Others sold all their remaining property, and at the same time implored the Lord to rescue those who had been sold by the ungodly Nicanor before he ever met them, [15] if not for their own sake, then for the sake of the covenants made with their ancestors, and because he had called them by his holy and glorious name. [16] But Maccabeus gathered his forces together, to the number six thousand, and exhorted them not to be frightened by the enemy and not to fear the great multitude of Gentiles who were wickedly coming against them, but to fight nobly, [17] keeping before their eyes the lawless outrage that the Gentiles[c] had committed against the holy place, and the torture of the derided city, and besides, the overthrow of their ancestral way of life. [18] "For they trust to arms and acts of daring," he said, "but we trust in the Almighty God, who is able with a single nod to strike down those who are coming against us, and even, if necessary, the whole world."

19 Moreover, he told them of the occasions when help came to their ancestors; how, in the time of Sennacherib, when one hundred eighty-five thousand perished, [20] and the time of the battle against the Galatians that took place in Babylonia, when eight thousand Jews[d] fought along with four thousand Macedonians; yet when the Macedonians were hard pressed, the eight thousand, by the help that came to them from heaven, destroyed one hundred twenty thousand Galatians[e] and took a great amount of booty.

21 With these words he filled them with courage and made them ready to die for their laws and their country; then he divided his army into four parts. [22] He appointed his brothers also, Simon and Joseph and Jonathan, each to command a division,

a Gk he  b Gk one of the first  c Gk they
d Gk lacks Jews  e Gk lacks Galatians

**8.8–29: First victory over Nicanor.** See 1 Macc 3.38–4.25. **8:** *Philip,* see 5.22n. *Ptolemy* (see 4.45n.), appointed by Lysias after Antiochus had left for Persia (1 Macc 3.38). **9:** *Gorgias,* not Nicanor, is the principal figure in 1 Macc 3.38–4.25. **10:** Since the battle of Magnesia (190 BCE), in which the Romans took from Antiochus III control of most of Asia Minor (see 1 Macc 1.10), the Seleucids had been forced to pay *tribute;* perhaps the *two thousand talents* represented the last installment. **11:** Slave traders accompanied the expedition (cf. 8.34 and 1 Macc 3.41). *Ninety slaves for a talent,* a very low price. **13:** Compare 1 Macc 3.56. **15:** The idea expressed by these words, echoing Dan 9.19, occurs often in later Jewish prayers. *Covenants,* with the patriarchs and at Sinai (see 1.24–29; Ex 19.5–6). *Called them by his . . . name,* as God's people (Deut 28.10). **17:** *Lawless outrage,* 5.15–16. *Ancestral way of life,* observance of the Torah. **19:** 2 Kings 19.35. **20:** *The Galatians* from Asia Minor often served as mercenaries. Jewish forces evidently aided Antiochus III and *the Macedonians.* This conflict is otherwise unknown. **22:** *Simon,* high priest from 142 to 134 BCE, and *Jonathan,* from 160 to 143 or 142. *Joseph,* called John in 1 Macc 2.2; 9.36. **23:** *Eleazar,* another brother, was killed at Beth-zechariah (1 Macc 2.5; 6.43–46). The motto putting fifteen hundred men under each. [23] Besides, he appointed Eleazar to read aloud[a] from the holy book, and gave the watchword, "The help of God"; then, leading the first division himself, he joined battle with Nicanor.

24 With the Almighty as their ally, they killed more than nine thousand of the enemy, and wounded and disabled most of Nicanor's army, and forced them all to flee. [25] They captured the money of those who had come to buy them as slaves. After pursuing them for some distance, they were obliged to return because the hour was late. [26] It was the day before the sabbath, and for that reason they did not continue their pursuit. [27] When they had collected the arms of the enemy and stripped them of their spoils, they kept the sabbath, giving great praise and thanks to the Lord, who had preserved them for that day and allotted it to them as the beginning of mercy. [28] After the sabbath they gave some of the spoils to those who had been tortured and to the widows and orphans, and distributed the rest among themselves and their children. [29] When they had done this, they made common supplication and implored the merciful Lord to be wholly reconciled with his servants.[b]

30 In encounters with the forces of Timothy and Bacchides they killed more than twenty thousand of them and got possession of some exceedingly high strongholds, and they divided a very large amount of plunder, giving to those who had been tortured and to the orphans and widows, and also to the aged, shares equal to their own. [31] They collected the arms of the enemy,[c] and carefully stored all of them in strategic places; the rest of the spoils they carried to Jerusalem. [32] They killed the commander of Timothy's forces, a most wicked man, and one who had greatly troubled the Jews. [33] While they were celebrating the victory in the city of their ancestors, they burned those who had set fire to the sacred gates, Callisthenes and some others, who had fled into one little house; so these received the proper reward for their impiety.[a]

34 The thrice-accursed Nicanor, who had brought the thousand merchants to buy the Jews, [35] having been humbled with the help of the Lord by opponents whom he regarded as of the least account, took off his splendid uniform and made his way alone like a runaway slave across the country until he reached Antioch, having succeeded chiefly in the destruction of his own army! [36] So he who had undertaken to secure tribute for the Romans by the capture of the people of Jerusalem proclaimed that the Jews had a Defender, and that therefore the Jews were invulnerable, because they followed the laws ordained by him.

9 About that time, as it happened, Antiochus had retreated in disorder from the region of Persia. [2] He had entered the city called Persepolis and attempted to rob the

a Meaning of Gk uncertain   b Gk slaves
c Gk their arms

"The help of God" is prescribed by the Qumran War Scroll for one of the banners of the army returning from battle. 25: Slaves, vv. 11,34. 26: Gorgias and his army were in the hills (cf. the explanation in 1 Macc 4.16–18). 27–29: The victory was a sign of God's favor, but the campaign had not yet been won (6.12–16; 1 Macc 4.19–25). For the principles underlying the division of spoils, see Num 31.25–47; 1 Sam 30.21–25.

8.30–36: Other victories. 30: 1 Macc 5.37–44 tells of a battle against Timothy at Raphon. Bacchides, 1 Macc 7.8. 33: City of their ancestors, Jerusalem, with its sacred gates, Judas's ancestral home (1 Macc 2.1). Callisthenes, otherwise unknown. 34: Thrice-accursed, 15.3; Add Esth 16.15. 36: A Defender, i.e., God.

9.1–12: Antiochus's illness (1 Macc 6.1–16). Here, in contrast to the sequence in 1 Maccabees, this story is placed before the purification of the Temple (10.1–8; 1 Macc 4.36–61), Judas's southern campaigns (10.14–38; 1 Macc 5), and Lysias's first expedition (11.1–15; 1 Macc 4.26–35). 1: Antiochus went to Persia to strengthen his authority there and to get funds. 2: Persepolis, near modern Shiraz, the capital of Persia, founded by Darius I. 3: Antiochus was on his way to Babylon (1 Macc 6.4) but temples and control the city. Therefore the people rushed to the rescue with arms, and Antiochus and his army were defeated,[a] with the result that Antiochus was put to flight by the inhabitants and beat a shameful retreat. 3 While he was in Ecbatana, news came to him of what had happened to Nicanor and the forces of Timothy. 4 Transported with rage, he conceived the idea of turning upon the Jews the injury done by those who had put him to flight; so he ordered his charioteer to drive without stopping until he completed the journey. But the judgment of heaven rode with him! For in his arrogance he said, "When I get there I will make Jerusalem a cemetery of Jews."

5 But the all-seeing Lord, the God of Israel, struck him with an incurable and invisible blow. As soon as he stopped speaking he was seized with a pain in his bowels, for which there was no relief, and with sharp internal tortures— 6 and that very justly, for he had tortured the bowels of others with many and strange inflictions. 7 Yet he did not in any way stop his insolence, but was even more filled with arrogance, breathing fire in his rage against the Jews, and giving orders to drive even faster. And so it came about that he fell out of his chariot as it was rushing along, and the fall was so hard as to torture every limb of his body. 8 Thus he who only a little while before had thought in his superhuman arrogance that he could command the waves of the sea, and had imagined that he could weigh the high mountains in a balance, was brought down to earth and carried in a litter, making the power of God manifest to all. 9 And so the ungodly man's body swarmed with worms, and while he was still living in anguish and pain, his flesh rotted away, and because of the stench the whole army felt revulsion at his decay. 10 Because of his intolerable stench no one was able to carry the man who a little while before had thought that he could touch the stars of heaven. 11 Then it was that, broken in spirit, he began to lose much of his arrogance and to come to his senses under the scourge of God, for he was tortured with pain every moment. 12 And when he could not endure his own stench, he uttered these words, "It is right to be subject to God; mortals should not think that they are equal to God."[b]

13 Then the abominable fellow made a vow to the Lord, who would no longer have mercy on him, stating 14 that the holy city, which he was hurrying to level to the ground and to make a cemetery, he was now declaring to be free; 15 and the Jews, whom he had not considered worth burying but had planned to throw out with their children for the wild animals and for the birds to eat, he would make, all of them, equal to citizens of Athens; 16 and the holy sanctuary, which he had formerly plundered, he would adorn with the finest offerings; and all the holy vessels he would give back, many times over; and the expenses incurred for the sacrifices he would provide from his own revenues; 17 and in addition to all this he also would become a Jew and would visit every inhabited place to proclaim the power of God. 18 But when his sufferings did not in any way abate, for the judgment of God had justly come upon him, he gave up all hope for himself and wrote to the Jews the following letter, in the form of a supplication. This was its content:

19 "To his worthy Jewish citizens, Anti-

a Gk they were defeated   b Or not think thoughts proper only to God

apparently went north by way of Ecbatana (modern Hamadan). 4: 5.11; 7.3. The word heaven is used as a substitute for "God" (see 1 Macc 3.18,22; 2 Macc 7.11n.). 5: Here Antiochus's illness seems to be physical; in 1 Macc 6.8–9 it is psychological. 8: Command the waves, Ps 89.9; Job 38.8–11. Weigh the high mountains, Isa 40.12. 10: An allusion to the fall of the Day Star in Isa 14.12–21 has influenced this description of Antiochus's demise (see also Dan 4.34–37).

9.13–29: Repentance and death of Antiochus. 15: Citizens of Athens were proud of their heritage, though the city no longer had actual power. 16: 5.16. 17: 7.37; Dan 4.31–35. 19–27: The letter is no ochus their king and general sends hearty greetings and good wishes for their health and prosperity. 20 If you and your children are well and your affairs are as you wish, I am glad. As my hope is in heaven, 21 I remember with affection your esteem and goodwill. On my way back from the region of Persia I suffered an annoying illness, and I have deemed it necessary to take thought for the general security of all. 22 I do not despair of my condition, for I have good hope of recovering from my illness, 23 but I observed that my father, on the occasions when he made expeditions into the upper country, appointed his successor, 24 so that, if anything unexpected happened or any unwelcome news came, the people throughout the realm would not be troubled, for they would know to whom the government was left. 25 Moreover, I understand how the princes along the borders and the neighbors of my kingdom keep watching for opportunities and waiting to see what will happen. So I have appointed my son Antiochus to be king, whom I have often entrusted and commended to most of you when I hurried off to the upper provinces; and I have written to him what is written here. 26 I therefore urge and beg you to remember the public and private services rendered to you and to maintain your present goodwill, each of you, toward me and my son. 27 For I am sure that he will follow my policy and will treat you with moderation and kindness."

28 So the murderer and blasphemer, having endured the more intense suffering, such as he had inflicted on others, came to the end of his life by a most pitiable fate, among the mountains in a strange land. 29 And Philip, one of his courtiers, took his body home; then, fearing the son of Antiochus, he withdrew to Ptolemy Philometor in Egypt.

10 Now Maccabeus and his followers, the Lord leading them on, recovered the temple and the city; 2 they tore down the altars that had been built in the public square by the foreigners, and also destroyed the sacred precincts. 3 They purified the sanctuary, and made another altar of sacrifice; then, striking fire out of flint, they offered sacrifices, after a lapse of two years, and they offered incense and lighted lamps and set out the bread of the Presence. 4 When they had done this, they fell prostrate and implored the Lord that they might never again fall into such misfortunes, but that, if they should ever sin, they might be disciplined by him with forbearance and not be handed over to blasphemous and barbarous nations. 5 It happened that on the same day on which the sanctuary had been profaned by the foreigners, the purification of the sanctuary took place, that is, on the twenty-fifth day of the same month,

supplication (v. 18); it is addressed to Jews loyal to the king and bids them support his *son Antiochus* V (vv. 25–27). **20:** *Heaven,* 9.4n. **23:** *My father,* Antiochus III (see 3.3n.), who *appointed* Seleucus IV as his *successor. The upper country,* Babylonia and Persia (1 Macc 3.37). **28:** Antiochus IV died *among the mountains,* perhaps (according to Polybius, *History* 31.11) at Gabae or Isfahan (see 1 Macc 6.5). **29:** *Philip* is introduced differently in 1 Macc 6.14–15. See 13.23n. *Fearing* Lysias, viceroy in the west, rather than *the son of Antiochus,* who was a child, he went over to Syria's enemy, *Ptolemy* VI (see 4.21n.). Josephus says that Philip took over the Seleucid government and was later killed (*Ant.* 2.9.7).

**10.1–9: Purification of the Temple** (cf. 1 Macc 4.36–61). **1:** They *recovered the temple,* desecrated by Antiochus (6.2–4; 1 Macc 1.54), *and the city,* except for the citadel (1 Macc 4.60; 6.18). **2:** *The altars* had been used for worship of other gods. **3:** They *purified the sanctuary* by removing the desecrated stones (1 Macc 1.44–46). The reference to *striking fire out of flint* differs from the legends of 1.19–2.1. *Two years,* according to 1 Macc 1.54 and 4.52 it was three years. The *incense, lamps,* and *bread of the Presence,* prescribed by Ex 30.7–8; 25.30. **4:** 5.17–20; 6.12–16. **5–6:** *Chislev,* December, 164 BCE. Judas set the rededication of the Temple on the anniversary of the day that it had been polluted (1 Macc 1.54). The Hanukkah festival, celebrated *for eight days* like Solomon's dedication of the first Temple (1 Kings 8.65–66) and Hezekiah's reconsecration (2 Chr 29.17), commemorates this event (see also 1 Macc 4.52–59). At the normal time of *the festival of booths,* in September, *they had been wandering* like their which was Chislev. 6 They celebrated it for eight days with rejoicing, in the manner of the festival of booths, remembering how not long before, during the festival of booths, they had been wandering in the mountains and caves like wild animals. 7 Therefore, carrying ivy-wreathed wands and beautiful branches and also fronds of palm, they offered hymns of thanksgiving to him who had given success to the purifying of his own holy place. 8 They decreed by public edict, ratified by vote, that the whole nation of the Jews should observe these days every year.

9 Such then was the end of Antiochus, who was called Epiphanes.

10 Now we will tell what took place under Antiochus Eupator, who was the son of that ungodly man, and will give a brief summary of the principal calamities of the wars. 11 This man, when he succeeded to the kingdom, appointed one Lysias to have charge of the government and to be chief governor of Coelesyria and Phoenicia. 12 Ptolemy, who was called Macron, took the lead in showing justice to the Jews because of the wrong that had been done to them, and attempted to maintain peaceful relations with them. 13 As a result he was accused before Eupator by the king's Friends. He heard himself called a traitor at every turn, because he had abandoned Cyprus, which Philometor had entrusted to him, and had gone over to Antiochus Epiphanes. Unable to command the respect due his office,*a* he took poison and ended his life.

14 When Gorgias became governor of the region, he maintained a force of mercenaries, and at every turn kept attacking the Jews. 15 Besides this, the Idumeans, who had control of important strongholds, were harassing the Jews; they received those who were banished from Jerusalem, and endeavored to keep up the war. 16 But Maccabeus and his forces, after making solemn supplication and imploring God to fight on their side, rushed to the strongholds of the Idumeans. 17 Attacking them vigorously, they gained possession of the places, and beat off all who fought upon the wall, and slaughtered those whom they encountered, killing no fewer than twenty thousand.

18 When at least nine thousand took refuge in two very strong towers well equipped to withstand a siege, 19 Maccabeus left Simon and Joseph, and also Zacchaeus and his troops, a force sufficient to besiege them; and he himself set off for places where he was more urgently needed. 20 But those with Simon, who were money-hungry, were bribed by some of those who were in the towers, and on receiving seventy thousand drachmas let some of them slip away. 21 When word of what had happened came to Maccabeus, he gathered the leaders of the people, and accused these men of having sold their kindred for money by setting their enemies free to fight against them. 22 Then he killed these men who had turned traitor, and immediately captured the two towers. 23 Having success at arms

a Cn: Meaning of Gk uncertain

ancestors (Lev 23.43) and could not celebrate it. **7:** *Ivy-wreathed wands,* here in honor of God (compare 6.7). *Branches* were carried in procession at the feast of booths. *Fronds of palm* symbolize victory (1 Macc 13.51).

**10.10–13: Antiochus V and Ptolemy Macron. 10–11:** *Antiochus V Eupator* (9.25), son of Antiochus IV, reigned from 164 to 162 BCE, when he was murdered by order of Demetrius I. He was about nine years old; his father had *appointed . . . Lysias* as regent (1 Macc 3.32–33). **12–13:** Ptolemy had changed allegiance from Egypt to Syria (see 4.45n.; 6.8n.); now he was friendly *to the Jews. Philometor,* see 4.21n.

**10.14–23: Attacks on the Idumeans** (1 Macc 5.1–3,9–54). **14:** *Gorgias* succeeded Ptolemy. **15:** *Idumeans,* the earlier Edomites, who controlled territory south of Judea (see 1 Macc 5.3); John Hyrcanus later forced them to adopt Judaism. *Those . . . banished,* supporters of Menelaus. **19:** *Urgently needed,* perhaps in Ammon and Gilead (1 Macc 5.6–13). **20:** *Drachma,* see 4.19n.

in everything he undertook, he destroyed more than twenty thousand in the two strongholds.

24 Now Timothy, who had been defeated by the Jews before, gathered a tremendous force of mercenaries and collected the cavalry from Asia in no small number. He came on, intending to take Judea by storm. 25 As he drew near, Maccabeus and his men sprinkled dust on their heads and girded their loins with sackcloth, in supplication to God. 26 Falling upon the steps before the altar, they implored him to be gracious to them and to be an enemy to their enemies and an adversary to their adversaries, as the law declares. 27 And rising from their prayer they took up their arms and advanced a considerable distance from the city; and when they came near the enemy they halted. 28 Just as dawn was breaking, the two armies joined battle, the one having as pledge of success and victory not only their valor but also their reliance on the Lord, while the other made rage their leader in the fight.

29 When the battle became fierce, there appeared to the enemy from heaven five resplendent men on horses with golden bridles, and they were leading the Jews. 30 Two of them took Maccabeus between them, and shielding him with their own armor and weapons, they kept him from being wounded. They showered arrows and thunderbolts on the enemy, so that, confused and blinded, they were thrown into disorder and cut to pieces. 31 Twenty thousand five hundred were slaughtered, besides six hundred cavalry.

32 Timothy himself fled to a stronghold called Gazara, especially well garrisoned, where Chaereas was commander. 33 Then Maccabeus and his men were glad, and they besieged the fort for four days. 34 The men within, relying on the strength of the place, kept blaspheming terribly and uttering wicked words. 35 But at dawn of the fifth day, twenty young men in the army of Maccabeus, fired with anger because of the blasphemies, bravely stormed the wall and with savage fury cut down everyone they met. 36 Others who came up in the same way wheeled around against the defenders and set fire to the towers; they kindled fires and burned the blasphemers alive. Others broke open the gates and let in the rest of the force, and they occupied the city. 37 They killed Timothy, who was hiding in a cistern, and his brother Chaereas, and Apollophanes. 38 When they had accomplished these things, with hymns and thanksgivings they blessed the Lord who shows great kindness to Israel and gives them the victory.

11 Very soon after this, Lysias, the king's guardian and kinsman, who was in charge of the government, being vexed at what had happened, 2 gathered about eighty thousand infantry and all his cavalry and came against the Jews. He intended to make the city a home for Greeks, 3 and to levy tribute on the temple as he did on the sacred places of the other nations, and to put up the high priesthood for sale every year. 4 He took no account whatever of the power of God, but was elated with his ten thousands of infantry, and his thousands of cavalry, and his eighty elephants. 5 Invading Judea, he approached

10.24–38: Victory over Timothy. 24: They met *Timothy* (8.30) at *dawn* (v. 28) at Dathema east of the Jordan (1 Macc 5.28–34). 26: Ex 23.22. 29: 3.24–26. 31: *Twenty thousand five hundred*, compare the number of fatalities mentioned in 8.30; 10.17,23. 32–38: The fort of *Gazara* (earlier Gezer, 1 Macc 4.15; 7.45) was well garrisoned; Simon captured it much later (1 Macc 13.43–48). In 1 Macc 5.8 the defeat of Timothy is associated with the taking of Jazer, not Gazara. 37: *They killed Timothy*; but a Timothy reappears in 12.2,18–25 (cf. 1 Macc 5.11–40).

11.1–15: Victory over Lysias at Beth-zur. This probably occurred before the dedication of the Temple (1 Macc 4.26–35). 1: *Lysias*, see 10.10–13n. 3: In the Hellenistic world *sale* of the *priesthood* was not unusual; Antiochus IV had twice disposed of the Jewish high priesthood (4.7,24). 4: *Elephants*, often used to force an opening in opposing ranks of soldiers; see 1 Macc 1.17; 6.34–35. 5: *Beth-zur*, about 25 km (16 mi) south-southeast of Jerusalem on the road to Hebron. 6: *Good angel*, 15.23; Ex 23.20; Josh

Beth-zur, which was a fortified place about five stadia[a] from Jerusalem, and pressed it hard.

6 When Maccabeus and his men got word that Lysias[b] was besieging the strongholds, they and all the people, with lamentations and tears, prayed the Lord to send a good angel to save Israel. 7 Maccabeus himself was the first to take up arms, and he urged the others to risk their lives with him to aid their kindred. Then they eagerly rushed off together. 8 And there, while they were still near Jerusalem, a horseman appeared at their head, clothed in white and brandishing weapons of gold. 9 And together they all praised the merciful God, and were strengthened in heart, ready to assail not only humans but the wildest animals or walls of iron. 10 They advanced in battle order, having their heavenly ally, for the Lord had mercy on them. 11 They hurled themselves like lions against the enemy, and laid low eleven thousand of them and sixteen hundred cavalry, and forced all the rest to flee. 12 Most of them got away stripped and wounded, and Lysias himself escaped by disgraceful flight.

13 As he was not without intelligence, he pondered over the defeat that had befallen him, and realized that the Hebrews were invincible because the mighty God fought on their side. So he sent to them 14 and persuaded them to settle everything on just terms, promising that he would persuade the king, constraining him to be their friend.[a] 15 Maccabeus, having regard for the common good, agreed to all that Lysias urged. For the king granted every request in behalf of the Jews which Maccabeus delivered to Lysias in writing.

16 The letter written to the Jews by Lysias was to this effect:

"Lysias to the people of the Jews, greetings. 17 John and Absalom, who were sent by you, have delivered your signed communication and have asked about the matters indicated in it. 18 I have informed the king of everything that needed to be brought before him, and he has agreed to what was possible. 19 If you will maintain your goodwill toward the government, I will endeavor in the future to help promote your welfare. 20 And concerning such matters and their details, I have ordered these men and my representatives to confer with you. 21 Farewell. The one hundred forty-eighth year,[c] Dioscorinthius twenty-fourth."

22 The king's letter ran thus:

"King Antiochus to his brother Lysias, greetings. 23 Now that our father has gone on to the gods, we desire that the subjects of the kingdom be undisturbed in caring for their own affairs. 24 We have heard that the Jews do not consent to our father's change to Greek customs, but prefer their own way of living and ask that their own customs be allowed them. 25 Accordingly, since we choose that this nation also should be free from disturbance, our decision is that their temple be restored to them and that they shall live according to the customs of their ancestors. 26 You will do well, therefore, to send word to them and give them pledges of friendship, so that they may know our policy and be of good cheer and go on happily in the conduct of their own affairs."

27 To the nation the king's letter was as follows:

a Meaning of Gk uncertain   b Gk he   c 164 B.C.

5.13–15; Judg 6.11; 2 Kings 19.35. **8:** For similar apparitions, see 3.25–26; 5.2–3; 10.29–30. **13–15:** According to 1 Macc 4.35 no peace was made, but Lysias returned to Antioch for reinforcements. He may have heard of Antiochus's death and hastened home to take control.

**11.16–38: Letters of Lysias, Antiochus V, and the Romans.** If Lysias heard of Philip's plot (see 9.29n.), he may have wished to gain time through friendly gestures to the Jews. **16–21:** Lysias's letter to the Jews. **16:** He wrote *to the people* rather than to Judas. **17:** *John,* perhaps the brother of Judas (1 Macc 2.2). *Absalom,* see 1 Macc 11.70; 13.11n. **21:** The date is early December, 164 BCE, before Judas rededicated the Temple (1 Macc 4.52). **22–26:** Antiochus's letter to Lysias. **23:** *Our father,* Antiochus IV, *has gone on to the gods;* in his lifetime he had been worshipped. **25:** 1 Macc 4.36–61 says nothing of this, but Lysias may have instructed the citadel garrison not to interfere with the Temple. **27–33:** Antiochus's letter

"King Antiochus to the senate of the Jews and to the other Jews, greetings. 28 If you are well, it is as we desire. We also are in good health. 29 Menelaus has informed us that you wish to return home and look after your own affairs. 30 Therefore those who go home by the thirtieth of Xanthicus will have our pledge of friendship and full permission 31 for the Jews to enjoy their own food and laws, just as formerly, and none of them shall be molested in any way for what may have been done in ignorance. 32 And I have also sent Menelaus to encourage you. 33 Farewell. The one hundred forty-eighth year,[a] Xanthicus fifteenth."

34 The Romans also sent them a letter, which read thus:

"Quintus Memmius and Titus Manius, envoys of the Romans, to the people of the Jews, greetings. 35 With regard to what Lysias the kinsman of the king has granted you, we also give consent. 36 But as to the matters that he decided are to be referred to the king, as soon as you have considered them, send some one promptly so that we may make proposals appropriate for you. For we are on our way to Antioch. 37 Therefore make haste and send messengers so that we may have your judgment. 38 Farewell. The one hundred forty-eighth year,[a] Xanthicus fifteenth."

12 When this agreement had been reached, Lysias returned to the king, and the Jews went about their farming.

2 But some of the governors in various places, Timothy and Apollonius son of Gennaeus, as well as Hieronymus and Demophon, and in addition to these Nicanor the governor of Cyprus, would not let them live quietly and in peace. 3 And the people of Joppa did so ungodly a deed as this: they invited the Jews who lived among them to embark, with their wives and children, on boats that they had provided, as though there were no ill will to the Jews;[b] 4 and this was done by public vote of the city. When they accepted, because they wished to live peaceably and suspected nothing, the people of Joppa[c] took them out to sea and drowned them, at least two hundred. 5 When Judas heard of the cruelty visited on his compatriots, he gave orders to his men 6 and, calling upon God, the righteous judge, attacked the murderers of his kindred. He set fire to the harbor by night, burned the boats, and massacred those who had taken refuge there. 7 Then, because the city's gates were closed, he withdrew, intending to come again and root out the whole community of Joppa. 8 But learning that the people in Jamnia meant in the same way to wipe out the Jews who were living among them, 9 he attacked the Jamnites by night and set fire to the harbor and the fleet, so that the glow of the light was seen in Jerusalem, thirty miles[d] distant.

10 When they had gone more than a mile[e] from there, on their march against Timothy, at least five thousand Arabs with

a 164 B.C.   b Gk to them   c Gk they   d Gk two hundred forty stadia   e Gk nine stadia

to the Jews. Like the letter of Lysias above, this letter is addressed *to the senate* (see 1.10n.) and not to Judas (see v. 16). **29:** *Menelaus* had gone to Antioch and advised the king to let the Jews *return* to Jerusalem. He was now sent back (v. 32), hoping to regain the high priesthood. **30:** *Xanthicus,* March–April. **31:** *Their own food and laws,* 1 Macc 1.47–49. The words *in ignorance* imply that the king still maintained his claims and merely granted pardon (1 Macc 13.39). **34–37:** Letter of the Romans to the Jews. The *envoys* acted as intermediaries in *matters . . . referred to the king* that were still under negotiation.

**12.1–16: Attacks on Joppa, Jamnia, and Caspin. 2:** *Timothy,* 8.30–33; 10.24–37. *Apollonius,* not the Apollonius of 4.21. *Nicanor* is called *governor of Cyprus;* it was under Egypt's rule until 58 BCE, but Syria may have claimed it after the defection of Ptolemy Macron (10.13). There may have been two Nicanors (see 14.11–14n.). **3:** *Joppa,* modern Jaffa, on the Mediterranean coast just south of modern Tel Aviv. **8:** *Jamnia,* about 23 km (14 mi) south of Joppa (1 Macc 5.58). **13:** *Caspin,* perhaps Chaspho in Gilead, east of the Sea of Galilee (1 Macc 5.36). **15:** Josh 6.1–21.

five hundred cavalry attacked them. [11] After a hard fight, Judas and his companions, with God's help, were victorious. The defeated nomads begged Judas to grant them pledges of friendship, promising to give him livestock and to help his people[a] in all other ways. [12] Judas, realizing that they might indeed be useful in many ways, agreed to make peace with them; and after receiving his pledges they went back to their tents.

[13] He also attacked a certain town that was strongly fortified with earthworks[b] and walls, and inhabited by all sorts of Gentiles. Its name was Caspin. [14] Those who were within, relying on the strength of the walls and on their supply of provisions, behaved most insolently toward Judas and his men, railing at them and even blaspheming and saying unholy things. [15] But Judas and his men, calling upon the great Sovereign of the world, who without battering rams or engines of war overthrew Jericho in the days of Joshua, rushed furiously upon the walls. [16] They took the town by the will of God, and slaughtered untold numbers, so that the adjoining lake, a quarter of a mile[c] wide, appeared to be running over with blood.

[17] When they had gone ninety-five miles[d] from there, they came to Charax, to the Jews who are called Toubiani. [18] They did not find Timothy in that region, for he had by then left there without accomplishing anything, though in one place he had left a very strong garrison. [19] Dositheus and Sosipater, who were captains under Maccabeus, marched out and destroyed those whom Timothy had left in the stronghold, more than ten thousand men. [20] But Maccabeus arranged his army in divisions, set men[a] in command of the divisions, and hurried after Timothy, who had with him one hundred twenty thousand infantry and two thousand five hundred cavalry.

[21] When Timothy learned of the approach of Judas, he sent off the women and the children and also the baggage to a place called Carnaim; for that place was hard to besiege and difficult of access because of the narrowness of all the approaches. [22] But when Judas's first division appeared, terror and fear came over the enemy at the manifestation to them of him who sees all things. In their flight they rushed headlong in every direction, so that often they were injured by their own men and pierced by the points of their own swords. [23] Judas pressed the pursuit with the utmost vigor, putting the sinners to the sword, and destroyed as many as thirty thousand.

[24] Timothy himself fell into the hands of Dositheus and Sosipater and their men. With great guile he begged them to let him go in safety, because he held the parents of most of them, and the brothers of some, to whom no consideration would be shown. [25] And when with many words he had confirmed his solemn promise to restore them unharmed, they let him go, for the sake of saving their kindred.

[26] Then Judas[e] marched against Carnaim and the temple of Atargatis, and slaughtered twenty-five thousand people. [27] After the rout and destruction of these, he marched also against Ephron, a fortified town where Lysias lived with multitudes of people of all nationalities.[b] Stalwart young men took their stand before the walls and made a vigorous defense; and great stores of war engines and missiles were there. [28] But the Jews[f] called upon the Sovereign who with power shatters the might of his enemies, and they got the town into their hands, and killed as many as twenty-five thousand of those who were in it.

a Gk them    b Meaning of Gk uncertain    c Gk two stadia    d Gk seven hundred fifty stadia    e Gk he    f Gk they

12.17–31: Battles in the northeast (the account supplements 1 Macc 5.9–32). 17: Charax, unknown. Toubiani, perhaps people of Tob (1 Macc 5.13). 18: One place, perhaps Bozrah; see 1 Macc 5.28. 21: Carnaim, in Gilead, exact location uncertain (Gen 14.5; 1 Macc 5.26). 22: Manifestation, see 2.21n; 3.24. 26: Atargatis, a Syrian goddess. 27: He marched south against Ephron, 13 km (8 mi) east of the Jordan, opposite Scythopolis (v. 29; 1 Macc 5.46–51). War engines were large catapults. 29: Scythopolis, ancient

29 Setting out from there, they hastened to Scythopolis, which is seventy-five miles[a] from Jerusalem. 30 But when the Jews who lived there bore witness to the goodwill that the people of Scythopolis had shown them and their kind treatment of them in times of misfortune, 31 they thanked them and exhorted them to be well disposed to their race in the future also. Then they went up to Jerusalem, as the festival of weeks was close at hand.

32 After the festival called Pentecost, they hurried against Gorgias, the governor of Idumea, 33 who came out with three thousand infantry and four hundred cavalry. 34 When they joined battle, it happened that a few of the Jews fell. 35 But a certain Dositheus, one of Bacenor's men, who was on horseback and was a strong man, caught hold of Gorgias, and grasping his cloak was dragging him off by main strength, wishing to take the accursed man alive, when one of the Thracian cavalry bore down on him and cut off his arm; so Gorgias escaped and reached Marisa.

36 As Esdris and his men had been fighting for a long time and were weary, Judas called upon the Lord to show himself their ally and leader in the battle. 37 In the language of their ancestors he raised the battle cry, with hymns; then he charged against Gorgias's troops when they were not expecting it, and put them to flight.

38 Then Judas assembled his army and went to the city of Adullam. As the seventh day was coming on, they purified themselves according to the custom, and kept the sabbath there.

39 On the next day, as had now become necessary, Judas and his men went to take up the bodies of the fallen and to bring them back to lie with their kindred in the sepulchres of their ancestors. 40 Then under the tunic of each one of the dead they found sacred tokens of the idols of Jamnia, which the law forbids the Jews to wear. And it became clear to all that this was the reason these men had fallen. 41 So they all blessed the ways of the Lord, the righteous judge, who reveals the things that are hidden; 42 and they turned to supplication, praying that the sin that had been committed might be wholly blotted out. The noble Judas exhorted the people to keep themselves free from sin, for they had seen with their own eyes what had happened as the result of the sin of those who had fallen. 43 He also took up a collection, man by man, to the amount of two thousand drachmas of silver, and sent it to Jerusalem to provide for a sin offering. In doing this he acted very well and honorably, taking account of the resurrection. 44 For if he were not expecting that those who had fallen would rise again, it would have been superfluous and foolish to pray for the dead. 45 But if he was looking to the splendid reward that is laid up for those who fall asleep in godliness, it was a

a Gk six hundred stadia

Beth-shan, about 26 km (16 mi) south of the Sea of Galilee (Judg 1.27; 1 Kings 4.12), then and later an important city (see 1 Macc 5.52). **31:** The *festival of weeks* or Pentecost was at the time of the wheat harvest, seven weeks after Passover, and was celebrated in Jerusalem (Ex 34.22–24; Deut 16.9–12).

**12.32–38: Battle with Gorgias. 32:** *Gorgias,* see 10.14–15. **35:** *Dositheus,* vv. 19,24. *Marisa,* earlier Maresha (Josh 15.44), in the foothills 32 km (20 mi) southwest of Jerusalem (see 1 Macc 5.66). **36:** *Esdris,* evidently a division leader (v. 20). **38:** *City of Adullam,* northeast of Marisa (Josh 12.15; 15.35). They *kept the sabbath,* when it was not necessary to fight (8.27; see 1 Macc 2.41, where the principle that one may profane one sabbath in order to keep all the others is implied).

**12.39–45: Prayers for the dead.** The author believed that many had been killed because they wore *sacred tokens* of gods *which the law forbids* (v. 40; Deut 7.25–26), but according to Josephus (*Ant.* 12.8.6) this reverse befell them because they had disobeyed Judas's instructions not to join battle before his arrival. See also 1 Macc 5.67. The *sin offering* could have been intended by Judas to protect the living soldiers from the guilt in their midst (see Lev 4–5). The author here makes the first known statement of the doctrine that prayer makes *atonement* for the sins of *the dead* (v. 45), and it is justified by the hope that *those who had fallen would rise again* (vv. 43–44; 7.11; 14.46; Dan 12.1–3). *Fall asleep,* die.

holy and pious thought. Therefore he made atonement for the dead, so that they might be delivered from their sin.

**13** In the one hundred forty-ninth year[a] word came to Judas and his men that Antiochus Eupator was coming with a great army against Judea, 2 and with him Lysias, his guardian, who had charge of the government. Each of them had a Greek force of one hundred ten thousand infantry, five thousand three hundred cavalry, twenty-two elephants, and three hundred chariots armed with scythes.

3 Menelaus also joined them and with utter hypocrisy urged Antiochus on, not for the sake of his country's welfare, but because he thought that he would be established in office. 4 But the King of kings aroused the anger of Antiochus against the scoundrel; and when Lysias informed him that this man was to blame for all the trouble, he ordered them to take him to Beroea and to put him to death by the method that is customary in that place. 5 For there is a tower there, fifty cubits high, full of ashes, and it has a rim running around it that on all sides inclines precipitously into the ashes. 6 There they all push to destruction anyone guilty of sacrilege or notorious for other crimes. 7 By such a fate it came about that Menelaus the lawbreaker died, without even burial in the earth. 8 And this was eminently just; because he had committed many sins against the altar whose fire and ashes were holy, he met his death in ashes.

9 The king with barbarous arrogance was coming to show the Jews things far worse than those that had been done[b] in his father's time. 10 But when Judas heard of this, he ordered the people to call upon the Lord day and night, now if ever to help those who were on the point of being deprived of the law and their country and the holy temple, 11 and not to let the people who had just begun to revive fall into the hands of the blasphemous Gentiles. 12 When they had all joined in the same petition and had implored the merciful Lord with weeping and fasting and lying prostrate for three days without ceasing, Judas exhorted them and ordered them to stand ready.

13 After consulting privately with the elders, he determined to march out and decide the matter by the help of God before the king's army could enter Judea and get possession of the city. 14 So, committing the decision to the Creator of the world and exhorting his troops to fight bravely to the death for the laws, temple, city, country, and commonwealth, he pitched his camp near Modein. 15 He gave his troops the watchword, "God's victory," and with a picked force of the bravest young men, he attacked the king's pavilion at night and killed as many as two thousand men in the camp. He stabbed[c] the leading elephant and its rider. 16 In the end they filled the camp with terror and confusion and withdrew in triumph. 17 This happened, just as day was dawning, because the Lord's help protected him.

18 The king, having had a taste of the daring of the Jews, tried strategy in attack-

a 163 B.C.   b Or the worst of the things that had been done   c Meaning of Gk uncertain

**13.1–8: Death of Menelaus. 1–2:** *Antiochus* and *Lysias,* see 10.10–11n. *Chariots armed with scythes* to cut down foot soldiers had been used since the days of the Persian Empire. **3:** *Menelaus,* see 4.23n. **4:** *The King of kings,* God (Deut 10.17; Ps 136.3). What *aroused* his *anger* is not known (but see 4.27). *Beroea,* now Aleppo in northern Syria. *The method* of execution (vv. 5–6) was Persian.
**13.9–17: Preliminary skirmish. 9:** *His father,* Antiochus IV; see 6.1–6. **12:** Jews employed such acts of penitence particularly when there was danger of sacrilege (3.15; 10.4; 1 Macc 4.40). **14:** The Syrian army had invaded Judea from the south, through Idumea (1 Macc 6.31). Judas first *pitched his camp near Modein,* his hometown (see 1 Macc 2.1n.), to watch the Syrian line along the coast. The first battle occurred at Beth-zechariah (1 Macc 6.32–47). **15:** *"God's victory,"* see 8.23n.; in 1 Macc 6.43–46 it is Eleazar who *stabbed the leading elephant.* **16:** According to 1 Macc 6.47 the Jews fled. **17:** Ps 46.6.
**13.18–26: Attack on Beth-zur. 19:** *Beth-zur,* see 11.5n. The Syrians were defeated in the first attempt

ing their positions. [19]He advanced against Beth-zur, a strong fortress of the Jews, was turned back, attacked again,[a] and was defeated. [20]Judas sent in to the garrison whatever was necessary. [21]But Rhodocus, a man from the ranks of the Jews, gave secret information to the enemy; he was sought for, caught, and put in prison. [22]The king negotiated a second time with the people in Beth-zur, gave pledges, received theirs, withdrew, attacked Judas and his men, was defeated; [23]he got word that Philip, who had been left in charge of the government, had revolted in Antioch; he was dismayed, called in the Jews, yielded and swore to observe all their rights, settled with them and offered sacrifice, honored the sanctuary and showed generosity to the holy place. [24]He received Maccabeus, left Hegemonides as governor from Ptolemais to Gerar, [25]and went to Ptolemais. The people of Ptolemais were indignant over the treaty; in fact they were so angry that they wanted to annul its terms.[b] [26]Lysias took the public platform, made the best possible defense, convinced them, appeased them, gained their goodwill, and set out for Antioch. This is how the king's attack and withdrawal turned out.

14 Three years later, word came to Judas and his men that Demetrius son of Seleucus had sailed into the harbor of Tripolis with a strong army and a fleet, [2]and had taken possession of the country, having made away with Antiochus and his guardian Lysias.

3 Now a certain Alcimus, who had formerly been high priest but had willfully defiled himself in the times of separation,[c] realized that there was no way for him to be safe or to have access again to the holy altar, [4]and went to King Demetrius in about the one hundred fifty-first year,[d] presenting to him a crown of gold and a palm, and besides these some of the customary olive branches from the temple. During that day he kept quiet. [5]But he found an opportunity that furthered his mad purpose when he was invited by Demetrius to a meeting of the council and was asked about the attitude and intentions of the Jews. He answered:

6 "Those of the Jews who are called Hasideans, whose leader is Judas Maccabeus, are keeping up war and stirring up sedition, and will not let the kingdom attain tranquility. [7]Therefore I have laid aside my ancestral glory—I mean the high priesthood—and have now come here, [8]first because I am genuinely concerned for the interests of the king, and second because I have regard also for my compatriots. For through the folly of those whom I have mentioned our whole nation is now in no small misfortune. [9]Since you are acquainted, O king, with the details of this matter, may it please you to take thought for our country and our hard-pressed nation with the gracious kindness that you show to all. [10]For as long as Judas lives, it is impossible for the government to find peace." [11]When he had said this, the rest of

---

a Or *faltered*   b Meaning of Gk uncertain   c Other ancient authorities read *of mixing*   d 161 B.C.

---

(1 Macc 6.31). **21–22:** The garrison surrendered because of lack of food (1 Macc 6.49); possibly this was the *secret information.* **23:** *Philip* is probably the official mentioned in 9.29, as 1 Macc 6.14–15,55–56 makes clear. The two books differ significantly in their treatment of Philip's role. **24:** *Ptolemais,* or Acco, north of Mt. Carmel to *Gerar,* south of Gaza, i.e., the entire coastal plain. **26:** 1 Macc 6.63.

**14.1–10: Accession of Demetrius I (1 Macc 7.1–7). 1:** *Three years later,* about 161 BCE. *Demetrius I Soter, son of Seleucus* IV, reigned 162–150. *Tripolis,* the town where Demetrius landed after his escape from Rome, and the place where he began to rule (see 1 Macc 7.1). **2:** *Antiochus . . . Lysias,* 1 Macc 7.3–4. **3:** *Alcimus* may not have *been high priest,* though it is possible he was appointed by Antiochus V after the execution of Menelaus. *Defiled,* 4.11–15. **4:** 1 Macc 7.5–7 may record an earlier visit. *Crown,* emblem of sovereignty; the *palm,* victory. **6:** *Hasideans,* "the pious," a group not concerned for Jewish nationalism but only for the religious law. At first they resisted passively, but later turned to violent action (1 Macc 1.62–63; 2.37; 2.42). **7:** *Ancestral glory,* he claimed legitimate succession (1 Macc 7.14).

the king's Friends,[a] who were hostile to Judas, quickly inflamed Demetrius still more. 12 He immediately chose Nicanor, who had been in command of the elephants, appointed him governor of Judea, and sent him off 13 with orders to kill Judas and scatter his troops, and to install Alcimus as high priest of the great[b] temple. 14 And the Gentiles throughout Judea, who had fled before[c] Judas, flocked to join Nicanor, thinking that the misfortunes and calamities of the Jews would mean prosperity for themselves.

15 When the Jews[d] heard of Nicanor's coming and the gathering of the Gentiles, they sprinkled dust on their heads and prayed to him who established his own people forever and always upholds his own heritage by manifesting himself. 16 At the command of the leader, they[e] set out from there immediately and engaged them in battle at a village called Dessau.[c] 17 Simon, the brother of Judas, had encountered Nicanor, but had been temporarily[f] checked because of the sudden consternation created by the enemy.

18 Nevertheless Nicanor, hearing of the valor of Judas and his troops and their courage in battle for their country, shrank from deciding the issue by bloodshed. 19 Therefore he sent Posidonius, Theodotus, and Mattathias to give and receive pledges of friendship. 20 When the terms had been fully considered, and the leader had informed the people, and it had appeared that they were of one mind, they agreed to the covenant. 21 The leaders[g] set a day on which to meet by themselves. A chariot came forward from each army; seats of honor were set in place; 22 Judas posted armed men in readiness at key places to prevent sudden treachery on the part of the enemy; so they duly held the consultation.

23 Nicanor stayed on in Jerusalem and did nothing out of the way, but dismissed the flocks of people that had gathered. 24 And he kept Judas always in his presence; he was warmly attached to the man. 25 He urged him to marry and have children; so Judas[e] married, settled down, and shared the common life.

26 But when Alcimus noticed their goodwill for one another, he took the covenant that had been made and went to Demetrius. He told him that Nicanor was disloyal to the government, since he had appointed that conspirator against the kingdom, Judas, to be his successor. 27 The king became excited and, provoked by the false accusations of that depraved man, wrote to Nicanor, stating that he was displeased with the covenant and commanding him to send Maccabeus to Antioch as a prisoner without delay.

28 When this message came to Nicanor, he was troubled and grieved that he had to annul their agreement when the man had done no wrong. 29 Since it was not possible to oppose the king, he watched for an opportunity to accomplish this by a stratagem. 30 But Maccabeus, noticing that Nicanor was more austere in his dealings with him and was meeting him more rudely than had been his custom, concluded that this austerity did not spring from the best motives. So he gathered not a few of his men, and went into hiding from Nicanor.

a Gk of the Friends   b Gk greatest   c Meaning of Gk uncertain   d Gk they   e Gk he   f Other ancient authorities read slowly   g Gk They

**14.11–14: Appointment of Nicanor and Alcimus.** This story omits the expedition of Bacchides (1 Macc 7.8–25). Josephus says that *Nicanor* (v. 12) had escaped from Rome with Demetrius (*Ant.* 12.10.4); if he is the person in 8.9–36 he must have gone from Syria to Rome to assist the escape. **11:** *Friends*, see 1.14n. **14.15–36: Nicanor seeks friendship with Judas. 15:** *Sprinkled dust*, Josh 7.6. **16:** *The leader*, Judas, or possibly Nicanor. *Dessau*, perhaps Adasa (1 Macc 7.40–45). **20–21:** *The leader*, Nicanor. *The people*, his army. Afterward *the leaders*, Nicanor and Judas, met. **22:** 1 Macc 7.12–18. **24:** *Warmly attached* only so long as things went well (cf. vv. 31–33). **26:** *Alcimus* failed to get civil power and feared that *Judas* would be made his *successor* as high priest. **28–33:** Cf. 1 Macc 7.30–38. **33:** *Stretched out his right hand . . . and swore*, 15.32–33. *Dionysus*, 6.7n. **35–36:** 1 Kings 8.27–30. *Purified*, 10.1–8.

31 When the latter became aware that he had been cleverly outwitted by the man, he went to the great[a] and holy temple while the priests were offering the customary sacrifices, and commanded them to hand the man over. 32 When they declared on oath that they did not know where the man was whom he wanted, 33 he stretched out his right hand toward the sanctuary, and swore this oath: "If you do not hand Judas over to me as a prisoner, I will level this shrine of God to the ground and tear down the altar, and build here a splendid temple to Dionysus."

34 Having said this, he went away. Then the priests stretched out their hands toward heaven and called upon the constant Defender of our nation, in these words: 35 "O Lord of all, though you have need of nothing, you were pleased that there should be a temple for your habitation among us; 36 so now, O holy One, Lord of all holiness, keep undefiled forever this house that has been so recently purified."

37 A certain Razis, one of the elders of Jerusalem, was denounced to Nicanor as a man who loved his compatriots and was very well thought of and for his goodwill was called father of the Jews. 38 In former times, when there was no mingling with the Gentiles, he had been accused of Judaism, and he had most zealously risked body and life for Judaism. 39 Nicanor, wishing to exhibit the enmity that he had for the Jews, sent more than five hundred soldiers to arrest him; 40 for he thought that by arresting[b] him he would do them an injury. 41 When the troops were about to capture the tower and were forcing the door of the courtyard, they ordered that fire be brought and the doors burned. Being surrounded, Razis[c] fell upon his own sword, 42 preferring to die nobly rather than to fall into the hands of sinners and suffer outrages unworthy of his noble birth. 43 But in the heat of the struggle he did not hit exactly, and the crowd was now rushing in through the doors. He courageously ran up on the wall, and bravely threw himself down into the crowd. 44 But as they quickly drew back, a space opened and he fell in the middle of the empty space. 45 Still alive and aflame with anger, he rose, and though his blood gushed forth and his wounds were severe he ran through the crowd; and standing upon a steep rock, 46 with his blood now completely drained from him, he tore out his entrails, took them in both hands and hurled them at the crowd, calling upon the Lord of life and spirit to give them back to him again. This was the manner of his death.

15 When Nicanor heard that Judas and his troops were in the region of Samaria, he made plans to attack them with complete safety on the day of rest. 2 When the Jews who were compelled to follow him said, "Do not destroy so savagely and barbarously, but show respect for the day that he who sees all things has honored and hallowed above other days," 3 the thrice-accursed wretch asked if there were a sovereign in heaven who had commanded the keeping of the sabbath day. 4 When they declared, "It is the living Lord himself, the Sovereign in heaven, who ordered us to observe the seventh day," 5 he replied, "But I am a sovereign also, on earth, and I command you to take up arms and finish the king's business." Nevertheless, he did not succeed in carrying out his abominable design.

6 This Nicanor in his utter boastfulness and arrogance had determined to erect a public monument of victory over Judas and his forces. 7 But Maccabeus did not cease to trust with all confidence that he would get

a Gk greatest    b Meaning of Gk uncertain
c Gk he

14.37–46: **Death of Razis.** A martyrology in the style of 6.18–7.42. **37:** *Elders,* 13.13. **42:** Cf. 1 Sam 31.4. **46:** He expected his body to be restored in the resurrection (7.11).

15.1–36: **Death of Nicanor** (1 Macc 7.39–50). **1:** *Nicanor* camped at Beth-horon, and *Judas* was at Adasa, between Beth-horon and Jerusalem. **2:** *The Jews* in Nicanor's army wished to honor the sabbath. **3:** *Thrice-accursed,* 8.34. **4–5:** Ex 20.8–11; Dan 3.16–18. **8:** 1 Macc 7.41. **9:** *The law and the prophets,* help from the Lord. 8He exhorted his troops not to fear the attack of the Gentiles, but to keep in mind the former times when help had come to them from heaven, and so to look for the victory that the Almighty would give them. 9Encouraging them from the law and the prophets, and reminding them also of the struggles they had won, he made them the more eager. 10When he had aroused their courage, he issued his orders, at the same time pointing out the perfidy of the Gentiles and their violation of oaths. 11He armed each of them not so much with confidence in shields and spears as with the inspiration of brave words, and he cheered them all by relating a dream, a sort of vision,*a* which was worthy of belief.

12 What he saw was this: Onias, who had been high priest, a noble and good man, of modest bearing and gentle manner, one who spoke fittingly and had been trained from childhood in all that belongs to excellence, was praying with outstretched hands for the whole body of the Jews. 13Then in the same fashion another appeared, distinguished by his gray hair and dignity, and of marvelous majesty and authority. 14And Onias spoke, saying, "This is a man who loves the family of Israel and prays much for the people and the holy city—Jeremiah, the prophet of God." 15Jeremiah stretched out his right hand and gave to Judas a golden sword, and as he gave it he addressed him thus: 16"Take this holy sword, a gift from God, with which you will strike down your adversaries."

17 Encouraged by the words of Judas, so noble and so effective in arousing valor and awaking courage in the souls of the young, they determined not to carry on a campaign*b* but to attack bravely, and to decide the matter by fighting hand to hand with all courage, because the city and the sanctuary and the temple were in danger.

18Their concern for wives and children, and also for brothers and sisters*c* and relatives, lay upon them less heavily; their greatest and first fear was for the consecrated sanctuary. 19And those who had to remain in the city were in no little distress, being anxious over the encounter in the open country.

20 When all were now looking forward to the coming issue, and the enemy was already close at hand with their army drawn up for battle, the elephants*d* strategically stationed and the cavalry deployed on the flanks, 21Maccabeus, observing the masses that were in front of him and the varied supply of arms and the savagery of the elephants, stretched out his hands toward heaven and called upon the Lord who works wonders; for he knew that it is not by arms, but as the Lord*e* decides, that he gains the victory for those who deserve it. 22He called upon him in these words: "O Lord, you sent your angel in the time of King Hezekiah of Judea, and he killed fully one hundred eighty-five thousand in the camp of Sennacherib. 23So now, O Sovereign of the heavens, send a good angel to spread terror and trembling before us. 24By the might of your arm may these blasphemers who come against your holy people be struck down." With these words he ended his prayer.

25 Nicanor and his troops advanced with trumpets and battle songs, 26but Judas and his troops met the enemy in battle with invocations to God and prayers. 27So, fighting with their hands and praying to God in their hearts, they laid low at least thirty-five thousand, and were greatly gladdened by God's manifestation.

28 When the action was over and they

a Meaning of Gk uncertain   b Or to remain in camp
c Gk for brothers   d Gk animals   e Gk he

the Torah (Pentateuch) and the prophetic books were now regarded as scripture (compare the Prologue to Sirach). **10:** *Violation of oaths,* 11.27–32; 14.20–28. **12:** *Onias,* 3.1–40. **15–16:** *Jeremiah,* see 2.1–8. The *golden sword* was a sign that God approved the Jews' self-defense on the sabbath (see Jer 50.35–38). Compare the treatment of the sabbath question in 1 Macc 2.39–41. On heavenly armaments of gold, see 3.25 and 5.2. **18:** *First fear,* cf. 14.33. **20:** *Elephants,* to break through the Jewish infantry; the *cavalry* protected the *flanks* of the Syrian infantry. **22–23:** See 11.6n.; 2 Kings 19.35. **29:** *Language of their* were returning with joy, they recognized Nicanor, lying dead, in full armor. 29 Then there was shouting and tumult, and they blessed the Sovereign Lord in the language of their ancestors. 30 Then the man who was ever in body and soul the defender of his people, the man who maintained his youthful goodwill toward his compatriots, ordered them to cut off Nicanor's head and arm and carry them to Jerusalem. 31 When he arrived there and had called his compatriots together and stationed the priests before the altar, he sent for those who were in the citadel. 32 He showed them the vile Nicanor's head and that profane man's arm, which had been boastfully stretched out against the holy house of the Almighty. 33 He cut out the tongue of the ungodly Nicanor and said that he would feed it piecemeal to the birds and would hang up these rewards of his folly opposite the sanctuary. 34 And they all, looking to heaven, blessed the Lord who had manifested himself, saying, "Blessed is he who has kept his own place undefiled!" 35 Judas[a] hung Nicanor's

head from the citadel, a clear and conspicuous sign to everyone of the help of the Lord. 36 And they all decreed by public vote never to let this day go unobserved, but to celebrate the thirteenth day of the twelfth month—which is called Adar in the Aramaic language—the day before Mordecai's day.

37 This, then, is how matters turned out with Nicanor, and from that time the city has been in the possession of the Hebrews. So I will here end my story. 38 If it is well told and to the point, that is what I myself desired; if it is poorly done and mediocre, that was the best I could do. 39 For just as it is harmful to drink wine alone, or, again, to drink water alone, while wine mixed with water is sweet and delicious and enhances one's enjoyment, so also the style of the story delights the ears of those who read the work. And here will be the end.

a Gk He

ancestors, Hebrew. Palestinian Jews spoke Aramaic, but formal prayer, using the language of scripture, was often in Hebrew. 30: 1 Sam 17.54. 31: *The citadel* on the Ophel hill was held by Syrians (1 Macc 1.33; 6.18), but the Jews had built another fort (1 Macc 4.60). 32: *Head . . . arm*, 14.33. 35: 1 Sam 31.9; Jdt 14.1; 1 Macc 7.47. 36: The *twelfth month* (February–March) was *called Adar in the Aramaic language* and also in Hebrew. *Mordecai's day*, the festival of Purim; see Esth 9. Nicanor's day was observed up to 70 CE.

**15.37–39: Epilogue.** The epitomist's conclusion to his work balances his introduction (2.19–32). The epitomist wrote some time before the Jewish war (66–70 CE), when Jerusalem was still in Jewish hands. **39:** The strong wine of Greece was usually tempered with water. *The style* will delight *the ears of those who read*, because in antiquity it was the custom to read literary works aloud, even to oneself.

(b) The books from 1 Esdras through 3 Maccabees are recognized as Deuterocanonical Scripture by the Greek and the Russian Orthodox Churches. They are not so recognized by the Roman Catholic Church, but 1 Esdras and the Prayer of Manasseh (together with 2 Esdras) are placed in an appendix to the Latin Vulgate Bible.

# 1 ESDRAS

First Esdras is one of several books bearing the name of Ezra (see Ezra-Nehemiah). Known in the Apocrypha as 1 Esdras, the book is called 3 Esdras in the Latin Vulgate Bible where (since the Council of Trent) it has been placed in an appendix after the New Testament. With one significant exception, the book repeats, with minor variations, sections from 2 Chronicles and Ezra-Nehemiah (see "Introduction to Chronicles" and "Introduction to Ezra-Nehemiah"). First Esdras begins with King Josiah's Passover celebration in Jerusalem in 622 BCE, reproducing the substance of 2 Chr 35.1–36.21. It continues directly with Ezra 1–10 (all of Ezra), followed with Nehemiah 8, which describes events that ostensibly transpired in 458. The only material unique to 1 Esdras is the story of the three young bodyguards in the court of King Darius (3.1–5.6). Although the book is largely copied from earlier biblical books, through its selection and organization of material, it offers a distinct perspective on the history it recounts. It traces a trajectory between two feasts (1.1–24 and 9.49–55), and thereby seems more upbeat than Ezra-Nehemiah's longer report about the difficulties of the return to the land and the restoration of worship and community.

The main divisions of the book are:

- 1.1–24: An ideal state of affairs: Josiah's Passover celebration (=2 Chr 35.1–27)
- 1.25–58: Decline and destruction (=2 Chr 36.1–21)
- 2.1–9.55: Stages of return and restoration (=Ezra 1–10 and Nehemiah 8)

The book begins and concludes with a feast in Jerusalem in front of the Temple—suggesting that the Temple, significant in other postexilic writings, is a central issue of 1 Esdras. The decline between the feasts is brief, followed immediately with a gradual but effective restoration of altar, Temple, and community. Whereas Ezra-Nehemiah highlights disjunctions between the past and the return, 1 Esdras, like Chronicles, underscores continuities, sometimes by conflating events.

First Esdras also contrasts with Ezra-Nehemiah in glorifying leaders, especially the Davidic heir Zerubbabel, whose role it expands significantly. In particular, the lengthy story of the three young men in Darius's court focuses the book upon Zerubbabel's achievements. This story portrays Zerubbabel as the wise hero who wins Darius's support and initiates the construction of the Temple. Ezra the priest also rises to a higher level, being called explicitly a high priest (but see Ezra 7.5n.). Ezra's prominence is further increased by the absence of collaboration with Nehemiah in the book. This highlights his prominence in the restoration and the climax of the entire story (8.1–9.55).

The book has been preserved in Greek and reflects Hellenistic values and vocabulary. Although the latest events it narrates are from the mid-fifth century, it probably dates in its current form from the second century BCE. It is unclear whether the book is a translation of an earlier Hebrew or Aramaic version (possibly as ancient as Ezra-Nehemiah) or a late adaptation of 2 Chronicles and Ezra-

Nehemiah composed originally in Greek. The work in Greek was used by Josephus in his *Antiquities,* written around 90 CE.

Since the book closely parallels Chronicles and Ezra-Nehemiah, see the notes to these books for fuller comments on parallel material.

1 Josiah kept the passover to his Lord in Jerusalem; he killed the passover lamb on the fourteenth day of the first month, [2] having placed the priests according to their divisions, arrayed in their vestments, in the temple of the Lord. [3] He told the Levites, the temple servants of Israel, that they should sanctify themselves to the Lord and put the holy ark of the Lord in the house that King Solomon, son of David, had built; [4] and he said, "You need no longer carry it on your shoulders. Now worship the Lord your God and serve his people Israel; prepare yourselves by your families and kindred, [5] in accordance with the directions of King David of Israel and the magnificence of his son Solomon. Stand in order in the temple according to the groupings of the ancestral houses of you Levites, who minister before your kindred the people of Israel, [6] and kill the passover lamb and prepare the sacrifices for your kindred, and keep the passover according to the commandment of the Lord that was given to Moses."

[7] To the people who were present Josiah gave thirty thousand lambs and kids, and three thousand calves; these were given from the king's possessions, as he promised, to the people and the priests and Levites. [8] Hilkiah, Zechariah, and Jehiel,[a] the chief officers of the temple, gave to the priests for the passover two thousand six hundred sheep and three hundred calves. [9] And Jeconiah and Shemaiah and his brother Nethanel, and Hashabiah and Ochiel and Joram, captains over thousands, gave the Levites for the passover five thousand sheep and seven hundred calves.

[10] This is what took place. The priests and the Levites, having the unleavened bread, stood in proper order according to kindred [11] and the grouping of the ancestral houses, before the people, to make the offering to the Lord as it is written in the book of Moses; this they did in the morning. [12] They roasted the passover lamb with fire, as required; and they boiled the sacrifices in bronze pots and caldrons, with a pleasing odor, [13] and carried them to all the people. Afterward they prepared the passover for themselves and for their kindred the priests, the sons of Aaron, [14] because the priests were offering the fat until nightfall; so the Levites prepared it for themselves and for their kindred the priests, the sons of Aaron. [15] The temple singers, the sons of Asaph, were in their place according to the arrangement made by David, and also Asaph, Zechariah, and Eddinus, who represented the king. [16] The gatekeepers were at each gate; no one needed to interrupt his daily duties, for their kindred the Levites prepared the passover for them.

[17] So the things that had to do with the sacrifices to the Lord were accomplished that day: the passover was kept [18] and the sacrifices were offered on the altar of the Lord, according to the command of King Josiah. [19] And the people of Israel who were

a Gk *Esyelus*

1.1–24: **An ideal state of affairs: Josiah's Passover celebration** (2 Chr 35.1–19). 1 Esdras begins with a celebration. This event constitutes a high point, with the holy ark duly installed in the Temple. According to 2 Kings 23.21–23 and 2 Chr 34.14–33, the Passover celebration concluded the religious reform of Josiah, king of Judah (640–609 BCE). In 1 Esdras the account of the reform itself is omitted. The author of 1 Esdras is interested in the continuity between the First and Second Temples, and thus does not depict Josiah as a reforming king. **3:** See 1 Chr 3.1–5.1. **5:** See 1 Chr 23; 28.13,21; 2 Chr 8.14. **6:** See Ex 12.1–13; Deut 16.1–8. **7–9:** The list of offerings differs slightly from that in 2 Chr 35.7–9. **20:** Cf. 2 Kings 23.22. **23–24:** The evaluation of Josiah in 1 Esdras elaborates on Chronicles.

present at that time kept the passover and the festival of unleavened bread seven days. 20 No passover like it had been kept in Israel since the times of the prophet Samuel; 21 none of the kings of Israel had kept such a passover as was kept by Josiah and the priests and Levites and the people of Judah and all of Israel who were living in Jerusalem. 22 In the eighteenth year of the reign of Josiah this passover was kept.

23 And the deeds of Josiah were upright in the sight of the Lord, for his heart was full of godliness. 24 In ancient times the events of his reign have been recorded— concerning those who sinned and acted wickedly toward the Lord beyond any other people or kingdom, and how they grieved the Lord[a] deeply, so that the words of the Lord fell upon Israel.

25 After all these acts of Josiah, it happened that Pharaoh, king of Egypt, went to make war at Carchemish on the Euphrates, and Josiah went out against him. 26 And the king of Egypt sent word to him saying, "What have we to do with each other, O king of Judea? 27 I was not sent against you by the Lord God, for my war is at the Euphrates. And now the Lord is with me! The Lord is with me, urging me on! Stand aside, and do not oppose the Lord."

28 Josiah, however, did not turn back to his chariot, but tried to fight with him, and did not heed the words of the prophet Jeremiah from the mouth of the Lord. 29 He joined battle with him in the plain of Megiddo, and the commanders came down

against King Josiah. 30 The king said to his servants, "Take me away from the battle, for I am very weak." And immediately his servants took him out of the line of battle. 31 He got into his second chariot; and after he was brought back to Jerusalem he died, and was buried in the tomb of his ancestors.

32 In all Judea they mourned for Josiah. The prophet Jeremiah lamented for Josiah, and the principal men, with the women,[b] have made lamentation for him to this day; it was ordained that this should always be done throughout the whole nation of Israel. 33 These things are written in the book of the histories of the kings of Judea; and every one of the acts of Josiah, and his splendor, and his understanding of the law of the Lord, and the things that he had done before, and these that are now told, are recorded in the book of the kings of Israel and Judah.

34 The men of the nation took Jeconiah[c] son of Josiah, who was twenty-three years old, and made him king in succession to his father Josiah. 35 He reigned three months in Judah and Jerusalem. Then the king of Egypt deposed him from reigning in Jerusalem, 36 and fined the nation one hundred talents of silver and one talent of gold. 37 The king of Egypt made his brother Jehoiakim king of Judea and Jerusalem. 38 Jehoiakim put the nobles in prison, and

a Gk him    b Or their wives    c 2 Kings 23.30; 2 Chr 36.1 Jehoahaz

1.25–58: Decline and destruction. 25–33: Josiah's death and the beginning of decline. 1 Esdras largely follows the account in 2 Chr 35.20–27, omitting the Pharaoh Neco's name, Josiah's disguising himself, and his being struck by an arrow. 28: The author of 1 Esdras probably found the Chronicler's account, in which the Pharaoh is depicted as a prophet, difficult, and revised it to suggest that Josiah's death results from ignoring the warning of Jeremiah. No passage in the book of Jeremiah clearly relates to the battle in which Josiah died. 33: Josiah is the last good king. His death marks the end of an era.

1.34–49: The last kings of Judah (2 Chr 36.1–14). Good king Josiah is followed by evil kings. 34: Jeconiah as successor to Josiah does not appear in 2 Chr or 2 Kings, and is probably an error for Jehoahaz (ruled briefly in 609 BCE; see 2 Kings 23.30–31; also called Shallum in Jer 22.11). Jeconiah was an alternate form of the name of Jehoiachin (see v. 43); see Jer 28.4; cf. Jer 22.24. The expression men of the nation corresponds to "the people of the land" of 2 Chr 36.1; in preexilic times these were probably landowners who often came to the support of reforming kings or who themselves instituted reforms (2 Kings 12.18,20; 21.24; 23.30). 36: A talent weighed about 34 kg (75 lb). 38: The author recasts 2 Chr 36.4, in which Neco of Egypt removed Jehoahaz from the throne and installed Josiah's elder son Eliakim seized his brother Zarius and brought him back from Egypt.

39 Jehoiakim was twenty-five years old when he began to reign in Judea and Jerusalem; he did what was evil in the sight of the Lord. 40 King Nebuchadnezzar of Babylon came up against him; he bound him with a chain of bronze and took him away to Babylon. 41 Nebuchadnezzar also took some holy vessels of the Lord, and carried them away, and stored them in his temple in Babylon. 42 But the things that are reported about Jehoiakim,*a* and his uncleanness and impiety, are written in the annals of the kings.

43 His son Jehoiachin*b* became king in his place; when he was made king he was eighteen years old, 44 and he reigned three months and ten days in Jerusalem. He did what was evil in the sight of the Lord. 45 A year later Nebuchadnezzar sent and removed him to Babylon, with the holy vessels of the Lord, 46 and made Zedekiah king of Judea and Jerusalem.

Zedekiah was twenty-one years old, and he reigned eleven years. 47 He also did what was evil in the sight of the Lord, and did not heed the words that were spoken by the prophet Jeremiah from the mouth of the Lord. 48 Although King Nebuchadnezzar had made him swear by the name of the Lord, he broke his oath and rebelled; he stiffened his neck and hardened his heart and transgressed the laws of the Lord, the God of Israel. 49 Even the leaders of the people and of the priests committed many acts of sacrilege and lawlessness beyond all the unclean deeds of all the nations, and polluted the temple of the Lord in Jerusalem—the temple that God had made holy. 50 The God of their ancestors sent his messenger to call them back, because he would have spared them and his dwelling place. 51 But they mocked his messengers, and whenever the Lord spoke, they scoffed at his prophets, 52 until in his anger against his people because of their ungodly acts he gave command to bring against them the kings of the Chaldeans. 53 These killed their young men with the sword around their holy temple, and did not spare young man or young woman,*c* old man or child, for he gave them all into their hands. 54 They took all the holy vessels of the Lord, great and small, the treasure chests of the Lord, and the royal stores, and carried them away to Babylon. 55 They burned the house of the Lord, broke down the walls of Jerusalem, burned their towers with fire, 56 and utterly destroyed all its glorious things. The survivors he led away to Babylon with the sword, 57 and they were servants to him and to his sons until the Persians began to reign, in fulfillment of the word of the Lord by the mouth of Jeremiah, 58 saying, "Until the land has enjoyed its sabbaths, it shall keep sabbath all the time of its desolation until the completion of seventy years."

2 In the first year of Cyrus as king of the Persians, so that the word of the Lord

*a* Gk *him*    *b* Gk *Jehoiakim*    *c* Gk *virgin*

as king, changing his name to Jehoiakim. Jehoahaz was taken to Egypt, where presumably he died (Jer 22.10–12). In the 1 Esdras account Jehoiakim brings up his brother Zarius from Egypt; the name Zarius may be a corruption of Jehoahaz or of Zedekiah, both of whom were brothers of Jehoiakim (2 Kings 24.17). **39:** According to 2 Chr 36.5, Jehoiakim reigned eleven years (608–598). **43:** 1 Esdras gives Jehoiakim rather than Jehoiachin (see note *b*) as the name of that king's son and successor; but the king's age at the beginning of his reign is correctly given (eighteen years; not eight, as in 2 Chr 36.9; cf. 2 Kings 24.8); he ruled in 597. **46:** *Zedekiah,* the last king of Judah, ruled 597–586.

**1.50–58: Jerusalem falls to the Babylonians** (2 Chr 36.15–21). **52:** *Chaldeans,* a biblical name for the Babylonians. **58:** To *keep sabbath* means that the land is to lie untended as in the seventh or sabbatical years until the exiles return (Jer 25.11–12; 29.10; cf. Lev 25.1–7; 26.27–39,43). Like Chronicles, 1 Esdras stresses the temporary nature of exile.

**2.1–9.55: Stages of return and restoration. 1–15:** Cyrus of Persia permits the exiles to return (Ezra 1.1–11). The text is almost identical with the end of 2 Chr and the beginning of Ezra, which are also nearly identical. **1:** *First year of Cyrus,* 538 BCE. **3–7:** The substance of the decree is consistent with by the mouth of Jeremiah might be accomplished— 2 the Lord stirred up the spirit of King Cyrus of the Persians, and he made a proclamation throughout all his kingdom and also put it in writing:

3 "Thus says Cyrus king of the Persians: The Lord of Israel, the Lord Most High, has made me king of the world, 4 and he has commanded me to build him a house at Jerusalem, which is in Judea. 5 If any of you, therefore, are of his people, may your Lord be with you; go up to Jerusalem, which is in Judea, and build the house of the Lord of Israel—he is the Lord who dwells in Jerusalem—6 and let each of you, wherever you may live, be helped by the people of your place with gold and silver, 7 with gifts and with horses and cattle, besides the other things added as votive offerings for the temple of the Lord that is in Jerusalem."

8 Then arose the heads of families of the tribes of Judah and Benjamin, and the priests and the Levites, and all whose spirit the Lord had stirred to go up to build the house in Jerusalem for the Lord; 9 their neighbors helped them with everything, with silver and gold, with horses and cattle, and with a very great number of votive offerings from many whose hearts were stirred.

10 King Cyrus also brought out the holy vessels of the Lord that Nebuchadnezzar had carried away from Jerusalem and stored in his temple of idols. 11 When King Cyrus of the Persians brought these out, he gave them to Mithridates, his treasurer, 12 and by him they were given to Sheshbazzar,[a] the governor of Judea. 13 The number of these was: one thousand gold cups, one thousand silver cups, twenty-nine silver censers, thirty gold bowls, two thousand four hundred ten silver bowls, and one thousand other vessels. 14 All the vessels were handed over, gold and silver, five thousand four hundred sixty-nine, 15 and they were carried back by Sheshbazzar with the returning exiles from Babylon to Jerusalem.

16 In the time of King Artaxerxes of the Persians, Bishlam, Mithridates, Tabeel, Rehum, Beltethmus, the scribe Shimshai, and the rest of their associates, living in Samaria and other places, wrote him the following letter, against those who were living in Judea and Jerusalem:

17 "To King Artaxerxes our lord, your servants the recorder Rehum and the scribe Shimshai and the other members of their council, and the judges in Coelesyria and Phoenicia: 18 Let it now be known to our lord the king that the Jews who came up from you to us have gone to Jerusalem and are building that rebellious and wicked city, repairing its market places and walls and laying the foundations for a temple. 19 Now if this city is built and the walls finished, they will not only refuse to pay tribute but will even resist kings. 20 Since the building of the temple is now going on,

a Gk Sanabassaros

Persian policy. **8:** *Judah and Benjamin,* the tribes that had constituted the Southern Kingdom of Judah. **10–15:** The inventory of the sacred vessels is smoother in 1 Esdras than in Ezra. **12:** *Sheshbazzar,* a Jewish leader and the first governor of the province of Judea (Yehud) appointed by the Persians. He may have been a descendant of David.

**2.16–30: Opposition to the rebuilding of the Temple and the city walls** (Ezra 4.7–24). A misplaced account of opposition to rebuilding the walls of Jerusalem in the time of Artaxerxes I (465–424 BCE). Cambyses (530–522) succeeded Cyrus and was followed by Darius I (522–486). Josephus (*Ant.* 11.2.1–3) substitutes Cambyses for Artaxerxes, thus providing the correct sequence of Persian kings. **16–20: The opponents' letter. 16:** The name *Beltethemus* is an error derived from the Greek transliteration of the Aramaic title ("be'el te'em") of the office held by Rehum. **17:** The persons named are officials of the region called "Beyond the River" (Ezra 4.10), which included the lands of (Coele-) Syria, Phoenicia, Samaria, and Judah. Rehum is designated "the royal deputy" in Ezra 4.8; the title *recorder* is supported by Josephus. **20:** The account differs considerably from that in Ezra 4.14, which contains no reference to the rebuilding of the Temple at this point. However, Ezra 4.24 states that work on the Temple stopped.

we think it best not to neglect such a matter, 21 but to speak to our lord the king, in order that, if it seems good to you, search may be made in the records of your ancestors. 22 You will find in the annals what has been written about them, and will learn that this city was rebellious, troubling both kings and other cities, 23 and that the Jews were rebels and kept setting up blockades in it from of old. That is why this city was laid waste. 24 Therefore we now make known to you, O lord and king, that if this city is built and its walls finished, you will no longer have access to Coelesyria and Phoenicia."

25 Then the king, in reply to the recorder Rehum, Beltethmus, the scribe Shimshai, and the others associated with them and living in Samaria and Syria and Phoenicia, wrote as follows:

26 "I have read the letter that you sent me. So I ordered search to be made, and it has been found that this city from of old has fought against kings, 27 that the people in it were given to rebellion and war, and that mighty and cruel kings ruled in Jerusalem and exacted tribute from Coelesyria and Phoenicia. 28 Therefore I have now issued orders to prevent these people from building the city and to take care that nothing more be done 29 and that such wicked proceedings go no further to the annoyance of kings."

30 Then, when the letter from King Artaxerxes was read, Rehum and the scribe Shimshai and their associates went quickly to Jerusalem, with cavalry and a large number of armed troops, and began to hinder the builders. And the building of the temple in Jerusalem stopped until the second year of the reign of King Darius of the Persians.

3 Now King Darius gave a great banquet for all that were under him, all that were born in his house, and all the nobles of Media and Persia, 2 and all the satraps and generals and governors that were under him in the hundred twenty-seven satrapies from India to Ethiopia. 3 They ate and drank, and when they were satisfied they went away, and King Darius went to his bedroom; he went to sleep, but woke up again.

4 Then the three young men of the bodyguard, who kept guard over the person of the king, said to one another, 5 "Let each of us state what one thing is strongest; and to

This revision and reworking of material is consistent with the focus of 1 Esdras on the Temple. **25–29:** The royal reply. **29:** Ezra 4.21 includes "until I make a decree," setting the stage for a reversal at a later date. **30:** *Until the second year of . . . Darius* implicitly refers to Darius I (522–486), the ruler in the subsequent narrative. It is unimaginable to these sources that construction stopped from lack of initiative, so external motivations are found.

**3.1–7.15: Return and restoration under Darius and Zerubbabel. 3.1–5.6: The three young bodyguards in the court of Darius.** This famous story, found only in 1 Esdras, magnifies the role of Zerubbabel, the last Davidic heir to have political power. In Ezra-Nehemiah, Zerubbabel is no more prominent than his coworker, Jeshua the priest. The story probably originated as a secular tale praising the relative strength of kings, wine, and women. The praise of the strength of truth (4.33–41) has close parallels in Greek thought and literature; since the third youth suggests the power of both women and truth (3.12), the praise of truth may be a secondary element in the story. The author of 1 Esdras, adopting the story, needed only to identify the third, wisest youth with Zerubbabel (4.13) and to add a sequel to the tale, relating how Darius rewarded Zerubbabel by supporting the rebuilding of Jerusalem and its Temple (4.42–5.6). Josephus's version (*Ant.* 11.3.2–9) differs significantly from the one given here.

**3.1–17a: The contest planned. 1–3:** Although the location is not explicitly mentioned, the Persian capital Susa may be implied (cf. Esth 1.2–3). *Media*, an important part of the Persian Empire, in northern Iran. **2:** During Darius's reign (522–486 BCE) there were actually only about twenty provinces (satrapies); this number was increased after 312 BCE, and the total one hundred twenty-seven became conventional in later Jewish literature (Esth 1.1; Josephus, *Ant.* 11.3.2). **4–12:** The three bodyguards decide of their own initiative to entertain the king, thereby bringing riches and honor to one of them. In Josephus (*Ant.*

the one whose statement seems wisest, King Darius will give rich gifts and great honors of victory. 6 He shall be clothed in purple, and drink from gold cups, and sleep on a gold bed,*a* and have a chariot with gold bridles, and a turban of fine linen, and a necklace around his neck; 7 and because of his wisdom he shall sit next to Darius and shall be called Kinsman of Darius."

8 Then each wrote his own statement, and they sealed them and put them under the pillow of King Darius, 9 and said, "When the king wakes, they will give him the writing; and to the one whose statement the king and the three nobles of Persia judge to be wisest the victory shall be given according to what is written." 10 The first wrote, "Wine is strongest." 11 The second wrote, "The king is strongest." 12 The third wrote, "Women are strongest, but above all things truth is victor."*b*

13 When the king awoke, they took the writing and gave it to him, and he read it. 14 Then he sent and summoned all the nobles of Persia and Media and the satraps and generals and governors and prefects, 15 and he took his seat in the council chamber, and the writing was read in their presence. 16 He said, "Call the young men, and they shall explain their statements." So they were summoned, and came in. 17 They said to them, "Explain to us what you have written."

Then the first, who had spoken of the strength of wine, began and said: 18 "Gentlemen, how is wine the strongest? It leads astray the minds of all who drink it. 19 It makes equal the mind of the king and the orphan, of the slave and the free, of the poor and the rich. 20 It turns every thought to feasting and mirth, and forgets all sorrow and debt. 21 It makes all hearts feel rich, forgets kings and satraps, and makes everyone talk in millions.*c* 22 When people

drink they forget to be friendly with friends and kindred, and before long they draw their swords. 23 And when they recover from the wine, they do not remember what they have done. 24 Gentlemen, is not wine the strongest, since it forces people to do these things?" When he had said this, he stopped speaking.

4 Then the second, who had spoken of the strength of the king, began to speak: 2 "Gentlemen, are not men strongest, who rule over land and sea and all that is in them? 3 But the king is stronger; he is their lord and master, and whatever he says to them they obey. 4 If he tells them to make war on one another, they do it; and if he sends them out against the enemy, they go, and conquer mountains, walls, and towers. 5 They kill and are killed, and do not disobey the king's command; if they win the victory, they bring everything to the king—whatever spoil they take and everything else. 6 Likewise those who do not serve in the army or make war but till the soil; whenever they sow and reap, they bring some to the king; and they compel one another to pay taxes to the king. 7 And yet he is only one man! If he tells them to kill, they kill; if he tells them to release, they release; 8 if he tells them to attack, they attack; if he tells them to lay waste, they lay waste; if he tells them to build, they build; 9 if he tells them to cut down, they cut down; if he tells them to plant, they plant. 10 All his people and his armies obey him. Furthermore, he reclines, he eats and drinks and sleeps, 11 but they keep watch around him, and no one may go away to attend to his own affairs, nor do they disobey him. 12 Gentlemen, why is not the king the strongest,

*a* Gk *on gold*   *b* Or *but truth is victor over all things*
*c* Gk *talents*

11.3.2), the king proposes the contest. **13–17a:** The entire court is assembled to hear the three men defend their respective answers; the scene is consonant with court practices in the ancient world.

**3.17b–24: In praise of the strength of wine.** Wine is the great leveler of society; it takes away the capacity for discernment and remembrance, overpowering king and commoner alike.

**4.1–12: In praise of the strength of kings.** The extreme power of ancient kings is accurately portrayed here. This passage is not a polemic against kingship.

since he is to be obeyed in this fashion?" And he stopped speaking.

13 Then the third, who had spoken of women and truth (and this was Zerubbabel), began to speak: 14 "Gentlemen, is not the king great, and are not men many, and is not wine strong? Who is it, then, that rules them, or has the mastery over them? Is it not women? 15 Women gave birth to the king and to every people that rules over sea and land. 16 From women they came; and women brought up the very men who plant the vineyards from which comes wine. 17 Women make men's clothes; they bring men glory; men cannot exist without women. 18 If men gather gold and silver or any other beautiful thing, and then see a woman lovely in appearance and beauty, 19 they let all those things go, and gape at her, and with open mouths stare at her, and all prefer her to gold or silver or any other beautiful thing. 20 A man leaves his own father, who brought him up, and his own country, and clings to his wife. 21 With his wife he ends his days, with no thought of his father or his mother or his country. 22 Therefore you must realize that women rule over you!

"Do you not labor and toil, and bring everything and give it to women? 23 A man takes his sword, and goes out to travel and rob and steal and to sail the sea and rivers; 24 he faces lions, and he walks in darkness, and when he steals and robs and plunders, he brings it back to the woman he loves. 25 A man loves his wife more than his father or his mother. 26 Many men have lost their minds because of women, and have become slaves because of them. 27 Many have perished, or stumbled, or sinned because of women. 28 And now do you not believe me?

"Is not the king great in his power? Do not all lands fear to touch him? 29 Yet I have seen him with Apame, the king's concubine, the daughter of the illustrious Bartacus; she would sit at the king's right hand 30 and take the crown from the king's head and put it on her own, and slap the king with her left hand. 31 At this the king would gaze at her with mouth agape. If she smiles at him, he laughs; if she loses her temper with him, he flatters her, so that she may be reconciled to him. 32 Gentlemen, why are not women strong, since they do such things?"

33 Then the king and the nobles looked at one another; and he began to speak about truth: 34 "Gentlemen, are not women strong? The earth is vast, and heaven is high, and the sun is swift in its course, for it makes the circuit of the heavens and returns to its place in one day. 35 Is not the one who does these things great? But truth is great, and stronger than all things. 36 The whole earth calls upon truth, and heaven blesses it. All God's works*a* quake and tremble, and with him there is nothing unrighteous. 37 Wine is unrighteous, the king is unrighteous, women are unrighteous, all human beings are unrighteous, all their works are unrighteous, and all such things. There is no truth in them and in their unrighteousness they will perish. 38 But truth endures and is strong forever, and lives and prevails forever and ever. 39 With it there is no partiality or preference, but it does what is righteous instead of anything that is un-

a Gk *All the works*

**4.13–32: In praise of the strength of women.** The third youth first depicts the strength of women, who give birth to kings, who receive from men the treasures won in warfare and heroic deeds, who can humiliate their masters, including kings, and yet are sought after and fawned upon even by those whom they humiliate. **13:** According to 1 Chr 3.19, *Zerubbabel* is a descendant of David. His name is added here as the older story is incorporated into 1 Esdras (see 3.1–5.6n.). **20:** Gen 2.24. **29:** The king's concubine, *Apame,* is not mentioned in other stories.

**4.33–41: In praise of the strength of truth.** An addition to the original story probably made prior to the story's adaptation to the Jewish author's purpose. Truth is portrayed in imagery familiar in Greek literature, though the Jewish adapter of the story may have modified the original somewhat to make truth more akin to ideas of truth and wisdom, emphasizing firmness and reliability. **40:** A clever maneuver by righteous or wicked. Everyone approves its deeds, 40 and there is nothing unrighteous in its judgment. To it belongs the strength and the kingship and the power and the majesty of all the ages. Blessed be the God of truth!" 41 When he stopped speaking, all the people shouted and said, "Great is truth, and strongest of all!"

42 Then the king said to him, "Ask what you wish, even beyond what is written, and we will give it to you, for you have been found to be the wisest. You shall sit next to me, and be called my Kinsman." 43 Then he said to the king, "Remember the vow that you made on the day when you became king, to build Jerusalem, 44 and to send back all the vessels that were taken from Jerusalem, which Cyrus set apart when he began[a] to destroy Babylon, and vowed to send them back there. 45 You also vowed to build the temple, which the Edomites burned when Judea was laid waste by the Chaldeans. 46 And now, O lord the king, this is what I ask and request of you, and this befits your greatness. I pray therefore that you fulfill the vow whose fulfillment you vowed to the King of heaven with your own lips."

47 Then King Darius got up and kissed him, and wrote letters for him to all the treasurers and governors and generals and satraps, that they should give safe conduct to him and to all who were going up with him to build Jerusalem. 48 And he wrote letters to all the governors in Coelesyria and Phoenicia and to those in Lebanon, to bring cedar timber from Lebanon to Jerusalem,

and to help him build the city. 49 He wrote in behalf of all the Jews who were going up from his kingdom to Judea, in the interest of their freedom, that no officer or satrap or governor or treasurer should forcibly enter their doors; 50 that all the country that they would occupy should be theirs without tribute; that the Idumeans should give up the villages of the Jews that they held; 51 that twenty talents a year should be given for the building of the temple until it was completed, 52 and an additional ten talents a year for burnt offerings to be offered on the altar every day, in accordance with the commandment to make seventeen offerings; 53 and that all who came from Babylonia to build the city should have their freedom, they and their children and all the priests who came. 54 He wrote also concerning their support and the priests' vestments in which[b] they were to minister. 55 He wrote that the support for the Levites should be provided until the day when the temple would be finished and Jerusalem built. 56 He wrote that land and wages should be provided for all who guarded the city. 57 And he sent back from Babylon all the vessels that Cyrus had set apart; everything that Cyrus had ordered to be done, he also commanded to be done and to be sent to Jerusalem.

58 When the young man went out, he lifted up his face to heaven toward Jerusalem, and praised the King of heaven, saying, 59 "From you comes the victory; from

a Cn: Gk vowed    b Gk in what priestly vestments

a Jewish adapter of the story to suggest that truth is virtually equivalent to the will of God. 41: The Vulgate translation of the people's response, "Magna est veritas et praevalet," became a famous proverb.

**4.42–57: Zerubbabel's reward.** Darius authorizes Zerubbabel to return to Jerusalem and rebuild the Temple, with generous support from the Persian treasury. **43:** This improbable vow of Darius to rebuild Jerusalem and its Temple upon his accession to kingship is not otherwise attested and is likely the creation of the author of 1 Esdras. **45:** The Edomites are not mentioned in 1.55 as having burned the Temple, but see Ob 11–14 and Ps 137.7. **48–57:** Darius magnificently supports the program outlined by Zerubbabel. The reality is reflected more accurately in the decree issued by Darius after the governor of Samaria had complained about the rebuilding of the Temple (Ezra 6.1–13; 1 Esd 6.23–34). The royal support depicted here is likely exaggerated. **50:** *Idumeans*, a later designation of the Edomites.

**4.58–60: Zerubbabel's prayer.** The language of this prayer is similar to a prayer of Daniel (Dan 2.20–23) and may be dependent upon it.

you comes wisdom, and yours is the glory. I am your servant. 60 Blessed are you, who have given me wisdom; I give you thanks, O Lord of our ancestors."

61 So he took the letters, and went to Babylon and told this to all his kindred. 62 And they praised the God of their ancestors, because he had given them release and permission 63 to go up and build Jerusalem and the temple that is called by his name; and they feasted, with music and rejoicing, for seven days.

5 After this the heads of ancestral houses were chosen to go up, according to their tribes, with their wives and sons and daughters, and their male and female servants, and their livestock. 2 And Darius sent with them a thousand cavalry to take them back to Jerusalem in safety, with the music of drums and flutes; 3 all their kindred were making merry. And he made them go up with them.

4 These are the names of the men who went up, according to their ancestral houses in the tribes, over their groups: 5 the priests, the descendants of Phinehas son of Aaron; Jeshua son of Jozadak son of Seraiah and Joakim son of Zerubbabel son of Shealtiel, of the house of David, of the lineage of Phares, of the tribe of Judah, 6 who spoke wise words before King Darius of the Persians, in the second year of his reign, in the month of Nisan, the first month.

7 These are the Judeans who came up out of their sojourn in exile, whom King Nebuchadnezzar of Babylon had carried away to Babylon 8 and who returned to Jerusalem and the rest of Judea, each to his own town. They came with Zerubbabel and Jeshua, Nehemiah, Seraiah, Resaiah, Eneneus, Mordecai, Beelsarus, Aspharasus,

Reeliah, Rehum, and Baanah, their leaders.

9 The number of those of the nation and their leaders: the descendants of Parosh, two thousand one hundred seventy-two. The descendants of Shephatiah, four hundred seventy-two. 10 The descendants of Arah, seven hundred fifty-six. 11 The descendants of Pahath-moab, of the descendants of Jeshua and Joab, two thousand eight hundred twelve. 12 The descendants of Elam, one thousand two hundred fifty-four. The descendants of Zattu, nine hundred forty-five. The descendants of Chorbe, seven hundred five. The descendants of Bani, six hundred forty-eight. 13 The descendants of Bebai, six hundred twenty-three. The descendants of Azgad, one thousand three hundred twenty-two. 14 The descendants of Adonikam, six hundred sixty-seven. The descendants of Bigvai, two thousand sixty-six. The descendants of Adin, four hundred fifty-four. 15 The descendants of Ater, namely of Hezekiah, ninety-two. The descendants of Kilan and Azetas, sixty-seven. The descendants of Azaru, four hundred thirty-two. 16 The descendants of Annias, one hundred one. The descendants of Arom. The descendants of Bezai, three hundred twenty-three. The descendants of Arsiphurith, one hundred twelve. 17 The descendants of Baiterus, three thousand five. The descendants of Bethlomon, one hundred twenty-three. 18 Those from Netophah, fifty-five. Those from Anathoth, one hundred fifty-eight. Those from Bethasmoth, forty-two. 19 Those from Kiriatharim, twenty-five. Those from Chephirah and Beeroth, seven hundred forty-three. 20 The Chadiasans and Ammidians, four hundred twenty-two. Those from Kirama and Geba, six hundred

**4.61–5.6: Preparations for the return.** Zerubbabel journeys (perhaps from Susa) to Babylon and there recruits leaders from the priestly and regal families for the returning exiles (5.4–6). The genealogies of the leaders are hopelessly confused. The material unique to 1 Esdras concludes here; the modified parallel with Ezra-Nehemiah resumes in the following chapters.

**5.7–46: A list of the returning exiles** (Ezra 2.1–70 and Neh 7.6–73a). The list in 1 Esdras differs from that in Ezra at many points, both as to names and to numbers. The totals, however, are almost identical. The numbers of the priests and Levites are almost identical in the three lists, an indication that priestly and Levitical genealogies were more carefully preserved than others. For comments on the list, see notes to Ezra 2. **24–25:** Only four divisions of priests are given, while in 1 Chr 24 twenty-four divisions appear.

twenty-one. ²¹Those from Macalon, one hundred twenty-two. Those from Betolio, fifty-two. The descendants of Niphish, one hundred fifty-six. ²²The descendants of the other Calamolalus and Ono, seven hundred twenty-five. The descendants of Jerechus, three hundred forty-five. ²³The descendants of Senaah, three thousand three hundred thirty.

24 The priests: the descendants of Jedaiah son of Jeshua, of the descendants of Anasib, nine hundred seventy-two. The descendants of Immer, one thousand and fifty-two. ²⁵The descendants of Pashhur, one thousand two hundred forty-seven. The descendants of Charme, one thousand seventeen.

26 The Levites: the descendants of Jeshua and Kadmiel and Bannas and Sudias, seventy-four. ²⁷The temple singers: the descendants of Asaph, one hundred twenty-eight. ²⁸The gatekeepers: the descendants of Shallum, the descendants of Ater, the descendants of Talmon, the descendants of Akkub, the descendants of Hatita, the descendants of Shobai, in all one hundred thirty-nine.

29 The temple servants: the descendants of Esau, the descendants of Hasupha, the descendants of Tabbaoth, the descendants of Keros, the descendants of Sua, the descendants of Padon, the descendants of Lebanah, the descendants of Hagabah, ³⁰the descendants of Akkub, the descendants of Uthai, the descendants of Ketab, the descendants of Hagab, the descendants of Subai, the descendants of Hana, the descendants of Cathua, the descendants of Geddur, ³¹the descendants of Jairus, the descendants of Daisan, the descendants of Noeba, the descendants of Chezib, the descendants of Gazera, the descendants of Uzza, the descendants of Phinoe, the descendants of Hasrah, the descendants of Basthai, the descendants of Asnah, the descendants of Maani, the descendants of Nephisim, the descendants of Acuph,ᵃ the

descendants of Hakupha, the descendants of Asur, the descendants of Pharakim, the descendants of Bazluth, ³²the descendants of Mehida, the descendants of Cutha, the descendants of Charea, the descendants of Barkos, the descendants of Serar, the descendants of Temah, the descendants of Neziah, the descendants of Hatipha.

33 The descendants of Solomon's servants: the descendants of Assaphioth, the descendants of Peruda, the descendants of Jaalah, the descendants of Lozon, the descendants of Isdael, the descendants of Shephatiah, ³⁴the descendants of Agia, the descendants of Pochereth-hazzebaim, the descendants of Sarothie, the descendants of Masiah, the descendants of Gas, the descendants of Addus, the descendants of Subas, the descendants of Apherra, the descendants of Barodis, the descendants of Shaphat, the descendants of Allon.

35 All the temple servants and the descendants of Solomon's servants were three hundred seventy-two.

36 The following are those who came up from Tel-melah and Tel-harsha, under the leadership of Cherub, Addan, and Immer, ³⁷though they could not prove by their ancestral houses or lineage that they belonged to Israel: the descendants of Delaiah son of Tobiah, and the descendants of Nekoda, six hundred fifty-two.

38 Of the priests the following had assumed the priesthood but were not found registered: the descendants of Habaiah, the descendants of Hakkoz, and the descendants of Jaddus who had married Agia, one of the daughters of Barzillai, and was called by his name. ³⁹When a search was made in the register and the genealogy of these men was not found, they were excluded from serving as priests. ⁴⁰And Nehemiah and Attharias᙮ told them not to share in the holy

a Other ancient authorities read *Acub* or *Acum*
b Or *the governor*

**40:** The name "Nehemiah" is not found in the parallel in Ezra-Nehemiah, and it is added here to compensate for the fact that he is missing later in the text, as Ezra's role is increased. *The governor* (see note *b*) orders the community to await the appearance of a high priest before participating in the holy things until a high priest should appear wearing Urim and Thummim.[a]

41 All those of Israel, twelve or more years of age, besides male and female servants, were forty-two thousand three hundred sixty; [42] their male and female servants were seven thousand three hundred thirty-seven; there were two hundred forty-five musicians and singers. [43] There were four hundred thirty-five camels, and seven thousand thirty-six horses, two hundred forty-five mules, and five thousand five hundred twenty-five donkeys.

44 Some of the heads of families, when they came to the temple of God that is in Jerusalem, vowed that, to the best of their ability, they would erect the house on its site, [45] and that they would give to the sacred treasury for the work a thousand minas of gold, five thousand minas of silver, and one hundred priests' vestments.

46 The priests, the Levites, and some of the people[b] settled in Jerusalem and its vicinity; and the temple singers, the gatekeepers, and all Israel in their towns.

47 When the seventh month came, and the Israelites were all in their own homes, they gathered with a single purpose in the square before the first gate toward the east.

[48] Then Jeshua son of Jozadak, with his fellow priests, and Zerubbabel son of Shealtiel, with his kinsmen, took their places and prepared the altar of the God of Israel, [49] to offer burnt offerings upon it, in accordance with the directions in the book of Moses the man of God. [50] And some joined them from the other peoples of the land. And they erected the altar in its place, for all the peoples of the land were hostile to them and were stronger than they; and they offered sacrifices at the proper times and burnt offerings to the Lord morning and evening. [51] They kept the festival of booths, as it is commanded in the law, and offered the proper sacrifices every day, [52] and thereafter the regular offerings and sacrifices on sabbaths and at new moons and at all the consecrated feasts. [53] And all who had made any vow to God began to offer sacrifices to God, from the new moon of the seventh month, though the temple of God was not yet built. [54] They gave money to the masons and the carpenters, and food and drink [55] and carts[c] to the Sidonians and the Tyrians, to bring cedar logs from Lebanon and convey them in rafts to the harbor

a Gk Manifestation and Truth  b Or those who were of the people  c Meaning of Gk uncertain

things. *Urim and Thummim* are the sacred lots used by the priests to receive oracular decisions (Ex 28.30; Lev 8.8; Deut 33.8; 1 Sam 14.41). **41:** The total exceeds the sum of the several groups listed; apparently others were present who are not specifically mentioned in the list.

**5.47–73: Work on the Temple commences and is interrupted** (Ezra 3.1–4.5; cf. Josephus, *Ant.* 11.4.1–3). Ezra-Nehemiah places the building of the Temple in both the reign of Cyrus (539–530 BCE) and that of Darius (522–486), deliberately merging several returns of exiles. 1 Esdras offers a more probable historical sequence, with Sheshbazzar beginning the work under Cyrus, and Zerubbabel working only under Darius. The likely sequence of events is that Sheshbazzar returned to Yehud (the Persian province of Judah) shortly after 538, restored the sacrificial altar, reestablished public worship, and laid the foundation of the Temple. The work on the Temple only resumed with the return of additional exiles under Zerubbabel and Jeshua, at which point opposition from Samaria quickly developed. Haggai and Zechariah encouraged the community to complete the Temple, and work was begun once more; it was finally dedicated in 516/515.

**5.47–55: Building the altar and resumption of sacrifices.** It is highly doubtful that Zerubbabel and Jeshua (v. 48) were involved in the initial work under Sheshbazzar. The author of 1 Esdras has conflated events. Those recorded here belong to the period of rebuilding begun in the second year of Darius, not Cyrus. **49:** *The book of Moses,* the Torah. **50:** Although the returnees elsewhere oppose marriages with peoples of the land, they do allow persons to join the community under certain conditions that are not specified in this text. **51:** The feast of booths is observed beginning on the fifteenth day of the seventh month (Lev 23.34). **52:** *New moons,* see Num 29.6.

of Joppa, according to the decree that they had in writing from King Cyrus of the Persians.

56 In the second year after their coming to the temple of God in Jerusalem, in the second month, Zerubbabel son of Shealtiel and Jeshua son of Jozadak made a beginning, together with their kindred and the levitical priests and all who had come back to Jerusalem from exile; 57 and they laid the foundation of the temple of God on the new moon of the second month in the second year after they came to Judea and Jerusalem. 58 They appointed the Levites who were twenty or more years of age to have charge of the work of the Lord. And Jeshua arose, and his sons and kindred and his brother Kadmiel and the sons of Jeshua Emadabun and the sons of Joda son of Iliadun, with their sons and kindred, all the Levites, pressing forward the work on the house of God with a single purpose.

So the builders built the temple of the Lord. 59 And the priests stood arrayed in their vestments, with musical instruments and trumpets, and the Levites, the sons of Asaph, with cymbals, 60 praising the Lord and blessing him, according to the directions of King David of Israel; 61 they sang hymns, giving thanks to the Lord, "For his goodness and his glory are forever upon all Israel." 62 And all the people sounded trumpets and shouted with a great shout, praising the Lord for the erection of the house of the Lord. 63 Some of the levitical priests and heads of ancestral houses, old men who had seen the former house, came to the building of this one with outcries and loud weeping, 64 while many came with trumpets and a joyful noise, 65 so that the people could not hear the trumpets because of the weeping of the people.

For the multitude sounded the trumpets loudly, so that the sound was heard far away; 66 and when the enemies of the tribe of Judah and Benjamin heard it, they came to find out what the sound of the trumpets meant. 67 They learned that those who had returned from exile were building the temple for the Lord God of Israel. 68 So they approached Zerubbabel and Jeshua and the heads of the ancestral houses and said to them, "We will build with you. 69 For we obey your Lord just as you do and we have been sacrificing to him ever since the days of King Esar-haddon[a] of the Assyrians, who brought us here." 70 But Zerubbabel and Jeshua and the heads of the ancestral houses in Israel said to them, "You have nothing to do with us in building the house for the Lord our God, 71 for we alone will build it for the Lord of Israel, as Cyrus, the king of the Persians, has commanded us." 72 But the peoples of the land pressed hard[b] upon those in Judea, cut off their supplies, and hindered their building; 73 and by plots and demagoguery and uprisings they prevented the completion of the building as long as King Cyrus lived. They were kept from building for two years, until the reign of Darius.

6 Now in the second year of the reign of Darius, the prophets Haggai and Zechariah son of Iddo prophesied to the Jews who were in Judea and Jerusalem; they prophesied to them in the name of the Lord

a Gk *Asbasareth*   b Meaning of Gk uncertain

5.56–65: **The Temple's foundation is laid. 56:** Apparently the second year of Cyrus is intended, but the second year of Darius is the correct date. **58:** The builders built the foundation of the Temple. **59–65:** The author transposed the ceremony described in Ezra 3.10–13, which occurred when the foundation of the Temple was laid, to the construction of the Temple in general.

5.66–73: **Enemies interrupt the work of the returned exiles. 69:** Instead of Esar-haddon, the Assyrian king who ruled 681–669 BCE, Josephus (*Ant.* 11.4.3) reads Shalmaneser (727–722; as in 2 Kings 17.3; 18.9). **73:** This verse (see parallel in Ezra 4.24) reflects a somewhat smoothed over rearrangement and merging of the different stages of return.

6.1–34: **Temple work resumes** (Ezra 4.24–6.12). Haggai and Zechariah encourage the resumption of work on the Temple and succeed in gaining support for Zerubbabel and Jeshua (Joshua; cf. Hag 1.1–4; 2.1–4; Zech 4.9; 6.15). **3:** Sisinnes is Tattenai; Sathrabuzanes is Shethar-bozenai (Ezra 5.3). **14:** *A king*

God of Israel. [2] Then Zerubbabel son of Shealtiel and Jeshua son of Jozadak began to build the house of the Lord that is in Jerusalem, with the help of the prophets of the Lord who were with them.

[3] At the same time Sisinnes the governor of Syria and Phoenicia and Sathrabuzanes and their associates came to them and said, [4] "By whose order are you building this house and this roof and finishing all the other things? And who are the builders that are finishing these things?" [5] Yet the elders of the Jews were dealt with kindly, for the providence of the Lord was over the captives; [6] they were not prevented from building until word could be sent to Darius concerning them and a report made.

[7] A copy of the letter that Sisinnes the governor of Syria and Phoenicia, and Sathrabuzanes, and their associates the local rulers in Syria and Phoenicia, wrote and sent to Darius:

[8] "To King Darius, greetings. Let it be fully known to our lord the king that, when we went to the country of Judea and entered the city of Jerusalem, we found the elders of the Jews, who had been in exile, [9] building in the city of Jerusalem a great new house for the Lord, of hewn stone, with costly timber laid in the walls. [10] These operations are going on rapidly, and the work is prospering in their hands and being completed with all splendor and care. [11] Then we asked these elders, 'At whose command are you building this house and laying the foundations of this structure?' [12] In order that we might inform you in writing who the leaders are, we questioned them and asked them for a list of the names of those who are at their head. [13] They answered us, 'We are the servants of the Lord who created the heaven and the earth. [14] The house was built many years ago by a king of Israel who was great and strong, and it was finished. [15] But when our ancestors sinned against the Lord of Israel who is

in heaven, and provoked him, he gave them over into the hands of King Nebuchadnezzar of Babylon, king of the Chaldeans; [16] and they pulled down the house, and burned it, and carried the people away captive to Babylon. [17] But in the first year that Cyrus reigned over the country of Babylonia, King Cyrus wrote that this house should be rebuilt. [18] And the holy vessels of gold and of silver, which Nebuchadnezzar had taken out of the house in Jerusalem and stored in his own temple, these King Cyrus took out again from the temple in Babylon, and they were delivered to Zerubbabel and Sheshbazzar[a] the governor [19] with the command that he should take all these vessels back and put them in the temple at Jerusalem, and that this temple of the Lord should be rebuilt on its site. [20] Then this Sheshbazzar, after coming here, laid the foundations of the house of the Lord that is in Jerusalem. Although it has been in process of construction from that time until now, it has not yet reached completion.' [21] Now therefore, O king, if it seems wise to do so, let search be made in the royal archives of our lord[b] the king that are in Babylon; [22] if it is found that the building of the house of the Lord in Jerusalem was done with the consent of King Cyrus, and if it is approved by our lord the king, let him send us directions concerning these things."

[23] Then Darius commanded that search be made in the royal archives that were deposited in Babylon. And in Ecbatana, the fortress that is in the country of Media, a scroll[c] was found in which this was recorded: [24] "In the first year of the reign of King Cyrus, he ordered the building of the house of the Lord in Jerusalem, where they sacrifice with perpetual fire; [25] its height to be sixty cubits and its width sixty cubits, with three courses of hewn stone and one

---

a Gk *Sanabassarus*    b Other ancient authorities read
*of Cyrus*    c Other authorities read *passage*

*of Israel,* namely Solomon (1 Kings 6). **15:** *Chaldeans,* see 1.52n. **18:** Zerubbabel, who is more prominent in 1 Esdras, is added here and in vv. 27,29; only Sheshbazzar is mentioned in Ezra 5.14 and in Josephus (*Ant.* 11.4.4). **23:** *Ecbatana* was the summer residence of Persian kings. **25:** A cubit is about 45 cm (18 in). **32:** Ezra 6.11 prescribes further that the houses of violators of the decree be made a dunghill.

course of new native timber; the cost to be paid from the treasury of King Cyrus; 26 and that the holy vessels of the house of the Lord, both of gold and of silver, which Nebuchadnezzar took out of the house in Jerusalem and carried away to Babylon, should be restored to the house in Jerusalem, to be placed where they had been."

27 So Darius[a] commanded Sisinnes the governor of Syria and Phoenicia, and Sathrabuzanes, and their associates, and those who were appointed as local rulers in Syria and Phoenicia, to keep away from the place, and to permit Zerubbabel, the servant of the Lord and governor of Judea, and the elders of the Jews to build this house of the Lord on its site. 28 "And I command that it be built completely, and that full effort be made to help those who have returned from the exile of Judea, until the house of the Lord is finished; 29 and that out of the tribute of Coelesyria and Phoenicia a portion be scrupulously given to these men, that is, to Zerubbabel the governor, for sacrifices to the Lord, for bulls and rams and lambs, 30 and likewise wheat and salt and wine and oil, regularly every year, without quibbling, for daily use as the priests in Jerusalem may indicate, 31 in order that libations may be made to the Most High God for the king and his children, and prayers be offered for their lives."

32 He commanded that if anyone should transgress or nullify any of the things herein written,[b] a beam should be taken out of the house of the perpetrator, who then should be impaled upon it, and all property forfeited to the king.

33 "Therefore may the Lord, whose name is there called upon, destroy every king and nation that shall stretch out their hands to hinder or damage that house of the Lord in Jerusalem.

34 "I, King Darius, have decreed that it be done with all diligence as here prescribed."

7 Then Sisinnes the governor of Coelesyria and Phoenicia, and Sathrabuzanes, and their associates, following the orders of King Darius, 2 supervised the holy work with very great care, assisting the elders of the Jews and the chief officers of the temple. 3 The holy work prospered, while the prophets Haggai and Zechariah prophesied; 4 and they completed it by the command of the Lord God of Israel. So with the consent of Cyrus and Darius and Artaxerxes, kings of the Persians, 5 the holy house was finished by the twenty-third day of the month of Adar, in the sixth year of King Darius. 6 And the people of Israel, the priests, the Levites, and the rest of those who returned from exile who joined them, did according to what was written in the book of Moses. 7 They offered at the dedication of the temple of the Lord one hundred bulls, two hundred rams, four hundred lambs, 8 and twelve male goats for the sin of all Israel, according to the number of the twelve leaders of the tribes of Israel; 9 and the priests and the Levites stood arrayed in their vestments, according to kindred, for the services of the Lord God of Israel in accordance with the book of Moses; and the gatekeepers were at each gate.

10 The people of Israel who came from exile kept the passover on the fourteenth day of the first month, after the priests and the Levites were purified together. 11 Not

---

a Gk he    b Other authorities read *stated above* or *added in writing*

**7.1–9: The Temple completed** (Ezra 6.13–18). **4:** Artaxerxes I (465–424 BCE) appears here anachronistically (see 8.1–9.36). This erroneous reference to him is taken from Ezra 6.14, where it functions ideologically, linking all the stages of the return. The verse is more problematic in 1 Esdras because, unlike Ezra-Nehemiah (see Neh 1–6), this book does not depict any building activities under Artaxerxes; Josephus omits the name. **5:** February-March, 516 BCE. **7–8:** Compare the account of the dedication of the first Temple (1 Kings 8.8,63). **9:** Compare Ezra 6.18.

**7.10–15: The Passover celebration** (Ezra 6.19–22). The celebration marks the restoration of Jewish life, resuming where Josiah's death in ch 1 left off. **11:** *Not all . . . were purified.* Not in Ezra 6, but perhaps borrowed from 2 Chr 30.18. **13:** Contrary to Ezra 6.21, the account here suggests that only the returned all of the returned captives were purified, but the Levites were all purified together,[a] 12 and they sacrificed the passover lamb for all the returned captives and for their kindred the priests and for themselves. 13 The people of Israel who had returned from exile ate it, all those who had separated themselves from the abominations of the peoples of the land and sought the Lord. 14 They also kept the festival of unleavened bread seven days, rejoicing before the Lord, 15 because he had changed the will of the king of the Assyrians concerning them, to strengthen their hands for the service of the Lord God of Israel.

8 After these things, when Artaxerxes, the king of the Persians, was reigning, Ezra came, the son of Seraiah, son of Azariah, son of Hilkiah, son of Shallum, 2 son of Zadok, son of Ahitub, son of Amariah, son of Uzzi, son of Bukki, son of Abishua, son of Phineas, son of Eleazar, son of Aaron the high[b] priest. 3 This Ezra came up from Babylon as a scribe skilled in the law of Moses, which was given by the God of Israel; 4 and the king showed him honor, for he found favor before the king[c] in all his requests. 5 There came up with him to Jerusalem some of the people of Israel and some of the priests and Levites and temple singers and gatekeepers and temple servants, 6 in the seventh year of the reign of Artaxerxes, in the fifth month (this was the king's seventh year); for they left Babylon on the new moon of the first month and arrived in Jerusalem on the new moon of

the fifth month, by the prosperous journey that the Lord gave them.[d] 7 For Ezra possessed great knowledge, so that he omitted nothing from the law of the Lord or the commandments, but taught all Israel all the ordinances and judgments.

8 The following is a copy of the written commission from King Artaxerxes that was delivered to Ezra the priest and reader of the law of the Lord:

9 "King Artaxerxes to Ezra the priest and reader of the law of the Lord, greeting. 10 In accordance with my gracious decision, I have given orders that those of the Jewish nation and of the priests and Levites and others in our realm, those who freely choose to do so, may go with you to Jerusalem. 11 Let as many as are so disposed, therefore, leave with you, just as I and the seven Friends who are my counselors have decided, 12 in order to look into matters in Judea and Jerusalem, in accordance with what is in the law of the Lord, 13 and to carry to Jerusalem the gifts for the Lord of Israel that I and my Friends have vowed, and to collect for the Lord in Jerusalem all the gold and silver that may be found in the country of Babylonia, 14 together with what is given by the nation for the temple of their Lord that is in Jerusalem, both gold and silver for bulls and rams and lambs and what goes with them, 15 so as to offer sacri-

a Meaning of Gk uncertain    b Gk the first
c Gk him    d Other authorities add for him or upon him

exiles participated in the Passover. **15:** *The king of the Assyrians,* see Ezra 6.22n. Josephus refers to the Persian king (*Ant.* 11.4.8).

**8.1–9.55: Final return and restoration under Ezra** (Ezra 7.1–10.44; Neh 7.73–8.12). Ezra, who like Zerubbabel is a key figure in 1 Esdras, is first introduced here. 1 Esdras closely parallels Ezra-Nehemiah on the matters they both discuss, though its author ignores the work of Nehemiah (Neh 1–7), as Sirach ignores the work of Ezra (Sir 49.13). Given the interest of the author of 1 Esdras in the Temple and its personnel, it is not surprising that Ezra the priest, rather than Nehemiah the governor, is highlighted. For the author of 1 Esdras, the restoration was accomplished by a Davidic heir—Zerubbabel—and by the priest Ezra. Ezra most likely came to Judah under Artaxerxes I (465–424 BCE).

**8.1–7: Ezra's credentials and mission** (Ezra 7.1–10). **1–2:** The genealogy is briefer than that in Ezra 7.1–5. **6:** *The seventh year . . . of Artaxerxes* I was 458 BCE. **7:** A paraphrase of Ezra 7.10.

**8.8–24: The letter of Artaxerxes authorizing Ezra** (Ezra 7.12–26). Artaxerxes's financial support for the Temple is extensive, as in Ezra. **11:** The seven *Friends* or counselors of the king (see Ezra 7.14) are referred to in Esth 1.14 and Herodotus 3.84. **20:** A talent was 34 kg (75 lb); a cor 230 l (6.5 bu); and fices on the altar of their Lord that is in Jerusalem. 16 Whatever you and your kindred are minded to do with the gold and silver, perform it in accordance with the will of your God; 17 deliver the holy vessels of the Lord that are given you for the use of the temple of your God that is in Jerusalem. 18 And whatever else occurs to you as necessary for the temple of your God, you may provide out of the royal treasury.

19 "I, King Artaxerxes, have commanded the treasurers of Syria and Phoenicia that whatever Ezra the priest and reader of the law of the Most High God sends for, they shall take care to give him, 20 up to a hundred talents of silver, and likewise up to a hundred cors of wheat, a hundred baths of wine, and salt in abundance. 21 Let all things prescribed in the law of God be scrupulously fulfilled for the Most High God, so that wrath may not come upon the kingdom of the king and his sons. 22 You are also informed that no tribute or any other tax is to be laid on any of the priests or Levites or temple singers or gatekeepers or temple servants or persons employed in this temple, and that no one has authority to impose any tax on them.

23 "And you, Ezra, according to the wisdom of God, appoint judges and justices to judge all those who know the law of your God, throughout all Syria and Phoenicia; and you shall teach it to those who do not know it. 24 All who transgress the law of your God or the law of the kingdom shall be strictly punished, whether by death or some other punishment, either fine or imprisonment."

25 Then Ezra the scribe said,[a] "Blessed be the Lord alone, who put this into the heart of the king, to glorify his house that is in Jerusalem, 26 and who honored me in the sight of the king and his counselors and all his Friends and nobles. 27 I was encouraged by the help of the Lord my God, and I gathered men from Israel to go up with me."

28 These are the leaders, according to their ancestral houses and their groups, who went up with me from Babylon, in the reign of King Artaxerxes: 29 Of the descendants of Phineas, Gershom. Of the descendants of Ithamar, Gamael. Of the descendants of David, Hattush son of Shecaniah. 30 Of the descendants of Parosh, Zechariah, and with him a hundred fifty men enrolled. 31 Of the descendants of Pahath-moab, Eliehoenai son of Zerahiah, and with him two hundred men. 32 Of the descendants of Zattu, Shecaniah son of Jahaziel, and with him three hundred men. Of the descendants of Adin, Obed son of Jonathan, and with him two hundred fifty men. 33 Of the descendants of Elam, Jeshaiah son of Gotholiah, and with him seventy men. 34 Of the descendants of Shephatiah, Zeraiah son of Michael, and with him seventy men. 35 Of the descendants of Joab, Obadiah son of Jehiel, and with him two hundred twelve men. 36 Of the descendants of Bani, Shelomith son of Josiphiah, and with him a hundred sixty men. 37 Of the descendants of Bebai, Zechariah son of Bebai, and with him twenty-eight men. 38 Of the descendants of Azgad, Johanan son of Hakkatan, and with him a hundred ten men. 39 Of the descendants of Adonikam, the last ones, their names being Eliphelet, Jeuel, and Shemaiah, and with them seventy men. 40 Of the descendants of Bigvai, Uthai son of Istalcurus, and with him seventy men.

41 I assembled them at the river called Theras, and we encamped there three days, and I inspected them. 42 When I found there

a Other ancient authorities lack Then Ezra the scribe said

a bath about 23 l (6 gal). 22: Temple personnel are exempt from all taxes. 23–24: Ezra is given authority to appoint judges throughout the entire province in order to maintain Jewish law.
8.25–60: Ezra's report: leading the exiles to Jerusalem (Ezra 7.27–8.30). 25–27: Ezra's prayer of thanksgiving (Ezra 7.27–28). 28–40: The list of exiles going to Jerusalem. The list of those who returned differs in a few particulars from that found in Ezra 8.1–14. 41–60: Communal preparations (Ezra 8.15–30). 41: The river … Theras is probably a tributary of the Euphrates. 42–49: Because neither priests nor Levites were among the group first assembled by Ezra, special measures had to be taken to

none of the descendants of the priests or of the Levites, [43] I sent word to Eliezar, Iduel, Maasmas, [44] Elnathan, Shemaiah, Jarib, Nathan, Elnathan, Zechariah, and Meshullam, who were leaders and men of understanding; [45] I told them to go to Iddo, who was the leading man at the place of the treasury, [46] and ordered them to tell Iddo and his kindred and the treasurers at that place to send us men to serve as priests in the house of our Lord. [47] And by the mighty hand of our Lord they brought us competent men of the descendants of Mahli son of Levi, son of Israel, namely Sherebiah[a] with his descendants and kinsmen, eighteen; [48] also Hashabiah and Annunus and his brother Jeshaiah, of the descendants of Hananiah, and their descendants, twenty men; [49] and of the temple servants, whom David and the leaders had given for the service of the Levites, two hundred twenty temple servants; the list of all their names was reported.

[50] There I proclaimed a fast for the young men before our Lord, to seek from him a prosperous journey for ourselves and for our children and the livestock that were with us. [51] For I was ashamed to ask the king for foot soldiers and cavalry and an escort to keep us safe from our adversaries; [52] for we had said to the king, "The power of our Lord will be with those who seek him, and will support them in every way." [53] And again we prayed to our Lord about these things, and we found him very merciful.

[54] Then I set apart twelve of the leaders of the priests, Sherebiah and Hashabiah, and ten of their kinsmen with them; [55] and I weighed out to them the silver and the gold and the holy vessels of the house of our Lord, which the king himself and his counselors and the nobles and all Israel had given. [56] I weighed and gave to them six hundred fifty talents of silver, and silver vessels worth a hundred talents, and a hundred talents of gold, [57] and twenty golden bowls, and twelve bronze vessels of fine bronze that glittered like gold. [58] And I said to them, "You are holy to the Lord, and the vessels are holy, and the silver and the gold are vowed to the Lord, the Lord of our ancestors. [59] Be watchful and on guard until you deliver them to the leaders of the priests and the Levites, and to the heads of the ancestral houses of Israel, in Jerusalem, in the chambers of the house of our Lord." [60] So the priests and the Levites who took the silver and the gold and the vessels that had been in Jerusalem carried them to the temple of the Lord.

[61] We left the river Theras on the twelfth day of the first month; and we arrived in Jerusalem by the mighty hand of our Lord, which was upon us; he delivered us from every enemy on the way, and so we came to Jerusalem. [62] When we had been there three days, the silver and the gold were weighed and delivered in the house of our Lord to the priest Meremoth son of Uriah; [63] with him was Eleazar son of Phinehas, and with them were Jozabad son of Jeshua and Moeth son of Binnui,[b] the Levites. [64] The whole was counted and weighed, and the weight of everything was recorded at that very time. [65] And those who had returned from exile offered sacrifices to the Lord, the God of Israel, twelve bulls for all Israel, ninety-six rams, [66] seventy-two lambs, and as a thank offering twelve male goats—all as a sacrifice to the Lord. [67] They delivered the king's orders to the royal stewards and to the governors of Coelesyria and Phoenicia; and these

a Gk *Asbebias*    b Gk *Sabannus*

secure the required number of both (Ezra 8 mentions only missing Levites). **45:** *The treasury* is not in Ezra 8. **50:** Fasting prior to an important undertaking was common, especially in the postexilic period (2 Chr 20.3; Esth 4.16). **56:** *Talents* weighed about 34 kg (75 lb) each. **58:** Holy objects could be entrusted only to those who were holy themselves.

**8.61–67:** Arrival in Jerusalem (Ezra 8.31–36). The treasures are placed in the Temple storehouses (chambers, v. 59); sacrifices are offered to God; and the king's orders are delivered to the provincial officers, who have no choice but to obey.

officials[a] honored the people and the temple of the Lord.

68 After these things had been done, the leaders came to me and said, 69 "The people of Israel and the rulers and the priests and the Levites have not put away from themselves the alien peoples of the land and their pollutions, the Canaanites, the Hittites, the Perizzites, the Jebusites, the Moabites, the Egyptians, and the Edomites. 70 For they and their descendants have married the daughters of these people,[b] and the holy race has been mixed with the alien peoples of the land; and from the beginning of this matter the leaders and the nobles have been sharing in this iniquity."

71 As soon as I heard these things I tore my garments and my holy mantle, and pulled out hair from my head and beard, and sat down in anxiety and grief. 72 And all who were ever moved at[c] the word of the Lord of Israel gathered around me, as I mourned over this iniquity, and I sat griefstricken until the evening sacrifice. 73 Then I rose from my fast, with my garments and my holy mantle torn, and kneeling down and stretching out my hands to the Lord 74 I said,

"O Lord, I am ashamed and confused before your face. 75 For our sins have risen higher than our heads, and our mistakes have mounted up to heaven 76 from the times of our ancestors, and we are in great sin to this day. 77 Because of our sins and the sins of our ancestors, we with our kindred and our kings and our priests were given over to the kings of the earth, to the sword and exile and plundering, in shame until this day. 78 And now in some measure

mercy has come to us from you, O Lord, to leave to us a root and a name in your holy place, 79 and to uncover a light for us in the house of the Lord our God, and to give us food in the time of our servitude. 80 Even in our bondage we were not forsaken by our Lord, but he brought us into favor with the kings of the Persians, so that they have given us food 81 and glorified the temple of our Lord, and raised Zion from desolation, to give us a stronghold in Judea and Jerusalem.

82 "And now, O Lord, what shall we say, when we have these things? For we have transgressed your commandments, which you gave by your servants the prophets, saying, 83 'The land that you are entering to take possession of is a land polluted with the pollution of the aliens of the land, and they have filled it with their uncleanness. 84 Therefore do not give your daughters in marriage to their descendants, and do not take their daughters for your descendants; 85 do not seek ever to have peace with them, so that you may be strong and eat the good things of the land and leave it for an inheritance to your children forever.' 86 And all that has happened to us has come about because of our evil deeds and our great sins. For you, O Lord, lifted the burden of our sins 87 and gave us such a root as this; but we turned back again to transgress your law by mixing with the uncleanness of the peoples of the land. 88 Were you not angry enough with us to destroy us without leaving a root or seed or name? 89 O Lord of Israel, you are faithful; for we are left as a root to this day. 90 See, we are now before

a Gk they    b Gk their daughters    c Or zealous for

8.68–9.36: **The crisis of mixed marriages in Judah** (Ezra 9.1–10.44; see comments there). Ezra and his supporters considered ethnic and religious cohesiveness to be essential for the survival of the community, and they urged a policy of separatism.
  8.68–70: **The nature of the crisis** (Ezra 9.1–2). The role of the leaders is particularly alarming to Ezra. **70:** *Race*, lit. "seed" (offspring).
  8.71–90: **Ezra's response to the crisis: mourning and prayer** (Ezra 9.3–15). Ezra interprets for the community the significance of mixed marriages, noting that they may again cause an exile. **71:** *Holy*, Ezra 9.3 does not ascribe holiness to Ezra's mantle; the addition in 1 Esdras stresses Ezra's significant position as high priest. **82–85:** The prophetic books contain no such statement; the author may have in mind such passages as Lev 18.24–30 and Deut 7.3–4, in the book of the prophet Moses.

you in our iniquities; for we can no longer stand in your presence because of these things."

91 While Ezra was praying and making his confession, weeping and lying on the ground before the temple, there gathered around him a very great crowd of men and women and youths from Jerusalem; for there was great weeping among the multitude. 92 Then Shecaniah son of Jehiel, one of the men of Israel, called out, and said to Ezra, "We have sinned against the Lord, and have married foreign women from the peoples of the land; but even now there is hope for Israel. 93 Let us take an oath to the Lord about this, that we will put away all our foreign wives, with their children, 94 as seems good to you and to all who obey the law of the Lord. 95 Rise up[a] and take action, for it is your task, and we are with you to take strong measures." 96 Then Ezra rose up and made the leaders of the priests and Levites of all Israel swear that they would do this. And they swore to it.

9 Then Ezra set out and went from the court of the temple to the chamber of Jehohanan son of Eliashib, 2 and spent the night there; and he did not eat bread or drink water, for he was mourning over the great iniquities of the multitude. 3 And a proclamation was made throughout Judea and Jerusalem to all who had returned from exile that they should assemble at Jerusalem, 4 and that if any did not meet there within two or three days, in accordance with the decision of the ruling elders, their livestock would be seized for sacrifice and the men themselves[b] expelled from the multitude of those who had returned from the captivity.

5 Then the men of the tribe of Judah and Benjamin assembled at Jerusalem within three days; this was the ninth month, on the twentieth day of the month. 6 All the multitude sat in the open square before the temple, shivering because of the bad weather that prevailed. 7 Then Ezra stood up and said to them, "You have broken the law and married foreign women, and so have increased the sin of Israel. 8 Now then make confession and give glory to the Lord the God of our ancestors, 9 and do his will; separate yourselves from the peoples of the land and from your foreign wives."

10 Then all the multitude shouted and said with a loud voice, "We will do as you have said. 11 But the multitude is great and it is winter, and we are not able to stand in the open air. This is not a work we can do in one day or two, for we have sinned too much in these things. 12 So let the leaders of the multitude stay, and let all those in our settlements who have foreign wives come at the time appointed, 13 with the elders and judges of each place, until we are freed from the wrath of the Lord over this matter."

14 Jonathan son of Asahel and Jahzeiah son of Tikvah[c] undertook the matter on these terms, and Meshullam and Levi and Shabbethai served with them as judges. 15 And those who had returned from exile acted in accordance with all this.

16 Ezra the priest chose for himself the leading men of their ancestral houses, all of them by name; and on the new moon of the

---

a Other ancient authorities read *as seems good to you." And all who obeyed the law of the Lord rose and said to Ezra,* 95 *"Rise up*   b Gk *he himself*   c Gk *Thocanos*

---

**8.91–9.36:** The people repent and dismiss their foreign wives (Ezra 10.1–44). As in Ezra 10, the account switches from a first-person report (so-called "Ezra Memoirs") to a third-person report about Ezra's reforms. **91–96:** A proposal to remove foreign wives is made. **9.1–17:** Ezra leads the communal process toward dismissing foreign wives. **4:** The ruling elders issue orders for the entire community to assemble within two or three days; Ezra exercises religious, not political, authority in the land. **7:** *The law,* e.g., Deut 7.3. **8:** To *give glory to the Lord* is to acknowledge themselves to be in the wrong (cf. Josh 7.19). **11–13:** Because of the severe winter weather and the complexity of the task, it is agreed that the separation should be handled by a committee, with the help of leaders from various districts. The multitude is dismissed. **16–17:** Three months are required to settle the cases, from the first of the tenth month (Tebet = December-January) to the first of the first month (Nisan = March-April). **18–36:** (Ezra tenth month they began their sessions to investigate the matter. [17] And the cases of the men who had foreign wives were brought to an end by the new moon of the first month.

18 Of the priests, those who were brought in and found to have foreign wives were: [19] of the descendants of Jeshua son of Jozadak and his kindred, Maaseiah, Eliezar, Jarib, and Jodan. [20] They pledged themselves to put away their wives, and to offer rams in expiation of their error. [21] Of the descendants of Immer: Hanani and Zebadiah and Maaseiah and Shemaiah and Jehiel and Azariah. [22] Of the descendants of Pashhur: Elioenai, Maaseiah, Ishmael, and Nathanael, and Gedaliah, and Salthas.

23 And of the Levites: Jozabad and Shimei and Kelaiah, who was Kelita, and Pethahiah and Judah and Jonah. [24] Of the temple singers: Eliashib and Zaccur.[a] [25] Of the gatekeepers: Shallum and Telem.[b]

26 Of Israel: of the descendants of Parosh: Ramiah, Izziah, Malchijah, Mijamin, and Eleazar, and Asibias, and Benaiah. [27] Of the descendants of Elam: Mattaniah and Zechariah, Jezrielus and Abdi, and Jeremoth and Elijah. [28] Of the descendants of Zamoth: Eliadas, Eliashib, Othoniah, Jeremoth, and Zabad and Zerdaiah. [29] Of the descendants of Bebai: Jehohanan and Hananiah and Zabbai and Emathis. [30] Of the descendants of Mani: Olamus, Mamuchus, Adaiah, Jashub, and Sheal and Jeremoth. [31] Of the descendants of Addi: Naathus and Moossias, Laccunus and Naidus, and Bescaspasmys and Sesthel, and Belnuus and Manasseas. [32] Of the descendants of Annan, Elionas and Asaias and Melchias and Sabbaias and Simon Chosamaeus. [33] Of the descendants of Hashum: Mattenai and Mattattah and Zabad and Eliphelet and Manasseh and Shimei. [34] Of the descendants of Bani: Jeremai, Momdius, Maerus, Joel, Mamdai and Bedeiah and Vaniah, Carabasion and Eliashib and Mamitanemus, Eliasis, Binnui, Elialis, Shimei, Shelemiah, Nethaniah. Of the descendants of Ezora: Shashai, Azarel, Azael, Samatus, Zambris, Joseph. [35] Of the descendants of Nooma: Mazitias, Zabad, Iddo, Joel, Benaiah. [36] All these had married foreign women, and they put them away together with their children.

37 The priests and the Levites and the Israelites settled in Jerusalem and in the country. On the new moon of the seventh month, when the people of Israel were in their settlements, [38] the whole multitude gathered with one accord in the open square before the east gate of the temple; [39] they told Ezra the chief priest and reader to bring the law of Moses that had been given by the Lord God of Israel. [40] So Ezra the chief priest brought the law, for all the multitude, men and women, and all the priests to hear the law, on the new moon of the seventh month. [41] He read aloud in the

a Gk Bacchurus    b Gk Tolbanes

10.18–44). The list of those who put away foreign wives, which includes priests, Levites, and the laity, may have been preserved in the Temple archives. **20:** An offering of a ram as a guilt offering (Ezra 10.19) was made *in expiation* of the sin. **22:** Gedaliah, Greek "Ocidelos." The parallel in Ezra 10.22 reads "Jozabad"; cf. Ezra 10.18. **36:** In contrast to 1 Esdras, the parallel in Ezra 10.44 does not specify that the wives and children were sent away. It only indicates that priests put away their wives. Many translators, however, append 1 Esd 9.36 to Ezra 10.44. On the conflict concerning foreign wives, see notes on Ezra 9–10.

**9.37–55: The restoration is complete: Ezra's public reading of the law** (Neh 7.73–8.12). 1 Esdras departs markedly from Ezra-Nehemiah at this juncture. In Ezra-Nehemiah the reading of the Torah (the law or teaching) follows the rebuilding of Jerusalem's walls under Nehemiah's leadership (Neh 1–6). For the author of 1 Esdras, the only important leaders are Zerubbabel and Ezra, who together restore (rather than transform) Israel's institutions and communal life. The book thus concludes, as it began, with the celebrating community in the Temple in Jerusalem. **37:** The new moon or first day of the seventh month was a day of holy convocation (Lev 23.23–24; Num 29.1), the day of the new year. **39:** Ezra is not explicitly identified elsewhere as the chief priest. **42:** The *platform* erected for Ezra probably continued the tradition open square before the gate of the temple from early morning until midday, in the presence of both men and women; and all the multitude gave attention to the law. [42] Ezra the priest and reader of the law stood on the wooden platform that had been prepared; [43] and beside him stood Mattathiah, Shema, Ananias, Azariah, Uriah, Hezekiah, and Baalsamus on his right, [44] and on his left Pedaiah, Mishael, Malchijah, Lothasubus, Nabariah, and Zechariah. [45] Then Ezra took up the book of the law in the sight of the multitude, for he had the place of honor in the presence of all. [46] When he opened the law, they all stood erect. And Ezra blessed the Lord God Most High, the God of hosts, the Almighty, [47] and the multitude answered, "Amen." They lifted up their hands, and fell to the ground and worshiped the Lord. [48] Jeshua and Anniuth and Sherebiah, Jadinus, Akkub, Shabbethai, Hodiah, Maiannas and Kelita, Azariah and Jozabad, Hanan, Pelaiah, the Levites, taught the law of the Lord,[a] at the same time explaining what was read.

[49] Then Attharates[b] said to Ezra the chief priest and reader, and to the Levites who were teaching the multitude, and to all, [50] "This day is holy to the Lord"—now they were all weeping as they heard the law— [51] "so go your way, eat the fat and drink the sweet, and send portions to those who have none; [52] for the day is holy to the Lord; and do not be sorrowful, for the Lord will exalt you." [53] The Levites commanded all the people, saying, "This day is holy; do not be sorrowful." [54] Then they all went their way, to eat and drink and enjoy themselves, and to give portions to those who had none, and to make great rejoicing; [55] because they were inspired by the words which they had been taught. And they came together.[c]

a Other ancient authorities add and read the law of the Lord to the multitude   b Or the governor
c The Greek text ends abruptly: compare Neh 8.13

whereby kings would appear before the people to reaffirm the covenant law on the festal occasion (cf. 2 Chr 20.5; 23.13; 29.4). It also served a practical need: to make the law (Torah) visible and audible to all. 48: The Levites explained the law to the people. Possibly translation into Aramaic was needed for those who may not have been familiar with Hebrew.

9.49–55: The concluding celebration. 49: Attharates is a corruption of "tirshatha" (governor) in Neh 8.9. The author of 1 Esdras does not intend to indicate that Nehemiah, the named governor in Neh 8.9, was a participant in the festivity. 50–55: The people are to rejoice even though the words of the law cause them to recognize their sin, because the law is associated with joy. 55: They came together, some consider the ending abrupt, with the continuation in the parallel in Neh 8 (a second gathering and the feast of booths in Neh 8.13–18) a more fitting conclusion. Nevertheless, coming together as a community around the law and celebrating in the Temple in Jerusalem constitute an appropriate ending for a book that began with a celebration under Josiah in the same location.

# THE PRAYER OF MANASSEH

The Prayer of Manasseh is a pseudepigraphical prayer characteristic of Second Temple Judaism. An anthological composition (i.e., a mosaic of biblical phrases and allusions), it is formally an individual lament for personal sin, with a petition for forgiveness. Similar to the "Penitential Psalms" in the Psalter, especially Ps 51, it differs from them in that an acknowledgment of divine justice and a confession of sin replace the complaint about God's inaction. Its closest biblical parallels are a number of late penitential prayers: Ezra 9.1–15; Neh 1.4–11; 9.6–37; Dan 9.4–19; Ps 106; Bar 1.15–3.8 (and cf. 1 Kings 8.48–52).

It is found in the *Didascalia Apostolorum,* a third-century CE Syriac translation of an original Greek work, and in the Apostolic Constitutions (fourth century, Greek). In the Codex Alexandrinus, it is one of the fourteen canticles appended to the Psalter. A composition of a Palestinian Jew, its original language may have been either Greek or Semitic (Hebrew or Aramaic). It is probably a work of the second or first century BCE. For the Eastern Orthodox churches, it is a deuterocanonical work.

Its title recalls the story of King Manasseh in 2 Chr 33; because of his idolatry (vv. 2–5), the Lord brought the Assyrians against Judah, and Manasseh was taken off, a captive in chains, to Babylon (10–11). In vv. 12–13 (and 18–19) the Chronicler states that Manasseh prayed in his distress. The Prayer of Manasseh was composed with 2 Chr 33 in mind (cf. Pr Man 10 and 2 Chr 33.10; Pr Man 9b–10 and 2 Chr 33.11; Pr Man 1,11 and 2 Chr 33.12) to fill a gap in 2 Chr, which lacks Manasseh's prayer. The major themes of the Prayer are the mercy that God extends even to the worst of sinners (see the sins of Manasseh in 2 Kings 21.2–17; 2 Chr 33.2–9,19) and the effectiveness of sincere contrition and repentance. It is a tripartite poem, consisting of an acknowledgment of God's infinite power, shown in his role as creator (vv. 1–4); a confession of sin, including divine mercy to repentant sinners (vv. 5–8) and a prayer for forgiveness (vv. 9–13); and a final petition for salvation and concluding doxology (vv. 14–15).

1 O Lord Almighty,
  God of our ancestors,
  of Abraham and Isaac and Jacob
  and of their righteous offspring;
2 you who made heaven and earth
  with all their order;
3 who shackled the sea by your word of
    command,
  who confined the deep
  and sealed it with your terrible and
    glorious name;
4 at whom all things shudder,
  and tremble before your power,
5 for your glorious splendor cannot be
    borne,
  and the wrath of your threat to
    sinners is unendurable;
6 yet immeasurable and unsearchable
  is your promised mercy,
7 for you are the Lord Most High,
  of great compassion, long-suffering,
    and very merciful,

**1–15: Invocation and praise of the creator;** cf. Neh 9.6–8. **1:** *God of our ancestors,* Ex 3.15–16; Dan 2.23; cf. Acts 3.13. **3:** The restraining of the sea by the creator is a common poetic theme of the Hebrew Bible (Ps 29.10; 104.7–9; 148.5–6; Job 38.8–11). *Your terrible and glorious name,* a hypostasis of the deity (Jer 10.6; 23.27; Ezek 20.39; 39.7; Zech 14.9). **7:** Cf. Ex 34.6–7; the Greek is very close to the LXX trans-

and you relent at human suffering.
O Lord, according to your great
    goodness
you have promised repentance and
    forgiveness
to those who have sinned against you,
and in the multitude of your mercies
you have appointed repentance for
    sinners,
so that they may be saved.[a]

8 Therefore you, O Lord, God of the
    righteous,
have not appointed repentance for the
    righteous,
for Abraham and Isaac and Jacob,
    who did not sin against you,
but you have appointed repentance
    for me, who am a sinner.

9 For the sins I have committed are
    more in number than the sand
    of the sea;
my transgressions are multiplied,
    O Lord, they are multiplied!
I am not worthy to look up and see
    the height of heaven
because of the multitude of my
    iniquities.

10 I am weighted down with many an
    iron fetter,
so that I am rejected[b] because of my
    sins,
and I have no relief;
for I have provoked your wrath

and have done what is evil in your
    sight,
setting up abominations and
    multiplying offenses.

11 And now I bend the knee of my
    heart,
imploring you for your kindness.

12 I have sinned, O Lord, I have sinned,
and I acknowledge my transgressions.

13 I earnestly implore you,
forgive me, O Lord, forgive me!
Do not destroy me with my
    transgressions!
Do not be angry with me forever or
    store up evil for me;
do not condemn me to the depths of
    the earth.
For you, O Lord, are the God of
    those who repent,

14 and in me you will manifest your
    goodness;
for, unworthy as I am, you will save
    me according to your great
    mercy,

15 and I will praise you continually all
    the days of my life.
For all the host of heaven sings your
    praise,
and yours is the glory forever. Amen.

a Other ancient authorities lack *O Lord, according . . .
be saved*    b Other ancient authorities read *so that I
cannot lift up my head*

lation of Joel 2.13 and Jon 4.21. The second part of this verse (*O Lord . . . may be saved*), preserved in the later Greek manuscripts and in the Latin and Syriac versions, is probably part of the original poem. It picks up on a major theme of Deuteronomy and related literature, the efficacy of repentance. **8:** *Not . . . for the righteous*, cf. Mk 2.17; Lk 5.32; 1 Tim 1.15. *For me . . . a sinner*, cf. Lk 15.7; 18.13. **10:** *I have done . . . in your sight*, Ps 51.4 (LXX 50.6). **13:** *The depths of the earth*, Sheol, the world of the dead (Ezek 26.20; 31.14,16,18; Ps 63.7). **15:** *Host of heaven*, the multitude of angelic beings (Job 38.7; Neh 9.6; cf. Lk 2.13).

# PSALM 151

❦

To the traditional Hebrew Psalter, the Septuagint (LXX) adds Ps 151, with a superscript describing it as "outside the number" (i.e., of the 150 Psalms); this is the basis of the NRSV translation. It is found in the fourth-century CE Greek Codex Sinaiticus with a different superscription and in the sixth-century Codex Alexandrinus (with a subscription, "The 151 Psalms of David"). In Syriac, Ps 151 is the first of a series of psalms (Ps 151–155) about the heroic exploits of David in 1 Sam 16–17.

A Hebrew version of the psalm is found in the Dead Sea Scrolls (11 QPsᵃ). This Hebrew version is made up of two distinct psalms: Ps 151A (= LXX Ps 151) is a poem based on 1 Sam 16.1–13, about David the shepherd becoming Israel's king, with a superscription; this psalm is truncated in the Greek and Syriac versions. Ps 151B is the fragmentary beginning of another psalm, also with a superscription, that must have followed Ps 151A in the original scroll; it apparently deals with David's contest with Goliath (1 Sam 17), a story that is also the subject of LXX Ps 151.6–7.

In form, Ps 151A is not a hymn or a petition, but a narrative (cf. Ps 78), an autobiographical poem in which David, the youngest of his brothers, speaks of his shepherding care for his father's flocks, of his psalms praising God, and of his anointment as Israel's king. It is probably to be dated to the Persian period, not later than the third century BCE (and therefore not composed at Qumran). Vv. 1–4 concern David the shepherd, and vv. 5–7 concern David the king. The superscription of the Hebrew poem ("A Hallelujah of David the son of Jesse") is similar to the superscriptions of Ps 145 ("Praise. Of David") and the introductory "Hallelujah" of Ps 111–113, 146–150, and thus serves to integrate this psalm into the end of Psalms.

*This psalm is ascribed to David as his own composition (though it is outside the number$^a$), after he had fought in single combat with Goliath.*

1 I was small among my brothers,
  and the youngest in my father's
      house;
  I tended my father's sheep.

2 My hands made a harp;
  my fingers fashioned a lyre.

3 And who will tell my Lord?
  The Lord himself; it is he who
      hears.$^b$

4 It was he who sent his messenger$^c$
  and took me from my father's
      sheep,

a Other ancient authorities add *of the one hundred fifty* (psalms)   b Other ancient authorities add *everything*; others add *me*; others read *who will hear me*   c Or *angel*

**1:** *Small . . . youngest,* 1 Sam 16.7,11; 17.14. A Syriac version of this psalm adds, "I discovered a lion and a wolf, and I killed and rent them" (cf. 1 Sam 17.34–35), an interpolation from Syriac Ps 152–153. **2:** 1 Sam 16.14–23; Am 6.5; Ps 144.9–10. **4:** *His messenger,* specified in 11 QPsᵃ as the prophet Samuel (see 1 Sam 16.1–13). **5:** 1 Sam 16.7. **6–7:** A reference to the Goliath story (1 Sam 17).

and anointed me with his anointing
oil.

5 My brothers were handsome and
tall,
but the Lord was not pleased with
them.

6 I went out to meet the Philistine,ᵃ

and he cursed me by his idols.

7 But I drew his own sword;
I beheaded him, and took away
disgrace from the people of
Israel.

a Or foreigner

# 3 MACCABEES

The title of the book known as 3 Maccabees is a misnomer, for it is not a historical account of the Maccabees, but a fictional story about Egyptian Jews under Ptolemy IV Philopator (221–204 BCE), half a century before the Maccabean period. The book is preserved in the Greek Septuagint and the Syriac Peshitta, as well as in most manuscripts of the Armenian Bible. It is not, however, included in the Latin Vulgate. This may explain why it was not included in the canon of the Roman Catholic Church or in the traditional Protestant apocrypha. It is included in the canon of the Eastern Orthodox churches.

Third Maccabees begins with a brief account of how Ptolemy was saved from assassination at the battle of Raphia by the intervention of a Jew (1.1–5). This brief story of Jewish loyalty provides a foil against which the king's hostility to the Jews must be seen. The second episode (1.6–2.24) tells of the king's unsuccessful attempt to enter the holy of holies in the Jerusalem Temple. The desecration is averted by divine intervention in response to the prayer of the high priest Simon. The third episode, which takes up most of the book, describes the persecution of the Jews in Egypt. Upon his return there, the king determines to take vengeance upon the Jews for his humiliation in Jerusalem. He radically alters their legal status and attempts to force them to worship the Greek god Dionysus, promising to those who comply full citizenship in Alexandria (2.25–33). The vast majority of Jews resists, and with great cruelty they are herded together to be registered, tortured, and put to death. Again divine intervention averts disaster, as after forty days the writing materials have been exhausted and the registration cannot be completed (3.1–4.21). Finally the king decrees that drugged elephants be turned upon the Jews, who have been detained in the city's arena. Twice this is providentially delayed, and the third miracle occurs in answer to the prayer of the aged priest Eleazar, paralleling the prayer of the high priest in the second episode. The elephants turn on the king's forces, and he repents, allowing the Jews to return to their homes (5.1–6.21). The book ends with a royal letter decreeing protection for the Jews, who punish those who had apostatized and rejoice at their providential deliverance (ch 7).

Third Maccabees belongs to a narrative genre that was especially popular among Jews who lived in the Diaspora, outside the land of Israel. Other examples are found in Esther and in Daniel 2–6. These stories tell of some great danger that threatens the Jewish community, which is then averted, either through heroic action (Esther) or, more typically, through divine intervention. Such stories provided both entertainment and edification, allowing the Jewish readers to indulge their fears of destruction and then allaying those fears by the happy ending.

The work was originally written in Greek by an unknown Alexandrian Jew. The change in the status of the Jews, and the promise of Alexandrian citizenship to those who abandoned their religion, reflect the situation of the Alexandrian Jews after Rome conquered Egypt in 30 BCE. Non-Jews were subjected to a new tax, called the "laographia" (the word used in connection with the change of status in 3 Macc 2.28). Citizenship normally required the worship of other gods, and so was unacceptable to most Jews. The book was most probably composed in the early first century CE, although it does depict some earlier historical events, such as the battle of Raphia, known from other sources.

Although the book is written in a rather bombastic style, it provides a colorful drama of danger and deliverance. It also conveys a strict message of the need for solidarity in the Jewish community and the contemptible nature of apostasy.

1 When Philopator learned from those who returned that the regions that he had controlled had been seized by Antiochus, he gave orders to all his forces, both infantry and cavalry, took with him his sister Arsinoë, and marched out to the region near Raphia, where the army of Antiochus was encamped. ² But a certain Theodotus, determined to carry out the plot he had devised, took with him the best of the Ptolemaic arms that had been previously issued to him,ᵃ and crossed over by night to the tent of Ptolemy, intending single-handed to kill him and thereby end the war. ³ But Dositheus, known as the son of Drimylus, a Jew by birth who later changed his religion and apostatized from the ancestral traditions, had led the king away and arranged that a certain insignificant man should sleep in the tent; and so it turned out that this man incurred the vengeance meant for the king.ᵇ ⁴ When a bitter fight resulted, and matters were turning out rather in favor of Antiochus, Arsinoë went to the troops with wailing and tears, her locks all disheveled, and exhorted them to defend themselves and their children and wives bravely, promising to give them each two minas of gold if they won the battle. ⁵ And so it came about that the enemy was routed in the action, and many captives also were taken. ⁶ Now that he had foiled the plot, Ptolemyᶜ decided to visit the neighboring cities and encourage them. ⁷ By doing this, and by endowing their sacred enclosures with gifts, he strengthened the morale of his subjects.

8 Since the Jews had sent some of their council and elders to greet him, to bring him gifts of welcome, and to congratulate him on what had happened, he was all the more eager to visit them as soon as possible. ⁹ After he had arrived in Jerusalem, he offered sacrifice to the supreme Godᵈ and made thank offerings and did what was fitting for the holy place.ᵉ Then, upon enter-

a Or *the best of the Ptolemaic soldiers previously put under his command*   b Gk *that one*   c Gk *he*
d Gk *the greatest God*   e Gk *the place*

**1.1–7: The battle of Raphia** (217 BCE). The abruptness with which the book opens and the use of the Greek conjunctive particle "de" may indicate that the introduction to 3 Maccabees has not survived (see also 2.25n.). Alternatively, the account of the battle may have been excerpted from a historical source. It resembles the account given by the second century BCE historian Polybius (book 5), who also reports a plot to kill the king, but not the role of Dositheus in foiling it. **1:** *Ptolemy IV* [Philopator] was king of Egypt 221–204. *From those who returned,* fugitives who had escaped. *Antiochus* III, later called the Great, was king of Syria 223–187. *Raphia,* a city of Palestine, three miles from Gaza and not far from the Egyptian frontier. *Arsinoë,* Ptolemy's sister, who became his wife, was later put to death at the instigation of her husband. **2:** *Theodotus* had been chief commander of the Egyptian forces in Syria, but subsequently became disaffected and deserted to Antiochus III (Polybius, 5.40). **3:** *Dositheus* is mentioned in Hibeh papyrus 90 as priest of Alexander in 222 BCE, a very exalted position, and he is also mentioned in earlier papyri as a Ptolemaic administrator. The papyri, however, do not identify him as Jewish. *A certain insignificant* man, Polybius identifies the man as Andreas, the king's physician. **5:** According to Polybius (5.86.5–6), Antiochus lost nearly 10,000 infantry, 300 cavalry, and 4,000 prisoners; Ptolemy lost 1,500 infantry and 700 cavalry.

**1.8–15: Ptolemy attempts to enter the sanctuary at Jerusalem. 9:** Reference to *the supreme God,* Greek "megistos theos," occurs frequently in 3 Maccabees (1.9,16; 3.11; 4.16; 5.25; 7.22) as well as in 2 Maccabees (3.36). The God of the Jews was often known as The Most High God in antiquity. Ptolemy's offering *sacrifice* to the God of the Jews was not an unusual practice in an age of religious syncretism. *The holy place,* an alternative term for "the Temple" in 3 Maccabees and other Jewish literature. **10:** No ing the place and being impressed by its excellence and its beauty, [10] he marveled at the good order of the temple, and conceived a desire to enter the sanctuary. [11] When they said that this was not permitted, because not even members of their own nation were allowed to enter, not even all of the priests, but only the high priest who was pre-eminent over all—and he only once a year—the king was by no means persuaded. [12] Even after the law had been read to him, he did not cease to maintain that he ought to enter, saying, "Even if those men are deprived of this honor, I ought not to be." [13] And he inquired why, when he entered every other temple,[a] no one there had stopped him. [14] And someone answered thoughtlessly that it was wrong to take that as a portent.[b] [15] "But since this has happened," the king[c] said, "why should not I at least enter, whether they wish it or not?"

16 Then the priests in all their vestments prostrated themselves and entreated the supreme God[d] to aid in the present situation and to avert the violence of this evil design, and they filled the temple with cries and tears; [17] those who remained behind in the city were agitated and hurried out, supposing that something mysterious was occurring. [18] Young women who had been secluded in their chambers rushed out with their mothers, sprinkled their hair with dust,[e] and filled the streets with groans and lamentations. [19] Those women who had recently been arrayed for marriage abandoned the bridal chambers[f] prepared for wedded union, and, neglecting proper modesty, in a disorderly rush flocked together in the city. [20] Mothers and nurses abandoned even newborn children here and there, some in houses and some in the streets, and without a backward look they crowded together at the most high temple. [21] Various were the supplications of those gathered there because of what the king was profanely plotting. [22] In addition, the bolder of the citizens would not tolerate the completion of his plans or the fulfillment of his intended purpose. [23] They shouted to their compatriots to take arms and die courageously for the ancestral law, and created a considerable disturbance in the holy place;[g] and being barely restrained by the old men and the elders,[h] they resorted to the same posture of supplication as the others. [24] Meanwhile the crowd, as before, was engaged in prayer, [25] while the elders near the king tried in various ways to change his arrogant mind from the plan that he had conceived. [26] But he, in his arrogance, took heed of nothing, and began now to approach, determined to bring the aforesaid plan to a conclusion. [27] When those who were around him observed this, they turned, together with our people, to call upon him who has all power to defend them in the present trouble and not to overlook this unlawful and haughty deed.

a Or entered the temple precincts   b Or to boast of this   c Gk he   d Gk the greatest God   e Other ancient authorities add and ashes   f Or the canopies   g Gk the place   h Other ancient authorities read priests

attempt by a Ptolemy to enter the holy of holies is otherwise known. The Roman general Pompey did enter it in 63 BCE, but the closest parallel to 3 Maccabees on this point is found in the story of Heliodorus in 2 Macc 3, although the details of the stories are different (Heliodorus was attempting to seize the Temple treasure). **11:** *High priest . . . once a year,* Lev 16.2,34.

**1.16–29:** Jewish reaction to Ptolemy's determination to enter the sanctuary. Compare the reaction to the attempt of Heliodorus in 2 Macc 3.14–21, and also the historical episodes when Pontius Pilate introduced the sacrilegious Roman standards into Jerusalem (Josephus, *War* 1.169–74; *Ant.* 18.55–59) and when Caligula attempted to have his statue installed in the Temple (*War* 2.184–203; *Ant.* 18.269–72). **18:** *Young women* were not permitted to appear in public before marriage; cf. 2 Macc 3.19. **19:** For other references to bridal chambers see Joel 2.16; 2 Esd 16.33–34; Bar 2.23. **23:** *Die courageously for the ancestral law,* 1 Macc 2.40; 3.21; 13.3–4; 2 Macc 8.21. It is noteworthy that the militants are restrained by the elders here, in contrast to the Maccabean rebellion and to the later Jewish revolt against Rome.

28 The continuous, vehement, and concerted cry of the crowds[a] resulted in an immense uproar; 29 for it seemed that not only the people but also the walls and the whole earth around echoed, because indeed all at that time[b] preferred death to the profanation of the place.

2 Then the high priest Simon, facing the sanctuary, bending his knees and extending his hands with calm dignity, prayed as follows:[c] 2 "Lord, Lord, king of the heavens, and sovereign of all creation, holy among the holy ones, the only ruler, almighty, give attention to us who are suffering grievously from an impious and profane man, puffed up in his audacity and power. 3 For you, the creator of all things and the governor of all, are a just Ruler, and you judge those who have done anything in insolence and arrogance. 4 You destroyed those who in the past committed injustice, among whom were even giants who trusted in their strength and boldness, whom you destroyed by bringing on them a boundless flood. 5 You consumed with fire and sulfur the people of Sodom who acted arrogantly, who were notorious for their vices;[d] and you made them an example to those who should come afterward. 6 You made known your mighty power by inflicting many and varied punishments on the audacious Pharaoh who had enslaved your holy people Israel. 7 And when he pursued them with chariots and a mass of troops, you overwhelmed him in the depths of the sea, but carried through safely those who had put their confidence in you, the Ruler over the whole creation. 8 And when they had seen works of your hands, they praised you, the Almighty. 9 You, O King, when you had created the boundless and immeasurable earth, chose this city and sanctified this place for your name, though you have no need of anything; and when you had glorified it by your magnificent manifestation,[e] you made it a firm foundation for the glory of your great and honored name. 10 And because you love the house of Israel, you promised that if we should have reverses and tribulation should overtake us, you would listen to our petition when we come to this place and pray. 11 And indeed you are faithful and true. 12 And because oftentimes when our fathers were oppressed you helped them in their humiliation, and rescued them from great evils, 13 see now, O holy King, that because of our many and great sins we are crushed with suffering, subjected to our enemies, and overtaken by helplessness. 14 In our downfall this audacious and profane man undertakes to violate the holy place on earth dedicated to your glorious name. 15 For your dwelling is the heaven of heavens, unapproachable by human beings.

a Other ancient authorities read *vehement cry of the assembled crowds*   b Other ancient authorities lack *at that time*   c Other ancient authorities lack verse 1   d Other ancient authorities read *secret in their vices*   e Or *epiphany*

**2.1–20: The prayer of Simon, the high priest.** Simon II, son of Onias II and called "the Just," was high priest about 219–196 BCE (see Sir 50.1n.). The prayer is in a classic Jewish form that, like Eleazar's prayer in 6.1–15, follows the pattern of Ps 105 and 106 in confessing the sins of the people but calling on God to deliver them as he did in the past. **2:** *Holy among the holy ones*, Isa 57.15 LXX. The *holy ones* are members of the divine council (see Deut 33.2; Ps 89.5), in this period understood as angels. **3:** Ex 18.11; Ps 31.23. **4:** *Giants*, the race of heroes whose origins are described in Gen 6.1–4, also mentioned in Wis 14.6; Sir 16.7; Bar 3.26; *1 Enoch* 7.2; 15.8. **5:** *Sodom*, Gen 19.24; Deut 29.23; Wis 10.7. *An example*, cf. 2 Pet 2.6. **6:** Exodus 5–12. *Your holy people Israel*, Ex 19.6; Wis 10.15. **7:** *Overwhelmed him*, Exodus 14. **8:** *They praised*, Ex 15.1–21; Wis 19.8–9. **9:** *This city*, Jerusalem. *Place*, see 1.9n. *No need of anything*, 2 Macc 14.35–36. **10:** *Promised . . . you would listen*, Deut 30.1–6; 1 Kings 8.33–34,48–50. **12:** *Our fathers . . . you . . . rescued*, 1 Sam 12.10–11; Ps 22.4–5; 106.43; Neh 9.28. **13:** *Because of our many and great sins*, even though the Jewish community has done nothing wrong in this instance, such confession of sin was a standard element in prayers of this type. **14:** *Glorious name*, Jdt 9.8. **15:** *The heaven of heavens*, 1 Kings 8.27; Isa 66.1. **18:** *Trampled down*, Isa 63.18; Dan 8.13; 1 Macc 3.45. **19:** *Wipe away our sins*, Ps 51.2,9. **20:** *Mercies*, Ps 79.8,13.

16 But because you graciously bestowed your glory on your people Israel, you sanctified this place. 17 Do not punish us for the defilement committed by these men, or call us to account for this profanation, otherwise the transgressors will boast in their wrath and exult in the arrogance of their tongue, saying, 18 'We have trampled down the house of the sanctuary as the houses of the abominations are trampled down.' 19 Wipe away our sins and disperse our errors, and reveal your mercy at this hour. 20 Speedily let your mercies overtake us, and put praises in the mouth of those who are downcast and broken in spirit, and give us peace."

21 Thereupon God, who oversees all things, the first Father of all, holy among the holy ones, having heard the lawful supplication, scourged him who had exalted himself in insolence and audacity. 22 He shook him on this side and that as a reed is shaken by the wind, so that he lay helpless on the ground and, besides being paralyzed in his limbs, was unable even to speak, since he was smitten[a] by a righteous judgment. 23 Then both friends and bodyguards, seeing the severe punishment that had overtaken him, and fearing that he would lose his life, quickly dragged him

out, panic-stricken in their exceedingly great fear. 24 After a while he recovered, and though he had been punished, he by no means repented, but went away uttering bitter threats.

25 When he arrived in Egypt, he increased in his deeds of malice, abetted by the previously mentioned drinking companions and comrades, who were strangers to everything just. 26 He was not content with his uncounted licentious deeds, but even continued with such audacity that he framed evil reports in the various localities; and many of his friends, intently observing the king's purpose, themselves also followed his will. 27 He proposed to inflict public disgrace on the Jewish community,[b] and he set up a stone[c] on the tower in the courtyard with this inscription: 28 "None of those who do not sacrifice shall enter their sanctuaries, and all Jews shall be subjected to a registration involving poll tax and to the status of slaves. Those who object to this are to be taken by force and put to death; 29 those who are registered are also to be branded on their bodies by fire with the ivy-leaf symbol of Dionysus, and they

a Other ancient authorities read *pierced*    b Gk *the nation*    c Gk *stele*

**2.21–24: The punishment of Ptolemy. 21:** *Holy ones*, v. 2n. **22:** *Paralyzed*, compare the punishment of Heliodorus (2 Macc 3.24–30) and of Antiochus (2 Macc 9.5–6). **23:** *Friends*, the higher officers and courtiers of the king (4 Macc 8.5n.). *Lose his life*, cf. 2 Macc 3.31. **24:** *By no means repented*, compare Antiochus Epiphanes in 2 Macc 9.7 (Antiochus is subsequently forced to repent).

**2.25–33: Hostile measures against the Jews of Alexandria. 25:** These *companions* have not, in fact, been *previously mentioned* in the present text of 3 Maccabees; this is additional evidence that the opening section has been lost (see 1.1–7n.). **26:** *Friends*, see v. 23n. **28:** The Jews are forbidden to *enter their sanctuaries*, that is, their synagogues. Synagogue worship was disrupted during a pogrom in Alexandria in 38 CE. *Registration*, for which the Greek term, "laographia," literally means census, is often used in connection with taxation. It is especially associated with the *poll tax* imposed by the Romans in 24 BCE. This is the only tax that is known to have entailed a reduction of the status of the Jews, since it classified them with the Egyptians, not with the Greeks. **29:** Ptolemy Philopator was in fact a devotee of the Greek god Dionysus. Branding was associated with the worship of Dionysus, and the king himself may have been branded. Judaism was sometimes thought by Gentile observers to be a form of the worship of Dionysus (see especially Plutarch, *Table Talk* 4.6.1–2). According to 2 Macc 6.7, Antiochus Epiphanes tried to make the people of Jerusalem observe the festival of Dionysus. Branding was also used to identify slaves in case they ran away. 3 Maccabees seems to confuse the two kinds of branding. *Their former limited status*, perhaps referring to the status of Jewish captives before they were released by Ptolemy II (see *Letter of Aristeas* 22). **32:** *Paying money*, as bribes. **33:** *Enemies of the Jewish nation*, renegade Jews are viewed with even greater opprobrium than the Gentile persecutors.

shall also be reduced to their former limited status." [30] In order that he might not appear to be an enemy of all, he inscribed below: "But if any of them prefer to join those who have been initiated into the mysteries, they shall have equal citizenship with the Alexandrians."

[31] Now some, however, with an obvious abhorrence of the price to be exacted for maintaining the religion of their city,[a] readily gave themselves up, since they expected to enhance their reputation by their future association with the king. [32] But the majority acted firmly with a courageous spirit and did not abandon their religion; and by paying money in exchange for life they confidently attempted to save themselves from the registration. [33] They remained resolutely hopeful of obtaining help, and they abhorred those who separated themselves from them, considering them to be enemies of the Jewish nation,[b] and depriving them of companionship and mutual help.

3 When the impious king comprehended this situation, he became so infuriated that not only was he enraged against those Jews who lived in Alexandria, but was still more bitterly hostile toward those in the countryside; and he ordered that all should promptly be gathered into one place, and put to death by the most cruel means. [2] While these matters were being arranged, a hostile rumor was circulated against the Jewish nation by some who conspired to do them ill, a pretext being given by a report that they hindered others[c] from the observance of their customs. [3] The Jews, however-

er, continued to maintain goodwill and unswerving loyalty toward the dynasty; [4] but because they worshiped God and conducted themselves by his law, they kept their separateness with respect to foods. For this reason they appeared hateful to some; [5] but since they adorned their style of life with the good deeds of upright people, they were established in good repute with everyone. [6] Nevertheless those of other races paid no heed to their good service to their nation, which was common talk among all; [7] instead they gossiped about the differences in worship and foods, alleging that these people were loyal neither to the king nor to his authorities, but were hostile and greatly opposed to his government. So they attached no ordinary reproach to them.

[8] The Greeks in the city, though wronged in no way, when they saw an unexpected tumult around these people and the crowds that suddenly were forming, were not strong enough to help them, for they lived under tyranny. They did try to console them, being grieved at the situation, and expected that matters would change; [9] for such a great community ought not be left to its fate when it had committed no offense. [10] And already some of their neighbors and friends and business associates had taken some of them aside privately and were pledging to protect them and to exert more earnest efforts for their assistance.

[11] Then the king, boastful of his present

a Meaning of Gk uncertain    b Gk the nation
c Gk them

**3.1–10: The Jews and their neighbors. 1:** The distinction between Jews in *Alexandria* and those in the *countryside* is made also in 4.11–12. The emphasis on Jews from the countryside is odd and may reflect a historical attempt by Ptolemy to take a census of the Jews in rural areas. **2:** The *rumor* maliciously represents the Jews as hostile to the best interests of the state (cf. Esth 3.8), whereas the author insists on their loyalty. **4:** *Separateness with respect to foods* was one of the barriers between Jew and Gentile, cf. 1 Macc 1.62–63; 2 Macc 11.30–31. Many Hellenistic Jewish writings avoid the subject. For a defense of the observance of Jewish dietary rules, by explaining them allegorically, see the *Letter of Aristeas*, 128–66. **5:** Deut 4.5–6. **7:** For similar charges see Esth 3.8; Add Esth 13.4–5. **8:** *The Greeks*, the elite, cultivated class, in distinction from *those of other races* (v. 6). The Alexandrian Greeks were bitter enemies of the Jews in the Roman period, but the author portrays a relationship of support and respect between the two groups.

**3.11–30: Ptolemy orders the arrest of all Jews in his kingdom. 11:** The king is *boastful*, and therefore good fortune, and not considering the might of the supreme God,[a] but assuming that he would persevere constantly in his same purpose, wrote this letter against them:

12 "King Ptolemy Philopator to his generals and soldiers in Egypt and all its districts, greetings and good health:

13 "I myself and our government are faring well. 14 When our expedition took place in Asia, as you yourselves know, it was brought to conclusion, according to plan, by the gods' deliberate alliance with us in battle, 15 and we considered that we should not rule the nations inhabiting Coelesyria and Phoenicia by the power of the spear, but should cherish them with clemency and great benevolence, gladly treating them well. 16 And when we had granted very great revenues to the temples in the cities, we came on to Jerusalem also, and went up to honor the temple of those wicked people, who never cease from their folly. 17 They accepted our presence by word, but insincerely by deed, because when we proposed to enter their inner temple and honor it with magnificent and most beautiful offerings, 18 they were carried away by their traditional arrogance, and excluded us from entering; but they were spared the exercise of our power because of the benevolence that we have toward all. 19 By maintaining their manifest ill-will toward us, they become the only people among all nations who hold their heads high in defiance of kings and their own benefactors, and are unwilling to regard any action as sincere.

20 "But we, when we arrived in Egypt victorious, accommodated ourselves to their folly and did as was proper, since we treat all nations with benevolence. 21 Among other things, we made known to all our amnesty toward their compatriots here, both because of their alliance with us and the myriad affairs liberally entrusted to them from the beginning; and we ventured to make a change, by deciding both to deem them worthy of Alexandrian citizenship and to make them participants in our regular religious rites.[b] 22 But in their innate malice they took this in a contrary spirit, and disdained what is good. Since they incline constantly to evil, 23 they not only spurn the priceless citizenship, but also both by speech and by silence they abominate those few among them who are sincerely disposed toward us; in every situation, in accordance with their infamous way of life, they secretly suspect that we may soon alter our policy. 24 Therefore, fully convinced by these indications that they are ill-disposed toward us in every way, we have taken precautions so that, if a sudden disorder later arises against us, we shall not have these impious people behind our backs as traitors and barbarous enemies. 25 Therefore we have given orders that, as soon as this letter arrives, you are to send to us those who live among you, together with their wives and children, with insulting and harsh treatment, and bound securely with iron fetters, to suffer the sure and shameful death that befits enemies. 26 For when all of these have been punished, we are sure that for the remaining time the government will be established for ourselves in good order and in the best state. 27 But those who shel-

a Gk the greatest God   b Other ancient authorities read partners of our regular priests

guilty of "hubris," the sin that leads to disaster in Greek tragedy. Assuming that he would persevere, an anticipatory reference to the calamity that came upon him by which he forgot his own previous commands (5.27–28). **15:** Coelesyria, western Syria. Phoenicia, modern Lebanon. Benevolence, Greek "philanthropia" (see vv. 18,20), was regarded as a major political virtue during the Hellenistic period. **21:** For the confidence placed in Jews, see 6.25 and Josephus, Ag. Ap. 2.49, who says that Ptolemy VI Philometor gave two Jewish generals, Onias and Dositheus, command of his whole army. Jews were often employed in Egypt as mercenaries. Alexandrian citizenship normally entailed participation in Greek religious ceremonies. Alexandrian Greeks, such as the first-century CE scholar Apion, complained that the Jews wanted the privileges of citizenship but were unwilling to fulfill the religious obligations that it usually entailed. **24:** Behind our backs, cf. Ex 1.10. **28:** Awarded their freedom, another rendering is "crowned ter any of the Jews, whether old people or children or even infants, will be tortured to death with the most hateful torments, together with their families. 28 Any who are willing to give information will receive the property of those who incur the punishment, and also two thousand drachmas from the royal treasury, and will be awarded their freedom.[a] 29 Every place detected sheltering a Jew is to be made unapproachable and burned with fire, and shall become useless for all time to any mortal creature."

30 The letter was written in the above form.

4 In every place, then, where this decree arrived, a feast at public expense was arranged for the Gentiles with shouts and gladness, for the inveterate enmity that had long ago been in their minds was now made evident and outspoken. 2 But among the Jews there was incessant mourning, lamentation, and tearful cries; everywhere their hearts were burning, and they groaned because of the unexpected destruction that had suddenly been decreed for them. 3 What district or city, or what habitable place at all, or what streets were not filled with mourning and wailing for them? 4 For with such a harsh and ruthless spirit were they being sent off, all together, by the generals in the several cities, that at the sight of their unusual punishments, even some of their enemies, perceiving the common object of pity before their eyes, reflected on the uncertainty of life and shed tears at the most miserable expulsion of these people. 5 For a multitude of gray-headed old men, sluggish and bent with age, was being led away, forced to march at a swift pace by the violence with which they were driven in such a shameful manner. 6 And young women who had just entered the bridal chamber[b] to share married life exchanged joy for wailing, their myrrh-perfumed hair sprinkled with ashes, and were carried away unveiled, all together raising a lament instead of a wedding song, as they were torn by the harsh treatment of the heathen.[c] 7 In bonds and in public view they were violently dragged along as far as the place of embarkation. 8 Their husbands, in the prime of youth, their necks encircled with ropes instead of garlands, spent the remaining days of their marriage festival in lamentations instead of good cheer and youthful revelry, seeing death immediately before them.[d] 9 They were brought on board like wild animals, driven under the constraint of iron bonds; some were fastened by the neck to the benches of the boats, others had their feet secured by unbreakable fetters, 10 and in addition they were confined under a solid deck, so that, with their eyes in total darkness, they would undergo treatment befitting traitors during the whole voyage.

11 When these people had been brought to the place called Schedia, and the voyage was concluded as the king had decreed, he commanded that they should be enclosed in the hippodrome that had been built with a monstrous perimeter wall in front of the city, and that was well suited to make them an obvious spectacle to all coming back into the city and to those from the city[e] going out into the country, so that they could neither communicate with the king's forces nor in any way claim to be inside the

a Gk *crowned with freedom*     b Or *the canopy*
c Other ancient authorities read *as though torn by heathen whelps*     d Gk *seeing Hades already lying at their feet*     e Gk *those of them*

at the Eleutheria" (a festival of Dionysus; see 2.29n.). **29:** *Useless for all time*, cf. Add Esth 16.24.

**4.1–21: The Jews brought to Alexandria and imprisoned. 1:** *Enmity* on the part of native-born Egyptians for the Jews is assumed in 3 Maccabees; contrast the depiction of the Greeks in 3.8. **2:** *Mourning, lamentation, and tearful cries*, cf. Esth 4.3. **11:** *Schedia*, a promontory about three miles from Alexandria. *The hippodrome* (arena) was situated at the east or Canobic gate of Alexandria; according to Strabo (17.1.10,16) a canal joined Schedia and the Canobic gate. *Inside . . . the city*, implies that Jews living in Alexandria (see v. 12, *compatriots from the city*) had been thus far unmolested (but cf. 3.1). 3 Maccabees may be adapting a story that originally dealt only with a census of the Jews of the countryside. **14:** *Mentioned before*, see 2.28. The registration for poll tax and slave status is transformed into an circuit of the city.[a] [12] And when this had happened, the king, hearing that the Jews' compatriots from the city frequently went out in secret to lament bitterly the ignoble misfortune of their kindred, [13] ordered in his rage that these people be dealt with in precisely the same fashion as the others, not omitting any detail of their punishment. [14] The entire race was to be registered individually, not for the hard labor that has been briefly mentioned before, but to be tortured with the outrages that he had ordered, and at the end to be destroyed in the space of a single day. [15] The registration of these people was therefore conducted with bitter haste and zealous intensity from the rising of the sun until its setting, coming to an end after forty days but still uncompleted.

16 The king was greatly and continually filled with joy, organizing feasts in honor of all his idols, with a mind alienated from truth and with a profane mouth, praising speechless things that are not able even to communicate or to come to one's help, and uttering improper words against the supreme God.[b] [17] But after the previously mentioned interval of time the scribes declared to the king that they were no longer able to take the census of the Jews because of their immense number, [18] though most of them were still in the country, some still residing in their homes, and some at the place;[c] the task was impossible for all the generals in Egypt. [19] After he had threatened them severely, charging that they had been bribed to contrive a means of escape, he was clearly convinced about the matter [20] when they said and proved that both the paper[d] and the pens they used for writing

had already given out. [21] But this was an act of the invincible providence of him who was aiding the Jews from heaven.

5 Then the king, completely inflexible, was filled with overpowering anger and wrath; so he summoned Hermon, keeper of the elephants, [2] and ordered him on the following day to drug all the elephants—five hundred in number—with large handfuls of frankincense and plenty of unmixed wine, and to drive them in, maddened by the lavish abundance of drink, so that the Jews might meet their doom. [3] When he had given these orders he returned to his feasting, together with those of his Friends and of the army who were especially hostile toward the Jews. [4] And Hermon, keeper of the elephants, proceeded faithfully to carry out the orders. [5] The servants in charge of the Jews[e] went out in the evening and bound the hands of the wretched people and arranged for their continued custody through the night, convinced that the whole nation would experience its final destruction. [6] For to the Gentiles it appeared that the Jews were left without any aid, [7] because in their bonds they were forcibly confined on every side. But with tears and a voice hard to silence they all called upon the Almighty Lord and Ruler of all power, their merciful God and Father, praying [8] that he avert with vengeance the evil plot against them and in a glorious manifestation rescue them from the fate now prepared for them. [9] So their entreaty ascended fervently to heaven.

a Or *claim protection of the walls*; meaning of Gk uncertain    b Gk *the greatest God*    c Other ancient authorities read *on the way*    d Or *paper factory*    e Gk *them*

---

instrument for the execution of *the entire race* of Jews. **16:** *Speechless things,* see Ps 115.3–7; Jer 10.5; Hab 2.18; Bar 6.7. *Supreme God,* see 1.9n. **17:** *Their immense number,* an obvious hyperbole. **19:** *Bribed,* see 2.32.

**5.1–51: Ptolemy orders the execution of the Jews, but is thwarted.** A variant of this story is told in Josephus, *Ag. Ap.* 2.53–55, but there the Ptolemy is Ptolemy VIII Euergetes II Physcon (144–117 BCE). **1:** *Hermon,* the name of the keeper of the elephants, recalls the figure of Haman in Esther. **2:** *Elephants—five hundred* is an exaggeration; according to Polybius, Ptolemy had seventy-three elephants at the battle of Raphia. After Alexander the Great encountered them in India, war-*elephants* were often a component of Hellenistic armies; see 1 Macc 1.17. Similar stimulation of war-elephants is reported in 1 Macc 6.34. **3:** *Returned to his feasting,* 4.16. **7:** *Father,* see Isa 63.16; Mal 2.10; Tob 13.4; Wis 11.10. **11:** The divine

10 Hermon, however, when he had drugged the pitiless elephants until they had been filled with a great abundance of wine and satiated with frankincense, presented himself at the courtyard early in the morning to report to the king about these preparations. [11] But the Lord[a] sent upon the king a portion of sleep, that beneficence that from the beginning, night and day, is bestowed by him who grants it to whomever he wishes. [12] And by the action of the Lord he was overcome by so pleasant and deep a sleep[b] that he quite failed in his lawless purpose and was completely frustrated in his inflexible plan. [13] Then the Jews, since they had escaped the appointed hour, praised their holy God and again implored him who is easily reconciled to show the might of his all-powerful hand to the arrogant Gentiles.

14 But now, since it was nearly the middle of the tenth hour, the person who was in charge of the invitations, seeing that the guests were assembled, approached the king and nudged him. [15] And when he had with difficulty roused him, he pointed out that the hour of the banquet was already slipping by, and he gave him an account of the situation. [16] The king, after considering this, returned to his drinking, and ordered those present for the banquet to recline opposite him. [17] When this was done he urged them to give themselves over to revelry and to make the present[c] portion of the banquet joyful by celebrating all the more. [18] After the party had been going on for some time, the king summoned Hermon and with sharp threats demanded to know why the Jews had been allowed to remain alive through the present day. [19] But when he, with the corroboration of the king's[d] Friends, pointed out that while it was still night he had carried out completely the order given him, [20] the king,[a] possessed by a savagery worse than that of Phalaris, said that the Jews[e] were benefited by today's sleep, "but," he added, "tomorrow without delay prepare the elephants in the same way for the destruction of the lawless Jews!" [21] When the king had spoken, all those present readily and joyfully with one accord gave their approval, and all went to their own homes. [22] But they did not so much employ the duration of the night in sleep as in devising all sorts of insults for those they thought to be doomed.

23 Then, as soon as the cock had crowed in the early morning, Hermon, having equipped[f] the animals, began to move them along in the great colonnade. [24] The crowds of the city had been assembled for this most pitiful spectacle and they were eagerly waiting for daybreak. [25] But the Jews, at their last gasp—since the time had run out—stretched their hands toward heaven and with most tearful supplication and mournful dirges implored the supreme God[g] to help them again at once. [26] The rays of the sun were not yet shed abroad, and while the king was receiving his Friends, Hermon arrived and invited him to come out, indicating that what the king desired was ready for action. [27] But he, on receiving the report and being struck by the unusual invitation to come out—since he had been completely overcome by incomprehension—inquired what the matter was for which this had been so zealously completed for him. [28] This was the act of God who rules over all things, for he had implanted in the king's mind a forgetfulness of the things he had previously devised. [29] Then Hermon and all the king's

a Gk he    b Other ancient authorities add *from evening until the ninth hour*    c Other ancient authorities read *delayed* (Gk *untimely*)    d Gk *his* e Gk *they*    f Or *armed*    g Gk *the greatest God*

gift of *sleep* is extolled by Roman poets (e.g., Seneca, *Hercules Furens* 1065–78; Statius, *Silvae* 5.4); see Ps 127.2. **14:** *Middle of the tenth hour*, 3:30 PM. **19:** *Friends*, see 2.23n. **20:** *Phalaris*, tyrant of Agrigentum in Sicily (ca. 570–554 BCE) whose cruelty was proverbial (Polybius 12.25). **28:** *The act of God*, cf. Prov 21.1. **29:** An addition in several Greek manuscripts indicates that though Ptolemy was moved by compassion and determined to release the Jews, Hermon influenced him to proceed with his plans to destroy them. **42:** *Phalaris*, see v. 20n. **45:** The *frightful devices* were probably scythes, knives, and other

Friends[a] pointed out that the animals and the armed forces were ready, "O king, according to your eager purpose."[b] 30 But at these words he was filled with an overpowering wrath, because by the providence of God his whole mind had been deranged concerning these matters; and with a threatening look he said, 31 "If your parents or children were present, I would have prepared them to be a rich feast for the savage animals instead of the Jews, who give me no ground for complaint and have exhibited to an extraordinary degree a full and firm loyalty to my ancestors. 32 In fact you would have been deprived of life instead of these, if it were not for an affection arising from our nurture in common and your usefulness." 33 So Hermon suffered an unexpected and dangerous threat, and his eyes wavered and his face fell. 34 The king's Friends one by one sullenly slipped away and dismissed[c] the assembled people to their own occupations. 35 Then the Jews, on hearing what the king had said, praised the manifest Lord God, King of kings, since this also was his aid that they had received.

36 The king, however, reconvened the party in the same manner and urged the guests to return to their celebrating. 37 After summoning Hermon he said in a threatening tone, "How many times, you poor wretch, must I give you orders about these things? 38 Equip[d] the elephants now once more for the destruction of the Jews tomorrow!" 39 But the officials who were at table with him, wondering at his instability of mind, remonstrated as follows: 40 "O king, how long will you put us to the test, as though we are idiots, ordering now for a third time that they be destroyed, and again revoking your decree in the matter?[e] 41 As a result the city is in a tumult because of its expectation; it is crowded with masses of people, and also in constant danger of being plundered."

42 At this the king, a Phalaris in everything and filled with madness, took no account of the changes of mind that had come about within him for the protection of the Jews, and he firmly swore an irrevocable oath that he would send them to death[f] without delay, mangled by the knees and feet of the animals, 43 and would also march against Judea and rapidly level it to the ground with fire and spear, and by burning to the ground the temple inaccessible to him[g] would quickly render it forever empty of those who offered sacrifices there. 44 Then the Friends and officers departed with great joy, and they confidently posted the armed forces at the places in the city most favorable for keeping guard.

45 Now when the animals had been brought virtually to a state of madness, so to speak, by the very fragrant draughts of wine mixed with frankincense and had been equipped with frightful devices, the elephant keeper 46 entered at about dawn into the courtyard—the city now being filled with countless masses of people crowding their way into the hippodrome— and urged the king on to the matter at hand. 47 So he, when he had filled his impious mind with a deep rage, rushed out in full force along with the animals, wishing to witness, with invulnerable heart and with his own eyes, the grievous and pitiful destruction of the aforementioned people.

48 When the Jews saw the dust raised by the elephants going out at the gate and by the following armed forces, as well as by the trampling of the crowd, and heard the loud and tumultuous noise, 49 they thought that this was their last moment of life, the end of their most miserable suspense, and giving way to lamentation and groans they kissed each other, embracing relatives and falling into one another's arms[h]—parents and children, mothers and daughters, and

a Gk all the Friends    b Other ancient authorities read pointed to the beasts and the armed forces, saying, "They are ready, O king, according to your eager purpose."    c Other ancient authorities read he dismissed    d Or Arm    e Other ancient authorities read when the matter is in hand    f Gk Hades    g Gk us    h Gk falling upon their necks

military equipment attached to different parts of the bodies of the elephants. 49: Embracing, but according to 6.27 they are still bound. 50–51: The author continues to build up his thesis that God was the only others with babies at their breasts who were drawing their last milk. [50] Not only this, but when they considered the help that they had received before from heaven, they prostrated themselves with one accord on the ground, removing the babies from their breasts, [51] and cried out in a very loud voice, imploring the Ruler over every power to manifest himself and be merciful to them, as they stood now at the gates of death.[a]

6 Then a certain Eleazar, famous among the priests of the country, who had attained a ripe old age and throughout his life had been adorned with every virtue, directed the elders around him to stop calling upon the holy God, and he prayed as follows: [2] "King of great power, Almighty God Most High, governing all creation with mercy, [3] look upon the descendants of Abraham, O Father, upon the children of the sainted Jacob, a people of your consecrated portion who are perishing as foreigners in a foreign land. [4] Pharaoh with his abundance of chariots, the former ruler of this Egypt, exalted with lawless insolence and boastful tongue, you destroyed together with his arrogant army by drowning them in the sea, manifesting the light of your mercy on the nation of Israel. [5] Sennacherib exulting in his countless forces, oppressive king of the Assyrians, who had already gained control of the whole world by the spear and was lifted up against your holy city, speaking grievous words with boasting and insolence, you, O Lord, broke in pieces, showing your power to many na-

tions. [6] The three companions in Babylon who had voluntarily surrendered their lives to the flames so as not to serve vain things, you rescued unharmed, even to a hair, moistening the fiery furnace with dew and turning the flame against all their enemies. [7] Daniel, who through envious slanders was thrown down into the ground to lions as food for wild animals, you brought up to the light unharmed. [8] And Jonah, wasting away in the belly of a huge, sea-born monster, you, Father, watched over and restored[b] unharmed to all his family. [9] And now, you who hate insolence, all-merciful and protector of all, reveal yourself quickly to those of the nation of Israel[c]—who are being outrageously treated by the abominable and lawless Gentiles.

10 "Even if our lives have become entangled in impieties in our exile, rescue us from the hand of the enemy, and destroy us, Lord, by whatever fate you choose. [11] Let not the vain-minded praise their vanities[d] at the destruction of your beloved people, saying, 'Not even their god has rescued them.' [12] But you, O Eternal One, who have all might and all power, watch over us now and have mercy on us who by the senseless insolence of the lawless are being deprived of life in the manner of traitors. [13] And let the Gentiles cower today in fear of your invincible might, O honored One, who have power to save the nation of

---

a Gk Hades    b Other ancient authorities read *rescued and restored*; others, *mercifully restored*
c Other ancient authorities read *to the saints of Israel*
d Or *bless their vain gods*

---

resort for the captives, and that their hope would not be frustrated. **51**: *Gates of death,* Ps 9.13; 107.18.

**6.1–15: The prayer of Eleazar.** Like Simon's prayer in 2.1–20, it is plainly Jewish in form and style, containing doxology, thanksgiving for God's earlier interventions in Israel's history, and petition for a new miracle. The emphasis is on the exclusiveness and separate standing of Israel before God (v. 3). Eleazar expects God's intervention, not on account of Israel's virtues or merits, but because of divine mercy. Unlike many Jewish prayers from this period, however, there is little confession of sin (but see v. 10). **1**: *Eleazar,* the name of one of Aaron's sons (Ex 6.23), of a martyr in 2 Macc 6 and 4 Macc 5–6, and of a high priest in the *Letter of Aristeas. Priests* were always numerous in the Jewish community. There was a Jewish temple at Leontopolis in Egypt, erected by an exiled high priest (Onias IV) in the second century BCE, in defiance of Deuteronomistic law (Deut 12). **4**: *Pharaoh,* Ex 14.28. **5**: *Sennacherib,* 2 Kings 18.13; 19.35–37. **6**: *Three companions in Babylon,* Dan 3.22,27; Song of Thr 22–27. **7**: *Daniel,* Dan 6.22. **8**: *Jonah,* Jon 2.10. **11**: Ps 115.2. **13**: *Let the Gentiles cower,* the prayer overlooks the exception made for the Greeks in 3.8. **15**: *As you have said,* Lev 26.44.

Jacob. 14 The whole throng of infants and their parents entreat you with tears. 15 Let it be shown to all the Gentiles that you are with us, O Lord, and have not turned your face from us; but just as you have said, 'Not even when they were in the land of their enemies did I neglect them,' so accomplish it, O Lord."

16 Just as Eleazar was ending his prayer, the king arrived at the hippodrome with the animals and all the arrogance of his forces. 17 And when the Jews observed this they raised great cries to heaven so that even the nearby valleys resounded with them and brought an uncontrollable terror upon the army. 18 Then the most glorious, almighty, and true God revealed his holy face and opened the heavenly gates, from which two glorious angels of fearful aspect descended, visible to all but the Jews. 19 They opposed the forces of the enemy and filled them with confusion and terror, binding them with immovable shackles. 20 Even the king began to shudder bodily, and he forgot his sullen insolence. 21 The animals turned back upon the armed forces following them and began trampling and destroying them.

22 Then the king's anger was turned to pity and tears because of the things that he had devised beforehand. 23 For when he heard the shouting and saw them all fallen headlong to destruction, he wept and angrily threatened his Friends, saying, 24 "You are committing treason and surpassing tyrants in cruelty; and even me, your benefactor, you are now attempting to deprive of dominion and life by secretly devising acts of no advantage to the kingdom. 25 Who has driven from their homes those who faithfully kept our country's fortresses, and foolishly gathered every one of them here?

26 Who is it that has so lawlessly encompassed with outrageous treatment those who from the beginning differed from[a] all nations in their goodwill toward us and often have accepted willingly the worst of human dangers? 27 Loose and untie their unjust bonds! Send them back to their homes in peace, begging pardon for your former actions![b] 28 Release the children of the almighty and living God of heaven, who from the time of our ancestors until now has granted an unimpeded and notable stability to our government." 29 These then were the things he said; and the Jews, immediately released, praised their holy God and Savior, since they now had escaped death.

30 Then the king, when he had returned to the city, summoned the official in charge of the revenues and ordered him to provide to the Jews both wines and everything else needed for a festival of seven days, deciding that they should celebrate their rescue with all joyfulness in that same place in which they had expected to meet their destruction. 31 Accordingly those disgracefully treated and near to death,[c] or rather, who stood at its gates, arranged for a banquet of deliverance instead of a bitter and lamentable death, and full of joy they apportioned to celebrants the place that had been prepared for their destruction and burial. 32 They stopped their chanting of dirges and took up the song of their ancestors, praising God, their Savior and worker of wonders.[d] Putting an end to all mourning

a Or excelled above    b Other ancient authorities read revoking your former commands    c Gk Hades
d Other ancient authorities read praising Israel and the wonder-working God; or praising Israel's Savior, the wonder-working God

6.16–29: The Jews are delivered, and the king now favors them. 18: Most glorious, Greek "megalodoxos," compare 1 Enoch 14.20 and Testament of Levi 3.4, where God is called "the Great Glory." Angels of fearful aspect, for similar terror-inspiring apparitions, see 2 Macc 3.25–29; 10.29. 21: The animals turned upon the king's own forces, a detail found also in Josephus's account (Ag. Ap. 2.5). For the principle, see Ps 7.15–16; 9.15–16; 35.8; 57.6. 25: Faithfully, see 3.21n.; contrast the king's language in 3.24. 28: Children of . . . God, Wis 18.13.

6.30–41: The Jews celebrate their deliverance. 32: The song of their ancestors, perhaps Ps 136, which often was used earlier as a hymn of thanksgiving (1 Chr 16.41; 2 Chr 5.13; 7.3; Ezra 3.11). 34: Food for and wailing, they formed choruses[a] as a sign of peaceful joy. 33 Likewise also the king, after convening a great banquet to celebrate these events, gave thanks to heaven unceasingly and lavishly for the unexpected rescue that he[b] had experienced. 34 Those who had previously believed that the Jews would be destroyed and become food for birds, and had joyfully registered them, groaned as they themselves were overcome by disgrace, and their fire-breathing boldness was ignominiously[c] quenched.

35 The Jews, as we have said before, arranged the aforementioned choral group[d] and passed the time in feasting to the accompaniment of joyous thanksgiving and psalms. 36 And when they had ordained a public rite for these things in their whole community and for their descendants, they instituted the observance of the aforesaid days as a festival, not for drinking and gluttony, but because of the deliverance that had come to them through God. 37 Then they petitioned the king, asking for dismissal to their homes. 38 So their registration was carried out from the twenty-fifth of Pachon to the fourth of Epeiph,[e] for forty days; and their destruction was set for the fifth to the seventh of Epeiph,[f] the three days 39 on which the Lord of all most gloriously revealed his mercy and rescued them all together and unharmed. 40 Then they feasted, being provided with everything by the king, until the fourteenth day,[g] on which also they made the petition for their dismissal. 41 The king granted their request at once and wrote the following letter for them to the generals in the cities, magnanimously expressing his concern:

7 "King Ptolemy Philopator to the generals in Egypt and all in authority in his government, greetings and good health:

2 "We ourselves and our children are faring well, the great God guiding our affairs according to our desire. 3 Certain of our friends, frequently urging us with malicious intent, persuaded us to gather together the Jews of the kingdom in a body and to punish them with barbarous penalties as traitors; 4 for they declared that our government would never be firmly established until this was accomplished, because of the ill-will that these people had toward all nations. 5 They also led them out with harsh treatment as slaves, or rather as traitors, and, girding themselves with a cruelty more savage than that of Scythian custom, they tried without any inquiry or examination to put them to death. 6 But we very severely threatened them for these acts, and in accordance with the clemency that we have toward all people we barely spared their lives. Since we have come to realize that the God of heaven surely defends the Jews, always taking their part as a father does for his children, 7 and since we have taken into account the friendly and firm goodwill that they had toward us and our ancestors, we justly have acquitted them of every charge of whatever kind. 8 We also have ordered all people to return to their own homes, with no one in any place[h] doing them harm at all or reproaching them for the irrational things that have happened. 9 For

a Or dances   b Other ancient authorities read they
c Other ancient authorities read completely   d Or
dance   e July 7—August 15   f August 16—18
g August 25   h Other ancient authorities read way

birds, Gen 40.19; Deut 28.26; Ezek 39.4; 2 Macc 9.15. **36:** The institution of Jewish festivals is a common feature in this period (Esth 9.20–23; 1 Macc 4.59; 7.49; 13.51–52).

**7.1–9: Ptolemy's letter on behalf of the Jews.** Compare the letters of Ahasuerus (Esth 8; Add Esth 16.1–24), of Nebuchadnezzar (Dan 4), and of Antiochus Epiphanes (2 Macc 9.19–27). **2:** *Children,* Philopator had only one legitimate son, born in 210 BCE, who reigned later as Ptolemy V Epiphanes (204–180). Either the author had no knowledge of Philopator's family life, or the king is using a general term for the members of his court. **3:** The king seeks to exonerate himself, blaming others (see 6.24). **4:** *Ill-will,* 3.2,7. **5:** *Scythian custom,* see 2 Macc 4.47n.; 4 Macc 10.7n. The Scythians were known for barbarism. **6:** *Threatened them,* that is, the enemies of the Jews. *Father,* 5.7n.; Ps 103.13. **8:** *In any place* through which the Jews might pass on their return.

you should know that if we devise any evil against them or cause them any grief at all, we always shall have not a mortal but the Ruler over every power, the Most High God, in everything and inescapably as an antagonist to avenge such acts. Farewell."

10 On receiving this letter the Jews[a] did not immediately hurry to make their departure, but they requested of the king that at their own hands those of the Jewish nation who had willfully transgressed against the holy God and the law of God should receive the punishment they deserved. 11 They declared that those who for the belly's sake had transgressed the divine commandments would never be favorably disposed toward the king's government. 12 The king[b] then, admitting and approving the truth of what they said, granted them a general license so that freely, and without royal authority or supervision, they might destroy those everywhere in his kingdom who had transgressed the law of God. 13 When they had applauded him in fitting manner, their priests and the whole multitude shouted the Hallelujah and joyfully departed. 14 And so on their way they punished and put to a public and shameful death any whom they met of their compatriots who had become defiled. 15 In that day they put to death more than three hundred men; and they kept the day as a joyful festival, since they had destroyed the profaners. 16 But those who had held fast to God even to death and had received the full enjoyment of deliverance began their departure from the city, crowned with all sorts of very fragrant flowers, joyfully and loudly giving thanks to the one God of their ancestors, the eternal Savior[c] of Israel, in words of praise and all kinds of melodious songs.

17 When they had arrived at Ptolemais, called "rose-bearing" because of a characteristic of the place, the fleet waited for them, in accordance with the common desire, for seven days. 18 There they celebrated their deliverance,[d] for the king had generously provided all things to them for their journey until all of them arrived at their own houses. 19 And when they had all landed in peace with appropriate thanksgiving, there too in like manner they decided to observe these days as a joyous festival during the time of their stay. 20 Then, after inscribing them as holy on a pillar and dedicating a place of prayer at the site of the festival, they departed unharmed, free, and overjoyed, since at the king's command they had all of them been brought safely by land and sea and river to their own homes. 21 They also possessed greater prestige among their enemies, being held in honor and awe; and they were not subject at all to confiscation of their belongings by anyone. 22 Besides, they all recovered all of their property, in accordance with the registration, so that those who held any of it restored it to them with extreme fear.[e] So the supreme God perfectly performed great deeds for their deliverance. 23 Blessed be the Deliverer of Israel through all times! Amen.

a Gk they  b Gk He  c Other ancient authorities read *the holy Savior*; others, *the holy one*  d Gk *they made a cup of deliverance*  e Other ancient authorities read *with a very large supplement*

**7.10–23: The Jews punish the renegades and return home. 10:** *They requested of the king,* in the Hellenistic and Roman periods the Jews were often obliged to seek permission from their foreign rulers to carry out their own laws pertaining to capital punishment (Deut 13.6–18; Esth 8.8–11). **13:** *Hallelujah,* see Ps 105n.; Tob 13.18. **17:** This *Ptolemais* was probably not the city of this name near Thebes in Upper Egypt, but "Ptolemais at the harbor" in the Arsinoite nome (province), about twelve miles from present-day Cairo. *Rose-bearing* is not elsewhere applied to Ptolemais. **22–23:** The book closes with a benediction to the *supreme God;* cf. 4 Macc 18.24.

(c) The following book is included in the Slavonic Bible as 3 Esdras, but is not found in the Greek. It is included in the Appendix to the Latin Vulgate Bible as 4 Esdras.

# 2 ESDRAS

The book known as 2 Esdras is actually a composite work made up of three separate writings: 5 Ezra (chs 1–2), 4 Ezra (chs 3–14), and 6 Ezra (chs 15–16).

Fourth Ezra, the longest and most complex of the three, is also the earliest. Written in Hebrew by an anonymous Jew in Israel near the end of the first century CE, it sets forth its author's anguished reflections on the destruction of Jerusalem and its Temple by the Romans in 70 CE. The author adopts the pseudonym of Ezra, whom he presents as living after the destruction of the First Temple by the Babylonians in 586 BCE, and also refers to Rome by a pseudonym, "Babylon." Thus he writes on two levels, comparing his own situation with that of his eponymous biblical hero. The book's central concern is the issue of theodicy: How could a just God allow such misfortunes to happen to God's chosen people?

The author of 4 Ezra is a deeply reflective and highly imaginative thinker, who is moreover skilled and sophisticated enough to present divergent theological viewpoints in different parts of the book. In the first three of the book's seven "visions," Ezra, the book's spirited and loquacious hero, argues persuasively a profoundly humanistic viewpoint that stresses the ideals of God's mercy, justice, and care for humanity, especially Israel. Ezra is rebuffed time and again, however, by his angelic interlocutor, who emphasizes the limitations of human reasoning.

In the fourth vision, the book's central and pivotal section, Ezra experiences a profound psychological shift (a "conversion" experience) from his previous attitude to a state of unquestioning acceptance of God's will. As a sign of this transition he receives a mystical vision of the heavenly Jerusalem. Equipped with his newly acquired state of mind, Ezra in the last section of the book receives two further mystical visions (the fifth and sixth), both indicating that the true solution to the problem of God's justice is an apocalyptic one: The suffering righteous will receive their reward at the end of the world. Finally, in the climactic seventh vision, the inspired Ezra is granted permission by God to rewrite the scriptures that had been burned by the "Babylonians," but with one variation: In addition to the traditional books of the Hebrew canon, he writes seventy secret books meant for the "wise" among his people. Fourth Ezra's author thus displays his penchant for mystical, esoteric, and apocalyptic modes of thinking and his conviction that these hold the answers to the ethical and theological dilemmas of Israel, and indeed of all humankind.

In the course of the second century CE, 4 Ezra was translated into Greek; from Greek it was rendered into a plethora of other languages. Although the Hebrew and Greek texts have been lost with time, the book is attested today in no less than eight versions: Latin, Syriac, Ethiopic, Georgian, Armenian, two independent Arabic versions, and a fragmentary Coptic version. This large number of translations attests to the book's immense popularity in the various regional Christian churches of the early Middle Ages.

Fifth Ezra, a Christian writing of the second or third century, is also pseudonymously ascribed to Ezra. It was composed in either Greek or Latin; its place of composition is uncertain. Fifth Ezra reflects the growing tension between Christian and Jewish communities. It indicts the people of

Israel for their sins and "predicts" the coming of a new people (the Christians) who will inherit Israel's patrimony.

Sixth Ezra is a Christian composition of the third century, probably from Asia Minor. In it an anonymous prophet predicts terrible catastrophes that will afflict the whole earth as a result of human iniquity and warns God's "elect" to abstain from sin if they wish to escape the calamities. The book reflects a situation in which its Christian community was experiencing persecution and strives to convince its audience to stand firm. Although 6 Ezra survives in full only in Latin, a fourth-century Greek parchment fragment of 15.57–59 found at Oxyrhynchus, Egypt, indicates that the book was composed in Greek.

At some time before 400 CE, a Latin form of 6 Ezra was appended to the end of 4 Ezra. In turn, a Latin form of 5 Ezra was later added to the end of that corpus, probably before 450. Then, prior to 800, 5 Ezra was moved to the head of the corpus, resulting in the form of the book known today.

Comprising what is sometimes
called 5 Ezra (chapters 1–2),
4 Ezra (chapters 3–14), and
6 Ezra (chapters 15–16)

1 The book*a* of the prophet Ezra son of Seraiah, son of Azariah, son of Hilkiah, son of Shallum, son of Zadok, son of Ahitub, 2 son of Ahijah, son of Phinehas, son of Eli, son of Amariah, son of Azariah, son of Meraimoth, son of Arna, son of Uzzi, son of Borith, son of Abishua, son of Phinehas, son of Eleazar, 3 son of Aaron, of the tribe of Levi, who was a captive in the country of the Medes in the reign of Artaxerxes, king of the Persians.*b*

4 The word of the Lord came to me, saying, 5 "Go, declare to my people their evil deeds, and to their children the iniquities that they have committed against me, so that they may tell*c* their children's children 6 that the sins of their parents have increased in them, for they have forgotten me and have offered sacrifices to strange gods. 7 Was it not I who brought them out of the land of Egypt, out of the house of bondage?

But they have angered me and despised my counsels. 8 Now you, pull out the hair of your head and hurl*d* all evils upon them, for they have not obeyed my law—they are a rebellious people. 9 How long shall I endure them, on whom I have bestowed such great benefits? 10 For their sake I have overthrown many kings; I struck down Pharaoh with his servants and all his army. 11 I destroyed all nations before them, and scattered in the east the peoples of two provinces,*e* Tyre and Sidon; I killed all their enemies.

12 "But speak to them and say, Thus says the Lord: 13 Surely it was I who brought you through the sea, and made

a Other ancient authorities read *The second book*
b Other ancient authorities, which place chapters 1 and 2 after 16.78, lack verses 1-3 and begin the chapter: *The word of the Lord that came to Ezra son of Chusi in the days of King Nebuchadnezzar, saying, "Go,*
c Other ancient authorities read *nourish*
d Other ancient authorities read *and shake out*
e Other ancient authorities read *Did I not destroy the city of Bethsaida because of you, and to the south burn two cities . . . ?*

**Chapters 1–2** comprise a separate literary composition also known as 5 Ezra. **1.1–3: Ascription.** Ezra is given a high-priestly genealogy similar to Ezra 7.1–5 and 1 Esd 8.1–2, but with several differences (see 1 Sam 14.3). **1:** *Prophet* is unusual; Ezra is usually called "priest" or "scribe" (Ezra 7.6,11; see 2 Esd 12.42n.). **3:** Probably *Artaxerxes* I (465–424 BCE). **1.4–2.9: A prophetic indictment against Israel. 4–23:** Prophetic historical recital of God's benefits during the Exodus. **4:** The expression, *The word of the Lord came . . . ,* is typical of prophetic address. **5:** Isa 58.1; Joel 1.3. **7:** *Was it not I . . . ?,* the Exodus was God's paradigmatic mighty act for Israel. **8:** The command to Ezra to *pull out* his *hair* is a prophetic act signaling Ezra's disgust with the people. **9:** *How long shall I endure them . . . ?,* frequent rhetorical questions like this one highlight God's exasperation. **10:** Ex 14.28. **11:** *Tyre and Sidon,* this action is not recorded in other Exodus traditions. **13:** Ex safe highways for you where there was no road; I gave you Moses as leader and Aaron as priest; [14] I provided light for you from a pillar of fire, and did great wonders among you. Yet you have forgotten me, says the Lord.

15 "Thus says the Lord Almighty:[a] The quails were a sign to you; I gave you camps for your protection, and in them you complained. [16] You have not exulted in my name at the destruction of your enemies, but to this day you still complain.[b] [17] Where are the benefits that I bestowed on you? When you were hungry and thirsty in the wilderness, did you not cry out to me, [18] saying, 'Why have you led us into this wilderness to kill us? It would have been better for us to serve the Egyptians than to die in this wilderness.' [19] I pitied your groanings and gave you manna for food; you ate the bread of angels. [20] When you were thirsty, did I not split the rock so that waters flowed in abundance? Because of the heat I clothed you with the leaves of trees.[c] [21] I divided fertile lands among you; I drove out the Canaanites, the Perizzites, and the Philistines[d] before you. What more can I do for you? says the Lord. [22] Thus says the Lord Almighty:[a] When you were in the wilderness, at the bitter stream, thirsty and blaspheming my name, [23] I did not send fire on you for your blasphemies, but threw a tree into the water and made the stream sweet.

24 "What shall I do to you, O Jacob? You, Judah, would not obey me. I will turn to other nations and will give them my name, so that they may keep my statutes. [25] Because you have forsaken me, I also will forsake you. When you beg mercy of me, I will show you no mercy. [26] When you call to me, I will not listen to you; for you have defiled your hands with blood, and your feet are swift to commit murder. [27] It is not as though you had forsaken me; you have forsaken yourselves, says the Lord.

28 "Thus says the Lord Almighty: Have I not entreated you as a father entreats his sons or a mother her daughters or a nurse her children, [29] so that you should be my people and I should be your God, and that you should be my children and I should be your father? [30] I gathered you as a hen gathers her chicks under her wings. But now, what shall I do to you? I will cast you out from my presence. [31] When you offer oblations to me, I will turn my face from you; for I have rejected your[e] festal days, and new moons, and circumcisions of the flesh.[f] [32] I sent you my servants the prophets, but you have taken and killed them and torn their bodies[g] in pieces; I will require their blood of you, says the Lord.[h]

33 "Thus says the Lord Almighty: Your house is desolate; I will drive you out as the

---

a Other ancient authorities lack *Almighty*
b Other ancient authorities read verse 16, *Your pursuer with his army I sank in the sea, but still the people complain also concerning their own destruction.*
c Other ancient authorities read *I made for you trees with leaves*    d Other ancient authorities read *Perizzites and their children*    e Other ancient authorities read *I have not commanded for you*
f Other ancient authorities lack *of the flesh*
g Other ancient authorities read *the bodies of the apostles*    h Other ancient authorities add *Thus says the Lord Almighty: Recently you also laid hands on me, crying out before the judge's seat for him to deliver me to you. You took me as a sinner, not as a father who freed you from slavery, and you delivered me to death by hanging me on the tree; these are the things you have done. Therefore, says the Lord, let my Father and his angels return and judge between you and me; if I have not kept the commandment of the Father, if I have not nourished you, if I have not done the things my Father commanded, I will contend in judgment with you, says the Lord.*

---

14.29. **14:** Ex 13.21. *You have forgotten me,* God indicts the people. **15:** Ex 16.13; Ps 105.40. **17–18:** Num 14.3. **19:** *The bread of angels,* Ps 78.24–25; Wis 16.20. **20:** Num 20.11; Wis 11.4. *I clothed you with leaves,* this is not mentioned in other Exodus traditions; protection from the *heat* is sometimes attributed to the pillar of cloud (Ex 13.21). **22–23:** Ex 15.22–25.

**1.24–37: Pronouncement of judgment against Israel. 24:** Isa 43.22. *I will turn to other nations,* the pivotal point of 5 Ezra, in which God decisively rejects the former nation (see Mt 21.43). **26:** Isa 1.15; 59.7. **29:** Jer 24.7; Heb 8.10. **30–33:** Compare Mt 23.30–38. This is the closest New Testament parallel in 5 Ezra, and it suggests Christian authorship. **31:** Isa 1.11–15. The rejection of circumcision also reveals wind drives straw; [34]and your sons will have no children, because with you[a] they have neglected my commandment and have done what is evil in my sight. [35]I will give your houses to a people that will come, who without having heard me will believe. Those to whom I have shown no signs will do what I have commanded. [36]They have seen no prophets, yet will recall their former state.[b] [37]I call to witness the gratitude of the people that is to come, whose children rejoice with gladness;[c] though they do not see me with bodily eyes, yet with the spirit they will believe the things I have said.

[38] "And now, father,[d] look with pride and see the people coming from the east; [39]to them I will give as leaders Abraham, Isaac, and Jacob, and Hosea and Amos and Micah and Joel and Obadiah and Jonah [40]and Nahum and Habakkuk, Zephaniah, Haggai, Zechariah and Malachi, who is also called the messenger of the Lord.[e]

2 "Thus says the Lord: I brought this people out of bondage, and I gave them commandments through my servants the prophets; but they would not listen to them, and made my counsels void. [2]The mother who bore them[f] says to them, 'Go, my children, because I am a widow and forsaken. [3]I brought you up with gladness; but with mourning and sorrow I have lost you, because you have sinned before the Lord God and have done what is evil in my sight.[g] [4]But now what can I do for you? For I am a widow and forsaken. Go, my children, and ask for mercy from the Lord.'

[5]Now I call upon you, father, as a witness in addition to the mother of the children, because they would not keep my covenant, [6]so that you may bring confusion on them and bring their mother to ruin, so that they may have no offspring. [7]Let them be scattered among the nations; let their names be blotted out from the earth, because they have despised my covenant.

[8] "Woe to you, Assyria, who conceal the unrighteous within you! O wicked nation, remember what I did to Sodom and Gomorrah, [9]whose land lies in lumps of pitch and heaps of ashes.[b] That is what I will do to those who have not listened to me, says the Lord Almighty."

[10] Thus says the Lord to Ezra: "Tell my people that I will give them the kingdom of Jerusalem, which I was going to give to Israel. [11]Moreover, I will take back to myself their glory, and will give to these others the everlasting habitations, which I had prepared for Israel.[i] [12]The tree of life shall give them fragrant perfume, and they shall

a Other ancient authorities lack *with you*
b Other ancient authorities read *their iniquities*
c Other ancient authorities read *The apostles bear witness to the coming people with joy*
d Other ancient authorities read *brother*
e Other ancient authorities read *and Jacob, Elijah and Enoch, Zechariah and Hosea, Amos, Joel, Micah, Obadiah, Zephaniah, [40]Nahum, Jonah, Mattia (or Mattathias), Habakkuk, and twelve angels with flowers*
f Other ancient authorities read *They begat for themselves a mother who*  g Other ancient authorities read *in his sight*  h Other ancient authorities read *Gomorrah, whose land descends to hell*  i Lat *for those*

the Christian identity of the author. **33:** Jer 13.24. **35–37:** Emphasis is placed on the untutored goodness of the *people that will come.* **35:** Zeph 3.12–13. **37:** *With bodily eyes,* Jn 20.29.

**1.38–40: Vision of the coming people. 38:** God addresses Ezra as *father,* a term of respect. The people coming *from the east* suggests a return from exile (see Bar 4.36–37; 5.5). **39–40:** The three patriarchs and the twelve minor prophets, arranged in the order of the Septuagint.

**2.1–9: Further pronouncement of judgment. 1:** Jer 7.25–26. **2:** *The mother who bore them,* Jerusalem (Isa 54.1). **2–4:** This section, like 1.38, draws on the last chapters of the book of Baruch (Bar 4.11–21). **5:** Ezra is again invoked as *father* (see 1.38), this time in conjunction with Jerusalem as *mother.* **6:** *Bring their mother to ruin,* a reference to the fall of Jerusalem in 70 or 135 CE. **8–9:** Woe against Assyria. The exact significance of this reference is uncertain; some scholars would view *Assyria* as a reference to Rome. *Sodom and Gomorrah,* Gen 19.

**2.10–41: Prophetic exhortation of the new people. 10–14: Blessing and instruction. 10:** *My people,* the newly chosen Christians. **11:** *Everlasting habitations,* postmortem dwelling places; see Lk 16.9. **12:** Rev neither toil nor become weary. [13] Go[a] and you will receive; pray that your days may be few, that they may be shortened. The kingdom is already prepared for you; be on the watch! [14] Call, O call heaven and earth to witness: I set aside evil and created good; for I am the Living One, says the Lord.

[15] "Mother, embrace your children; bring them up with gladness, as does a dove; strengthen their feet, because I have chosen you, says the Lord. [16] And I will raise up the dead from their places, and bring them out from their tombs, because I recognize my name in them. [17] Do not fear, mother of children, for I have chosen you, says the Lord. [18] I will send you help, my servants Isaiah and Jeremiah. According to their counsel I have consecrated and prepared for you twelve trees loaded with various fruits, [19] and the same number of springs flowing with milk and honey, and seven mighty mountains on which roses and lilies grow; by these I will fill your children with joy.

[20] "Guard the rights of the widow, secure justice for the ward, give to the needy, defend the orphan, clothe the naked, [21] care for the injured and the weak, do not ridicule the lame, protect the maimed, and let the blind have a vision of my splendor. [22] Protect the old and the young within your walls. [23] When you find any who are dead, commit them to the grave and mark it,[b] and I will give you the first place in my resurrection. [24] Pause and be quiet, my people, because your rest will come.

[25] "Good nurse, nourish your children; strengthen their feet. [26] Not one of the servants[c] whom I have given you will perish, for I will require them from among your

number. [27] Do not be anxious, for when the day of tribulation and anguish comes, others shall weep and be sorrowful, but you shall rejoice and have abundance. [28] The nations shall envy you, but they shall not be able to do anything against you, says the Lord. [29] My power will protect[d] you, so that your children may not see hell.[e]

[30] "Rejoice, O mother, with your children, because I will deliver you, says the Lord. [31] Remember your children that sleep, because I will bring them out of the hiding places of the earth, and will show mercy to them; for I am merciful, says the Lord Almighty. [32] Embrace your children until I come, and proclaim mercy to them; because my springs run over, and my grace will not fail."

[33] I, Ezra, received a command from the Lord on Mount Horeb to go to Israel. When I came to them they rejected me and refused the Lord's commandment. [34] Therefore I say to you, O nations that hear and understand, "Wait for your shepherd; he will give you everlasting rest, because he who will come at the end of the age is close at hand. [35] Be ready for the rewards of the kingdom, because perpetual light will shine on you forevermore. [36] Flee from the shadow of this age, receive the joy of your glory; I publicly call on my savior to witness.[f] [37] Receive what the Lord has entrusted to you and be joyful, giving thanks to him who has called you to the celestial king-

a Other ancient authorities read Seek    b Or seal it; or mark them and commit them to the grave
c Or slaves    d Lat hands will cover    e Lat Gehenna
f Other ancient authorities read I testify that my savior has been commissioned by the Lord

2.7; 22.2,14; 1 Enoch 24.4–25.7. **13:** Mt 7.7–8; 24.22; 25.34; Mk 13.37. **14:** Heaven and earth, Deut 4.26; Isa 1.2. Living One, Rev 1.18.

**2.15–32:** Exhortation of the mother. In distinction to 2.2–6, it is now the church, not Jerusalem, that is addressed as mother. **16:** Resurrection is promised; see Ezek 37.12. **18:** Twelve trees, Rev 22.2. **19:** Springs . . . mountains, 1 Enoch 18.6; 24.2–3; 32.1; 48.1. **20–23:** A recital of the traditional "works of mercy" of the church (see Isa 58.6–10; Tob 1.17–19; Mt 25.35–45; Hermas Mand. 8.10). **26:** Jn 17.12. **27–31:** The author emphasizes eschatology and resurrection.

**2.33–41:** Encouragement of the "nations." **33:** On Mount Horeb, depicting Ezra as a second Moses (Ex 3.1). **34:** Nations, Gentiles; cf. Acts 13.46–47. **34–41:** Portrays the eschatological feast of God as a celestial banquet, with participants clothed in white. **38:** Sealed, Rev 7.4. **39:** Glorious garments, 1 Enoch doms. 38 Rise, stand erect and see the number of those who have been sealed at the feast of the Lord. 39 Those who have departed from the shadow of this age have received glorious garments from the Lord. 40 Take again your full number, O Zion, and close the list of your people who are clothed in white, who have fulfilled the law of the Lord. 41 The number of your children, whom you desired, is now complete; implore the Lord's authority that your people, who have been called from the beginning, may be made holy."

42 I, Ezra, saw on Mount Zion a great multitude that I could not number, and they all were praising the Lord with songs. 43 In their midst was a young man of great stature, taller than any of the others, and on the head of each of them he placed a crown, but he was more exalted than they. And I was held spellbound. 44 Then I asked an angel, "Who are these, my lord?" 45 He answered and said to me, "These are they who have put off mortal clothing and have put on the immortal, and have confessed the name of God. Now they are being crowned, and receive palms." 46 Then I said to the angel, "Who is that young man who is placing crowns on them and putting palms in their hands?" 47 He answered and said to me, "He is the Son of God, whom they confessed in the world." So I began to praise those who had stood valiantly for the name of the Lord.[a] 48 Then the angel said to me, "Go, tell my people how great and how many are the wonders of the Lord God that you have seen."

3 In the thirtieth year after the destruction of the city, I was in Babylon—I, Salathiel, who am also called Ezra. I was troubled as I lay on my bed, and my thoughts welled up in my heart, 2 because I saw the desolation of Zion and the wealth of those who lived in Babylon. 3 My spirit was greatly agitated, and I began to speak anxious words to the Most High, and said, 4 "O sovereign Lord, did you not speak at the beginning when you planted[b] the earth—and that without help—and commanded the dust[c] 5 and it gave you Adam, a lifeless body? Yet he was the creation of your hands, and you breathed into him the breath of life, and he was made alive in your presence. 6 And you led him into the garden that your right hand had planted before the earth appeared. 7 And you laid upon him one commandment of yours; but he transgressed it, and immediately you appointed death for him and for his descen-

a Other ancient authorities read to praise and glorify the Lord    b Other ancient authorities read formed    c Syr Ethiop: Lat people or world

62.15–16. **40:** *Full number,* see 4.36–37; Rev 6.11. *O Zion,* the church is identified as Zion; cf. Heb 12.22–23. *Clothed in white,* Rev 3.4; 6.11; 7.14; 1 Enoch 71.1. **41:** 1 Enoch 47.4.

**2.42–48:** *Ezra's vision of a great multitude* (cf. Rev 7.9–17). **42:** *Mount Zion,* contrasted here with the *Mount Horeb* of 2.33. *Great multitude,* Rev 7.9; 1 Enoch 39.12–40.1. **43:** *Young man,* a messianic figure, here depicting Jesus. **47:** *Son of God,* here a Christian designation, can also be Jewish (see 7.28–29; 13.32,37,52). *Confessed in the world,* signifying Christian martyrs.

**Chapters 3–14** comprise a separate literary composition also known as 4 Ezra.

**3.1–5.20:** *The first vision.* **1–3:** *Introduction.* **1:** *The thirtieth year after the destruction* of Jerusalem by Nebuchadnezzar in 586 BCE (2 Kings 25.1–21) would be 556. The date specified may imply that the author was writing about 100 CE (i.e., thirty years after the fall of Jerusalem in 70 CE). The historical Ezra lived almost a century after the claimed setting of the book. *Salathiel* is the Greek form of "Shealtiel" (Ezra 3.2; 5.2; Neh 12.1), appropriately meaning "I asked God" in Hebrew. The identification of Salathiel with Ezra has never been adequately explained. *On my bed,* cf. Dan 7.1.

**3.4–36:** *Addressing God, the author raises perplexing questions.* Whence comes sin with its consequent misery? How can Israel's continuing affliction be reconciled with God's justice? **4–5:** *The creation of Adam,* based on Gen 2.7, and drawing on the concept of creation by divine speech in Gen 1. **6–8:** *Adam's disobedience gives rise to sin and death for all humans.* **7:** The words *immediately you appointed death* imply that Adam was not originally intended to be mortal (see Gen 3.22; cf. Wis 1.13–14; 2.23–24).

dants. From him there sprang nations and tribes, peoples and clans without number. [8] And every nation walked after its own will; they did ungodly things in your sight and rejected your commands, and you did not hinder them. [9] But again, in its time you brought the flood upon the inhabitants of the world and destroyed them. [10] And the same fate befell all of them: just as death came upon Adam, so the flood upon them. [11] But you left one of them, Noah with his household, and all the righteous who have descended from him.

[12] "When those who lived on earth began to multiply, they produced children and peoples and many nations, and again they began to be more ungodly than were their ancestors. [13] And when they were committing iniquity in your sight, you chose for yourself one of them, whose name was Abraham; [14] you loved him, and to him alone you revealed the end of the times, secretly by night. [15] You made an everlasting covenant with him, and promised him that you would never forsake his descendants; and you gave him Isaac, and to Isaac you gave Jacob and Esau. [16] You set apart Jacob for yourself, but Esau you rejected; and Jacob became a great multitude. [17] And when you led his descendants out of Egypt, you brought them to Mount Sinai. [18] You bent down the heavens and shook[a] the earth, and moved the world, and caused the depths to tremble, and troubled the times. [19] Your glory passed through the four gates of fire and earthquake and wind

and ice, to give the law to the descendants of Jacob, and your commandment to the posterity of Israel.

[20] "Yet you did not take away their evil heart from them, so that your law might produce fruit in them. [21] For the first Adam, burdened with an evil heart, transgressed and was overcome, as were also all who were descended from him. [22] Thus the disease became permanent; the law was in the hearts of the people along with the evil root; but what was good departed, and the evil remained. [23] So the times passed and the years were completed, and you raised up for yourself a servant, named David. [24] You commanded him to build a city for your name, and there to offer you oblations from what is yours. [25] This was done for many years; but the inhabitants of the city transgressed, [26] in everything doing just as Adam and all his descendants had done, for they also had the evil heart. [27] So you handed over your city to your enemies.

[28] "Then I said in my heart, Are the deeds of those who inhabit Babylon any better? Is that why it has gained dominion over Zion? [29] For when I came here I saw ungodly deeds without number, and my soul has seen many sinners during these thirty years.[b] And my heart failed me, [30] because I have seen how you endure those who sin, and have spared those who act wickedly, and have destroyed your peo-

a Syr Ethiop Arab 1 Georg: Lat *set fast*
b Ethiop Arab 1 Arm: Lat Syr *in this thirtieth year*

8: Gen 6.12. **9–11:** The flood (Gen 6.11–8.22). **12–15:** The choice of and covenant with Abraham (Gen 12.1; 17.5). **14:** *The end of the times* is not the topic of Gen 15. See, however, *The Apocalypse of Abraham*, roughly contemporary with chs 3–14. *By night*, Gen 15.5,12,17. **17–19:** The Exodus and the giving of the law. **18:** Compare Ex 19.16–18; Ps 68.7–8. **19:** *Four gates*, according to certain early Jewish cosmological models, meteorological phenomena passed from heaven to earth through *gates* in the heavenly firmament, here enumerated as *four*. See *1 Enoch* 36.1,76; cf. Ps 78.23; 1 Kings 19.11–12. Here God's *glory* descends through these *gates* to *give the law* on Mt. Sinai. **20–27:** The tendency to sin is universal and permanent. **20:** *You did not take away*, here, as in v. 8 (*you did not hinder them*), Ezra implies that God bears some responsibility for human sinfulness. *Evil heart*, possibly, in the Hebrew (now lost), the evil "yetser," an inclination or tendency to sin (Gen 6.5; 2 Esd 4.30–31). The "yetser" can also be an inclination to good (Isa 26.3; 1 Chr 29.18). **23–27:** The *city* is Jerusalem. **27:** *Handed over your city*, the Babylonian conquest of Jerusalem in 586 BCE (2 Kings 25.1–21). **28–36:** Ezra questions whether the deeds of Babylon are any better than those of Israel. **28:** *Babylon*, here, as regularly in the book, stands for Rome (compare Rev 14.8). **30–31:** Here the author expresses the essence of the problem: God permits ple, and protected your enemies, [31] and have not shown to anyone how your way may be comprehended.[a] Are the deeds of Babylon better than those of Zion? [32] Or has another nation known you besides Israel? Or what tribes have so believed the covenants as these tribes of Jacob? [33] Yet their reward has not appeared and their labor has borne no fruit. For I have traveled widely among the nations and have seen that they abound in wealth, though they are unmindful of your commandments. [34] Now therefore weigh in a balance our iniquities and those of the inhabitants of the world; and it will be found which way the turn of the scale will incline. [35] When have the inhabitants of the earth not sinned in your sight? Or what nation has kept your commandments so well? [36] You may indeed find individuals who have kept your commandments, but nations you will not find."

4 Then the angel that had been sent to me, whose name was Uriel, answered [2] and said to me, "Your understanding has utterly failed regarding this world, and do you think you can comprehend the way of the Most High?" [3] Then I said, "Yes, my lord." And he replied to me, "I have been sent to show you three ways, and to put before you three problems. [4] If you can solve one of them for me, then I will show you the way you desire to see, and will teach you why the heart is evil."

[5] I said, "Speak, my lord."

And he said to me, "Go, weigh for me the weight of fire, or measure for me a blast[b] of wind, or call back for me the day that is past."

[6] I answered and said, "Who of those that have been born can do that, that you should ask me about such things?"

[7] And he said to me, "If I had asked you, 'How many dwellings are in the heart of the sea, or how many streams are at the source of the deep, or how many streams are above the firmament, or which are the exits of Hades, or which are the entrances[c] of paradise?' [8] perhaps you would have said to me, 'I never went down into the deep, nor as yet into Hades, neither did I ever ascend into heaven.' [9] But now I have asked you only about fire and wind and the day—things that you have experienced and from which you cannot be separated, and you have given me no answer about them." [10] He said to me, "You cannot understand the things with which you have grown up; [11] how then can your mind comprehend the way of the Most High? And how can one who is already worn out[d] by the corrupt world understand incorruption?"[e] When I heard this, I fell on my face[f] [12] and said to him, "It would have been better for us not to be here than to come here and live in ungodliness, and to suffer and not understand why."

[13] He answered me and said, "I went into a forest of trees of the plain, and they made a plan [14] and said, 'Come, let us go

---

a Syr; compare Ethiop: Lat *how this way should be forsaken*    b Syr Ethiop Arab 1 Arab 2 Georg *a measure*    c Syr Compare Ethiop Arab 2 Arm: Lat lacks *of Hades, or which are the entrances*    d Meaning of Lat uncertain    e Syr Ethiop *the way of the incorruptible?*    f Syr Ethiop Arab 1: Meaning of Lat uncertain

---

evildoers to continue in their wickedness, does not spare the suffering people of God, and does not let anyone understand why this should be so. **33–36:** Ezra claims that God's judgment regarding the present world order has been faulty. **36:** *Individuals* among the Gentiles.

**4.1–25: Dialogic dispute between Ezra and the angel Uriel.** The message is that God's ways are beyond human understanding. **1–12:** Three riddles illustrate the limitations of human knowledge. **1:** *Angel*, representing the viewpoint of God. The name *Uriel* in Hebrew means "God is my fire" (or "my light"). According to *1 Enoch* 20.2, Uriel is a watcher over the world and over Tartarus, the lowest part of hell (cf. 2 Pet 2.4 note c). **7:** *How many dwellings . . . ?*, in many apocalypses, these types of questions are in fact issues of proper concern. **8:** See Deut 30.11–13. **10–11:** See Job 38–41; Jn 3.12. **12:** For the seer, to live without understanding of life's meaning is intolerable. **13–21:** Parable of the conflict between the forest and the sea. **21:** Isa 55.8–9; Ps 104.5–9. **22–25:** Ezra protests that he is inquiring only about the and make war against the sea, so that it may recede before us and so that we may make for ourselves more forests.' 15 In like manner the waves of the sea also made a plan and said, 'Come, let us go up and subdue the forest of the plain so that there also we may gain more territory for ourselves.' 16 But the plan of the forest was in vain, for the fire came and consumed it; 17 likewise also the plan of the waves of the sea was in vain,[a] for the sand stood firm and blocked it. 18 If now you were a judge between them, which would you undertake to justify, and which to condemn?"

19 I answered and said, "Each made a foolish plan, for the land has been assigned to the forest, and the locale of the sea a place to carry its waves."

20 He answered me and said, "You have judged rightly, but why have you not judged so in your own case? 21 For as the land has been assigned to the forest and the sea to its waves, so also those who inhabit the earth can understand only what is on the earth, and he who is[b] above the heavens can understand what is above the height of the heavens."

22 Then I answered and said, "I implore you, my lord, why[c] have I been endowed with the power of understanding? 23 For I did not wish to inquire about the ways above, but about those things that we daily experience: why Israel has been given over to the Gentiles in disgrace; why the people whom you loved has been given over to godless tribes, and the law of our ancestors has been brought to destruction and the written covenants no longer exist. 24 We pass from the world like locusts, and our life is like a mist,[d] and we are not worthy

to obtain mercy. 25 But what will he do for his[e] name that is invoked over us? It is about these things that I have asked."

26 He answered me and said, "If you are alive, you will see, and if you live long,[f] you will often marvel, because the age is hurrying swiftly to its end. 27 It will not be able to bring the things that have been promised to the righteous in their appointed times, because this age is full of sadness and infirmities. 28 For the evil about which[g] you ask me has been sown, but the harvest of it has not yet come. 29 If therefore that which has been sown is not reaped, and if the place where the evil has been sown does not pass away, the field where the good has been sown will not come. 30 For a grain of evil seed was sown in Adam's heart from the beginning, and how much ungodliness it has produced until now—and will produce until the time of threshing comes! 31 Consider now for yourself how much fruit of ungodliness a grain of evil seed has produced. 32 When heads of grain without number are sown, how great a threshing floor they will fill!"

33 Then I answered and said, "How long?[g] When will these things be? Why are our years few and evil?" 34 He answered me and said, "Do not be in a greater hurry than the Most High. You, indeed, are in a hurry for yourself,[h] but the Highest is in a hurry on behalf of many. 35 Did not the souls of the righteous in their chambers ask

a Lat lacks *was in vain*   b Or *those who are*
c Syr Ethiop Arm: Meaning of Lat uncertain
d Syr Ethiop Arab Georg: Lat *a trembling*
e Ethiop adds *holy*   f Syr: Lat *live*
g Syr Ethiop: Meaning of Lat uncertain
h Syr Ethiop Arab Arm: Meaning of Lat uncertain

meaning of earthly, historical happenings, not about cosmic events. **24:** Ps 109.23; Hos 13.3; Wis 2.4.

**4.26–52: Dialogic prediction regarding the future. 26–32:** The angel's concern shifts to the end of the present, evil age and the distinction between this age and the next. **29:** Compare the fourth vision, 9.26–10.59. **30:** The *grain of evil seed*, or evil "yetser," (see 3.20n.) *sown in Adam's heart*, introduced in 3.7–27, must ripen and be harvested before the coming, righteous age can appear. **33–52:** Ezra's questions concerning the time of the end. **33:** *How long?*, the question is a prophetic and apocalyptic commonplace; see Isa 6.11; Dan 8.13; 12.6; Zech 1.12. Ezra's concerns, like the angel's, also move to the end of the age. **35:** *Souls of the righteous in their chambers*, according to Jewish thought of the time, the souls of the righteous dead are placed in "chambers," or "treasuries," to await the last judgment (see 2.31; 4.41; 7.32,80,95,101; 2 Apoc. Bar. 21.23). **36:** *Archangel Jeremiel*, see 1 Enoch 20.8, Apoc. Zeph. 6.11–17;

about these matters, saying, 'How long are we to remain here?[a] And when will the harvest of our reward come?' 36 And the archangel Jeremiel answered and said, 'When the number of those like yourselves is completed;[b] for he has weighed the age in the balance, 37 and measured the times by measure, and numbered the times by number; and he will not move or arouse them until that measure is fulfilled.' "

38 Then I answered and said, "But, O sovereign Lord, all of us also are full of ungodliness. 39 It is perhaps on account of us that the time of threshing is delayed for the righteous—on account of the sins of those who inhabit the earth."

40 He answered me and said, "Go and ask a pregnant woman whether, when her nine months have been completed, her womb can keep the fetus within her any longer."

41 And I said, "No, lord, it cannot."

He said to me, "In Hades the chambers of the souls are like the womb. 42 For just as a woman who is in labor makes haste to escape the pangs of birth, so also do these places hasten to give back those things that were committed to them from the beginning. 43 Then the things that you desire to see will be disclosed to you."

44 I answered and said, "If I have found favor in your sight, and if it is possible, and if I am worthy, 45 show me this also: whether more time is to come than has passed, or whether for us the greater part has gone by. 46 For I know what has gone by, but I do not know what is to come."

47 And he said to me, "Stand at my right side, and I will show you the interpretation of a parable."

48 So I stood and looked, and lo, a flaming furnace passed by before me, and when the flame had gone by I looked, and lo, the smoke remained. 49 And after this a cloud full of water passed before me and poured down a heavy and violent rain, and when the violent rainstorm had passed, drops still remained in the cloud.[c]

50 He said to me, "Consider it for yourself; for just as the rain is more than the drops, and the fire is greater than the smoke, so the quantity that passed was far greater; but drops and smoke remained."

51 Then I prayed and said, "Do you think that I shall live until those days? Or who will be alive in those days?"

52 He answered me and said, "Concerning the signs about which you ask me, I can tell you in part; but I was not sent to tell you concerning your life, for I do not know.

5 "Now concerning the signs: lo, the days are coming when those who inhabit the earth shall be seized with great terror,[d] and the way of truth shall be hidden, and the land shall be barren of faith. 2 Unrighteousness shall be increased beyond what you yourself see, and beyond what you heard of formerly. 3 And the land that you now see ruling shall be a trackless waste, and people shall see it desolate. 4 But if the Most High grants that you live, you shall see it thrown into confusion after the third period;[e]

and the sun shall suddenly begin to shine at night,

a Syr Ethiop Arab 2 Georg: Lat *How long do I hope thus?*   b Syr Ethiop Arab 2: Lat *number of seeds is completed for you*   c Lat *in it*
d Syr Ethiop: Meaning of Lat uncertain
e Literally *after the third*; Ethiop *after three months*; Arm *after the third vision*; Georg *after the third day*

2 Baruch chs 53–74. In *1 Enoch* 20.8 the angel, called Remeiel, is "in charge of those who rise." *When the number . . . is completed*, cf. 2.40–41; Rev 6.11. **36–37:** *Weighed . . . measured . . . numbered*, God has determined the times and periods of history (see Sir 36.10n.). **40–43:** The analogy of *a woman who is in labor* explains the inevitability of the end (cf. 16.38–39; 1 Thess 5.3). **41:** *Chambers*, see v. 35n. **44–50:** The seer asks what proportion of time remains; he is told by a parable that the end is near.

**5.1–13: Direct prediction of the future by the angel**, who uses classical apocalyptic *signs* to describe the end of this age (cf. the "synoptic apocalypse" in Mt 24.4–31; Mk 13.5–27; Lk 21.8–28). **2:** Mt 24.12. **4–9:** The natural order, mirroring the moral order, will be confused and overturned. **4:** The reference to *the third period* is cryptic (cf. 14.11–13). **5:** *The stone shall utter its voice*, Hab 2.11; Lk 19.40.

and the moon during the day.

5 Blood shall drip from wood,
and the stone shall utter its voice;
the peoples shall be troubled,
and the stars shall fall.[a]

6 And one shall reign whom those who inhabit the earth do not expect, and the birds shall fly away together; 7 and the Dead Sea[b] shall cast up fish; and one whom the many do not know shall make his voice heard by night, and all shall hear his voice.[c] 8 There shall be chaos also in many places, fire shall often break out, the wild animals shall roam beyond their haunts, and menstruous women shall bring forth monsters. 9 Salt waters shall be found in the sweet, and all friends shall conquer one another; then shall reason hide itself, and wisdom shall withdraw into its chamber, 10 and it shall be sought by many but shall not be found, and unrighteousness and unrestraint shall increase on earth. 11 One country shall ask its neighbor, 'Has righteousness, or anyone who does right, passed through you?' And it will answer, 'No.' 12 At that time people shall hope but not obtain; they shall labor, but their ways shall not prosper. 13 These are the signs that I am permitted to tell you, and if you pray again, and weep as you do now, and fast for seven days, you shall hear yet greater things than these."

14 Then I woke up, and my body shuddered violently, and my soul was so troubled that it fainted. 15 But the angel who had come and talked with me held me and strengthened me and set me on my feet.

16 Now on the second night Phaltiel, a chief of the people, came to me and said, "Where have you been? And why is your face sad? 17 Or do you not know that Israel has been entrusted to you in the land of their exile? 18 Rise therefore and eat some bread, and do not forsake us, like a shepherd who leaves the flock in the power of savage wolves."

19 Then I said to him, "Go away from me and do not come near me for seven days; then you may come to me."

He heard what I said and left me. 20 So I fasted seven days, mourning and weeping, as the angel Uriel had commanded me.

21 After seven days the thoughts of my heart were very grievous to me again. 22 Then my soul recovered the spirit of understanding, and I began once more to speak words in the presence of the Most High. 23 I said, "O sovereign Lord, from every forest of the earth and from all its trees you have chosen one vine, 24 and from all the lands of the world you have chosen for yourself one region,[d] and from all the flowers of the world you have chosen for yourself one lily, 25 and from all the depths of the sea you have filled for yourself one river, and from all the cities that have been built you have consecrated Zion for yourself, 26 and from all the birds that have been created you have named for yourself one

a Ethiop Compare Syr and Arab: Meaning of Lat uncertain   b Lat Sea of Sodom   c Cn: Lat fish; and it shall make its voice heard by night, which the many have not known, but all shall hear its voice.
d Ethiop: Lat pit

7: Cf. Ezek 47.8–10. 8a: Syriac, "There shall be chasms also in many places" (cf. Zech 14.4). 9–11: Wisdom, personified as in the wisdom literature, shall withdraw, another classic apocalyptic theme (cf. Isa 59.14–15; 2 Apoc. Bar. 48.36). 13: For the author, fasting prepared one to receive a divine revelation; he refers to three fasts, each lasting seven days (5.20; 6.35; 12.51).

5.14–20: Conclusion of the vision. 14: Then I woke up, from the dream vision. My soul . . . fainted, cf. Dan 7.28; 8.27; 10.9–10,17b–19. 16–19: Phaltiel, a chief of the people, named only here, tries unsuccessfully to dissuade Ezra from his solitary visionary quest.

5.21–6.34: The second vision. 21–22: Introduction; cf. 3.1–3.

5.23–30: Addressing God, the seer reiterates his complaints of divine injustice in dealing with Israel. 23–28: In this series of comparisons, most of the chosen elements are biblical figures representing Israel: the vine (v. 23), Ps 80.8–15; Jer 2.21; the lily (v. 24), Song 2.2 (interpreted allegorically); Hos 14.5; the river (v. 25), Isa 8.6; the city of Zion (v. 25), Ps 132.13; the dove (v. 26), Ps 74.19; the sheep (v. 26), Ps dove, and from all the flocks that have been made you have provided for yourself one sheep, 27 and from all the multitude of peoples you have gotten for yourself one people; and to this people, whom you have loved, you have given the law that is approved by all. 28 And now, O Lord, why have you handed the one over to the many, and dishonored[a] the one root beyond the others, and scattered your only one among the many? 29 And those who opposed your promises have trampled on those who believed your covenants. 30 If you really hate your people, they should be punished at your own hands."

31 When I had spoken these words, the angel who had come to me on a previous night was sent to me. 32 He said to me, "Listen to me, and I will instruct you; pay attention to me, and I will tell you more."

33 Then I said, "Speak, my lord." And he said to me, "Are you greatly disturbed in mind over Israel? Or do you love him more than his Maker does?"

34 I said, "No, my lord, but because of my grief I have spoken; for every hour I suffer agonies of heart, while I strive to understand the way of the Most High and to search out some part of his judgment."

35 He said to me, "You cannot." And I said, "Why not, my lord? Why then was I born? Or why did not my mother's womb become my grave, so that I would not see the travail of Jacob and the exhaustion of the people of Israel?"

36 He said to me, "Count up for me those who have not yet come, and gather for me the scattered raindrops, and make the withered flowers bloom again for me; 37 open for me the closed chambers, and bring out for me the winds shut up in them, or show me the picture of a voice; and then I will explain to you the travail that you ask to understand."[b]

38 I said, "O sovereign Lord, who is able to know these things except him whose dwelling is not with mortals? 39 As for me, I am without wisdom, and how can I speak concerning the things that you have asked me?"

40 He said to me, "Just as you cannot do one of the things that were mentioned, so you cannot discover my judgment, or the goal of the love that I have promised to my people."

41 I said, "Yet, O Lord, you have charge of those who are alive at the end, but what will those do who lived before me, or we, ourselves, or those who come after us?"

42 He said to me, "I shall liken my judgment to a circle;[c] just as for those who are last there is no slowness, so for those who are first there is no haste."

43 Then I answered and said, "Could you not have created at one time those who have been and those who are and those who will be, so that you might show your judgment the sooner?"

44 He replied to me and said, "The creation cannot move faster than the Creator, nor can the world hold at one time those who have been created in it."

45 I said, "How have you said to your servant that you[d] will certainly give life at one time to your creation? If therefore all

a Syr Ethiop Arab: Lat *prepared*    b Lat *see*
c Or *crown*    d Syr Ethiop Arab 1: Meaning of Lat uncertain

79.13; Isa 53.7; the *root* (v. 28), *1 Enoch* 93.8. **27:** The claim that God has *loved* Israel (see Deut 7.8) is contrasted with the idea of *hate* in v. 30.

**5.31–40: Dialogic dispute with the angel.** The issue of contention is the same as in the first vision. **31:** *The angel who had come to me,* see 4.1n. **33:** The angel answers Ezra's concern for God's *love* for Israel. **35:** Job 3.11; 10.18–19; Jer 20.17. **36–40:** As in the first vision (4.5), the angel poses unanswerable riddles from nature. **40:** *My . . . I,* the angel speaks in God's name.

**5.41–6.10: Dialogic prediction concerning the future. 41–49:** Ezra's concern is for fair treatment of all at the judgment. **41:** *You have charge,* Ezra immediately resumes his questioning about the details of the end. The problem of the faithful who die before the end time was also an issue in early Christianity (1 Thess 4.13–15). **45:** *How have you said . . . ?,* Ezra points out an apparent contradiction in the logic:

creatures will live at one time[a] and the creation will sustain them, it might even now be able to support all of them present at one time."

46 He said to me, "Ask a woman's womb, and say to it, 'If you bear ten[b] children, why one after another?' Request it therefore to produce ten at one time."

47 I said, "Of course it cannot, but only each in its own time."

48 He said to me, "Even so I have given the womb of the earth to those who from time to time are sown in it. 49 For as an infant does not bring forth, and a woman who has become old does not bring forth any longer, so I have made the same rule for the world that I created."

50 Then I inquired and said, "Since you have now given me the opportunity, let me speak before you. Is our mother, of whom you have told me, still young? Or is she now approaching old age?"

51 He replied to me, "Ask a woman who bears children, and she will tell you. 52 Say to her, 'Why are those whom you have borne recently not like those whom you bore before, but smaller in stature?' 53 And she herself will answer you, 'Those born in the strength of youth are different from those born during the time of old age, when the womb is failing.' 54 Therefore you also should consider that you and your contemporaries are smaller in stature than those who were before you, 55 and those who come after you will be smaller than you, as born of a creation that already is aging and passing the strength of youth."

56 I said, "I implore you, O Lord, if I have found favor in your sight, show your servant through whom you will visit your creation."

6 He said to me, "At the beginning of the circle of the earth, before[c] the portals of the world were in place, and before the assembled winds blew, 2 and before the rumblings of thunder sounded, and before the flashes of lightning shone, and before the foundations of paradise were laid, 3 and before the beautiful flowers were seen, and before the powers of movements[d] were established, and before the innumerable hosts of angels were gathered together, 4 and before the heights of the air were lifted up, and before the measures of the firmaments were named, and before the footstool of Zion was established, 5 and before the present years were reckoned and before the imaginations of those who now sin were estranged, and before those who stored up treasures of faith were sealed— 6 then I planned these things, and they were made through me alone and not through another; just as the end shall come through me alone and not through another."

7 I answered and said, "What will be the dividing of the times? Or when will be the end of the first age and the beginning of the age that follows?"

8 He said to me, "From Abraham to Isaac,[e] because from him were born Jacob and Esau, for Jacob's hand held Esau's heel from the beginning. 9 Now Esau is the end of this age, and Jacob is the beginning of the age that follows. 10 The beginning of a

a Lat lacks *If . . . one time*    b Syr Ethiop Arab 2 Arm: Meaning of Lat uncertain    c Meaning of Lat uncertain: Compare Syr *The beginning by the hand of humankind, but the end by my own hands. For as before the land of the world existed there, and before*; Ethiop: *At first by the Son of Man, and afterwards I myself. For before the earth and the lands were created, and before*    d Or *earthquakes* e Other ancient authorities read *to Abraham*

All *will live at one time*, namely at the resurrection. **48:** *The womb of the earth*, see Job 1.21. **50–55:** As in the first vision (4.44–46), Ezra asks about the timing of the end. **54:** Ezra's generation being *smaller in stature* shows that the end is near. Various traditions refer to an ancient race of giants (Gen 6.4; Num 13.33; Deut 3.11). **5.56–6.6:** To Ezra's question concerning an eschatological agent, the angel responds that God alone will act. **6.1:** *Portals of the world*, here, as elsewhere, the author shows a fascination with natural phenomena and their origins (vv. 1–5). **4:** *Footstool*, see Ps 99.5; 132.7. **7–10:** The division of the ages. In allegorical language the seer is told that the present corrupt age (symbolized by *Esau*) will be followed immediately, without a break, by the glorious age to come (symbolized by *Jacob*). **8:** *Heel*, see Gen 25.26.

person is the hand, and the end of a person is the heel;[a] seek for nothing else, Ezra, between the heel and the hand, Ezra!"

11 I answered and said, "O sovereign Lord, if I have found favor in your sight, 12 show your servant the last of your signs of which you showed me a part on a previous night."

13 He answered and said to me, "Rise to your feet and you will hear a full, resounding voice. 14 And if the place where you are standing is greatly shaken 15 while the voice is speaking, do not be terrified; because the word concerns the end, and the foundations of the earth will understand 16 that the speech concerns them. They will tremble and be shaken, for they know that their end must be changed."

17 When I heard this, I got to my feet and listened; a voice was speaking, and its sound was like the sound of mighty[b] waters. 18 It said, "The days are coming when I draw near to visit the inhabitants of the earth, 19 and when I require from the doers of iniquity the penalty of their iniquity, and when the humiliation of Zion is complete. 20 When the seal is placed upon the age that is about to pass away, then I will show these signs: the books shall be opened before the face of the firmament, and all shall see my judgment[c] together. 21 Children a year old shall speak with their voices, and pregnant women shall give birth to premature children at three and four months, and these shall live and leap about. 22 Sown places shall suddenly appear unsown, and full storehouses shall suddenly be found to be empty; 23 the trumpet shall sound aloud, and when all hear it, they shall suddenly be terrified. 24 At that time friends shall make war on friends like enemies, the earth and those who inhabit it shall be terrified, and the springs of the fountains shall stand still, so that for three hours they shall not flow.

25 "It shall be that whoever remains after all that I have foretold to you shall be saved and shall see my salvation and the end of my world. 26 And they shall see those who were taken up, who from their birth have not tasted death; and the heart of the earth's[d] inhabitants shall be changed and converted to a different spirit. 27 For evil shall be blotted out, and deceit shall be quenched; 28 faithfulness shall flourish, and corruption shall be overcome, and the truth, which has been so long without fruit, shall be revealed."

29 While he spoke to me, little by little the place where I was standing began to rock to and fro.[e] 30 And he said to me, "I have come to show you these things this night.[f] 31 If therefore you will pray again and fast again for seven days, I will again declare to you greater things than these,[g] 32 because your voice has surely been heard by the Most High; for the Mighty One has seen your uprightness and has also observed the purity that you have maintained from your youth. 33 Therefore he sent me to show you all these things, and to say to you: 'Believe and do not be afraid! 34 Do not be quick to think vain thoughts con-

---

a Syr: Meaning of Lat uncertain    b Lat many
c Syr: Lat lacks my judgment    d Syr Compare Ethiop
Arab 1 Arm: Lat lacks earth's    e Syr Ethiop Compare
Arab Arm: Meaning of Lat uncertain
f Syr Compare Ethiop: Meaning of Lat uncertain
g Syr Ethiop Arab 1 Arm: Lat adds by day

---

6.11–29: **Direct prediction of the future**, this time in response to Ezra's query (6.11–12). As in 5.1–13, the author uses classical apocalypic signs. **17:** A voice . . . like the sound of mighty waters signifies direct address by God. The image is developed from the vision of Ezekiel (Ezek 1.24–25). Compare Rev 1.15; 14.2; 19.6. **20:** The books shall be opened, the heavenly books in which are written the deeds of humankind (Dan 7.10; 12.1; Mal 3.16; cf. Ex 32.32; Ps 69.28). The motif is also common in Christian writings roughly contemporary with chs 3–14 (Lk 10.20; Heb 12.23; Rev 20.12). **23:** The trumpet shall sound, a common eschatological motif (1 Cor 15.52; 1 Thess 4.16). **26:** Those who were taken up, such as Enoch (Gen 5.24; Sir 44.16) and Elijah (2 Kings 2.11–12); cf. 14.9. **26–28:** The transition from evil to truth.

6.30–34: **The conclusion of the vision** (compare 5.14–20). **34:** The seer is cautioned against being presumptuous.

cerning the former times; then you will not act hastily in the last times.' "

35 Now after this I wept again and fasted seven days in the same way as before, in order to complete the three weeks that had been prescribed for me. 36 Then on the eighth night my heart was troubled within me again, and I began to speak in the presence of the Most High. 37 My spirit was greatly aroused, and my soul was in distress.

38 I said, "O Lord, you spoke at the beginning of creation, and said on the first day, 'Let heaven and earth be made,' and your word accomplished the work. 39 Then the spirit was blowing, and darkness and silence embraced everything; the sound of human voices was not yet there.[a] 40 Then you commanded a ray of light to be brought out from your store-chambers, so that your works could be seen.

41 "Again, on the second day, you created the spirit of the firmament, and commanded it to divide and separate the waters, so that one part might move upward and the other part remain beneath.

42 "On the third day you commanded the waters to be gathered together in a seventh part of the earth; six parts you dried up and kept so that some of them might be planted and cultivated and be of service before you. 43 For your word went forth, and at once the work was done. 44 Immediately fruit came forth in endless abundance and of varied appeal to the taste, and flowers of inimitable color, and odors of inexpressible fragrance. These were made on the third day.

45 "On the fourth day you commanded the brightness of the sun, the light of the moon, and the arrangement of the stars to come into being; 46 and you commanded them to serve humankind, about to be formed.

47 "On the fifth day you commanded the seventh part, where the water had been gathered together, to bring forth living creatures, birds, and fishes; and so it was done. 48 The dumb and lifeless water produced living creatures, as it was commanded, so that therefore the nations might declare your wondrous works.

49 "Then you kept in existence two living creatures;[b] the one you called Behemoth[c] and the name of the other Leviathan. 50 And you separated one from the other, for the seventh part where the water had been gathered together could not hold them both. 51 And you gave Behemoth[c] one of the parts that had been dried up on the third day, to live in it, where there are a thousand mountains; 52 but to Leviathan you gave the seventh part, the watery part; and you have kept them to be eaten by whom you wish, and when you wish.

53 "On the sixth day you commanded the earth to bring forth before you cattle, wild animals, and creeping things; 54 and

a Syr Ethiop: Lat *was not yet from you*
b Syr Ethiop: Lat *two souls*   c Other Lat authorities read *Enoch*

**6.35–9.25:** The third vision. **6.35–7.44:** The first section of the third vision. **35–37:** Introduction (cf. 3.1–3 and 5.21–22). **35:** *I . . . fasted seven days*, see 5.13n. *The three weeks* (cf. Dan 10.2–3), so far only two fasts of seven days have been mentioned (here and at 5.20). The author may be referring to this as Ezra's third vision.

**6.38–59:** Addressing God, the seer recounts God's work in six days of creation. If the world was created for Israel (v. 55), why has the nation not possessed its inheritance? This is similar in theme and content to the addresses in 3.4–36 and 5.23–30. **38–54:** Gen 1. **42:** *A seventh part . . . six parts,* although there is no exact parallel to this division in Genesis or other literature, explorers like Christopher Columbus took this verse as an indicator of the world's layout. **49–52:** The land creature *Behemoth* and the sea creature *Leviathan* are two primeval monsters frequently found in Israelite mythology (see Job 7.12; 26.12–13; Ps 74.12–15; 89.10–11; Isa 30.7; 51.9–10). Their eschatological function is to serve as food for the elect. **55:** *For us* (Israel) *that you created this world,* a notion developed from such passages as Ex 4.22; Deut 10.15; 14.2. See 7.11. **56:** *A drop from a bucket,* Isa 40.15 (note especially the Septuagint version).

over these you placed Adam, as ruler over all the works that you had made; and from him we have all come, the people whom you have chosen.

55 "All this I have spoken before you, O Lord, because you have said that it was for us that you created this world.[a] 56 As for the other nations that have descended from Adam, you have said that they are nothing, and that they are like spittle, and you have compared their abundance to a drop from a bucket. 57 And now, O Lord, these nations, which are reputed to be as nothing, domineer over us and devour us. 58 But we your people, whom you have called your firstborn, only begotten, zealous for you,[b] and most dear, have been given into their hands. 59 If the world has indeed been created for us, why do we not possess our world as an inheritance? How long will this be so?"

7 When I had finished speaking these words, the angel who had been sent to me on the former nights was sent to me again. 2 He said to me, "Rise, Ezra, and listen to the words that I have come to speak to you."

3 I said, "Speak, my lord." And he said to me, "There is a sea set in a wide expanse so that it is deep and vast, 4 but it has an entrance set in a narrow place, so that it is like a river. 5 If there are those who wish to reach the sea, to look at it or to navigate it, how can they come to the broad part unless they pass through the narrow part? 6 Another example: There is a city built and set on a plain, and it is full of all good things; 7 but the entrance to it is narrow and set in a precipitous place, so that there is fire on the right hand and deep water on the left. 8 There is only one path lying between them, that is, between the fire and the water, so that only one person can walk on the path. 9 If now the city is given to someone

as an inheritance, how will the heir receive the inheritance unless by passing through the appointed danger?"

10 I said, "That is right, lord." He said to me, "So also is Israel's portion. 11 For I made the world for their sake, and when Adam transgressed my statutes, what had been made was judged. 12 And so the entrances of this world were made narrow and sorrowful and toilsome; they are few and evil, full of dangers and involved in great hardships. 13 But the entrances of the greater world are broad and safe, and yield the fruit of immortality. 14 Therefore unless the living pass through the difficult and futile experiences, they can never receive those things that have been reserved for them. 15 Now therefore why are you disturbed, seeing that you are to perish? Why are you moved, seeing that you are mortal? 16 Why have you not considered in your mind what is to come, rather than what is now present?"

17 Then I answered and said, "O sovereign Lord, you have ordained in your law that the righteous shall inherit these things, but that the ungodly shall perish. 18 The righteous, therefore, can endure difficult circumstances while hoping for easier ones; but those who have done wickedly have suffered the difficult circumstances and will never see the easier ones."

19 He said to me, "You are not a better judge than the Lord,[c] or wiser than the Most High! 20 Let many perish who are now living, rather than that the law of God that is set before them be disregarded! 21 For the Lord[d] strictly commanded those who came into the world, when they came,

a Syr Ethiop Arab 2: Lat *the firstborn world* Compare Arab 1 *first world*    b Meaning of Lat uncertain    c Other ancient authorities read *God*; Ethiop Georg *the only One*    d Other ancient authorities read *God*

7.1–25: **Dispute between Ezra and the angel.** It is necessary first to undergo the trials of this world before one can receive the rewards of the next. **1:** The *former nights*, 4.1; 5.31. **3–9:** The angel tells two parables, of a sea and a city, to illustrate his point. **11:** By implication, the *world* was created entirely good for Israel's *sake, and when Adam transgressed*, that inheritance was despoiled (see 3.7,21). **12–13:** *This world* of evil is contrasted with the *greater world* to come. **17:** Deut 8.1; Ps 37.9. **17–18:** The seer exhibits a characteristic concern for *the ungodly*, but is told that their punishment is deserved (vv. 19–25).

what they should do to live, and what they should observe to avoid punishment. 22 Nevertheless they were not obedient, and spoke against him;

> they devised for themselves vain
> > thoughts,
> 23 and proposed to themselves wicked
> > frauds;
> they even declared that the Most
> > High does not exist,
> and they ignored his ways.
> 24 They scorned his law,
> and denied his covenants;
> they have been unfaithful to his
> > statutes,
> and have not performed his works.

25 That is the reason, Ezra, that empty things are for the empty, and full things are for the full.

26 "For indeed the time will come, when the signs that I have foretold to you will come to pass, that the city that now is not seen shall appear,[a] and the land that now is hidden shall be disclosed. 27 Everyone who has been delivered from the evils that I have foretold shall see my wonders. 28 For my son the Messiah[b] shall be revealed with those who are with him, and those who remain shall rejoice four hundred years. 29 After those years my son the Messiah shall die, and all who draw human breath.[c] 30 Then the world shall be turned back to primeval silence for seven days, as it was at the first beginnings, so that no one shall be left. 31 After seven days the world that is not yet awake shall be roused, and that which is corruptible shall perish.

32 The earth shall give up those who are asleep in it, and the dust those who rest there in silence; and the chambers shall give up the souls that have been committed to them. 33 The Most High shall be revealed on the seat of judgment, and compassion shall pass away, and patience shall be withdrawn.[d] 34 Only judgment shall remain, truth shall stand, and faithfulness shall grow strong. 35 Recompense shall follow, and the reward shall be manifested; righteous deeds shall awake, and unrighteous deeds shall not sleep.[e] 36 The pit[f] of torment shall appear, and opposite it shall be the place of rest; and the furnace of hell[g] shall be disclosed, and opposite it the paradise of delight. 37 Then the Most High will say to the nations that have been raised from the dead, 'Look now, and understand whom you have denied, whom you have not served, whose commandments you have despised. 38 Look on this side and on that; here are delight and rest, and there are fire and torments.' Thus he will[h] speak to them on the day of judgment— 39 a day that has no sun or moon or stars, 40 or cloud or thunder or lightning, or wind or water or air, or darkness or evening or morning, 41 or summer or spring or heat or

a Arm: Lat Syr *that the bride shall appear, even the city appearing*    b Syr Arab 1: Ethiop *my Messiah*; Arab 2 *the Messiah*; Arm *the Messiah of God*; Lat *my son Jesus*    c Arm *all who have continued in faith and in patience*    d Lat *shall gather together*
e The passage from verse 36 to verse 105, formerly missing, has been restored to the text
f Syr Ethiop: Lat *place*    g Lat Syr Ethiop *Gehenna*
h Syr Ethiop Arab 1: Lat *you shall*

**7.26–44: Direct prediction of the future by the angel,** again using classical apocalyptic *signs* (cf. 5.1–13; 6.11–29). In this section the focus is on God's judgment (cf. Mt 25.31–46). **26:** *The city,* the heavenly Jerusalem; see 10.25–54. **28:** *My son the Messiah,* a term used often in this book (see 13.32,37,52; 14.9). The precise connection between this term and Christian notions of Jesus "the Messiah" as "son of God" is uncertain, and in any event is indirect. *Those who are with him,* 13.52; 14.9. **29:** *My son the Messiah shall die,* this idea is unparalleled in other Jewish sources. **30:** *Primeval silence,* as before creation. **32:** Dan 12.2. *Chambers,* see 4.35n. Resurrection precedes the day of judgment. **33–34:** On the day of judgment, *only judgment shall remain;* mercy is put aside (see 7.104–105). **36–105:** These verses are lacking from the standard editions of the Latin Vulgate, and from the King James Version. They are present in the Syriac, Ethiopic, Arabic, and Armenian versions, and in seven Latin manuscripts. The section was probably deliberately cut out of an ancestor of most surviving Latin manuscripts because of dogmatic reasons, for the passage contains an emphatic denial of the value of prayers for the dead (v. 105). **36:** *Pit,* Isa 38.17–18; Rev 9.2. **39–43:** A description of the day of judgment;

winter[a] or frost or cold, or hail or rain or dew, 42or noon or night, or dawn or shining or brightness or light, but only the splendor of the glory of the Most High, by which all shall see what has been destined. 43It will last as though for a week of years. 44This is my judgment and its prescribed order; and to you alone I have shown these things."

45 I answered and said, "O sovereign Lord, I said then and[b] I say now: Blessed are those who are alive and keep your commandments! 46But what of those for whom I prayed? For who among the living is there that has not sinned, or who is there among mortals that has not transgressed your covenant? 47And now I see that the world to come will bring delight to few, but torments to many. 48For an evil heart has grown up in us, which has alienated us from God,[c] and has brought us into corruption and the ways of death, and has shown us the paths of perdition and removed us far from life—and that not merely for a few but for almost all who have been created."

49 He answered me and said, "Listen to me, Ezra,[d] and I will instruct you, and will admonish you once more. 50For this reason the Most High has made not one world but two. 51Inasmuch as you have said that the righteous are not many but few, while the ungodly abound, hear the explanation for this.

52 "If you have just a few precious stones, will you add to them lead and clay?"[e] 53I said, "Lord, how could that be?" 54And he said to me, "Not only that, but ask the earth and she will tell you; defer to her, and she will declare it to you. 55Say to her, 'You produce gold and silver and bronze, and also iron and lead and clay; 56but silver is more abundant than gold, and bronze than silver, and iron than bronze, and lead than iron, and clay than lead.' 57Judge therefore which things are precious and desirable, those that are abundant or those that are rare?"

58 I said, "O sovereign Lord, what is plentiful is of less worth, for what is more rare is more precious."

59 He answered me and said, "Consider within yourself[f] what you have thought, for the person who has what is hard to get rejoices more than the person who has what is plentiful. 60So also will be the judgment[g] that I have promised; for I will rejoice over the few who shall be saved, because it is they who have made my glory to prevail now, and through them my name has now been honored. 61I will not grieve over the great number of those who perish; for it is they who are now like a mist, and are similar to a flame and smoke—they are set on fire and burn hotly, and are extinguished."

62 I replied and said, "O earth, what have you brought forth, if the mind is made out of the dust like the other created things? 63For it would have been better if the dust itself had not been born, so that the mind might not have been made from it. 64But now the mind grows with us, and therefore we are tormented, because we perish and we know it. 65Let the human race lament, but let the wild animals of the

a Or storm  b Syr: Lat And I answered, "I said then, O Lord, and  c Cn: Lat Syr Ethiop from these  d Syr Arab 1 Georg: Lat Ethiop lack Ezra  e Arab 1: Meaning of Lat Syr Ethiop uncertain  f Syr Ethiop Arab 1: Meaning of Lat uncertain  g Syr Arab 1: Lat creation

cf. Gen 8.22; Zech 14.6–7. **42:** Isa 60.19–20; Rev 21.23. **43:** *A week of years,* seven years; cf. Dan 9.24,26.

**7.45–8.3:** The second section of the third vision. **45–74:** Dispute between Ezra and the angel. God rejoices over the few who will be saved and does not lament the many wicked who perish. **45–48:** Ezra again bemoans the fate of sinners. **46:** 1 Kings 8.46; Prov 20.9. **48:** *An evil heart,* see 3.20n. **52–57:** Precious as opposed to common metals and substances; see the similar arguments in 9.14–16. **62–69:** Ezra's heated lament (*better if . . . had not been born*) is typical of his reactions to the angel's arguments (see 4.12; 5.35). **64–68:** The *human race,* aware of their sins and their fate, are worse off than the blissfully ignorant *wild animals.* **72:** Humans who are sinful deserve their fate.

field be glad; let all who have been born lament, but let the cattle and the flocks rejoice. 66 It is much better with them than with us; for they do not look for a judgment, and they do not know of any torment or salvation promised to them after death. 67 What does it profit us that we shall be preserved alive but cruelly tormented? 68 For all who have been born are entangled in[a] iniquities, and are full of sins and burdened with transgressions. 69 And if after death we were not to come into judgment, perhaps it would have been better for us."

70 He answered me and said, "When the Most High made the world and Adam and all who have come from him, he first prepared the judgment and the things that pertain to the judgment. 71 But now, understand from your own words—for you have said that the mind grows with us. 72 For this reason, therefore, those who live on earth shall be tormented, because though they had understanding, they committed iniquity; and though they received the commandments, they did not keep them; and though they obtained the law, they dealt unfaithfully with what they received. 73 What, then, will they have to say in the judgment, or how will they answer in the last times? 74 How long the Most High has been patient with those who inhabit the world!— and not for their sake, but because of the times that he has foreordained."

75 I answered and said, "If I have found favor in your sight, O Lord, show this also to your servant: whether after death, as soon as everyone of us yields up the soul, we shall be kept in rest until those times come when you will renew the creation, or whether we shall be tormented at once?"

76 He answered me and said, "I will show you that also, but do not include yourself with those who have shown scorn, or number yourself among those who are tormented. 77 For you have a treasure of works stored up with the Most High, but it will not be shown to you until the last times. 78 Now concerning death, the teaching is: When the decisive decree has gone out from the Most High that a person shall die, as the spirit leaves the body to return again to him who gave it, first of all it adores the glory of the Most High. 79 If it is one of those who have shown scorn and have not kept the way of the Most High, who have despised his law and hated those who fear God— 80 such spirits shall not enter into habitations, but shall immediately wander about in torments, always grieving and sad, in seven ways. 81 The first way, because they have scorned the law of the Most High. 82 The second way, because they cannot now make a good repentance so that they may live. 83 The third way, they shall see the reward laid up for those who have trusted the covenants of the Most High. 84 The fourth way, they shall consider the torment laid up for themselves in the last days. 85 The fifth way, they shall see how the habitations of the others are guarded by angels in profound quiet. 86 The sixth way, they shall see how some of them will cross over[b] into torments. 87 The seventh way, which is worse[c] than all the ways that have been mentioned, because they shall utterly waste away in confusion and be consumed with shame,[d] and shall wither with fear at seeing the glory of the Most High in whose presence they sinned while they were alive, and in whose presence they are to be judged in the last times.

88 "Now this is the order of those who have kept the ways of the Most High, when they shall be separated from their mortal

a Syr *defiled with*   b Cn: Meaning of Lat uncertain
c Lat Syr Ethiop *greater*   d Syr Ethiop: Meaning of Lat uncertain

**7.75–101:** Dialogic prediction of the future. The state of souls after death and before the judgment. **76–77:** *Do not include yourself*, the angel repeatedly asserts that Ezra is specially favored by God (see 6.32–33; 8.19,47–54; 13.53–56; 14.9). **77:** *A treasure of works*, 8.33,36. **79–99:** The fates of two different types of souls, good and evil, are laid out in parallel fashion. **80–87:** Seven kinds of torment for the wicked; cf. Lk 16.19–31. **80:** *Habitations*, elsewhere called "chambers," see 4.35n. **88–99:** Seven kinds of joyous rest for the righteous. Compare the teaching regarding death in Dan 12.2–3; Wis 3–5. **92:**

body.[a] 89 During the time that they lived in it,[b] they laboriously served the Most High, and withstood danger every hour so that they might keep the law of the Lawgiver perfectly. 90 Therefore this is the teaching concerning them: 91 First of all, they shall see with great joy the glory of him who receives them, for they shall have rest in seven orders. 92 The first order, because they have striven with great effort to overcome the evil thought that was formed with them, so that it might not lead them astray from life into death. 93 The second order, because they see the perplexity in which the souls of the ungodly wander and the punishment that awaits them. 94 The third order, they see the witness that he who formed them bears concerning them, that throughout their life they kept the law with which they were entrusted. 95 The fourth order, they understand the rest that they now enjoy, being gathered into their chambers and guarded by angels in profound quiet, and the glory waiting for them in the last days. 96 The fifth order, they rejoice that they have now escaped what is corruptible and shall inherit what is to come; and besides they see the straits and toil[c] from which they have been delivered, and the spacious liberty that they are to receive and enjoy in immortality. 97 The sixth order, when it is shown them how their face is to shine like the sun, and how they are to be made like the light of the stars, being incorruptible from then on. 98 The seventh order, which is greater than all that have been mentioned, because they shall rejoice with boldness, and shall be confident without confusion, and shall be glad without fear, for they press forward to see the face of him whom they served in life and from whom they are to receive their reward when glorified. 99 This is the order of the souls of the righteous, as henceforth is announced;[d] and the previously mentioned are the ways of torment that those who would not give heed shall suffer hereafter."

100 Then I answered and said, "Will time therefore be given to the souls, after they have been separated from the bodies, to see what you have described to me?"

101 He said to me, "They shall have freedom for seven days, so that during these seven days they may see the things of which you have been told, and afterwards they shall be gathered in their habitations."

102 I answered and said, "If I have found favor in your sight, show further to me, your servant, whether on the day of judgment the righteous will be able to intercede for the ungodly or to entreat the Most High for them— 103 fathers for sons or sons for parents, brothers for brothers, relatives for their kindred, or friends for those who are most dear."

104 He answered me and said, "Since you have found favor in my sight, I will show you this also. The day of judgment is decisive[e] and displays to all the seal of truth. Just as now a father does not send his son, or a son his father, or a master his servant, or a friend his dearest friend, to be ill[f] or sleep or eat or be healed in his place, 105 so no one shall ever pray for another on that day, neither shall anyone lay a burden on another;[g] for then all shall bear their own righteousness and unrighteousness."

36 106 I answered and said, "How then do we find that first Abraham prayed for the people of Sodom, and Moses for our ancestors who sinned in the desert,

a Lat *the corruptible vessel*   b Syr Ethiop: Meaning of Lat uncertain   c Syr Ethiop: Lat *fullness*   d Syr: Meaning of Lat uncertain   e Lat *bold*   f Syr Ethiop Arm: Lat *to understand*   g Syr Ethiop: Lat lacks *on that . . . another*

*The evil thought*, the evil "yetser" (see 3.20n.). **97**: *Sun . . . stars*, v. 125; Dan 12.3; Mt 13.43. **98**: *To see the face* of God (Ex 33.20; 1 Jn 3.2; Rev 22.4). *Reward*, cf. Rev 22.12.

**7.102–115**: **Dispute between Ezra and the angel**, mainly concerning the idea that there will be no intercession for the evil on the day of judgment (cf. Deut 24.16; Jer 31.30; Ezek 18.1–32). **104**: *Decisive*, 7.33–34. **106**: At v. 106 we come to the continuation of ch 7 as preserved in the standard editions of the Latin Vulgate; NRSV resumes the Latin numbering here, designating verses *106–140* as 36–70, but with the numbers *106–140* in italics added as well. *Abraham*, Gen 18.23; *Moses*, Ex 32.11. **107**: *Joshua*, Josh

37 107 and Joshua after him for Israel in the days of Achan, 38 108 and Samuel in the days of Saul,ᵃ and David for the plague, and Solomon for those at the dedication, 39 109 and Elijah for those who received the rain, and for the one who was dead, that he might live, 40 110 and Hezekiah for the people in the days of Sennacherib, and many others prayed for many? 41 111 So if now, when corruption has increased and unrighteousness has multiplied, the righteous have prayed for the ungodly, why will it not be so then as well?"

42 112 He answered me and said, "This present world is not the end; the full glory does notᵇ remain in it;ᶜ therefore those who were strong prayed for the weak. 43 113 But the day of judgment will be the end of this age and the beginningᵈ of the immortal age to come, in which corruption has passed away, 44 114 sinful indulgence has come to an end, unbelief has been cut off, and righteousness has increased and truth has appeared. 45 115 Therefore no one will then be able to have mercy on someone who has been condemned in the judgment, or to harmᵉ someone who is victorious."

46 116 I answered and said, "This is my first and last comment: it would have been better if the earth had not produced Adam, or else, when it had produced him, had restrained him from sinning. 47 117 For what good is it to all that they live in sorrow now and expect punishment after death? 48 118 O Adam, what have you done? For though it was you who sinned, the fall was not yours alone, but ours also who are your descendants. 49 119 For what good is it to us, if an immortal time has been promised to us, but we have done deeds that bring death? 50 120 And what good is it that an

everlasting hope has been promised to us, but we have miserably failed? 51 121 Or that safe and healthful habitations have been reserved for us, but we have lived wickedly? 52 122 Or that the glory of the Most High will defend those who have led a pure life, but we have walked in the most wicked ways? 53 123 Or that a paradise shall be revealed, whose fruit remains unspoiled and in which are abundance and healing, but we shall not enter it 54 124 because we have lived in perverse ways?ᶠ 55 125 Or that the faces of those who practiced self-control shall shine more than the stars, but our faces shall be blacker than darkness? 56 126 For while we lived and committed iniquity we did not consider what we should suffer after death."

57 127 He answered and said, "This is the significance of the contest that all who are born on earth shall wage: 58 128 if they are defeated they shall suffer what you have said, but if they are victorious they shall receive what I have said.ᵍ 59 129 For this is the way of which Moses, while he was alive, spoke to the people, saying, 'Choose life for yourself, so that you may live!' 60 130 But they did not believe him or the prophets after him, or even myself who have spoken to them. 61 131 Therefore there shall not beʰ grief at their destruction, so much as joy over those to whom salvation is assured."

62 132 I answered and said, "I know, O Lord, that the Most High is now called

a Syr Ethiop Arab 1: Lat Arab 2 Arm lack *in the days of Saul*   b Lat lacks *not*   c Or *the glory does not continuously abide in it*   d Syr Ethiop: Lat lacks *the beginning*   e Syr Ethiop: Lat *overwhelm*   f Cn: Lat Syr *places*   g Syr Ethiop Arab 1: Lat *what I say*   h Syr: Lat *there was not*

7.6–7. **108**: *Samuel*, 1 Sam 7.9; 12.23. *David*, 2 Sam 24.17. *Solomon*, 1 Kings 8.22–23,30. **109**: *Elijah*, 1 Kings 18.42,45; 17.20–21. **110**: *Hezekiah*, 2 Kings 19.15–19. **112–115**: The angel again contrasts the present and future ages. **7.116–8.3**: Further dispute between Ezra and the angel, returning to the issue of the seeming unfairness of the human condition. **116–126**: Ezra again laments the fate of humans (cf. 4.12,22–24; 5.35; 7.62–69). **116**: *My first . . . comment*, 3.5–7. **118**: 3.7–10; 4.30–31. **123**: *Fruit*, cf. Ezek 47.12; Rev 22.2. **125**: *Shine more than the stars*, see 7.97n. *Darkness*, 1 Enoch 62.10. **127–131**: The idea of life as a *contest*, in which one can be *defeated* or *victorious*. **129**: *Moses*, Deut 30.19. **130**: *Prophets*, 2 Chr 36.15–16; cf. Mt 5.17; 23.31–37. **132–140**: As the angel had quoted scripture (Deut 30.19), the seer responds with a rabbinic exegesis, or "midrash," of Ex 34.6–7. He pleads that God *is now* merciful, because he has mercy on those who have not yet come into the world; 63 133 and gracious, because he is gracious to those who turn in repentance to his law; 64 134 and patient, because he shows patience toward those who have sinned, since they are his own creatures; 65 135 and bountiful, because he would rather give than take away;ᵃ 66 136 and abundant in compassion, because he makes his compassions abound more and more to those now living and to those who are gone and to those yet to come— 37 137 for if he did not make them abound, the world with those who inhabit it would not have life— 68 138 and he is called the giver, because if he did not give out of his goodness so that those who have committed iniquities might be relieved of them, not one ten-thousandth of humankind could have life; 69 139 and the judge, because if he did not pardon those who were created by his word and blot out the multitude of their sins,ᵇ 70 140 there would probably be left only very few of the innumerable multitude."

8 He answered me and said, "The Most High made this world for the sake of many, but the world to come for the sake of only a few. 2 But I tell you a parable, Ezra. Just as, when you ask the earth, it will tell you that it provides a large amount of clay from which earthenware is made, but only a little dust from which gold comes, so is the course of the present world. 3 Many have been created, but only a few shall be saved."

4 I answered and said, "Then drink your fill of understanding,ᶜ O my soul, and drink wisdom, O my heart. 5 For not of your own will did you come into the world,ᵈ and against your will you depart, for you have been given only a short time to live. 6 O Lord above us, grant to your servant that we may pray before you, and give us a seed for our heart and cultivation of our understanding so that fruit may be produced, by which every mortal who bears the likenessᵉ of a human being may be able to live. 7 For you alone exist, and we are a work of your hands, as you have declared. 8 And because you give life to the body that is now fashioned in the womb, and furnish it with members, what you have created is preserved amid fire and water, and for nine months the wombᶠ endures your creature that has been created in it. 9 But that which keeps and that which is kept shall both be kept by your keeping.ᵈ And when the womb gives up again what has been created in it, 10 you have commanded that from the members themselves (that is, from the breasts) milk, the fruit of the breasts, should be supplied, 11 so that what has been fashioned may be nourished for a time; and afterwards you will still guide it in your mercy. 12 You have nurtured it in your righteousness, and instructed it in your law, and reproved it in your wisdom. 13 You put it to death as your creation, and make it live as your work. 14 If then you will suddenly and quicklyᵍ destroy what with so great labor was fashioned by your command, to what purpose was it made? 15 And now I will speak out: About all humankind you know best; but I will speak about your people, for whom I am grieved, 16 and about your inheritance, for whom I lament, and about Israel, for whom I am sad, and about the seed of Jacob, for whom I am

a Or he is ready to give according to requests b Lat contempts c Syr: Lat Then release understanding d Syr: Meaning of Lat uncertain e Syr: Lat place f Lat what you have formed g Syr: Lat will with a light command

called merciful . . . and gracious . . . and patient. **138:** Life, eternal life. **8.1–3:** The angel repeats the arguments and parable used in 7.52–61.

**8.4–9.25: The third section of the third vision. 4–19a: Monologue of Ezra:** Why should God wonderfully fashion and sustain all humankind, only to destroy a great majority? **6:** Ezra seeks a seed . . . so that fruit may be produced that will counteract the effect of the evil seed . . . sown in Adam's heart (4.30). **7:** Deut 4.35; 6.4; Isa 44.6; 45.11; 60.21. **8–14:** The enigma of God's creative activity and providential care followed by destruction recalls Job 10.8–13. **15–16:** The seer leaves the fate of humankind in God's hands, and speaks particularly about Israel, God's inheritance (Ps 28.9). **17:** I will pray, in 8.19b–36.

troubled. 17 Therefore I will pray before you for myself and for them, for I see the failings of us who inhabit the earth; 18 and now also[a] I have heard of the swiftness of the judgment that is to come. 19 Therefore hear my voice and understand my words, and I will speak before you."

The beginning of the words of Ezra's prayer,[b] before he was taken up. He said: 20 "O Lord, you who inhabit eternity,[c] whose eyes are exalted[d] and whose upper chambers are in the air, 21 whose throne is beyond measure and whose glory is beyond comprehension, before whom the hosts of angels stand trembling 22 and at whose command they are changed to wind and fire,[e] whose word is sure and whose utterances are certain, whose command is strong and whose ordinance is terrible, 23 whose look dries up the depths and whose indignation makes the mountains melt away, and whose truth is established[f] forever— 24 hear, O Lord, the prayer of your servant, and give ear to the petition of your creature; attend to my words. 25 For as long as I live I will speak, and as long as I have understanding I will answer. 26 O do not look on the sins of your people, but on those who serve you in truth. 27 Do not take note of the endeavors of those who act wickedly, but of the endeavors of those who have kept your covenants amid afflictions. 28 Do not think of those who have lived wickedly in your sight, but remember those who have willingly acknowledged

that you are to be feared. 29 Do not will the destruction of those who have the ways of cattle, but regard those who have gloriously taught your law.[g] 30 Do not be angry with those who are deemed worse than wild animals, but love those who have always put their trust in your glory. 31 For we and our ancestors have passed our lives in ways that bring death;[h] but it is because of us sinners that you are called merciful. 32 For if you have desired to have pity on us, who have no works of righteousness, then you will be called merciful. 33 For the righteous, who have many works laid up with you, shall receive their reward in consequence of their own deeds. 34 But what are mortals, that you are angry with them; or what is a corruptible race, that you are so bitter against it? 35 For in truth there is no one among those who have been born who has not acted wickedly; among those who have existed[i] there is no one who has not done wrong. 36 For in this, O Lord, your righteousness and goodness will be declared, when you are merciful to those who have no store of good works."

37 He answered me and said, "Some

a Syr: Lat *but*    b Syr Ethiop; Lat *beginning of Ezra's words*    c Or *you who abide forever*
d Another Lat text reads *whose are the highest heavens*
e Syr: Lat *they whose service takes the form of wind and fire*    f Arab 2: Other authorities read *truth bears witness*    g Syr *have received the brightness of your law*    h Syr Ethiop: Meaning of Lat uncertain
i Syr: Meaning of Lat uncertain

**8.19b–36: Ezra's prayer,** a beautiful and liturgically structured piece (invocation to God, whose attributes are recalled, vv. 20–23; petitions, interspersed with confession and intercessions, vv. 24–35; concluding ascription of praise, v. 36). This prayer also occurs separately, with the title "Confessio Esdrae," in the section of canticles and hymns contained in many manuscripts of the Latin Vulgate Bible. This circumstance probably accounts for the presence (in v. 19b) of a superscription in the third person. **19b:** The words, *before he was taken up,* point to the belief that Ezra, like Enoch and Elijah, was taken up to heaven without dying (see 14.9). **21:** *Hosts of angels* are a traditional element in the description of the heavenly throne room; see 1 Kings 22.19; Isa 6.2–3; Dan 7.9–10. **22:** *Wind and fire,* Ps 104.4; Heb 1.7. **23:** *Dries up,* Isa 50.2; 51.10. *Mountains melt,* Mic 1.4; Sir 16.18–19. **26–36:** A strikingly developed series of rhetorical contrasts between sinners and the righteous introduces an appeal to the mercy of God, the quality highlighted in the influential liturgical formula found in Ex 34.6–7. **33–36:** Ezra is concerned not for those who have *many works laid up* with God (see 7.77), but for those who have *no store of good works* (v. 36).

**8.37–62a: Dispute between Ezra and the angel. 37–40:** God's reply to Ezra's prayer is characteristic (see 7.60–61; 7.127–131). As after 7.132–140, Ezra's plea for mercy goes unacknowledged. In stating things you have spoken rightly, and it will turn out according to your words. 38 For indeed I will not concern myself about the fashioning of those who have sinned, or about their death, their judgment, or their destruction; 39 but I will rejoice over the creation of the righteous, over their pilgrimage also, and their salvation, and their receiving their reward. 40 As I have spoken, therefore, so it shall be.

41 "For just as the farmer sows many seeds in the ground and plants a multitude of seedlings, and yet not all that have been sown will come up[a] in due season, and not all that were planted will take root; so also those who have been sown in the world will not all be saved."

42 I answered and said, "If I have found favor in your sight, let me speak. 43 If the farmer's seed does not come up, because it has not received your rain in due season, or if it has been ruined by too much rain, it perishes.[b] 44 But people, who have been formed by your hands and are called your own image because they are made like you, and for whose sake you have formed all things—have you also made them like the farmer's seed? 45 Surely not, O Lord[c] above! But spare your people and have mercy on your inheritance, for you have mercy on your own creation."

46 He answered me and said, "Things that are present are for those who live now, and things that are future are for those who will live hereafter. 47 For you come far short of being able to love my creation more than I love it. But you have often compared yourself[d] to the unrighteous. Never do so! 48 But even in this respect you will be praiseworthy before the Most High, 49 be-

cause you have humbled yourself, as is becoming for you, and have not considered yourself to be among the righteous. You will receive the greatest glory, 50 for many miseries will affect those who inhabit the world in the last times, because they have walked in great pride. 51 But think of your own case, and inquire concerning the glory of those who are like yourself, 52 because it is for you that paradise is opened, the tree of life is planted, the age to come is prepared, plenty is provided, a city is built, rest is appointed,[e] goodness is established and wisdom perfected beforehand. 53 The root of evil[f] is sealed up from you, illness is banished from you, and death[g] is hidden; Hades has fled and corruption has been forgotten;[h] 54 sorrows have passed away, and in the end the treasure of immortality is made manifest. 55 Therefore do not ask any more questions about the great number of those who perish. 56 For when they had opportunity to choose, they despised the Most High, and were contemptuous of his law, and abandoned his ways. 57 Moreover, they have even trampled on his righteous ones, 58 and said in their hearts that there is no God—though they knew well that they must die. 59 For just as the things that I have predicted await[i] you, so the thirst and torment that are prepared await them. For the Most High did not intend that anyone

a Syr Ethiop will live; Lat will be saved
b Cn: Compare Syr Arab 1 Arm Georg 2: Meaning of Lat uncertain   c Ethiop Arab Compare Syr: Lat lacks O Lord   d Syr Ethiop: Lat brought yourself near
e Syr Ethiop: Lat allowed   f Lat lacks of evil
g Syr Ethiop Arm: Lat lacks death   h Syr: Lat Hades and corruption have fled into oblivion; or corruption has fled into Hades to be forgotten   i Syr: Lat will receive

that God will not concern himself with sinners but will rejoice over the righteous, the angel playfully admits that Ezra has ironically spoken rightly about some things, namely, in Ezra's plea (vv. 26–36) that God ignore the wicked and pay attention only to the righteous. 41–45: To God's analogy of seeds (cf. Mt 13.3–9), Ezra protests that surely humans are more valuable than plants. 46–62a: The final divine reply: The seer is assured that his lot is with the blessed and is advised to think no more about sinners, who deserve their doom because they have despised the Most High (v. 56). 46: 7.14–18,25. 47: See 5.33; 7.76–77n. 48–54: The angel praises Ezra's character and offers a list of delights awaiting those who are like him (see 14.9). 52: Paradise, 7.123; tree of life, Gen 2.9; Rev 2.7; 22.2. City, the heavenly Jerusalem; see 10.27,44,54. 53: Hades, the realm of the dead. 58: Ps 14.1; 53.1. 59: Torment, 7.80–87. 61: Drawing near, see 4.50; 5.55. 62: A few like you, see 8.51; 14.9,46.

should be destroyed; [60] but those who were created have themselves defiled the name of him who made them, and have been ungrateful to him who prepared life for them now. [61] Therefore my judgment is now drawing near; [62] I have not shown this to all people, but only to you and a few like you."

Then I answered and said, [63] "O Lord, you have already shown me a great number of the signs that you will do in the last times, but you have not shown me when you will do them."

**9** He answered me and said, "Measure carefully in your mind, and when you see that some of the predicted signs have occurred, [2] then you will know that it is the very time when the Most High is about to visit the world that he has made. [3] So when there shall appear in the world earthquakes, tumult of peoples, intrigues of nations, wavering of leaders, confusion of princes, [4] then you will know that it was of these that the Most High spoke from the days that were of old, from the beginning. [5] For just as with everything that has occurred in the world, the beginning is evident,[a] and the end manifest; [6] so also are the times of the Most High: the beginnings are manifest in wonders and mighty works, and the end in penalties[b] and in signs.

[7] "It shall be that all who will be saved and will be able to escape on account of their works, or on account of the faith by which they have believed, [8] will survive the dangers that have been predicted, and will see my salvation in my land and within my borders, which I have sanctified for myself from the beginning. [9] Then those who have now abused my ways shall be amazed, and those who have rejected them with con-

tempt shall live in torments. [10] For as many as did not acknowledge me in their lifetime, though they received my benefits, [11] and as many as scorned my law while they still had freedom, and did not understand but despised it[c] while an opportunity of repentance was still open to them, [12] these must in torment acknowledge it[c] after death. [13] Therefore, do not continue to be curious about how the ungodly will be punished; but inquire how the righteous will be saved, those to whom the age belongs and for whose sake the age was made."[d]

[14] I answered and said, [15] "I said before, and I say now, and will say it again: there are more who perish than those who will be saved, [16] as a wave is greater than a drop of water."

[17] He answered me and said, "As is the field, so is the seed; and as are the flowers, so are the colors; and as is the work, so is the product; and as is the farmer, so is the threshing floor. [18] For there was a time in this age when I was preparing for those who now exist, before the world was made for them to live in, and no one opposed me then, for no one existed; [19] but now those who have been created in this world, which is supplied both with an unfailing table and an inexhaustible pasture,[e] have become corrupt in their ways. [20] So I considered my world, and saw that it was lost. I saw that my earth was in peril because of the devices of those who[f] had come into it. [21] And I saw and spared some[g] with great difficul-

---

a Syr: Ethiop *is in the word*; Meaning of Lat uncertain
b Syr: Lat Ethiop *in effects*    c Or *me*
d Syr: Lat *saved, and whose is the age and for whose sake the age was made and when*    e Cn: Lat *law*
f Cn: Lat *devices that*    g Lat *them*

---

**8.62b–9.22**: Direct prediction of the future by the angel, now in response to Ezra's request, and again using the key word *signs* (v. 63) (cf. 5.1–13; 6.11–29; 7.26–44). **63**: *When*, see 4.33; Mk 13.4. **9.1–3**: The author uses classical apocalyptic signs (see Mk 13.7–8,29). **7**: *Able to escape*, cf. Mk 13.14–16. The author counts both *works* and *faith* as valid criteria for salvation. **8**: *See my salvation*, cf. Mk 13.13. *Within my borders*, 12.34; 13.48. **9**: *Torments*, 7.79–87. **11**: *Scorned . . . despised*, 7.22–24,37,72,79–81; 8.56–60. **13**: 8.38–39,55. *For whose sake*, 6.59; 7.11. **14–22**: The final explanation of why so few are saved: The many *have become corrupt in their ways*. Cf. Gen 6.5, where the corruption of humankind provokes the flood, which kills all but Noah and his family. **22**: *Let the multitude perish*, God disclaims responsibility for the fates of the mass of humanity.

ty, and saved for myself one grape out of a cluster, and one plant out of a great forest.[a] 22 So let the multitude perish that has been born in vain, but let my grape and my plant be saved, because with much labor I have perfected them.

23 "Now, if you will let seven days more pass—do not, however, fast during them, 24 but go into a field of flowers where no house has been built, and eat only of the flowers of the field, and taste no meat and drink no wine, but eat only flowers— 25 and pray to the Most High continually, then I will come and talk with you."

26 So I went, as he directed me, into the field that is called Ardat;[b] there I sat among the flowers and ate of the plants of the field, and the nourishment they afforded satisfied me. 27 After seven days, while I lay on the grass, my heart was troubled again as it was before. 28 Then my mouth was opened, and I began to speak before the Most High, and said, 29 "O Lord, you showed yourself among us, to our ancestors in the wilderness when they came out from Egypt and when they came into the untrodden and unfruitful wilderness; 30 and you said, 'Hear me, O Israel, and give heed to my words, O descendants of Jacob. 31 For I sow my law in you, and it shall bring forth fruit in you, and you shall be glorified through it forever.' 32 But though our ancestors received the law, they did not keep it and did not observe the[c] statutes; yet the fruit of the law did not perish—for it could not, because it was yours. 33 Yet those who received it perished, because they did not keep what had been sown in them. 34 Now this is the general rule that, when the ground has received seed, or the sea a ship, or any dish food or drink, and when it comes about that what was sown or what was launched or what was put in is destroyed, 35 they are destroyed, but the things that held them remain; yet with us it has not been so. 36 For we who have received the law and sinned will perish, as well as our hearts that received it; 37 the law, however, does not perish but survives in its glory."

38 When I said these things in my heart, I looked around,[d] and on my right I saw a woman; she was mourning and weeping with a loud voice, and was deeply grieved at heart; her clothes were torn, and there were ashes on her head. 39 Then I dismissed the thoughts with which I had been engaged, and turned to her 40 and said to her, "Why are you weeping, and why are you grieved at heart?"

41 She said to me, "Let me alone, my lord, so that I may weep for myself and continue to mourn, for I am greatly embittered in spirit and deeply distressed."

42 I said to her, "What has happened to you? Tell me."

43 And she said to me, "Your servant was barren and had no child, though I lived with my husband for thirty years. 44 Every hour and every day during those thirty

a Syr Ethiop Arab 1: Lat *tribe*    b Syr Ethiop *Arpad*; Arm *Ardab*    c Lat *my*    d Syr Arab Arm: Lat *I looked about me with my eyes*

9.23–25: **Conclusion and injunctions.** Ezra's prescribed diet of *flowers* recalls Dan 1.8–16 (cf. 2 Macc 5.27).

9.26–10.59: **The fourth vision. 26–28: Introduction. 26:** *Ardat*, an unknown location. **27:** *As it was before*, before each of the first three visions.

9.29–37: **Ezra's address.** Instead of challenging God, as he had done in the first three visions, Ezra praises the *law*, which *survives in its glory* despite the perishing of humankind, its vessel. **29:** An allusion to the theophany at Mt. Sinai, Ex 19.9; 24.10; Deut 4.12. **30–37:** Unlike the normal case, where the container outlasts what is placed in it, with humankind it is just the opposite: We perish, while God's law, implanted within us, survives intact. **31:** See 3.20.

9.38–10.4: **The first part of the vision.** Ezra converses with a disconsolate woman. The sudden departure from the pattern of the first three visions, wherein the angel had appeared, signals a shift in tone. **38:** *Clothes were torn, ashes*, signs of mourning; Josh 7.6; Job 2.12–13. **40:** Now it is the woman who is *weeping* and *grieved*, as Ezra had been during the first three visions. **45:** *After thirty years*, see 3.1. Like years I prayed to the Most High, night and day. 45 And after thirty years God heard your servant, and looked upon my low estate, and considered my distress, and gave me a son. I rejoiced greatly over him, I and my husband and all my neighbors;ᵃ and we gave great glory to the Mighty One. 46 And I brought him up with much care. 47 So when he grew up and I came to take a wife for him, I set a day for the marriage feast.

10 "But it happened that when my son entered his wedding chamber, he fell down and died. 2 So all of us put out our lamps, and all my neighborsᵃ attempted to console me; I remained quiet until the evening of the second day. 3 But when all of them had stopped consoling me, encouraging me to be quiet, I got up in the night and fled, and I came to this field, as you see. 4 And now I intend not to return to the town, but to stay here; I will neither eat nor drink, but will mourn and fast continually until I die."

5 Then I broke off the reflections with which I was still engaged, and answered her in anger and said, 6 "You most foolish of women, do you not see our mourning, and what has happened to us? 7 For Zion, the mother of us all, is in deep grief and great distress. 8 It is most appropriate to mourn now, because we are all mourning, and to be sorrowful, because we are all sorrowing; you are sorrowing for one son, but we, the whole world, for our mother.ᵇ 9 Now ask the earth, and she will tell you that it is she who ought to mourn over so many who have come into being upon her. 10 From the beginning all have been born of her, and others will come; and, lo, almost all goᶜ to perdition, and a multitude of them will come to doom. 11 Who then ought to mourn the more, she who lost so great a multitude, or you who are grieving for one alone? 12 But if you say to me, 'My lamentation is not like the earth's, for I have lost the fruit of my womb, which I brought forth in pain and bore in sorrow; 13 but it is with the earth according to the way of the earth—the multitude that is now in it goes as it came'; 14 then I say to you, 'Just as you brought forth in sorrow, so the earth also has from the beginning given her fruit, that is, humankind, to him who made her.' 15 Now, therefore, keep your sorrow to yourself, and bear bravely the troubles that have come upon you. 16 For if you acknowledge the decree of God to be just, you will receive your son back in due time, and will be praised among women. 17 Therefore go into the town to your husband."

18 She said to me, "I will not do so; I will not go into the city, but I will die here."

19 So I spoke again to her, and said, 20 "Do not do that, but let yourself be persuaded—for how many are the adversities of Zion?—and be consoled because of the sorrow of Jerusalem. 21 For you see how

a Literally all my citizens    b Compare Syr: Meaning of Lat uncertain    c Literally walk

Sarah (Gen 18.11–14), Hannah (1 Sam 1.20), and Elizabeth (Lk 1.24), the woman conceives a child in her old age. **10.1:** Cf. Tob 7.11; 8.10. **4:** *Mourn and fast,* as Ezra had done previously.
**10.5–24: The second part of the vision.** Ezra tries to convince the woman of the relative insignificance of her own sorrows in relation to the broader concerns of *the whole world* (v. 8), just as the angel had done with Ezra in the earlier visions. **5:** *Broke off the reflections:* As before (*dismissed the thoughts,* 9.39), Ezra is forced to leave aside his prior concerns. **5–6:** *In anger . . . you most foolish,* Ezra's highly emotional disposition, evident in the first three visions, continues here, but is redirected. **7:** *Zion, the mother of us all,* Bar 4.8–5.9. **9:** *Ask the earth,* who is also the mother of all humankind (v. 10). Thus, the figure of the mother functions on three levels: Ezra's interlocutor, Zion (Jerusalem), and the whole earth. **10:** This is the perspective Ezra refused to accept in the third vision. **16:** *If you acknowledge,* as the angel had earlier encouraged Ezra to do. *You will receive your son back in due time,* perhaps in the resurrection; 2 Macc 7.29. **18:** *I will not,* the woman's stubbornness recalls Ezra's earlier attitude. **21–23:** Ezra sadly recalls the desolation of Jerusalem (cf. Lam 1.10; 2.7; 1 Macc 1.36–40; 2.7–13); ultimately, this refers to the destruction of the city in 70 CE. **22:** *Harp* symbolizes the service of praise. The extinction

our sanctuary has been laid waste, our altar thrown down, our temple destroyed; 22 our harp has been laid low, our song has been silenced, and our rejoicing has been ended; the light of our lampstand has been put out, the ark of our covenant has been plundered, our holy things have been polluted, and the name by which we are called has been almost profaned; our children[a] have suffered abuse, our priests have been burned to death, our Levites have gone into exile, our virgins have been defiled, and our wives have been ravished; our righteous men[b] have been carried off, our little ones have been cast out, our young men have been enslaved and our strong men made powerless. 23 And, worst of all, the seal of Zion has been deprived of its glory, and given over into the hands of those that hate us. 24 Therefore shake off your great sadness and lay aside your many sorrows, so that the Mighty One may be merciful to you again, and the Most High may give you rest, a respite from your troubles."

25 While I was talking to her, her face suddenly began to shine exceedingly; her countenance flashed like lightning, so that I was too frightened to approach her, and my heart was terrified. While[c] I was wondering what this meant, 26 she suddenly uttered a loud and fearful cry, so that the earth shook at the sound. 27 When I looked up, the woman was no longer visible to me, but a city was being built,[d] and a place of huge foundations showed itself. I was afraid, and cried with a loud voice and said, 28 "Where is the angel Uriel, who came to

me at first? For it was he who brought me into this overpowering bewilderment; my end has become corruption, and my prayer a reproach."

29 While I was speaking these words, the angel who had come to me at first came to me, and when he saw me 30 lying there like a corpse, deprived of my understanding, he grasped my right hand and strengthened me and set me on my feet, and said to me, 31 "What is the matter with you? And why are you troubled? And why are your understanding and the thoughts of your mind troubled?"

32 I said, "It was because you abandoned me. I did as you directed, and went out into the field, and lo, what I have seen and can still see, I am unable to explain."

33 He said to me, "Stand up like a man, and I will instruct you."

34 I said, "Speak, my lord; only do not forsake me, so that I may not die before my time.[e] 35 For I have seen what I did not know, and I hear[f] what I do not understand 36 —or is my mind deceived, and my soul dreaming? 37 Now therefore I beg you to give your servant an explanation of this bewildering vision."

38 He answered me and said, "Listen to me, and I will teach you, and tell you about the things that you fear; for the Most High

---

a Ethiop *free men*   b Syr *our seers*
c Syr Ethiop Arab 1: Lat lacks *I was too . . . terrified. While*   d Lat: Syr Ethiop Arab 1 Arab 2 Arm *but there was an established city*   e Syr Ethiop Arab: Lat *die to no purpose*   f Other ancient authorities read *have heard*

---

of the perpetually burning lamp marked the cessation of Temple services. *Our holy things* are enumerated in 1 Macc 4.49–51. *The name* "Israel" was bestowed by God (Gen 32.28). **24:** In Ezra's final words to the woman, he has fully become a consoler to her, just as the angel earlier had been to him.

**10.25–27a: A vision of the transformed Jerusalem. 25:** *Suddenly began to shine,* the figure of the woman had only been a foil for the inner transformation of Ezra, who is now worthy to receive the vision. **27:** *A city was being built,* Zech 2.1–5; Rev 21.9–21. Jerusalem, whose destruction was movingly described in vv. 21–23, is being transformed or rebuilt in a way open only to visionary experience.

**10.27b–37: The appearance of the angel. 28:** *At first,* 4.1. Although the angel (Uriel; 4.1) has had no part in this vision, it is he upon whom Ezra immediately calls for guidance. **30:** *Like a corpse,* cf. Dan 8.18; 10.9; Rev 1.17. **32:** *And can still see,* the vision is still before the seer's eyes. The seer is *unable to explain* the vision, much as he had earlier been unable to come to terms with the angel's more rational explanations. **33:** Cf. Job 38.3; 40.7; see 5.15; 6.13,17; 7.2.

**10.38–54: Interpretation of the vision. 38–39:** See 7.76–77n. **44:** *Zion,* the transformed Jerusalem.

has revealed many secrets to you. 39 He has seen your righteous conduct, and that you have sorrowed continually for your people and mourned greatly over Zion. 40 This therefore is the meaning of the vision. 41 The woman who appeared to you a little while ago, whom you saw mourning and whom you began to console 42 (you do not now see the form of a woman, but there appeared to you a city being built)ᵃ 43 and who told you about the misfortune of her son—this is the interpretation: 44 The woman whom you saw is Zion, which you now behold as a city being built.ᵇ 45 And as for her telling you that she was barren for thirty years, the reason is that there were three thousandᶜ years in the world before any offering was offered in it.ᵈ 46 And after three thousandᵉ years Solomon built the city, and offered offerings; then it was that the barren woman bore a son. 47 And as for her telling you that she brought him up with much care, that was the period of residence in Jerusalem. 48 And as for her saying to you, 'My son died as he entered his wedding chamber,' and that misfortune had overtaken her,ᶠ this was the destruction that befell Jerusalem. 49 So you saw her likeness, how she mourned for her son, and you began to console her for what had happened.ᵍ 50 For now the Most High, seeing that you are sincerely grieved and profoundly distressed for her, has shown you the brilliance of her glory, and the loveliness of her beauty. 51 Therefore I told you to remain in the field where no house had been built, 52 for I knew that the Most High

would reveal these things to you. 53 Therefore I told you to go into the field where there was no foundation of any building, 54 because no work of human construction could endure in a place where the city of the Most High was to be revealed.

55 "Therefore do not be afraid, and do not let your heart be terrified; but go in and see the splendor orʰ the vastness of the building, as far as it is possible for your eyes to see it, 56 and afterward you will hear as much as your ears can hear. 57 For you are more blessed than many, and you have been called to be withⁱ the Most High as few have been. 58 But tomorrow night you shall remain here, 59 and the Most High will show you in those dream visions what the Most High will do to those who inhabit the earth in the last days."

So I slept that night and the following one, as he had told me.

11 On the second night I had a dream: I saw rising from the sea an eagle that had twelve feathered wings and three heads. 2 I saw it spread its wings overʲ the whole earth, and all the winds of heaven blew upon it, and the clouds were gathered around it.ᵏ 3 I saw that out of its wings there grew opposing wings; but they be-

a Lat: Syr Ethiop Arab 1 Arab 2 Arm *an established city*    b Cn: Lat *an established city*    c Most Lat Mss read *three*    d Cn: Lat Syr Arab Arm *her*    e Syr Ethiop Arab Arm: Lat *three*    f Or *him*    g Most Lat Mss and Arab 1 add *These were the things to be opened to you*    h Other ancient authorities read *and*    i Or *been named by*    j Arab 2 Arm: Lat Syr Ethiop *in*    k Syr: Compare Ethiop Arab: Lat lacks *the clouds* and *around it*

**46:** *A son,* the historical Jerusalem. *Solomon,* although David established Jerusalem as an Israelite city, Solomon built the Temple (1 Kings 5–6). **48:** *The destruction,* see 10.21–23 and note. In its context, this passage refers to the destruction of Jerusalem in 586 BCE. **49:** *Zion,* in the universal sense, *mourned for* the destruction of her physical manifestation, the earthly city. **49–50:** Ezra's vision is a direct reward for his sincere consolation of the mourning woman.

**10.55–59: Conclusion and injunctions. 55–56:** *Go in and see,* the city is conceived as still present to Ezra (see vv. 32,44). **59:** The remainder of the book will consist of "dream visions" rather than argumentation.

**11.1–12.51: The fifth vision (the eagle vision). 11.1–12.3a: Description of the vision. 1:** The interpretation of the fifth vision that is set forth in the notes to 11.1–12.3a anticipates that given in the text of 2 Esdras itself in 12.10–36. *From the sea,* Dan 7.3; Rev 13.1. *An eagle,* symbol of the Roman Empire. **2:** *Spread its wings,* asserted its dominion. *The winds,* 13.2; Dan 7.2. At the time of 4 Ezra's composition, the Romans ruled almost the *whole* inhabited *earth.* **3:** *Opposing wings,* symbolizing usurpers who came little, puny wings. 4 But its heads were at rest; the middle head was larger than the other heads, but it too was at rest with them. 5 Then I saw that the eagle flew with its wings, and it reigned over the earth and over those who inhabit it. 6 And I saw how all things under heaven were subjected to it, and no one spoke against it—not a single creature that was on the earth. 7 Then I saw the eagle rise upon its talons, and it uttered a cry to its wings, saying, 8 "Do not all watch at the same time; let each sleep in its own place, and watch in its turn; 9 but let the heads be reserved for the last."

10 I looked again and saw that the voice did not come from its heads, but from the middle of its body. 11 I counted its rival wings, and there were eight of them. 12 As I watched, one wing on the right side rose up, and it reigned over all the earth. 13 And after a time its reign came to an end, and it disappeared, so that even its place was no longer visible. Then the next wing rose up and reigned, and it continued to reign a long time. 14 While it was reigning its end came also, so that it disappeared like the first. 15 And a voice sounded, saying to it, 16 "Listen to me, you who have ruled the earth all this time; I announce this to you before you disappear. 17 After you no one shall rule as long as you have ruled, not even half as long."

18 Then the third wing raised itself up, and held the rule as the earlier ones had done, and it also disappeared. 19 And so it went with all the wings; they wielded power one after another and then were never seen again. 20 I kept looking, and in due time the wings that followed[a] also rose up on the right[b] side, in order to rule. There were some of them that ruled, yet disappeared suddenly; 21 and others of them rose up, but did not hold the rule.

22 And after this I looked and saw that the twelve wings and the two little wings had disappeared, 23 and nothing remained on the eagle's body except the three heads that were at rest and six little wings.

24 As I kept looking I saw that two little wings separated from the six and remained under the head that was on the right side; but four remained in their place. 25 Then I saw that these little wings[c] planned to set themselves up and hold the rule. 26 As I kept looking, one was set up, but suddenly disappeared; 27 a second also, and this disappeared more quickly than the first. 28 While I continued to look the two that remained were planning between themselves to reign together; 29 and while they were planning, one of the heads that were at rest (the one that was in the middle) suddenly awoke; it was greater than the other two heads. 30 And I saw how it allied the two heads with itself, 31 and how the head turned with those that were with it and devoured the two little wings[c] that were planning to reign. 32 Moreover this head gained control of the whole earth, and with much oppression dominated its inhabitants; it had greater power over the world than all the wings that had gone before.

33 After this I looked again and saw the head in the middle suddenly disappear, just as the wings had done. 34 But the two heads remained, which also in like manner ruled over the earth and its inhabitants. 35 And while I looked, I saw the head on the right side devour the one on the left.

36 Then I heard a voice saying to me, "Look in front of you and consider what you see." 37 When I looked, I saw what seemed to be a lion roused from the forest, roaring; and I heard how it uttered a human voice to the eagle, and spoke, saying, 38 "Listen and I will speak to you. The Most High says to you, 39 'Are you not the

a Syr Arab 2 *the little wings*   b Some Ethiop Mss read *left*   c Syr: Lat *underwings*

revolted against the Roman emperors. *But they became little,* they were subdued. **11:** *Rival wings,* the *opposing wings* of v. 3. **13:** *Its reign came to an end,* the ruler symbolized by the wing perished. **35:** At this point, only the *head on the right* and the two little wings under it remain. **37:** The *lion* is a symbol of the messiah; cf. Rev 5.5. **39:** *Four beasts,* Dan 7. In Daniel, however, the fourth beast is not an eagle but a horned monster. **40:** *With grievous oppression,* at this time in history, after the Romans had one that remains of the four beasts that I had made to reign in my world, so that the end of my times might come through them? [40] You, the fourth that has come, have conquered all the beasts that have gone before; and you have held sway over the world with great terror, and over all the earth with grievous oppression; and for so long you have lived on the earth with deceit.[a] [41] You have judged the earth, but not with truth, [42] for you have oppressed the meek and injured the peaceable; you have hated those who tell the truth, and have loved liars; you have destroyed the homes of those who brought forth fruit, and have laid low the walls of those who did you no harm. [43] Your insolence has come up before the Most High, and your pride to the Mighty One. [44] The Most High has looked at his times; now they have ended, and his ages have reached completion. [45] Therefore you, eagle, will surely disappear, you and your terrifying wings, your most evil little wings, your malicious heads, your most evil talons, and your whole worthless body, [46] so that the whole earth, freed from your violence, may be refreshed and relieved, and may hope for the judgment and mercy of him who made it.' "

12 While the lion was saying these words to the eagle, I looked [2] and saw that the remaining head had disappeared. The two wings that had gone over to it rose up and[b] set themselves up to reign, and their reign was brief and full of tumult. [3] When I looked again, they were already vanishing. The whole body of the eagle was burned, and the earth was exceedingly terrified.

Then I woke up in great perplexity of mind and great fear, and I said to my spirit,

[4] "You have brought this upon me, because you search out the ways of the Most High. [5] I am still weary in mind and very weak in my spirit, and not even a little strength is left in me, because of the great fear with which I have been terrified tonight. [6] Therefore I will now entreat the Most High that he may strengthen me to the end."

7 Then I said, "O sovereign Lord, if I have found favor in your sight, and if I have been accounted righteous before you beyond many others, and if my prayer has indeed come up before your face, [8] strengthen me and show me, your servant, the interpretation and meaning of this terrifying vision so that you may fully comfort my soul. [9] For you have judged me worthy to be shown the end of the times and the last events of the times."

10 He said to me, "This is the interpretation of this vision that you have seen: [11] The eagle that you saw coming up from the sea is the fourth kingdom that appeared in a vision to your brother Daniel. [12] But it was not explained to him as I now explain to you or have explained it. [13] The days are coming when a kingdom shall rise on earth, and it shall be more terrifying than all the kingdoms that have been before it. [14] And twelve kings shall reign in it, one after another. [15] But the second that is to reign shall hold sway for a longer time than any other one of the twelve. [16] This is the interpretation of the twelve wings that you saw.

17 "As for your hearing a voice that spoke, coming not from the eagle's[c] heads but from the midst of its body, this is the

a Syr Arab Arm: Lat Ethiop *The fourth came, however, and conquered . . . and held sway . . . and for so long lived*    b Ethiop: Lat lacks *rose up and*    c Lat *his*

destroyed Jerusalem and its Temple, they were considered evil oppressors by the Jews. **44:** God's judgment of the fourth beast is a sign that the *ages have reached completion.*

**12.3b–9: The seer's response.** Ezra, terrified, seeks an explanation of the vision (cf. 10.27–37; 13.13b–20).

**12.10–36: The interpretation. 11:** *The fourth kingdom* in Daniel's vision (Dan 7.7) symbolized the Greek or Macedonian Empire; here, however, it is reinterpreted (cf. v. 12) to refer to the Roman Empire (see 11.1n.; 11.39n.). **13:** *The days are coming,* since the seer is represented as prophesying during the exile, the rise of the Roman Empire is depicted as a future event. **15:** *The second* king is Caesar Augustus (ruled 27 BCE–14 CE). **18:** There is nothing in the vision that corresponds to what is said in this verse.

interpretation: [18] In the midst of[a] the time of that kingdom great struggles shall arise, and it shall be in danger of falling; nevertheless it shall not fall then, but shall regain its former power.[b] [19] As for your seeing eight little wings[c] clinging to its wings, this is the interpretation: [20] Eight kings shall arise in it, whose times shall be short and their years swift; [21] two of them shall perish when the middle of its time draws near; and four shall be kept for the time when its end approaches, but two shall be kept until the end.

22 "As for your seeing three heads at rest, this is the interpretation: [23] In its last days the Most High will raise up three kings,[d] and they[e] shall renew many things in it, and shall rule the earth [24] and its inhabitants more oppressively than all who were before them. Therefore they are called the heads of the eagle, [25] because it is they who shall sum up his wickedness and perform his last actions. [26] As for your seeing that the large head disappeared, one of the kings[f] shall die in his bed, but in agonies. [27] But as for the two who remained, the sword shall devour them. [28] For the sword of one shall devour him who was with him; but he also shall fall by the sword in the last days.

29 "As for your seeing two little wings[g] passing over to[h] the head which was on the right side, [30] this is the interpretation: It is these whom the Most High has kept for the eagle's[i] end; this was the reign which was brief and full of tumult, as you have seen.

31 "And as for the lion whom you saw rousing up out of the forest and roaring and speaking to the eagle and reproving him for his unrighteousness, and as for all his words that you have heard, [32] this is the Messiah[j] whom the Most High has kept until the end of days, who will arise from the offspring of David, and will come and speak[k] with them. He will denounce them for their ungodliness and for their wickedness, and will display before them their contemptuous dealings. [33] For first he will bring them alive before his judgment seat, and when he has reproved them, then he will destroy them. [34] But in mercy he will set free the remnant of my people, those who have been saved throughout my borders, and he will make them joyful until the end comes, the day of judgment, of which I spoke to you at the beginning. [35] This is the dream that you saw, and this is its interpretation. [36] And you alone were worthy to learn this secret of the Most High. [37] Therefore write all these things that you have seen in a book, put it[l] in a hidden place; [38] and you shall teach them to the wise among your people, whose hearts you know are able to comprehend and keep these secrets. [39] But as for you, wait here seven days more, so that you may be shown whatever it pleases the Most High to show you." Then he left me.

40 When all the people heard that the

a Syr Arm: Lat After    b Ethiop Arab 1 Arm: Lat Syr its beginning    c Syr: Lat underwings
d Syr Ethiop Arab Arm: Lat kingdoms
e Syr Ethiop Arm: Lat he    f Lat them
g Arab 1: Lat underwings    h Syr Ethiop: Lat lacks to
i Lat his    j Literally anointed one    k Syr: Lat lacks
of days . . . and speak    l Ethiop Arab 1 Arab 2 Arm:
Lat Syr them

The author may refer to the time of great struggles for power that followed the death of Nero in 68 CE. 19: Little wings, 11.3,11. 20–21: These apparently represent imperial usurpers or pretenders; they cannot be identified precisely. 22: Three heads, the Flavian emperors (Vespasian, 69–79 CE; Titus, 79–81; and Domitian, 81–96). 23–24: 11.30–32. 26: The large head, Vespasian. Vespasian did die in his bed, perhaps a rarity for Roman emperors, but the attendant agonies are otherwise unattested. 30: As you have seen, vv. 2–3. 32: Messiah, 7.28–29n.; 1 Enoch 62.7. 33: Here, unlike earlier in the book (6.6; 7.28–44), the Messiah functions as eschatological judge. 34: Throughout my borders, 9.8; 13.48. He will make them joyful, 7.28. This verse envisions a second day of judgment after that described in v. 33.

12.37–39: Conclusion and injunctions. 37–38: The angel's command to write a secret book for the wise anticipates 14.23–26,37–48 (cf. Isa 8.16; Dan 12.3–4; Rev 1.11; 22.10).

12.40–51: The seer comforts those who were grieved because of his absence (cf. 5.16–19). 40: The seven days were past and I had not returned to the city, they all gathered together, from the least to the greatest, and came to me and spoke to me, saying, 41 "How have we offended you, and what harm have we done you, that you have forsaken us and sit in this place? 42 For of all the prophets you alone are left to us, like a cluster of grapes from the vintage, and like a lamp in a dark place, and like a haven for a ship saved from a storm. 43 Are not the disasters that have befallen us enough? 44 Therefore if you forsake us, how much better it would have been for us if we also had been consumed in the burning of Zion. 45 For we are no better than those who died there." And they wept with a loud voice.

Then I answered them and said, 46 "Take courage, O Israel; and do not be sorrowful, O house of Jacob; 47 for the Most High has you in remembrance, and the Mighty One has not forgotten you in your struggle. 48 As for me, I have neither forsaken you nor withdrawn from you; but I have come to this place to pray on account of the desolation of Zion, and to seek mercy on account of the humiliation of our*a* sanctuary. 49 Now go to your homes, every one of you, and after these days I will come to you." 50 So the people went into the city, as I told them to do. 51 But I sat in the field seven days, as the angel*b* had commanded me; and I ate only of the flowers of the field, and my food was of plants during those days.

13 After seven days I dreamed a dream in the night. 2 And lo, a wind arose from the sea and stirred up*c* all its waves. 3 As I kept looking the wind made something like the figure of a man come up out of the heart of the sea. And I saw*d* that this man flew*e* with the clouds of heaven; and wherever he turned his face to look, everything under his gaze trembled, 4 and whenever his voice issued from his mouth, all who heard his voice melted as wax melts*f* when it feels the fire.

5 After this I looked and saw that an innumerable multitude of people were gathered together from the four winds of heaven to make war against the man who came up out of the sea. 6 And I looked and saw that he carved out for himself a great mountain, and flew up on to it. 7 And I tried to see the region or place from which the mountain was carved, but I could not.

8 After this I looked and saw that all who had gathered together against him, to wage war with him, were filled with fear, and yet they dared to fight. 9 When he saw the onrush of the approaching multitude, he neither lifted his hand nor held a spear or any weapon of war; 10 but I saw only how he sent forth from his mouth something like a stream of fire, and from his lips a flaming breath, and from his tongue he shot forth a storm of sparks.*g* 11 All these were mingled together, the stream of fire and the flaming breath and the great storm, and fell on the onrushing multitude that was prepared to fight, and burned up all of them, so that suddenly nothing was seen of the innumerable multitude but only the dust of ashes and the smell of smoke. When I saw it, I was amazed.

12 After this I saw the same man come

---

*a* Syr Ethiop: Lat *your*  *b* Literally *he*
*c* Other ancient authorities read *I saw a wind arise from the sea and stir up*  *d* Syr: Lat lacks *the wind . . . I saw*  *e* Syr Ethiop Arab Arm: Lat *grew strong*
*f* Syr: Lat *burned as the earth rests*
*g* Meaning of Lat uncertain

---

*seven days,* 9.23,27. **42:** Only here and in 1.1 in the biblical and apocryphal literature is Ezra called a prophet. **44–45:** The people's lament recalls Ezra's earlier words (4.12; 5.35; 7.63). **46–47:** Ezra's reply in turn recalls the earlier encouragement of the angel. **51:** 9.24–26. Ezra's vegetarian diet is clearly linked to the onset of his dream visions.

**13.1–58:** The sixth vision (the man from the sea). **1–13a:** Description of the vision. **2:** *A wind . . . from the sea,* 11.1–2; Dan 7.2. **3:** *Something like the figure of a man,* a messianic figure (cf. Dan 7.13), later in the vision called God's *Son* (13.32). *Flew with the clouds,* Isa 19.1; Dan 7.13; Mk 13.26; Rev 1.7. **4:** *As wax melts,* Mic 1.4; Jdt 16.15. **5:** *Four winds of heaven,* Dan 7.2. **6:** *Carved out,* Dan 2.45. **10:** Isa down from the mountain and call to himself another multitude that was peaceable. [13] Then many people[a] came to him, some of whom were joyful and some sorrowful; some of them were bound, and some were bringing others as offerings.

Then I woke up in great terror, and prayed to the Most High, and said, [14] "From the beginning you have shown your servant these wonders, and have deemed me worthy to have my prayer heard by you; [15] now show me the interpretation of this dream also. [16] For as I consider it in my mind, alas for those who will be left in those days! And still more, alas for those who are not left! [17] For those who are not left will be sad [18] because they understand the things that are reserved for the last days, but cannot attain them. [19] But alas for those also who are left, and for that very reason! For they shall see great dangers and much distress, as these dreams show. [20] Yet it is better[b] to come into these things,[c] though incurring peril, than to pass from the world like a cloud, and not to see what will happen in the last days."

He answered me and said, [21] "I will tell you the interpretation of the vision, and I will also explain to you the things that you have mentioned. [22] As for what you said about those who survive, and concerning those who do not survive,[d] this is the interpretation: [23] The one who brings the peril at that time will protect those who fall into peril, who have works and faith toward the Almighty. [24] Understand therefore that those who are left are more blessed than those who have died.

[25] "This is the interpretation of the vision: As for your seeing a man come up from the heart of the sea, [26] this is he whom the Most High has been keeping for many ages, who will himself deliver his creation; and he will direct those who are left. [27] And as for your seeing wind and fire and a storm coming out of his mouth, [28] and as for his not holding a spear or weapon of war, yet destroying the onrushing multitude that came to conquer him, this is the interpretation: [29] The days are coming when the Most High will deliver those who are on the earth. [30] And bewilderment of mind shall come over those who inhabit the earth. [31] They shall plan to make war against one another, city against city, place against place, people against people, and kingdom against kingdom. [32] When these things take place and the signs occur that I showed you before, then my Son will be revealed, whom you saw as a man coming up from the sea.[e]

[33] "Then, when all the nations hear his voice, all the nations shall leave their own lands and the warfare that they have against one another; [34] and an innumerable multitude shall be gathered together, as you saw, wishing to come and conquer him. [35] But he shall stand on the top of Mount Zion. [36] And Zion shall come and be made manifest to all people, prepared and built, as you saw the mountain carved out without hands. [37] Then he, my Son, will reprove the assembled nations for their ungodliness (this was symbolized by the storm), [38] and will reproach them to their face with their evil thoughts and the torments with which they are to be tortured (which were symbolized by the flames), and will destroy

a Lat Syr Arab 2 literally *the faces of many people*
b Ethiop Compare Arab 2: Lat *easier*    c Syr: Lat *this*
d Syr Arab 1: Lat lacks *and . . . not survive*
e Syr and most Lat Mss lack *from the sea*

11.4; 2 Thess 2.8. **11**: *Burned up*, 12.3; Rev 20.9. **13a**: *Some . . . were bound*, Jews who came from captivity. *Others as offerings*, Isa 66.20.

**13.13b–20a**: The seer prays that God will interpret the vision to him. **14**: *My prayer*, 9.25–37.

**13.20b–55**: The interpretation. **21**: *Things . . . mentioned*, in vv. 16–20. **23**: *The one who brings the peril*, the Messiah; vv. 3–13a. *Works and faith*, see 9.7n. **24**: Contrast 5.41–42. **26**: *He whom the Most High has been keeping for many ages*, the Messiah, v. 52; 12.32. **31**: Isa 19.2; Mt 24.7. **32**: 6.20; 7.26–28; 9.1–2; Mk 13.29. **33–34**: Rev 16.14–16; 19.19; 20.7–9. **36**: *Zion shall come and be made manifest*, 7.26; 10.25–54; Rev 21.2,9–14. *Without hands*, Dan 2.34,45. **37–38**: *Reprove . . . reproach . . . destroy*, as in 11.37–46; 12.31–33. **40**: 2 Kings 17.1–6. *The nine tribes*, the Northern Kingdom them without effort by means of the law[a] (which was symbolized by the fire).

39 "And as for your seeing him gather to himself another multitude that was peaceable, [40] these are the nine[b] tribes that were taken away from their own land into exile in the days of King Hoshea, whom Shalmaneser, king of the Assyrians, made captives; he took them across the river, and they were taken into another land. [41] But they formed this plan for themselves, that they would leave the multitude of the nations and go to a more distant region, where no human beings had ever lived, [42] so that there at least they might keep their statutes that they had not kept in their own land. [43] And they went in by the narrow passages of the Euphrates river. [44] For at that time the Most High performed signs for them, and stopped the channels of the river until they had crossed over. [45] Through that region there was a long way to go, a journey of a year and a half; and that country is called Arzareth.[c]

46 "Then they lived there until the last times; and now, when they are about to come again, [47] the Most High will stop[d] the channels of the river again, so that they may be able to cross over. Therefore you saw the multitude gathered together in peace. [48] But those who are left of your people, who are found within my holy borders, shall be saved.[e] [49] Therefore when he destroys the multitude of the nations that are gathered together, he will defend the people who remain. [50] And then he will show them very many wonders."

51 I said, "O sovereign Lord, explain this to me: Why did I see the man coming up from the heart of the sea?"

52 He said to me, "Just as no one can explore or know what is in the depths of the sea, so no one on earth can see my Son or those who are with him, except in the time of his day.[f] [53] This is the interpretation of the dream that you saw. And you alone have been enlightened about this, [54] because you have forsaken your own ways and have applied yourself to mine, and have searched out my law; [55] for you have devoted your life to wisdom, and called understanding your mother. [56] Therefore I have shown you these things; for there is a reward laid up with the Most High. For it will be that after three more days I will tell you other things, and explain weighty and wondrous matters to you."

57 Then I got up and walked in the field, giving great glory and praise to the Most High for the wonders that he does[g] from time to time, [58] and because he governs the times and whatever things come to pass in their seasons. And I stayed there three days.

14 On the third day, while I was sitting under an oak, suddenly a voice came out of a bush opposite me and said, "Ezra, Ezra!" [2] And I answered, "Here I am, Lord," and I rose to my feet. [3] Then he said to me, "I revealed myself in a bush and spoke to Moses when my people were in bondage in Egypt; [4] and I sent him and led[h] my people out of Egypt; and I led him up on Mount Sinai, where I kept him with me many days. [5] I told him many wondrous

a Syr: Lat *effort and the law*   b Other Lat Mss *ten*; Syr Ethiop Arab 1 Arm *nine and a half*
c That is *Another Land*   d Syr: Lat *stops*
e Syr: Lat lacks *shall be saved*   f Syr: Ethiop *except when his time and his day have come.* Lat lacks *his*
g Lat *did*   h Syr Arab 1 Arab 2 *he led*

(usually "ten tribes"; see note b). *The river*, the Euphrates. **44**: *Stopped . . . the river*, Josh 3.14–16. **45**: *Arzareth*, Hebrew for "Another Land" (see note c; cf. Deut 29.28). **47**: *Will stop . . . the river*, Isa 11.15–16. **48**: *Within my . . . borders*, presumably the borders of Israel (cf. 9.8; 12.34). This answers the seer's previous questions about the fate of Israel. **52**: *Those who are with him*, perhaps "those who were taken up," 6.26. Cf. 8.51; 14.9. **53–55**: See 7.76–77n.

**13.56–58**: Conclusion and injunctions. Ezra's giving *great glory and praise* to God shows the change in attitude that he has experienced since his earlier petulance.

**14.1–48**: The seventh vision (the legend of Ezra and the holy scriptures). **1–18**: God speaks to Ezra. **1–2**: *A bush . . . Here I am*, cf. Ex 3.4. **2**: *I rose*, in contrast to previous occasions, when Ezra was asked to rise (6.13; 7.2; 10.33). **3**: This chapter explicitly parallels Ezra and *Moses*. **4**: Ex 34.28. **5–6**: The things, and showed him the secrets of the times and declared to him[a] the end of the times. Then I commanded him, saying, 6'These words you shall publish openly, and these you shall keep secret.' 7 And now I say to you: 8 Lay up in your heart the signs that I have shown you, the dreams that you have seen, and the interpretations that you have heard; 9 for you shall be taken up from among humankind, and henceforth you shall live with my Son and with those who are like you, until the times are ended. 10 The age has lost its youth, and the times begin to grow old. 11 For the age is divided into twelve parts, and nine[b] of its parts have already passed, 12 as well as half of the tenth part; so two of its parts remain, besides half of the tenth part.[c] 13 Now therefore, set your house in order, and reprove your people; comfort the lowly among them, and instruct those that are wise.[d] And now renounce the life that is corruptible, 14 and put away from you mortal thoughts; cast away from you the burdens of humankind, and divest yourself now of your weak nature; 15 lay to one side the thoughts that are most grievous to you, and hurry to escape from these times. 16 For evils worse than those that you have now seen happen shall take place hereafter. 17 For the weaker the world becomes through old age, the more shall evils be increased upon its inhabitants. 18 Truth shall go farther away, and falsehood shall come near. For the eagle[e] that you saw in the vision is already hurrying to come."

19 Then I answered and said, "Let me speak[f] in your presence, Lord. 20 For I will go, as you have commanded me, and I will reprove the people who are now living; but who will warn those who will be born hereafter? For the world lies in darkness, and its inhabitants are without light. 21 For your law has been burned, and so no one knows the things which have been done or will be done by you. 22 If then I have found favor with you, send the holy spirit into me, and I will write everything that has happened in the world from the beginning, the things that were written in your law, so that people may be able to find the path, and that those who want to live in the last days may do so."

23 He answered me and said, "Go and gather the people, and tell them not to seek you for forty days. 24 But prepare for yourself many writing tablets, and take with you Sarea, Dabria, Selemia, Ethanus, and Asiel—these five, who are trained to write rapidly; 25 and you shall come here, and I will light in your heart the lamp of understanding, which shall not be put out until what you are about to write is finished. 26 And when you have finished, some things you shall make public, and some you shall deliver in secret to the wise; tomorrow at this hour you shall begin to write."

27 Then I went as he commanded me, and I gathered all the people together, and

---

a Syr Ethiop Arab Arm: Lat lacks *declared to him*
b Cn: Lat Ethiop *ten*  c Syr lacks verses 11, 12: Ethiop *For the world is divided into ten parts, and has come to the tenth, and half of the tenth remains. Now . . .*  d Lat lacks *and . . . wise*  e Syr Ethiop Arab Arm: Meaning of Lat uncertain  f Most Lat Mss lack *Let me speak*

biblical Moses was never instructed to *keep* some teachings *secret*. **9:** *You shall be taken up*, see 6.26n. *My Son*, the Messiah (7.28–29; 13.32,37,52). *Those who are like you*, 8.51; cf. 13.52. **10:** 5.50–55. **11:** See 2 *Baruch* chs 53–70 for a similar division of world history into twelve parts. **16–18:** Mk 13.7–8. **18:** 5.9–11. *The eagle*, chs 11–12.

**14.19–26:** Ezra's prayer for inspiration to restore the holy scriptures is granted. **20:** *Who will warn?*, Ezra's characteristic concern for his fellow Jews finally bears fruit in his desire to rewrite the scriptures. *Without light*, without the light of God's law (Ps 19.8b). **21:** According to one tradition, the *law had been burned* by the Babylonians when they destroyed Jerusalem (4.23). **22:** *The holy spirit* will guide Ezra in rewriting the law. **23:** *Forty days*, Ex 24.18; 34.28; Deut 9.9,18. **26:** *Some things . . . make public*, namely, the rewritten books of the Jewish scriptures. *Some . . . deliver in secret*, namely, certain extracanonical books (see 12.37–38; 14.5–6,45–47).

**14.27–36:** Ezra reproves the people (14.13,20), reminding them of the reasons for their state of said, [28]"Hear these words, O Israel. [29]At first our ancestors lived as aliens in Egypt, and they were liberated from there [30]and received the law of life, which they did not keep, which you also have transgressed after them. [31]Then land was given to you for a possession in the land of Zion; but you and your ancestors committed iniquity and did not keep the ways that the Most High commanded you. [32]And since he is a righteous judge, in due time he took from you what he had given. [33]And now you are here, and your people[a] are farther in the interior.[b] [34]If you, then, will rule over your minds and discipline your hearts, you shall be kept alive, and after death you shall obtain mercy. [35]For after death the judgment will come, when we shall live again; and then the names of the righteous shall become manifest, and the deeds of the ungodly shall be disclosed. [36]But let no one come to me now, and let no one seek me for forty days."

[37] So I took the five men, as he commanded me, and we proceeded to the field, and remained there. [38]And on the next day a voice called me, saying, "Ezra, open your mouth and drink what I give you to drink." [39]So I opened my mouth, and a full cup was offered to me; it was full of something like water, but its color was like fire. [40]I took it and drank; and when I had drunk it, my heart poured forth understanding, and wisdom increased in my breast, for my spirit retained its memory, [41]and my mouth

was opened and was no longer closed. [42]Moreover, the Most High gave understanding to the five men, and by turns they wrote what was dictated, using characters that they did not know.[c] They sat forty days; they wrote during the daytime, and ate their bread at night. [43]But as for me, I spoke in the daytime and was not silent at night. [44]So during the forty days, ninety-four[d] books were written. [45]And when the forty days were ended, the Most High spoke to me, saying, "Make public the twenty-four[e] books that you wrote first, and let the worthy and the unworthy read them; [46]but keep the seventy that were written last, in order to give them to the wise among your people. [47]For in them is the spring of understanding, the fountain of wisdom, and the river of knowledge." [48]And I did so.[f]

15 [g]Speak in the ears of my people the words of the prophecy that I will

---

a Lat brothers    b Syr Ethiop Arm: Lat are among you    c Syr Compare Ethiop Arab 2 Arm: Meaning of Lat uncertain    d Syr Ethiop Arab 1 Arm: Meaning of Lat uncertain    e Syr Arab 1: Lat lacks twenty-four    f Syr adds in the seventh year of the sixth week, five thousand years and three months and twelve days after creation. At that time Ezra was caught up, and taken to the place of those who are like him, after he had written all these things. And he was called the scribe of the knowledge of the Most High for ever and ever. Ethiop Arab 1 Arm have a similar ending    g Chapters 15 and 16 (except 15.57-59, which has been found in Greek) are extant only in Lat

---

exile. **28:** See 9.30; Deut 6.4. **33:** *Farther,* apparently referring to the ten northern tribes (13.39–45).

**14.37–48: The revelation of scriptures. 37:** *The five men,* v. 24. *The field,* the same one in which Ezra has received the fourth through the seventh visions (see 9.24). **39:** *A full cup* of inspiration, containing the fire of the spirit (v. 22). **42:** *Using characters that they did not know,* in a new script for Hebrew, the Aramaic square characters. **45:** *Twenty-four books* is one traditional reckoning of the Hebrew canon: the five books of the Law (Gen, Ex, Lev, Num, Deut), eight books of the Prophets (the former prophets: Josh; Judg; 1 and 2 Sam [as one book]; 1 and 2 Kings [as one book]; the latter prophets: Isa; Jer; Ezek; and the Twelve [as one book]), and eleven books of the Writings (Ps; Prov; Job; Song; Ruth; Lam; Eccl; Esth; Dan; Ezra-Neh [as one book]; 1 and 2 Chr [as one book]). **46:** *The seventy* are esoteric, apocryphal books (see 12.37–38; 14.26). **48:** The original version of 4 Ezra probably ended with an account of Ezra's being taken up into heaven and functioning as a heavenly scribe (see note *f*). This ending was apparently dropped from the Latin version to make way for the prophecies of chs 15–16 when they were added at a later time.

**Chapters 15–16** comprise a separate literary composition also known as 6 Ezra.

**15.1–4: The commissioning of the prophet,** who in this context is not named. See Jer 1.7–9; Hab 2.2.

put in your mouth, says the Lord, 2 and cause them to be written on paper; for they are trustworthy and true. 3 Do not fear the plots against you, and do not be troubled by the unbelief of those who oppose you. 4 For all unbelievers shall die in their unbelief.[a]

5 Beware, says the Lord, I am bringing evils upon the world, the sword and famine, death and destruction, 6 because iniquity has spread throughout every land, and their harmful doings have reached their limit. 7 Therefore, says the Lord, 8 I will be silent no longer concerning their ungodly acts that they impiously commit, neither will I tolerate their wicked practices. Innocent and righteous blood cries out to me, and the souls of the righteous cry out continually. 9 I will surely avenge them, says the Lord, and will receive to myself all the innocent blood from among them. 10 See, my people are being led like a flock to the slaughter; I will not allow them to live any longer in the land of Egypt, 11 but I will bring them out with a mighty hand and with an uplifted arm, and will strike Egypt with plagues, as before, and will destroy all its land.

12 Let Egypt mourn, and its foundations, because of the plague of chastisement and castigation that the Lord will bring upon it. 13 Let the farmers that till the ground mourn, because their seed shall fail to grow[b] and their trees shall be ruined by blight and hail and by a terrible tempest. 14 Alas for the world and for those who live in it! 15 For the sword and misery draw near them, and nation shall rise up to fight against nation, with swords in their hands. 16 For there shall be unrest among people; growing strong against one another, they shall in their might have no respect for their king or the chief of their leaders. 17 For a person will desire to go into a city, and shall not be able to do so. 18 Because of their pride the cities shall be in confusion, the houses shall be destroyed, and people shall be afraid. 19 People shall have no pity for their neighbors, but shall make an assault upon[c] their houses with the sword, and plunder their goods, because of hunger for bread and because of great tribulation.

20 See how I am calling together all the kings of the earth to turn to me, says God, from the rising sun and from the south, from the east and from Lebanon; to turn and repay what they have given them. 21 Just as they have done to my elect until this day, so I will do, and will repay into their bosom. Thus says the Lord God: 22 My right hand will not spare the sinners, and my sword will not cease from those who shed innocent blood on earth. 23 And a fire went forth from his wrath, and consumed the foundations of the earth and the sinners, like burnt straw. 24 Alas for those who sin and do not observe my commandments, says the Lord;[d] 25 I will not spare them. Depart, you faithless children! Do not pollute my sanctuary. 26 For God[e] knows all who sin against him; therefore he will hand them over to death and slaughter. 27 Already calamities have come upon the whole earth, and you shall remain in them; God[e] will not deliver you, because you have sinned against him.

28 What a terrifying sight, appearing from the east! 29 The nations of the dragons of Arabia shall come out with many chariots, and from the day that they set out, their hissing shall spread over the earth, so that all who hear them will fear and trem-

a Other ancient authorities add and all who believe shall be saved by their faith   b Lat lacks to grow   c Cn: Lat shall empty   d Other ancient authorities read God   e Other ancient authorities read the Lord

15.5–16.34: Prediction of worldwide catastrophes. 5–27: God will destroy the world because of human sinfulness. 8: Innocent and righteous blood cries out, Gen 4.10; Rev 6.9–10. 10–11: Egypt and the plagues are probably symbols for the author's own situation of crisis. Compare Ps 44.22; Isa 53.7. 14: The destruction will be universal. 15: Nation . . . against nation, Mk 13.8. 18: Lk 21.26. 22–27: Woes against sinners.

15.28–33: A vision of warfare in the east. This section may reflect conflicts between Odaenathus of Palmyra (dragons of Arabia) and Shapur I of Persia (Carmonians) that took place on the eastern borders ble. [30] Also the Carmonians, raging in wrath, shall go forth like wild boars[a] from the forest, and with great power they shall come and engage them in battle, and with their tusks they shall devastate a portion of the land of the Assyrians with their teeth. [31] And then the dragons,[b] remembering their origin, shall become still stronger; and if they combine in great power and turn to pursue them, [32] then these shall be disorganized and silenced by their power, and shall turn and flee.[c] [33] And from the land of the Assyrians an enemy in ambush shall attack them and destroy one of them, and fear and trembling shall come upon their army, and indecision upon their kings.

[34] See the clouds from the east, and from the north to the south! Their appearance is exceedingly threatening, full of wrath and storm. [35] They shall clash against one another and shall pour out a heavy tempest on the earth, and their own tempest;[d] and there shall be blood from the sword as high as a horse's belly [36] and a man's thigh and a camel's hock. [37] And there shall be fear and great trembling on the earth; those who see that wrath shall be horror-stricken, and they shall be seized with trembling. [38] After that, heavy storm clouds shall be stirred up from the south, and from the north, and another part from the west. [39] But the winds from the east shall prevail over the cloud that was[e] raised in wrath, and shall dispel it; and the tempest[d] that was to cause destruction by the east wind shall be driven violently toward the south and west. [40] Great and mighty clouds, full of wrath and tempest, shall rise and destroy all the earth and its inhabitants, and shall pour out upon every high and lofty place[f] a terrible tempest, [41] fire and hail and flying swords and floods of water, so that all the fields and all the streams shall be filled with the abundance of those waters. [42] They shall destroy cities and walls, mountains and hills, trees of the forests, and grass of the meadows, and their grain. [43] They shall go on steadily to Babylon and blot it out. [44] They shall come to it and surround it; they shall pour out on it the tempest[d] and all its fury;[g] then the dust and smoke shall reach the sky, and all who are around it shall mourn for it. [45] And those who survive shall serve those who have destroyed it.

[46] And you, Asia, who share in the splendor of Babylon and the glory of her person— [47] woe to you, miserable wretch! For you have made yourself like her; you have decked out your daughters for prostitution to please and glory in your lovers, who have always lusted after you. [48] You have imitated that hateful one in all her deeds and devices.[h] Therefore God[i] says, [49] I will send evils upon you: widowhood, poverty, famine, sword, and pestilence, bringing ruin to your houses, bringing destruction and death. [50] And the glory of your strength shall wither like a flower when the heat shall rise that is sent upon you. [51] You shall be weakened like a wretched woman who is beaten and wounded, so that you cannot receive your mighty lovers. [52] Would I have dealt with you so violently, says the Lord, [53] if you had not killed my chosen people continually, exulting and clapping your hands and

---

a Other ancient authorities lack *like wild boars*
b Cn: Lat *dragon*   c Other ancient authorities read *turn their face to the north*   d Meaning of Lat uncertain   e Literally *that he*   f Or *eminent person*
g Other ancient authorities add *until they destroy it to its foundations*   h Other ancient authorities read *devices, and you have followed after that one about to gratify her magnates and leaders so that you may be made proud and be pleased by her fornications*
i Other ancient authorities read *the Lord*

---

of the Roman Empire between 261 and 267 CE. **30:** *The Carmonians,* from Carmania (Kirman), a southern province of the Parthian Empire.

**15.34–63: A vision of destructive storm clouds.** The exact historical referents of this section, if any, are unclear. **35:** *As high as . . . ,* Rev 14.20. **43:** *Babylon,* Rome. **43–44:** Rev 18.9–10,15; 19.3. **46–63:** Polemic against *Asia,* imitator of the corrupt *splendor of Babylon* (Rome). *Asia,* here and in 16.1, probably designates the whole of Asia Minor. **47–48:** Rev 14.8; 17.2–5; 18.3. **49:** Rev 18.7–8. **50:** Rev 17.16. **51:** Jer 3.1, etc.; Rev 18.9–10. **52–53:** Rev 17.6; 18.24. **56:** Rev 19.2. **57–59:** This section survives talking about their death when you were drunk? 54 Beautify your face! 55 The reward of a prostitute is in your lap; therefore you shall receive your recompense. 56 As you will do to my chosen people, says the Lord, so God will do to you, and will hand you over to adversities. 57 Your children shall die of hunger, and you shall fall by the sword; your cities shall be wiped out, and all your people who are in the open country shall fall by the sword. 58 Those who are in the mountains and highlands[a] shall perish of hunger, and they shall eat their own flesh in hunger for bread and drink their own blood in thirst for water. 59 Unhappy above all others, you shall come and suffer fresh miseries. 60 As they pass by they shall crush the hateful[b] city, and shall destroy a part of your land and abolish a portion of your glory, when they return from devastated Babylon. 61 You shall be broken down by them like stubble,[c] and they shall be like fire to you. 62 They shall devour you and your cities, your land and your mountains; they shall burn with fire all your forests and your fruitful trees. 63 They shall carry your children away captive, plunder your wealth, and mar the glory of your countenance.

16 Woe to you, Babylon and Asia! Woe to you, Egypt and Syria! 2 Bind on sackcloth and cloth of goats' hair,[d] and wail for your children, and lament for them; for your destruction is at hand. 3 The sword has been sent upon you, and who is there to turn it back? 4 A fire has been sent upon you, and who is there to quench it? 5 Calamities have been sent upon you, and who is there to drive them away? 6 Can one drive off a hungry lion in the forest, or quench a fire in the stubble once it has started to burn?[e] 7 Can one turn back an arrow shot by a strong archer? 8 The Lord God sends calamities, and who will drive them away? 9 Fire will go forth from his wrath, and who is there to quench it? 10 He will flash lightning, and who will not be afraid? He will thunder, and who will not be terrified? 11 The Lord will threaten, and who will not be utterly shattered at his presence? 12 The earth and its foundations quake, the sea is churned up from the depths, and its waves and the fish with them shall be troubled at the presence of the Lord and the glory of his power. 13 For his right hand that bends the bow is strong, and his arrows that he shoots are sharp and when they are shot to the ends of the world will not miss once. 14 Calamities are sent forth and shall not return until they come over the earth. 15 The fire is kindled, and shall not be put out until it consumes the foundations of the earth. 16 Just as an arrow shot by a mighty archer does not return, so the calamities that are sent upon the earth shall not return. 17 Alas for me! Alas for me! Who will deliver me in those days?

18 The beginning of sorrows, when there shall be much lamentation; the beginning of famine, when many shall perish; the beginning of wars, when the powers shall be terrified; the beginning of calamities, when all shall tremble. What shall they do, when the calamities come? 19 Famine and plague, tribulation and anguish are sent as scourges for the correction of humankind. 20 Yet for all this they will not turn from their iniquities, or ever be mindful of the scourges. 21 Indeed, provisions will be so cheap upon earth that people will imagine that peace is assured for them, and then

---

a Gk: Lat omits *and highlands*   b Another reading is *idle* or *unprofitable*   c Other ancient authorities read *like dry straw*   d Other ancient authorities lack *cloth of goats' hair*   e Other ancient authorities read *fire when dry straw has been set on fire*

in Greek in a parchment fragment from Oxyrhynchus, Egypt. **60:** Rev 18.21. *The hateful city*, Babylon/Rome. **63:** Rev 18.14.

**16.1–17: The inevitability of God's judgment** (cf. Am 3.3–8). **1–2:** A reprise of ch 15. **2:** *Sackcloth and cloth of goats' hair*, signs of mourning. **12–13:** Ps 18.14–15. **15:** Deut 32.22; 2 Pet 3.10. **17:** A personal interlude by the prophet.

**16.18–34: Prediction of desolation on the earth. 28:** Am 5.3. **29–31:** Isa 17.6. **32:** Isa 7.23–25.

calamities shall spring up on the earth—the sword, famine, and great confusion. 22 For many of those who live on the earth shall perish by famine; and those who survive the famine shall die by the sword. 23 And the dead shall be thrown out like dung, and there shall be no one to console them; for the earth shall be left desolate, and its cities shall be demolished. 24 No one shall be left to cultivate the earth or to sow it. 25 The trees shall bear fruit, but who will gather it? 26 The grapes shall ripen, but who will tread them? For in all places there shall be great solitude; 27 a person will long to see another human being, or even to hear a human voice. 28 For ten shall be left out of a city; and two, out of the field, those who have hidden themselves in thick groves and clefts in the rocks. 29 Just as in an olive orchard three or four olives may be left on every tree, 30 or just as, when a vineyard is gathered, some clusters may be left[a] by those who search carefully through the vineyard, 31 so in those days three or four shall be left by those who search their houses with the sword. 32 The earth shall be left desolate, and its fields shall be plowed up,[b] and its roads and all its paths shall bring forth thorns, because no sheep will go along them. 33 Virgins shall mourn because they have no bridegrooms; women shall mourn because they have no husbands; their daughters shall mourn, because they have no help. 34 Their bridegrooms shall be killed in war, and their husbands shall perish of famine.

35 Listen now to these things, and understand them, you who are servants of the Lord. 36 This is the word of the Lord; receive it and do not disbelieve what the Lord says.[c] 37 The calamities draw near, and are not delayed. 38 Just as a pregnant woman, in the ninth month when the time of her delivery draws near, has great pains around her womb for two or three hours beforehand, but when the child comes forth from the womb, there will not be a moment's delay, 39 so the calamities will not delay in coming upon the earth, and the world will groan, and pains will seize it on every side.

40 Hear my words, O my people; prepare for battle, and in the midst of the calamities be like strangers on the earth. 41 Let the one who sells be like one who will flee; let the one who buys be like one who will lose; 42 let the one who does business be like one who will not make a profit; and let the one who builds a house be like one who will not live in it; 43 let the one who sows be like one who will not reap; so also the one who prunes the vines, like one who will not gather the grapes; 44 those who marry, like those who will have no children; and those who do not marry, like those who are widowed. 45 Because of this, those who labor, labor in vain; 46 for strangers shall gather their fruits, and plunder their goods, overthrow their houses, and take their children captive; for in captivity and famine they will produce their children.[d] 47 Those who conduct business, do so only to have it plundered; the more they adorn their cities, their houses and possessions, and their persons, 48 the more angry I will be with them for their sins, says the Lord. 49 Just as a respectable and virtuous woman abhors a prostitute, 50 so righteousness shall abhor iniquity, when she decks herself out, and shall accuse her to her face when he comes who will defend the one who searches out every sin on earth.

51 Therefore do not be like her or her works. 52 For in a very short time iniquity will be removed from the earth, and righteousness will reign over us. 53 Sinners must

a Other ancient authorities read a cluster may remain exposed   b Other ancient authorities read be for briers   c Cn: Lat do not believe the gods of whom the Lord speaks   d Other ancient authorities read therefore those who are married may know that they will produce children for captivity and famine

16.35–78: Exhortation of God's people. 35–52: Advice and instruction. 38–39: 4.40–42. 41–47: Every form of worldly activity is useless. See Deut 28.30–33,38–42; 1 Cor 7.29–31. 53: Prov 25.22.
16.53–67: The impossibility of hiding sins from God. 55–62: This recital of God's acts of creation

not say that they have not sinned;[a] for God[b] will burn coals of fire on the head of everyone who says, "I have not sinned before God and his glory." [54]The Lord[c] certainly knows everything that people do; he knows their imaginations and their thoughts and their hearts. [55]He said, "Let the earth be made," and it was made, and "Let the heaven be made," and it was made. [56]At his word the stars were fixed in their places, and he knows the number of the stars. [57]He searches the abyss and its treasures; he has measured the sea and its contents; [58]he has confined the sea in the midst of the waters;[d] and by his word he has suspended the earth over the water. [59]He has spread out the heaven like a dome and made it secure upon the waters; [60]he has put springs of water in the desert, and pools on the tops of the mountains, so as to send rivers from the heights to water the earth. [61]He formed human beings and put a heart in the midst of each body, and gave each person breath and life and understanding [62]and the spirit[e] of Almighty God,[f] who surely made all things and searches out hidden things in hidden places. [63]He knows your imaginations and what you think in your hearts! Woe to those who sin and want to hide their sins! [64]The Lord will strictly examine all their works, and will make a public spectacle of all of you. [65]You shall be put to shame when your sins come out before others, and your own iniquities shall stand as your accusers on that day. [66]What will you do? Or how will you hide your sins before the Lord and his glory? [67]Indeed, God[g] is the judge; fear him! Cease from your sins, and forget your iniquities, never to commit them again; so God[g] will lead you forth and deliver you from all tribulation.

[68]The burning wrath of a great multitude is kindled over you; they shall drag some of you away and force you to eat what was sacrificed to idols. [69]And those who consent to eat shall be held in derision and contempt, and shall be trampled under foot. [70]For in many places[h] and in neighboring cities there shall be a great uprising against those who fear the Lord. [71]They shall[i] be like maniacs, sparing no one, but plundering and destroying those who continue to fear the Lord.[j] [72]For they shall destroy and plunder their goods, and drive them out of house and home. [73]Then the tested quality of my elect shall be manifest, like gold that is tested by fire.

[74]Listen, my elect ones, says the Lord; the days of tribulation are at hand, but I will deliver you from them. [75]Do not fear or doubt, for God[g] is your guide. [76]You who keep my commandments and precepts, says the Lord God, must not let your sins weigh you down, or your iniquities prevail over you. [77]Woe to those who are choked by their sins and overwhelmed by their iniquities! They are like a field choked with underbrush and its path[k] overwhelmed with thorns, so that no one can pass through. [78]It is shut off and given up to be consumed by fire.

a Other ancient authorities add or the unjust done injustice    b Lat for he    c Other ancient authorities read Lord God    d Other ancient authorities read confined the world between the waters and the waters    e Or breath    f Other ancient authorities read of the Lord Almighty    g Other ancient authorities read the Lord    h Meaning of Lat uncertain    i Other ancient authorities read For people, because of their misfortunes, shall    j Other ancient authorities read fear God    k Other ancient authorities read seed

underscores God's omniscience; cf. Job 38; Sir 43. **55**: See Gen 1.6,9. **59**: Isa 40.22; Ps 104.2. **60**: Isa 41.18. **62**: Rev 2.23.

**16.68–73: Prediction of persecutions.** These descriptions have close parallels with third- and early fourth-century Roman persecutions of Christians. **68**: Eating food *sacrificed to idols* was forbidden for many Jewish and early Christian groups. See Ex 34.15; Acts 15.20,29; 1 Cor 8.1–13; 10.14–22; Rev 2.14,20; 4 Macc 5.2. **73**: Zech 13.9; 1 Pet 1.7.

**16.74–78: Concluding instructions to the elect. 77–78**: 2 Sam 23.6–7; Heb 6.8.

# 4 MACCABEES

❧ ❧

Although not a part of the canon of scripture of any religious community, 4 Maccabees is included in some important manuscripts of the Septuagint (the Greek Bible), and its particularly vivid, sometimes morbid, presentation of unflinching commitment to one's faith was a source of inspiration for Jews during the Hellenistic era. Despite its title, 4 Maccabees has little to do with the Maccabean family or their armed revolt against Seleucid rule during the second century BCE (see the Introductions to 1 and 2 Maccabees). The focus instead is on heroes of a different sort, a group of Jewish martyrs who endure torture and execution out of loyalty to their God and their people. According to the interpretation advanced by the book, it was their noble sacrifice, not any military or political exploits, that ultimately secured God's favor for the Jews and rescued them from apostasy and foreign oppression (18.3–5).

Part moral treatise, part funeral oration, 4 Maccabees is a classic example of the interpretation of Jewish religion in terms of Greco-Roman intellectual and rhetorical conventions. Indeed, Judaism is even presented as "a philosophy in accordance with devout reason" (8.1; see also 1.1; 5.4,7,11, 22,35; 7.7,9,21; 8.15). As such, its adherents are trained to exercise control over the ruinous influence of irrational emotions such as desire and fear, to prevail over the cruel injustices of tyranny, and to embody moral virtues, especially piety, wisdom, and courage. The book's underlying contention is that strict adherence to Judaism actually fulfills the highest ideals of Hellenistic civilization, a pointed message for Jews under constant pressure to assimilate into the dominant, pagan culture.

The book has two major parts. The first (1.1–3.18) presents the philosophical thesis that "reason rules the emotions" (1.5), linking reason especially with "a way of life in accordance with the [Mosaic] law" (2.8). The second, longer part (3.19–18.19) dramatizes this thesis through a series of narratives that describe the brutal tortures inflicted by the Seleucid ruler Antiochus IV Epiphanes (ruled 175–164 BCE) on Eleazar, seven brothers, and their mother. These heroic stories, based on the much shorter accounts of 2 Maccabees 6–7, are meant to advocate loyalty to Judaism even in the most trying circumstances. Ultimately, the martyrs are meant as exemplars for anyone who would "fight the sacred and noble battle for religion" (9.24; cf. 16.16). Conversely, Antiochus, portrayed as a shameless, impious, and bloodthirsty tyrant (e.g., 11.3–6; 12.11–14), represents the epitome of Gentile vice.

The book's theology, emphasizing veneration of the patriarchs, obedience to the law, and the sovereignty of God, is fully Jewish, with two distinctive features. First, the martyrdoms are interpreted as a substitutionary atonement that expiates the nation's sin and purifies the land (see 17.21–22n.). Second, in contrast to 2 Maccabees with its emphasis on bodily resurrection, 4 Maccabees speaks of God's final reward for the martyrs in terms of the immortality of the soul, reflecting Hellenistic ideas (see 9.22n.).

Written in Greek by an unknown author, 4 Maccabees has sometimes been assigned to the period 20–54 CE, when Cilicia was joined to Syria and Phoenicia as a single province (see 4.2), although it in fact could have been written at any time during the late first century BCE or the first century CE.

The book's place of origin is similarly uncertain. Jerusalem is a likely candidate, though Antioch (see 5.1n.), Alexandria, and other cities have been proposed. While it is unlikely that 4 Maccabees was known to any New Testament authors, the book's interpretation of martyrdom is representative of the theological milieu in which early Christians attached atoning significance to the suffering and death of Jesus (e.g., Mt 26.28; Mk 10.45; Rom 3.24–25; Heb 9.11–14; 1 Jn 1.7).

1 The subject that I am about to discuss is most philosophical, that is, whether devout reason is sovereign over the emotions. So it is right for me to advise you to pay earnest attention to philosophy. [2] For the subject is essential to everyone who is seeking knowledge, and in addition it includes the praise of the highest virtue—I mean, of course, rational judgment. [3] If, then, it is evident that reason rules over those emotions that hinder self-control, namely, gluttony and lust, [4] it is also clear that it masters the emotions that hinder one from justice, such as malice, and those that stand in the way of courage, namely anger, fear, and pain. [5] Some might perhaps ask, "If reason rules the emotions, why is it not sovereign over forgetfulness and ignorance?" Their attempt at argument is ridiculous![a] [6] For reason does not rule its own emotions, but those that are opposed to justice, courage, and self-control;[b] and it is not for the purpose of destroying them, but so that one may not give way to them.

[7] I could prove to you from many and various examples that reason[c] is dominant over the emotions, [8] but I can demonstrate it best from the noble bravery of those who died for the sake of virtue, Eleazar and the seven brothers and their mother. [9] All of these, by despising sufferings that bring death, demonstrated that reason controls the emotions. [10] On this anniversary[d] it is fitting for me to praise for their virtues those who, with their mother, died for the sake of nobility and goodness, but I would also call them blessed for the honor in which they are held. [11] All people, even their torturers, marveled at their courage and endurance, and they became the cause of the downfall of tyranny over their nation. By their endurance they conquered the tyrant, and thus their native land was purified through them. [12] I shall shortly have an opportunity to speak of this; but, as my custom is, I shall begin by stating my main principle, and then I shall turn to their story, giving glory to the all-wise God.

a Or They are attempting to make my argument ridiculous! b Other ancient authorities add and rational judgment c Other ancient authorities read devout reason d Gk At this time

**1.1–3.18: A philosophical introduction** states the book's principal thesis, that reason rules over the emotions, and gives a number of basic definitions and descriptions. **1.1–6:** Statement of the thesis. **1:** *Reason*, a major theme of Hellenistic philosophy (e.g., Plutarch, *On Moral Virtue* 440D), is specified here as *devout* (see 6.31; 7.4,16; 8.1; 13.1; 15.23; 16.1,4; 18.2), correlating it with devotion to God and God's law (see 1.15–17). **2–4:** *Rational judgment, self-control, justice, courage,* the four cardinal virtues of the Platonic and Stoic traditions (see 1.18; 5.23–24; 15.10; Wis 8.7; Cicero, *On Moral Duties* 1.5.15–17). **2:** *Praise*, anticipating the book's main purpose, to honor virtue, especially as embodied by the martyrs (1.10; 2.2; 7.9; 13.3,17; 18.13). **5:** The objection is answered in 2.24–3.5. **7–12:** The thesis will be demonstrated principally through the *examples* of the martyrs. **8:** The example of *Eleazar* is elaborated in chs 5–7, and that of the *seven brothers* in chs 8–12. **10:** *On this anniversary*, the phrase (see text note d) has suggested to some that the book was originally an oration meant to be delivered at a festival commemorating the martyrs, though it could just as easily be a literary device (see 3.19; 14.9; 17.8–10). *For the sake of nobility*, the martyrs' character is manifest in their determination to preserve the honor of their country and ancestors (6.22; 7.8; 9.24; 10.3,15; 11.22; 12.14; 13.25; 15.9; 16.16; cf. Philo, *On the Virtues* 187–227). **11:** *The downfall of tyranny*, through their endurance and deaths the martyrs not only cause God to deliver the land but also to execute judgment on Antiochus IV Ephiphanes (see 8.15; 9.9,24,30; 11.25; 16.14; 17.20; 18.4–5; cf. Rev 12.10–11). **13–35:** The author's analysis of the *emotions*

13 Our inquiry, accordingly, is whether reason is sovereign over the emotions. 14 We shall decide just what reason is and what emotion is, how many kinds of emotions there are, and whether reason rules over all these. 15 Now reason is the mind that with sound logic prefers the life of wisdom. 16 Wisdom, next, is the knowledge of divine and human matters and the causes of these. 17 This, in turn, is education in the law, by which we learn divine matters reverently and human affairs to our advantage. 18 Now the kinds of wisdom are rational judgment, justice, courage, and self-control. 19 Rational judgment is supreme over all of these, since by means of it reason rules over the emotions. 20 The two most comprehensive types[a] of the emotions are pleasure and pain; and each of these is by nature concerned with both body and soul. 21 The emotions of both pleasure and pain have many consequences. 22 Thus desire precedes pleasure and delight follows it. 23 Fear precedes pain and sorrow comes after. 24 Anger, as a person will see by reflecting on this experience, is an emotion embracing pleasure and pain. 25 In pleasure there exists even a malevolent tendency, which is the most complex of all the emotions. 26 In the soul it is boastfulness, covetousness, thirst for honor, rivalry, and malice; 27 in the body, indiscriminate eating, gluttony, and solitary gormandizing.

28 Just as pleasure and pain are two plants growing from the body and the soul, so there are many offshoots of these plants,[b] 29 each of which the master cultivator, reason, weeds and prunes and ties up and waters and thoroughly irrigates, and so tames the jungle of habits and emotions. 30 For reason is the guide of the virtues, but over the emotions it is sovereign.

Observe now, first of all, that rational judgment is sovereign over the emotions by virtue of the restraining power of self-control. 31 Self-control, then, is dominance over the desires. 32 Some desires are mental, others are physical, and reason obviously rules over both. 33 Otherwise, how is it that when we are attracted to forbidden foods we abstain from the pleasure to be had from them? Is it not because reason is able to rule over appetites? I for one think so. 34 Therefore when we crave seafood and fowl and animals and all sorts of foods that are forbidden to us by the law, we abstain because of domination by reason. 35 For the emotions of the appetites are restrained, checked by the temperate mind, and all the impulses of the body are bridled by reason.

2 And why is it amazing that the desires of the mind for the enjoyment of beauty are rendered powerless? 2 It is for this reason, certainly, that the temperate Joseph is praised, because by mental effort[c] he over-

a Or sources    b Other ancient authorities read these emotions    c Other ancient authorities add in reasoning

appropriates concepts from Greek ethics and psychology (see 6.31–35; 13.1–7). **15:** *Sound logic,* a technical term of Greek ethics for the process of rationally choosing virtue over vice (cf. Epictetus, *Discourses* 4.8.12). **16:** This definition of *wisdom* is philosophical in origin (see Seneca, *Moral Epistles* 89.5). **17:** *Education in the law,* i.e., the law of Moses, cf. 2.1–23; 5.14–38; 18.1–19; Sir 1.26; 19.20. **18:** See 1.2–4n. **20:** The division of *the emotions* into two *types—pleasure and pain—*is familiar from Aristotle's *Rhetoric* 2.1.8. **24:** This definition of *anger* is similar to Aristotle's in *Rhetoric* 2.2.1–2. **25:** On the perils of *pleasure,* see Prov 21.17; Isa 47.8–9. **26–27:** Such catalogs of vices were popular in Greco-Roman moral literature (see 2 Tim 3.2–4; Titus 3.3). **28–29:** The work of *reason* in the *soul* was frequently likened to that of a gardener, e.g., Philo, *The Worse Attacks the Better* 105. **30b–31:** *Self-control,* see 5.23–24; 13.16; Prov 25.28; Sir 18.30–19.3. **33–34:** *Forbidden foods,* see Lev 11.1–47; Deut 14.3–21. **35:** Emotions are not to be extirpated but mastered, as Stoics like Posidonius (ca. 135–ca. 50 BCE) taught (cf. 2.21n.; 3.2–5).

**2.1–23:** Fellowship of reason with the law. The *way of life* established by the law is *temperate* and just. **2–3:** Joseph resisted the temptations of Potiphar's wife (Gen 39.7–12); his piety and temperance are extolled also in the apocryphal Jewish romance, *Joseph and Aseneth.* **5:** Ex 20.17; Deut 5.21. **2.6b–14:**

came sexual desire. [3] For when he was young and in his prime for intercourse, by his reason he nullified the frenzy[a] of the passions. [4] Not only is reason proved to rule over the frenzied urge of sexual desire, but also over every desire.[b] [5] Thus the law says, "You shall not covet your neighbor's wife or anything that is your neighbor's." [6] In fact, since the law has told us not to covet, I could prove to you all the more that reason is able to control desires.

Just so it is with the emotions that hinder one from justice. [7] Otherwise how could it be that someone who is habitually a solitary gormandizer, a glutton, or even a drunkard can learn a better way, unless reason is clearly lord of the emotions? [8] Thus, as soon as one adopts a way of life in accordance with the law, even though a lover of money, one is forced to act contrary to natural ways and to lend without interest to the needy and to cancel the debt when the seventh year arrives. [9] If one is greedy, one is ruled by the law through reason so that one neither gleans the harvest nor gathers the last grapes from the vineyard.

In all other matters we can recognize that reason rules the emotions. [10] For the law prevails even over affection for parents, so that virtue is not abandoned for their sakes. [11] It is superior to love for one's wife, so that one rebukes her when she breaks the law. [12] It takes precedence over love for children, so that one punishes them for misdeeds. [13] It is sovereign over the relationship of friends, so that one rebukes friends when they act wickedly. [14] Do not consider it paradoxical when reason, through the law, can prevail even over enmity. The fruit trees of the enemy are not cut down, but one preserves the property of enemies from marauders and helps raise up what has fallen.[c]

15 It is evident that reason rules even[d] the more violent emotions: lust for power, vainglory, boasting, arrogance, and malice. [16] For the temperate mind repels all these malicious emotions, just as it repels anger—for it is sovereign over even this. [17] When Moses was angry with Dathan and Abiram, he did nothing against them in anger, but controlled his anger by reason. [18] For, as I have said, the temperate mind is able to get the better of the emotions, to correct some, and to render others powerless. [19] Why else did Jacob, our most wise father, censure the households of Simeon and Levi for their irrational slaughter of the entire tribe of the Shechemites, saying, "Cursed be their anger"? [20] For if reason could not control anger, he would not have spoken thus. [21] Now when God fashioned human beings, he planted in them emotions and inclinations, [22] but at the same time he enthroned the mind among the senses as a sacred governor over them all. [23] To the mind he gave the law; and one who lives subject to this will rule a kingdom that is temperate, just, good, and courageous.

24 How is it then, one might say, that if reason is master of the emotions, it does not control forgetfulness and ignorance?

a Or gadfly    b Or all covetousness    c Or the beasts that have fallen    d Other ancient authorities read through

These examples emphasize the law's humanitarian principles. **8:** *Lend without interest,* to fellow Jews, Ex 22.25; Lev 25.36–37; Deut 23.19–20. *Seventh year,* Deut 15.1–3. **9:** On gleanings for the poor, see Ex 23.10–11; Lev 19.9–10; Deut 24.20–21; Ruth 2. **10–13:** Assertions regarding the precedence of *the law* over natural *affections* and *love* anticipate the stories of martyrdom that follow (e.g., 13.19–14.1; 14.13–15.28). **12:** Cf. Deut 21.18–21; Prov 13.24; 19.18; 29.15,17. **14:** *Fruit trees . . . are not cut down,* Deut 20.19 (cf. Josephus, *Ag. Ap.* 2.211–12). *Raise up,* Deut 22.4. **17:** Num 16.1–35; Sir 45.18–19. **19:** Gen 34; 49.7. **21:** According to different Jewish traditions, God *planted* the good and evil *inclinations* in *human beings;* the latter is to be controlled, and in itself is not essentially evil (cf. Sir 37.3). **23:** *Will rule a kingdom,* according to the Stoics, the sage is the only true king because only he rules his moral purpose with complete freedom and integrity (cf. 14.2); an example of such a "king" is given in the next passage.

**2.24–3.18:** The example of King David's thirst, 2 Sam 23.13–17; 1 Chr 11.15–19. Because of his

**3** [1] But this argument is entirely ridiculous; for it is evident that reason rules not over its own emotions, but over those of the body. [2] No one of us[a] can eradicate that kind of desire, but reason can provide a way for us not to be enslaved by desire. [3] No one of us can eradicate anger from the mind, but reason can help to deal with anger. [4] No one of us can eradicate malice, but reason can fight at our side so that we are not overcome by malice. [5] For reason does not uproot the emotions but is their antagonist.

[6] Now this can be explained more clearly by the story of King David's thirst. [7] David had been attacking the Philistines all day long, and together with the soldiers of his nation had killed many of them. [8] Then when evening fell, he[b] came, sweating and quite exhausted, to the royal tent, around which the whole army of our ancestors had encamped. [9] Now all the rest were at supper, [10] but the king was extremely thirsty, and though springs were plentiful there, he could not satisfy his thirst from them. [11] But a certain irrational desire for the water in the enemy's territory tormented and inflamed him, undid and consumed him. [12] When his guards complained bitterly because of the king's craving, two staunch young soldiers, respecting[c] the king's desire, armed themselves fully, and taking a pitcher climbed over the enemy's ramparts. [13] Eluding the sentinels at the gates, they went searching throughout the enemy camp [14] and found the spring, and from it boldly brought the king a drink. [15] But David,[d] though he was burning with thirst, considered it an altogether fearful danger to his soul to drink what was regarded as equivalent to blood. [16] Therefore, opposing reason to desire, he poured out the drink as an offering to God. [17] For the temperate mind can conquer the drives of the emotions and quench the flames of frenzied desires; [18] it can overthrow bodily agonies even when they are extreme, and by nobility of reason spurn all domination by the emotions.

[19] The present occasion now invites us to a narrative demonstration of temperate reason.

[20] At a time when our ancestors were enjoying profound peace because of their observance of the law and were prospering, so that even Seleucus Nicanor, king of Asia, had both appropriated money to them for the temple service and recognized their commonwealth— [21] just at that time certain persons attempted a revolution against the public harmony and caused many and various disasters.

**4** Now there was a certain Simon, a political opponent of the noble and good man, Onias, who then held the high priesthood for life. When despite all manner of slander he was unable to injure Onias in the eyes of the nation, he fled the country with the purpose of betraying it. [2] So he came to Apollonius, governor of Syria, Phoenicia, and Cilicia, and said, [3] "I have come here

a Gk you  b Other ancient authorities read he hurried and  c Or embarrassed because of  d Gk he

temperate mind and nobility of reason David was not enslaved by desire. **3.2–5:** See 1.35n. **11:** The author emphasizes that David's desire is not simply physical thirst but an irrational desire. **16:** David's action is one of both piety and justice, of not taking for oneself what rightly belongs to God. Poured out . . . an offering, cf. Deut 12.23–24; 1 Sam 7.6. **19:** This verse provides a transition from philosophical discourse to dramatic narrative, which occupies the remainder of the book. The present occasion, see 1.10n.

**3.20–4.14:** Apollonius's attempt on the temple treasury, 2 Macc 3.1–40. The author briefly describes the historical background of the persecution (compare the story of Ptolemy IV Philopator in 3 Macc 1.8–2.24). **20–21:** The author establishes the story's political context; internal rivalry threatens the public harmony of the Jewish commonwealth which was secured by obedience to the law (see 5.16; 15.29; 18.4–5). **20:** The author has confused Seleucus I Nicator (ruled 305–281 BCE) with Seleucus IV Philopator (ruled 187–175) who was king during the events described. **4.1:** Simon, captain of the temple, 2 Macc 3.4. Onias, 2 Macc 3.1. **2:** Apollonius, 2 Macc 3.5. **3:** Private funds in the Jerusalem Temple, see because I am loyal to the king's government, to report that in the Jerusalem treasuries there are deposited tens of thousands in private funds, which are not the property of the temple but belong to King Seleucus." 4 When Apollonius learned the details of these things, he praised Simon for his service to the king and went up to Seleucus to inform him of the rich treasure. 5 On receiving authority to deal with this matter, he proceeded quickly to our country accompanied by the accursed Simon and a very strong military force. 6 He said that he had come with the king's authority to seize the private funds in the treasury. 7 The people indignantly protested his words, considering it outrageous that those who had committed deposits to the sacred treasury should be deprived of them, and did all that they could to prevent it. 8 But, uttering threats, Apollonius went on to the temple. 9 While the priests together with women and children were imploring God in the temple to shield the holy place that was being treated so contemptuously, 10 and while Apollonius was going up with his armed forces to seize the money, angels on horseback with lightning flashing from their weapons appeared from heaven, instilling in them great fear and trembling. 11 Then Apollonius fell down half dead in the temple area that was open to all, stretched out his hands toward heaven, and with tears begged the Hebrews to pray for him and propitiate the wrath of the heavenly army. 12 For he said that he had committed a sin deserving of death, and that if he were spared he would praise the blessedness of the holy place before all people. 13 Moved by these words, the high priest

Onias, although otherwise he had scruples about doing so, prayed for him so that King Seleucus would not suppose that Apollonius had been overcome by human treachery and not by divine justice. 14 So Apollonius,[a] having been saved beyond all expectations, went away to report to the king what had happened to him.

15 When King Seleucus died, his son Antiochus Epiphanes succeeded to the throne, an arrogant and terrible man, 16 who removed Onias from the priesthood and appointed Onias's[b] brother Jason as high priest. 17 Jason[c] agreed that if the office were conferred on him he would pay the king three thousand six hundred sixty talents annually. 18 So the king appointed him high priest and ruler of the nation. 19 Jason[c] changed the nation's way of life and altered its form of government in complete violation of the law, 20 so that not only was a gymnasium constructed at the very citadel[d] of our native land, but also the temple service was abolished. 21 The divine justice was angered by these acts and caused Antiochus himself to make war on them. 22 For when he was warring against Ptolemy in Egypt, he heard that a rumor of his death had spread and that the people of Jerusalem had rejoiced greatly. He speedily marched against them, 23 and after he had plundered them he issued a decree that if any of them were found observing the ancestral law they should die. 24 When, by means of his decrees, he had not been able in any way to put an end to the people's observance of the law, but saw that all his threats and punishments were being disre-

a Gk he   b Gk his   c Gk He   d Or high place

Josephus, *War* 6.5.2. **5:** Compare 2 Macc 3.7–8, where Heliodorus, not Apollonius, is put in command. **10:** *Angels on horseback*, a common image of divine judgment (2 Macc 3.25–26; 5.2–3; 10.29; 11.8; Rev 9.13–19).
   **4.15–26: Antiochus's persecution of the Jews** (2 Macc 4.7–6.11; cf. 1 Macc 1.20–64). **15:** *Antiochus IV Epiphanes* (ruled 175–164 BCE) was the brother of *Seleucus* IV, and son of Antiochus III (see 1 Macc 1.10). **16:** *Jason* served as high priest ca. 175–172. **20:** *Gymnasium*, a basic institution for imparting Greek culture to young men (1 Macc 1.14–15; 2 Macc 4.9,12). *At the very citadel,* (see text note d) more probably "under the citadel," as in 2 Macc 4.12. **21:** *Antiochus* is an instrument of *divine justice*, punishing the people for their apostasy (compare the curse for breach of covenant in Deut 28.47–50). **22:** *Ptolemy* VI Philometor (180–145), 1 Macc 1.16–19. **26:** The tests of fidelity to Judaism

garded [25]—even to the extent that women, because they had circumcised their sons, were thrown headlong from heights along with their infants, though they had known beforehand that they would suffer this— [26] when, I say, his decrees were despised by the people, he himself tried through torture to compel everyone in the nation to eat defiling foods and to renounce Judaism.

5 The tyrant Antiochus, sitting in state with his counselors on a certain high place, and with his armed soldiers standing around him, [2] ordered the guards to seize each and every Hebrew and to compel them to eat pork and food sacrificed to idols. [3] If any were not willing to eat defiling food, they were to be broken on the wheel and killed. [4] When many persons had been rounded up, one man, Eleazar by name, leader of the flock, was brought[a] before the king. He was a man of priestly family, learned in the law, advanced in age, and known to many in the tyrant's court because of his philosophy.[b]

[5] When Antiochus saw him he said, [6] "Before I begin to torture you, old man, I would advise you to save yourself by eating pork, [7] for I respect your age and your gray hairs. Although you have had them for so long a time, it does not seem to me that you are a philosopher when you observe the religion of the Jews. [8] When nature has granted it to us, why should you abhor eating the very excellent meat of this animal? [9] It is senseless not to enjoy delicious things that are not shameful, and wrong to spurn the gifts of nature. [10] It seems to me that you will do something even more senseless if, by holding a vain opinion concerning the truth, you continue to despise me to your own hurt. [11] Will you not awaken from your foolish philosophy, dispel your futile reasonings, adopt a mind appropriate to your years, philosophize according to the truth of what is beneficial, [12] and have compassion on your old age by honoring my humane advice? [13] For consider this: if there is some power watching over this religion of yours, it will excuse you from any transgression that arises out of compulsion."

a Or was the first of the flock to be brought
b Other ancient authorities read his advanced age

that follow will concern *defiling foods* (5.3,19,25,27,36; 6.19; 7.6; 8.2,12,29; 11.16,25; 13.2); non-Jews often ridiculed Jewish dietary restrictions (e.g., Tacitus, *Histories* 5.4).

**5.1–7.23: Martyrdom of Eleazar** (see 2 Macc 6.18–31). The stories about Eleazar and the youths (5.1–14.10) follow a similar pattern: the king's demand for apostasy; a defiant reply; torture, last words, and death of the hero; an encomium, that is, a speech praising the martyr and his virtue. The mother's story (14.11–17.6) has a somewhat different structure. **5.1:** *Sitting in state,* presumably in Jerusalem (see 18.5), though later tradition placed the martyrs' tombs in Antioch. **2:** *Pork and food sacrificed to idols,* Lev 11.7; Deut 14.8 (cf. 2 Macc 6.7–9; 2 Esd 16.68; Acts 15.29; 1 Cor 8, 10). **4:** *Eleazar,* in 2 Macc 6.18 he is described as "one of the scribes in high position," not as a priest. His *advanced . . . age,* which makes his courage all the more remarkable (5.31–33; 7.16) is specified in 2 Macc 6.24 as ninety. Since Eleazar is *known to many . . . because of his philosophy,* the arguments the king poses to him (5.7–13) are philosophical in character.

**5.5–13: Antiochus's exhortation to apostasy.** This speech, like the one in 8.5–14, reflects the dominant culture's assessment of Judaism, expressing enticements to assimilation with which the readers themselves were probably familiar; the martyrs' speeches to the tyrant and each other provide them with appropriate counter-arguments. **7–8:** Typically, a Greek *philosopher* regarded the distinctions of national religions and laws, such as those of Judaism, as inconsequential (e.g., Dio Chrysostom, *Orations* 80.3–7), whereas Jews considered the Mosaic law to be the highest philosophy. Philosophers also taught the merit of living according to *nature* (e.g., Epictetus, *Discourses* 3.1.1–9,25–26). **13:** *Some power watching over,* a Greek philosophical expression (cf. 2 Macc 7.35; 9.5; 3 Macc 2.21). *Out of compulsion,* the same argument is made in 8.14,22,24 (cf. Aristotle, *Nicomachean Ethics* 3.1.7–12); Eleazar's answer comes in 5.16. Philosophers insisted on the sage's freedom from such external pressures (e.g., Epictetus, *Discourses* 3.24.66–72).

14 When the tyrant urged him in this fashion to eat meat unlawfully, Eleazar asked to have a word. 15 When he had received permission to speak, he began to address the people as follows: 16 "We, O Antiochus, who have been persuaded to govern our lives by the divine law, think that there is no compulsion more powerful than our obedience to the law. 17 Therefore we consider that we should not transgress it in any respect. 18 Even if, as you suppose, our law were not truly divine and we had wrongly held it to be divine, not even so would it be right for us to invalidate our reputation for piety. 19 Therefore do not suppose that it would be a petty sin if we were to eat defiling food; 20 to transgress the law in matters either small or great is of equal seriousness, 21 for in either case the law is equally despised. 22 You scoff at our philosophy as though living by it were irrational, 23 but it teaches us self-control, so that we master all pleasures and desires, and it also trains us in courage, so that we endure any suffering willingly; 24 it instructs us in justice, so that in all our dealings we act impartially,*a* and it teaches us piety, so that with proper reverence we worship the only living God.

25 "Therefore we do not eat defiling food; for since we believe that the law was established by God, we know that in the nature of things the Creator of the world in giving us the law has shown sympathy toward us. 26 He has permitted us to eat what will be most suitable for our lives,*b* but he has forbidden us to eat meats that would be contrary to this. 27 It would be tyrannical for you to compel us not only to transgress the law, but also to eat in such a way that you may deride us for eating defiling foods, which are most hateful to us. 28 But you shall have no such occasion to laugh at me, 29 nor will I transgress the sacred oaths of my ancestors concerning the keeping of the law, 30 not even if you gouge out my eyes and burn my entrails. 31 I am not so old and cowardly as not to be young in reason on behalf of piety. 32 Therefore get your torture wheels ready and fan the fire more vehemently! 33 I do not so pity my old age as to break the ancestral law by my own act. 34 I will not play false to you, O law that trained me, nor will I renounce you, beloved self-control. 35 I will not put you to shame, philosophical reason, nor will I reject you, honored priesthood and knowledge of the law. 36 You, O king,*c* shall not defile the honorable mouth of my old age, nor my long life lived lawfully. 37 My ancestors will receive me as pure, as one who does not fear your violence even to death. 38 You may tyrannize the ungodly, but you shall not dominate my religious principles, either by words or through deeds."

*a Or so that we hold in balance all our habitual inclinations    b Or souls    c Gk lacks O king*

**5.14–38:** Eleazar's reply mentions many of the book's key themes; his allegiance to God, the law, and virtue make assimilation to the Greek way of life impossible. In his determination to preserve his integrity rather than his life, he resembles Socrates (cf. Plato's *Crito*). **15:** *The people,* the public setting of the martyrdoms is noted, lending them a sense of national importance (cf. 15.29; 17.14). **18:** *Piety,* demonstrated in the history of Jewish loyalty to the divine and embodied in the martyrs themselves (5.24,31; 6.2; 7.16; 9.6,29; 10.15; 13.10; 15.2–3,12; 16.13,17; 17.5; 18.1). Piety is sometimes included among the cardinal virtues (see 1.2–4n.), e.g., Philo, *Life of Moses* 2.216 (cf. Titus 1.8; 2.12). **20:** Even minor or symbolic transgressions against *the law* are serious (cf. Pirke Abot 2.1). The Stoic philosophers argued a similar position. **23–24:** *Teaches us . . . trains us . . . instructs us,* virtue comes only through education and discipline (cf. 1.17; 5.23–24,34; 9.6; 10.2,10; 13.22,24; 18.18). **25:** *Creator,* cf. 11.5. **26:** *Most suitable for our lives,* (see text note b) the law promotes what is beneficial for people in accordance with their created nature (see Philo, *Special Laws* 4.100). **37:** *Will receive me,* see 9.22n. The martyr's death must be a *pure,* sacred sacrifice (1.11; 6.29; 7.4,6; 13.13; 17.19–21). **38:** *You may tyrannize the ungodly,* Greco-Roman philosophers maintained that tyrants have no power over a sage's integrity (e.g., Epictetus, *Discourses* 1.18.17).

6 When Eleazar in this manner had made eloquent response to the exhortations of the tyrant, the guards who were standing by dragged him violently to the instruments of torture. 2First they stripped the old man, though he remained adorned with the gracefulness of his piety. 3After they had tied his arms on each side they flogged him, 4while a herald who faced him cried out, "Obey the king's commands!" 5But the courageous and noble man, like a true Eleazar, was unmoved, as though being tortured in a dream; 6yet while the old man's eyes were raised to heaven, his flesh was being torn by scourges, his blood flowing, and his sides were being cut to pieces. 7Although he fell to the ground because his body could not endure the agonies, he kept his reason upright and unswerving. 8One of the cruel guards rushed at him and began to kick him in the side to make him get up again after he fell. 9But he bore the pains and scorned the punishment and endured the tortures. 10Like a noble athlete the old man, while being beaten, was victorious over his torturers; 11in fact, with his face bathed in sweat, and gasping heavily for breath, he amazed even his torturers by his courageous spirit.

12 At that point, partly out of pity for his old age, 13partly out of sympathy from their acquaintance with him, partly out of admiration for his endurance, some of the king's retinue came to him and said, 14"Eleazar, why are you so irrationally destroying yourself through these evil things? 15We will set before you some cooked meat; save yourself by pretending to eat pork."

16 But Eleazar, as though more bitterly tormented by this counsel, cried out: 17"Never may we, the children of Abraham,[a] think so basely that out of cowardice we feign a role unbecoming to us! 18For it would be irrational if having lived in accordance with truth up to old age and having maintained in accordance with law the reputation of such a life, we should now change our course 19and ourselves become a pattern of impiety to the young by setting them an example in the eating of defiling food. 20It would be shameful if we should survive for a little while and during that time be a laughingstock to all for our cowardice, 21and be despised by the tyrant as unmanly by not contending even to death for our divine law. 22Therefore, O children of Abraham, die nobly for your religion! 23And you, guards of the tyrant, why do you delay?"

24 When they saw that he was so courageous in the face of the afflictions, and that he had not been changed by their compassion, the guards brought him to the fire. 25There they burned him with maliciously contrived instruments, threw him down, and poured stinking liquids into his nostrils. 26When he was now burned to his very bones and about to expire, he lifted up his eyes to God and said, 27"You know, O God, that though I might have saved myself, I am dying in burning torments for the sake of the law. 28Be merciful to your people, and let our punishment suffice for them. 29Make my blood their purification, and take my life in exchange for theirs." 30After he said this, the holy man died nobly in his tortures; even in the tortures of

a Or O children of Abraham

6.1–35: Eleazar's torture and death. 2: Although physically disgraced, Eleazar reveals the *gracefulness of his piety;* as Plato argued (*Gorgias* 523A–525A), it is the soul, not the body, that is ultimately judged for virtue. 5: *A true Eleazar,* compare Num 20.25–28; 2 Macc 8.23; 3 Macc 6.1–15. The name "Eleazar" means "God has helped." 6: *Eyes . . . raised to heaven,* in prayer (cf. 6.26; Acts 7.55). 10: *A noble athlete,* see 17.11–16n. 17: *The children of Abraham,* the patriarch's memory is venerated because of his willingness to obey God's command, even to the point of sacrificing his son (6.22; 7.19; 9.21; 13.12,17; 14.20; 15.28; 16.20,25; 17.6; 18.1,11,20,23). 19: Eleazar is aware of his role as a *pattern* and *example* for others; therefore he will not even pretend to eat pork (cf. 7.9; 9.6,23n.; 17.23–24). 28–29: Eleazar prays that his faithful death is sufficient *punishment* for the nation's apostasy (see 17.21–22n.). 31–35: Eleazar's heroism is held up as proof of the book's opening thesis (1.1–12; cf. 13.1–5).

death he resisted, by virtue of reason, for the sake of the law.

31 Admittedly, then, devout reason is sovereign over the emotions. 32 For if the emotions had prevailed over reason, we would have testified to their domination. 33 But now that reason has conquered the emotions, we properly attribute to it the power to govern. 34 It is right for us to acknowledge the dominance of reason when it masters even external agonies. It would be ridiculous to deny it.[a] 35 I have proved not only that reason has mastered agonies, but also that it masters pleasures and in no respect yields to them.

7 For like a most skillful pilot, the reason of our father Eleazar steered the ship of religion over the sea of the emotions, 2 and though buffeted by the stormings of the tyrant and overwhelmed by the mighty waves of tortures, 3 in no way did he turn the rudder of religion until he sailed into the haven of immortal victory. 4 No city besieged with many ingenious war machines has ever held out as did that most holy man. Although his sacred life was consumed by tortures and racks, he conquered the besiegers with the shield of his devout reason. 5 For in setting his mind firm like a jutting cliff, our father Eleazar broke the maddening waves of the emotions. 6 O priest, worthy of the priesthood, you neither defiled your sacred teeth nor profaned your stomach, which had room only for reverence and purity, by eating defiling foods. 7 O man in harmony with the law and philosopher of divine life! 8 Such should be those who are administrators of the law, shielding it with their own blood and noble sweat in sufferings even to death. 9 You, father, strengthened our loyalty to the law through your glorious endurance, and you did not abandon the holiness that you praised, but by your deeds you made your words of divine[b] philosophy credible. 10 O aged man, more powerful than tortures; O elder, fiercer than fire; O supreme king over the passions, Eleazar! 11 For just as our father Aaron, armed with the censer, ran through the multitude of the people and conquered the fiery[c] angel, 12 so the descendant of Aaron, Eleazar, though being consumed by the fire, remained unmoved in his reason. 13 Most amazing, indeed, though he was an old man, his body no longer tense and firm,[d] his muscles flabby, his sinews feeble, he became young again 14 in spirit through reason; and by reason like that of Isaac he rendered the many-headed rack ineffective. 15 O man of blessed age and of venerable gray hair and of law-abiding life, whom the faithful seal of death has perfected!

16 If, therefore, because of piety an aged man despised tortures even to death, most certainly devout reason is governor of the emotions. 17 Some perhaps might say, "Not all have full command of their emotions, because not all have prudent reason." 18 But as many as attend to religion with a whole heart, these alone are able to control the passions of the flesh, 19 since they believe that they, like our patriarchs Abraham and Isaac and Jacob, do not die to God, but live to God. 20 No contradiction therefore

a Syr: Meaning of Gk uncertain   b Other ancient authorities lack *divine*   c Other ancient authorities lack *fiery*   d Gk *the tautness of the body already loosed*

**7.1–23: An encomium on Eleazar.** In keeping with the style and function of the typical funeral oration (e.g., Pericles's speech in Thucydides, *The Peloponnesian War* 2.34–46), the author praises both the deceased and his virtue, implicitly encouraging the audience to follow the example he set in both life and death (cf. 13.1–14.10; 15.1–32; 17.2–18.24). **1–3:** The metaphor of the *pilot* and the *ship,* common in Greek literature, recurs in 13.6–7; 15.31–32 (cf. Jas 3.4; 1 Pet 3.20; Philo, *Allegorical Interpretation* 3.223–224). **4:** *City besieged,* Stoics popularized the image of the sage and his reason as an impregnable fortress (cf. 2 Cor 10.3–6). **11:** Num 16.46–50 (cf. Wis 18.20–25). **14:** *Isaac,* Gen 22.1–14. **15:** *The faithful seal,* like the other martyrs, Eleazar's virtuous life is *perfected* in the honorable manner of his *death.* **17–23:** The author concedes that *only the wise* rule the emotions, but contends that everyone is able to overcome them by living as a philosopher. **18:** See 9.18n. **19:** *Like our patriarchs,* the martyrdoms are not isolated events but belong to Israel's sacred history (cf. 6.17n.; 7.11–12,14; 16.20–23; 18.10–19).

arises when some persons appear to be dominated by their emotions because of the weakness of their reason. 21 What person who lives as a philosopher by the whole rule of philosophy, and trusts in God, 22 and knows that it is blessed to endure any suffering for the sake of virtue, would not be able to overcome the emotions through godliness? 23 For only the wise and courageous are masters of their emotions.

8 For this is why even the very young, by following a philosophy in accordance with devout reason, have prevailed over the most painful instruments of torture. 2 For when the tyrant was conspicuously defeated in his first attempt, being unable to compel an aged man to eat defiling foods, then in violent rage he commanded that others of the Hebrew captives be brought, and that any who ate defiling food would be freed after eating, but if any were to refuse, they would be tortured even more cruelly.

3 When the tyrant had given these orders, seven brothers—handsome, modest, noble, and accomplished in every way—were brought before him along with their aged mother. 4 When the tyrant saw them, grouped about their mother as though a chorus, he was pleased with them. And struck by their appearance and nobility, he smiled at them, and summoned them nearer and said, 5 "Young men, with favorable feelings I admire each and every one of you, and greatly respect the beauty and the number of such brothers. Not only do I advise you not to display the same madness as that of the old man who has just been tortured, but I also exhort you to yield to me and

enjoy my friendship. 6 Just as I am able to punish those who disobey my orders, so I can be a benefactor to those who obey me. 7 Trust me, then, and you will have positions of authority in my government if you will renounce the ancestral tradition of your national life. 8 Enjoy your youth by adopting the Greek way of life and by changing your manner of living. 9 But if by disobedience you rouse my anger, you will compel me to destroy each and every one of you with dreadful punishments through tortures. 10 Therefore take pity on yourselves. Even I, your enemy, have compassion for your youth and handsome appearance. 11 Will you not consider this, that if you disobey, nothing remains for you but to die on the rack?"

12 When he had said these things, he ordered the instruments of torture to be brought forward so as to persuade them out of fear to eat the defiling food. 13 When the guards had placed before them wheels and joint-dislocators, rack and hooks[a] and catapults[b] and caldrons, braziers and thumbscrews and iron claws and wedges and bellows, the tyrant resumed speaking: 14 "Be afraid, young fellows; whatever justice you revere will be merciful to you when you transgress under compulsion."

15 But when they had heard the inducements and saw the dreadful devices, not only were they not afraid, but they also opposed the tyrant with their own philosophy, and by their right reasoning nullified

a Meaning of Gk uncertain   b Here and elsewhere in 4 Macc an instrument of torture

---

*Abraham and Isaac and Jacob* are living (Mk 12.26). *Live to God,* similar expressions are found in Lk 20.38; Rom 6.10; 14.8; Gal 2.19 (cf. 4 Macc 16.25).

**8.1–14.10: The martyrdom of the seven brothers** (see 2 Macc 7).
**8.1–14: Antiochus confronts the seven brothers.** He exhorts them to apostasy (cf. 5.5–13; 2 Macc 7.1,24–25). **1:** The brothers' reason and courage are remarkable because they are *very young* (see 8.20). **2:** The king's *violent rage* contrasts with the martyrs' self-control (cf. 9.10). **4:** *Chorus,* in Greek plays the chorus, speaking its lines in unison, commented on the action; see 13.8; 14.7–8; 18.23; 3 Macc 6.35. **5–11:** Antiochus's remarks are laced with sexual innuendo. **5:** *Friendship* with the king was a highly prized, official relationship (1 Macc 2.18; 7.8; 10.15–20,65; 11.26–27,57; 13.36; 15.32). **6:** *Benefactor,* a title popular with Hellenistic monarchs (3 Macc 3.19; 6.24; Lk 22.25). **14:** *Justice,* a philosophical way of speaking of God (see 4.13,21; 8.22; 9.9,15,24; 11.3; 12.12; 18.22).

**8.15–9.9: The brothers' reply** (see 2 Macc 7.2). **16–26:** An imaginary speech presents false arguments his tyranny. [16] Let us consider, on the other hand, what arguments might have been used if some of them had been cowardly and unmanly. Would they not have been the following? [17] "O wretches that we are and so senseless! Since the king has summoned and exhorted us to accept kind treatment if we obey him, [18] why do we take pleasure in vain resolves and venture upon a disobedience that brings death? [19] O men and brothers, should we not fear the instruments of torture and consider the threats of torments, and give up this vain opinion and this arrogance that threatens to destroy us? [20] Let us take pity on our youth and have compassion on our mother's age; [21] and let us seriously consider that if we disobey we are dead! [22] Also, divine justice will excuse us for fearing the king when we are under compulsion. [23] Why do we banish ourselves from this most pleasant life and deprive ourselves of this delightful world? [24] Let us not struggle against compulsion[a] or take hollow pride in being put to the rack. [25] Not even the law itself would arbitrarily put us to death for fearing the instruments of torture. [26] Why does such contentiousness excite us and such a fatal stubbornness please us, when we can live in peace if we obey the king?"

27 But the youths, though about to be tortured, neither said any of these things nor even seriously considered them. [28] For they were contemptuous of the emotions and sovereign over agonies, [29] so that as soon as the tyrant had ceased counseling them to eat defiling food, all with one voice together, as from one mind, said:

9 "Why do you delay, O tyrant? For we are ready to die rather than transgress our ancestral commandments; [2] we are ob-

viously putting our forebears to shame unless we should practice ready obedience to the law and to Moses[b] our counselor. [3] Tyrant and counselor of lawlessness, in your hatred for us do not pity us more than we pity ourselves.[c] [4] For we consider this pity of yours, which insures our safety through transgression of the law, to be more grievous than death itself. [5] You are trying to terrify us by threatening us with death by torture, as though a short time ago you learned nothing from Eleazar. [6] And if the aged men of the Hebrews because of their religion lived piously[d] while enduring torture, it would be even more fitting that we young men should die despising your coercive tortures, which our aged instructor also overcame. [7] Therefore, tyrant, put us to the test; and if you take our lives because of our religion, do not suppose that you can injure us by torturing us. [8] For we, through this severe suffering and endurance, shall have the prize of virtue and shall be with God, on whose account we suffer; [9] but you, because of your bloodthirstiness toward us, will deservedly undergo from the divine justice eternal torment by fire."

10 When they had said these things, the tyrant was not only indignant, as at those who are disobedient, but also infuriated, as at those who are ungrateful. [11] Then at his command the guards brought forward the eldest, and having torn off his tunic, they bound his hands and arms with thongs on each side. [12] When they had worn themselves out beating him with scourges, without accomplishing anything, they placed

a Or fate   b Other ancient authorities read knowledge   c Meaning of Gk uncertain   d Other ancient authorities read died

that the brothers might have used but reject; the mother gives a similar speech in 16.6–11. **29:** *With one voice,* see 13.19–27n. **9.2:** *Shame,* this test of the brothers' integrity reflects on that of the Jewish people and their ancestors (see 5.9,35; 6.20; 13.18; 16.17). **5:** *Eleazar,* see 5.4–6.30. **6:** *Aged men,* the plural may refer to Hebrew prophets such as Isaiah, who, according to Jewish tradition, were also martyred (see Heb 11.32–37; *The Lives of the Prophets*). **7:** *Do not suppose that you can injure us,* a Stoic principle; injuries and insults cannot affect the sage's virtue (e.g., Seneca, *On the Firmness of the Wise Man* 2.1–3). **9:** *Divine justice* means *eternal torment* for the tyrant (9.15,24,30,32; 10.11,15,21; 11.3,23; 12.12,14,18; 13.15; 17.21; 18.5,22).

**9.10–25: Martyrdom of the eldest** (see 2 Macc 7.3–6). **17:** See 9.7n. **18:** *Children of the Hebrews* him upon the wheel. 13 When the noble youth was stretched out around this, his limbs were dislocated, 14 and with every member disjointed he denounced the tyrant, saying, 15 "Most abominable tyrant, enemy of heavenly justice, savage of mind, you are mangling me in this manner, not because I am a murderer, or as one who acts impiously, but because I protect the divine law." 16 And when the guards said, "Agree to eat so that you may be released from the tortures," 17 he replied, "You abominable lackeys, your wheel is not so powerful as to strangle my reason. Cut my limbs, burn my flesh, and twist my joints; 18 through all these tortures I will convince you that children of the Hebrews alone are invincible where virtue is concerned." 19 While he was saying these things, they spread fire under him, and while fanning the flames*a* they tightened the wheel further. 20 The wheel was completely smeared with blood, and the heap of coals was being quenched by the drippings of gore, and pieces of flesh were falling off the axles of the machine. 21 Although the ligaments joining his bones were already severed, the courageous youth, worthy of Abraham, did not groan, 22 but as though transformed by fire into immortality, he nobly endured the rackings. 23 "Imitate me, brothers," he said. "Do not leave your post in my struggle*b* or renounce our courageous family ties. 24 Fight the sacred and noble battle for religion. Thereby the just Providence of our

ancestors may become merciful to our nation and take vengeance on the accursed tyrant." 25 When he had said this, the saintly youth broke the thread of life.

26 While all were marveling at his courageous spirit, the guards brought in the next eldest, and after fitting themselves with iron gauntlets having sharp hooks, they bound him to the torture machine and catapult. 27 Before torturing him, they inquired if he were willing to eat, and they heard his noble decision.*c* 28 These leopard-like beasts tore out his sinews with the iron hands, flayed all his flesh up to his chin, and tore away his scalp. But he steadfastly endured this agony and said, 29 "How sweet is any kind of death for the religion of our ancestors!" 30 To the tyrant he said, "Do you not think, you most savage tyrant, that you are being tortured more than I, as you see the arrogant design of your tyranny being defeated by our endurance for the sake of religion? 31 I lighten my pain by the joys that come from virtue, 32 but you suffer torture by the threats that come from impiety. You will not escape, you most abominable tyrant, the judgments of the divine wrath."

10 When he too had endured a glorious death, the third was led in, and many repeatedly urged him to save himself

a Meaning of Gk uncertain   b Other ancient authorities read *post forever*   c Other ancient authorities read *having heard his noble decision, they tore him to shreds*

*alone,* the author's strongest claim for Judaism as the path to virtue (cf. 2.23; 7.18). **22:** The author emphasizes not bodily resurrection, but *immortality* of the soul, in accord with Greek views (5.37; 7.19; 9.8; 10.15; 13.17; 14.5–6; 15.3; 16.13,25; 17.18; 18.23; see Wis 3.4n.); cf. 2 Macc 7.11,14 where resurrection of the body is anticipated. *Transformed,* cf. 1 Cor 15.53; 2 Cor 3.18; 5.4; Phil 3.21. **23:** *Imitate me,* like Eleazar (see 6.19n.), the eldest brother is aware of his example to others (see 10.15; 12.16; 13.9). **24:** *Fight,* given the story's context (see 4.21–23), it is not surprising that the author often employs martial imagery to describe the struggle between Antiochus and the martyrs (see also 1.11; 3.4,17–18; 6.33; 7.4,11; 8.2; 9.23,30; 11.20–21,25; 13.2–3,7,16; 16.14,16; 17.23–24). *Providence,* see 5.13; 13.19; 17.22; 1 Esd 6.5; 3 Macc 4.21; 5.30.

**9.26–32:** Martyrdom of the second brother (see 2 Macc 7.7–9). **30:** *By our endurance,* the author repeatedly draws attention to the martyrs' capacity to overcome physical torment (1.11; 5.23; 6.13; 7.9,22; 9.8; 11.12; 13.27; 15.30; 16.19; 17.7,10,12,17,23). **31:** *Joys that come from virtue,* these contrast with the worldly delights of 8.23 (cf. 1.22); that the virtuous alone are happy was a philosophical commonplace (e.g., Plato, *Gorgias* 507B–C).

**10.1–11:** Martyrdom of the third brother (see 2 Macc 7.10–12). **4:** *You cannot touch my soul,* this by tasting the meat. 2 But he shouted, "Do you not know that the same father begot me as well as those who died, and the same mother bore me, and that I was brought up on the same teachings? 3 I do not renounce the noble kinship that binds me to my brothers."[a] 5 Enraged by the man's boldness, they disjointed his hands and feet with their instruments, dismembering him by prying his limbs from their sockets, 6 and breaking his fingers and arms and legs and elbows. 7 Since they were not able in any way to break his spirit,[b] they abandoned the instruments[c] and scalped him with their fingernails in a Scythian fashion. 8 They immediately brought him to the wheel, and while his vertebrae were being dislocated by this, he saw his own flesh torn all around and drops of blood flowing from his entrails. 9 When he was about to die, he said, 10 "We, most abominable tyrant, are suffering because of our godly training and virtue, 11 but you, because of your impiety and bloodthirstiness, will undergo unceasing torments."

12 When he too had died in a manner worthy of his brothers, they dragged in the fourth, saying, 13 "As for you, do not give way to the same insanity as your brothers, but obey the king and save yourself." 14 But he said to them, "You do not have a fire hot enough to make me play the coward. 15 No—by the blessed death of my brothers, by the eternal destruction of the tyrant, and by the everlasting life of the pious, I will not renounce our noble family ties. 16 Contrive tortures, tyrant, so that you may learn from them that I am a brother to those who have just now been tortured." 17 When he heard this, the bloodthirsty,

murderous, and utterly abominable Antiochus gave orders to cut out his tongue. 18 But he said, "Even if you remove my organ of speech, God hears also those who are mute. 19 See, here is my tongue; cut it off, for in spite of this you will not make our reason speechless. 20 Gladly, for the sake of God, we let our bodily members be mutilated. 21 God will visit you swiftly, for you are cutting out a tongue that has been melodious with divine hymns."

11 When he too died, after being cruelly tortured, the fifth leaped up, saying, 2 "I will not refuse, tyrant, to be tortured for the sake of virtue. 3 I have come of my own accord, so that by murdering me you will incur punishment from the heavenly justice for even more crimes. 4 Hater of virtue, hater of humankind, for what act of ours are you destroying us in this way? 5 Is it because[d] we revere the Creator of all things and live according to his virtuous law? 6 But these deeds deserve honors, not tortures."[e] 9 While he was saying these things, the guards bound him and dragged him to the catapult; 10 they tied him to it on his knees, and fitting iron clamps on them, they twisted his back[f] around the wedge on the wheel,[g] so that he was completely curled back like a scorpion, and all his

a Other ancient authorities add verse 4, *So if you have any instrument of torture, apply it to my body; for you cannot touch my soul, even if you wish."*
b Gk *to strangle him*    c Other ancient authorities read *they tore off his skin*    d Other ancient authorities read *Or does it seem evil to you that*
e Other authorities add verses 7 and 8, 7*If you but understood human feelings and had hope of salvation from God—* 8*but, as it is, you are a stranger to God and persecute those who serve him."*    f Gk *loins*
g Meaning of Gk uncertain

verse is probably a later addition to the book (see text note *a*); cf. 9.7; 13.14–15. **5:** *Boldness of speech* in adversity was a prized philosophical virtue, especially in Stoic and Cynic circles (cf. 15.19; Acts 4.13,29,31). **7:** *Scythian fashion,* cf. 2 Macc 4.47; 3 Macc 7.5. The Scythians were notorious for barbarism.

**10.12–21: Martyrdom of the fourth brother** (2 Macc 7.13–14). **19:** *Here is my tongue,* a similar story is told in Diogenes Laertius, *Lives of Eminent Philosophers* 9.59.

**11.1–12: Martyrdom of the fifth brother** (2 Macc 7.15–17). **3:** The fifth brother volunteers for torture so that the tyrant will receive even greater *punishment;* philosophers often contended that it was more injurious to perpetrate injustice than to suffer it (e.g., Plato, *Gorgias* 508C–E). **7–8:** These verses are a later addition to the text (see text note *e*).

members were disjointed. 11 In this condition, gasping for breath and in anguish of body, 12 he said, "Tyrant, they are splendid favors that you grant us against your will, because through these noble sufferings you give us an opportunity to show our endurance for the law."

13 When he too had died, the sixth, a mere boy, was led in. When the tyrant inquired whether he was willing to eat and be released, he said, 14 "I am younger in age than my brothers, but I am their equal in mind. 15 Since to this end we were born and bred, we ought likewise to die for the same principles. 16 So if you intend to torture me for not eating defiling foods, go on torturing!" 17 When he had said this, they led him to the wheel. 18 He was carefully stretched tight upon it, his back was broken, and he was roasted[a] from underneath. 19 To his back they applied sharp spits that had been heated in the fire, and pierced his ribs so that his entrails were burned through. 20 While being tortured he said, "O contest befitting holiness, in which so many of us brothers have been summoned to an arena of sufferings for religion, and in which we have not been defeated! 21 For religious knowledge, O tyrant, is invincible. 22 I also, equipped with nobility, will die with my brothers, 23 and I myself will bring a great avenger upon you, you inventor of tortures and enemy of those who are truly devout. 24 We six boys have paralyzed your tyranny. 25 Since you have not been able to persuade us to change our mind or to force us to eat defiling foods, is not this your downfall? 26 Your fire is cold to us, and the catapults painless, and your violence powerless. 27 For it is not the guards of the tyrant but those of the divine law that are set over us;

therefore, unconquered, we hold fast to reason."

12 When he too, thrown into the caldron, had died a blessed death, the seventh and youngest of all came forward. 2 Even though the tyrant had been vehemently reproached by the brothers, he felt strong compassion for this child when he saw that he was already in fetters. He summoned him to come nearer and tried to persuade him, saying, 3 "You see the result of your brothers' stupidity, for they died in torments because of their disobedience. 4 You too, if you do not obey, will be miserably tortured and die before your time, 5 but if you yield to persuasion you will be my friend and a leader in the government of the kingdom." 6 When he had thus appealed to him, he sent for the boy's mother to show compassion on her who had been bereaved of so many sons and to influence her to persuade the surviving son to obey and save himself. 7 But when his mother had exhorted him in the Hebrew language, as we shall tell a little later, 8 he said, "Let me loose, let me speak to the king and to all his friends that are with him." 9 Extremely pleased by the boy's declaration, they freed him at once. 10 Running to the nearest of the braziers, 11 he said, "You profane tyrant, most impious of all the wicked, since you have received good things and also your kingdom from God, were you not ashamed to murder his servants and torture on the wheel those who practice religion? 12 Because of this, justice has laid up for you intense and eternal fire and tortures, and these throughout all time[b] will never

a Other ancient authorities add by fire
b Gk throughout the whole age

**11.13–27:** Martyrdom of the sixth brother (2 Macc 7.18–19). **13–14:** *A mere boy,* the youth of the sixth and seventh brothers is emphasized; see 12.1–2. **20:** *Contest,* see 17.11–16n. **25:** *Your downfall,* see 9.9n.,24n.

**12.1–19:** Martyrdom of the youngest brother (see 2 Macc 7.24–40). **6–7:** Summoning *the boy's mother* gives an unexpected twist to the narrative pattern of the martyrdoms. The promise to *tell a little later* what she said creates dramatic tension (see 16.16–23; 18.6–19). *In the Hebrew language,* speaking in the law's original language, perhaps so that the tyrant will not understand (cf. 16.15; 2 Macc 7.8,21,27). **7:** See 16.15–23; 18.6–19. **12:** *Eternal fire,* the speech in 12.11–18 stresses the king's punishment for persecuting the faithful. **13:** *Feelings like yours,* Hellenistic moralists often emphasized human-let you go. [13] As a man, were you not ashamed, you most savage beast, to cut out the tongues of men who have feelings like yours and are made of the same elements as you, and to maltreat and torture them in this way? [14] Surely they by dying nobly fulfilled their service to God, but you will wail bitterly for having killed without cause the contestants for virtue." [15] Then because he too was about to die, he said, [16] "I do not desert the excellent example[a] of my brothers, [17] and I call on the God of our ancestors to be merciful to our nation;[b] [18] but on you he will take vengeance both in this present life and when you are dead." [19] After he had uttered these imprecations, he flung himself into the braziers and so ended his life.[c]

13 Since, then, the seven brothers despised sufferings even unto death, everyone must concede that devout reason is sovereign over the emotions. [2] For if they had been slaves to their emotions and had eaten defiling food, we would say that they had been conquered by these emotions. [3] But in fact it was not so. Instead, by reason, which is praised before God, they prevailed over their emotions. [4] The supremacy of the mind over these cannot be overlooked, for the brothers[d] mastered both emotions and pains. [5] How then can one fail to confess the sovereignty of right reason over emotion in those who were not turned back by fiery agonies? [6] For just as towers jutting out over harbors hold back the threatening waves and make it calm for those who sail into the inner basin, [7] so the seven-towered right reason of the youths, by fortifying the harbor of religion,

conquered the tempest of the emotions. [8] For they constituted a holy chorus of religion and encouraged one another, saying, [9] "Brothers, let us die like brothers for the sake of the law; let us imitate the three youths in Assyria who despised the same ordeal of the furnace. [10] Let us not be cowardly in the demonstration of our piety." [11] While one said, "Courage, brother," another said, "Bear up nobly," [12] and another reminded them, "Remember whence you came, and the father by whose hand Isaac would have submitted to being slain for the sake of religion." [13] Each of them and all of them together looking at one another, cheerful and undaunted, said, "Let us with all our hearts consecrate ourselves to God, who gave us our lives,[e] and let us use our bodies as a bulwark for the law. [14] Let us not fear him who thinks he is killing us, [15] for great is the struggle of the soul and the danger of eternal torment lying before those who transgress the commandment of God. [16] Therefore let us put on the full armor of self-control, which is divine reason. [17] For if we so die,[f] Abraham and Isaac and Jacob will welcome us, and all the fathers will praise us." [18] Those who were left behind said to each of the brothers who were being dragged away, "Do not put us to shame, brother, or betray the brothers who have died before us."

[19] You are not ignorant of the affection of family ties, which the divine and all-wise

---

a Other ancient authorities read *the witness*
b Other ancient authorities read *my race*
c Gk *and so gave up*; other ancient authorities read *gave up his spirit* or *his soul*     d Gk *they*
e Or *souls*     f Other ancient authorities read *suffer*

ity's common bonds (cf. Wis 7.1–6; Acts 14.15; Jas 5.17; Epictetus, *Discourses* 1.13.3–5). **19:** *Flung himself,* Jews, like Stoics, sometimes approved of suicide (cf. 17.1; 1 Sam 31.1–6; 2 Macc 14.41–46).

**13.1–14.10: An encomium** (see 7.1–23n.), praising the brothers' courage, integrity, and concord, opens with a philosophical meditation (13.1–5), similar in tone and content to 1.1–3.18; 6.31–35. The brothers' true opponent was not the tyrant but their own *emotions and pains;* their martyrdoms attest the supremacy of *devout reason.* **6–7:** Cf. 7.5. **8:** *Chorus,* see 8.4n. *They . . . encouraged one another,* as Aristotle observes (*Nicomachean Ethics* 8.8.5), true friends restrain one another from doing anything shameful (cf. 9.23–24; 15.12). **9:** Dan 3. **12:** Isa 51.1–2; Gen 22.1–19 (cf. Heb 11.17–19; Jas 2.21–23). **13:** *All of them together,* as a chorus, see 8.4n. **14–15:** See 10.4n. **16:** *Armor,* compare Wis 5.17–20; Rom 13.12; Eph 6.11–17. **19–27:** The explanation of the brothers' *affection* and *concord* (see also 8.29; 10.2–3; 13.13; 14.1,3,7–8n.) draws on philosophical concepts (cf. Plutarch's *On Brotherly Love*). Their

Providence has bequeathed through the fathers to their descendants and which was implanted in the mother's womb. 20 There each of the brothers spent the same length of time and was shaped during the same period of time; and growing from the same blood and through the same life, they were brought to the light of day. 21 When they were born after an equal time of gestation, they drank milk from the same fountains. From such embraces brotherly-loving souls are nourished; 22 and they grow stronger from this common nurture and daily companionship, and from both general education and our discipline in the law of God.

23 Therefore, when sympathy and brotherly affection had been so established, the brothers were the more sympathetic to one another. 24 Since they had been educated by the same law and trained in the same virtues and brought up in right living, they loved one another all the more. 25 A common zeal for nobility strengthened their goodwill toward one another, and their concord, 26 because they could make their brotherly love more fervent with the aid of their religion. 27 But although nature and companionship and virtuous habits had augmented the affection of family ties, those who were left endured for the sake of religion, while watching their brothers being maltreated and tortured to death.

14 Furthermore, they encouraged them to face the torture, so that they not only despised their agonies, but also mastered the emotions of brotherly love.

2 O reason,[a] more royal than kings and freer than the free! 3 O sacred and harmonious concord of the seven brothers on behalf of religion! 4 None of the seven youths proved coward or shrank from death, 5 but all of them, as though running the course toward immortality, hastened to death by torture. 6 Just as the hands and feet are moved in harmony with the guidance of the mind, so those holy youths, as though moved by an immortal spirit of devotion, agreed to go to death for its sake. 7 O most holy seven, brothers in harmony! For just as the seven days of creation move in choral dance around religion, 8 so these youths, forming a chorus, encircled the sevenfold fear of tortures and dissolved it. 9 Even now, we ourselves shudder as we hear of the suffering of these young men; they not only saw what was happening, not only heard the direct word of threat, but also bore the sufferings patiently, and in agonies of fire at that. 10 What could be more excruciatingly painful than this? For the power of fire is intense and swift, and it consumed their bodies quickly.

11 Do not consider it amazing that reason had full command over these men in their tortures, since the mind of woman despised even more diverse agonies, 12 for the mother of the seven young men bore up under the rackings of each one of her children.

13 Observe how complex is a mother's love for her children, which draws everything toward an emotion felt in her inmost parts. 14 Even unreasoning animals, as well as human beings, have a sympathy and parental love for their offspring. 15 For example, among birds, the ones that are tame protect their young by building on the housetops, 16 and the others, by building in precipitous chasms and in holes and tops of trees, hatch the nestlings and ward off the

a Or O minds

---

conduct sets an example for the *public harmony* of the whole Jewish nation (3.21). **14.1:** *They . . . mastered the emotions of brotherly love,* true commitment to the law is stronger than natural affections (cf. 2.10–13). **5:** See 9.22n. **7–8:** *Chorus,* see 8.4; 13.8; 18.23; 3 Macc 6.35. **9:** *Even now,* see 1.10n.

**14.11–20: Reason and maternal affection.** The author's assertions (as in ch 15) are based on ancient constructions of gender. **11:** *The mind of woman,* the presence of reason and courage, generally understood as male virtues, in an old woman is seen as remarkable (see 15.5,23,30; 16.1–2). **13–19:** The author asserts that maternal affection is instinctual, not rational (see also Aristotle, *Nicomachean Ethics* 8.12.2–3). Analogies like this between human life and the animal world were common in ancient moral discourse (e.g., Plutarch, *On Affection for Offspring* 493C). **20:** See 13.12n.

intruder. [17] If they are not able to keep the intruder[a] away, they do what they can to help their young by flying in circles around them in the anguish of love, warning them with their own calls. [18] And why is it necessary to demonstrate sympathy for children by the example of unreasoning animals, [19] since even bees at the time for making honeycombs defend themselves against intruders and, as though with an iron dart, sting those who approach their hive and defend it even to the death? [20] But sympathy for her children did not sway the mother of the young men; she was of the same mind as Abraham.

**15** O reason of the children, tyrant over the emotions! O religion, more desirable to the mother than her children! [2] Two courses were open to this mother, that of religion, and that of preserving her seven sons for a time, as the tyrant had promised. [3] She loved religion more, the religion that preserves them for eternal life according to God's promise.[b] [4] In what manner might I express the emotions of parents who love their children? We impress upon the character of a small child a wondrous likeness both of mind and of form. Especially is this true of mothers, who because of their birth pangs have a deeper sympathy toward their offspring than do the fathers. [5] Considering that mothers are the weaker sex and give birth to many, they are more devoted to their children.[c] [6] The mother of the seven boys, more than any other mother, loved her children. In seven pregnancies she had implanted in herself tender love toward them, [7] and because of the many pains she suffered with each of them she had sympathy for them; [8] yet because of the fear of God she disdained the temporary safety of her children. [9] Not only so, but also because of the nobility of her sons and their ready obedience to the law, she felt a greater tenderness toward them. [10] For they were righteous and self-controlled and brave and magnanimous, and loved their brothers and their mother, so that they obeyed her even to death in keeping the ordinances.

11 Nevertheless, though so many factors influenced the mother to suffer with them out of love for her children, in the case of none of them were the various tortures strong enough to pervert her reason. [12] But each child separately and all of them together the mother urged on to death for religion's sake. [13] O sacred nature and affection of parental love, yearning of parents toward offspring, nurture and indomitable suffering by mothers! [14] This mother, who saw them tortured and burned one by one, because of religion did not change her attitude. [15] She watched the flesh of her children being consumed by fire, their toes and fingers scattered[d] on the ground, and the flesh of the head to the chin exposed like masks.

16 O mother, tried now by more bitter pains than even the birth pangs you suffered for them! [17] O woman, who alone gave birth to such complete devotion! [18] When the firstborn breathed his last, it did not turn you aside, nor when the second in torments looked at you piteously nor when the third expired; [19] nor did you weep when you looked at the eyes of each one in his tortures gazing boldly at the same agonies, and saw in their nostrils the signs of the approach of death. [20] When you saw the flesh of children burned upon the flesh of other children, severed hands upon hands, scalped heads upon heads, and corpses fallen on other corpses, and when you saw the place filled with many spectators of the torturings, you did not shed

a Gk it  b Gk according to God  c Or For to the degree that mothers are weaker and the more children they bear, the more they are devoted to their children. d Or quivering

**15.1–32: An encomium praising the mother** (see 7.1–23n.), whose words and deeds have shown that religious love is stronger than parental love. In contrast to Eleazar and the brothers, her suffering is principally affective and psychological in nature. **2–3:** The mother wisely opts for *God's promise* of *eternal life* for her sons over the *temporary safety* (v. 8) they would gain from apostasy (see vv. 25–28). **5:** *The weaker sex,* cf. 14.11–12; 15.23,30; 16.1–2,14. **10:** See 1.2–4n. **17:** Cf. 16.13; 17.6. **21:** *Melodies* tears. 21 Neither the melodies of sirens nor the songs of swans attract the attention of their hearers as did the voices of the children in torture calling to their mother. 22 How great and how many torments the mother then suffered as her sons were tortured on the wheel and with the hot irons! 23 But devout reason, giving her heart a man's courage in the very midst of her emotions, strengthened her to disregard, for the time, her parental love.

24 Although she witnessed the destruction of seven children and the ingenious and various rackings, this noble mother disregarded all these[a] because of faith in God. 25 For as in the council chamber of her own soul she saw mighty advocates—nature, family, parental love, and the rackings of her children— 26 this mother held two ballots, one bearing death and the other deliverance for her children. 27 She did not approve the deliverance that would preserve the seven sons for a short time, 28 but as the daughter of God-fearing Abraham she remembered his fortitude.

29 O mother of the nation, vindicator of the law and champion of religion, who carried away the prize of the contest in your heart! 30 O more noble than males in steadfastness, and more courageous than men in endurance! 31 Just as Noah's ark, carrying the world in the universal flood, stoutly endured the waves, 32 so you, O guardian of the law, overwhelmed from every side by the flood of your emotions and the violent winds, the torture of your sons, endured nobly and withstood the wintry storms that assail religion.

16 If, then, a woman, advanced in years and mother of seven sons, endured seeing her children tortured to death,

it must be admitted that devout reason is sovereign over the emotions. 2 Thus I have demonstrated not only that men have ruled over the emotions, but also that a woman has despised the fiercest tortures. 3 The lions surrounding Daniel were not so savage, nor was the raging fiery furnace of Mishael so intensely hot, as was her innate parental love, inflamed as she saw her seven sons tortured in such varied ways. 4 But the mother quenched so many and such great emotions by devout reason.

5 Consider this also: If this woman, though a mother, had been fainthearted, she would have mourned over them and perhaps spoken as follows: 6 "O how wretched am I and many times unhappy! After bearing seven children, I am now the mother of none! 7 O seven childbirths all in vain, seven profitless pregnancies, fruitless nurturings and wretched nursings! 8 In vain, my sons, I endured many birth pangs for you, and the more grievous anxieties of your upbringing. 9 Alas for my children, some unmarried, others married and without offspring![b] I shall not see your children or have the happiness of being called grandmother. 10 Alas, I who had so many and beautiful children am a widow and alone, with many sorrows.[c] 11 And when I die, I shall have none of my sons to bury me."

12 Yet that holy and God-fearing mother did not wail with such a lament for any of them, nor did she dissuade any of them from dying, nor did she grieve as they were dying. 13 On the contrary, as though having

a Other ancient authorities read *having bidden them farewell, surrendered them*    b Gk *without benefit*
c Or *much to be pitied*

*of sirens*, irresistible songs that would have lured Odysseus and his men to their deaths had he not stopped their ears with wax and lashed himself to the ship's mast (*Odyssey* 12.39–58,154–200). *Songs of swans*, the beautiful songs that, according to tradition, swans utter just before they die. **29**: *Mother of the nation*, her faith and virtue have political implications, helping to save the country (see 17.21–22n.). *The contest*, see 17.11–16 n. **31–32**: Gen 6.11–8.22 (cf. Philo, *Questions on Genesis* 2.18).

**16.1–17.1: The mother's martyrdom** (see 2 Macc 7.20–29,41). After a restatement of the thesis (16.1–4), we hear a speech the mother might have made but rejected (16.5–11; cf. 8.16–26), offset by her actual words of encouragement to her sons (16.12–25; cf. 18.6–19), and a brief account of her death (17.1). **3**: *Daniel*, Dan 6.1–24. *Mishael*, i.e., Meshach, Dan 3.19–30. **13**: *Giving rebirth for immortality*, a mind like adamant and giving rebirth for immortality to the whole number of her sons, she implored them and urged them on to death for the sake of religion. [14] O mother, soldier of God in the cause of religion, elder and woman! By steadfastness you have conquered even a tyrant, and in word and deed you have proved more powerful than a man. [15] For when you and your sons were arrested together, you stood and watched Eleazar being tortured, and said to your sons in the Hebrew language, [16] "My sons, noble is the contest to which you are called to bear witness for the nation. Fight zealously for our ancestral law. [17] For it would be shameful if, while an aged man endures such agonies for the sake of religion, you young men were to be terrified by tortures. [18] Remember that it is through God that you have had a share in the world and have enjoyed life, [19] and therefore you ought to endure any suffering for the sake of God. [20] For his sake also our father Abraham was zealous to sacrifice his son Isaac, the ancestor of our nation; and when Isaac saw his father's hand wielding a knife[a] and descending upon him, he did not cower. [21] Daniel the righteous was thrown to the lions, and Hananiah, Azariah, and Mishael were hurled into the fiery furnace and endured it for the sake of God. [22] You too must have the same faith in God and not be grieved. [23] It is unreasonable for people who have religious knowledge not to withstand pain."

24 By these words the mother of the seven encouraged and persuaded each of her sons to die rather than violate God's commandment. [25] They knew also that those who die for the sake of God live to God, as do Abraham and Isaac and Jacob and all the patriarchs.

17 Some of the guards said that when she also was about to be seized and put to death she threw herself into the flames so that no one might touch her body.

2 O mother, who with your seven sons nullified the violence of the tyrant, frustrated his evil designs, and showed the courage of your faith! [3] Nobly set like a roof on the pillars of your sons, you held firm and unswerving against the earthquake of the tortures. [4] Take courage, therefore, O holy-minded mother, maintaining firm an enduring hope in God. [5] The moon in heaven, with the stars, does not stand so august as you, who, after lighting the way of your star-like seven sons to piety, stand in honor before God and are firmly set in heaven with them. [6] For your children were true descendants of father Abraham.[b]

7 If it were possible for us to paint the history of your religion as an artist might, would not those who first beheld it have shuddered as they saw the mother of the seven children enduring their varied tortures to death for the sake of religion? [8] In-

a Gk sword  b Gk For your childbearing was from Abraham the father; other ancient authorities read For . . . Abraham the servant

cf. 9.22n.; 15.16; Ignatius, Romans 6.1–2. **15:** You stood and watched, yet according to 8.3 the mother and her sons were brought before Antiochus only after Eleazar was killed. **20:** Abraham, see Gen 22.1–19; 4 Macc 13.12n.). Genesis does not record Isaac's reaction. **21:** See 16.3 n. **17.1:** The mother's suicide (see 12.19 n.), which is not mentioned in 2 Maccabees, prevents the guards from violating her, preserving her honor. A similar story is told in Plutarch, On the Bravery of Women 253D–E.

**17.2–6: A second encomium** (cf. 15.1–32) praises the mother; in death she demonstrates unity with her sons. **5:** Star-like, cf. Dan 12.3; Sir 44.21; 50.6–7; Phil 2.15.

**17.7–18.5: A final encomium** (see 7.1–23n.) explains the meaning of the martyrdoms. The section contains several elements familiar from ancient funeral orations, such as reference to an epitaph (17.8–10), the image of the contest (17.11–16), the benefits of the heroes' death (17.20–22; 18.4–5), the example set by the deceased (17.23–24; 18.3), and a direct appeal to the audience (18.1–2). **17.8–10:** To inscribe on their tomb, while this speech may have actually been delivered at the site of the martyrs' grave (see 1.10n.), it is more likely that the epitaph is fictional, exemplifying a common device of Greco-Roman literature (cf. Demosthenes, Funeral Speech 60.1). **11–16:** For the motif of the divine contest, see 6.10;

deed it would be proper to inscribe on their tomb these words as a reminder to the people of our nation:[a]

9 "Here lie buried an aged priest and an aged woman and seven sons, because of the violence of the tyrant who wished to destroy the way of life of the Hebrews. [10] They vindicated their nation, looking to God and enduring torture even to death."

11 Truly the contest in which they were engaged was divine, [12] for on that day virtue gave the awards and tested them for their endurance. The prize was immortality in endless life. [13] Eleazar was the first contestant, the mother of the seven sons entered the competition, and the brothers contended. [14] The tyrant was the antagonist, and the world and the human race were the spectators. [15] Reverence for God was victor and gave the crown to its own athletes. [16] Who did not admire the athletes of the divine[b] legislation? Who were not amazed?

17 The tyrant himself and all his council marveled at their[c] endurance, [18] because of which they now stand before the divine throne and live the life of eternal blessedness. [19] For Moses says, "All who are consecrated are under your hands." [20] These, then, who have been consecrated for the sake of God,[d] are honored, not only with this honor, but also by the fact that because of them our enemies did not rule over our nation, [21] the tyrant was punished, and the homeland purified—they having become, as it were, a ransom for the sin of our nation. [22] And through the blood of those devout ones and their death as an atoning

sacrifice, divine Providence preserved Israel that previously had been mistreated.

23 For the tyrant Antiochus, when he saw the courage of their virtue and their endurance under the tortures, proclaimed them to his soldiers as an example for their own endurance, [24] and this made them brave and courageous for infantry battle and siege, and he ravaged and conquered all his enemies.

18 O Israelite children, offspring of the seed of Abraham, obey this law and exercise piety in every way, [2] knowing that devout reason is master of all emotions, not only of sufferings from within, but also of those from without.

3 Therefore those who gave over their bodies in suffering for the sake of religion were not only admired by mortals, but also were deemed worthy to share in a divine inheritance. [4] Because of them the nation gained peace, and by reviving observance of the law in the homeland they ravaged the enemy. [5] The tyrant Antiochus was both punished on earth and is being chastised after his death. Since in no way whatever was he able to compel the Israelites to become pagans and to abandon their ancestral customs, he left Jerusalem and marched against the Persians.

6 The mother of seven sons expressed also these principles to her children: [7] "I was a pure virgin and did not go outside my father's house; but I guarded the rib from

a Or *as a memorial to the heroes of our people*
b Other ancient authorities read *true*
c Other ancient authorities add *virtue and*
d Other ancient authorities lack *for the sake of God*

7.3; 11.20; 12.14; 15.29; 16.16; 18.23; 1 Cor 9.24–27; 2 Tim 2.5; Heb 12.1. Athletic imagery of this kind was common in ancient moral discourse (e.g., Philo, *Every Good Man is Free* 26–27). **14:** *The world and the human race,* the author emphasizes the public setting of the martyrdoms (cf. 5.15), suggesting their national, even global significance. Stoics taught that the sage's life was a public "spectacle" (Seneca, *On Providence* 2.9; cf. 1 Cor 4.9). **18:** *Stand before the . . . throne,* cf. Rev 7.15. **19:** The quotation is from Deut 33.3. **21–22:** *Atoning sacrifice,* the virtuous martyrdoms are taken as sufficient punishment for the nation's apostasy, so that divine favor is restored (1.11; 6.28–29; 9.24; 12.17; 17.10; 18.4); cf. Lev 16.1–34; Num 28.16–29.11; Sir 28.5; for a similar idea in early Christianity, see Rom 3.25; Heb 2.17; 1 Jn 4.10. **23–24:** The martyrs are even a moral *example* to their pagan adversaries. **18.1:** See 5.18n. **4–5:** *Because of them,* the nation is indebted to the martyrs for its political and religious welfare. The defeat of tyranny was a popular theme in Hellenistic literature, e.g., Lucian's *The Tyrannicide.*

**18.6–19:** The mother's last words (cf. 2 Macc 7.22–29). **7:** *Rib,* Gen 2.22. **8:** *Desert plain,* Deut which woman was made.[a] [8]No seducer corrupted me on a desert plain, nor did the destroyer, the deceitful serpent, defile the purity of my virginity. [9]In the time of my maturity I remained with my husband, and when these sons had grown up their father died. A happy man was he, who lived out his life with good children, and did not have the grief of bereavement. [10]While he was still with you, he taught you the law and the prophets. [11]He read to you about Abel slain by Cain, and Isaac who was offered as a burnt offering, and about Joseph in prison. [12]He told you of the zeal of Phinehas, and he taught you about Hananiah, Azariah, and Mishael in the fire. [13]He praised Daniel in the den of the lions and blessed him. [14]He reminded you of the scripture of Isaiah, which says, 'Even though you go through the fire, the flame shall not consume you.' [15]He sang to you songs of the psalmist David, who said, 'Many are the afflictions of the righteous.' [16]He recounted to you Solomon's proverb, 'There is a tree of life for those who do his will.' [17]He confirmed the query of Ezekiel, 'Shall these dry bones live?' [18]For he did not forget to teach you the song that Moses taught, which says, [19]'I kill and I make alive: this is your life and the length of your days.'"

[20] O bitter was that day—and yet not bitter—when that bitter tyrant of the Greeks quenched fire with fire in his cruel caldrons, and in his burning rage brought those seven sons of the daughter of Abraham to the catapult and back again to more[b] tortures, [21]pierced the pupils of their eyes and cut out their tongues, and put them to death with various tortures. [22]For these crimes divine justice pursued and will pursue the accursed tyrant. [23]But the sons of Abraham with their victorious mother are gathered together into the chorus of the fathers, and have received pure and immortal[c] souls from God, [24]to whom be glory forever and ever. Amen.

a Gk *the rib that was built*    b Other ancient authorities read *to all his*    c Other ancient authorities read *victorious*

22.25–27. **10–19:** An explanation of the religious education that cultivated the martyrs' virtue; on the obligation to teach children the law, see Deut 4.9; 6.7; 11.19; 31.12–13. **11:** *Abel*, Gen 4.2–15. *Isaac*, Gen 22.1–19. *Joseph*, Gen 39.1–23. **12:** *Phinehas*, Num 25.1–13. *Hananiah, Azariah, and Mishael*, Daniel 3. **13:** *Daniel*, Dan 6.1–24. **14:** Isa 43.2. **15:** Ps 34.19. **16:** Prov 3.18. **17:** Ezek 37.2–3. **19:** Deut 32.39; 30.20.

   **18.20–24: The conclusion** consists of a final lament (vv. 20–21) and consolation (vv. 22–24), both typical elements of a funeral oration. The section summarizes several of the book's key themes, especially justice and immortality. **23:** *Chorus*, see 8.4n. **24:** Cf. 2 Tim 4.18; Heb 13.21.

The Near East
in the
Hellenistic Period
Ptolemaic & Seleucid Empires

0   100   200 Miles

0   100   200 Kilometres